Scotlan **D1581583**

SELF CATERING 2009

Published by VisitScotland, 2008   Photography Paul Tomkins / VisitScotland / Scottish Viewpoint / Alistair Firth / Kelburn Castle / Joan Stewart / Iain Sarjeant / Nae Limits / Laurie Campbell / Hazel Marr   visitscotland.com 0845 22 55 121

Eilean Donan Castle, Highlands

WELCOME TO SCOTLAND

Once you've enjoyed a holiday in Scotland, it is easy to see why so many people from all over the world visit time and again. Scotland is a wonderful place for holidaymakers. From the briefest of breaks to annual vacations, Scotland has so much to offer that you'll never run out of options.

Flick through the pages of this guide and you'll immediately get a flavour of Scotland's diversity. You'll discover an inspiring array of fascinating places, each with its own unique attractions.

The best small country in the world

Though it's a relatively small country, Scotland is remarkably varied. You can climb mountains in the morning and still be on the beach in the afternoon. You can canoe across a remote loch and never see another soul all day long or you can sip coffee in a city centre pavement café and watch the whole world go by. You can get dressed up to the nines and go to a world premier on a balmy summer's evening or you can join in with some traditional music round a welcoming log fire in a quaint little pub on a cold winter's night.

Because of its remarkable diversity, Scotland is a world-class holiday destination all year round. There's always something on the go, and when you get to where you're going, you'll be spoiled for choice for somewhere to stay

With a self-catering holiday, you'll have the flexibility to enjoy your holiday at your own pace. Whether you're off on an adventure with all the family or a romantic weekend break just for two, you'll find your ideal home from home in the pages ahead.

So what's it going to be? A charming cottage by the sea or lovely little house in a tranquil Highland glen. Or what about something more ostentatious? A historic hunting lodge or castle fit for a king? How about an old croft or former lighthouse? The list is endless.

When you're camping or caravanning, you can get close to nature and explore a wilder side of Scotland. Though many of Scotland's caravan sites are now very sophisticated with a wide range of home comforts, others have retained that degree of simplicity that makes camping and caravanning so enjoyable.

So if it's adventure you're looking for, this is the way to go. With a tent on your back or mobile home at your disposal, you're free to tour around and explore.

There's an excellent range of holiday parks and sites all over the country – often in quite stunning locations.

When you've found the ideal place, you can look forward to a rousing welcome in a country that is renowned for its hospitality. Nobody loves a good time like the Scots. Whether it's bringing in the New Year with a wee dram, swirling your partner at a ceilidh or enjoying a sumptuous dinner for two in an exclusive restaurant with a stunning view, unforgettable experiences are never far away.

There's always the likelihood too that you'll meet some great folk – locals and visitors alike – some of whom could well become friends for life. That's all just part of a visit to Scotland.

As they say in the Gaelic tongue, *ceud mille failte* – 'a hundred thousand welcomes'. Come and enjoy our beautiful country.

The Brig o' Dee, Royal Deeside, Aberdeenshire

Join the Homecoming Scotland celebrations throughout 2009

HOMECOMING 2009

Join us in 2009 when Scotland will host its first ever Homecoming year which has been created and timed to mark the 250th anniversary of the birth of Scotland's national poet, the international cultural icon Robert Burns. From Burns Night to St Andrew's Day 2009 a country-wide programme of exciting and inspirational Homecoming events and activities will celebrate some of Scotland's great contributions to the world: Burns himself, Whisky, Golf, Great Scottish Minds and Innovations and our rich culture and heritage which lives on at home and through our global family. The best small country in the world.

From Orkney to Aberdeen, from Oban to the Scottish Borders, there will be a packed calendar of over 200 events and activities to choose from.

Here's a taste of what's on next year:

January 2009

Heralded by Scotland's internationally renowned Hogmanay Celebrations, the Homecoming Scotland 2009 programme will officially kick off on the weekend of Robert Burns' 250th anniversary (24-25 January) with a programme of high profile Burns events planned in key locations across Scotland.

To find out more, call 0845 22 55 121 or go to visitscotland.com

May is Whisky Month with an invitation extended to come to the Home of Whisky to explore and appreciate the expertise of the stillsmen and master blenders whose diligence has created one of Scotland's biggest exports and extensions of its culture. Kicking off at the biggest ever Spirit of Speyside Whisky Festival (1-10 May), the distilleries open their doors to visitors and locals alike. From a tasting session at The Scotch Whisky Experience in Edinburgh to a 3 day whisky course in Fife, there are a range of ways to sample Scotland's national tipple. New for 2009, The Spirit of the West event (16-17 May) in the beautiful surroundings of Inveraray Castle will provide a showcase for the 16 distilleries that make up the Whisky Coast. The month concludes with Feis Ile, Islay's Annual Malt and Music Festival.

Summer 2009

Over the summer months, Homecoming Scotland 2009 will present some brand new and enhanced major international events: The Gathering 2009 in Edinburgh (25-26 July) has been created especially for the Homecoming year to celebrate the contribution that Scottish clans have made to the history and culture of the world, whilst some of Scotland's stellar international events including The Edinburgh International Festival, The Edinburgh Military Tattoo, The Edinburgh International Book Festival and The Open Golf Championship will be celebrating the year with special Homecoming activity.

Autumn 2009

In October the Highlands will present a fortnight long festival (15-30 October, provisional dates) celebrating the best of traditional Highland Culture. Built around a major international conference exploring Scotland's Global Impact, regional and fringe events will take place across the region.

Closing Celebrations

In November around St Andrew's Day and as a sensational finale to the year, Homecoming Scotland will present a major celebration of Scottish Music (28-30 November, across Scotland). From traditional Scottish folk heroes to the cutting edge of contemporary Scottish bands currently making their mark internationally, expect a truly unique St Andrews Day celebration.

2009 is a special year for Scots and for those who love Scotland.

Look out for Homecoming events throughout this guide.

Go to homecomingscotland2009.com to find out more about all the different events.

Enjoy a dram in May, Homecoming Scotland's Whisky month

Top left: Two Hillwalkers take in the view from Sgurr A Ghreadaidh on the Black Cuillin Ridge towards Loch Curuisk, Isle of Skye. Top right: A puffin perches on a cliff edge, the Treshnish Isles, Inner Hebrides. Above: Sandy beach near Durness, Sutherland.

DON'T MISS

Walking

From the rolling hills in the south to the mountainous north, Scotland is perfect for walkers - whether it's a gentle stroll with the kids or a serious trek through the wilderness.

Beaches

Scotland's beaches are something special whether it's for a romantic stroll, or to try some surfing. Explore Fife's Blue Flag beaches or the breathtaking stretches of sand in the Outer Hebrides.

Wildlife

From dolphins in the Moray Firth to capercaillie in the Highlands and seals and puffins on the coastline, you never know what you might spot.

Culture & Heritage

From the mysterious standing stones in Orkney and the Outer Hebrides to Burns Cottage and Rosslyn Chapel, Scotland's fascinating history can be encountered throughout the country.

Rosslyn Chapel, Roslin, Midlothian

To find out more, call 0845 22 55 121 or go to visitscotland.com

Adventure

From rock climbing to sea kayaking, you can do it all. Try Perthshire for unusual adventure activities or the south of Scotland for some serious mountain biking.

Kayaking around the island of Vatersay, Outer Hebrides

Shopping

From designer stores to unique boutiques, from Glasgow's stylish city centre to Edinburgh's eclectic Old Town, Scotland is a shopper's paradise with lots of hidden gems to uncover.

Victoria Street, Edinburgh.

Golf

The country that gave the world the game of golf is still the best place to play it. With more than 500 courses in Scotland, take advantage of one of the regional golf passes on offer.

The Golf Course at Cruden Bay, Aberdeenshire.

Castles

Wherever you are in Scotland you are never far from a great Scottish icon, whether it's an impressive ruin or an imposing fortress, a fairytale castle or country estate.

Eilean Donan Castle, Loch Duich, Highlands.

Highland Games

From the famous Braemar Gathering in Aberdeenshire to the spectacular Cowal Highland Gathering in Argyll, hot foot it to some Highland Games action for pipe bands, dancers, and tossing the caber.

The sword dance at the Cowal Highland Gathering, Dunoon

Events & Festivals

In Scotland there's so much going on with fabulous events and festivals throughout the year, from the biggest names to the quirky and traditional.

The Royal Mile during the Festival, Edinburgh

If you love food, get a taste of Scotland. Scotland's natural larder offers some of the best produce in the world. Scotland's coastal waters are home to an abundance of lobster, prawns, oysters and more, whilst the land produces world famous beef, lamb and game.

There's high quality food and drink on menus all over the country often cooked up by award-winning chefs in restaurants where the view is second to none. You'll find home cooking, fine dining, takeaways and tearooms. Whether you're looking for a family-friendly pub or a romantic Highland restaurant there's the perfect place to dine. And there's no better time to indulge than when you're on holiday!

Live it. Visit *Scotland.*
eatscotland.com 0845 22 55 121

Traditional fare

Haggis and whisky might be recognised as traditional Scottish fare but why not add cullen skink, clapshot, cranachan, and clootie dumpling to the list…discover the tastes that match such ancient names. Sample some local hospitality along with regional specialities such as the Selkirk Bannock or Arbroath Smokies. Or experience the freedom of eating fish and chips straight from the wrapper while breathing in the clear evening air. Visit **eatscotland.com** and see our 'Food & Drink' section to find out more.

Farmers' markets

Scotland is a land renowned for producing ingredients of the highest quality. You can handpick fresh local produce at farmers' markets in towns and cities across the country. Create your own culinary delights or learn from the masters at the world famous Nick Nairn Cook School in Stirling. Savour the aroma, excite your taste buds and experience the buzz of a farmers' market. To find out more visit the Farmers Market information on the **eatscotland.com** website that can be found in the 'Food & Drink' section.

EATING AND DRINKING

Events

Scotland serves up a full calendar of food and drink festivals. Events like Taste of Edinburgh and Highland Feast are a must for foodies. Whisky fans can share their passion at the Islay Malt Whisky Festival, the Highland Whisky Festival, or the Spirit of Speyside Whisky Festival. Visit **eatscotland.com** to find out more about the events and festivals that are on in the 'What's on' section.

Tours and trails

If you're a lover of seafood spend some time exploring the rugged, unspoilt coastline of mid-Argyll following The Seafood Trail. Or if you fancy a wee dram visit the eight distilleries and cooperage on the world's only Malt Whisky Trail in Speyside. Visit visitscotland.com/cafedays to find out more about some great cafés that our visitors have discovered and enjoy a cup of something lovely surrounded by amazing scenery.

EatScotland Quality Assurance Scheme

EatScotland is a nationwide Quality Assurance Scheme from VisitScotland. The scheme includes all sectors of the catering industry from chip shops, pubs and takeaways to restaurants.

A trained team of assessors carry out an incognito visit to assess quality, standards and ambience. Only those operators who meet the EatScotland quality standards are accredited to the scheme so look out for the logo to ensure you visit Scotland's best quality establishments.

The newly launched EatScotland Silver and Gold Award Scheme recognises outstanding standards, reflecting that an establishment offers an excellent eating out experience in Scotland.

To find great EatScotland places to dine throughout the country visit **eatscotland.com**

Beach at Elie in Fife

GREEN TOURISM

Scotland is a stunning destination and we want to make sure it stays that way. That's why we encourage all tourism operators including accommodation providers to take part in our Green Tourism Business Scheme. It means you're assured of a great quality stay at an establishment that's trying to minimise its impact on the environment.

VisitScotland rigorously assesses accommodation providers against measures as diverse as energy use, using local produce on menus, or promoting local wildlife walks or cycle hire. Environmentally responsible businesses can achieve Bronze, Silver or Gold awards, to acknowledge how much they are doing to help conserve the quality of Scotland's beautiful environment.

Look out for the Bronze, Silver and Gold Green Tourism logos throughout this guide to help you decide where to stay and do your bit to help protect our environment.

For a quick reference see our directory at the back of the book which highlights all quality assured accommodation that has been awarded with the Gold, Silver or Bronze award.

green-business.co.uk

Bronze Green Tourism Award

SilverGreen Tourism Award

GoldGreen Tourism Award

Friendly faces... a wealth of helpful advice... loads of local knowledge... get the most out of your stay...

Visitor Information Centres are staffed by people 'in the know', offering friendly advice, helping to make your stay in Scotland the most enjoyable ever... whatever your needs!

LOCAL KNOWLEDGE • WHERE TO STAY • ACCOMMODATION BOOKING PLACES TO VISIT THINGS TO DO • MAPS AND GUIDES TRAVEL ADVICE • ROUTE PLANNING • WHERE TO SHOP AND EAT LOCAL CRAFTS AND PRODUCE • EVENT INFORMATION • TICKETS

Live it. Visit *Scotland.*
visitscotland.com/wheretofindus

To find out more, call 0845 22 55 121 or go to visitscotland.com

VisitScotland, under the Scottish Tourist Board brand, administers the 5-star grading schemes which assess the quality and standards of all types of visitor accommodation and attractions from castles and historic houses to garden centres and arts venues. We grade around 80 per cent of the accommodation in Scotland and 90 per cent of the visitor attractions – so wherever you want to stay or visit, we've got it covered. The schemes are monitored all year round each establishment is reviewed once a year. We do the hard work so you can relax and enjoy your holiday.

The promise of the stars:

★
It is clean, tidy and an acceptable, if basic, standard

★★
It is a good, all round standard

★★★
It is a very good standard, with attention to detail in every area

★★★★
It is excellent – using high quality materials, good food (except self-catering) and friendly, professional service

★★★★★
An exceptional standard where presentation, ambience, food (except self-catering) and service are hard to fault.

IT'S WRITTEN IN THE STARS...

How does the system work?

Our advisors visit and assess establishments on up to 50 areas from quality, comfort and cleanliness to welcome, ambience and service. If an establishment scores less than 60 per cent it will not be graded. The same star scheme now runs in England and Wales, so you can follow the stars wherever you go.

Graded visitor attractions

Visitor attractions from castles and museums to leisure centres and tours are graded with 1-5 stars depending on their level of customer care. The focus is on the standard of hospitality and service as well as presentation, quality of shop or café (if there is one) and toilet facilities.

 The Thistle symbol recognises a high standard of caravan holiday home.

We want you to feel welcome

Walkers Welcome and Cyclists Welcome. Establishments that carry the symbols below pay particular attention to the specific needs of walkers and cyclists.

 Cyclists Welcome

 Walkers Welcome

There are similar schemes for Anglers, Bikers, Classic Cars, Golfers, Children and Ancestral Tourism. Check with establishment when booking.

Access all areas

The following symbols will help visitors with physical disabilities to decide whether accommodation is suitable. The directory at the back of this book will highlight all quality assured establishments that have suitable accommodation.

 Unassisted wheelchair access

 Assisted wheelchair access

 Access for visitors with mobility difficulties

Further information:

Quality Assurance
Tel: 01463 244111
Fax: 01463 244161
Email: qainfo@visitscotland.com

The Glenfinnan Viaduct, near Fort William, Highlands

TRAVEL TO SCOTLAND

It's really easy to get to Scotland whether you choose to travel by car, train, plane, coach or ferry. And once you get here travel is easy as Scotland is a compact country.

By Air

Flying to Scotland couldn't be simpler with flight times from London, Dublin and Belfast only around one hour. There are airports at Edinburgh, Glasgow, Glasgow Prestwick, Aberdeen, Dundee and Inverness. The following airlines operate flights to Scotland (although not all airports) from within the UK and Ireland:

bmi
Tel: 0870 60 70 555
From Ireland: 1332 64 8181
flybmi.com

bmi baby
Tel: 0871 224 0224
From Ireland: 1 890 340 122
bmibaby.com

British Airways
Tel: 0844 493 0787
From Ireland: 1890 626 747
ba.com

Eastern Airways
Tel: 08703 669 100
easternairways.com

easyJet
Tel: 0905 821 0905
From Ireland: 1890 923 922
easyjet.com

Flybe
Tel: 0871 700 2000
From Ireland: 1392 268 529
flybe.com

Ryanair
Tel: 0871 246 0000
From Ireland: 0818 30 30 30
ryanair.com

Air France
Tel: 0870 142 4343
airfrance.co.uk

Aer Arann
Tel: 0870 876 76 76
From Ireland: 0818 210 210
aerarann.com

To find out more, call 0845 22 55 121 or go to visitscotland.com

Jet2
Tel: 0871 226 1737
From Ireland: 0818 200017
jet2.com

AirBerlin
Tel: 0871 5000 737
airberlin.com

Aer Lingus
Tel: 0870 876 5000
From Ireland: 0818 365 000
aerlingus.com

By Rail

Scotland has major rail stations in Aberdeen, Edinburgh Waverley and Edinburgh Haymarket, Glasgow Queen Street and Glasgow Central, Perth, Stirling, Dundee and Inverness. There are regular cross border railway services from England and Wales, and good city links. You could even travel on the First ScotRail Caledonian Sleeper overnight train service from London and wake up to the sights and sounds of Scotland.

First ScotRail
Tel: 08457 55 00 33
scotrail.co.uk

Virgin Trains
Tel: 08457 222 333
virgintrains.co.uk

National Express East Coast
Tel: 08457 225 225
nationalexpresseastcoast.com

National Rail
Tel: 08457 484950
nationalrail.co.uk

By Road

Scotland has an excellent road network from motorways and dual carriageway linking cities and major towns, to remote single-track roads with passing places to let others by. Whether you are coming in your own car from home or hiring a car once you get here, getting away from traffic jams and out onto Scotland's quiet roads can really put the fun back into driving. Branches of the following companies can be found throughout Scotland:

Arnold Clark
Tel: 0845 607 4500
arnoldclarkrental.com

easyCar
Tel: 08710 500444
easycar.com

Hertz
Tel: 08708 44 88 44
hertz.co.uk

Avis Rent A Car
Tel: 08445 818 181
avis.co.uk

Enterprise Rent-A-Car
Tel: 0870 350 3000
enterprise.co.uk

National Car Rental
Tel: 0870 400 4560
nationalcar.com

Budget
Tel: 0845 581 9998
budget.co.uk

Europcar
Tel: 0870 607 5000
europcarscotland.co.uk

Sixt rent a car
Tel: 0844 499 3399
sixt.co.uk

By Ferry

Scotland has over 130 inhabited islands so ferries are important. And whether you are coming from Ireland or trying to get to the outer islands, you might be in need of a ferry crossing. Ferries to and around the islands are regular and reliable and most carry vehicles. These companies all operate ferry services around Scotland:

Stena Line
Tel: 08705 204 204
stenaline.co.uk

Caledonian MacBrayne
Tel: 08000 665000
calmac.co.uk

Northlink Ferries
Tel: 08456 000 449
northlinkferries.co.uk

P&O Irish Sea
Tel: 0870 24 24 777
poirishsea.com

Western Ferries
Tel: 01369 704 452
western-ferries.co.uk

By Coach

Coach connections include express services to Scotland from all over the UK, and there is a good network of coach services once you get here too. You could even travel on the Postbus – a special feature of the Scottish mail service which carries fare-paying passengers along with the mail in rural areas where there is no other form of transport, bringing a new dimension to travel.

National Express
Tel: 08705 80 80 80
nationalexpress.com

City Link
Tel: 08705 50 50 50
citylink.co.uk

Postbus
Tel: 08457 740 740
royalmail.com/postbus

Distances are given in miles (M, upper figure) and kilometres (KM, lower figure).

From \ To	ABERDEEN	BIRMINGHAM	CARDIFF	DOVER	DUMFRIES	DUNDEE	EDINBURGH	FORT WILLIAM	GLASGOW	HARWICH	HAWICK	HULL	INVERNESS	KYLE OF LOCHALSH	LONDON	MANCHESTER	NEWCASTLE	OBAN	PERTH	PRESTWICK	ROSYTH	STIRLING	STRANRAER	THURSO	TROON	ULLAPOOL
BIRMINGHAM	421 687																									
CARDIFF	529 851	113 182																								
DOVER	617 993	200 322	224 361																							
DUMFRIES	214 344	234 376	335 539	436 700																						
DUNDEE	71 114	357 575	465 749	553 890	149 240																					
EDINBURGH	131 210	290 467	398 641	486 782	80 128	62 99																				
FORT WILLIAM	161 258	396 637	504 811	592 952	179 288	123 197	138 221																			
GLASGOW	152 243	286 461	394 634	482 776	76 122	84 134	45 72	108 173																		
HARWICH	604 972	187 300	242 390	130 210	370 595	540 869	473 761	578 931	469 754																	
HAWICK	178 287	243 391	344 554	417 671	53 86	113 182	50 81	185 298	85 137	370 596																
HULL	387 619	137 221	251 405	255 411	205 330	318 509	255 408	384 614	275 440	214 346	206 331															
INVERNESS	118 189	446 717	553 890	641 1032	289 385	134 214	162 259	69 110	178 285	628 1011	209 337	444 710														
KYLE OF LOCHALSH	200 320	469 755	577 929	665 1070	253 407	179 286	207 331	76 122	184 294	652 1049	254 408	459 734	82 131													
LONDON	549 878	118 190	150 242	75 122	349 561	481 770	412 659	514 822	406 650	78 126	358 576	216 346	573 917	590 944												
MANCHESTER	345 556	93 150	201 324	281 453	157 252	214 345	320 515	210 338	268 431	166 267	95 154	370 595	393 633	201 322												
NEWCASTLE	244 390	208 336	323 519	350 563	91 147	175 280	112 179	267 427	159 254	309 498	64 102	148 237	274 438	343 549	288 461	147 237										
OBAN	190 304	385 620	493 794	581 935	168 270	121 194	125 200	50 80	96 154	568 914	175 281	371 594	180 125	200 502	803 309	498 310	496									
PERTH	86 139	348 560	449 723	550 884	128 205	21 34	43 69	104 166	64 104	484 778	96 155	319 513	114 183	158 254	463 744	271 436	152 245	94 151								
PRESTWICK	177 285	304 489	411 662	500 804	61 98	113 182	79 127	131 210	32 52	486 783	105 168	279 449	201 324	204 329	418 673	228 366	168 271	120 193	96 155							
ROSYTH	115 185	324 522	425 684	477 768	104 170	48 77	14 23	124 200	47 76	430 692	67 108	265 426	145 233	189 304	437 703	247 398	114 183	31 49	79 127							
STIRLING	120 193	313 503	414 666	514 823	92 149	55 89	38 61	97 157	29 47	448 722	87 141	284 456	145 234	172 277	427 688	236 379	143 231	87 140	37 60	61 99	26 42					
STRANRAER	241 386	297 478	404 651	489 787	71 115	172 275	133 213	196 314	89 142	475 765	125 202	284 454	265 424	272 435	664 205	358 224	161 259	172 277	149 240	54 87	131 211	114 611				
THURSO	234 374	555 893	663 1066	750 1208	348 560	250 400	278 445	183 293	293 469	737 1186	319 513	559 894	112 180	177 283	559 894	391 798	233 373	221 311	355 500	254 409	252 406	382 183				
TROON	183 295	314 505	415 668	516 830	64 104	119 191	82 132	126 203	35 56	450 724	106 171	285 459	209 336	200 322	429 690	237 381	171 276	116 186	101 162	5 8	80 129	63 101	60 96	316 508		
ULLAPOOL	179 286	499 803	607 976	695 1118	293 472	194 310	222 355	119 190	238 381	681 1097	263 424	504 806	63 101	91 146	635 1006	444 710	335 536	169 270	168 270	255 411	199 320	128 205	327 523	263 423		
YORK	343 552	132 212	246 396	273 439	151 243	279 449	191 308	318 511	208 335	233 374	41 65	367 591	630 208	391 70	113 90	146 307	495 237	382 226	363 212	341 230	370 477	767 218	352 231	372 421	678	

M
KM

To find out more, call 0845 22 55 121 or go to visitscotland.com

MAPS

MAP 1

These maps show locations of establishments appearing in the Main Advertising Section of this guide. For route planning and touring please use a current road atlas.

MAP 2

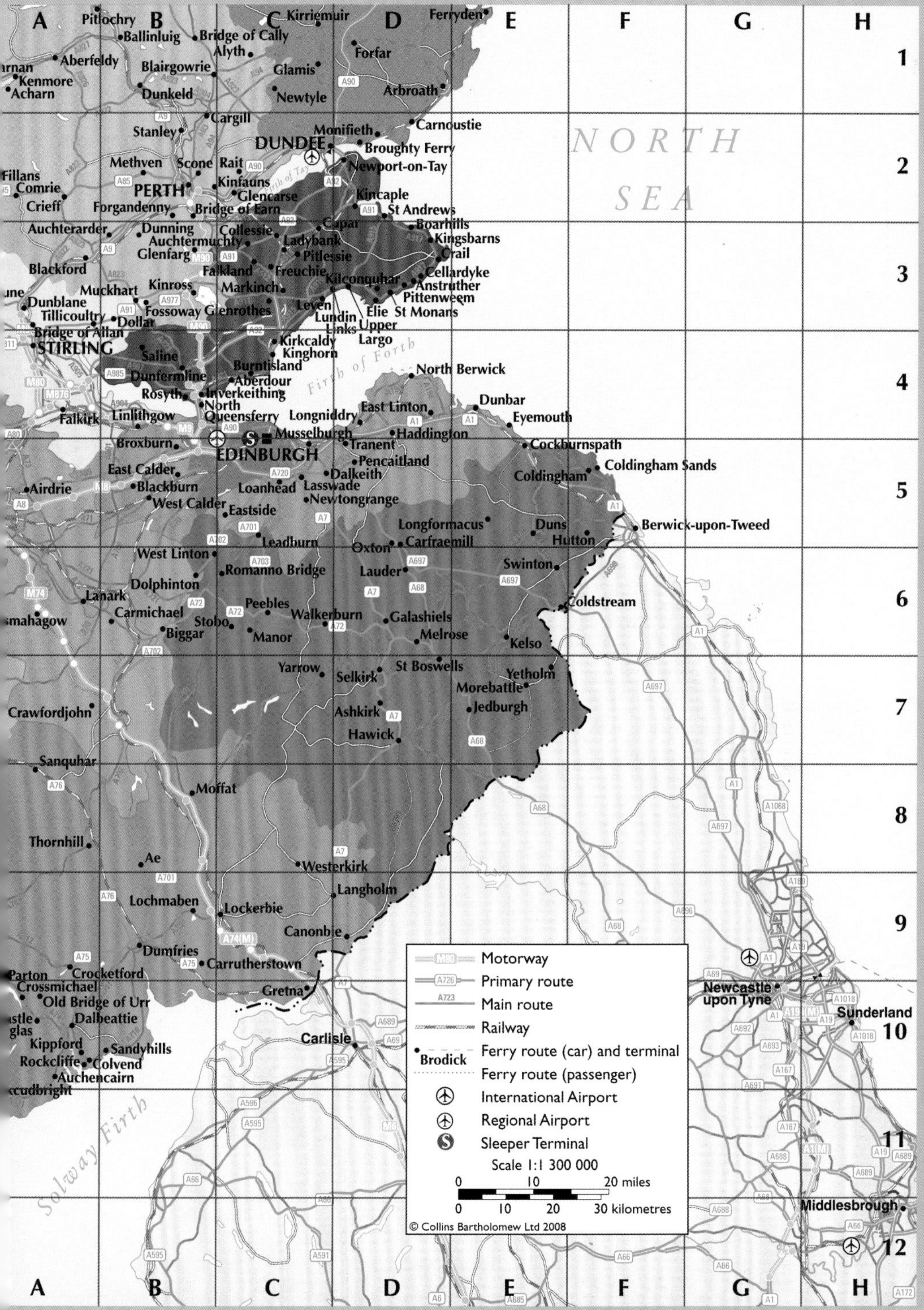

Grid columns: A B C D E F G H
Grid rows: 1 2 3 4 5 6 7 8 9 10 11 12

NORTH SEA

Pitlochry • Ballinluig • Bridge of Cally • C.Kirriemuir • Ferryden
Aberfeldy • Alyth • Forfar
Kenmore • Blairgowrie • Glamis
Acharn • Dunkeld • Newtyle • Arbroath
arnan • Cargill
Stanley • Carnoustie
Fillans • Methven Scone Rait • Monifieth • DUNDEE • Broughty Ferry
Comrie • PERTH • Kinfauns • Newport-on-Tay
Crieff • Forgandenny • Glencarse • Kincaple
Auchterarder • Dunning • Collessie • St Andrews
Blackford • Auchtermuchty • Ladybank • Boarhills
Glenfarg • Capar • Kingsbarns
Dunblane • Glenfarg • Pitlessie • Crail
Tillicoultry • Kinross • Freuchie • Kilconquhar • Cellardyke
Bridge of Allan • Muckhart • Markinch • Anstruther
STIRLING • Dollar • Fossoway Glenrothes • Leven • Pittenweem
Saline • Lundin • Elie St Monans
Falkirk • Dunfermline • Kirkcaldy • Links Upper
Broxburn • Aberdour • Kinghorn • Largo
Linlithgow • North Queensferry • Burntisland
Rosyth • Inverkeithing • North Berwick
EDINBURGH • Musselburgh • Longniddry • East Linton • Dunbar
Tranent • Haddington • Eyemouth
East Calder • Pencaitland • Cockburnspath
Blackburn • Dalkeith • Coldingham • Coldingham Sands
West Calder • Loanhead Lasswade
Eastside • Newtongrange
Airdrie • Leadburn • Longformacus • Duns
Blackburn • Oxton • Carfraemill • Hutton
West Linton • Lauder • Berwick-upon-Tweed
Dolphinton • Romanno Bridge • Swinton
Lanark • Peebles • Coldstream
Carmichael • Walkerburn • Galashiels
Stobo • Manor • Melrose • Kelso
maghagow • Biggar • Yarrow • St Boswells • Yetholm
Selkirk • Morebattle
Ashkirk • Jedburgh
Crawfordjohn • Hawick
Sanquhar • Moffat
Thornhill • Ae • Westerkirk
Lochmaben • Langholm • Newcastle upon Tyne
Lockerbie • Sunderland
Canonbie
Dumfries • Carrutherstown
Parton • Crocketford • Gretna
Crossmichael • Carlisle • Middlesbrough
Old Bridge of Urr • Dalbeattie
Kippford • Sandyhills
Rockcliffe • Colvend
Auchencairn
ccudbright

Solway Firth
Firth of Tay
Firth of Forth

Legend

M80	Motorway
A726	Primary route
A723	Main route
	Railway
●	Ferry route (car) and terminal — Brodick
	Ferry route (passenger)
✈	International Airport
⊕	Regional Airport
S	Sleeper Terminal

Scale 1:1 300 000

0   10   20 miles
0   10   20   30 kilometres

© Collins Bartholomew Ltd 2008

MAP 3

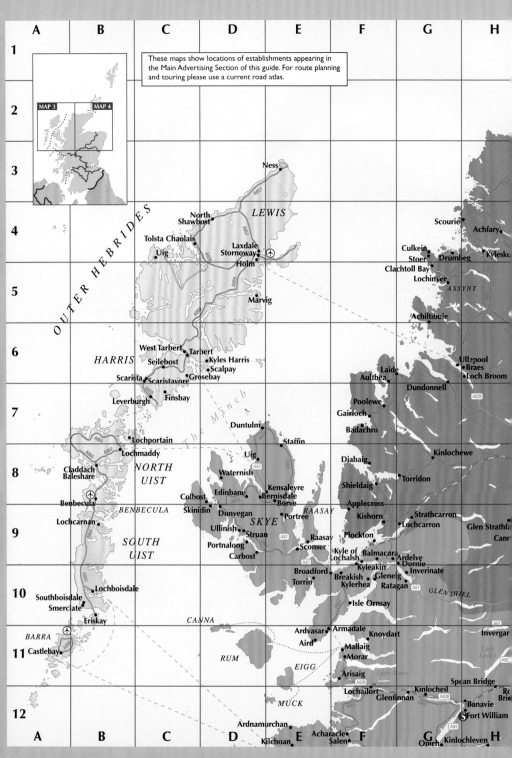

These maps show locations of establishments appearing in the Main Advertising Section of this guide. For route planning and touring please use a current road atlas.

MAP 3 MAP 4

Ness

LEWIS

North Shawbost
Tolsta Chaolais
Uig
Laxdale
Stornoway
Holm

Scourie
Achfary
Culkein
Stoer
Drumbeg
Kylesku
Clachtoll Bay
Lochinver
ASSYNT

Marvig

Achiltibuie

West Tarbert Tarbert
Seilebost Kyles Harris
Scalpay
Scarista Scaristavore Grosebay
Leverburgh Finsbay

HARRIS

Ullapool
Braes
Laide Loch Broom
Aultbea
Dundonnell
Poolewe
Gairloch
Badachro

Duntulm
Staffin

Kinlochewe

Lochportain
Lochmaddy

Uig
Waternish

Djabaig
Torridon

Shieldaig

Claddach
Baleshare

NORTH
UIST

Colbost
Skinidin Dunvegan
Ullinish Struan
Portnalong
Carbost

Edinbane
Bernisdale
Borve

Kensaleyre

RAASAY

Applecross
Kishorn Strathcarron
Lochcarron

Glen Strath
Canr

Benbecula
Lochcarnan

BENBECULA

SKYE Portree

Raasay
Sconser

Plockton

SOUTH
UIST

Kyle of Balmacara
Lochalsh
Broadford Kyleakin Glenelg
Torrin Kylerhea Ratagan

Ardelve
Dornie
Inverinate
GLEN SHIEL

Lochboisdale
Southboisdale
Smerclate
Eriskay

Isle Ornsay

BARRA
Castlebay

CANNA

RUM

Ardvasar Armadale
Aird Knoydart
Mallaig
Morar

Arisaig

Invergar

Spean Bridge

EIGG

MUCK

Lochailort Kinlocheil
Glenfinnan

Banavie
Fort William

Ardnamurchan
Kilchoan

Acharacle
Salen

Onich Kinlochleven

MAP 4

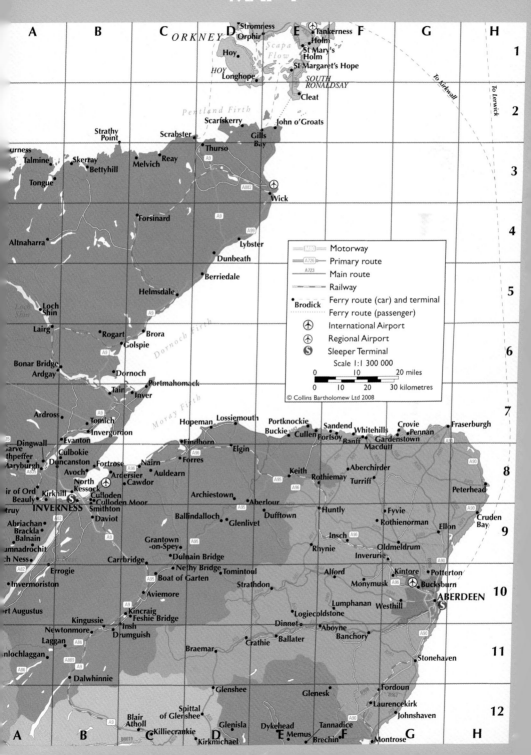

ORKNEY

Stromness
Orphir
Tankerness
Holm
St Mary's Holm
St Margaret's Hope
Hoy
HOY
Longhope
Scapa Flow
SOUTH RONALDSAY
Cleat
To Kirkwall
To Lerwick

Scarfskerry
John o'Groats
Scrabster
Gills Bay
Strathy Point
Thurso
Melvich
Reay
Skerray
Talmine
Bettyhill
Tongue
Wick
Forsinard
Altnaharra
Lybster
Dunbeath
Berriedale
Helmsdale
Loch Shin
Lairg
Rogart
Brora
Golspie
Dornoch Firth
Bonar Bridge
Ardgay
Dornoch
Tain
Inver
Portmahomack
Ardross
Tomich
Invergordon
Moray Firth
Hopeman
Lossiemouth
Portknockie
Buckie
Cullen
Sandend
Whitehills
Crovie
Pennan
Fraserburgh
Dingwall
Findhorn
Portsoy
Banff
Gardenstown
Macduff
Culbokie
Duncanston
Forres
Elgin
Maryburgh
Fortrose
Nairn
Keith
Aberchirder
Peterhead
Avoch
Ardersier
Cawdor
Auldearn
Rothiemay
Turriff
North Kessock
Culloden
Archiestown
Aberlour
Huntly
Fyvie
Cruden Bay
Kirkhill
INVERNESS
Smithton
Culloden Moor
Ballindalloch
Glenlivet
Dufftown
Rothienorman
Ellon
Abriachan
Brackla
Balnain
Daviot
Grantown-on-Spey
Dulnain Bridge
Insch
Rhynie
Oldmeldrum
Potterton
Errogie
Carrbridge
Nethy Bridge
Tomintoul
Alford
Kintore
Bucksburn
Invermoriston
Boat of Garten
Strathdon
Monymusk
ABERDEEN
Aviemore
Lumphanan
Westhill
Kingussie
Kincraig
Feshie Bridge
Insh
Logiecoldstone
Newtonmore
Drumguish
Dinnet
Aboyne
Banchory
Laggan
Stonehaven
Dalwhinnie
Braemar
Crathie
Ballater
Glenshee
Glenesk
Fordoun
Laurencekirk
Johnshaven
Blair Atholl
Spittal of Glenshee
Killiecrankie
Glenisla
Dykehead
Memus
Tannadice
Montrose
Kirkmichael
Brechin

Legend

Motorway	
A726	Primary route
A723	Main route
Railway	
Brodick	Ferry route (car) and terminal
	Ferry route (passenger)
International Airport	
Regional Airport	
S	Sleeper Terminal

Scale 1:1 300 000

0   10   20 miles
0   10   20   30 kilometres

© Collins Bartholomew Ltd 2008

MAP 5

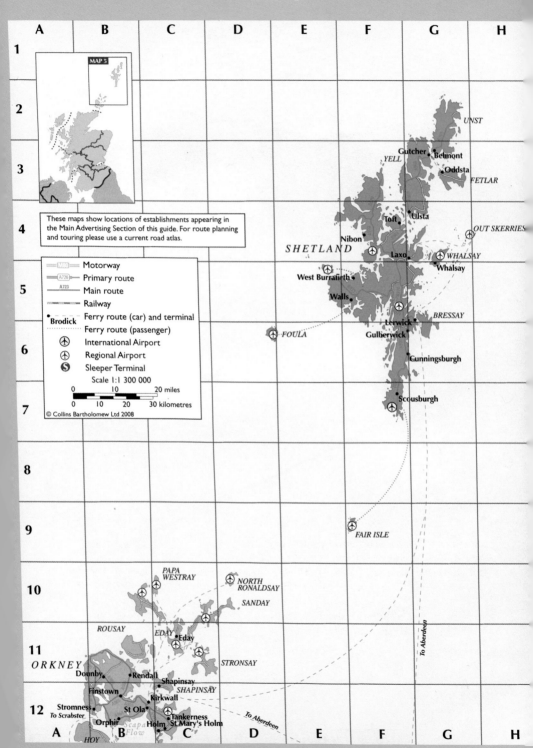

MAP 5

These maps show locations of establishments appearing in the Main Advertising Section of this guide. For route planning and touring please use a current road atlas.

▭M80▭	Motorway
▭A726▭	Primary route
A723	Main route
	Railway
•Brodick	Ferry route (car) and terminal
	Ferry route (passenger)
✈	International Airport
✈	Regional Airport
Ⓢ	Sleeper Terminal

Scale 1:1 300 000

0   10   20 miles
0   10   20   30 kilometres

© Collins Bartholomew Ltd 2008

UNST

YELL

Gutcher • Belmont

• Oddsta

FETLAR

Toft • Ulsta

OUT SKERRIES

Nibon

SHETLAND

Laxo

✈ WHALSAY

Whalsay

West Burrafirth •

Walls •

BRESSAY

Lerwick

FOULA

Gulberwick

Cunningsburgh

Scousburgh

FAIR ISLE

PAPA WESTRAY

NORTH RONALDSAY

SANDAY

ROUSAY

EDAY • Eday

STRONSAY

ORKNEY

Dounby •

• Rendall

Shapinsay

SHAPINSAY

Finstown

Kirkwall

Stromness •
To Scrabster

St Ola •

Tankerness

St Mary's Holm

Orphir •

Holm

Scapa Flow

To Aberdeen

To Aberdeen

To Aberdeen

HOY

Elgol, Isle of Skye

ACCOMMODATION LISTINGS

- Self Catering/Caravan & Camping accommodation listings for all of Scotland.

- Establishments are listed by location in alphabetical order.

- At the back of this book there is a directory showing:
  – VisitScotland quality assured self catering accommodation
  – VisitScotland quality assured caravan and camping accommodation.
  These directories show you which establishments have accessible accommodation for visitors with mobility difficulties, and establishments that have obtained a Green Award
  - Also directories showing Caravan holiday homes that have been awarded a Thistle Award and Hostel Accommodation through Scotland

- You will also find an Index by location which will tell you where to look if you already know where you want to go.

- Inside the back cover flap you will find a key to the symbols.

A family enjoy the snow at Castle Fraser – south west of Inverurie

To find out more, call 0845 22 55 121 or go to visitscotland.com

The town of Melrose, showing Abbey and River Tweed, Scottish Borders

SOUTH OF SCOTLAND

Ayrshire & Arran,
Dumfries & Galloway,
Scottish Borders

No matter how many times you holiday in the Scottish Borders, Ayrshire & Arran or Dumfries & Galloway, you'll always find something new and interesting to do.

The proud heritage, distinct traditions and enthralling history of Scotland's most southerly places are sure to capture your imagination.

Explore the region's imposing castles and ruined abbeys and follow the trail of an often bloody and turbulent past. It's a story of battles and skirmishes - from all out war to cattle rustling cross-border raids.

Living history

Though you'd be hard pushed to find a more peaceful part of the country these days, the legacy of these more unsettled times can still be experienced in many a Scottish Borders town during the Common Ridings. Throughout the summer months hundreds of colourful riders on horseback commemorate the days when their ancestors risked their lives patrolling town boundaries and neighbouring villages.

The South is alive with history. Traquair House, near Innerleithen, is Scotland's oldest continuously inhabited house, dating back to 1107. In Selkirk the whole town is transformed in early December as locals step back to the days when Sir Walter Scott presided over the local courtroom, by partaking in the Scott's Selkirk celebrations.

Beautiful beaches

Southern Scotland isn't just about rolling hills and lush farmland, both coasts are well worth a visit. To the east you can see the rocky cliffs and picturesque harbours at St Abbs Head and Eyemouth, while over on the west, there are the beautiful Ayrshire beaches and more than 200 miles of the lovely Solway Coast to explore.

To find out more, call 0845 22 55 121 or go to visitscotland.com

And off the Ayrshire coast is the Isle of Arran – one of Scotland's finest islands and everything a holidaymaker could want.

Whatever your interests, you'll be spoiled for choice in southern Scotland. If you love angling, there's world-class salmon fishing on the River Tweed. If golf's your game, Turnberry, Prestwick and Royal Troon are up with the best.

If you're a mountain biker, you won't find better than Glentress or Kirroughtree, two of the 7stanes mountain bike routes. Enjoy reading? Head for Wigtown, Scotland's National Book Town and home to more than 20 bookshops. Ice cream? Who can resist Cream o' Galloway at Gatehouse of Fleet?

If you're a gardener, you'll be inspired all year round by the flourishing collection of rare plants at the Logan Botanic Garden near Stranraer and Dawyck Botanic Gardens near Peebles.

What's more, 2009 is a big year for Scotland – we're celebrating the 250th anniversary of the birth of Robert Burns. There's over 200 special events taking place throughout the year, all over Scotland. Go to homecomingscotland2009.com to find out about events in this area.

That's the South of Scotland. Bursting with brilliant places, including some excellent parks for caravanning and camping, waiting with a hearty Scottish welcome and ready to captivate you with a holiday experience you will never forget.

Enjoy an ice cream at Cream o' Galloway, Gatehouse of Fleet

What's On?

Burns Light
25 January 2009
Homecoming on your Doorstep.

Melrose 7's Rugby Tournament
11 April 2009
The Greenyards, Melrose, April 2009
Melrose is the home of rugby 7's and this popular and expanding tournament is certain to be a big crowd puller!
melrose7s.com

Spring Fling
May Bank Holiday weekend 2009
Arts and crafts open studio event.
spring-fling.co.uk

Burns an 'a' That! Festival
16 – 24 May 2009
Celebrate the 250th anniversary of Rabbie Burns' birth: more than 100 events across Ayrshire will bring together the biggest names in music, comedy and the arts.
burnsfestival.com

Ayr Flower Show
2 – 9 August 2009
Scotland's answer to the Chelsea Flower Show, the Ayr Flower Show takes place in the beautiful grounds of Rozelle Park.
ayrflowershow.org

Return To The Ridings:
Border Common Ridings
7 -30 August 2009
across the Scottish Borders

Marymass
13 - 24 August 2009
A local Queen is crowned and the oldest horse racing event in the world takes place on the moor.
marymass.org

In the Footsteps of
the Reivers
5 – 12 September 2009
Throughout Jedburdh and Hawick.

Wigtown Book Festival
25 September – 4 October 2009
Meet famous writers and broadcasters in the idyllic Galloway countryside.
wigtownbookfestival.com

All dates correct at time of publication. Please check before booking. VisitScotland cannot be held responsible for any inaccuracies

25

MAP

©Collins Bartholomew Ltd 2008

To find out more, call 0845 22 55 121 or go to visitscotland.com

VISITOR INFORMATION CENTRES

Visitor Information Centres are staffed by people 'in the know' offering friendly advice, helping to make your stay in Scotland the most enjoyable ever . . . whatever your needs!

Ayrshire & Arran

Ayr	22 Sandgate, Ayr, KA7 1BW	Tel: 01292 290300
Brodick	The Pier, Brodick, Isle of Arran, KA27 8AU	Tel: 01770 303774/776

Dumfries & Galloway

Dumfries	64 Whitesands, Dumfries DG1 2RS	Tel: 01387 253862
Gretna	Unit 38, Gretna Gateway Outlet Village, Glasgow Road, Gretna, DG16 5GG	Tel: 01461 337834
Kirkcudbright	Harbour Square, Kirkcudbright DG6 4HY	Tel: 01557 330494
Southwaite	M6 Service Area, Southwaite, CA4 0NS	Tel: 01697 473445
Stranraer	Burns House, 28 Harbour Street, Stranraer, Dumfries DG9 7RA	Tel: 01776 702595

Scottish Borders

Hawick	Tower Mill, Heart of Hawick Campus, Kirkstile, Hawick, TD9 0AE	Tel: 01450 373993
Jedburgh	Murray's Green, Jedburgh, TD8 6BE	Tel: 01835 863171/864099
Kelso	Town House, The Square, Kelso, TD5 7HF	Tel: 01573 228055
Melrose	Abbey House, Abbey Street, TD6 9LGR	Tel: 01896 822283
Peebles	23 High Street, Peebles, EH45 8AG	Tel: 01721 723159

LOCAL KNOWLEDGE • WHERE TO STAY • ACCOMMODATION BOOKING • PLACES TO VISIT • THINGS TO DO • MAPS AND GUIDES TRAVEL ADVICE • ROUTE PLANNING • WHERE TO SHOP AND EAT LOCAL CRAFTS AND PRODUCE • EVENT INFORMATION • TICKETS

For information and ideas about exploring Scotland in advance of your trip, call our booking and information service **0845 22 55 121** or go to **visitscotland.com**

If calling from outside the UK and Ireland **+44 1506 832 121**   From Ireland **1800 932 510**

A £4 booking fee applies for accommodation bookings made via a Visitor Information Centre and through our booking and information service.

Canyoning in North Glen Sannox on the Isle of Arran

Ayrshire & Arran

Ayrshire is home to 80 miles of unspoiled coastline and rolling green hills. Southwest of Glasgow, the area is steeped in history from Bronze Age standing stones to Medieval Viking battles and the majestic splendour of some of the best-preserved castles in the UK.

Not forgetting it is also the birthplace of world-renowned poet Robert Burns, to whom homage is paid on January 25th throughout the world. Why not experience Burns night surrounded by the scenery and culture that inspired the Bard himself.

Arran offers everything that is good about Scotland in one small and easily accessible island. It has mountains and lochs in the north, and rolling hills and meadows in the south. With fantastic walks, seven golf courses, breathtaking scenery and delicious food and drink, Arran has something for everyone.

Brodick Highland Games

To find out more, call 0845 22 55 121 or go to visitscotland.com

DON'T MISS

1 See what happens when you bring 4 of the world's best graffiti artists to Scotland and provide them with a castle as a canvas. This is exactly what the owners of Kelburn Castle did. Kelburn is the ancient home of the Earls of Glasgow and dates back to the 13th century. The graffiti project on the castle is a spectacular piece of artwork, surrounded by a beautiful country estate and wooden glen. There is plenty to interest all the family.

2 The island of Great Cumbrae, accessible via a 10-minute ferry crossing from Largs, has an undeniable charm and a fabulous setting on the Clyde with views towards Arran. The capital, Millport, is every inch the model Victorian resort, with its own museum and aquarium, as well as the Cathedral of the Isles, Europe's smallest cathedral. The sportscotland National Centre Cumbrae is perfect for thrill seekers, while Country & Western fans will enjoy the week-long festival in late summer.

3 Opened in 1995, the Isle of Arran Distillery at Lochranza enjoys a spectacular location and is among the most recent to begin production in Scotland. The distillery has a visitor centre that offers fully guided tours, and the opportunity to pour your own bottle. Peat and artificial colourings aren't used in Arran whisky, which the distillers proudly claim offers 'the true spirit of nature'.

4 Dean Castle lies in Kilmarnock, East Ayrshire. Known for its astounding collection of medieval instruments and armoury, the castle sits in a glorious country park. Dean Castle is a family favourite, with a pet corner, an adventure playground and many different woodland walks and cycle routes. Contact the castle ahead of your visit to confirm seasonal opening hours for the Castle and its facilities.

5 For some crazy outdoor fun, head to Loudoun Castle, in Galston, Ayrshire. Loudoun Castle is a terrific day out for younger kids with swashbuckling fun in the Pirates' Cove, and pony treks and tractor rides at McDougal's Farm.

6 One of the finest collections of Bronze Age standing stones in Scotland can be found at scenic Machrie Moor on Arran. Around seven separate rings of stones have been discovered on the moor, with many still laying undiscovered beneath the peat which now grows in the vicinity. Visit during the summer solstice for a truly atmospheric experience.

FOOD AND DRINK

eatscotland.com

7   With excellent local produce such as cheese, ale, honey, ice cream and chocolate made to the highest standard, the Ayrshire & Arran kitchen will delight the palate and ignite culinary creativity.

8   Being on the west coast, seafood is delicious and could not be fresher. Take advantage of the opportunity to visit an up-market fish and chip shop or order the seafood at one of the excellent restaurants.

9   With such a range of natural & local ingredients to inspire, it is no wonder that Ayrshire & Arran has such fabulous restaurants. From Michelin Star and AA rosette winning restaurants to the best that gastro pubs have to offer, Ayrshire & Arran will satisfy the biggest gourmet's appetite.

GOLF

visitscotland.com/golf

10   Scotland is not only the Home of Golf, it is the home of links golf, the original form of the game that had its beginnings in Scotland over 600 years ago. Ayrshire & Arran have some of the finest and most famous links golf courses in the world; Western Gailes, Glasgow Gailes, West Kilbride, Royal Troon, Prestwick, Prestwick St Nicholas, Turnberry Alisa (pictured) and Shiskine on the Isle of Arran are all part of the Great Scottish Links collection.

11   However, it is not just the championship courses that Ayrshire is famous for. It is the good value and spectacular play of some of the lesser renowned courses. The charm and challenge of hidden gems like Belleisle, Brodick, Prestwick St. Cuthbert, Routenburn, Lochgreen and Largs, to name just a few, offer brilliant golf at a very reasonable price.

12   Ayrshire & Arran offer 3 different golf passes which are great value for money. By spending less on the course, you will have more to spend at the 19th hole. Visit ayrshire-arran.com for more information.

13   The Open returns to Ayrshire in 2009. It will see the world's best professional golfers flock to the legendry links of Turnberry to take on the greatest challenge in professional golf. If previous years are anything to go by, the competition will be fierce and the sun will be shining.

To find out more, call 0845 22 55 121 or go to visitscotland.com

WALKS

14   Going through forest, along the beach and across fields, the Kings Cave Forest Walk offers beautiful views across the sea to Kintyre. You also get the chance to explore the cave where reputedly Robert the Bruce hid from the English and was inspired by a spider to try, try and try again.

15   If you are looking for a short and pleasant walk with a combination of forest and open hills Dinmurchie Trail is ideal. Look out for local wildlife including deer, foxes, hares, kestrels and buzzards.

16   The Isle of Arran Coastal Way allows you to walk around the island. It is 75 miles long, but can be broken down into 7 more manageable sections. This route offers spectacular scenery and enjoyable challenges. Guide books are available at Brodick Visitor Information Centre.

17   The River Ayr Way is the first source to sea path network, which follows the river (66km) from its source at Glenbuck to the sea at Ayr. With beautiful scenery and abundant wildlife it is enjoyable to walk all or part of this route.

HISTORY

18   Robert Adam's fairytale Culzean Castle, perched on a clifftop overlooking Ailsa Craig and the Firth of Clyde, is a study in extravagance. A favourite of President Eisenhower, he was given his own apartment here by its previous owner, the Kennedy's. Fans of military history should explore the Armoury, filled with antique pistols and swords. 565 acres of country park surround the castle, with woodland walks, a walled garden and even a beach.

19   On 25th January 1759, Scotland's National Bard was born in the picturesque village of Alloway, a must for admirers of the man and his work. Here, you can visit Burns Cottage and a museum containing prized artefacts such as an original manuscript of Auld Lang Syne. Numerous surrounding sites, including the Brig O' Doon and Kirk Alloway, are familiar from Burns' epic poem Tam O'Shanter, which even has an entire visitor attraction dedicated to it.

20   The Isle of Arran Heritage Museum can be found on the main road at Rosaburn, just north of Brodick. The present group of buildings was once a working croft and smiddy, and include a farmhouse, cottage, bothy, milk house, laundry, stable, coach house and harness room. The fascinating exhibits reflect the social history, archaeology and geology of the island.

21   To visit Dalgarven Mill, and the Museum of Ayrshire Country life and Costume, is to step back in time. The comprehensive exhibition of tools, machinery, horse and harness, churns, fire irons and furnishings, evokes a powerful sense of the past, which cannot fail to leave an impression. The costume collection is constantly changing, and demonstrates how fashion has changed from 1780. The grind and splash of the wooden mill ensures the museum has an authentic ambience.

22   Dumfries House, the Georgian masterpiece designed by the renowned Scottish architect Robert Adam, opened to the public on 6th June 2008. The house, which sits in 2000 acres of East Ayrshire countryside, is opening its doors for the first time in 250 years. The former home of the Marquises of Bute, it was saved for the nation at the eleventh hour by a consortium of organisations and individuals brought together by HRH The Duke of Rothesay.

Ayrshire & Arran

Kildonan, Isle of Arran
Mrs M Stewart
Map Ref: 1F7

Open: All year
Craigdhu, East Bennan, Isle of Arran KA27 8SH
T: 01770 820225
E: mmwrstewart@supanet.com
W: cottageguide.co.uk/craigdhu

20900

2 Cottages	2 Public Rooms	Sleeps 4-5
Prices from:		
£260.00		**Per week**
£50.00		**Per night**

Lamlash, Isle of Arran
Mrs J Schofield
Map Ref: 1F7

Open: All year
Craig Dhu Cottage, Shore Road,
Lamlash, Isle of Arran KA27 8LH
T: 01770 600276
E: craigdhu1@hotmail.com
W: craigdhuholidaycottages.co.uk

30147

1 Cottage	1 Public Room	Sleeps 4
Prices from:		
£325.00		**Per week**
£50.00		**Per night**

Lamlash, Isle of Arran
Sunnybank
Map Ref: 1F7

Open: All year
Hazeldean, 38 Spring Hill Road,
Sheffield, South Yorkshire S10 1ES
T: 01142 680019
E: sunny.arran@hotmail.co.uk
W: sunnybank-arran.co.uk

68472

1 Bungalow	1 Public Room	Sleeps 4
Prices from:		
£250.00-390.00		**Per week**
On application		**Per night**

Ballantrae, Ayrshire
Mrs M Drummond
Map Ref:1F9

Open: All year
81 Main Street, Ballantrae, Ayrshire KA26 0NA
T: 01465 831343
M: 0776 5107373
E: marti@ardstinchar.freeserve.co.uk

12683

1 Cottage	1 Public Room	Sleeps 1-6
Prices from:		
£180.00		**Per week**
£40.00		**Per night**

Colmonell, by Girvan
Stinchar Cottages
Map Ref: 1F9

Open: All year
19 Main Street, Colmonell,
by Girvan, Ayrshire KA26 0RY
T: 01465 881265
E: shankland@colmonell.freeserve.co.uk
W: stincharcottages.co.uk

18084

3 Cottages	1-2 Public Rooms	Sleeps 2-6
1 Cabin	1 Public Room	Sleeps 2-4
Prices from:		
Cottage:	£200.00-400.00	**Per week**
	£50.00	**Per night**
Cabin:	£200.00-350.00	**Per week**
	£50.00	**Per night**

IMPORTANT: Prices stated are estimates and may be subject to change. Awards correct as of beginning of October 2008.

Galston, Ayrshire
Miss Audrey McCreight
Map Ref: 1H6

WAITING RADING

Open: All year

Fo reservations contact:
T: 07802 975949/07841 214164
E: keith@smfs.co.uk or
    audrey@smfs.co.uk

Located in beautiful Ayrshire countryside, this recently renovated cottage offers a very cosy stay. Situated just 30 minutes from Glasgow Airport and 20 minutes from Troon Harbour. Ideal location for touring Ayrshire, enjoying outdoor pursuits or visiting many tourist attractions.

83999

1 Cottage	2 Public Rooms	Sleeps 4

Prices from:
£55.00-65.00   **Per night**

Largs, Ayrshire
Kelburn Court
Map Ref: 1F5

★★★
SELF CATERING

Open: All year

55 Greenock Road, Largs KA30 8PL

T: 01475 686369
E: info@seger.co.uk

A very well appointed flat on the ground floor. Fine views over to Cumbrae. A short walk to town centre. Private parking. Ideal for a relaxing break in Largs and for touring this beautiful part of Scotland.

33482

1 Flat	1 Public Room	Sleeps 1-4

Prices from:
£250.00-425.00   **Per week**
£40.00   **Per night**

Maybole, Ayrshire
Culzean Castle Camping & Caravaning Club Site
Map Ref: 1G8

★★★
TOURING PARK

Open: 2 April-2 November

Culzean, Maybole, Ayrshire KA19 8JX

T: 0845 130 7633
E: vb@thefriendlyclub.co.uk
W: campingandcaravanningclub.co.uk/culzeancastle

This site is beautifully situated in the grounds of a fairytale castle. This fantastic example of Robert Adams' architecture stands dramatically on a cliff and our club site has amazing views across the sea to the Isle of Arran.

17831

From south on A77 turn left onto A719, site 4 miles on left. From north on A77 turn right onto B7023 in Maybole. After 100 yards turn left, site 4 miles on right.

Park accommodates 90

Total Touring Pitches: 90

Prices from:
£17.90-£23.30 per couple per night per pitch.

Ayrshire & Arran

Millport, Isle of Cumbrae
Mrs B McLuckie

Map Ref:1F6

★★ UP TO
★★★★
SELF
CATERING

Open: All year
Muirhall Farm, Larbert, Stirlingshire FK5 4EW
T: 01324 551570
E: b@l-guildford-street.co.uk
W: l-guildford-street.co.uk

⬛🖥️📺🖨️🛏️💺📻📠✝☺☺⚓⛵🎣📦🖊️⚡🔥⚙️🅿️📮♿£

42593

| 1 House | 2 Public Rooms | Sleeps 8 |
| 5 Apartments | 1 Public Room | Sleeps 2-10 |

Prices from:	
House £365.00-675.00	**Per week**
Apartment £155.00-406.00	**Per week**

The pier at Largs (a resort on the Firth of Clyde) with the ferry to Great Cumbrae in the background

IMPORTANT: Prices stated are estimates and may be subject to change. Awards correct as of beginning of October 2008.

Carsphairn View, Dumfries and Galloway

Dumfries & Galloway

Dumfries & Galloway is a naturally inspiring place, where landscapes, people and atmosphere conspire to make this a holiday experience you'll never forget.

Poets and artists have found inspiration here, capturing the look and feel of this beautiful region where 200 miles of coastline meet the tide and impressive hills rise up to greet the vast clear sky.

Remember to visit Kirkcudbright Artists' Town with its thriving artistic community, studios and galleries. From the Galloway Forest Park to the Solway Coast, there are so many picturesque places to explore and an abundance of wildlife habitats.

Look out for red deer, rare red kites, wild goats and even ospreys at Wigtown, Scotland's Book Town.

For those looking for adventure, there's world class mountain biking, challenging golf courses and many activity centres waiting to offer an adrenaline rush.

Whatever you choose to do, you'll find Dumfries & Galloway the perfect setting for a great holiday adventure.

Picnic, Priorwood Gardens, Melrose

DON'T MISS

1   As you travel through Dumfries & Galloway taking in the breathtaking scenery, you will come face to face with some amazing **environmental artworks** set in the landscape: head carvings in a sheep pen in the Galloway Forest Park, sculpture within Creetown town square, Andy Goldsworthy's Striding Arches near Moniaive. You never know what intriguing works you'll discover around the next corner!

2   Set in the pretty village of New Abbey, you'll find the origin of the word sweetheart at the splendid remains of this Cistercian Abbey, **Sweetheart Abbey**, established by Lady Devorgilla in memory of her husband John Balliol. Lady Devorgilla's love for her departed husband extended to carrying his embalmed heart around with her in an ivory box. Devorgilla and the heart are now buried together before the high altar. Be sure to pop in to the welcoming Abbey Cottage tearoom after your visit.

3   **Logan Botanic Garden**, under the care of the Royal Botanic Garden, Edinburgh is Scotland's most exotic garden where a fabulous array of bizarre and exotic plants and trees flourish outdoors. Warmed by the Gulf Stream, the climate provides ideal growing conditions for many plants from the southern hemisphere including a number of palm trees, which means you may forget where you are!

4   Built in the 17th century as a home for the first Duke of Queensberry, surrounded by the 120,000 acre Queensberry Estate, Country Park and grand Victorian Gardens, **Drumlanrig Castle** houses one of the finest private art collections in the UK. Join a Castle tour, a Land Rover Tour of the Estate, stroll through beautiful gardens and woodland walks enjoying the wildlife or take to your bike on a mountain bike trail. Kids are sure to enjoy the adventure playground, and the only museum in Scotland devoted to the history of cycling.

5   Set in a beautiful woodland location at Shambellie House, New Abbey, **The National Museum of Costume** opens the door on fashion and society from the 1850s to 1950s using lifelike room settings, in conjunction with a programme of special exhibitions, workshops and children's events.

6   Painters, artists and craftsmen have flocked to this area for centuries, no place more so than **Kirkcudbright** with its pastel coloured houses and traditional working harbour, now known as the Artists' Town for its historic artistic heritage. During the summer of 2009, the annual art exhibition, in the Town Hall, provides another chance to view the successful exhibition of 2000, '**The Homecoming**', featuring works by many of the artists who made Kirkcudbright famous as an artists' town.

HERITAGE

historic-scotland.gov.uk

7 **Caerlaverock Castle** is everyone's idea of a medieval fortress, with its moat, twin towered gatehouse and imposing battlements. Britain's only triangular castle, close to Dumfries, has a turbulent history which is brought back to life with a medieval re-enactment each summer.

8 An amazing exhibition at Eastriggs tells the story of the greatest munitions factory on earth. **Devil's Porridge** was the highly explosive mixture of nitro-glycerine and nitro-cotton, hand mixed in HM Factory Gretna during World War 1. The exhibition tells the story of over 30,000 brave men and women who worked in the factory. Get an insight into their work and social life through sight and sound. Why not follow in the footsteps of runaway couples and visit nearby romantic Gretna Green?

9 **Homecoming Scotland 2009** is inspired by the 250th anniversary of the birth of Scotland's National Bard, **Robert Burns**. Pay a visit to **Ellisland Farm**, just north of Dumfries, where he wrote the famous song Auld Lang Syne, sung all over the world at New Year celebrations, **Robert Burns House**, in Dumfries where he spent the last years of his life, **The Globe Inn** his favourite "howff" (pub) and his final resting place, The Mausoleum in **St Michael's Churchyard**.

10 Dating back to about 2000 BC, the impressive remains of 2 chambered cairns at **Cairnholy** are surrounded by hills on three sides, but open to the sea to the south. With glorious views across Wigtown Bay to the Machars and the Isle of Man, just relax and enjoy the tranquillity of this historic setting.

WALKS

visitscotland.com/walking

11 Scotland's longest waymarked walking route, the **Southern Upland Way**, runs 212 miles from Portpatrick in the west to Cockburnspath on the east coast, traversing some beautiful hill scenery. If this is too challenging, there are several sections which can be enjoyed as part of shorter walks. The coastal section from Portpatrick to Killantringan Lighthouse is a great place to start or why not try the 7½ mile section between Wanlockhead and Sanquhar for a completely different experience of the Way.

12 There are many great walks around **Moffat**, Scotland's first "Walkers are Welcome" town, where a warm welcome is guaranteed. **The Grey Mare's Tail**, in the care of the National Trust for Scotland, just a short drive from Moffat along the Selkirk Road, provides a glorious walk up the side of this impressive 61m waterfall. At the top of the falls you will reach its source, Loch Skene, whose clear waters are populated by vendace, Britain's rarest freshwater fish. Join an experienced walk leader to discover more great walks during the **Moffat Walking Festival**, held in October each year.

13 The **River Annan** walk, takes you along one side of the river from Battery Park, Annan to the village of Brydekirk, some 3 miles away, and returns along the opposite bank. This calm and peaceful walk never takes you far from the river. Should you require a shorter walk, there are 2 additional bridges over the river, allowing shorter walks of 1½ and 3 miles.

14 Enjoy a leisurely stroll along the **Jubilee Path**, linking the picturesque coastal villages of Kippford and Rockcliffe. This 2 mile walk can be made from either village as you return by the same route, although some detours can be made on other minor paths. All the walks within this section have been taken from **"Dumfries & Galloway 12 Walks"** guide which can be requested via visitdumfriesandgalloway.co.uk/walking.

WILDLIFE   visitscotland.com/wildlife

15 The graceful red kite has been successfully reintroduced to Galloway, in an area around Loch Ken. The **Galloway Red Kite Trail** takes a circular route through some impressive scenery, designed to take you closer to this elusive raptor with observation points and interpretation boards. Visit the feeding station at Bellymack Farm, near Laurieston where up to 30 have been seen at once - feeding time, 2pm.

16 **Ospreys** are back in Galloway after a break of over 100 years. Visit the County Buildings in Wigtown where you can watch live CCTV coverage of the ospreys, or edited highlights once the birds have left for Africa. Nesting ospreys can also be seen via a live video link at WWT Caerlaverock. Get an unparalleled view of ospreys sitting on their eggs and bringing up their young, the male coming back with fish to share with the female and taking over nesting duties while she eats.

17 Dumfries & Galloway is home to 20% of the Scottish population of **red squirrel**, making them easier to spot here than anywhere else. Red squirrels are well adapted to the woodland habitat in which they live, and you can even follow a waymarked Red Squirrel Walk within Dalbeattie Forest for a good chance of seeing these endearing mammals.

18 Thousands of **barnacle geese** return every year from Norway to winter on the wetlands of the Solway Firth. Dumfries & Galloway is an ornithologist's paradise, and places such as **WWT Caerlaverock** and **Mersehead Nature Reserve** make it easy to get up close. Why not join an expert on a guided walk to find out more about the birds and wildlife? Events take place from Mull of Galloway to Wanlockhead – pick up your free Countryside Events booklet at Visitor Information Centres.

ACTIVITIES

19 Scotland's Biking Heaven – world class mountain biking at the **7stanes** centres across southern Scotland offering mile upon mile of exhilarating fast flowing single track. The highlight at **Kirroughtree** is 'McMoab' with its huge slabs and ridges of exposed granite linked by boulder causeways. **Dalbeattie's** most talked about section is 'The Slab', sheer granite lying at an extreme angle. Are you brave enough to tackle 'The Dark Side', expert level northshore at **Mabie** or the 'Omega Man' descent at **Ae**, do you have the stamina to tackle the 58km 'Big Country Ride' at **Glentrool?** If this all sounds too much, don't worry, as these centres offer trails for beginners up to the most expert riders, and coupled with some stunning scenery you'll want to return again and again.

20 Explore Dumfries & Galloway using our extensive network of quiet B Roads. Take your time to discover the hidden treasures along the **Solway Coast Heritage Trail**, the **Border Reiver Trail** or **The Burns Heritage Trail**. For an extra special tour, hire a vintage car from Motorparty, near Dumfries and take to these quiet routes in style. Kirkpatrick McMillan invented the bicycle in Dumfries & Galloway and there's still no better place to travel on two wheels with over 400 miles of **signposted cycle routes**.

21 Dumfries' new state of the art leisure centre, **DG One** has a three separate swimming pool areas, one with a moveable floor, leisure water and flumes. The 80 station fitness suite is furnished with state-of-the-art equipment, and the sports hall is the biggest in Dumfries & Galloway. With a 1200 seating capacity, DG One is the ideal venue with a great programme of events and arts and entertainment performances.

22 Enjoy a fun packed break with attractions that are **great for all the family**. Show your artistic side by painting a pot at **Dalton Pottery Art Café** near Lockerbie, shoot down the astroslide at **Mabie Farm Park**, near New Abbey, take a trip on the flying fox followed by some delicious ice cream at **Cream o' Galloway**, Gatehouse of Fleet or take to the zip slide at **Dalscone Farm** on the outskirts of Dumfries. You will be spoiled for choice!

Ae, near Dumfries
Ae Forest Cottages
Map Ref: 2B8

★★ UP TO ★★★
SELF CATERING

Open: All year

Gubhill Farm, Ae Forest, Dumfries DG1 1RL

T: 01387 860648
E: gill@gubhill.co.uk
W: aefarmcottages.co.uk

Homely apartments on traditional farm in quiet valley with easy access to hill and forest yet in easy reach of Dumfries, Moffat and Thornhill. Rivers, ponds, meadows, paths and bike tracks to explore. Or just sit back and relax.

11162

	1 Public Room	Sleeps 8
1 Cottage		
2 Apartments	1 Public Room	Sleeps 4
Prices from:		
Cottage:	£398.00-780.00	**Per week**
	£64.00-125.00	**Per night**
Apartment:	£240.00-470.00	**Per week**
	£40.00-75.00	**Per night**

Auchencairn, by Castle Douglas
Mrs G Holland
Map Ref: 2A10

★★★
SELF CATERING

Open: All year

Craigshall, Shore Road, Auchencairn,
Castle Douglas, Kirkcudbrightshire DG7 1QY
T: 01556 640028
E: gail@craigshall.com   W: craigshall-cottage.co.uk

75997

1 Cottage	1 Public Room	Sleeps 2-6
Prices from:		
£350.00		**Per week**
£250.00		**Per 3 nights**

Borgue, Kirkcudbrightshire
Mrs L Brown
Map Ref: 1H10

★★★
SELF CATERING

Open: All year

Scottish Coastal Cottages, Roberton,
Borgue, Kirkcudbrightshire DG6 4UB

T: 01557 870217
E: brown@robertonhouse.co.uk
W: scottishcoastalcottages.co.uk

Craig is wonderfully situated in a stunning coastal location near its own beach. This traditional cottage stands alone in a field and has breathtaking views over the sea to the Isle of Man.

56740

1 Cottage	1 Public Room	Sleeps 1-4
Prices from:		
£320.00-600.00		**Per week**
£180.00		**Per 2 nights**

Castle Douglas, Kirkcudbrightshire
Airds Farm
Map Ref: 2A10

★★★
SELF CATERING

Open: All year

Airds Farmhouse, Crossmichael,
Castle Douglas, Kirkcudbrightshire DG7 3BG
T: 01556 670418
E: enquiries@airds.com
W: airds.com

70151

1 Cottage	1 Public Room	Sleeps 5
Prices from:		
£180.00		**Per week**

For a full listing of quality assured non-serviced establishments please see pages 229-385.

39

Castle Douglas, Kirkcudbrightshire
Barncrosh Leisure Company Ltd Map Ref: 2A10

★★ UP TO ★★★ SELF CATERING

14321

Open: All year
Barncrosh Farm, Castle Douglas,Kirkcudbright DG7 1TX
T: 01556 680216
E: enq@barncrosh.co.uk
W: barncrosh.co.uk

6 Houses	1-2 Public Rooms	Sleeps 7-12
1 Bungalow	1 Public Room	Sleeps 8
9 Apartments	1 Public Room	Sleeps 2-4

Prices from:	
£130.00	**Per week**
£65.00	**Per 2 nights**

Castle Douglas, Kirkcudbrightshire
Lochside Caravan & Camping Site Map Ref: 2A10

★★★ TOURING PARK

36135

Open: Easter-October
c/o Leisure and Sport, Community Centre,Cotton Street,
Castle Douglas DG7 1AJ
T: 01556 502949   01556 503806 (out of season)
E: scott.grant@dumgal.gov.uk
W: dumgal.gov.uk/caravanandcamping

Off A75 towards Castle Douglas by Carlingwark Loch

Park accommodates 108 pitches

Total Touring Pitches: 108
Prices from:
(108) £11.00   (53) £11.00   (108) £11.00

Castle Douglas, Kirkcudbrightshire
Mrs A Nelson (45 Academy Street) Map Ref:2A10

★★ SELF CATERING

42395

Open: April-October
11 Barnton Park Place, Edinburgh EH4 6ET
T: 0131 336 4779
E: f.nelson@blueyonder.co.uk

| 1 House | 2 Public Rooms | Sleeps 1-7 |

| **Prices from:** | |
| £300.00-340.00 | **Per week** |

Colvend, Kirkcudbrightshire
Oakwood & Ashwood Lodges Map Ref: 2A10

★★★★ SELF CATERING

19639

Open: All year
Mrs Anne Bell, Clifton Farm,
Southwick, Dumfries DG2 8AR
T: 01387 780206
E: anne@bellcliftonfarm.co.uk
W: bellcliftonfarm.co.uk

| 2 Cabins | 2 Public Rooms | Sleeps 2-6 |

Prices from:	
£425.00-750.00	**Per week**
£POA	**Per night**

Dalbeattie, Kirkcudbrightshire
Glenearly Caravan Park Map Ref: 2A10

★★★★ HOLIDAY PARK

28126

Open: All year
Glenearly, Dalbeattie, Dumfries & Galloway DG5 4NE
T: 01556 611393 E: glenearlycaravan@btconnect.com

*Take A711 from Dumfries to Dalbeattie. As approaching
Dalbeattie see brown tourist board signs. Turn right into
entrance adjacent to bungalow.*

Park accommodates 39 pitches

Total Touring Pitches: 39
Prices from:
£13.00-14.00   £13.00-14.00   £13.00-14.00
(2) £235.00-410.00 per week. Sleeps 2-6.

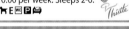

by Drummore, Wigtownshire
James & Christine McClymont Map Ref: 1F11

★★★★ SELF CATERING

76673

Open: All year
2 Low Currochtrie, Drummore,
Stranraer, Wigtownshire DG9 9QS
T: 01776 840242
E: mail@aulddairy.co.uk
W: aulddairy.co.uk

| 1 Cottage | 1 Public Room | Sleeps 2-6 |

Prices from:	
£400.00-595.00	**Per week**
3 nights short break - 70% weekly rate	

IMPORTANT: Prices stated are estimates and may be subject to change. Awards correct as of beginning of October 2008.

Gatehouse-of-Fleet, Kirkcudbrightshire
Mr Martin Howe
Map Ref: 1H10

★★
SELF
CATERING

Open: All year

41 Hotspur Street,
Tynemouth, Tyne & Wear NE30 4EN
T: 07968 873485
E: martin@martinhouse.com

74504

1 Cottage	4 Public Rooms	Sleeps 2-7
Prices from:		
£350.00-475.00		**Per week**
£55.00		**Per night**

Gatehouse-of-Fleet, Kirkcudbrightshire
Carrick Holiday Cottages
Map Ref: 1H10

★★★
SELF
CATERING

Open: All year

Owl Cote Byre, Carrick Shore,
Gatehouse-of-Fleet, Kirkcudbrightshire DG7 2DT
T: 01557 870010/01557 814130
M: 07719 263098
E: cathie@carrick-cottages.co.uk
W: carrickcottages.com

Single storey cottages 100 yards from the unspoilt
natural beauty of Carrick Bay with its safe sandy
beaches. Ideal location for sailing, cycling, golf,
bird-watching, coastal walks and relaxing. Sky,
Freeview. Kirkcudbright 10 miles. Pets welcome.
Real fires.

18279

2 Cottages	1 Public Room	Sleeps 2-8
Prices from:		
£260.00-470.00		**Per week**
£45.00 per night		**3 nights minimum**

The garden at Broughton House (NTS) in Kirkcudbright, Dumfries and Galloway

For a full listing of quality assured non-serviced establishments please see pages 229-385.

41

Gatehouse of Fleet, Kirkcudbrightshire
Rusko Holidays
Map Ref: 1H10

★★★
SELF
CATERING

Open: All year

Rusko, Gatehouse of Fleet,
Castle Douglas, Dumfries & Galloway DG7 2BS
T: 01557 814215
E: info@ruskoholidays.co.uk
W: ruskoholidays.co.uk

Beautiful large house and three charming cottages set amid magnificent Scottish scenery. Near historic town, golf course, coast, hills and sub-tropical gardens. The perfect getaway break. Walking, cycling, bird watching, or just relaxing.

52646

3 Cottages 1 House	1-2 Public Rooms 2 Public Rooms	Sleeps 1-6 Sleeps 2-12
Prices from:		
Cottage:	£225.00-660.00	**Per week**
	£135.00-372.00	**Per 3 nights**
House:	£794.00-1925.00	**Per week**
	£476.00-682.00	**Per 3 nights**

nr Gretna Green, Dumfriesshire
Cove Estate
Map Ref: 2C10

★★★★
SELF
CATERING

Open: All year

Jan & Andy Ritchie, Cove Estate, Kirkpatrick Fleming, by Lockerbie, Dumfries & Galloway DG11 3AT
T: 01461 800285   M: 07779 138694
E: jan534@btinternet.co.uk   W: brucescave.co.uk and coveestate.co.uk

83629

2 Suites	1 Public Room	Sleeps 2-6
Prices from:		
£350.00-600.00		**Per week**
£75.00-90.00 Per night		**Min 3 nights**

Kippford, nr Dalbeattie
Mr Alistair Richardson
Map Ref: 2A10

★★
SELF
CATERING

Open: All year excl Xmas and New Year

Croft Corner, Meikle Richorn, Dalbeattie DG5 4QT
T: 01556 611549

Secluded position with panoramic views. Only a short drive to the popular coastal villages of Rockcliffe, Kippford and Sandyhills where sailing and fishing are well catered for. Forest walks and cycle trails (including 7Stanes) and golf courses all within easy reach.

79872

1 House	1 Public Room	Sleeps 6
Prices from:		
£425.00-550.00		**Per week**
£100.00 per night		**Min 3 nights**

Kirkcudbright
Brighouse Bay Holiday Cottages
Map Ref: 2A10

★★★★
SELF
CATERING

Open: All year

Brighouse, Borgue, Kirkcudbright DG6 4TS
T: 01557 870606   M: 07923 374756
E: margaret@brighouse.wanadoo.co.uk
W: brighousebayholidaycottages.com

81313

1 Cottage	1 Public Room	Sleeps 1-6
Prices from:		
£300.00-595.00		**Per week**
£180.00		**Per 3 nights**

IMPORTANT: Prices stated are estimates and may be subject to change. Awards correct as of beginning of October 2008.

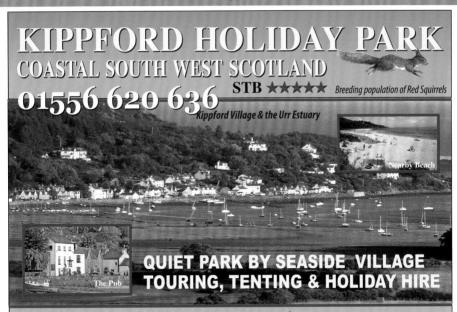
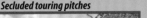

For a full listing of quality assured non-serviced establishments please see pages 229-385.

43

Dumfries & Galloway

Kirkcudbright
Silvercraigs Caravan & Camping Site — Map Ref: 1A10

★★★★ TOURING PARK

Open: Easter-October

c/o Leisure & Sport, Community Centre, Cotton St, Castle Douglas, Dumfries & Galloway DG7 1AJ

T: 01557 330123 (Easter-Oct) 01556 503806 (Oct-Easter)
E: scott.grant@dumgal.gov.uk W: dumgal.gov.uk/caravanandcamping

In Kirkcudbright off Silvercraigs Road. Access via A711, follow signs to site.

54708

Park accommodates 50 pitches		
Total Touring Pitches: 37		
Prices from:		
(37) £11.00	(13) £11.00	(37) £11.00

near Langholm, Dumfriesshire
Mrs L Luescher — Map Ref: 2C8

★★★★ SELF CATERING

Open: All year

The Kerr, Canonbie, Dumfriesshire DG14 0XP
T: 013873 71420
E: glendinningfarms@btopenworld.com
W: glendinningfarms.btinternet.co.uk

Charming traditional stone-built cottage situated on 3700 acre working hill farm. Beautifully furnished accommodation, equipped to a high standard. Double glazed and electrically heated throughout. Open log fire. Lovely peaceful location, ideal for walking, cycling or touring southern Scotland.

32728

1 Cottage	1 Public Room	Sleeps 1-5
Prices from:		
£350.00-425.00		**Per week**
£75.00		**Per night**

Lochmaben, Dumfriesshire
Kirk Loch Caravan & Camping Site — Map Ref: 2B9

★★★ TOURING PARK

Open: Easter-October

c/o Leisure & Sport, Community Centre, Cotton St, Castle Douglas, Dumfries & Galloway DG7 1AJ
T: 07746 123783 (Easter-Oct) 01556 503806 (Oct-Easter)
E: scott.grant@dumgal.gov.uk W: dumgal.gov.uk/caravanandcamping

In Lochmaben enter via Kirkloch Brae.

34339

Park accommodates 30 pitches		
Total Touring Pitches: 30		
Prices from:		
£8.90	£8.90	£8.90

New Galloway, Castle Douglas
Glenlee Holiday Houses — Map Ref: 1H9

★★★ SELF CATERING

Open: March-December

Mrs C Agnew, Glenlee Holiday Houses, New Galloway, Castle Douglas, Kirkcudbrightshire DG7 3SF
T: 01644 430212
E: agnew@glenlee-holidays.co.uk
W: glenlee-holidays.co.uk

Five charming cottages round a central courtyard beautifully converted from the former home farm. Wonderful woodland walks and waterfalls. Free fishing. Pets welcome. Open fires. An excellent base for exploring Galloway.

28233

5 Cottages	1-2 Public Rooms	Sleeps 1-7
Prices from:		
£320.00-500.00		**Per week**
£50.00-75.00		**Per night**

IMPORTANT: Prices stated are estimates and may be subject to change. Awards correct as of beginning of October 2008.

Newton Stewart, Wigtownshire
Creebridge Holiday Park
Map Ref: 1H10

21233

★★★ HOLIDAY PARK

Open: All year

Minnigaff, Newton Stewart DG8 6AJ
T/F: 01671 402324
W: creebridgecaravanpark.com

Five minute walk to Newton Stewart. Plenty to see and do. Golf, fishing, walking, cycling nearby. Ideal base for touring. Additional charge for electricity.

Located off the A75 in Minnigaff outside Newton Stewart.

Park accommodates 18 pitches
Total Touring Pitches: 18
Prices from:

🚐 + car £10.00-16.00   ⛺ + car £10.00-16.00
⛺ £8.00-12.00

Parton, Kirkcudbrightshire
Loch Ken Holiday Park
Map Ref: 2A9

35849

★★★ HOLIDAY PARK

Open: March-November

Parton, Castle Douglas, Dumfries & Galloway DG7 3NE
T: 01644 470282 E: penny@lochkenholidaypark.co.uk
W: lochkenholidaypark.co.uk

Located on the A713, 7 miles north-west of Castle Douglas at Parton.

Park accommodates 81 pitches
Total Touring Pitches: 81
Prices from:

🚐 (25) £16.00-19.00   ⛺ (50) £13.00-17.00
🚐 (6) £16.00-19.00
🏠 (10) £280.00-480.00 per week.

Port Logan, Wigtownshire
Matthew & Aileen Caughie
Map Ref: 1F11

79919

★★★★ SELF CATERING

Open: All year

Kirkbride Farm, Port Logan, DG9 9NP
T: 07769 806259
E: stay@kirkbridecottages.co.uk
W: kirkbridecottages.co.uk

Set in the heart of our large farm with superb elevated position and magnificent panoramic sea views. Our well appointed cottages are equipped and furnished to the highest standard to ensure a comfortable stay. Ideal choice for a family holiday.

2 Cottages	2-3 Public Rooms	Sleeps 1-13

Prices from:	
£350.00-1650.00	**Per week**
£45.00-300.00	**Per night**

For a full listing of quality assured non-serviced establishments please see pages 229-385.

45

Portpatrick, Wigtownshire
Mrs S McCaig
Map Ref: 1F10

★★★★
SELF CATERING

Open: All year
North Port-O-Spittal, Portpatrick,
Stranraer, Wigtownshire DG9 9AD
T: 01776 810412

50211

1 Bungalow	1 Public Room	Sleeps 6
Prices from:		
£200.00-460.00		**Per week**

Portpatrick, Wigtownshire
Portpatrick Holidays
Map Ref: 1F10

★★★★
SELF CATERING

Open: All year
47 Main Street, Portpatrick, DG9 8JW
T: 01776 810555
E: info@portpatrickholidays.co.uk
W: portpatrickholidays.co.uk

Portpatrick Holidays currently have six 4 star holiday units ranging from one to five bedrooms. All houses are fully equipped to a very high standard and benefit from magnificent views over the sea to Ireland and Dunskey Glen.

26986

3 Cottages	2 Public Rooms	Sleeps 4-9
2 Houses	2 Public Rooms	Sleeps 10-12
1 Apartment	1 Public Room	Sleeps 2
Prices from:		
£16.00		**Per person per night**

Sandhead, Stranraer
Culmorebridge Cottages
Map Ref: 1F10

★★★★
SELF CATERING

Open: All year
Mr & Mrs J Sime, Oak Cottage,
Sandhead, Stranraer DG9 9DX
T: 01776 830539
E: jandmsime@aol.com
W: culmorebridge.co.uk

Spacious, warm, comfortable three bedroom, two bathroom bungalows. Excellent furnishings and fittings. Situated in beautiful peaceful location, close to sea, but only short distance from main routes. Nine acres woodland, garden areas, viewpoints and ponds. Cottages/paths wheelchair friendly throughout.

68427

4 Cottages	1 Public Room	Sleeps 1-6
Prices from:		
£390.00		**Per week**

IMPORTANT: Prices stated are estimates and may be subject to change. Awards correct as of beginning of October 2008.

nr Stranraer, Wigtownshire
Mrs J Waugh (Self Catering)　　Map Ref: 1F10

Open: All year

East Challoch Farmhouse,
Dunragit, Near Stranraer, DG9 8PY
T:　01581 400391

Traditional semi detached former dairy house on edge of farm. Comfortably furnished and well equipped with part sea views and close to nearby beaches. Ideally situated for visiting local gardens, birdwatching, golf and fishing and touring the unspoilt south-west Scotland coast.

70742

★★★ SELF CATERING

1 House	2 Public Rooms	Sleeps 1-6
Prices from:		
£210.00		**Per week**
£100.00		**Per 2 nights**

---

near Thornhill, Dumfriesshire
Mrs M Craig　　Map Ref: 2A8

Open: All year

The Garth, Tynron, Thornhill
Dumfriesshire DG3 4JY
T:　01848 200364
E:　chrisandmimi@supanet.com
W:　visitscotland.com

★★★ SELF CATERING

58295

1 Cottage	1 Public Room	Sleeps 1-2
Prices from:		
£243.00		**Per week**
£130.00		**Per 3 nights**

Whithorn, Wigtownshire
Mrs Morag Forsyth　　Map Ref: 1H11

Open: Easter-end October

Old Bishopton, Whithorn, Wigtownshire DG8 8DE
T:　01988 500754
E:　morag@whithorn.net

★★★ SELF CATERING

48237

1 Bungalow	4 Public Rooms	Sleeps 2-4
Prices from:		
£180.00		**Per week**
£30.00		**Per night**

Isle of Whithorn, Wigtownshire
Seagulls　　Map Ref: 1H11

Open: All year

Mrs A Hammond, 58 Sunderton Lane,
Clanfield, Waterlooville, Hampshire PO8 0NT
T:　02392593468
E:　ann@thehammonds.freeserve.co.uk
W:　laighisle.co.uk

★★ SELF CATERING

10261

1 Chalet	1 Public Room	Sleeps 2-6
Prices from:		
£200.00-250.00		**Per week**
£30 per night (excl. Summer)		**Min 2 nights**

For a full listing of quality assured non-serviced establishments please see pages 229-385.

47

St Abbs Head

Scottish Borders

The Scottish Borders stretches from rolling hills and moorland in the west, through gentler valleys to the high agricultural plains of the east, and on to the rocky Berwickshire coastline with its secluded coves and picturesque fishing villages.

In the bright spring months, fresh new growth fills the valleys and forests of the Scottish Borders. Enjoy the lure of long summer days or relax in more mellow shades of autumn when mauves and purples tint the moors. The Scottish Borders is truly 'A Destination for all seasons'.

There are many lovely towns to visit in the Scottish Borders and a huge amount to see. Take the four great Borders abbeys of Dryburgh, Kelso, Jedburgh and Melrose. They were founded by King David I

in the 12th century and though each is in ruins, a strong impression of their former glory remains.

Hawick is the centre of the local textile industry and you can still pick up bargain knitwear, tartans and tweeds at the many outlets and mills in the area.

Abbotsford, the former home of Sir Walter Scott, is now a visitor attraction just west of Melrose and you can also visit his old courtroom in Selkirk, preserved as it was in the 1800s when he presided over trials.

There's some great walking in the Scottish Borders with over 1500 miles of designated walking routes. The St Cuthbert's Way stretches 62 miles from Melrose to Lindisfarne; the Southern Upland Way is a 212 mile coast to coast trek taking in forest, farmland and hills while the Borders Abbeys Way is a very pleasant 65 mile circular route visiting all four historic abbeys.

DON'T MISS

1   Take the B6404 St Boswells to Kelso road and turn onto the B6356, signposted Dryburgh Abbey. About 1 mile along this road there is a junction signposting **Scott's View** to the right. Follow this road for about 2 miles for panoramic views of the Eildon Hills and the Scottish Borders countryside stretched out before you. Great spot for a picnic.

2   **Traquair House**, near Innerleithen, dates back to the 12th century and is said to be the oldest continuously inhibited house in Scotland. Discover the Traquair Maze, one of the largest hedged mazes in Scotland. Watch out for the Medieval Fayre in May and the Summer Fair in August.

3   The **Berwickshire Coastal Path** combines great natural beauty, with magnificent birdlife. There are spectacular views with sandstone cliffs, small coves, sandy beaches and natural harbours. The 15 mile (24km) route is way-marked and strong walkers may manage it in one day. Most people prefer to break it down into shorter stretches and stop off at the pretty villages along the way. Eyemouth is the largest town on this route – enjoy fresh fish and chips from Giacopazzi's by the harbour and watch out for the family of seals in the harbour!

4   The four great **Borders Abbeys** of Kelso, Melrose, Jedburgh and Dryburgh are a must see for any visitor to the area. Melrose Abbey is said to be the resting place of the casket containing the heart of King Robert the Bruce. Dryburgh is the burial place of Field Marshall Earl Haig and Sir Walter Scott. All of the Abbeys are under the care of Historic Scotland. Kelso is the most incomplete and has free access. For access to Melrose, Jedburgh and Dryburgh an admission charge applies.

5   **Floors Castle** in Kelso is the largest inhabited castle in Scotland and home to the Roxburghe family. The house has 365 windows, one for every day of the year. The castle, grounds, gardens and restaurant are open from Easter to October with The Terrace Restaurant, walled gardens, playground and garden centre open all year. The castle hosts an extensive events calendar throughout the year.

RETAIL, CRAFTS & TEXTILES   visitscottishborders.com

6   There are still **independent artists and craftsmen** working in wool in the Borders - spinners, weavers, knitwear designers and tapestry makers - but they have also been joined by workers in other crafts, potters, glass makers, workers in stone and wood and many more, who are more than willing to welcome the visitor into their workshop and demonstrate their skills. Many sell direct to the public. A visit to the Scottish Borders will allow you to enjoy the beautiful scenery of rolling hills, meandering rivers and romantic landscapes, which provide a source of inspiration to the artists.

7   In many towns throughout the Scottish Borders, high streets are a vibrant mix of independent specialists and boutiques. Bakers carrying on the tradition of the Selkirk Bannock, a fruited tea bread; butchers winning plaudits for their haggis recipes; confectioners satisfying the Scottish sweet tooth for Soor Plooms and Hawick Balls; each add to the pleasure of shopping here. Of particular note is **Peebles**, recently voted the **'Top Independent Retailing Town in Scotland'** for its quality range of individual shops.

8   The Scottish Borders knitwear business is world famous, take a look at the catwalks each season and it is clear that top designers around the world are increasingly turning to Scotland for inspiration and materials. **Tartan, tweed, wool and cashmere**; all strut their stuff down the runway. The Scottish Borders is at the very hub of the world's woollen industry, creating colours and garments for the ever changing and exacting fashion houses. **Lochcarron of Scotland** has recently opened a new retail outlet in Selkirk and **Hawick Cashmere, Peter Scott** and **Pringle of Scotland** are all found in Hawick.

WALKS   visitscottishborders.com

9   The life and progress of St Cuthbert provided the inspiration for the **St Cuthbert's Way** walking route. Starting in Melrose and ending on Holy Island (Lindisfarne) it passes through rolling farmland, river valleys, sheltered woods, hills and moorland culminating in The Holy Island Causeway, passable only at low tide. The full route is 100km / 60 miles in length but this can be broken down into shorter stages.

10   The **Borders Abbeys Way** is a circular route linking the four great ruined Border Abbeys in Kelso, Jedburgh, Dryburgh and Melrose. The full route is 105km / 65 miles in length and can easily be broken down into stages.

11   The **Southern Upland Way** is Britain's first official coast to coast long distance footpath. It runs 212 miles (340km) from Portpatrick in the west to Cockburnspath on the Berwickshire coast. This route takes in some of the finest scenery in Southern Scotland and, of the total route, 130km / 82 miles is in the Scottish Borders. The Way goes through many remote uplands areas, providing a real challenge for the experienced walker, while some parts lie within easy reach of towns and villages and are more suitable for families and the less ambitious.

12   The **John Buchan Way** is named after the writer and diplomat who had many associations with the Scottish Borders. The 22km / 13 mile route takes you from Peebles to Broughton and ends at the John Buchan centre, which houses a collection of photographs, books and other memorabilia.

To find out more, call 0845 22 55 121 or go to visitscotland.com

ACTIVITIES

13   Glentress and **Innerleithen** in the Tweed Valley and **Newcastleton** to the south have a massive reputation for some of the best **mountain biking** in the UK and beyond. Glentress is probably the best biking centre in Britain, with brilliant trails of all grades, a top-notch cafe, a bike shop with bike hire, changing and showering facilities, and a great atmosphere. Innerleithen, situated just a few miles south east of Glentress, is quite different from its better-known sister. It's a venue for the more experienced rider and home to the Traquair XC Black run – not for the faint-hearted! All three centres are part of the **7Stanes** – 7 mountain biking centres of excellence across the South of Scotland.

14   'Freedom of the Fairways' is Scotland's best selling **golf** pass. This pass offers access to 21 superb courses ranging from the coastal course at Eyemouth to the winner of the 'most friendly' 9-hole course, St Boswells to the championship The Roxburghe and Cardrona. The Freedom of the Fairways scheme runs between April and October and offers both senior and junior passes, available to book online at visitscottishborders.com

15   Along with mountain biking the Scottish Borders offers some superb road **cycle** routes through the peaceful Borders countryside. The **Borderloop** is a magnificent 250 mile way-marked circular route linking Peebles in the west with the Berwickshire coast at Eyemouth. The **Tweed Cycleway** starts 650 feet above sea level near Biggar and runs close by to the River Tweed through the Scottish Borders to the finish at Berwick upon Tweed. This 89 mile way-marked route can be broken down into sections and it takes in some of the key Borders towns en-route, including Peebles, Melrose, Kelso and Coldstream.

16   The Scottish Borders has everything for the angler. From the internationally famous salmon **fishing** on the **River Tweed** to the excellent sea trout fishing on its tributaries; from the rainbow trout in the local lochs to wild brown trout in the rivers; and from the course fishing of the lower Tweed to the sea fishing off the Berwickshire coast; there is plenty to choose from.

WILDLIFE   visitscotland.com/wildlife

17   The elusive, native **red squirrel** can still be found in pockets throughout the Scottish Borders. Try Paxton House, nr Berwick, Tweed Valley Forest Park and Floors Castle Estate. Anywhere with plenty of trees and peace and quiet, be sure to keep your eyes peeled!

18   The **Tweed Valley Osprey Watch** has two centres; Glentress and Kailzie Gardens. Both are open from Easter until mid-August and September respectively. Enjoy live camera action from an osprey nest within The Tweed Valley Forest Park. Follow the progress of the family, from nest building in spring to chicks hatching in May, to fledglings in August. Both centres have a variety of interpretative materials and volunteer guides. A small admission charge applies.

19   On the Berwickshire Coast, **St Abbs Head** is a National Nature Reserve. It is a landmark site for birdwatchers and wildlife enthusiasts. Thousands of breeding seabirds can be seen between April and August and migrating birds in October. The scenery is stunning with wide-sweeping views from the lighthouse on 'The Head' north towards Edinburgh and the Fife coast and south towards Holy Island, Bamburgh and the Farne Islands. There are a number of way-marked trails around the reserve which all start from the car park and information centre.

Ashkirk, Selkirkshire
Mr Nicholas Brown
Map Ref: 2D7

★★★★
SELF
CATERING

41505

Open: All year
New Woll Estate, Ashkirk, Selkirkshire, TD7 4PE
T: 01750 32799
E: wollgolf@tiscali.co.uk
W: wollgolf.co.uk

5 Houses	1-2 Public Rooms	Sleeps 4-6

Prices from:

£343.00-913.00	Per week
£95.00-171.00	Per night

Carfraemill, nr Lauder
Lauder Camping & Caravanning Club Site
Map Ref: 2D5

★★★★★
TOURING
PARK

17833

Open: 2 April-2 November 2009

Carfraemill, Oxton, Lauder TD2 6RA
T: 0845 130 7633
E: vb@thefriendlyclub.co.uk
W: campingandcaravanningclub.co.uk/lauder

There is something for everyone around this peaceful, relaxing club site. The river runs the full length of the site and there is plenty to see in the area – including Edinburgh, Scotland's capital city.

From Lauder, turn right at roundabout onto A697, then left at the Lodge hotel (signposted). Site on right, behind the Lodge Hotel.

Park accommodates pitches 63

Total Touring Pitches: 63
Prices from:
£16.30-£21.90 per couple per night per pitch.

(4) From £309.00-457.00 per week. Sleeps 4.

Thistle

Cockburnspath, Berwickshire
Cloverknowe & Dovecothall
Map Ref: 2E5

★★★ UP TO
★★★★
SELF
CATERING

44383

Open: All year

Pathhead Farm, Cockburnspath,
Berwickshire, TD13 5XB
T: 01368 830318   M: 07980 877481
E: mlauder@supanet.com
W: cloverknowecottages.co.uk

Two traditional stone built cottages, each with self-contained garden and carefully renovated to provide comfortable and flexible accommodation. Located on a working farm on the Berwickshire coast, they provide an ideal base for the Scottish Borders, Edinburgh, Northumberland and beyond.

3 Cottages	1 Public Room	Sleeps 2-8

Prices from:

£280.00-850.00	Per week
£60.00-200.00	Per night

IMPORTANT: Prices stated are estimates and may be subject to change. Awards correct as of beginning of October 2008.

Cockburnspath, Berwickshire
Red Gauntlet, Tower Farm

Map Ref: 2E5

★★★
SELF
CATERING

Open: All year

Tower Farm Holiday Homes,
3 Gardener Street, Dunbar, East Lothian, EH42 1AP
T: 01368 864782   M: 0778 979 1667
E: info@tower-farm.co.uk
W: tower-farm.co.uk

Enjoy sea views at this old farm steading location, only 50 minutes south of Edinburgh; an ideal spot to explore the Scottish Borders and surrounding area. A perfect holiday house equipped to a high standard with comfort in mind.

73383

1 House	1 Public Room	Sleeps 4-10
Prices from:		
£1400.00		**Per week**
£840.00		**3 nights**

Coldstream, Berwickshire
Mrs Sheila Letham

Map Ref: 2E6

★★
SELF
CATERING

Open: All year

Fireburn Mill, Coldstream, Berwickshire, TD12 4LN
T: 01890 882124
E: andrewletham@tiscali.co.uk

37989

2 Cottages	1 Public Room	Sleeps 2-6
Prices from:		
£170.00		**Per week**

Jedburgh, Roxburghshire
Mrs A Fraser

Map Ref: 2E7

★★★
SELF
CATERING

Open: All year

Overwells Country Cottages,
Overwells, Jedburgh, Roxburghshire TD8 6LT
T: 01835 863020
E: abfraser@btinternet.com
W: overwells.co.uk

A converted mill on a farm three miles from Jedburgh. Maintained to the highest standard. Millhouse has a stunning view to the Cheviot Hills. An ideal base for sporting activities or exploring the beautiful Borders countryside.

48862

1 Cottage	2 Public Rooms	Sleeps 1-4
Prices from:		
£250.00-400.00		**Per week**
£160.00		**2 nights minimum**

Jedburgh, Roxburghshire
Old Bridge End Self Catering

Map Ref: 2E7

★★
SELF
CATERING

Open: All year

69 High Street, Innerleithen, Peeblesshire EH44 6HD
T: 01896 831544
E: m.dbrand@btinternet.com
W: old-bridge-end-self-catering.co.uk

82544

1 Apartment	1 Public Room	Sleeps 1-4
Prices from:		
£200.00-350.00		**Per week**
£33.00-55.00		**Per night**

For a full listing of quality assured non-serviced establishments please see pages 229-385.

53

eee

Scottish Borders

eeeeeeeeeeeeeeeeeeeeeeeeeeeeeeeeeeeeeeeeeeeeeeeeeee

Kelso, Roxburghshire
Burnbrae Holidays

Map Ref: 2E6

★★★★
SELF
CATERING

Open: All year

Burnbrae Mill, Nenthorn,
Kelso, Roxburghshire TD5 7RY

T: 01573 225570
E: vsn@burnbraehol.co.uk
W: burnbraehol.co.uk

Three peaceful cottages. Light, airy, each generously equipped, comfortable accommodation for two. Extra beds. Log fire. Heating throughout. Level access to all rooms. South-facing conservatory, open views to Cheviots. 12ha. river margin, pasture, large pond, trees, wildlife. Walks from site.

3 Cottages	2 Public Rooms	Sleeps 2

Prices from:	
£260.00-410.00	**Per week**
£58.00-97.00	**Per night**

Melrose, Roxburghshire
Mrs Rosemary Dale

Map Ref: 2D6

★★★
SELF
CATERING

Open: April-November

The Holmes, St Boswells,
Melrose, Roxburghshire TD6 0EL

T: 01334 653628
E: enquiries@holidayholmes.co.uk
W: holidayholmes.co.uk

Large self catering holiday accommodation on a private estate set on the banks of the River Tweed. Spacious wing of Victorian mansion house set in grounds of a delightful estate ideal for families and large groups.

1 House	2 Public Rooms	Sleeps 10-11

Prices from:	
£450.00	**Per week**

Melrose, Roxburghshire
Eildon Holiday Cottages

Map Ref: 2D6

★★★ UP TO
★★★★
SELF
CATERING

Open: All year

Dingleton Mains, Melrose, Roxburghshire, TD6 9HS

T: 01896 823258
E: info@eildon.co.uk
W: eildon.co.uk

Eildon Holiday Cottages comprises 6 award-winning, modern, self catering holiday "cottages", five of which are Category 1 (unassisted wheelchair access). Walking, riding, fishing, cycling and golf are available nearby. Magnificent views over Tweed valley and Lammermuir hills. One hour from Edinburgh.

6 Cottages		Sleeps 2-6

Prices from:	
£290.00-670.00	**Per week**
£45.00	**Per night**

eeeeeeeeeeeeeeeeeeeeeeeeeeeeeeeeeeeeeeeeeeeeeeeeeee

IMPORTANT: Prices stated are estimates and may be subject to change. Awards correct as of beginning of October 2008.

Peebles
Glenrath Holiday Homes
Map Ref: 2C6

28319

Open: All year

Glenrath Farm, Kirkton Manor, Peebles,
Peeblesshire, EH45 9JW

T: 01721 740221/ 01721 740226
E: langhaugh@glenrathfarms.co.uk
W: aboutscotland.com/langhaugh/farm.html

Peebles luxury 4 bedroomed house with lovely enclosed garden on a quiet residential estate in Peebles. Also tranquil very comfortable country cottages on a private estate in picturesque Manor Valley 10 minutes from Peebles. Excellent base for Edinburgh, hillwalking, fishing, biking and golfing.

3 Cottages	1 Public Room	Sleeps 2-8
1 House	1 Public Room	Sleeps 2-8
Prices from:		
Cottage:	£250.00	**Per week**
House:	£300.00-750.00	**Per week**

Peebles
Mrs J Holmes
Map Ref: 2C6

33622

Open: March-November

Kerfield Coach House,
Innerleithen Road, Peebles EH45 8BG

T: 01721 720264
E: ph.kerfield@tiscali.co.uk
W: kerfieldcoachhouse.co.uk

1 Cottage	1 Public Room	Sleeps 4
Prices from:		
£300.00-450.00		**Per week**

Peebles
Lyne Cottage
Map Ref: 2C6

70045

Open: All year

Lyne Farmhouse, Peebles, EH45 8NR

T: 01721 740255
E: lynefarmhouse@btinternet.com
W: lynefarm.co.uk

1 Cottage	2 Public Rooms	Sleeps 2-8
Prices from:		
£350.00		**Per week**
£25.00	**Per person per night min 2 nights**	

Nr Peebles
Chapelhill Farm Cottages
Map Ref: 2C6

13106

Open: All year

Mr John Smith, Chapel Hill Farm, EH45 8PQ

T: 01721 720188
F: 01721 729734

3 Cottages	Sleeps 5-6
Prices from:	
£320.00	**Per week**

West Linton, Peeblesshire
Slipperfield Loch Cottages
Map Ref: 2B6

54972

Open: All year

Slipperfield House,
West Linton, Peeblesshire EH46 7AA

T: 01968 660401
E: cottages@slipperfield.com **W:** slipperfield.com

1 Cottage	1 Public Room	Sleeps 2-4
1 Bungalow	1 Public Room	Sleeps 2-6
Prices from:		
Cottage:	£360.00-530.00	**Per week**
Bungalow:	£450.00-670.00	**Per week**

For a full listing of quality assured non-serviced establishments please see pages 229-385.

55

The Old Town skyline at dusk, Edinburgh

EDINBURGH AND THE LOTHIANS

Each year, more than three and a half million visitors arrive in Scotland's capital and discover one of the finest cities in the world.

Whether you're partying at the biggest Hogmanay celebrations on Earth or taking your seat in the audience at the planet's largest arts festival, Edinburgh always offers more than you could ever hope to take on in one visit.

Streets steeped in history

No trip to Edinburgh is complete without a visit to the world famous Castle. Over a million people take to its ramparts every year. Many then set off down the Esplanade and onto the Royal Mile, touching history with every step. During the Festival weeks, hundreds of performers take to the Mile in an explosion of colour and sound, creating an exciting mêlée that changes every day.

Although the trappings of modern life are never far away in the shops, cafés and bars, the Old Town's fascinating history is impossible to ignore. Edinburgh's ghosts whisper in the closes: grave robbers and thieves rubbing shoulders with poets, philosophers, kings and queens – each conjured up and colourfully interpreted in the museums, exhibitions and visitor attractions you'll pass along the way.

A city of beauty

The city's rich history is matched by its beauty. Architecturally, Edinburgh is a stunning city. That beauty extends to its parks, gardens and wild places. Don't miss the Royal Botanic Garden, the view from the top of majestic Arthur's Seat or the Water of Leith walkway, which brings a touch of the countryside right into the city.

Edinburgh is also a city by the sea with a rapidly changing seafront. The busy port of Leith has been transformed in recent years and it boasts a wonderful selection of bars and restaurants.

Get out of town

Further out of town, there's much to explore. Take a trip down the coast to places like Aberlady, Gullane, Longniddry, Dirleton, North Berwick and Dunbar. Play golf on top class courses, watch the seabirds on beautiful sandy beaches or take a boat trip around the Bass Rock.

You could cycle for miles along the Union Canal towpath, visit Roslin Glen and the mysterious Rosslyn Chapel, head for Linlithgow and its ruined Palace or enjoy a thrilling day out at the Musselburgh races.

What's more, 2009 is a big year for Scotland – we're celebrating the 250th anniversary of the birth of Robert Burns. There's over 200 special events taking place throughout the year, all over Scotland. Go to homecomingscotland2009.com to find out about events in this area.

So what is it you'd like to do on your visit to Edinburgh and the Lothians? And where would you like to stay? From luxury apartments to city flats, trendy aparthotels to seaside cottages, you've got so much to choose from. While most people wouldn't associate the capital city with caravans and camping, there are some fine options within Edinburgh itself as well as a splendid array of parks throughout the Lothians. So whether you fancy a seaside location or country park you're sure to find a superb holiday base in an area that will continue to inspire you and leave you longing for more.

Ceilidh Culture

What's On?

Ceilidh Culture
27 March – 19 April 2009
A vibrant celebration of traditional Scottish arts.
ceilidhculture.co.uk

Edinburgh International Science Festival
6 – 18 April 2009
Stir the curiosity of inquiring minds.
sciencefestival.co.uk

Mary King's Ghost Fest
8 - 18 May 2009 (dates provisional)
Explore Edinburgh's haunted places.
edinburghghostfest.com

Edinburgh International Film Festival
17- 28 June 2009
The festival where the films are the stars.
edfilmfest.org.uk

The Gathering 2009
25 – 26 July 2009
Edinburgh will witness one of the largest clan gatherings in history as part of the Homecoming 2009 celebrations.
clangathering.org

Edinburgh Military Tattoo
7 – 29 August 2009
This military extravaganza is an international favourite.
edinburgh-tattoo.co.uk

Edinburgh Festival Fringe
7 – 31 August 2009
The largest arts festival on the planet.
edfringe.com

Edinburgh International Festival
7 – 30 August 2009
The very best of opera, theatre, music and dance.
eif.org.uk

East Lothian Food & Drink Festival
25 – 27 September 2009
Food and entertainment for all ages.
foodanddrinkeastlothian.com

Edinburgh's Christmas
24 November – 25 December 2009
Edinburgh becomes a winter wonderland.
edinburghschristmas.com

Edinburgh's Hogmanay
29 December – 1 January 2010
The world's favourite place to celebrate Hogmanay.
edinburghshogmanay.com

All dates correct at time of publication. Please check before booking. VisitScotland cannot be held responsible for any inaccuracies

57

DON'T MISS

1   Stroll down the **Royal Mile**, so-called because it boasts Edinburgh Castle at the top and the Palace of Holyroodhouse at the bottom. Browse through the wide range of quirky, independent gift shops and stop off in one of the many tea rooms or cafés along the way. Upon reaching the Canongate, you will find the new Scottish Parliament, famed for its striking contemporary architecture.

2   Never a month passes without a major event or **festival** in Edinburgh, the International Science Festival in April, the Heineken Cup, the Rugby Sevens World Series and Children's Theatre in May, International Film Festival in June, Jazz and Blues in July, Christmas or Hogmanay. And of course, there's the world's largest international arts festival in August, taking in the Fringe, the Tattoo, the Book and International Festivals.

3   **The National Galleries of Scotland** exhibit work by some of the world's most influential artists in five galleries across Edinburgh. From Rembrandt and Monet, to Picasso and Bacon, not to mention major touring exhibitions.

4   **Linlithgow Palace**, once an important royal residence and birthplace of Mary, Queen of Scots, is now a magnificent ruin. Set beside a loch, with a huge number of rooms, passages and stairways, you can imagine what life must have been like in this vast palace.

5   Within minutes of Edinburgh, you can stroll along the white sands of **East Lothian**, with only the sound of water lapping on the shore. Head for Gullane, Yellowcraig or North Berwick. The sheer expanse of each beach is truly breathtaking.

6   Set amidst the beauty of Roslin Glen, the mysterious **Rosslyn Chapel** is undoubtedly Scotland's most outstanding Gothic church. According to Dan Brown's The Da Vinci Code, this chapel is on the trail of the Holy Grail, which only adds to the intrigue.

FOOD AND DRINK   eatscotland.com

7   **Farmers' markets** are great ways to get the freshest quality, local produce. Held on every Saturday morning on Castle Terrace and the last Saturday of each month in Haddington (except December) in East Lothian, be sure to pop along early to pick up the very best supplies.

8   For the story of whisky, try either the **Scotch Whisky Experience** in Edinburgh or **Glenkinchie Distillery**, by Pencaitland. The former tells how the amber nectar is made and how best to enjoy it, while the latter is ideal for warming you up on your return from walking the East Lothian beaches.

9   For restaurants with the best views in Edinburgh, visit **Oloroso** on Castle Street or the **Forth Floor Restaurant** at Harvey Nichols in Edinburgh. Combine fine dining with panoramic cityscapes. Don't forget your camera!

10 **East Lothian** holds its annual **Food and Drink Festival** in late September each year, giving you ample opportunity to savour the best of the region's produce and hospitality.

HISTORY AND HERITAGE

11 **The Scottish Mining Museum** is located at the former Lady Victoria Colliery at Newtongrange in Midlothian. The five-star attraction has turned the story of Scotland's coal into a fascinating tour and exhibition. With every guide an ex-miner, you'll see and hear the authentic stories of a working mine.

12 **The Royal Yacht** *Britannia*, former floating home of the monarchy, offers a superb visitor experience that will guide you through 40 years of royal life, including private quarters, the sick bay and the laundry!

13 Edinburgh is one of Europe's most haunted cities, surrounded by myth and legend. Take a journey back in time and experience the narrow underground closes at **Real Mary King's Close** or try one of the many walking ghost tours, if you dare!

14 With fantastic views over the Firth of Forth, the imposing 15th century **Blackness Castle** looks almost poised to set sail. Explore its darkened corridors, which still capture the atmosphere of a garrison fortress and state prison.

SHOPPING

15   **Multrees Walk** is located at the heart of the city and is headed by Scotland's flagship Harvey Nichols. Known locally as The Walk, shops include Louis Vuitton, Links of London, Azendi, Calvin Klein Underwear and Reiss. The focal point for luxury shopping, this is a must-see for all shoppers.

16   Surrounding the city centre, Edinburgh has a number of urban villages where you'll find **specialist shops**, from up-and-coming designers to crafts, jewellery, food and gifts. In the centre, try the West End, Victoria Street and Royal Mile, while Bruntsfield and Stockbridge are a little further from the city centre.

17   Only a short bus ride from the city centre, take a refreshing stroll along the waterfront in **Leith**, where you'll find independent shops and galleries, alongside contemporary bars and cafes.

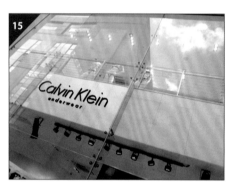

ACTIVITIES AND ATTRACTIONS

18   Edinburgh and the Lothians is a superb base for **golf**, whether you choose to play some of the city's fine courses or go east to the coast. Stay in the city for the challenges of Bruntsfield Links, Prestonfield or Duddingston. Or head to the Lothians for the perfect mixture of parkland and links courses. You can enjoy inspirational views across to Fife from some courses in East Lothian.

19   There is a fantastic range of **walks and trails** throughout the scenic and historic countryside of Edinburgh and the Lothians. Through the heart of the city runs the Water of Leith where a peaceful path offers a handy escape from the vibrant centre. In East Lothian the stretch of beach from Gullane to Yellowcraig is perfect for a walk or a picnic, whilst Roslin Glen in Midlothian and Avon River in West Lothian are exhilarating walks to make best use of an afternoon.

20   The area is home to some of Scotland's most impressive visitor attractions. From interactive exhibits to wonders of the natural world, there is something for everyone. Head to the **Scottish Seabird Centre** in North Berwick or **Edinburgh Zoo** to see wildlife up close, travel back in time at **Our Dynamic Earth** or try rock climbing at the **Edinburgh International Climbing Arena**.

21   With free entry to over 30 top attractions, free return airport and city centre bus transport, a free comprehensive guidebook as well as many exclusive offers, the **Edinburgh Pass** is the best way to discover all that Edinburgh has to offer. Buy a 1, 2 or 3 day Pass from edinburghpass.com or from one of the Visitor Information Centres in Edinburgh (see next page).

To find out more, call 0845 22 55 121 or go to visitscotland.com

MAP

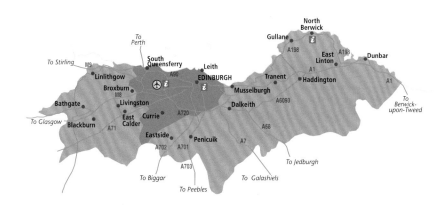

©Collins Bartholomew Ltd 2008

VISITOR INFORMATION CENTRES

Visitor Information Centres are staffed by people 'in the know' offering friendly advice, helping to make your stay in Scotland the most enjoyable ever . . . whatever your needs!

Edinburgh and Lothians

Edinburgh	3 Princes Street, Edinburgh, EH2 2QP	Tel: 0131 473 3820
Edinburgh Airport	Main Concourse, Edinburgh International Airport, EH12 9DN	Tel: 0131 344 3120
North Berwick	1 Quality Street, North Berwick, EH39 4HJ	Tel: 01620 892197

LOCAL KNOWLEDGE • WHERE TO STAY • ACCOMMODATION BOOKING • PLACES TO VISIT • THINGS TO DO • MAPS AND GUIDES TRAVEL ADVICE • ROUTE PLANNING • WHERE TO SHOP AND EAT LOCAL CRAFTS AND PRODUCE • EVENT INFORMATION • TICKETS

For information and ideas about exploring Scotland in advance of your trip, call our booking and information service **0845 22 55 121** or go to **visitscotland.com**

If calling from outside the UK and Ireland **+44 1506 832 121**   From Ireland **1800 932 510**

A £4 booking fee applies for accommodation bookings made via a Visitor Information Centre and through our booking and information service.

Live it. Visit *Scotland.*
visitscotland.com/wheretofindus

Edinburgh and the Lothians

Broxburn, West Lothian
Bankhead Farm
Map Ref: 2B5

★★★★★
SELF
CATERING

Open: All year
Bankhead Farm, Dechmont,
Broxburn, West Lothian EH52 6NB
T: 01506 811209
E: bankheadbb@aol.com
W: bankheadfarm.com

2 Cottages	2 Public Rooms	Sleeps 4-6
Prices from:		
£600.00-800.00		**Per week**
£150.00		**Per night**

72170

Dunbar, East Lothian
Belhaven Bay Caravan Park
Map Ref: 2E4

★★★★
HOLIDAY
PARK

Open: all Mar-Oct, then hol. homes w/ends-Jan
Edinburgh Road, Dunbar, East Lothian EH42 1TU
T: 01368 865956 **E:** belhaven@meadowhead.co.uk
W: meadowhead.co.uk

Exit A1 at Thistley Cross roundabout, turn east onto A1087 at Beltonford roundabout. The park is ½ mile along A1087 on the left hand side of the road

67622

Park accommodates 59 pitches		
Total Touring Pitches: 27		
Prices from:		
(27) £13.75	(25) £8.50	(27) £13.75
(7) £280.00 per week.		

Dunbar, East Lothian
David Gilchrist
Map Ref: 2E4

★★★
SELF
CATERING

Open: All year
West Meikle Pinkerton, Dunbar, East Lothian EH42 1RX
T: 07866 164021
E: mail@goldenoakchalet.com
W: goldenoakchalet.com

78083

1 Chalet	1 Public Room	Sleeps 1-6
Prices from:		
£300.00-490.00		**Per week**
£70.00		**Per night**

East Calder, nr Edinburgh
Linwater Caravan Park
Map Ref: 2B5

★★★★
TOURING
PARK

Open: 13 March-1 November 2009
West Clifton, East Calder, West Lothian EH53 0HT
T: 0131 333 3326
E: linwater@supanet.com **W:** linwater.co.uk

Signposted from junction 1 of M9 or from Wilkieston on A71 along B7030.

63596

Park accommodates 60 pitches		
Total Touring Pitches: 50		
Prices are From:		
(50) £12.00-16.00	(10) £10.00-14.00	
(50) £12.00-16.00	Timber Tents (3) From £22.00.	

Eastside, Penicuik, nr Edinburgh
Susan Cowan
Map Ref: 2C5

★★★★
SELF
CATERING

Open: All year

Eastside Farm, Penicuik, Midlothian EH26 9LN
T: 01968 677842
E: info@eastsidecottages.co.uk
W: eastsidecottages.co.uk

Escape to a hilltop hideaway! Three charming
cottages on working family farm in Pentland Park.
Hillside location with spectacular views. Edinburgh
eight miles. See www.eastsidecottages.co.uk for
details.

24293

3 Cottages	1 Public Room	Sleeps 2-6
Prices from:		
£250.00-720.00		**Per week**

Edinburgh
AJEM, 142 Easter Road
Map Ref: 2C5

Open: All year
AJEM Self Catering Edinburgh,
132/4 Easter Road, Edinburgh EH7 5RJ
T: 07828 122904
E: info@selfcateringedinburgh.eu
W: selfcateringedinburgh.eu

77748

2 Apartments	1 Public Room	Sleeps 1-6
Prices from:		
£350.00		**Per week**
£50.00		**Per night**

Edinburgh
Calton Apartments
Map Ref: 2C5

Open: All year
HO: Abbey Hotel,
9 Royal Terrace, Edinburgh EH7 5AB
T: 0131 556 3221
E: caltonapts@ednet.co.uk
W: townhousehotels.co.uk

City centre location. Short walk to Princes Street,
Calton Hill, Playhouse Theatre and Edinburgh Castle.
Furnished to a high standard. An ideal base to
explore historic Edinburgh. Free Wi-Fi internet access.
Freeview digital TV. Free private car parking.

17678

8 Apartments	1 Public Room	Sleeps 2-6
Prices from:		
£300.00		**Per week**
£50.00		**Per night**

Edinburgh
City Nights
Map Ref: 2C5

Open: All year
97 Market Street, Musselburgh EH21 6PY
T: 0131 665 7140
E: simpson@edinburgh-nights.co.uk
W: edinburgh-nights.co.uk

43154

2 Apartments	1 Public Room	Sleeps 1-4
Prices from:		
£260.00-640.00		**Per week**
£52.00-88.00		**Per night**

Edinburgh
45 Cumberland Street
Map Ref: 2C5

Open: All year
Margaret Kingan, Blairshinnoch,
Kirkgunzeon, Dumfries DG2 8JJ
T: 01387 760230
E: info@45cumberlandstreet.co.uk
W: 45cumberlandstreet.co.uk

Lovely ground floor apartment for up to three
people. City centre. Great base for exploring
Edinburgh. Double bedroom (ensuite) and smaller
single bedroom (ensuite). Very comfortable.
Restaurants, galleries and shops all within strolling
distance. Short breaks from three nights.

15425

1 Apartment	1 Public Room	Sleeps 1-3
Prices from:		
£490.00-980.00		**Per week**
£70.00-140.00		**Per night**

For a full listing of quality assured non-serviced establishments please see pages 229-385.

63

Edinburgh and the Lothians

Edinburgh
Mrs J Cumming   Map Ref: 2C5

★★★★
SELF CATERING

Open: All year
Smithfield Garden Cottage, Peebles EH45 8QG
T: 07762 180229
E: apartmentbyroyalmile@hotmail.com
W: apartmentbyroyalmile.com

1 Apartment	2 Public Rooms	Sleeps 2
Prices from:		
£315.00-650.00		**Per week**
£40.00		**Per night**

Edinburgh
Edinburgh First (Self Catering)   Map Ref: 2C5

★
SELF CATERING

Open: July-September
The University of Edinburgh,
18 Holyrood Park Road, Edinburgh EH16 5AY
T: 0131 651 2184
E: edinburgh.first@ed.ac.uk
W: edinburghfirst.com

104 Flats	1 Public Room	Sleeps 3-6
Prices from:		
£350.00		**Per week**

Edinburgh
Edinburgh Flats   Map Ref: 2C5

★★★ UP TO
★★★★★
SELF CATERING

Open: All year
27 Queen Street, Edinburgh EH2 1JX
T: 07973 345559
E: info@edinburghflats.co.uk
W: edinburghflats.co.uk

Beautifully renovated superbly furnished apartments in Georgian townhouses only metres from central Princes Street. Period elegance with hi-tech specifications (plasma TVs, integrated sound systems, wireless internet). Combining hotel facilities with home comforts. 24 hour on-call service.

3 Apartments	1 Public Room	Sleeps 1-6
Prices from:		
£300.00-1250.00		**Per week**
£50.00-150.00		**Per night**

Edinburgh
Fairnington Premier Properties   Map Ref: 2C5

★★★ UP TO
★★★★
SELF CATERING

Open: All year
Office, 152 Dalkeith Road,
Edinburgh, Midlothian EH16 5DX
T: 01890 820590/0131 667 7042 **M:** 07721853940
E: muriel@fairnington.com
W: fairnington.com

Superb apartments viewing Holyrood Park with access to pool and leisure centre. Five minutes Royal Mile. Plus luxury villa in exclusive area with panoramic views of city and castle. Double garage, electronic doors.

1 House	2 Public Rooms	Sleeps 2-12
3 Apartments	1-2 Public Rooms	Sleeps 2-6
Prices from:		
House:	£800.00-2100.00	**Per week**
	POA	**Per night**
Apartment:	£290.00-900.00	**Per week**
	POA	**Per night**

IMPORTANT: Prices stated are estimates and may be subject to change. Awards correct as of beginning of October 2008.

Edinburgh
Fountain Court Apartments
Map Ref: 2C5

★★★
SELF
CATERING

26652

Open: All year
123 Grove Street, Fountain Bridge,
Edinburgh EH3 8AA
T: 0131 622 6677
E: enq@fcapartments.com
W: fcapartments.com

Apartments 122		Sleeps 2-6
Prices per apartment from:		
£700.00		**Per week**
£69.00		**Per night**

Edinburgh
Merchiston Apartment
Map Ref: 2C5

★★
SELF
CATERING

38104

Open: All year
Invermark, 60 Polwarth Terrace, Edinburgh EH11 1NJ
T: 0131 337 1066
M: 07799690323
E: merchistonapartment@hotmail.co.uk

1 Apartment	2 Public Rooms	Sleeps 5
Prices from:		
£500.00-750.00		**Per week**

Edinburgh
Mr & Mrs A Morrison
Map Ref: 2C5

★★★
SELF
CATERING

75059

Open: All year
Albern Holiday Lets, 10/2 Ettrick Road,
Edinburgh EH10 5BJ
T: 07914 639962/0131 228 3232
E: albernholidaylets@btinternet.com
W: albernholidaylets.co.uk

1 Apartment	1 Public Room	Sleeps 4
Prices per apartment from:		
£350.00-690.00		**Per week**
£55.00-110.00		**Per night**

Edinburgh
Mortonhall Caravan & Camping Park
Map Ref: 2C5

★★★
HOLIDAY
PARK

39087

Open: March-January
38 Mortonhall Gate, Frogston Road East, Edinburgh EH16 6TJ
T: 0131 664 1533 **E:** mortonhall@meadowhead.co.uk
W: meadowhead.co.uk

Leisure facilities:
Exit the A720 Edinburgh city bypass at either the Straiton or
Lothianburn junctions and follow the signs to Mortonhall.

Park accommodates 274 pitches		
Total Touring Pitches: 250 Prices from:		
£13.50	£13.50	£13.50
Wigwam (4) £14.00pppn. Sleeps max. 5		
(20) £295.00 per week. Sleeps max. 8		

Edinburgh
One O'Clock Gunn
Map Ref: 2C5

★ UP TO
★★★
SELF
CATERING

66868

Open: All year
30 Spylaw Street, Colinton, Edinburgh EH13 0JT
T: 0131 441 2373
E: oneoclockgunn@aol.com
W: oneoclockgunn.com

4 York Place -City centre location,
sleeping up to four people.

5 Coates Place- City centre location,
sleeping from two up to eight people.

8 Woodhall Road, Colinton, Edinburgh.
Village location sleeping up to six people.

3 Apartments	2 Public Rooms	Sleeps 4-8 max.
Prices from:		
£500.00-550.00		**Per week**

For a full listing of quality assured non-serviced establishments please see pages 229-385.

65

Edinburgh and the Lothians

Edinburgh
Rossie Place, Mrs Julie Reynolds   Map Ref: 2C5

★★★
SELF
CATERING

Open: All year
11 Paisley Gardens, Willowbrae, Edinburgh EH8 7JN
T: 0131 661 1934   **M:** 07939523580
E: julie@edinburghlets.org
W: edinburghlets.org

52217

1 Apartment	1 Public Room	Sleeps 7

Prices from:	
£400.00-900.00	**Per week**
£60.00-140.00	**Per night**

Edinburgh
Dr Julie Watt   Map Ref: 2C5

★★★★
SELF
CATERING

Open: All year
630 Lanark Road, Edinburgh EH14 5EW
T: 0131 538 0352
E: julie@candlemaker.fsnet.co.uk
W: edinburghselfcatering.webeden.co.uk

17886

1 Apartment	1 Public Room	Sleeps 2-4

Prices per apartment from:	
£310.00-680.00	**Per week**
£55.00	**Per night**

Edinburgh
The Wright Place in the City   Map Ref: 2C5

★★★★
SELF
CATERING

Open: All year
73 Easter Drylaw Place, Edinburgh EH4 2QH
T: 0131 467 9844
E: wrightplace@blueyonder.co.uk
W: the-wright-place-in-the-city.com

70336

1 Apartment	2 Public Rooms	Sleeps 2

Prices per apartment from:	
£315.00	**Per week**
£60.00	**Per night**

Lasswade, Midlothian
Gorton House and Cottages   Map Ref: 2C5

★★ UP TO
★★★
SELF
CATERING

Open: All year
Gorton House, Lasswade,
Edinburgh, Midlothian EH18 1EH
T: 0131 440 4332
E: info@gorton.plus.com   **W:** gorton.plus.com

28683

4 Cottages	1 Public Room	Sleeps 4-5
3 Houses	1 Public Room	Sleeps 5-7

Prices from:		
Cottage:	£355.00-505.00	**Per week**
	£60.00-90.00	**Per night**
House:	£450.00-785.00	**Per week**
	£100.00-200.00	**Per night**

Linlithgow, West Lothian
Beecraigs Caravan & Camping Site   Map Ref: 2B4

★★★★
TOURING
PARK

Open: All year
West Lothian Council, Beecraigs Country Park,
The Park Centre, Linlithgow EH49 6PL

T: 01506 844516   **E:** mail@beecraigs.com
W: beecraigs.com

14668

Open all year. Ideal countryside retreat. Many
walks and activities within country park. Modern
toilet facilities. Hard standing for caravans and
motorhomes. Under five year-olds go free. Pets free.

Leisure Facilities: ✪

*J3 or J4 off M9 motorway to Linlithgow. Follow signs for
Beecraigs Country Park – two miles along Preston Road,
turn left, first right to reception situated within the Beecraigs
Restaurant.*

Park accommodates 42 pitches	
Total Touring Pitches: 30	

Prices are From:	
🚐 (30) £14.00-18.00	⛺ (12) £12.00-21.00
🚍 (30) £14.00-18.00	

66

North Berwick, East Lothian
Fishermen's Hall
Map Ref: 2D4

★★★★
SELF
CATERING

Open: All year
Mrs J. M. Boggon, The Banks, Hopetoun,
South Queensferry, West Lothian EH30 9SL
T: 0131 331 3878
E: boggon@lineone.net
W: fishermenshall.com

58142

1 Cottage	2 Public Rooms	Sleeps 6-8
Prices from:		
£475.00-850.00		**Per week**
3 nights short breaks at 60% of weekly charge		

North Berwick, East Lothian
Mrs Gillian Hunter
Map Ref: 2D4

★★ UP TO
★★★★
SELF
CATERING

Open:
Stonelaws Farm, East Linton, East Lothian EH40 3DX
T: 01620 870606
E: colin.hunter54@btinternet.com
W: stonelawsholidaycottages.co.uk

73558

2 Cottages	1 Public Room	Sleeps 1-4
Prices from:		
£250.00-550.00		**Per week**
£50.00		**Per night**

North Berwick, East Lothian
Kirkpatrick Self Catering
Map Ref: 2D4

★
SELF
CATERING

Open: All year
2 Hillview Road, Edinburgh EH12 8QN
T: 0131 334 5951
E: ian-g-kirkpatrick@hotmail.com

40770

1 Flat	1 Public Room	Sleeps 1-4
Prices from:		
£165.00-295.00		**Per week**
£105.00-180.00		**Per 3 nights**

North Berwick, East Lothian
Tantallon Caravan and Camping Park
Map Ref: 2D4

★★★★
HOLIDAY
PARK

Open: March-October
North Berwick, East Lothian EH39 5NJ
T: 01620 893348
E: tantallon@meadowhead.co.uk
W: meadowhead.co.uk

37916

*From South - exit A1 at Thistley Cross onto A1087 and follow signs to
North Berwick. Turn right onto A198. Park is one mile past Tantallon
Castle. From North - exit A1 onto A198 and follow signs to North
Berwick. Then follow signs to Tantallon Park.*

Park accommodates 158 pitches

Total Touring Pitches: 89 Prices from:
🚐 (89) £13.50 ⛺ (55) £13.50 🚐 (89) £13.50
Wigwam (4) £16.50 Sleeps 5 max.

(10) £310.00 per week. Sleeps 8 max.

For a full listing of quality assured non-serviced establishments please see pages 229-385.

67

IMPORTANT: Prices stated are estimates and may be subject to change. Awards correct as of beginning of October 2008.

The Victorian Temperate Palm House in the Royal Botanic Garden ('The Botanics'), Edinburgh

For a full listing of quality assured non-serviced establishments please see pages 229-385.

69

The Clyde Auditorium, Glasgow

GREATER GLASGOW AND CLYDE VALLEY

Glasgow is one of Europe's most exciting destinations, with all the energy and sophistication of a great international city.

There's so much choice it's difficult to know where to start and even harder to know when to stop.

And wherever you go in Scotland's largest city, you'll be overwhelmed by the irresistible friendliness of its inhabitants.

Shop 'til you drop

It's easy to get caught up in Glasgow's fast-moving social whirl – especially if you like shopping. Outside of London, there isn't a UK city that can touch Glasgow for quantity and quality.

If you're in need of retail therapy you'll revel in the elegance of Princes Square, the diversity of the Buchanan Galleries and the classy opulence of the Italian Centre in the chic Merchant City.

Glasgow is easily Scotland's most fashion-conscious city and its passion for all things stylish brings an exciting edge to its boutiques and malls.

That passion spills over into the cafés and bars, boutique hotels, restaurants, nightclubs, theatres and music venues. Glasgow nightlife is always exhilarating whether you're checking out the next hit band at King Tut's, watching groundbreaking theatre at Oran Mor or just sipping a pint in Ashton Lane.

The Glasgow Platter

Glasgow has one of the best restaurant scenes in the UK. From traditional afternoon tea at One Devonshire Gardens or the Willow Tearooms to every major culinary style in the world, Glasgow's restaurants have a rapidly growing international reputation.

For a selection of eating establishments available in and around Glasgow go to eatscotland.com

To find out more, call 0845 22 55 121 or go to visitscotland.com

An Art Lover's Paradise

Glasgow is an outstanding city to step out in. The impressive legacy of its most eminent architectural sons, Charles Rennie Mackintosh and Alexander 'Greek' Thomson, can be seen in the city's streets, while its galleries and museums host one of Europe's biggest collections of civic art.

The Kelvingrove Art Gallery and Museum, restored in 2006 at a cost of £27.9 million, is a must see. This popular visitor attraction is free to enter and hosts some 8,000 exhibits.

Don't spend so long there that you miss the Burrell Collection in Pollok Country Park or the University of Glasgow's Hunterian Museum & Art Gallery.

The Great Outdoors

Despite the endless hustle and bustle, peace and tranquillity are never far away. Glasgow is known as the 'dear green place' and there are over 70 parks and gardens in the city where you can escape for a while.

Beyond the city limits, you can trace the river through the Clyde Valley all the way to the picturesque Falls of Clyde in Lanarkshire, just beside the immaculately preserved village of New Lanark which is a World Heritage Site.

On the Clyde coast you can take a trip 'doon the watter' in the P.S. Waverley, the world's last sea-going paddle steamer. At Strathclyde Country Park in Motherwell and Mugdock Country Park near Milngavie you'll enjoy a wide range of outdoor activities including walking, cycling, horse riding and much more.

Glasgow's maritime history can be explored at The Scottish Maritime Museum in Braehead and in Paisley you'll find an impressive Abbey dating back to 1163. Both places are just a short journey away from the city of Glasgow.

What's more, 2009 is a big year for Scotland – we're celebrating the 250th anniversary of the birth of Robert Burns. There's over 200 special events taking place throughout the year, all over Scotland. Go to homecomingscotland2009.com to find out about events in this area.

Whatever you choose to do, wherever you stay, a visit to Glasgow and Clyde Valley will be a revelation and you'll be very glad you came.

Christmas lights are turned on, George Square, Glasgow

What's On?

Celtic Connections
15 January – 1 February 2009
Recognised as the principal Celtic Festival in the UK, this event is a must for any traditional music lover.
celticconnections.com

Glasgow Film Festival
12 – 22 February 2009
Premiers and previews galore as Glasgow celebrates its 5th festival celebrating the city's love of the movies.
glasgowfilmfestival.org.uk

Aye Write!
The Bank of Scotland Book Festival
6 – 14 March 2009
An annual literature festival celebrating both Scottish and international writers.
ayewrite.com

Glasgow Art Fair
23 – 26 April 2009
With over 50 galleries and art organisations in one place, the 14th national fair is THE place to view, buy and sell art in Scotland.
glasgowartfair.com

Paisley Beer Festival
29 April – 2 May 2009
Scotland's largest real ale festival, with well over 100 real ales on tap.
paisleybeerfestival.org.uk

Glasgow River Festival
Mid July 2009
A weekend of land and water-based entertainment for the whole family on the banks of the River Clyde.
glasgowriverfestival.co.uk

Kirkintilloch Canal Festival
29 – 30 August 2009
Two days of fun in the 'Canal Capital of Scotland'.
kirkintillochcanalfestival.org.uk

World Pipe Band Championships
15 August 2009
Piping Live: International Piping Festival, August 10 - 16 2009
A piping spectacular, with Music of the Clans – a special series of Homecoming events dedicated to Scottish heritage and piping.
pipinglive.co.uk

Merchant City Festival, Glasgow
24 – 27 September 2009
Festival celebrating the cultural richness of the city's old commercial quarter.
merchantcityfestival.com

Glasgow's Hogmanay
31 December 2009 – 1 January 2010
Bring in the New Year with live bands.
winterfestglasgow.com

All dates correct at time of publication. Please check before booking. VisitScotland cannot be held responsible for any inaccuracies

71

DON'T MISS

1   **Kelvingrove Art Gallery and Museum** - Scotland's most visited museum re-opened in 2006 following a three-year, £27.9 million restoration project. It now has a collection of 8,000 objects on display over three floors – 4,000 more than ever before. Old favourites and exciting new arrivals are waiting to welcome you. Forget everything you think you know about museums, Kelvingrove is different.

2   Located within the World Heritage Site of **New Lanark**, the Falls of Clyde Wildlife Reserve covers 59 hectares, has woodland along the River Clyde gorge and 4 spectacular waterfalls. Breeding peregrine falcons, tawny owls and sparrowhawks rule the air while badgers, foxes and roe deer can also be seen. The river is home to otters, dippers, herons and kingfishers. The recently refurbished visitor centre includes interactive interpretation highlighting these key species.

3   It's all about fun when you're on holidays but what if at the same time you could sneak in a bit of learning? **Glasgow Science Centre** has the answer. Easily accessible from Glasgow city centre by car, subway, train or bus, the Centre stands tall and instantly recognisable on the River Clyde. The interactive exhibits can keep not only the children entertained but the adults too and that's before you hit the IMAX cinema and the ScottishPower Planetarium.

4   Glasgow University's **Hunterian Art Gallery & Museum** hosts an extensive art collection of superb quality, with outstanding works by Rembrandt, Whistler, Chardin, Stubbs, the Scottish Colourists and many more. See the most significant collection of original Charles Rennie Mackintosh works in the world and visit the Mackintosh House – his Glasgow home.

5   One of Scotland's most magnificent medieval buildings, **Glasgow Cathedral**, is one of the few Scottish medieval churches to survive the reformation of 1560 intact. The tomb of St. Mungo, Glasgow's patron saint and founder, is located within the church. Beside the Cathedral is Glasgow Necropolis, the "City of the Dead". This Victorian garden cemetery is a real hidden gem and offers a unique insight into Glasgow's social and economic heritage.

6   The **Gallery of Modern Art** opened in 1996 and is housed in an elegant, neo-classical building in the heart of the city centre. The building was refurbished to house the city's contemporary art collection, and is an appealing combination of old and new architecture. GoMA is now the second most visited contemporary gallery outside London, offering an outstanding programme of temporary exhibitions and workshops.

FOOD AND DRINK

eatscotland.com

7 In the Merchant City, **Rogano** (11 Exchange Place) is a must. Since 1935 Rogano has been preparing the finest Scottish seafood and serving it in its unique Art Deco surroundings with the wonderful flair of that bygone era. Rogano is a Glasgow institution.

8 With a motto like "Think global, eat local" it is not surprising that the menu at **Stravaigin** (28 Gibson St) has been built from diverse world influences while focusing on the best of Scottish ingredients. The result is a collection of eclectic and globe trotting dishes. Stravaigin is an excellent example of West End dining.

9 Special occasions will go off nicely at **Brian Maule at Chardon d'Or** (176 West Regent St). Brian Maul was head chef at Le Gavroche for 7 years. He combines his French culinary skill with Scottish produce to create a taste sensation! Since opening, the restaurant has been extended to include private dining rooms and a bar in the basement.

10 If Indian food is your thing, try **The Dhabba**, (44 Candleriggs) which specialises in authentic North Indian cuisine, or the Dakhin, (First Floor, 89 Candleriggs) where the focus is on South Indian cuisine. Both restaurants are situated in the fashionable Merchant City area, and both use only the freshest ingredients to create many unusual regional dishes. Perfect for the seasoned Indian food fan and novice alike.

ACTIVITIES

11 Just north of Glasgow, near Loch Lomond, is **Glengoyne Distillery**. The distillery is open all year round and offers the most in-depth range of tours in the industry, from the Masterblender Tour, where guests create their very own blended whisky, to the Cask Tasting Tour, specially designed for guests who enjoy tasting, and learning about, cask strength whisky.

12 Enjoy a seaplane flight from Glasgow to Oban Bay on Scotland's west coast with **Loch Lomond Seaplanes**. The journey, which takes approximately 25 minutes, will take you over areas of outstanding natural beauty. Once in Oban, there's time for a bite to eat and a spot of sightseeing before the return journey. Or if you prefer, extend your stay and return at a later date.

13 As you enter through the main doors of **Xscape** you can watch brave souls hanging from the ceiling as they have a go on the state of the art aerial adventure course. The Centre houses numerous outdoor shops, restaurants, bars, bowling, rock climbing, a cinema and much more. However, without a doubt the piece-de-résistance is the incredible SNO!zone which allows you to experience indoor skiing, snowboarding or sledging on the UK's biggest indoor real snow slope.

14 Charles Rennie Mackintosh is considered the father of the 'Glasgow Style', with his motifs instantly recognisable to visitors. He was a true visionary who worked almost exclusively in the city. His legacy lives on and can be enjoyed with the help of a **Mackintosh Trail** ticket giving admission to all associated attractions in and around Glasgow including the School of Art, Scotland Street School Museum, House for an Art Lover and the Mackintosh Church. The ticket can be purchased at Glasgow Visitor Information Centres, SPT Travel Centres, all participating Mackintosh venues or online at crmsociety.com.

SHOPPING

15   **Buchanan Street** is arguably one of the classiest major shopping thoroughfares in Britain. With a tempting mix of big high street names, alternative retailers and designer outlets, it's deservedly popular. **Buchanan Galleries** at the top of the street offers a choice of over 80 shops including John Lewis. A must visit.

16   The true highlight of Buchanan Street is **Princes Square**: a speciality shopping centre in a beautifully restored listed building dating from 1841. The architects have preserved many original features whilst transforming the interior to create a venue for shopping where designer boutiques and stylish eateries are linked by escalators criss-crossing over a central courtyard.

17   Visitors in search of the city's chic and modern side should head to the **Merchant City**. Originally landscaped for the homes and warehouses of 18th century tobacco barons, it is now the city's main style quarter. Wander around its innovative boutiques in search of that must-have item.

18   With strong Italian heritage, it's only fitting that there should be somewhere to purchase the latest fashions from Milan. With designer boutiques such as Versace Collections and Emporio Armani the **Italian Centre** may be easier on the eye than on the pocket, but it's ideal for a treat.

19   Glasgow is often complimented for its European flavour, and nowhere is this more in evidence than on **Byres Road**, with its fruit and veg stalls, butchers, fishmongers, flanking hip record stores and clothing retailers. Head to the West End for some wonderful eateries in the mews lanes off Byres Road.

20   Out of town there's **Braehead Shopping Centre** near Glasgow Airport, Silverburn Shopping Centre in Pollock, which opened its doors in late 2007, and Glasgow Fort located east of the city at junction 10 on the M8.

HERITAGE AND CULTURE

21   Take in a **football** match for 90 minutes you'll never forget. It would be an understatement to say that Glaswegians have a passion for the beautiful game, and Glasgow is the only city in the UK to support three 50,000+ capacity football stadiums. Situated within the national stadium of Hampden, the Scottish Football Museum is an essential attraction for all football fans.

22   From Celtic Connections each January to the Magners International Comedy Festival in March and Piping Live! in August, the Glasgow calendar is filled with live performances, **events and festivals** and entertainment throughout the year.

23   Situated within beautiful Bellahouston Park, **House for an Art Lover** was inspired by Charles Rennie Mackintosh designs from 1901. Its restaurant houses changing art exhibitions and visitors are entertained throughout the year with a programme of dinner concerts and afternoon music recitals.

24   Built in 1898 for the people of Glasgow's East End, the **People's Palace** and **Winter Gardens** tells the story of Glasgow from 1750 to the present day. Outside the museum stands the spectacular Doulton Fountain – the largest terracotta fountain in the world. Gifted to Glasgow by Henry Doulton, it has recently been restored.

MAP

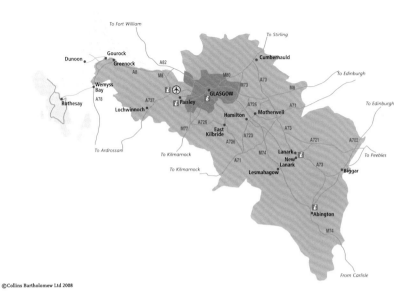

©Collins Bartholomew Ltd 2008

VISITOR INFORMATION CENTRES

Visitor Information Centres are staffed by people 'in the know' offering friendly advice, helping to make your stay in Scotland the most enjoyable ever . . . whatever your needs!

Greater Glasgow & Clyde Valley		
Abington	Welcome Break, Motorway Service Area, Junction 13, M74 Abington, ML12 6RG	Tel: 01864 502436
Glasgow	11 George Square, Glasgow G2 1DY	Tel: 0141 204 4400
Glasgow Airport	International Arrivals Hall, Glasgow International Airport, PA3 2ST	Tel: 0141 848 4440
Lanark	Horsemarket, Ladyacre Road, Lanark, ML11 7QD	Tel: 01555 661661
Paisley	9A Gilmour Street, Paisley, PA1 1DD	Tel: 0141 889 0711

LOCAL KNOWLEDGE • WHERE TO STAY • ACCOMMODATION BOOKING • PLACES TO VISIT • THINGS TO DO • MAPS AND GUIDES TRAVEL ADVICE • ROUTE PLANNING • WHERE TO SHOP AND EAT LOCAL CRAFTS AND PRODUCE • EVENT INFORMATION • TICKETS

For information and ideas about exploring Scotland in advance of your trip, call our booking and information service **0845 22 55 121** or go to **visitscotland.com**

If calling from outside the UK and Ireland **+44 1506 832 121**   From Ireland **1800 932 510**

A £4 booking fee applies for accommodation bookings made via a Visitor Information Centre and through our booking and information service.

Live it. Visit *Scotland.*
visitscotland.com/wheretofindus

Glasgow
City Apartments & Embassy Suites   Map Ref: 1H5

★★★★
SELF CATERING

Open: All year
401 North Woodside Road, Glasgow G20 6NN
T: 0141 342 4060
F: 0141 334 8159
E: city@mcquadehotels.com
W: mcquadehotels.com

19296

10 Apartments	Sleeps 1-7
Prices from:	
£355.00	**Per week**
£58	**Per night**

Glasgow
Embassy Apartments   Map Ref: 1H5

★★★★
SELF CATERING

Open: All year
8 Kelvin Drive, Glasgow
T: 0141 946 6698
E: embassy@mcquadehotels.com
W: mcquadehotels.com

24903

6 Apartments	1 Public Room	Sleeps 1-7
Prices from:		
£450.00		**Per week**
£60		**Per night**

Glasgow
Kelvin Apartment   Map Ref: 1H5

★★★★
SELF CATERING

Open: All year
14 Buckingham Terrace,
Great Western Road, Glasgow G12 8EB
T: 0141 339 7143
E: enquiries@kelvinhotel.com
W: kelvinhotel.com

33516

1 Apartment	3 Public Rooms	Sleeps 1-5
Prices from:		
£450.00-800.00		**Per week**
£70.00-120.00		**Per night**

Glasgow
My Place in Glasgow   Map Ref: 1H5

★★★★
SELF CATERING

Open: All year
Reservations by phone or e.mail
T: 07858 381583
E: info@myplaceinglasgow.co.uk
W: myplaceinglasgow.co.uk

74971

Located within the restored mid-19th Century Greek Revival building, formerly used as the Sheriff Court, our luxury apartments provide the perfect holiday location. At the heart of the Merchant City (G1) they are perfectly placed for the all Glasgow's attractions.

3 Apartments	2 Public Rooms	Sleeps 2
Prices from:		
£420.00		**Per week**
£70		**Per night**

IMPORTANT: Prices stated are estimates and may be subject to change. Awards correct as of beginning of October 2008.

Glasgow
University of Glasgow
Map Ref: 1H5

★★★
HOSTEL

65588

Open: All year

Residential Services,
73 Great George Street, Glasgow G12 8RR
T: 00 44 (0)141 330 4116/2318
E: vacationaccom@gla.ac.uk
W: glasgow.ac.uk/cvso

The University of Glasgow's self catering accommodation is not only comfortable, well furnished and ideally located to enjoy our wonderful city, but also includes access to amenities such as free of charge laundry facilities and free parking.

Prices from:		
Standard University Residence:		
£129.50		Per week
£18.50		Per night
Ensuite University Residence:		
£240.45		Per week
£34.35		Per night

Glasgow
University of Strathclyde
Map Ref: 1H5

★
SELF CATERING

62602

Open: June-September

Residence & Catering Services,
50 Richmond Street, Glasgow G1 1XP
T: 0141 553 4148
E: accommodationglasgow@strath.ac.uk
W: rescat.strath.ac.uk

44 Apartments	1 Public Room	Sleeps 4-6
Prices from:		
£350.00		**Per week**

Lochwinnoch, Renfrewshire
East Lochhead Holiday Cottages
Map Ref: 1G5

★★★★
SELF CATERING

24152

Open: All year

c/o The Studio, East Lochhead,
Kilburnie Road, Lochwinnoch, Renfrewshire PA12 4DX
T: 01505 842610
E: admin@eastlochhead.co.uk
W: eastlochhead.co.uk

Four carefully restored and comfortable cottages set in countryside but easy access to trains, motorways and airports. Ideally situated for Glasgow's cultural attractions, outdoor activities and the scenery of the Clyde estuary, Loch Lomond and the Trossachs.

4 Cottages	1 Public Room	Sleeps 3-6
Prices from:		
£280.00-700.00		**Per week**
£70.00-110.00		**Per night**

For a full listing of quality assured non-serviced establishments please see pages 229-385.

Oban waterfront at night

WEST HIGHLANDS AND ISLANDS, LOCH LOMOND, STIRLING AND TROSSACHS

Contrast is the word that best sums up an area that spans Scotland from the shores of the Forth in the east to the very tip of Tiree in the west. Here the Highlands meet the Lowlands and geography and cultures diverge.

For the visitor, the endlessly changing landscape means a rich and varied holiday experience.

There are rugged high mountains, spectacular freshwater lochs, fascinating islands and dramatic seascapes. You'll find pretty villages, mill towns, not to mention one of Scotland's newest cities, Stirling.

Discover the birthplace of the Scots nation and visit places that witnessed some of the most dramatic scenes in Scotland's history.

On the eastern side of the country the flat plain of the Forth Valley stretches up from the River Forth towards the little towns of the Hillfoots, which enjoy

the spectacular backdrop of the Ochil Hills.

Elsewhere in the Forth Valley, you can visit Scotland's smallest county, Clackmannanshire, or the Wee County as it is known. Head for Dollar Glen and the magnificent Castle Campbell, once the Lowland stronghold of the Clan Campbell.

Moving to the Hillfoot towns you'll be tracing the roots of Scotland's textile industry which has thrived here for many years. Learn the history of the local woollen industry at the Mill Trail Visitor Centre in Alva.

New city, ancient history

Beyond Alva to the west lies Stirling – a city since 2002 and one of the most important places in Scottish history thanks to its strategically important location as the gateway to the Highlands.

Once, whoever controlled Stirling, controlled Scotland. Its impressive castle stands guard over all it surveys and was the capital for the Stewart Kings. It's

To find out more, call 0845 22 55 121 or go to visitscotland.com

a relatively quiet spot these days but no fewer than seven battle sites can be seen from the Castle ramparts – including Stirling Bridge, a scene of triumph for William Wallace and Bannockburn where Robert the Bruce led the Scots to victory in 1314.

A National Park on your doorstep

Scotland's first national park Loch Lomond and the Trossachs National Park, takes advantage of the natural treasures of this area and that means 20 Munros (mountains over 3,000ft) to climb, 50 rivers to fish, 22 lochs to sail and thousands of miles of road and track to cycle. When you've had your fill of activities, head for Loch Lomond Shores for a cultural and retail experience.

You can also cruise on Loch Lomond. It's Britain's biggest freshwater expanse and there's no better way to see the surrounding countryside than from the water.

Heading west the Whisky Coast round Islay and Jura are waiting to be explored – Islay alone has eight working distilleries!

A place in history

Further west still, The Cowal Peninsula with its sea lochs and deep forests is beautiful and relaxing. To get there, just jump aboard the ferry at Gourock and sail for Dunoon. While you're there, don't miss the nearby Benmore Botanic Gardens.

Explore Lochgilphead and beyond to Kilmartin where you can trace the very roots of the nation where the Scots arrived from Ireland in the 6th century.

What's more, 2009 is a big year for Scotland – we're celebrating the 250th anniversary of the birth of Robert Burns. There's over 200 special events taking place throughout the year, all over Scotland. Go to homecomingscotland2009.com to find out about events in this area.

Choosing a holiday destination in an area as diverse as this will always be difficult but the stunning array of self catering or caravan and camping accommodation will help firm up your thoughts. There are some wonderful holiday parks with splendid facilities in superb, unspoiled locations, as well as loch shore boathouses, luxury lodges, holiday parks and perfect cottages. You'll easily find somewhere to enjoy a perfect holiday.

The Mishnish Hotel, Tobermory, Isle of Mull

What's On?

Big in Falkirk
2 – 3 May 2009
Scotland's largest streets arts festival features music, outdoor theatre and art in Callendar Park. A two-day extravaganza not to be missed!
biginfalkirk.co.uk

The Loch Lomond Food & Drink Festival
30 – 31 May 2009
A showcase for local food and great chefs, giving the visitor a chance to sample the delicious servings amongst the stunning backdrop of Loch Lomond.
lochlomondfoodanddrinkfestival.com

Scottish Pipe Band Championship
May 2009
For one day in May, Dumbarton will be alive to the skirl of pipes. A world-class competition with competitors from all over the globe.
rspba.org

World Fly Fishing Championships
5 – 12 June 2009
Welcoming anglers from over 25 countries over 7 days of competition, showcasing the fishing sites and surrounding landscapes of Stirling & Perthshire to an international audience.
worldflyfishingchampionships2009.com

Helensburgh and Loch Lomond Highland Games
14 June 2009
Come experience the Highland Games with traditional events such as tossing the caber, putting the stone, throwing the hammer and many more making this a fun-filled day out.
helensburghandlomondgames.co.uk

Cowal Highland Gathering
27 – 29 August 2009
Dating back to 1894, the Gathering is described as 'the largest and most spectacular Highland Games in the world'
cowalgathering.com

Connect Festival, Inveraray
28 – 30 August 2009
Pack your campervan and head for connect at Inveraray Castle. It's simply one of the best summer rock festivals in the UK.
connectmusicfestival.com

Off the Page – The Stirling Book Festival
13 – 20 September 2009
A celebration of writing in its various forms for adults, children and families. Lots of exciting events throughout the area in the library-organised festival that celebrates its fourth year.
stirling.gov.uk/offthepage

Cowalfest
9 – 18 October 2009
Scotland's largest walking festival with cycling, wildlife, the arts, film, music and drama thrown in.
cowalfest.org

MAP

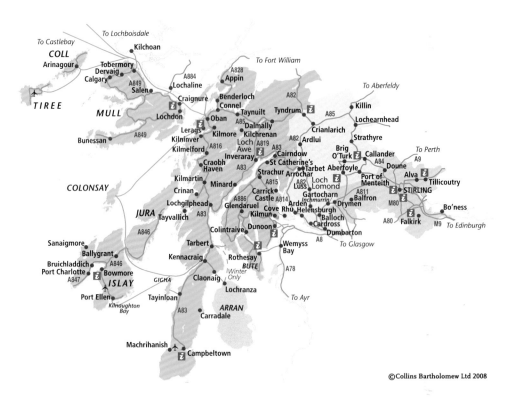

©Collins Bartholomew Ltd 2008

To find out more, call 0845 22 55 121 or go to visitscotland.com

VISITOR INFORMATION CENTRES

Visitor Information Centres are staffed by people 'in the know' offering friendly advice, helping to make your stay in Scotland the most enjoyable ever . . . whatever your needs!

West Highlands

Bowmore	The Square, Bowmore, Isle of Islay, PA43 7JP	Tel: 01496 810254
Campbeltown	Mackinnon House, The Pier, Campbeltown, PA28 6EF	Tel: 01586 552056
Craignure	The Pier, Craignure, Isle of Mull, PA65 6AY	Tel: 01680 812377
Dunoon	7 Alexander Place, Dunoon, PA23 8AB	Tel: 01369 703785
Inveraray	Front Street, Inveraray, PA32 8UY	Tel: 01499 302063
Oban	Argyll Square, Oban, PA34 4AR	Tel: 01631 563122
Rothesay	Winter Gardens, Rothesay, Isle of Bute, PA20 0AJ	Tel: 01700 502151

Loch Lomond

Aberfoyle	Trossachs Discovery Centre, Main Street, Aberfoyle, FK8 3UQ	Tel: 01877 382352
Callander	Ancaster Square, Callander, FK17 8ED	Tel: 01877 330342
Tyndrum	Main Street, Tyndrum, FK20 8RY	Tel: 01838 400324

Stirling & Trossachs

Falkirk	The Falkirk Wheel, Lime Road, Tamfourhill, Falkirk, FK1 4RS	Tel: 01324 620244
Stirling (Dumbarton Rd)	41 Dumbarton Road, Stirling, FK8 2LQ	Tel: 01786 475019
Stirling (Pirnhall)	Motorway Service Area, Junction 9, M9	Tel: 01786 814111
Tillicoultry	Unit 22, Sterling Mills Outlet Village, Devondale, Tillicoultry, Clackmannanshire, FK13 6HQ	Tel: 01259 769696

LOCAL KNOWLEDGE • WHERE TO STAY • ACCOMMODATION BOOKING • PLACES TO VISIT • THINGS TO DO • MAPS AND GUIDES TRAVEL ADVICE • ROUTE PLANNING • WHERE TO SHOP AND EAT LOCAL CRAFTS AND PRODUCE • EVENT INFORMATION • TICKETS

For information and ideas about exploring Scotland in advance of your trip, call our booking and information service **0845 22 55 121** or go to **visitscotland.com**

If calling from outside the UK and Ireland **+44 1506 832 121**   From Ireland **1800 932 510**

A £4 booking fee applies for accommodation bookings made via a Visitor Information Centre and through our booking and information service.

Live it. Visit *Scotland.*
visitscotland.com/wheretofindus

Island of Tiree, Inner Hebrides

West Highlands and Islands

Savour the atmosphere of the rugged west coast and take a journey around some of Scotland's most magical isles and peninsulas. The pace of island life is a powerful draw for visitors and, while there are parts of the mainland around Kintyre which feel more like island than mainland, if you're looking for the genuine island experience, you'll be spoiled for choice.

The many islands to explore include Gigha, Jura, Islay and Colonsay. And no trip to these parts would be complete without visiting Oban, the gateway to the isles, from where boats make their way to and from the likes of Mull, Coll, Tiree and Colonsay.

They all have their own special allure. Visit Islay for the whisky, deeply spiritual Iona, and Mull, where you can see colourful Tobermory (or Balamory as families with young children will recognise it). On your way to the isles stop off in Oban, its harbour is always bustling and the area around the port has a great selection of shops, bars and restaurants.

Sambayabamba at the Connect Music Festival, Inveraray

To find out more, call 0845 22 55 121 or go to visitscotland.com

DON'T MISS

1   Wherever you travel in this area, you're never far from one of the **whisky distilleries**. Islay alone is home to eight working distilleries, producing world-famous whiskies such as Laphroaig and Bowmore, renowned for their peaty qualities. Here, you'll also find Kilchoman, a recently opened farm distillery. The neighbouring Isle of Jura manufactures its own popular malt, while Campbeltown on Kintyre now boasts two local whiskies, Springbank and Glengyle, the latter dating from only 2004. Facilities and opening hours vary.

2   **Island Exploring** is a must in the West Highlands and with such a diversity of locations all linked by ferry, it's a popular choice. Iona Abbey is considered the origin for the spread of Christianity throughout Scotland and is a must-visit on Iona. Explore Fingal's Cave on Staffa, the surfing on Tiree and the whiskies of Islay. White beaches, tasty organic food and spectacular scenery welcome you and urge your return.

3   Any trip which takes in the breathtaking Argyll coastline or Argyll's Atlantic Islands, known as **Scotland's Sea Kingdom**, promises a memorable experience. Negotiate the Gulf of Corryvreckan with its famous whirlpool and travel round Scarba while looking out for whales, dolphins, deer and eagles, or venture further to the remote Garvellachs. You can sail from Ardfern with Craignish Cruises, from Craobh Haven with Farsain Cruises, from Crinan with Gemini Cruises or from Easdale with Seafari Adventures or Sealife Adventures.

4   **Mount Stuart** on the Isle of Bute was the ancestral home of the Marquess of Bute. Today it is a high quality, award-winning, four-star attraction featuring magnificent Victorian Gothic architecture and design together with contemporary craftsmanship. Mount Stuart is surrounded by 300 acres of gloriously maintained grounds and gardens.

5   **Kilmartin Glen** is home to a myriad of Neolithic and Bronze Age monuments, coupled with early Christian carved stones and ruined castles. South of Oban, this site was capital of the ancient Celtic kingdom of Dalriada, as evidenced at Dunadd Fort, where a footprint in the stone is thought to have featured in royal inauguration ceremonies.

6   The common characteristic of the **Glorious Gardens of Argyll & Bute** is their individuality. Each garden has a variety of terrain; many are mainly level with smooth paths, while some are steep and rocky. The gardens range from informal woodland gardens to beautiful classic examples of 18th century design.

FOOD AND DRINK   eatscotland.com

7   The original **Loch Fyne Oyster Bar** and shop started in a small shed in the lay-by at the head of Loch Fyne in the early 1980s. In 1985 it moved into the old cow byre at Clachan Farm. It has been listed in the Good Food Guide every year since then.

8   Among the many fine restaurants across the West Highlands, **Coast** in Oban stands out with its clean, calming feel and contemporary approach to food. Both light bite and a la carte menus are brimming with the fresh seafood synonymous in the area. You can let your food go down while watching the sunset across Oban Bay.

9   **The Seafood Trail** takes you through some of the most spectacular coastal scenery Scotland has to offer, and enables seafood lovers to sample, share and enjoy seafood and shellfish from a wide variety of waterfront establishments.

10 The **Whisky Coast** blends incredible Scottish scenery with arguably the best sixteen single malt whiskies for a truly memorable experience. Getting to and around the Whisky Coast is surprisingly easy for the independent traveller in search of stunning landscapes and the finest whiskies, as the area is well served by road, rail, air and ferry.

WILDLIFE   visitscotland.com/wildlife

11 There are numerous operators that offer **sea trip safaris** around **Oban** and **Mull** where you can spot majestic wildlife against a backdrop of spectacular scenery. The wildlife in this area is magnificent and you may well spot the majestic sea eagle, golden eagle, or a range of seabirds along with seals, dolphins, porpoises and the occasional minke whale.

12 The extensive **Argyll Forest Park** offers a perfect introduction to Loch Lomond & The Trossachs National Park. Start at the Ardgartan Visitor Centre on the A83 at the north of Loch Long, where the Boathouse and Riverside walks provide options for pushchairs. You'll also find cycle paths, a play area and refreshments. With its spectacular mountains, glens, lochs and woodlands, many claim that Britain's first forest park is also the finest.

13 The islands of **Islay and Jura** are something of a mecca for **wildlife** lovers. With well over a hundred breeding bird species in summer, and some of Europe's largest populations of wintering wildfowl, they are a year round destination for ornithologists. Add to this some exceptional marine wildlife, including minke whales, common and bottlenose dolphins, basking sharks and literally thousands of seals, alongside some of Britain's best opportunities to spy otters, red deer and golden eagles, and you have a natural paradise. A particular highlight is the arrival of around 50,000 barnacle and white-fronted geese from the Arctic Circle each autumn.

14 **Wildlife and bird watching safaris** offer the chance to explore the remote areas of Mull with experienced guides to help you spot and learn about the wildlife which inhabits the island. This is your chance to see golden eagles, otters, harriers and merlin to name a few.

WALKS   visitscotland.com/walking

15   **Lismore** is a lovely location to get away from it all and is easy to reach by boat from Oban. The island is just 12 miles long and 1.5 miles at its widest point, and offers many interesting walks with spectacular views of the sea and mountains. Kerrera is a beautiful island where it is also possible to walk round the entire island although this walk is about 10 miles and will take some time.

16   The wonderfully unexplored Kintyre Peninsula boasts hidden coves, deserted beaches, tiny fishing communities, gentle hills, fabulous local produce and welcoming friendly people. Stretching from Tarbert to Southend, the waymarked **Kintyre Way** criss-crosses the peninsula, connecting communities and landscape, people and produce. At 89 miles long (142 kms), and with 4 to 7 days worth of walking, there's serious hiking and gentle rambles, all of which bring home the beautiful reality that is Kintyre.

17   The **West Island Way**, which opened in September 2000, is the first long distance way-marked path on a Scottish island. It encompasses some of the best walking that the Isle of Bute has to offer, runs the length of the island and embraces a variety of landscapes.

18   **The Cowal Way** follows a route running the length of Argyll's Cowal peninsula. It starts in the south-west at Portavadie beside Loch Fyne, and finishes in the north-east at Ardgartan by Loch Long, and involves walking on roads and on lochside, hill and woodland terrains. The way-marked route is 75 kms/47 miles in length and is divided into six shorter, more manageable sections.

ACTIVITIES

19   Tiny Port Askaig on Islay is something of a ferry hub, serving Colonsay, the mainland and Jura. Its proximity to the last makes it an ideal location to view the **Paps of Jura**, three rounded mountains rising out of the sea to over 730m. Relax with a drink outside the Port Askaig Hotel and soak up the view.

20   The village of Carradale on the eastern side of Kintyre makes an excellent base from which to explore the peninsula. The delightful beach and harbour area offer stunning views over the Kilbrannan Sound to the dramatic hills of **Arran**.

21   One of Scotland's most romanticised stretches of water, the narrow straits known as the **Kyles of Bute**, more than live up to their reputation. The Kyles are best admired from the viewpoint on the A886 above Colintraive, where the view to their namesake island is truly awe-inspiring. Remember to bring along your picnic so you can really make the most of this view and open space.

22   The steep 10-minute climb from the centre of Oban to **McCaig's Tower** is well worth it for the view of Oban Bay, Kerrera and the Isle of Mull. The Tower was built by a local banker in the late 19th century in an effort to replicate Rome's Colosseum. The view of the town and the islands to the west is breathtaking.

Appin, Argyll
Appin House Lodges

Map Ref: 1E1

★★★★
SELF
CATERING

12330

Open: All year excl 1 November-mid December & 5 January-10 February

Appin House, Appin, Argyll PA38 4BN

T: 01631 730207
E: denys@appinhouse.co.uk
W: appinhouse.co.uk

A tranquil and relaxing break is assured in Gate Lodge and Tigh An Lios. Spacious, warm, well equipped, both offer fantastic views across Loch Linnhe towards Lismuire. Enjoy our large fragrant garden with abundant wild life. Well placed for touring.

| 1 House | 1 Public Room | Sleeps 2-8 |
| 1 Lodge | 1 Public Room | Sleeps 2-6 |

Prices from:		
House:	£565.00-1150.00	Per week
	£140.00	Per night
Lodge:	£565.00-950.00	Per week
	£140.00	Per night

Appin, Argyll
Inverboat House

Map Ref: 1E1

★★★ UP TO
★★★★
SELF
CATERING

31888

Open: All year

Mackay's Agency, Cairncross House,
25 Union Street, Edinburgh EH1 3LR

T: 0131 550 1180
E: bookings@mackays-scotland.co.uk
W: inverboathouse.co.uk

Spectacular sea loch/mountain setting. Private beach, slipway, spa bath, sauna, pool table, log fires. Walking, sailing, diving, wild life, fishing. Surrounded by nature reserve, Glasdrum wood (slopes of Ben Churalain) and Loch Creran with it's biogenic reefs (special area of conservation).

| 1 Cottage | 1 Public Room | Sleeps 4 |
| 1 House | 3 Public Rooms | Sleeps 8-10 |

Prices from:		
Cottage:	£264.00	Per week
House:	£539.00	Per week

Rothesay, Isle of Bute
Ardencraig House Apartments

Map Ref: 1F5

★★★★
SELF
CATERING

12529

Open: All year

Ardencraig House, Ardencraig Road,
High Craigmore, Rothesay, Isle of Bute PA20 9EP

T: 01700 505077
E: ebdan10@aol.com
W: ardencraig.org.uk

| 4 Apartments | 1 Public Room | Sleeps 2-7 |

Prices from:	
£325.00-575.00	Per week
£195.00-325.00	3/4 day short breaks

Rothesay, Isle of Bute
Arranview

Map Ref: 1F5

★★★★★
SELF
CATERING

12996

Open: All year

Stewart Hall, Rothesay, Isle of Bute PA20 0QE

T: 01700 500006
E: donald@stewarthall-isle-of-bute.co.uk
W: visitbute.co.uk

| 1 Cottage | 1 Public Room | Sleeps 2-6 |

Prices from:	
£500.00	Per week
£100.00	Per night

IMPORTANT: Prices stated are estimates and may be subject to change. Awards correct as of beginning of October 2008.

Rothesay, Isle of Bute
Morningside
Map Ref: 1F5

★★★
SELF
CATERING

Open: All year
Mrs Patricia Lyon, Serpentine Road,
Rothesay, Isle of Bute PA20 9HD
T: 01700 504237 **M:** 07732 324387
E: info@isleofbuteholidayflats.co.uk
W: isleofbuteholidayflats.co.uk

33751

4 Apartments (contained in 1 house)	1 Public Room	Sleeps 1-5
Prices from:		
£200.00		**Per week**
£60.00		**Per night**

Rothesay, Isle of Bute
Prospect House
Map Ref: 1F5

★★★
SELF
CATERING

Open: All year
Eastbay, 21 Battery Place,
Rothesay, Isle of Bute PA20 9DU
T: 01700 503526
E: ta.shaw@zen.co.uk
W: prospecthouse-bute.co.uk

43368

1 Cottage	1-2 Public Rooms	Sleeps 4
5 Apartments	1-2 Public Rooms	Sleeps 4-6
Prices from:		
Cottage:	£257.00-477.00	**Per week**
	£56.00-85.00	**Per night**
Apartments:	£257.00-477.00	**Per week**
	£56.00-85.00	**Per night**

Carradale, Argyll
Torrisdale Estate
Map Ref: 1E6

★ UP TO
★★★
SELF
CATERING

Open: All year
Torrisdale Castle, Carradale, Kintyre, Argyll PA28 6QT
T: 01583 431233
E: machall@torrisdalecastle.com
W: torrisdalecastle.com

61596

3 Cottages	1 Public Room	Sleeps 2-4
2 Houses	2 Public Rooms	Sleeps 7-10
3 Apartments	1 Public Room	Sleeps 4-6
Prices from:		
Cottage:	£190.00	**Per week**
	£133.00	**Per 3 nights**
House:	£310.00	**Per week**
	£217.00	**Per 3 nights**
Apartment:	£280.00	**Per week**
	£196.00	**Per 3 nights**

Carrick Castle, Loch Goil
Darroch Mhor Chalets
Map Ref: 1F4

★★
SELF
CATERING

Open: All year
Carrick Castle, Loch Goil, Argyll and Bute PA24 8AF
T: 01301 703249
E: mail@argyllchalets.com
W: argyllchalets.com

22198

3 Chalets	1 Public Room	Sleeps 4
Prices from:		
£120.00		**Per week**
£40.00		**Per night**

Crinan, by Lochgilphead
Mrs D Murray
Map Ref: 1E4

★★
SELF
CATERING

Open: All year
Kilmahumaig Barn Flats, Kilmahumaig,
Crinan, Lochgilphead, Argyll PA31 8SW
T: 01546 830238
E: murray104@btinternet.com

33832

3 Apartments	1- 2 Public Rooms	Sleeps 2-6
Prices from:		
£150.00-400.00		**Per week**
£45.00		**Per night**

Dunoon, Argyll
Clyde Cottage
Map Ref: 1F5

★★★★
SELF
CATERING

Open: All year
Ri Cruin, Kilmartin, by Lochgilphead,
Argyll and Bute PA31 8QF
T: 01546 510316
E: gordon@ri-cruin.freeserve.co.uk

19757

1 House	2 Public Rooms	Sleeps 1-6
Prices from:		
£215.00-544.00		**Per week**
£50.00		**Per night**

For a full listing of quality assured non-serviced establishments please see pages 229-385.

87

Dunoon, Argyll
4 Deercroft
Map Ref: 1F5

★★★ SELF CATERING

Open: April-September
15 Deercroft, Hafton,
by Dunoon, Argyll and Bute PA23 8HP
T: 01369 703586
E: gwpursley@aol.com

73401

1 Lodge	1 Public Room	Sleeps 2-4
Prices from:		
£325.00		**Per week**
£47.00		**Per night**

Dunoon, Argyll
Lyall Cliff
Map Ref: 1F5

★★★ SELF CATERING

Open: All year
141 Alexandra Parade,
East Bay, Dunoon, Argyll PA23 8AW
T: 01369 702041
E: info@lyallcliff.co.uk
W: lyallcliff.co.uk

Beautifully situated direct on the Dunoon promenade, our spacious 'Firthview House' (capacity 8) and cosy cottage (capacity 4) enjoy magnificent sea views, a large garden, and all modern comforts. Short breaks available. Flexible booking system.

36612

1 Cottage	2 Public Rooms	Sleeps 2-4
1 House	3 Public Rooms	Sleeps 2-8
Prices from:		
Cottage:	£220.00	**Per week**
	£50.00	**Per night**
House:	£410.00	**Per week**
	£94.00	**Per night**

Dunoon, Argyll
Sebright Self Catering
Map Ref: 1F5

★★★ SELF CATERING

Open: All year
145A Alexandra Parade, Dunoon PA23 8AW
T: 07887 793274
E: iain@sebright.eu
W: sebright.eu

73262

1 Apartment	1 Public Room	Sleeps 2-8
Prices from:		
£420.00		**Per week**
£60.00		**Per night**

Dunoon, Argyll
Serendipity
Map Ref: 1F5

★★★ SELF CATERING

Open: All year
Blythewood Place, Port Elphinstone,
Inverurie, Aberdeenshire AB51 3XE
T: 01467 626071
E: stanmroczek@btinternet.com
W: dunoonselfcatering.co.uk

54187

1 Maisonette	2 Public Rooms	Sleeps 2-4
Prices from:		
£295.00-395.00		**Per week**

nr Dunoon, Argyll
Mrs W Buffey
Map Ref: 1F5

AWAITING GRADING

Open: All year
Balmoral, 189 Marine Parade, Hunters Quay
Dunoon PA23 8HJ
T: 01664 501744   **M:** 07949 672967
E: wanda@thebuffeys.wanadoo.co.uk
W: balmoral189.com

81299

1 Apartment	2 Public Rooms	Sleeps 2-6
Prices from:		
£250.00-450.00		**Per week**
£50.00-80.00		**Per night**

IMPORTANT: Prices stated are estimates and may be subject to change. Awards correct as of beginning of October 2008.

Glendaruel, Argyll
Ardachearnbeg Cottages
Map Ref: 1F4

75378

WAITING GRADING

Open: All year
Ardachearnbeg Farmhouse,
Glendaruel, Argyll and Bute PA22 3AE
T: 01369 820272
E: info@ardachearnbeg.co.uk
W: ardachearnbeg.co.uk

4 Cottages	1 Public Room	Sleeps 4-20
Prices from:		
£230.00-630.00		**Per week**
£60.00		**Per night**

Glendaruel, Argyll
Mr & Mrs M Webster
Map Ref: 1F4

83852

★★★ SELF CATERING

Open: All year excl February
The Watermill, Glendaruel, Argyll and Bute PA22 3AB
T: 01369 820203
E: michael.webster18@btinternet.com

2 Apartments	1 Public Room	Sleeps 4
Prices from:		
Sawmill:	£250.00-450.00	**Per week**
	£90.00	**Per night**
Joiner Shop:	£190.00-380.00	**Per week**
	£75.00	**Per night**

Inverary, Argyll
Argyll Caravan Park
Map Ref: 1F3

68793

★★★★ HOLIDAY PARK

Open: April-October
Inverary, Argyll PA32 8XT
T: 01499 302285 **E:** enquiries@argyllcaravanpark.com
W: argyllcaravanpark.com
Leisure Facilities:

From Inverary the park is situated two miles south, along the A83

Park accommodates 100 pitches
Total Touring Pitches: 100 (Sorry no tents)
Prices from:
(60) £20.00   (40) £20.00
(4) £385.00 per week

Thistle

Inverary, Argyll
Mr C R Elkin
Map Ref: 1F3

16548

★★ SELF CATERING

Open: All year
Inverae, Minard, Inverary, Argyll PA32 8YF
T: 01546 886655
E: colum.elkin@virgin.net
W: brondeg.co.uk

1 Cottage	2 Public Rooms	Sleeps 2-6
Prices from:		
Cottage: £185.00-420.00		**Per week**

Ballygrant, Isle of Islay
Mrs C Bell
Map Ref: 1C5

20877

UP TO ★★★ SELF CATERING

Open: All year
Craigard Holiday Accommodation,
Traigh Cill an Rubha, Bridgend, Isle of Islay PA44 7NY
T: 01496 810728 **E:** holidays@craigard-islay.co.uk
W: craigard-islay.co.uk

1 Cottage	1 Public Room	Sleeps 5
3 Apartments	1 Public Room	Sleeps 2-6
Prices from:		
Cottage:	£540.00-640.00	**Per week**
Apartment	£210.00-350.00	**Per week**

Bruichladdich, Isle of Islay
Coull Farm
Map Ref: 1B5

20633

★★ SELF CATERING

Open: All year
Kilchoman, Bruichladdich,
Isle of Islay, Argyll PA49 7UT
T: 01496 850317
E: pjones@mail2world.com
W: coull-farm-holidays.co.uk

1 Cottage	1 Public Room	Sleeps 4
1 Apartment	1 Public Room	Sleeps 4
Prices from:		
Cottage:	£200.00-420.00	**Per week**
Apartment	£200.00-420.00	**Per week**
	Short break prices on application	

For a full listing of quality assured non-serviced establishments please see pages 229-385.

89

Port Charlotte, Isle of Islay
Port Charlotte Hall   Map Ref: 1B6

74246

★★★★
SELF
CATERING

Open: All year
Mrs Margaret McCallum, Port Charlotte Homes Ltd.,
27 Southview Drive, Bearsden, Glasgow G61 4HQ
T: 0141 943 2529   **M:**   07979023021
E: enquiries@portcharlotteholidays.com
W: portcharlotteholidays.com

3 Apartments	1-2 Public Rooms	Sleeps 2-8

Prices from:

£275.00-795.00	**Per week**

Short break prices available on request

Sanaigmore, Gruinart, Isle of Islay
Stable Cottage   Map Ref: 1B5

82637

★★★★
SELF
CATERING

Open: All year
Sanaigmore, Gruinart, Isle of Islay, PA44 7PT
T: 01496 850259
E: petra.pearce@tiscali.co.uk
W: sanaigmore.com

Stable Cottage is in a stunning location enjoying
peace, tranquility and exceptional sea views. It
has been sympathetically restored retaining a
traditional stone finish outside while creating a
contemporary, airy and spacious feel inside. Superior
accommodation surrounded by natural beauty.

1 Cottage	2 Public Rooms	Sleeps 1-4

Prices from:

£350.00-600.00	**Per week**
£70.00	**Per night**

Kilchrenan, Argyll
Ardabhaigh   Map Ref: 1F2

12459

★★★★
SELF
CATERING

Open: All year
Dundorran, Kilbride Cottage,
Inverary, Argyll PA32 8XT
T: 01499 302736
E: gmoncrieff@btinternet.com

1 Bungalow	2 Public Rooms	Sleeps 2-7

Prices from:

£350.00-800.00	**Per week**

Kilmartin, by Lochgilphead
The Bullock Shed and The Stable, Kilmartin Map Ref: 1E4

19756

★★★★
SELF
CATERING

Open: All year
Ri Cruin, Kilmartin, Lochgilphead, Argyll PA31 8QF
T: 01546 510316
E: gordon@ri-cruin.freeserve.co.uk
W: ri-cruin.co.uk

Two very comfortable tastefully renovated stable
buildings on 100 acre sheep farm in historic Kilmartin
Glen. Sandy beaches and Crinan Canal nearby. Ideal
base for walking, cycling, fishing, nature watching,
day trips to nearby islands or simply relaxing.

1 Cottage	1 Public Room	Sleeps 4
1 Wing of Large House	1 Public Room	Sleeps 6

Prices from:

Cottage:	£215.00-544.00	**Per week**
	£50.00	**Per night**
House:	£234.00-644.00	**Per week**
	£60.00	**Per night**

IMPORTANT: Prices stated are estimates and may be subject to change. Awards correct as of beginning of October 2008.

Kilmelford, by Oban
Melfort Village
Map Ref: 1E3

★★★★
SELF
CATERING

Open: All year excl 2nd/3rd weeks in January
Kilmelford, Oban, Argyll PA34 4XD
T: 01852 200257
E: rentals@melfortvillage.co.uk
W: melfortvillage.co.uk

38024

26 cottages	Sleeps 2-6
6 houses	Sleeps 2-8

Prices from:		
Cottage	– £370.00	Per week
Cottage	– £65.00	Per night
House	– £500.00	Per week
House	– £100.00	Per night

Kilmore, by Oban
Clan Cottages
Map Ref:1E2

★★★★
SELF
CATERING

Open: All year

John & Mary MacKinnon, Kilmore, by Oban
Argyll PA34 4XU
T/F: 01631 770372 **M:** 07785 221217
E: info@clancottages.com
W: clancottages.com

Five newly built thatched holiday cottages situated on the shores of Loch Nell and the River Nell, six minutes drive from Oban. Perfect base to explore Argyll and the Islands. Ideal location for walking, cycling and fishing. Abundance of wildlife.

71460

5 Cottages	1-2 Public Rooms	Sleeps 1-6

Prices from:	
£625.00	**Per week**
£120.00	**Per night**

Kilmun, by Dunoon
Fintry
Map Ref: 1F4

★★★
SELF
CATERING

Open: All year
The Martin Nichol Partnership,
1 Myrtle Avenue, Lenzie, Glasgow G66 4HW
T: 0141 776 3158
E: nichol@abel.co.uk
W: argyllholiday.co.uk

26022

1 Bungalow	2 Public Rooms	Sleeps 2-6

Prices from:	
£395.00-650.00	**Per week**
Short breaks available at 75% of weekly tariff	

Kilninver, by Oban
Mrs Macdonald
Map Ref: 1E2

★★★
SELF
CATERING

Open: All year
21 Lindisfarne Road, Newcastle Upon Tyne, NE2 2HE
T: 0191 281 1695
E: dacmac@hotmail.co.uk
W: blaran.com

Relax in this comfortable, well equipped cottage twelve miles south of Oban. Enjoy magnificent views of the "Braes of Lorne" and a trout stream (with fishing). Fully fenced garden, two bathrooms, wireless broadband. Explore Crinan Canan, Kilmartin Glen, the islands.

15438

1 Cottage	2 Public Rooms	Sleeps 6

Prices from:	
£395.00-745.00	**Per week**
Short breaks available at 1/2 weekly tariff for first 2 nights, 1/5 weekly tariff thereon.	

For a full listing of quality assured non-serviced establishments please see pages 229-385.

91

Lerags, by Oban
Mrs Margaret Whitton
Map Ref: 1E2

★★ SELF CATERING

Open: All year
Kilbride Farm, Lerags, Oban, Argyll PA34 4SE
T: 01631 562878

33723

1 House	1 Public Room	Sleeps 1-8

Prices from:		
£210.00-360.00		**Per week**
£70.00		**Per night**

Loch Awe, Inveraray
Ardbrecknish House
Map Ref: 1F2

★★ SELF CATERING

Open: All year
South Lochaweside, by Dalmally, Argyll PA33 1BH
T: 01866 833223/07767 306345
E: enquiries@loch-awe.co.uk
W: loch-awe.co.uk

12489

Historic house on banks of Loch Awe with ten self catering properties. Friendly licensed bar on site, bar meals. Boat hire/launch nearby, fishing, walking, bird watching. Near Oban, Mull and the Isles, Glen Coe and Fort William. Glasgow airport 1½ hours.

1 Cottage	1-2 Public Rooms	Sleeps 4-5
9 Apartments	1-2 Public Rooms	Sleeps 2-12

Prices from:		
Cottage:	£190.00-450.00	**Per week**
	£48.00	**Per night**
Apartment:	£175.00-1100.00	**Per week**
	£44.00	**Per night**

---

by Lochgilphead, Argyll
Ellary Estate - Castle Sween Bay (Holiday) Ltd
Map Ref: 1E4

★★ UP TO ★★★★ SELF CATERING

Open: Cottages all year, Chalets March-November
Ellary Estate, Ellary, Lochgilphead, Argyll PA31 8PA
T: 01880 770232
E: info@ellary.com
W: ellary.com

24799

8 Cottages	1-2 Public Rooms	Sleeps 6-8
4 Chalets	1-2 Public Rooms	Sleeps 4

Prices from:		
Cottage:	£325.00-650.00	**Per week**
Chalet:	£310.00-485.00	**Per week**
Short break prices on application		

Machrihanish, Kintyre, Argyll
Carraig
Map Ref: 1D7

★★★★ SELF CATERING

Open: All year
For reservations please contact: Mrs H Edge
T: 07778 036137
E: h.edge@virgin.net
W: carraig.net

18256

1 Bungalow	2 Public Rooms	Sleeps 7

Prices from:		
£425.00-850.00		**Per week**
Short breaks available at 70% of weekly cost		

Machrihanish, Kintyre
Mrs M Craig
Map Ref: 1D7

★★ SELF CATERING

Open: All year
The Garth, Tynron, Thornhill, Dumfriesshire DG3 4JY
T: 01848 200364
E: chrisandmimi@supanet.com
W: visitscotland.com

14504

1 House	3 Public Rooms	Sleeps 5/6

Prices from:		
£385.00-480.00		**Per week**

IMPORTANT: Prices stated are estimates and may be subject to change. Awards correct as of beginning of October 2008.

Minard, nr Inverary
The Anchorage
Map Ref: 1E4

Open: All year
Ms M Muir, Flat 1 Scott's Land, Main Street, Inverkip, Greenock, Renfrewshire PA16 0AU
T: 07751 105345
E: scottishholidays@yahoo.co.uk
W: scottishholidays.co.uk

26220

1 Bungalow	2 Public Rooms	Sleeps 2-6
Prices from:		
£250.00-450.00		**Per week**
£60.00-80.00		**Per night**

Bunessan, Isle of Mull
Mr D Black
Map Ref: 1C3

Open: All year
21 Montgomery Crescent, Dunblane FK15 9FB
T: 01786 825510
E: donald@blackshouse.demon.co.uk
W: blackshouse.demon.co.uk

34456

1 Cottage	1 Public Room	Sleeps 1-5
Prices from:		
£145.00		**Per week**
£50.00		**Per night**

Bunessan, Isle of Mull
Mrs A MacNeill
Map Ref: 1C3

Open: All year
Ardness House, Tiraghoil,
Bunessan, Isle of Mull, PA67 6UD
T: 01681 700260
E: enquiries@isleofmullholidays.com
W: isleofmullholidays.com

12550

2 Cottages	2 Public Rooms	Sleeps 2-7
Prices from:		
£300.00-750.00		**Per week**

Calgary, Isle of Mull
Mrs Ann Harvey
Map Ref: 1C1

Open: All year
Frachadil Farm, Calgary, Isle of Mull PA75 6QQ
T: 01688 400265

Frachadil Farm was a traditional Hebridean croft set in lovely surroundings near the white sandy beach of Calgary Bay. The apartment is warm, comfortable and fully equipped. Calgary is a wonderful, peaceful part of Mull, full of birds and wildlife.

26708

1 Apartment	1 Public Room	Sleeps 4-5
Prices from:		
£250.00-450.00		**Per week**
£50.00-65.00		**Per night**

For a full listing of quality assured non-serviced establishments please see pages 229-385.

93

West Highlands and Islands

Craignure, Isle of Mull
Shieling Cottage
Map Ref:1D2

54549

★★★
SELF
CATERING

Open: All year
Craignure, Isle of Mull, Argyll PA65 6AY
T: 01680 812496
E: available on website
W: shielingholidays.co.uk

1 Cottage	2 Public Rooms	Sleeps 1-6
Prices from:		
£330.00		**Per week**
£65.00		**Per night**

Craignure, Isle of Mull
Shieling Holidays
Map Ref: 1D2

54549

★★★★★
CAMPING
PARK

Open: March-October inclusive
Craignure, Isle of Mull, Argyll PA65 6AY
T: 01680 812496 **E:** available on website
W: shielingholidays.co.uk   Leisure Facilities: 🔍

From the ferry, left on the A849 to Iona. After 400 metres, left again and follow the campsite signs out to the sea, only 800 metres in all. OS Map 49 grid ref 724369

Park accommodates 106 pitches
Total Touring Pitches: 90 **Prices from:**
🚐 (30) £20.00 ⛺ (60) £17.00 🚍 (30) £20.00
Shieling (16) £241.00 per week,
£47.00 per night. Sleeps 1-6

Dervaig, Isle of Mull
Mrs Sally Marsh
Map Ref: 1C1

47137

★★★
SELF
CATERING

Open: Easter-end October
New Barns, 18 High Street, Ravensthorpe,
Northampton, Northamptonshire NN6 8EH
T: 01604 770868
E: sally@newbarns.org.uk
W: penmorebeg.co.uk

1 Bungalow	1 Public Room	Sleeps 6-8
Prices from:		
£400.00-500.00		**Per week**

Dervaig, Isle of Mull
The Old Mill
Map Ref: 1C1

59676

★★★★
SELF
CATERING

Open: All year
Penmore, Dervaig, Isle of Mull, PA75 6QS
T: 01688 400242
E: info@turusmara.com
W: mull-self-catering.co.uk

1 House	2 Public Rooms	Sleeps 9
Prices from:		
£500.00-850.00		**Per week**

Lochdon, Isle of Mull
Mr A Carew-Hunt
Map Ref: 1D2

16959

Open: All year
6 Alverstone Avenue,
Wimbledon Park, London SW19 8BE
T: 020 8947 3181
E: racarew-hunt@tiscali.co.uk
W: assc.co.uk

1 Bungalow	5 Public Rooms	Sleeps 4
Prices from:		
£210.00-500.00		**Per week**

Salen, Isle of Mull
Mrs E. MacPhail
Map Ref: 1D1

61132

Open: All year
Callachally Farm, Salen, Isle of Mull PA72 6JN
T: 01680 300424
E: macphail@tiscali.co.uk
W: holidaysonmull.co.uk

1 Bungalow	2 Public Rooms	Sleeps 8
Prices from:		
£250.00		**Per week**

IMPORTANT: Prices stated are estimates and may be subject to change. Awards correct as of beginning of October 2008.

Tobermory, Isle of Mull
Mrs Hands
Map Ref: 1C1

Open: March(Easter)-October
19 Orwell Road, Walsall WS1 2PJ
T: 01922 624091
E: royhands@talktalk.net

61849

1 Cottage	1 Public Room	Sleeps 1-5
Prices from:		
£375.00-495.00		**Per week**

Tobermory, Isle of Mull
Oxlip Cottage
Map Ref: 1C1

Open: All year
Aileen Gallagher, Gordondale Cottage, Kendal Road, Kemnay, Aberdeenshire AB51 5RN
T: 01467 641584
E: lgallagher1979@yahoo.co.uk

79189

1 Cottage	1 Public Room	Sleeps 2
Prices from:		
£150.00-310.00		**Per week**
£50.00		**Per night**

Oban, Argyll
An Cladach
Map Ref: 1E2

Open: All year
Mrs Sarah Anderson, Carr House, High Stittenham, Sheriff Hutton, York YO60 7TW
T: 01347 878418
E: awaspa@aol.com

On it's own foreshore on Loch Etive there are two spacious and comfortable houses with large gardens. One house sleeps four and the other six people. From its secluded position there are extensive views over the loch to the mountains beyond.

68208

1 Cottage	2 Public Rooms	Sleeps 2-6
1 Bungalow	1 Public Room	Sleeps 2-6
Prices from:		
Cottage:	£250.00-450.00	**Per week**
Bungalow:	£250.00-450.00	**Per week**

Oban, Argyll
Ardoran Marine Ltd
Map Ref: 1E2

Open: March-December
Ardoran Marine, Lerags, Oban, Argyll PA34 4SE
T: 01631 566123
E: helen@ardoran.co.uk
W: ardoran.co.uk

12660

3 Chalets	1 Public Room	Sleeps 4-6
Prices from:		
£250.00		**Per week**
£50.00		**Per night**

Oban, Argyll
Esplanade Court Apartments
Map Ref: 1E2

Open: April-November
Esplanade Court Apartments, Corran Esplanade, Oban, Argyll PA34 5PW
T: 01631 562067
E: enquiries@esplanadecourt.co.uk
W: esplanadecourt.co.uk

46055

45 Apartments	1 Public Room	Sleeps 1-6
Prices from:		
£330.00-645.00		**Per week**

For a full listing of quality assured non-serviced establishments please see pages 229-385.

95

Oban, Argyll
Mr W. McDicken
Map Ref: 1E2

★★★
SELF
CATERING

44880

Open: All year
5 Shillingworth Steadings,
Kilgraston Road, Bridge of Weir PA11 3RP
T: 0790 3366 757
E: billmcdicken@fsmail.net

1 Apartment	1 Public Room	Sleeps 4
Prices from:		
£250.00-380.00		**Per week**

Oban, Argyll
North Ledaig Caravan Park
Map Ref: 1E2

★★★★★
TOURING
PARK

47704

Open: March-October
Connel, Oban PA37 1RU
T: 01631 710291

Beautiful sea shore location on Ardmucknish Bay with breathtaking views to the islands. Conveniently situated near Oban it is an ideal place to explore the area, relax, watch sunsets, enjoy watersports, explore local gardens and walk the nearby hills.

Leisure Facilities: ✎

From east on A85; in Connel turn left onto A828 signposted Fort William. Site on left in one mile. From north on A82; in Ballachulish turn onto A828. Site on right in 24 miles.

Park accommodates 240 pitches
Total Touring Pitches: 240
(120 for Caravan Club only)
Prices, including hook up, from:
🚐 £14.00-22.25   🚍 £14.00-22.25

Oban, Argyll
Oban Seil Croft Cottages
Map Ref: 1E2

★★★★
SELF
CATERING

48095

Open: All year
Oban Seil Croft, Isle of Seil, Oban, Argyll PA34 4TN
T: 01852 300457
E: obanseilcroft@btinternet.com
W: obanseilcroft.co.uk

Superb self catering cottages of individual character situated in peaceful surroundings. The town of Oban is 20 minutes away by car and is a good touring base and the main ferry departure point for the islands including Mull and Iona.

2 Cottages	2 Public Rooms	Sleeps 1-4
Prices from:		
£375.00-540.00		**Per week**
£95.00		**Per night**

St Catherine's, Cowal
Halftown Cottages
Map Ref: 1F3

★★★★
SELF
CATERING

21346

Open: All year
Westfield, Letters Way,
Strachur, Argyll and Bute PA27 8DP
T: 01369 860750   **M:** 07876 085110
E: info@argyllcottages.com
W: argyllcottages.com

2 Cottages	1 Public Room	Sleeps 4
Prices from:		
£290.00		**Per week**
£50.00 per night		**Min 3 nights**

IMPORTANT: Prices stated are estimates and may be subject to change. Awards correct as of beginning of October 2008.

Strachur, Argyll
Mrs M. Cove
Map Ref: 1F3

83610

Open: All year

Bayview, Raineachan, The Bay, Strachur
Argyll PA27 8DE

T: 01369 860043
E: johnandmoya@gmail.com
W: raineachancottageargyll.com

Attractive luxury cottage in peaceful village with panoramic views of Loch Fyne. Spacious accommodation. Two double bedrooms. Wood burning stove. Excellent walking, good range of outdoor activities, area attractions, local events. Real haven in stunning area. Easy distance from Edinburgh and Glasgow.

1 Cottage	1 Public Room	Sleeps 4

Prices from:

£350.00-772.00	**Per week**

Taynuilt, Argyll
Airdeny Chalets
Map Ref: 1F2

11265

Open: All year

Airdeny Chalets, Glen Lonan,
Taynuilt, Argyll PA35 1HY

T: 01866 822648
E: jenifer@airdenychalets.co.uk
W: airdenychalets.co.uk

Small chalet park in a peaceful natural habitat, with spectacular views. Furnished to a very high standard and immaculately maintained by the resident owner. Ideal for walking, cycling, fishing, bird watching, touring the Western Highlands and Islands or just relaxing.

7 Chalets	1 Public Room	Sleeps 4-6

Prices from:

£275.00-705.00	**Per week**

Short breaks available on request

Taynuilt, Argyll
Mr and Mrs F Beaton
Map Ref: 1F2

22102

Open: All year

Dalry, Kirkton, Taynuilt, Argyll PA35 1HW

T: 01866 822657
E: mail@kirktoncroft.co.uk
W: kirktoncroft.co.uk

1 Cottage	1 Public Room	Sleeps 2-4
1 Wooden Chalet	1 Public Room	Sleeps 2

Prices from:

Cottage:	£250.00-420.00	**Per week**
	£60.00	**Per night**
Chalet:	£200.00-320.00	**Per week**
	£45.00	**Per night**

Taynuilt, Argyll
Cuilreoch Caravans
Map Ref: 1F2

21636

Open: March-October inclusive

Kilchrenan, Taynuilt, Argyll PA35 1HG

T: 01866 833236
E: joyce@cuilreoch.freeserve.co.uk
W: cuilreochcaravans.com

(3) £170.00-200.00 per week. Sleeps 1-6.

From Glasgow/Edinburgh to Crianlarich : then take A82 to Tyndrum; at Tyndrum take A85 to Taynuilt (Oban); before Taynuilt village turn left on B845; on entering Kilchrenan, turn right at Kilchrenan Inn and right at next junction; Cuilreoch is about ¼ mile further on.

For a full listing of quality assured non-serviced establishments please see pages 229-385.

97

West Highlands and Islands

Tayvallich, Argyll
The Steadings

Map Ref: 1D4

★★★★
SELF
CATERING

60522

Open: All year

Inchjura, Carsaig Bay, Tayvallich, Argyll PA31 8PN
T: 01546 870294/698
E: jamesb@riddellj.freeserve.co.uk
W: the-steadings-tayvallich.co.uk

Luxurious cottage close to Tayvallich and Carsaig
Bay on the Sound of Jura. Ensuite master bedroom,
bathroom, sitting room, dining area, opens to patio
by private brook. Two twin bedrooms upstairs.
Tayvallich is famous for yachting and near numerous
forestry walks.

1 Cottage	1 Public Room	Sleeps 6

Prices from:

£350.00-575.00	Per week
£75.00	Per night

Strachur on the east side of Loch Fyne, Argyll

IMPORTANT: Prices stated are estimates and may be subject to change. Awards correct as of beginning of October 2008.

Canoeing on Loch Lomond, Argyll

Loch Lomond and The Trossachs

Whatever road you take to the bonny banks of Loch Lomond, you'll arrive at one of the most picturesque places in all of Scotland. This vast National Park is, indeed, one of the most beautiful places in the world.

Towns like Callander, Balloch, Killin and Aberfoyle make a great base to explore different corners of the park. And once you're there, you'll find so much to do, from watersports to mountain climbing, angling to gentle strolls in the stunning countryside.

You can even integrate the sedate with the active – catch the SS Sir Walter Scott from the Trossachs Pier and cruise Loch Katrine to Stronachlachar, then enjoy the 12-mile shore hike back.

Falls of Dochart, Killin

DON'T MISS

1   **Loch Lomond and The Trossachs National Park** has its Gateway Centre on the southern shore of the loch in Balloch. From here and elsewhere on the loch, boat trips offer visitors the chance to explore the largest body of freshwater in Britain. To the west, Argyll Forest Park provides secluded waymarked trails, while the Trossachs to the east have provided inspiration for poets and novelists throughout the centuries.

2   The main visitor centre of the **Queen Elizabeth Forest Park** is on the A821 north of Aberfoyle. An integral part of the National Park, it offers a host of walking, wildlife and photography opportunities from the foot of Loch Lomond to Strathyre Forest, north of Loch Lubnaig. Here, you'll find a multitude of waymarked paths, a forest shop, wildlife viewing station and Liz MacGregor's Coffee Shop.

3   The dramatic scenery of the Trossachs is said to be the inspiration behind Sir Walter Scott's The Lady of the Lake. It is fitting then that the historic steamship which regularly sets sail on Loch Katrine is named after him. The **SS Sir Walter Scott** cruises up to Stronachlachar and will return you to the Trossachs Pier.

4   At **Go Ape!** in Aberfoyle, you can take to the trees and experience a new, exhilarating course of rope bridges, tarzan swings and zip slides (including the longest in the UK) up to 37 metres above the forest floor. Approximately three hours of fun and adventure await.

5   For a fun family day out, visit the **Scottish Wool Centre** in Aberfoyle, where you can enjoy a light-hearted look at 2,000 years of Scottish history portrayed by human and animal actors, plus spinning and weaving demonstrations. The live animal show features sheepdogs rounding up both sheep and Indian Runner Ducks, whilst younger visitors can enjoy the lambs and baby goats in springtime.

FOOD AND DRINK   eatscotland.com

6   Whilst touring around Loch Lomond, be sure to stop at the **Coach House Coffee Shop** in the conservation village of Luss. Accompany a bumper homemade scone with a Lomond Latte or a Clyde Cappuccino!

7   The **Village Inn** at Arrochar is a charming country inn on the edge of Loch Long. Offering traditional Scottish home-cooking, it proves to be a great favourite with walkers exploring the adjacent 'Arrochar Alps'.

8   The family friendly **Forth Inn** at Aberfoyle is known for its good food and atmosphere. Its award-winning bar and restaurant are favourites with locals and visitors alike.

9   **The Kilted Skirlie** is a modern Scottish restaurant with a sense of theatre that caters for every taste and pocket at Loch Lomond Shores. Rain or shine, the view of Loch Lomond and the towering Ben Lomond is the perfect setting to enjoy a delicious meal.

9

11

HISTORY AND HERITAGE

10   The **islands of Loch Lomond** are home to many ancient ruins including a 7th-century monastery and the remains of a former Victorian whisky distilleries.

11   The Lake of Menteith is the only 'lake' in Scotland, all others being known as lochs. Sail from the Port of Menteith, off the A81 south of Callander, to the island that is home to **Inchmahome Priory**, an 18th century Augustinian monastery.

12   The historic village of Killin, with the spectacular Falls of Dochart, is the setting for the **Breadalbane Forklore Centre** which is housed in a beautifully restored mill with a working waterwheel. Dedicated to exploring the rich myths and legends prevalent in these parts, you can follow the stories of the local clans and learn about St Fillan and the arrival of Christianity in Scotland. Open April to October.

VIEWS

13   The beauty of **Loch Lomond** is undisputed but the finest vantage point is more open to debate. Everyone has their favourite spot and no doubt you will too. Take a cruise on the loch itself from Luss, Balloch or Tarbet or head to Inversnaid on the west bank for more rugged views.

14   'The Dumpling' is the nickname for **Duncryne Hill**, a volcanic plug, situated just off the A811 at the east end of Gartocharn. At about 465ft high and accessible by a short steep path, it is an astounding vantage point overlooking Loch Lomond's islands.

15   **Conic Hill** is located just north of Balmaha on the B837. A 358m ascent, it offers superb views of Loch Lomond and its islands. From here, you can also see the dramatic changes to the landscape caused by the Highland Boundary Fault.

16   From the Stronachlachar junction on the Inversnaid road (B829), the wild landscape of **Loch Arklet** leads down towards Loch Lomond and its surrounding hills.

WALKS   **visitscotland.com/walking**

17   To walk along the shore of **Loch Katrine**, start at the Trossachs Pier (A821 west of Callander). Here you can choose to walk the 12 mile route to Stronachlachar and get the steamer back or you can walk as far as you like and then re-trace your steps. Cycle hire is also available here.

18   The village hall in Balquhidder is your starting point for one of Breadalbane's most glorious views. Head along the Kirkton Burn and upwards onto a forest road. Soon you'll reach **Creag an Tuirc** where you can absorb the beauty of Balquhidder Glen, Loch Voil and little Loch Doine. Including a short climb, this 2½ mile walk should take you about 2 hours.

19   **Rowardennan** (B837 from Drymen) on the eastern edge of Loch Lomond is a wonderful starting and finishing point for a gentle walk along the shores, following part of the famous West Highland Way.

Loch Lomond and the Trossachs

Aberfoyle, Stirlingshire
Trossachs Holiday Park
Map Ref: 1H3

Open: Self Catering, all year. Caravan and Camping, 1 March-31 October

By Aberfoyle, Stirlingshire FK8 3SA

T: 01877 382614
E: info@trossachsholidays.co.uk
W: trossachsholidays.co.uk

The Trossachs Holiday Park offers the perfect base to explore the Trossachs National Park – walking, cycling, photography, fishing, golf or just relax in this area of outstanding beauty. Our holiday caravans offer peace and quiet with views to the hills.

We are situated 3 miles south of Aberfoyle on the east side of the A81.

Park accommodates 46 pitches

Total Touring Pitches: 46

Prices from:
(46) from £14.00   (20) from £14.00   (46) from £14.00
(10) From £259 pw or from £35 pn. Sleeps 4-6.

Arden, by Loch Lomond
The Gardeners Cottages
Map Ref: 1G4

Open: All year
Arden House Estate, Arden, Loch Lomond G83 8RD
T: 01389 850601
E: amacleod@gardeners-cottages.com
W: gardeners-cottages.com

3 Cottages	1 Public Rooms	Sleeps 2-5
Prices from:		
£273.00-617.00		**Per week**
£60.00-113.00		**Per night**

Ardlui, Loch Lomond
Ardlui Luxury Lodges
Map Ref: 1G3

Open: All year
Ardlui Hotel, Ardlui, Loch Lomond G83 7EB
T: 01301 704243/704269
E: info@ardlui.co.uk
W: ardlui.co.uk

2 Cabins	1 Public Room	Sleeps 6
Prices from:		
£575.00		**Per week**
£380.00		**Per 3 nights**

Balfron
The Stables & Ploughmans Cottage
Map Ref: 1H4

Open: All year

Meikle Camoquhill Farm, Balfron G63 0QW
T: 01360 440325
E: enquiries@lochlomond-farmcottages.com
W: lochlomond-farmcottages.com

Beautifully renovated courtyard cottages on a working farm. Spacious, bright and comfortable two and three bedroom homes. Private gardens to relax and enjoy the beautiful surroundings. Situated in the stunning countryside between Loch Lomond and the Trossachs.

2 Cottages	2 Public Rooms	Sleeps 1-6
Prices from:		
£295.00-645.00		**Per week**
£190.00-365.00		**Short Breaks**

For a full listing of quality assured non-serviced establishments please see pages 229-385.

103

Loch Lomond and the Trossachs

Balloch, Loch Lomond
Lomond Woods Holiday Park
Map Ref: 1G4

★★★★ SELF CATERING

★★★★★ HOLIDAY PARK

68185

Open: All year

Tullichewan, Balloch, Loch Lomond G83 8QP
T: 01389 755000
E: lomondwoods@holiday-parks.co.uk
W: holiday-parks.co.uk

Nestling in the hills and woodlands surrounding Loch Lomond, Lomond Woods Holiday Park is at the gateway to the National Park and next to Lomond Shores Visitor Experience. Pine lodges and caravans for family holidays and relaxing short breaks.

6 Pine Lodges	1 Public Room	Sleeps 2-8

Prices from:
£295.00   **Per week**

Brig O'Turk, Callander
Frennich House
Map Ref: 1H3

★★★★ SELF CATERING

70376

Open: March-November

Frennich House, Brig O'Turk, Callander, FK17 8HT
T: 01877 376274
E: frennich.house@virgin.net
W: frennich-house.co.uk

1 Apartment	1 Public Room	Sleeps 2

Prices from:
£230.00-250.00   **Per week**

Callander, Perthshire
Gart Caravan Park
Map Ref: 1H3

★★★★★ HOLIDAY PARK

27321

Open: Easter-15th October

Stirling Road, Callander, Perthshire FK17 8LE

T: 01877 330002
E: enquiries@theholidaypark.co.uk
W: theholidaypark.co.uk

Peaceful and spacious, this outstanding award winning family run park is maintained to very high standards with modern heated shower and toilet facilities. Callander is an ideal base for walking, cycling, golf and fishing or to just simply relax.

Situated on A84. From south; one mile before Callander town centre. From north; one mile south of Callander

Park accommodates 128 pitches

Total Touring Pitches: 128
Prices from:
(128) £19.50

Callander, Perthshire
Mrs Greenfield
Map Ref: 1H3

★★★ SELF CATERING

12216

Open: All year

Norlea, Ancaster Road, Callander, Perthshire, FK17 8EL
T: 01877 330234
E: james772greenfield@btinternet.com

1 Bungalow	1 Public Room	Sleeps 3

Prices from:
£200.00-320.00   **Per week**

Short breaks available by request

IMPORTANT: Prices stated are estimates and may be subject to change. Awards correct as of beginning of October 2008.

Callander, Perthshire
Mr Andrew Little

Map Ref: 1H3

★★ UP TO ★★★★
SELF CATERING

Open: All year

Riverview, Leny Road, Callander, Perthshire FK17 8AL
T: 01877 330635
E: drew@visitcallander.co.uk
W: visitcallander.co.uk

We offer a wide choice of excellent accommodation to suit all tastes with Auld Toll in a rural location, Lochview Barn overlooking Loch Lubnaig and Craigard in Callander. Your choice to enjoy. The picture is of Auld Toll Cottages.

13496

2 Cottages	1 Public Room	Sleeps 2-4
1 Apartment	1 Public Room	Sleeps 2
1 Converted Barn	1 Public Room	Sleeps 3

Prices from:
Cottage:	£150.00-400.00	Per week
	£40.00 **Per night (3 nights min) low season**	
Apartment:	£150.00-250.00	Per week
	£40.00 **Per night (3 nights min) low season**	
Barn:	£150.00-400.00	Per week
	£50.00 **Per night (3 nights min) low season**	

📺🗄🔲🍽️🚲🎵✳️Ⓜ☺◎🛩🅿📱✲🎞✿♨🐾🅿†

Drymen, Stirlingshire
Ballat Smithy Cottage

Map Ref: 1H4

★★★★
SELF CATERING

Open: All year

Mrs Anne Currie, Ballat Smithy, Balfron Station, by Drymen, Stirlingshire G63 0SE
T: +44 (0) 1360 440269
 E: a.h.currie@btopenworld.com
W: ballatsmithycottage.com

A charming and very high quality cottage surrounded by beautiful countryside and lovely views, ideally situated for exploring Loch Lomond, the Trossachs and central Scotland. Price all inclusive, with welcome pack of Scottish and Fair Trade provisions. Short breaks available.

13952

| 1 Cottage | 1 Public Room | Sleeps 1-4 |

Prices from:
| £275.00-465.00 | **Per week** |
| £70.00 | **Per night** |

📺🗄🔲🍽️🚲🎵🎞🖥️✳️☺◎🛩🅿📱🎞✿♨🐾🅿⛷✉

Drymen, Loch Lomond
Elmbank

Map Ref: 1H4

★★
SELF CATERING

Open: All year

10 Stirling Road, Drymen, G63 0BN
T: 01360 661016   **M:** 07977 756226
E: enquiries@elmbank-drymen.co.uk
W: elmbank-drymen.co.uk

80038

| 2 Apartments | 1-2 Public Rooms | Sleeps 6-8 |

Prices from:
| £450.00 | **Per week** |
| £120.00 | **Per night** |

🎵🗄📺🔲🍽️🖥️Ⓜ☺🛩🅿📱🎞✿♨🐾🅿
✳️🅿⛷†

Drymen, Loch Lomond
Foxglove Cottages

Map Ref: 1H4

★★★★
SELF CATERING

Open: All year

Gartness Road, Drymen, Stirlingshire G63 0DW
T: 01360 661128
E: admin@foxglovecottages.co.uk
W: foxglovecottages.co.uk

68133

| 3 Cottages | 2 Public Rooms | Sleeps 2-8 |

Prices from:
| £560.00-1260.00 | **Per week** |
| £80.00-180.00 | **Per night** |

📺🗄🔲🍽️☺◎🛩🅿📱🎞✿🐾♨⛷🅿📷♿🐕🛁📺 SP

For a full listing of quality assured non-serviced establishments please see pages 229-385.

105

Loch Lomond and the Trossachs

Helensburgh, Argyll
Pier View
Map Ref: 1G4

Open: All year
Arran View, 32 Barclay Drive,
Helensburgh, Argyll and Bute G84 9RA
T: 01436 673713
E: bookings@pier-view.co.uk
W: pier-view.co.uk

49786

1 Apartment   1 Public Room   Sleeps 4-6

Prices from:

£205.00-375.00   **Per week**

£35.00-60.00   **Per night**

Helensburgh, Argyll
Rhu Lodge
Map Ref: 1G4

Open: All year
Rhu, by Helensburgh, Argyll and Bute G84 8NF
T: 01436 821315
E: dmmcgowan@btinternet.com
W: rhulodge.co.uk

67491

1 Apartment   1 Public Room   Sleeps 1-2

Prices from:

£320.00-420.00   **Per week**

Helensburgh, Argyll
Shandonbank Cottage
Map Ref: 1G4

Open: All year
Inverallt, Shandon,
Helensburgh, Argyll and Bute G84 8NR
T: 01436 820314
E: shandoncooks@btinternet.com
W: shandonbank.com

31908

This renovated listed building with three bedrooms
and large flat enclosed garden dates from 1840.
Living areas and main bedroom face the sea with
spectacular views across Gareloch. The garden wall
has a towered summerhouse and provides access to
the beach.

1 Cottage   2 Public Rooms   Sleeps 6

Prices from:

£450.00   **Per week**

£65.00   **Per night**

Helensburgh, Argyll
Mrs Angela Stanton
Map Ref: 1G4

Open: All year
Rosebank Cottage, 28A Campbell Street,
Helensburgh, Argyll and Bute G84 8BQ
T: 01436 675372
E: angelagardencottage@hotmail.co.uk

27211

1 Cottage   1 Public Room   Sleeps 1-7

Prices from:

£525.00-595.00   **Per week**

£75.00-85.00   **Per night**

Helensburgh, Argyll
Crosskeys Cottage
Map Ref: 1G4

Open: All year
Mrs Joyce Sykes, Crosskeys, Glen Fruin,
nr Helensburgh, Argyll and Bute G84 9EE
T: 01389 850595
E: joyce_sykes@hotmail.co.uk

75025

1 Cottage   2 Public Rooms   Sleeps 2-4

Prices from:

£280.00-550.00   **Per week**

£45.00-60.00   **Per night**

IMPORTANT: Prices stated are estimates and may be subject to change. Awards correct as of beginning of October 2008.

Inchmurrin Island, Loch lomond
Inchmurrin Island Self Catering

Map Ref: 1G4

★★★
SELF CATERING

Open: All year
Inchmurrin Hotel, Inchmurrin Island, Loch Lomond G63 0JY
T: 01389 850245
E: scotts@inchmurrin-lochlomond.com
W: inchmurrin-lochlomond.com

31548

1 Cottage	1 Public Room	Sleeps 2-8
3 Apartments	1 Public Room	Sleeps 4-6
Prices from:		
Cottage:	£440.00	Per week
	£341.00	Per ½ week
Apartment:	£407.00	Per week
	£275.00	Per ½ week

Killin, Perthshire
Mrs L Frost

Map Ref: 1H2

★★★
SELF TERING

Open: All year
Kennels Cottage, Boreland,
by Killin, Perthshire, FK21 8UA
T: 01567 820562

13989

1 Bungalow	2 Public Rooms	Sleeps 6
Prices from:		
£170.00-380.00		**Per week**
£90.00-190.00		**Per night**

Killin, Perthshire
Gracedieu

Map Ref: 1H2

★★★
SELF TERING

Open: All year
Mrs J. M. Huntley, c/o Rowanbank,
Dochart Road, Killin, Perthshire, FK21 8SN
T/F: 01567 820396

43890

1 Cottage	3 Public Rooms	Sleeps 1-6
Prices from:		
£250.00-400.00		**Per week**
£50.00		**Per night**

by Killin, Perthshire
Dr K Chew

Map Ref: 1H2

★★★
SELF TERING

Open: All year
Morenish Mews, by Killin, FK21 8TX
T: 01567 820527
E: stay@morenishmews.com
W: morenishmews.com

72535

Two semi-detached cottage apartments and Coach House apartment within four acres of secluded garden overlooking Loch Tay in Highland Perthshire. Centrally situated for touring and outdoor activities. The village of Killin and picturesque Falls of Dochart are 3 miles away.

2 Cottages	1 Public Room	Sleeps 1-3
1 Apartment	1 Public Room	Sleeps 1-2
Prices from:		
Cottage:	£225.00-375.00	Per week
	£45.00-75.00	Per night
Apartment:	£225.00-375.00	Per week
	£45.00-75.00	Per night

For a full listing of quality assured non-serviced establishments please see pages 229-385.

Loch Lomond and the Trossachs

Lochearnhead, Perthshire
Mr Cameron
Map Ref: 1H2

★★★ SELF CATERING

Open: All year
Lochside Cottages, Lochearnhead, Perthshire FK19 8PT
T: 01567 830268
E: gus.dundhu@btinternet.com
W: lochsidecottages.net

Family run chalet and cottage business on the edge of beautiful Lochearn. Ideal centre for touring, golfing and water skiing (we have our own jetty, slipway and moorings). All chalets are kitted out for a self catering holiday made easy.

36146

| 9 Cabins | 4 Public Rooms | Sleeps 4-6 |

Prices from:

| £180.00 | **Per week** |
| £90.00 | **Per 3 nights** |

Luss, Loch Lomond
Shemore Farm Cottage
Map Ref: 1G4

★★★ SELF CATERING

Open: All year
Shantron Farm, Luss, Argyll and Bute, G83 8RH
T: 01389 850231
E: anne@farmstay-lochlomond.co.uk
W: farmstay-lochlomond.co.uk

54303

| 1 Cottage | 1 Public Room | Sleeps 5 |

Prices from:

| £375.00 | **Per week** |
| £70.00 | **Per night** |

Luss, Loch Lomond
Shegarton Farm Cottages
Map Ref: 1G4

★★★★ SELF CATERING

Open: All year
Shegarton Farm, Luss, Argyll & Bute, G83 8RH
T: 01389 850269
E: shegarton@supanet.com
W: shegartonfarmcottages.com

54426

| 2 Cottages | 2 Public Rooms | Sleeps 2-4 |

Prices from:

| £200.00-450.00 | **Per week** |
| £40.00 | **Per night** |

Port of Menteith, Perthshire
Archie and Nicola Orr Ewing
Map Ref: 1H3

★★★ SELF CATERING

Open: All year
Cardross Holiday Homes, Cardross House, Port of Menteith, Perthshire FK8 3JY
T: 01877 385223
E: adoewing@cardrossestate.demon.co.uk
W: cardrossholidayhomes.com

18045

| 5 Cottages | 1 Public Room | Sleeps 2-8 |

Prices from:

| £325.00 | **Per week** |
| £195.00 | **Per 3 nights** |

Tyndrum, Perthshire
Burnbrae Cottage
Map Ref: 1G2

★★★ SELF CATERING

Open: All year
East Cottage, Auchertyre, Tyndrum, Perthshire, FK20 8RU
T: 01838 400331
E: info@stayburnbrae.co.uk **W:** stayburnbrae.co.uk

67877

| 2 Cottages | 2 Public Rooms | Sleeps 4-5 |

Prices from:

| £200.00 | **Per week** |
| £60.00 | **Per night** |

IMPORTANT: Prices stated are estimates and may be subject to change. Awards correct as of beginning of October 2008.

Tyndrum, Perthshire
Strathfillan Wigwams

Map Ref: 1G2

Open: All year
Auchtertyre, Tyndrum, Perthshire FK20 8RU
T: 01838 400251
E: wigwam@sac.ac.uk
W: sac.ac.uk/wigwams

⊙◎👣🔲✏🔲♿📺🐾🔆💺E🚽🗡❄🛋🚐💷♨

We are three miles north of Crianlarich on the A82 - travelling from south. And two miles south of Tyndrum - travelling from the north.

56909

Park accommodates 39 pitches

Total Touring Pitches: 5 **Prices from:**

⛺ (10) £12.00   🚐 (5) £14.00
Wigwam (20) £25.00pn (2 people sharing)

🛖 (4) £50.00 per night.
Ⓜ◎👣🔲♿📺🐾E🚽🗡❄🅿🚐

Looking down to the bridge at the Falls of Dochart (at the confluence of Rivers Dochart and Lochay), Killin

For a full listing of quality assured non-serviced establishments please see pages 229-385.

109

Stirling Castle at Dusk

Stirling and Forth Valley

Stirling and the Forth Valley offer a huge range of visitor attractions but a recent addition to the list is proving extremely popular. Built to celebrate the new Millennium and opened in 2002, The Falkirk Wheel is a triumph of engineering. It's the world's only rotating boatlift and, standing an impressive 24 metres high, it has reconnected the Forth & Clyde Canal with the Union Canal.

Scotland's industrial heritage is well represented locally at the Bo'ness and Kinneil Steam Railway, Birkhill Fireclay Mine and Callendar House, while you can see traces of Scotland's woollen industry on the shores of the Forth in Clackmannan.

History is everywhere around Stirling. Don't miss Stirling Castle and the National Wallace Monument but remember to leave enough time to take a walk round the town and enjoy a spot of shopping too.

Port Street, Stirling

To find out more, call 0845 22 55 121 or go to visitscotland.com

DON'T MISS

1   **Stirling Castle**, undoubtedly one of the finest in Scotland, sits high on its volcanic rock towering over the stunning countryside known as 'Braveheart Country'. A favourite royal residence over the centuries and a key military stronghold, visit the Great Hall, the Chapel Royal, and the Renaissance Palace. From the castle esplanade the sites of no less than seven historic battles can be seen, as can the majestic **National Wallace Monument** built in tribute to William Wallace.

2   The world's only rotating boatlift, **The Falkirk Wheel**, was constructed in 2002 to link the Forth & Clyde and Union canals. It is now possible for boats to traverse Central Scotland by canal for the first time in more than 40 years. Learn about Scotland's canal network in the visitor centre or board a vessel to take a trip on the mechanical marvel itself.

3   The **Antonine Wall** dates back to the 2nd century and once marked the northern frontier of the Roman Empire. Substantial lengths have been preserved and can still be seen at various sites around Falkirk. The site was awarded UNESCO World Heritage Status in July 2008. Follow the wall for a relaxed walk along the towpath on the north of the canal, taking you past the Falkirk Wheel to Bonnybridge.

4   Just a few miles north west of Stirling on the A84 you will find **Blair Drummond Safari Park**. Here you can drive through wild animal reserves and get close to lions and zebras, and a whole host of other animals. Or you can park and walk around the pet farm, see the only elephants in Scotland, watch a sea lion display, find out what it's like to hold a bird of prey and take a boat to Chimp Island. There is also an adventure play area, pedal boats for hire and for the more adventurous – the flying fox!

FOOD AND DRINK   eatscotland.com

5 The **Gargunnock Inn** is situated in the small village of Gargunnock on the A811 west of Stirling. A welcoming, friendly establishment, it serves freshly prepared, local produce in its restaurant and has a more informal bar adjoining for relaxing in after dinner.

6 **Harviestoun Country Hotel & Restaurant** in Tillicoultry is the perfect place to stop, whether it is for lunch, high tea or an evening meal. The restored 18th century steading, with the backdrop of the stunning Ochil Hills, is the ideal setting for relaxing with good food and fine wine.

7 The lovely Victorian spa town of Bridge of Allan is home to the **Bridge of Allan Brewery** where you can see how traditional Scottish handcrafted ales are produced and even have a free tasting session!

HISTORY AND HERITAGE

8 Built in tribute to Scotland's national hero Sir William Wallace, the **National Wallace Monument**, by Stirling, can be seen for miles around. The Monument exhibition tells of Sir Wallace's epic struggle for a free Scotland.

9 **Castle Campbell** is beautifully sited at the head of Dollar Glen, immediately north of Dollar. Sitting in lofty isolation and overlooked by the Ochil Hills, the castle became the chief lowland stronghold of the Campbell clan, upon whose members the successive titles of Earl, Marquis, and Duke of Argyll were bestowed. There are excellent walks through Dollar Glen to enjoy too.

10 On the site of the original battlefield, the **Bannockburn Heritage Centre** on the southern outskirts of Stirling, tells the story of the greatest victory of Scotland's favourite monarch King Robert the Bruce. Walk the battlefield and then enjoy the audio-visual presentation in the centre, recounting the battle. A re-enactment of the battle takes place over two days every September.

11 Open the door to **Callendar House** in Falkirk, and you open the door to 600 years of Scottish history. Journey through time from the days of the Jacobites to the advent of the railway, and don't forget to stop at the Georgian kitchens for some refreshments prepared using authentic Georgian recipes.

12 Discover what life was like for unfortunate inmates within the authentic Victorian **Stirling Old Town Jail**. You might well run into Jock Rankin, the notorious town hangman, and even witness an attempted jail break!

WALLS

13   Walk around Muiravon Country Park along the River Avon and you'll pass the Avon Aqueduct, Scotland's longest and tallest, which carries the Union Canal above the river. Near Bo'Ness, the River Avon flows through the **Avon Gorge**, a well known local beauty spot where you can stroll through ancient woodlands, home to a variety of wildlife including deer and otters.

14   Not far from Dollar where the A823 meets the A977, it's worth stopping to explore the delightful **Rumbling Bridge**, so named because of the continuous rumbling sound of the falls and the river below. The unusual double bridge spans a narrow gorge and you'll find a network of platforms and paths that take you over the river and deep into the gorge with spectacular views of waterfalls and swirling pools.

15   The **Darn Walk** from Bridge of Allan to Dunblane is a beautiful walk which can be enjoyed at any time of the year. Highlights include a scenic stretch alongside the River Allan and the cave which was Robert Louis Stevenson's inspiration for Ben Gunn's cave in Treasure Island. The walk can be completed in 1½ to 2 hours.

16   At the heart of Clackmannanshire's 300-acre **Gartmorn Dam Country Park**, visitors can enjoy a short walk with gentle gradients suitable for wheelchairs or pushchairs. Gartmorn Dam is the oldest man-made reservoir still in use in Scotland, and is a nature reserve which is the winter home of thousands of migratory ducks.

ATTRACTIONS

17   Dating back to the 14th century, **Alloa Tower** is one of the largest surviving medieval tower houses in Scotland. The tower has been recently restored and has amazing features.

18   Situated by the banks of the River Teith, **Doune Castle** was once the ancestral home of the Earls of Moray. At one time occupied by the Jacobite troops, this castle can now be explored and makes a great picnic spot. Film lovers may also recognise the castle from scenes from 'Monty Python and the Holy Grail'.

19   Just north of Stirling, **Argaty Red Kites** is one of Scotland's red kite feeding stations. After 130 years of Scottish Natural Heritage, the RSPB has reintroduced these exciting, acrobatic birds to central Scotland. Spend a day and you can enjoy a guided walk or just watch the birds from the hide.

Stirling
Mr T Harris
Map Ref: 2A4

Open: All year

Wellsfield Farm Holiday Lodges, Health Club, Trout Fishery &
Equestrian Centre, Stirling Road, Denny, Stirlingshire, FK6 6QZ
T: 01324 822800   **W:** wellsfield.co.uk
E: enquiries@touristholidays.demon.co.uk

4 Cabin	1 Public Room	Sleeps 4

Prices from:		
£420.00		**Per week**
£60.00		**Per night**

63548

Stirling
Stirling Flexible Lettings
Map Ref: 2A4

Open: All year

Mackeanston House, Doune, Perthshire, FK16 6AX
T: 01786 850213
E: info@stirling-flexible-lettings.co.uk
W: stirling-flexible-lettings.co.uk

1 Cottage	1 Public Room	Sleeps 4-5
3 Apartments	1 Public Room	Sleeps 2-4

Prices from:		
Cottage:	£350.00-£600.00	**Per week**
	£70.00	**Per night**
Apartment:	£350.00-£585.00	**Per week**

16292

Stirling
Witches Craig Caravan and Camping Park
Map Ref: 2A4

Open: April-October

Witches Craig, Blairlogie, Stirling FK9 5PX
T: 01786 474947   **E:** info@witchescraig.co.uk
W: witchescraig.co.uk

An attractive and exceptionally well maintained 5 star
touring park with award winning facilities. Peacefully
situated below the picturesque Ochil Hills. An ideal
place to relax and unwind but also a great base for
travelling. A warm welcome awaits you.

3 miles north east of Stirling on A91 Stirling - St Andrews road.

64425

Park accommodates 60 pitches

Total Touring Pitches: 60
Prices from:
🚐 £13.50-17.50 ⛺£13.50-17.50 🚎 £13.50-17.50

IMPORTANT: Prices stated are estimates and may be subject to change. Awards correct as of beginning of October 2008.

The Pots of Gartness, near Killearn, Stirling

For a full listing of quality assured non-serviced establishments please see pages 229-385.

115

Carnoustie Golf Links, Carnoustie, Angus

PERTHSHIRE, ANGUS AND DUNDEE AND THE KINGDOM OF FIFE

Scotland's heartlands are the perfect holiday destination in many ways. There's so much to discover in this part of the world that you're sure to find something that suits you perfectly. Golfing, fishing, walking, sightseeing, there's an abundance of choice and there are some wonderful places to stay.

You'll find former fishermen's cottages in the charming little towns or villages in the East Neuk, farmhouses in glorious Perthshire and delightful little places in the idyllic Angus glens. There's also an excellent selection of touring and holiday parks in the area – many with exceptional facilities like swimming pools, games rooms, play areas and even salmon and trout fishing on site!

The countryside is so varied too. Fife has an enviable coastline with a number of perfect little harbour towns, Perthshire is unspoiled and magnificent, with some of Scotland's finest woodlands and stunning lochs and hills. And then there's Dundee – the area's largest city. There's always another fascinating place waiting to be explored.

This is a holiday destination that can be as active as you want it to be. For the outdoor enthusiast, there's anything from hill walking to whitewater rafting and pretty much everything in between. Anglers love the thrill of pursuing salmon and trout on some of the country's greatest river beats or heading out to sea where the catch can be bountiful.

Golfers love this area too. Some of the world's finest courses are here, from the home of golf at St Andrews to championship quality greats Gleneagles and Carnoustie.

If wildlife's your thing, the opportunities are endless. In the countryside of Perthshire and the Angus Glens there are ospreys, eagles, otters and deer. By the sea from Fife to Angus spot a wide variety of seabirds – especially around the Montrose Basin which attracts thousands of migrant species.

You don't have to be escaping civilisation to enjoy these parts, however. There are towns and cities that you'll enjoy enormously, each with their own unique attractions. Perth has specialist shops and high street retailers. St Andrews is a fine university town with a fascinating history. Dunfermline was once the seat of Scotland's Kings while Dundee, the City of Discovery, is enjoying something of a renaissance these days and is a great place for a big day out.

What's more, 2009 is a big year for Scotland – we're celebrating the 250th anniversary of the birth of Robert Burns. There's over 200 special events taking place throughout the year, all over Scotland. Go to homecomingscotland2009.com to find out about events in this area.

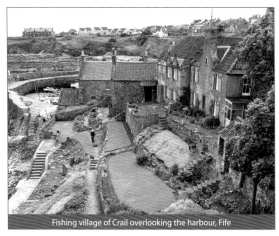
Fishing village of Crail overlooking the harbour, Fife

Canadian canoeing on Loch Tay at Kenmore, Perthshire

What's On?

Snowdrop Festival 2009
February/March 2009
visitscotland.com/snowdrops

StAnza 2009
Scotland's Poetry Festival
18 - 22 March 2009
stanzapoetry.org

Angus Glens Walking Festival
28 – 31 May 2009, Angus Glens
angusanddundee.co.uk/walkingfestival

Perth Festival of the Arts
21 -31 May 2009, Perth
The Festival features world-class artists.
perthfestival.co.uk

Game Conservancy Scottish Fair
3 - 5 July 2009, Scone Palace, Perth
One of the main countryside events of the year in Scotland.
www.scottishfair.com

The 34th Scottish Transport Extravaganza
11 – 12 July 2009
Glamis Castle, Angus
svvc.co.uk

Arbroath Seafest
8 –9 August 2009
Arbroath Harbour, Arbroath
angusahead.com

Culross Music & Arts Festival
August 2009
culrossfestival.com

Blair Castle International Horse Trials & Country Fair
Blair Castle, Blair Atholl
27 – 30 August 2009
Equestrian sport on an international scale!
blairhorsetrials.co.uk

Dundee Flower and Food Festival
4 – 6 September 2009
dundeeflowerandfoodfestival.com

The Enchanted Forest
16 October – 1 November 2009
Faskally Wood, by Pitlochry
A spectacular journey of light and sound in Perthshire's Big Tree Country.
enchantedforest.org.uk

MAP

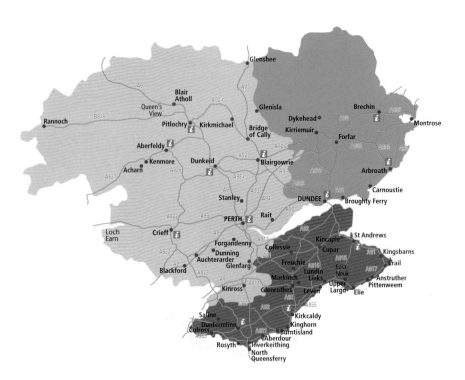

©Collins Bartholomew Ltd

To find out more, call 0845 22 55 121 or go to visitscotland.com

VISITOR INFORMATION CENTRES

Visitor Information Centres are staffed by people 'in the know' offering friendly advice, helping to make your stay in Scotland the most enjoyable ever . . . whatever your needs!

Perthshire		
Aberfeldy	The Square, Aberfeldy, PH15 2DD	Tel: 01887 820276
Blairgowrie	26 Wellmeadow, Blairgowrie PH10 6AS	Tel: 01250 872960
Crieff	High Street, Crieff, PH7 3HU	Tel: 01764 652578
Dunkeld	The Cross, Dunkeld, PH8 0AN	Tel: 01350 727688
Perth	Lower City Mills, West Mill Street, Perth, PH1 5QP	Tel: 01736 450600
Pitlochry	22 Atholl Road, Pitlochry, PH16 5BX	Tel: 01796 472215

Angus and Dundee		
Arbroath	Harbour Visitor Centre, Fishmarket Quay, Arbroath, DD11 1PS	Tel: 01241 872609
Brechin	Pictavia Centre, Haughmuir, Brechin	Tel: 01356 623050
Dundee	Discovery Point, Discovery Quay, Dundee DD1 4XA	Tel: 01382 527527

Fife		
Dunfermline	1 High Street, Dunfermline, KY12 7DL	Tel: 01383 720999
Kirkcaldy	The Merchant's House, 339 High Street, Kirkcaldy, KY1 1JL	Tel: 01592 267775
St Andrews	70 Market St St Andrews Fife FY16 9NU	Tel: 01334 472021

LOCAL KNOWLEDGE • WHERE TO STAY • ACCOMMODATION BOOKING • PLACES TO VISIT • THINGS TO DO • MAPS AND GUIDES TRAVEL ADVICE • ROUTE PLANNING • WHERE TO SHOP AND EAT LOCAL CRAFTS AND PRODUCE • EVENT INFORMATION • TICKETS

For information and ideas about exploring Scotland in advance of your trip, call our booking and information service **0845 22 55 121** or go to **visitscotland.com**

If calling from outside the UK and Ireland **+44 1506 832 121**   From Ireland **1800 932 510**

A £4 booking fee applies for accommodation bookings made via a Visitor Information Centre and through our booking and information service.

Schiehallion and Loch Tummel from The Queen's View, by Pitlochry

Perthshire

Perthshire is one of the most strikingly picturesque parts of Scotland. It ranges from wild and mountainous to sophisticated and cultured, from the wilderness of Rannoch Moor to the lap of luxury at the 5-star Gleneagles Hotel.

You can experience everything here, from traditional activities like golf, fishing and horse riding to more recent innovations like sphereing and white water rafting. Whatever you pursue, it will be against a backdrop of spectacular scenery; high mountains, deep forests, sparkling lochs and wide rivers.

But you don't have to spend the day pushing yourself to the limits; a walk through the forests of Big Tree Country may suffice. Take a romantic stroll through the Birks o' Aberfeldy, visit one of nine great gardens, marvel at a reconstructed Iron Age crannog on Loch Tay or simply enjoy the Queen's View near Pitlochry.

Sphereing

To find out more, call 0845 22 55 121 or go to visitscotland.com

DON'T MISS

1   The Scottish Crannog Centre at Kenmore on Loch Tay is an authentic recreation of an ancient loch-dwelling. Imagine a round house in the middle of a loch with a thatched roof, on stilts. You can tour the Crannog to see how life used to be 2,600 years ago. Upon your return to shore, have a go at a variety of Iron Age crafts; see if you can grind the grain, drill through stone or make fire through wood friction.

2   Scone Palace, near Perth, was renowned as the traditional crowning place of Scottish kings, as the capital of the Pictish kingdom and centre of the ancient Celtic Church. Nowadays, the great house and its beautiful accompanying grounds are home to the Earls of Mansfield, and offer an ideal day out.

3   Blair Castle, the stunningly situated ancient seat of the Dukes and Earls of Atholl, is a five-star castle experience. The unmistakeable white façade is visible from the A9 just north of Blair Atholl. Dating back 740 years, the castle has played a part in some of Scotland's most tumultuous events but today it is a relaxing and fascinating place to visit.

4   The Famous Grouse Experience is housed within Glenturret Distillery, Scotland's oldest malt whisky distillery. It is an interactive attraction where visitors can familiarise themselves with this renowned tipple and the brand that accompanies it! As well as a tour of the production areas, you can enjoy a unique audio-visual presentation which gives a grouse's eye view of Scotland, and delicious food.

5   Among its many other attractions, Perthshire – known as Big Tree Country - can boast some of the most remarkable trees and woodlands anywhere in Europe. The 250 miles of way-marked paths give you an excellent opportunity to explore the area and, if you're lucky, catch a glimpse of the many different species of wildlife which make Perthshire their home. Here you'll discover Europe's oldest tree in Fortingall Churchyard, the world's highest hedge and one of Britain's tallest trees at The Hermitage by Dunkeld.

6   You'll find some of Scotland's most beautiful parks and gardens in Perthshire, ranging from small privately owned gardens to formal sumptuous gardens, containing examples of native Scottish plants and rare and exotic species from around the world. The Perthshire Gardens Collection brings together 9 spectacular examples of the gardener's art such as Kinross House, Drummond Castle and Branklyn Gardens. Heather, wild woodlands and Himalayan treasures will inspire you whether you're a horticultural enthusiast or someone who simply loves beautiful gardens.

FOOD AND DRINK

eatscotland.com

7   Farmers' markets have seen a resurgence in recent years in the UK and Perth's Farmers' Market is arguably the best known in Scotland. Taking place throughout the year on the first Saturday of each month, it is something of a showcase for local producers and growers and is a rewarding visit in its own right. Look out for fish, meat and game, baked goods, fruit wines and liqueurs, honeys and preserves, fruit and vegetables, sweets and herbs. Sound tempting? Many stallholders also offer free tastings.

8   The area around Blairgowrie is Europe's centre for soft fruit production and a particular feature of the area are the signs at farms inviting you to 'pick your own' strawberries, raspberries, gooseberries, redcurrants, and tayberries. Sample the local produce of field and hedgerow at Cairn O' Mohr Wines in Errol. A family-run business it produces Scottish fruit wines made from local berries, flowers and leaves - a truly unique end product. Explore the winery through one of the on site tours before undertaking a tasting session!

9   Edradour Distillery – Scotland's smallest malt whisky distillery - can be found in the Highland foothills just to the east of Pitlochry. Built in the early 19th century Edradour is the only remaining 'farm' distillery in Perthshire and seems to have hardly changed in the 170 years of its existence. Visitors can enjoy a guided tour of the production areas, before relaxing with a wee dram of the amber nectar.

10 In addition to outstanding restaurant facilities, Baxters at Blackford offers a fantastic Scottish showcase of inspirational fine food, gifts and much, much more. Visitors are invited to taste a variety of products, from specialist chocolate in The Chocolate Parlour to tasting what Baxters is most famous for, specialty soups, in The Baxters Hub. Whether making a quick stop or for those wishing to stay a little bit longer, Baxters is ideal for the perfect day out.

WALKS

visitscotland.com/walking

11 A 63 mile (101 km) circular waymarked walking route through the scenic Perthshire and Angus Glens, The Cateran Trail follows paths used by the 15th century Caterans (cattle rustlers). Complete the whole route in a leisurely five days or enjoy a shorter section on a day's walk. Take in the soft contours of Strathardle on the Bridge of Cally to Kirkmichael section or head for the hills between Kirkmichael and the Spittal of Glenshee.

12 Revered in poetry by the national bard, Robert Burns, the Birks of Aberfeldy ('birks' being the old Scots for birch trees) line a short walk alongside the Moness Burn, reached from a car park on the Crieff Road. A circular path leads to a beautiful waterfall, where birds and flowers are abundant.

13 Lady Mary's Walk in Crieff is one of the most popular in Perthshire and provides a peaceful stroll beside the beautiful River Earn, along an avenue of mature oak, beech, lime and sweet chestnut trees. Partly accessible for wheelchairs and pushchairs, the walk is particularly photogenic in the late autumn when the beech trees are a riot of rust and gold.

14 On the A9 just north of Dunkeld, you'll find The Hermitage. A beautiful walk along the banks of the River Braan takes you to the focal point, Ossian's Hall set in a picturesque gorge and overlooking Black Linn Falls. Ask the local rangers for advice or read the display panels as you pass amidst the huge Douglas Firs en route.

WILDLIFE
visitscotland.com/wildlife

15 Glengoulandie Country Park is located in the beautiful shelter of Schiehallion, one of Scotland's best known and most popular mountains. The park is home to a beautiful herd of red deer and is a lovely escape for the whole family. It's also an ideal location for setting up camp with a site right next door.

16 Visit Loch of the Lowes between April and August and there's every chance you'll encounter its famous nesting ospreys. The Scottish Wildlife Trust's visitor centre provides interpretation on the birds, which migrate to Scotland from their winter homes in West Africa. There are also telescopes and binoculars on hand to give you a better view. Between October and March, the nature reserve is worth visiting for the sheer numbers of wildfowl which are present.

17 The Black Wood of Rannoch is one of the few remaining areas of the original Caledonian pine forest that covered the majority of Scotland. After being hunted to extinction, the capercaillie was reintroduced to Scotland at Drummond Hill, Kenmore in the 1830s. The Black Wood is an important site for capercaillie and Scottish Natural Heritage aims to extend it by removing the non-native trees to encourage a return to its natural state.

18 Each year between April and October an average of 5,400 salmon fight their way upstream from Atlantic feeding grounds to spawn in the upper reaches of the River Tummel. They must by-pass the Hydro-Electric dam at Pitlochry by travelling through the interconnected pools that form the Pitlochry 'fish ladder' – a very special attraction.

ADVENTURE
visitscotland.com/adventure

In this area you'll find over 35 different adventure activities! Here's a selection:

19 Perthshire is renowned for its stunning lochs and rivers, many of which are excellent for white water rafting. A truly unforgettable experience awaits you with a spectacular combination of rugged Highland scenery and the adrenaline rush of this activity - it's easy to understand why it's one of the most popular. Get some friends together and go for it!

20 Perthshire is the only place in Scotland where you can try sphereing. Like so many unique adventure activities, this one originated in New Zealand and is described as a 'truly amazing adrenaline buzz'. It involves a huge 12 ft inflatable ball which the willing participants strap themselves safely into and then take a wild and bouncy tumble down the hill.

21 Wet, wild and wonderful - canyoning is all this and more! Unleash your adrenaline streak as you swim through rapids, cliff jump into deep clear pools, abseil through waterfalls and slide down natural stone 'flumes'. This one is awesome and not to be missed!

22 If you enjoy wide-open spaces try a microlight flight for the nearest experience to flying like a bird. With the latest microlight technology, enjoy up to sixty miles of spectacular views and scenery in one hour. This is a great way to enjoy the Perthshire landscape as well as being the experience of a lifetime.

23 Not only can you enjoy river bugging in Perthshire but also the new innovation of Adventure Tubing at Nae Limits. The idea is simple. Take a specially designed reinforced inner tyre tube with handles and navigate your way through steep gorges, white-water runs, and jump off cliffs into deep pools below. It's truly pulse quickening stuff!

Aberfeldy, Perthshire
Aberfeldy Cottages
Map Ref: 2A1

35049

★★★★
SELF CATERING

Open: All year

5 Templars, Cramond, Edinburgh EH4 6BY
T: 0131 339 6548
E: geoff@aberfeldycottages.co.uk
W: aberfeldycottages.co.uk

Aberfeldy Cottages offer seven 4 star self catering holiday cottages in this charming, traditional market town on the River Tay, surrounded by stunningly beautiful majestic Scottish hills. Every conceivable recreational facility available locally. 22 free discount vouchers provided with every reservation.

3 Cottages	1-2 Public Rooms	Sleeps 5-6
3 Houses	2-3 Public Rooms	Sleeps 6-8
1 Apartment	1 Public Room	Sleeps 4

Prices from:

Cottage	£275.00-595.00	per week	£175.00	per night
House	£275.00-895.00	per week	£175.00	per night
Apartment	£275.00-450.00	per week	£175.00	per night

Aberfeldy, Perthshire
Drumcroy Lodges
Map Ref: 2A1

23274

★★★★
SELF CATERING

Open: All year

Mains of Murthly, Aberfeldy, Perthshire PH15 2EA
T: 01887 820978
E: info@highland-lodges.com
W: highland-lodges.com

Six beautiful lodges situated in stunning rural setting on family farm. Spectacular views over the River Tay. Furnished to the highest standards. Heating, double glazing. Just one mile from Aberfeldy. Ideal base to explore Central Scotland. Walks, fishing, and mountain biking.

| 6 Lodges | 1 Public Room | Sleeps 4-6 |

Prices from:

£225.00-495.00 — **Per week**
£65.00 per night — **Min 3nights, Nov-Mar**

Aberfeldy, Perthshire
Loch Tay Lodges
Map Ref: 2A1

35959

★★★
SELF CATERING

Open: All year

Remony, Aberfeldy, Perthshire PH15 2HR
T: 01887 830209
E: remony@btinternet.com
W: lochtaylodges.co.uk

Escape the rat race, enjoy the tranquility, grandeur, beauty and comfort of Highland Perthshire. Lots to do including hill walking, fishing, sailing, golf. Central location at heart of Scotland, ideal for touring. Modernised stone building listed for its architectural interest. Log fires.

| 4 Cottages | 1 Public Room | Sleeps 4-8 |
| 2 Apartments | 1 Public Room | Sleeps 6 |

Prices from:

Cottage	£225.00-605.00	**Per week**
	£112.50-287.50	**Per 2 nights**
Apartment	£225.00-530.00	**Per week**
	£112.50-242.50	**Per 2 nights**

IMPORTANT: Prices stated are estimates and may be subject to change. Awards correct as of beginning of October 2008.

Aberfeldy, Perthshire
Luxury Self Catering Cottages at Moness   Map Ref: 2A1

Open: All year

38837

Moness House Hotel and Country Club,
Crieff Road, Aberfeldy, Perthshire PH15 2DY
T: 0845 330 2838
E: info@moness.com
W: moness.com

Set within 35 acres of woodland overlooking the picturesque town Aberfeldy, Moness Country Club offers a choice of superb fully equipped self-catering accommodation. Cottages range in size to include one, two and three bedroom cottages sleeping from 2-8 guests. All cottages are furnished to the high standard required for STB 4 star rating. Guests receive free membership to the onsite leisure club during their stay, which includes an indoor heated pool, steam room, solarium and snooker room. No need to self cater all holiday as Moness has onsite restaurant and bar facilities open for both lunch and evening dinner.

18 Cottages	1 Public Room	Sleeps 1-8
Prices from:		
£334.00-1250.00		**Per week**
£129.00-499.00		**Per night**

Aberfeldy, Perthshire
Struan House   Map Ref: 2A1

Open: All year

83501

AWAITING GRADING

18 Twaite Close, Erith, Kent, DA8 1DP
T: 01322 333618
E: feldyboy@hotmail.com

Stay in beautiful town of Aberfeldy. First floor flat with outstanding views of town and countryside. One double bedroom, second bedroom will sleep three. Newly fitted throughout. Ideal for touring by foot, vehicle or public transport. In main town square.

1 Apartment	1 Public Room	Sleeps 1-5
Prices from:		
£250.00		**Per week**

Short breaks available with first night costing £100.00 then £50.00 per night thereon

Perthshire

by Abefeldy, Perthshire
Glengoulandie Country Park
Map Ref: 2A1

Open: Easter-Mid October

Glengoulandie, by Aberfeldy, Perthshire PH16 5NL

T: 01887 830495   E: info@glengoulandie.co.uk
W: glengoulandie.co.uk

Set at the foot of Schiehallion our camping site has stunning views onto the deer park. Facilities include toilets, showers, laundry, dishwashing area. We also have a small coffee shop onsite serving breakfasts and homemade food. Great spot for hillwalkers.

From the A9 turn off at Ballinluig on the A827 towards Aberfeldy. Turn left at the traffic lights/crossroads in town, straight over the Wades Bridge onto the B846, we are eight miles from Aberfeldy on the left hand side.

Park accommodates 25 pitches

Prices are From:
Δ (25) £8.00-14.00

Acharn, by Kenmore
Bracken Lodges, Loch Tay
Map Ref: 2A1

Open: All year

Loch Tay, by Acharn, Aberfeldy, Perthshire PH15 2HX

T: 01567 820169
E: info@bracken-lodges.com
W: bracken-lodges.com

If you are looking for a relaxing self catering holiday with breathtaking scenery, then look no further. The perfect location for touring Highland Perthshire, with wonderful walks, fishing, castles, distilleries and picturesque villages nearby.

Welcome To
Bracken Lodges

8 Lodges	1 Public Room	Sleeps 2-6

Prices from:
£300.00-750.00   **Per week**

Blair Atholl, Perthshire
Blair Castle Caravan Park
Map Ref: 4C12

Open: March-November inclusive

Blair Atholl, Perthshire PH18 5SR

T: 01796 481263
E: mail@blaircastlecaravanpark.co.uk
W: atholl-estates. co.uk

Blair Castle Caravan Park is part of the historic Atholl Estates set in 145,000 acres of beautiful Highland Perthshire. Red squirrels and other wildlife live around the park. Visit our website for wonderful images of spectacular scenery, wildlife and activities.

Leisure facilities: 🎣

Blair Castle Caravan park is just off the main A9 road at Blair Atholl in Highland Perthshire between Perth and Inverness.

Park accommodates 290 pitches

Total Touring Pitches: 199
Prices from:
🚐 (182) £15.00   Δ (64) £15.00   🚛 (17) £15.00
🏠 (27) £280.00-495.00

IMPORTANT: Prices stated are estimates and may be subject to change. Awards correct as of beginning of October 2008.

Blair Atholl, Perthshire
The Firs Self Catering
Map Ref: 4C12

★★★
SELF
CATERING

Open: All year

St Andrews Crescent, Blair Atholl, Perthshire PH18 5TA
T: 01796 481256
E: kirstie@firs-blairatholl.co.uk
W: firs-blairatholl.co.uk

Firs Lodge - top quality fully equipped timber lodge providing very comfortable year-round accommodation with secluded garden/patio area and verandah. Greenlea Cottage offers similar accommodation and facilities with excellent views of the surrounding mountains. Both properties have off street parking.

1 Cottage	1 Public Room	Sleeps 2-5
1 Cabin	1 Public Room	Sleeps 2-5
Prices from:		
Cottage:	£195.00	**Per week**
	£150.00	**Per 3 nights**
Cabin:	£195.00	**Per week**
	£150.00	**Per 3 nights**

Blair Atholl, Perthshire
The River Tilt Park
Map Ref: 2A1

★★★★
HOLIDAY
PARK

Open: Beginning March-end October

Blair Atholl, Perthshire PH18 5TE
T: 01796 481467
E: stuart@rivertilt.co.uk   W: rivertilt.co.uk

This family-owned and operated holiday park offers the very highest service and best of facilities, with an indoor level deck pool, jacuzzi, toddlers' pool, steam room, sauna, standing tan, new multi gym and the renowned Loft Restaurant. 5 Stars.
Leisure Facilities:

A9 5 miles N of Pitlochry take B8079 signed Blair Atholl, in village, turn left at Tilt Hotel. We are 50 metres down the road with golf course on right

Park accommodates 35

Total Touring Pitches: 35
Prices from:
£10.00-17 per night, £330.00-435.00 per week

(5) £330.00-435.00 per week. Sleeps 2-6.

 Thistle

Blairgowrie, Perthshire
Blairgowrie Holiday Park
Map Ref: 2B1

★★★★
HOLIDAY
PARK

★★★
SELF
CATERING

Open: All year

Rattray, Blairgowrie, Perthshire PH10 7AL
T: 01250 876666
E: blairgowrie@holiday-parks.co.uk
W: holiday-parks.co.uk

Superb pine lodges set in beautiful landscaped grounds on this family run holiday park. Whether you choose a romantic break in luxury accommodation, a sightseeing tour of Perthshire's great outdoors or a big family adventure holiday, we have a lodge just right for you.

9 Lodges	1 Public Room	Sleeps 2-8

Prices from:
£250.00   **Per week**

 Thistle

For a full listing of quality assured non-serviced establishments please see pages 229-385.

127

Blairgowrie, Perthshire
Glenshieling Lodge
Map Ref: 2B1

★★★ SELF CATERING

Open: All year

Hatton Road, Blairgowrie, Perthshire PH10 7HZ
T: 01250 874605
E: rosemary.catherine@btinternet.com
W: glenshielinghouse.co.uk

Well appointed Victorian lodge with its own south facing garden. Centrally located for exploring a wealth of interesting places and activities. Comprising of: fully equipped kitchen/diner, sitting room, family bedroom, twin bedded room, bathroom and shower room. Utilities, linens included in price.

28343

1 Lodge	2 Public Rooms	Sleeps 5
Prices from:		
£220.00-460.00		**Per week**
£120.00		**Per 3 nights**

Blairgowrie, Perthshire
Mr Fraser Mackay
Map Ref: 2B1

★★★ SELF CATERING

Open: All year

Kinwreaton, Brucefield Road, Rosemount, Perthshire PH10 6LA
T: 01250 874246
E: fraser.mackay@sbcglobal.net

70000

1 Apartment	1 Public Room	Sleeps 1-4
Prices from:		
£250.00		**Per week**
£50.00 per night		**Min 3 nights**

Bridge of Cally, Blairgowrie
Corriefodly Holiday Park
Map Ref: 2B1

★★★★★ HOLIDAY PARK

Open: All year

Bridge of Cally, by Blairgowrie, Perthshire PH10 7JG
T: 01250 876666   E: corriefodly@holiday-parks.co.uk
W: holiday-parks.co.uk

Nestling in hills and woodlands in the fir-lined Strathmore valley this family run riverside park is ideal for touring or simply relaxing. On park fishing, bar, games room. Caravans for hire and private ownership. Touring caravans welcome

Leisure facilities: ✆

Five miles north of Blairgowrie on A93, turn left onto Pitlochry road at Post Office on north side of the bridge. Park is on the left approximately 200 yards.

20529

Park accommodates 17 pitches
Total Touring Pitches: 15
Prices from:
(15) £16.00
(2) £190.00-450.00 per week. Sleeps 2-4.

Crieff, Perthshire
Loch Monzievaird Norwegian Lodges   Map Ref: 2A2

35910

★★★
SELF
CATERING

Open: All year

Ochtertyre, Crieff, Perthshire PH7 4JR
T: 01764 652586
E: stay@monzievaird.co.uk
W: monzievaird.co.uk

Norwegian Lodges and Gamekeeper's Cottage in
beautiful, mature, spacious grounds. Wonderful
views over the Loch, elevated positions. Many walks
from your door. Trout fishing on the Loch, river
fishing, tennis, 10 golf courses within 10 miles, horse
riding. Pets welcome.

1 Cottage	2 Public Rooms	Sleeps 6
23 Lodges	2 Public Rooms	Sleeps 2-8
Prices from:		
Cottage	£520.00	**Per week**
	£105.00	**Per night**
Lodge	£410.00	**Per week**
	£95.00	**Per night**

Dunkeld, Perthshire
Laighwood Holidays   Map Ref: 2B1

63155

★★ UP TO
★★★
SELF
CATERING

Open: All year (3 properties)
March-October (3 properties)

Laighwood, Dunkeld, Perthshire PH8 0HB
T: 01350 724241
E: holidays@laighwood.co.uk
W: laighwood.co.uk

One house, three cottages and two apartments all
in idyllic tranquil settings. Central for touring. Ideal
for walking and fishing. Personal attention to your
comfort. Please request colour brochure.

3 Cottages	1-2 Public Rooms	Sleeps 2-6
1 House	3 Public Rooms	Sleeps 8
2 Apartments	1 Public Room	Sleeps 3-4
Prices from:		
Cottage:	£200.00	**Per week**
	20% of weekly rate	**Per night**
House:	£490.00	**Per week**
	£120.00	**Per night**
Apartment:	£210.00	**Per week**
	20% of weekly rate	**Per night**

Dunning, Perthshire
Duncrub Holidays Ltd   Map Ref: 2B3

23613

★★ UP TO
★★★★
SELF
CATERING

Open: All year

Dalreoch, Dunning, Perthshire PH2 0QJ
T: 01764 684100
E: info@duncrub-holidays.com
W: duncrub-holidays.com

1 House	2 Public Rooms	Sleeps 4
1 Apartment	1 Public Room	Sleeps 2
Prices from:		
House:	£360.00-600.00	**Per week**
	£180.00	**Per night**
Apartment:	£320.00-490.00	**Per week**
	£160.00	**Per night**

For a full listing of quality assured non-serviced establishments please see pages 229-385.

129

Perthshire

Glenfarg, Perthshire
Colliston Cottages
Map Ref: 2B3

Open: All year

Colliston, Glenfarg, Perth, Perthshire PH2 9PE
T: 01577 830434
E: colliston_cottages@hotmail.co.uk
W: perthshire-selfcatering.com

Situated on Colliston overlooking Lomond Hills and Loch Leven. Occupying picturesque spot with lovely views. Perth, Edinburgh, Stirling, St Andrews easily accessed. Lovely walks, fishing, swimming, horse riding, children's play park, tennis, cycling, golf, historic interest (Falkland Palace). Good food available locally.

35048

2 Cottages	1 Public Room	Sleeps 2-4
Prices from:		
£220.00-511.00		**Per week**
£55.00-100.00		**Per night**

Glenisla, Perthshire
Mr and Mrs Gammell
Map Ref: 4D12

Open: All year

Ardargie Farms,
c/o Laguna House, Murthly, Perth PH1 4HE
T: 01738 710440
E: sarah.gammell@btconnect.com

Our cottages offer spacious, bright, well appointed accommodation set in this outstandingly beautiful and peaceful Highland Glen within the Cairngorms National Park. Chill in spectacular scenery. Tour surrounding lochs and glens. Five golf courses and numerous castles within one hours drive.

12464

2 Houses	2 Public Rooms	Sleeps 2-6
1 Bungalow	2 Public Rooms	Sleeps 2-8
Prices from:		
House:	£180.00-700.00	**Per week**
	£50.00-100.00	**Per night**
Bungalow:	£250.00-550.00	**Per week**
	£52.00-90.00	**Per night**

Glenshee, Perthshire
Dalmunzie Ltd
Map Ref: 4D12

Open: All year

Spittal O'Glenshee, Blairgowrie, Perthshire PH10 7QE
T: 01250 885226
E: enquiries@dalmunziecottages.com
W: dalmunziecottages.com

7 stone built traditional cottages of individual style and character on 6000 acre sporting estate. Ideal base for touring Royal Deeside and the Highlands or for a sporting holiday with our own 9 hole golf course, shooting, fishing, tennis, hillwalking.

22074

7 Cottages	1-2 Public Rooms	Sleeps 2-6
Prices from:		
£230.00-530.00		**Per week**

IMPORTANT: Prices stated are estimates and may be subject to change. Awards correct as of beginning of October 2008.

Glenshee, Perthshire
Dalnoid Holiday Cottages
Map Ref: 4D12

★★★
SELF CATERING

Open: All year

Dalnoid Farmhouse, Glenshee, Blairgowrie PH10 7LR
T: 01250 882200
E: info@dalnoid.co.uk
W: dalnoid.co.uk

Set in spectacular Glenshee. Both cottages, fully refurbished in 2007, have ground floor king-size double bedroom ensuite, twin bedroom, open plan living area with wood-burning stove, private garden. Stunning views. Ideally located for outdoor activities and exploring Perthshire and Royal Deeside.

2 Cottages	1 Public Room	Sleeps 1-4
Prices from:		
£300.00-520.00		**Per week**
£50.00-87.00		**Per night**

Glenshee, Perthshire
Finegand Estate Ltd
Map Ref: 4D12

★ UP TO
★★★
SELF CATERING

Open: All year

Finegand, Glenshee, Perthshire PH10 7QB
T: 01250 885234
W: finegandestate.com

4 Cottages	1-2 Public Rooms	Sleeps 2-7
Prices from:		
£195.00-450.00		**Per week**
£100.00		**Per night**

By Kenmore, Perthshire
Mrs M I Pugh
Map Ref: 2A1

★★★
SELF CATERING

Open: All year

Stanton House, Stanton,
Morpeth, Northumberland NE65 8PS
T: 01670 772234
E: moragpugh@hotmail.com

Close to a small village with magnificent views over Loch Tay towards Ben Lawers, this spacious single storey house offers a relaxing haven with all modern conveniences. Ideal base for touring, outdoor pursuits or just enjoying the beautiful Perthshire countryside. Brochure provided.

1 Bungalow	2 Public Rooms	Sleeps 7
Prices from:		
£440.00-770.00		**Per week**

Kinross, Perthshire
Gateside Farm Cottage
Map Ref: 2B3

★★
SELF CATERING

Open: All year

Gateside Farm, Fossoway, Kinross KY13 0QL
T: 01577 840223
E: sallyanndath@aol.com
W: gatesidefarmcottage.com

1 Cottage	1 Public Room	Sleeps 1-3
Prices from:		
£180.00-350.00		**Per week**
£120.00-300.00		**3 night short break**

For a full listing of quality assured non-serviced establishments please see pages 229-385.

131

Perthshire

Methven, nr Perth
Cloag Farm Cottages
Map Ref: 2B2

40414

Open: All year

Cloag Farm, Methven, Perthshire PH1 3RR
T: 01738 840239
E: info@cloagfarm.co.uk
W: cloagfarm.co.uk

Three comfortable family run farm cottages. In a peaceful setting and with panoramic views, this is a great base for visiting east and central Scotland or for visiting family and friends. All inclusive pricing. Special offers for couples all year.

3 Cottages	1 Public Room	Sleeps 4

Prices from:
£240.00-385.00 **Per week**
Short breaks from £150.00

By Perth
Old Smiddy Cottage
Map Ref: 2B2

59939

Open: All year

Kinclaven, Stanley, Perth PH1 4QJ
T: 07703540932/01250 883236
E: oldsmiddy@yahoo.co.uk
W: oldsmiddy.com

'Home from home'. Relaxing country cottage with charm and character (sleeps six plus two zedbeds). Ten miles Perth. Beautiful countryside. Antique lounge. Ingle-nook log fire. Country kitchen with Aga. Large fenced garden. Pets welcome. Parking. Ideal base for touring or relaxing.

1 Cottage	3 Public Rooms	Sleeps 6-8

Prices from:
£550.00-650.00 **Per week**
£100.00-150.00 **Per night**

By Perth
Towerview Coach Houses
Map Ref: 2B2

57345

Open: All year

The Nurseries, St. Madoes, Glencarse, Perthshire PH2 7NF
T: 01738 446577
E: susan@towerviewscotland.co.uk
W: towerviewscotland.co.uk

Set in the magnificent Kinnoull area of the Perthshire Tay Valley, secluded newly imaginatively converted coach houses in an attractive courtyard offering exceptional accommodation with rural tranquility and swift access to the fair city of Perth.

6 Houses	1 Public Room	Sleeps 2-6

Prices from:
£270.00-940.00 **Per week**
Contact for short breaks.

IMPORTANT: Prices stated are estimates and may be subject to change. Awards correct as of beginning of October 2008.

Pitlochry, Perthshire
Atholl Highland Lodges
Map Ref: 2A1

★ UP TO
★★★★
SELF
CATERING

Open: All year

77640

Atholl Palace Hotel, Perth Road, Pitlochry PH16 5LY
T: 01796 472400
E: info@scottishholidaylodges.com
W: scottishholidaylodges.com

Overlooking Pitlochry we offer a small collection of
country lodges, cottages and apartments. Choose
a spacious modern lodge in the garden or the
characterful Gate Lodge. During your visit enjoy
full use of Atholl Palace leisure facilities inccluding
swimming pools.

1 Cottage	1 Public Room	Sleeps 4
3 Apartments	1-2 Public Rooms	Sleeps 2-8
6 Lodges	1-2 Public Rooms	Sleeps 6

Prices from:	
Cottage: £445.00	Per week
Apartment: £340.00	Per week
Lodge: £800.00	Per week

Pitlochry, Perthshire
Mr and Mrs James
Map Ref: 2A1

★★
SELF
CATERING

Open: All year

60794

The Yellow House, 1 Springhill,
Eastington, Stonehouse, Gloucestershire GL10 3AT
T: 01453 823992
E: jamesth9@aol.com

| 1 Cottage | 2 Public Rooms | Sleeps 6 |

Prices from:	
£185.00-550.00	Per week
£40.00	Per night

Pitlochry, Perthshire
Lavalette
Map Ref: 2A1

★★
SELF
CATERING

Open: March-October

44940

Manse Road, Moulin, Pitlochry, Perthshire PH16 5EP
T: 01796 472364
E: barrypheonix@aol.com
W: visitscotland.com

| 1 Cottage | 3 Public Rooms | Sleeps 4 |

Prices from:	
£200.00-270.00	Per week

Pitlochry, Perthshire
Milton of Fonab Caravan Site
Map Ref: 2A1

★★★
HOLIDAY
PARK

Open: Easter-mid October

38495

Bridge Road, Pitlochry, Perthshire PH16 5NA
T: 01796 472882
E: info@fonab.co.uk   W: fonab.co.uk

½ mile south of Pitlochry, opposite Bell's Distillery. Ten minute
walk from Pitlochry Festival Theatre.

Park accommodates 210 pitches
Total Touring Pitches: 210
Prices are From:
🚐 £15.00-18.00   ⛺ £15.00-18.00   🚐 £15.00-18.00
(36) £246.00-460.00 per week. Sleeps 6.

For a full listing of quality assured non-serviced establishments please see pages 229-385.

Pitlochry, Perthshire
Mrs K Yates
Map Ref: 2A1

Open: All year excl Xmas and New Year

19041

Cherry Cottage, Ballinluig, Perthshire PH9 0LG
T: 01796 482409
E: kathleenyates@btinternet.com
W: cherrycottage.net

Cherry Cottage, in Ballinluig village, offers delightful accommodation for four people. This 200 year old stone built cottage has a wealth of character and charm, and retains some of the original features including pine shutters and a cast iron range.

★★★★
SELF CATERING

1 Cottage	1-2 Public Rooms	Sleeps 2-4

Prices from:	
£300.00	**Per week**
£55.00	**Per night**

Rait, Perthshire
Fingask Cottages
Map Ref: 2C2

Open: All year

25989

Fingask Castle, Rait, Perthshire PH2 7SA
T: 01821 670777
E: cottages@fingaskcastle.com
W: fingaskcastle.com

★★★
SELF CATERING

5 Cottage	1 Public Room	Sleeps 4-14

Prices from:	
£240.00-1500.00	**Per week**

Stanley, by Perth
Mrs Christine Jeffrey
Map Ref: 2B2

Open: All year

14642

Lomond View, Airntully, Stanley, Perth PH1 4PH
T: 01738 828463
E: enquiries@strathmoreholidayproperties.co.uk
W: strathmoreholidayproperties.co.uk

★★★ UP TO
★★★★
SELF CATERING

1 Cottage	1 Public Room	Sleeps 5-6
1 House	1 Public Room	Sleeps 4-5

Prices from:		
Cottage	£290.00	**Per week**
House	£280.00	**Per week**

IMPORTANT: Prices stated are estimates and may be subject to change. Awards correct as of beginning of October 2008.

RRS Discovery at Discovery Point, Dundee

Angus and Dundee

The Angus and Dundee area boasts some of Scotland's best beaches – wonderful unspoiled stretches of sand which are at times windswept and dramatic, but more frequently warm and inviting, with the peace only occasionally shattered by the cries of the seabirds.

Dundee, you'll discover, has a proud maritime history. Captain Scott's polar research ship the RRS Discovery has returned to the city that built it and is now a top tourist attraction. The city's industrial past also features high on the tourist trail – don't miss the Verdant Works where you can learn about the jute trade that was once a mainstay of the city's economy. Today Dundee has a thriving cosmopolitan feel and dynamic cultural quarter.

For a complete contrast to city life, explore the Angus Glens. There are five: Glen Isla, Glen Prosen, Glen Lethnot, Glen Clova and Glen Esk. Each has its own unique features but all are exceptionally beautiful and wonderfully peaceful places to explore.

Lunan Bay, Angus

1   Perhaps Scotland's finest fairytale castle, **Glamis Castle** is famed for its Macbeth connections, as well as being the birthplace of the late Princess Margaret and childhood home of the late Queen Mother. Set against the backdrop of the Grampian Mountains, Glamis is an L-shaped castle built over 5-storeys in striking pink sandstone. The grounds host the Grand Scottish Proms in August each year, complete with spectacular fireworks display.

2   Little more than half an hour's drive north of the bustling city of Dundee, a series of picturesque valleys runs north into the heart of the Grampians. Collectively known as the **Angus Glens**, they offer the perfect escape for those seeking a walk, a spot of wildlife watching, a scenic picnic or a pub lunch. Ranging from gentle and wooded (Glen Isla) to the truly awe-inspiring (Glen Clova and neighbouring Glen Doll), there is more to discover here than you can fit into a single trip.

3   Discover Dundee's polar past at **Discovery Point**. Step aboard Captain Scott's famous ship that took Scott and Shackleton to Antarctica in 1901 and come face to face with the heroes of the ice in the award winning visitor centre.

4   Dundee is the perfect place for a city break, with great shopping, restaurants and nightlife. Spend a day at Dundee's vibrant and cool **Cultural Quarter** where you can indulge in speciality shopping at the Westport, visit Sensation, Dundee's Science Centre which explores the world of the senses, take in a film or an exhibition at Dundee Contemporary Arts, visit Dundee's acclaimed Rep Theatre, and round it all off with a meal at one of the many restaurants and a drink at one of the area's contemporary bars.

5   For the chance to see bottlenose dolphins at close proximity, why not book a trip on one of the **River Tay Dolphin Trips**. If you prefer to stay on dry land the dolphins can sometimes be seen from Broughty Ferry Beach. The best time to see them is from March-September.

6   Angus was the heartland of the Picts, a warrior people who lived in Scotland around 2,000 years ago and left behind many intriguing monuments. **Pictavia**, at Brechin, provides a fascinating insight including hands-on exhibits and a themed play area for all the family. The small hamlet of Aberlemno, 6 miles north-east of Forfar, is famous for its intricately sculptured Pictish cross-slab in the churchyard.

7   For an excellent view of the City and beyond, take a trip to the top of **The Law** – Dundee's highest point – an extinct volcano. Enjoy magnificent views over the River Tay, and to the hills of Angus and beyond on a clear day.

FOOD AND DRINK

eatscotland.com

8   The **But 'n Ben** in Auchmithie, just 5 miles north of Arbroath, is one of the best seafood restaurants in the area and serves as its speciality the 'smokie pancake'.

9   **Jute Café Bar** is situated on the ground floor of Dundee Contemporary Arts Centre. Its menu ranges widely, with the emphasis on informality, while the ambience goes from a relaxing morning coffee venue to a stylish evening hotspot. Eat, drink and enjoy yourself with freshly cooked contemporary dishes, everything from a light snack to a full meal.

10   **The Roundhouse Restaurant** at Lintrathen, by Kirriemuir, is an award-winning restaurant offering innovative modern menus using Angus and Perthshire produce in a peaceful rural setting. The chef is a former Master Chef of Great Britain, whose specialities include local Angus beef and game.

11   No visit to the area would be complete without stopping off to pick up some of the area's best local produce to take home. **Milton Haugh Farm Shop** specialises in the freshest seasonal potatoes, own reared beef and free range chickens. The Corn Kist Coffee Shop also serves up some delicious home made meals and tempting treats.

WALKS

visitscotland.com/walking

12   Scenic **Glen Doll** is one of the famous Angus Glens, north of Dundee. Follow one of the waymarked forest walks from the car park, or more ambitious hikers can take any of three rights of way leading over the surrounding hills into the neighbouring valleys of Glen Shee and Royal Deeside.

13   Situated five miles North West of Carnoustie, **Crombie Country Park** covers 100 hectares of mixed woodland around a picturesque reservoir. Great opportunities for wildlife watching including butterflies, water and woodland birds.

14   **Seaton Cliffs Nature Trail** is a self guided trail which goes from Arbroath into Sites of Special Scientific Interest, and the sea cliffs are spectacular. There are 15 interpretative points of interest and a wide variety of sea bird species can be seen including puffins, guillemots, razorbill and eider duck to name but a few. Allow approximately 2 hours and 30 minutes.

15   If you want to get out and about in the fresh air, see some of what Dundee has to offer, and get fit at the same time, why not try out one of the themed **Dundee city centre walks** in the Dundee Walking Guide available from the Visitor Information Centre. The trails include buildings of historical significance, examples of both 19th and 20th century architecture, plus explorations of Dundee's maritime and industrial heritage. You will also pass many of Dundee's visitor attractions where you can stop en route.

GOLF
visitscotland.com/golf

16   If you want to experience the very best in Scottish golf, a visit to the **Carnoustie Championship Course** is a must. Venue of the 2007 Open Golf Championship, the course has been deemed the 'toughest links course in the world'.

17   **Montrose Medal Golf Course**, established in 1562, is the fifth oldest golf course in the world with a traditional links layout.

18   **Downfield Golf Club** is an attractive parkland course that has played host to many golfing tournaments and has an excellent reputation as a challenging course.

19   **Kirriemuir Golf Course** is a gem of a parkland course designed by the renowned James Braid. Look out for the notorious oak tree at the 18th!

HISTORY AND HERITAGE

20   **JM Barrie's Birthplace** at Kirriemuir has been carefully restored to reflect how it might have looked in the 1860s. The exhibition next door details the life and work of this hugely talented and celebrated author, whose books include Peter Pan.

21   In 1178 William the Lion founded the now ruined Tironensian monastery that is **Arbroath Abbey**, near the harbour in Arbroath. The abbey is famously associated with the Declaration of Arbroath, signed here in 1320, which asserted Scotland's independence from England. An adjacent visitor centre tells the building's story.

22   **Edzell Castle** is an elegant 16th century residence with tower house that was home to the Lindsays. The beautiful walled garden was created by Sir David Lindsay in 1604 and features an astonishing architectural framework. The 'Pleasance' is a delightful formal garden with walls decorated with sculptured stone panels, flower boxes and niches for nesting birds.

Brechin, Angus
Greenden Farmhouse Holiday Lets Map Ref: 4F12

Open: All year

Greenden Farmhouse, Farnell, by Brechin DD9 6TS
T: 01356 625354   M: 07831 333 333
E: enquiries@parkersgreenden.com
W: parkersgreenden.com

Enjoying an enchanting rural location this beautifully imaginative barn conversion offers luxury living with a contemporary twist. Providing a perfect base to explore a County of contrasts - breathtaking beaches, magnificent mountains. Castles, distilleries, Championship golf courses and fishing close by.

28995

1 Converted Steading	2 Public Rooms	Sleeps 6

Prices from:	
£350.00-825.00	**Per week**
£95.00	**Per night**

Broughty Ferry, Angus
Forbes of Kingennie Country Resort   Map Ref: 2D2

Open: All year excl 26th, 27th December and 12th-18th January

Kingennie, Dundee DD5 3RD
T: 01382 350777
E: bpark@forbesofkingennie.com
W: forbesofkingennie.com

Discover Forbes of Kingennie Country Resort luxury lodge accommodation. Lakeside and woodland, bar restaurant and function facilities. Maze play area, fishing and nine hole golf course open all year round, 8 am till late.

48427

12 Lodges	1-2 Public Rooms	Sleeps 4-10

Prices from:	
£525.00	**Per week**
£340.00	**Per night**

Dundee, Angus
Seabraes Flats   Map Ref: 2C2

Open: July-August
Sanctuary Management Services,
Management Office, Heathfield, Dundee DD1 5EN
T: 01382 383111
E: enquiries-dundee@sanctuary-housing.co.uk
W: scotland2000.com/seabraes

16 Apartments	1 Public Room	Sleeps 2-8
7 Rms in shared flat	1 Public Room	Sleeps 1

70027

Prices from:		
Apartment	£434.00-728.00	**Per week**
	£186.00-312.00	**Per 3 nights**
Shared Flat	£25.00-36.00	**Per night**

Angus and Dundee

Forfar, Angus
Foresterseat Caravan Park
Map Ref: 2D1

26502

★★★★
TOURING PARK

Open: 20 March-20 November
Burnside, Arbroath Road, Forfar, Angus DD8 2RY
T: 01307 818880 E: emma@foresterseat.co.uk
W: foresterseat.co.uk   Leisure Facilities: ✿

From market town, Forfar, in the heart of Angus, take the A932 to Arbroath, pass town border and 'Cunninghill' Golf Course on your right. Foresterseat is one mile from the golf course on the right.

Park accommodates 44 pitches

Total Touring Pitches: 34
Prices from:
🚐 (34) £14.00-16.00   ⚑ (10) £10.00-14.00
🚎 (34) £14.00-16.00

Forfar, Angus
Mrs Laird
Map Ref: 2D1

76820

★★★
SELF CATERING

Open: All year
Broom Farm, Tannadice, by Forfar, Angus DD8 3SJ
T: 01307 850267
E: laird.at.broom@btinternet.com

1 Cottage	2 Public Rooms	Sleeps 1-4

Prices from:

£150.00	**Per week**
£28.00	**Per night**

Kirriemuir, Angus
Purgavie Farm
Map Ref: 2C1

50669

★★★ UP TO ★★★★
SELF CATERING

Open: All year
Lintrathen, Kirriemuir, Angus DD8 5HZ
T: 01575 560213
E: purgavie@aol.com
W: purgavie.co.uk

1 Bungaow	1 Public Room	Sleeps 4
1 Cabin	1 Public Room	Sleeps 6

Prices from:

Bungalow	£250.00	**Per week**
Cabin	£300.00	**Per week**

---

nr Kirriemuir, Angus
Crawford Cottages
Map Ref: 2C1

71907

★★★★
SELF CATERING

Open: All year
Mrs Kathleen Smith, Crawford Cottages,
Mid Road, North Muir, Kirriemuir, Angus DD8 4PJ
T: 01575 572655   M: 07801492531
E: kathleen@crawfordcottages.co.uk
W: crawfordcottages.co.uk

Enjoy peaceful surroundings with spectacular views of Angus Glens. Three miles A90, supermarket. Secluded garden, barbecue, WiFi, payphone. Easy reach of Glamis Castle, picturesque harbours, beaches, theatres, museums, golf courses, river and loch fishing, walking, climbing, horse riding. Linen and fuel provided.

3 Cottages	1-2 Public Rooms	Sleeps 1-8

Prices from:
£250.00-550.00   **Per week**
Short breaks prices on application.

140

IMPORTANT: Prices stated are estimates and may be subject to change. Awards correct as of beginning of October 2008.

Looking down the main driveway to Glamis Castle, north of Dundee

For a full listing of quality assured non-serviced establishments please see pages 229-385.

141

The golf course at Aberdour, Fife

Kingdom of Fife

If you're a golfer, the ancient Kingdom of Fife will be a powerful draw. Every serious golfer wants to play the Old Course at St Andrews at least once in a lifetime and, thanks to a public allocation of rounds each day, you can. There are also 45 other fabulous courses in Fife to put your game to the test.

For keen walkers, one of the great ways to explore Fife is on foot. The Fife Coastal Path takes in some truly delightful places and you'll get to relax on some of the best beaches in the country – with five Fife beaches achieving the top standard Blue Flag status in 2008.

Fife's seaside communities have their roots in fishing and the North Sea herring fleet used to land its catch in the East Neuk's ports. The harbour at Anstruther is still busy but the halcyon days of deep sea fishing have been consigned to the fascinating exhibitions in the Scottish Fisheries Museum in the town.

Harbour at Anstruther Fife, Fisheries Museum behind

To find out more, call 0845 22 55 121 or go to visitscotland.com

1   Travel through the quaint fishing villages of the **East Neuk** of Fife and you travel back through time. This corner of Fife is filled with traditional cottages with red pantile roofs and crow-stepped gable ends which appear unchanged from a bygone age. Fishing boats lie at rest in the harbours follows the bustle of unloading their catch. Between communities lie unspoilt stretches of sandy beaches, perfect for walks and picnics. Visit Pittenweem for art, Crail for crafts or Anstruther for a trip to the Isle of May, followed by some of Britain's finest fish and chips.

2   Fife boasts some of Scotland's finest and cleanest sandy **beaches**, great for peaceful strolls or quiet contemplation. The area is home to five of Scotland's six Blue Flag award-winning strands at Aberdour, Burntisland, Elie Harbour, Leven East and St Andrews West Sands.

3   Stretching for 150 kms around much of Fife's coastline from North Queensferry to the Tay Bridge, the **Fife Coastal Path** can be experienced in short bite-sized walks or as a long distance route to bring your senses to life. Listen to the seabirds soaring above the waves, smell the salt sea air and savour the sea breezes on this wonderful stretch of coastline.

4   The **Royal Palace of Falkland** was the countryside residence of Stuart Kings and Queens when they hunted deer and wild boar in the forests of Fife, and was a favourite childhood playground of Mary, Queen of Scots. Built in the 1500s, the spacious garden houses the original Royal Tennis Court – the oldest in Britain still in use – built in 1539.

FOOD AND DRINK

eatscotland.com

5   **Balbirnie House**, a Georgian Mansion set in its own 416 acre country estate, is recognised as one of Scotland's finest Grade A listed historic houses. Dining in either the Orangery or the Balbirnie Bistro provides a delightful way to experience the natural larder that Scotland has to offer and both have built up a deserved reputation as some of the best restaurants in Fife.

6   The renowned **Peat Inn**, 3 miles from Cupar, offers top quality modern Scottish cuisine. Only the very best of local produce is used and dishes are prepared with great skill and flair. A mouth-watering wine list is available and visitors wishing to sleep off a hearty meal can stay over in the indulgent 5-star accommodation.

7   No trip to Fife is complete without a trip to the multi-award winning **Anstruther Fish Bar & Restaurant**. Voted Scotland's Fish & Chip Shop of the Year 2006/07, they serve only the freshest prime quality seafood, offering a true taste of Scotland.

8   **The Inn at Lathones**, near St Andrews, is a coaching inn with a history spanning back 400 years. The restaurant here continues to welcome travellers with a tempting menu featuring the best of local produce transformed into à la carte, gourmet delights.

BEACHES AND GOLF

visitscotland.com/golf

9   Recognised worldwide as the Home of Golf – the **Old Course** in St Andrews is where it all began and still remains a favourite of today's champions. To play on these hallowed fairways and greens is a dream come true for the golfing fan and an experience which will not be forgotten.

10 As well as the iconic Old Course, the small peninsula of the Kingdom of Fife boasts over 45 other wonderful **golf courses** each offering something different for the visiting golfer. Try the testing challenges of the Open Qualifying courses or an enjoyable, relaxing game, links or parklands, 9 or 18 hole – golf is a way of life in the Kingdom of Fife and there is something for everyone.

11 The long stretches of golden sandy beaches at **Elie** are undoubtedly some of the best in the East Neuk. From summer cricket on the beach to long, peaceful strolls, this is an idyllic spot not to be missed.

12 The sand dunes and beach at the mouth of the Tay estuary are one of the fastest growing parts of Scotland and home to **Tentsmuir** – one of Scotland's National Nature Reserves. This dynamic coastline is important for waders and wildfowl, common and grey seals, ducks and seaduck. It is truly one of Scotland's most magical coastlines and well worth a visit.

WALKING AND WILDLIFE   visitscotland.com/walking

13   Dominating the skyline of central Fife, the **Lomond Hills** are one of the area's most popular walking destinations. The regional park, which encompasses the hills extends over 65 square miles and provides ample opportunity for all levels of walker, with spectacular vistas over the surrounding countryside.

14   The **Scottish Deer Centre**, near Cupar, allows visitors to spot nine species of deer in over 55 acres of scenic parkland as well as its very own pack of wolves. There are daily falconry displays, featuring native Scottish species, a range of shops and a cosy café.

15   For keen bird watchers, the **Fife Ness Muir Wildlife Reserve** on the outskirts of Crail is excellent for migrant and breeding birds. Over 150 species of bird have been seen from the reserve, including 7 species of warbler and migrant butterflies.

16   Culross and the immediate vicinity are rich in historical interest. **The Culross Town Walk**, starting west of the town, passes by a malthouse, tollbooth, mercat cross, abbey house and various other historical buildings. All are worth further exploration.

HERITAGE AND GARDENS

17   **Cambo Gardens** is a romantic 'Secret Garden' nestled on the coast between St Andrews and the East Neuk of Fife. Created around Cambo Burn, the garden boasts everything from spectacular snowdrops to glowing autumn borders, a wild array of woodland plants and animals, waterfalls and rose-clad wrought-iron bridges. This truly is a plantsman's paradise.

18   **Aberdour Castle** was built by the Douglas family in the 13th century and has been added to throughout the centuries, to create a wonderful mix of styles. Situated in the delightful village of Aberdour, the castle boasts fine interior painted ceilings, galleries, a doocot and a recently-uncovered walled garden.

19   **Dunfermline's** royal and monastic past dominates the town. This former capital of Scotland, birthplace of James I and Charles I, boasts a royal palace and a 12th century abbey, which is the final resting place of Robert the Bruce and the burial site of eleven other Scottish kings and queens.

Aberdour, Fife
The Farmhouse Flat
Map Ref: 2C4

★★★
SELF
CATERING

Open: All year

Dalachy Farm, Aberdour, Fife KY3 0RL
T: 01383 860340
E: info@dalachy.co.uk
W: dalachy.co.uk

Enjoy panoramic views over River Forth towards Edinburgh. In character ground floor apartment on working farm. On bus route. Scenic walks with links to coastal path. Picturesque Aberdour one mile. Ideal for golf, beaches, railway station and restaurants. Short breaks available.

1 Apartment	1 Public Room	Sleeps 4

Prices from:
£60.00 — **Per night**

Aberdour, Fife
Mr Alan Fleming
Map Ref: 2C4

★★★★
SELF
CATERING

Open: All year

Cullaloe Lodge, Aberdour, Fife KY3 0LU
T: 01383 860575
E: cullaloelodge@excite.com

Cullaloe Lodge is an ideal place to stay, whether you're a walker, golfer or day tripper. Edinburgh, Dundee and Perth are accessible by train from Aberdour Station one mile away. A large garden for bird watching and relaxing in.

1 Lodge	1 Public Room	Sleeps 2-3

Prices from:
£220.00-300.00 — **Per week**
Short breaks available on request.

Crail, Fife
The Cottage, Craighead Farmhouse
Map Ref: 2D3

★★★★
SELF
CATERING

Open: All year

Peter and Sue Griffiths, The East Fife Letting Company, Craigforth Cottage, Earlsferry, Elie, Fife KY9 1AD
T: 01333 330241
E: info@eastfifeletting.co.uk
W: crailholidaycottage.com

1 Cottage	1 Public Room	Sleeps 4

Prices from:
£355.00-495.00 — **Per week**
£71.00-132.00 — **Per night**

IMPORTANT: Prices stated are estimates and may be subject to change. Awards correct as of beginning of October 2008.

lie, Fife
Kilconquhar Castle Estate Ltd
Map Ref: 2D3

★★UP TO ★★★★ SELF CATERING

Open: All year
Kilconquhar, Elie, Fife KY9 1EZ
T: 01333 340501
E: rentals@kilconquharcastle.co.uk
W: kilconquharcastle.co.uk

Close to Edinburgh and St Andrews our 130 acre country estate is home to 58 units which are a selection of detached villas, castle suites and historic cottages. Minimum two night stay required. Complimentary use of leisure facilities.

33747

58 Units	1 Public Room	Sleeps 2-8
Prices from:		
£700.00-2280.00		**Per week**
£135.00-380.00 per night		**Min 2 nights**

---

lie, Fife
Mrs Jessie Stirling
Map Ref: 2D3

★★ SELF CATERING

Open: All year
42 Fairies Road, Perth PH1 1LZ
T: 01738 442953
E: jessie@stentoncottage.com
W: stentoncottage.com

56475

1 House	1 Public Room	Sleeps 2-6
Prices from:		
£293.00-637.00		**Per week**
£100.00-212.00		**Per night**

Kincaple, nr St Andrews
Woodland Holiday Lodges
Map Ref: 2D2

AWAITING GRADING

Open: All year
Kincaple Lodge, Kincaple, St Andrews KY16 9SH
T: 01334 850217
E: stay@woodlandholidays.co.uk
W: woodlandholidays.co.uk

Nine Scandinavian lodges in peaceful garden grounds with panoramic views towards the sea and golf courses. Space to relax and unwind. Tennis court and play areas. Ideal base for golf, walking, birdwatching and touring. Groups welcome.

83640

9 Log Cabins	1 Public Room	Sleeps up to 4
Prices from:		
£250.00-500.00		**Per week**
POA		**Per night**

Lundin Links, Fife
Tweedbank
Map Ref: 2C3

★★★ SELF CATERING

Open: All year
Ms Wendy Steele, Kirklea, Durie Street, Leven KY8 4HA
T: 07505 007754
E: wendysteele9@aol.com

78835

1 Apartment	3 Public Rooms	Sleeps 5
Prices from:		
£270.00 Oct-Mar, £500.00 Apr-Sept		**Per week**
£38.50 Oct-Mar, £71.40 Apr-Sept		**Per night**

For a full listing of quality assured non-serviced establishments please see pages 229-385.

147

Kingdom of Fife

Lundin Links, Fife
White Pillars Apartment
Map Ref: 2C3

★★★★
SELF CATERING

77862

Open: All year
Mrs D. McLachlan, 8 Hillhead Lane,
Lundin Links, Fife KY8 6DE
T: 01333 329536
E: whitepillars@hotmail.com

1 Apartment	1 Public Room	Sleeps 1-2
Prices from:		
£196.00		**Per week**
£45.00		**Per night**

North Queensferry, Fife
Northcliff
Map Ref: 2B4

★★ UP TO ★★★
SELF CATERING

47757

Open: All year
Mrs E Anderson, 1 Inverkeithing Road,
Crossgates, Fife KY4 8AL
T/F: 01383 510666
E: enquiries@northcliff.co.uk
W: northcliff.co.uk

3 Cottages	1 Public Room	Sleeps 1-6
6 Apartments	1 Public Room	Sleeps 1-8
Prices from:		
Cottage:	£230.00	**Per week**
Apartment:	£220.00	**Per week**

Pittenweem, Fife
Mrs H MacGillivray
Map Ref: 2D3

★★
SELF CATERING

33780

Open: April-October
4 Meadowbank Avenue,
Strathaven, Lanarkshire ML10 6JS
T: 01357 520463
E: john.macgillivray@btopenworld.com

1 Cottage	1 Public Room	Sleeps 2-3
Prices from:		
£225.00-260.00		**Per week**
£33.00-35.00		**Per night**

St Andrews, Fife
Albany Apartments
Map Ref: 2D2

★★★★★
SELF CATERING

11410

Open: All year

c/o 2 Easter Belmont Road, Edinburgh EH12 6EX
T: 0131 346 8662
E: alastair.loudon@btconnect.com
W: albany-apartments.com

Located in the heart of traditional St Andrews only two minutes walk to the Old Course and close to shops. Suitable for a family of five or two couples. A luxury 'home from home'.

1 Apartment	2 Public Rooms	Sleeps 5
Prices from:		
£980.00		**Per week**
£140.00		**Per night**

St Andrews, Fife
Clayton Caravan Park
Map Ref: 2D2

★★★★★
HOLIDAY PARK

19585

Open: mid March-end October
Clayton, St Andrews, Fife KY16 9YE
T: 01334 870242 **E:** enquiries@clayton-caravan-park.com
W: clayton-caravan-park.com

4.5 miles west of St Andrews on A91 between Dairsie and Guardbridge.

Park accommodates: 31	
Total Touring Pitches: 26	
Prices from:	
(26) £20.00	
(5) £296.00-518.00 Sleeps 6	

St Andrews, Fife
Mrs Judy Crichton
Map Ref: 2D2

★★★
SELF
CATERING

43951

Open: All year
20 Belgrave Crescent, Edinburgh EH4 3AJ
T: 0131 332 9499
E: j.crichton@zen.co.uk
W: scotland2000.com/northstreet/

1 House	1 Public Room	Sleeps 5
Prices from:		
£525.00		**Per week**
£80.00 per night		**Min 3 nights**

St Andrews, Fife
Dron Court
Map Ref: 2D2

★ UP TO
★★★
SELF
CATERING

23207

Open: All year

Mrs Joan Inglis, 8 Dunure Place,
Newton Mearns, Glasgow G77 5TZ
T: 0141 616 3491
E: jinglis@dron8.freeserve.co.uk
W: droncourt.com

Dron Court is a farm steading conversion set in
two acres of gardens overlooking the Eden Valley.
Five miles from St Andrews there are seven houses
and cottages ranging from one to four bedrooms,
sleeping two to eight persons.

5 Cottages	1-2 Public Rooms	Sleeps 2-5
2 Houses	2 Public Rooms	Sleeps 8
Prices from:		
Cottage	£290.00-495.00	**Per week**
House	£440.00-650.00	**Per week**

St Andrews, Fife
Heart of St Andrews
Map Ref: 2D2

★★★
SELF
CATERING

26632

Open: All year

Fortrenn, St Fillans, Perthshire PH6 2NG
T: 01764 685482
E: enquiries@heartofstandrews.co.uk
W: heartofstandrews.co.uk

Cobwebs offers luxury accommodation with a
unique St Andrews walled garden. Scribbles, newly
refurbished, emphasises modern intimate comfort.
On the university's door step in the residential
North Street you are close to the 'Auld Toon' centre,
fabulous beaches and famous golf courses.

1 House	1 Public Room	Sleeps 1-5
1 Apartment	1 Public Room	Sleeps 1-2
Prices from:		
House:	£400.00-760.00	**Per week**
	£80.00	**Per night**
Apartment:	£300.00-520.00	**Per week**
	£60.00	**Per night**

For a full listing of quality assured non-serviced establishments please see pages 229-385.

149

Kingdom of Fife

St Andrews, Fife
Inchdairnie Properties
Map Ref: 2D2

★★★ UP TO ★★★★
SELF CATERING

Open: All year

50 Argyle Street, St Andrews, Fife KY16 9BU
T: 01334 477011
E: gillian@inchdairnieproperties.co.uk
W: standrewsletting.com

A small and select choice of charming apartments, maisonnettes, town houses and country cottages in and around the historic town of St Andrews. Colour brochure available.

1 House	2 Public Rooms	Sleeps 8
4 Apartments	1 Public Room	Sleeps 1-6

Prices from:		
House:	£600.00-800.00	**Per week**
	£100.00-150.00	**Per night**
Apartment:	£300.00-840.00	**Per week**
	£55.00-120.00	**Per night**

St Andrews, Fife
Kingsbarns Holidays
Map Ref: 2D2

★★★★
SELF CATERING

Open: All year

Daisybank and The Smithy, 2 Smiddyburn, Kingsbarns, St Andrews, Fife KY16 8SN
T: 07802 756551/07816 621450
E: accommodation@caeltd.co.uk
W: kingsbarnsholidays.co.uk

Set in the idyllic village of Kingsbarns, both properties offer the highest standard of accommodation and provide the ideal base to enjoy the many attractions of nearby St Andrews and the East Neuk of Fife.

1 Cottage	3 Public Rooms	Sleeps 5
1 House	1 Public Room	Sleeps 6

Prices from:		
Cottage	£300.00-550.00	**Per week**
House	£395.00-800.00	**Per Week**

St Andrews, Fife
116h Market Street
Map Ref: 2D2

★★★ UP TO ★★★★
SELF CATERING

Open: All year

Sir Peter and Lady Erskine, Cambo House, Kingsbarns, by St Andrews, Fife KY16 8QD
T: 01333 450054
E: cambo@camboestate.com
W: camboestate.com

Tucked away in it's charming, secluded courtyard in the heart of St Andrews this compact and convenient two bedroom cottage is the ideal base to explore this ancient city and its fascinating surrounds, play golf or visit the University.

1 Cottage	1 Public Room	Sleeps 1-3

Prices from:	
£343.00-597.00	**Per week**
£43.00 per night	**(midweek min 4 nights)**

150

IMPORTANT: Prices stated are estimates and may be subject to change. Awards correct as of beginning of October 2008.

Kingdom of Fife

St Andrews, Fife
Mrs Anne Newell
Map Ref: 2D2

Open: June-mid September
Kildonan House, 4B Links Crescent,
St Andrews, Fife KY16 9HP
T: 01334 473446
E: ann.newell@btinternet.com
W: standrews-selfcatering.com

71429

1 Flat	1 Public Room	Sleeps 2

Prices from:	
£360.00-380.00	**Per week**

St Andrews, Fife
Sandmill House
Map Ref: 2D2

Open: All year
For reservations contact: Charles and Mary
T: 01333 450549
E: mail@sandmillhouse.com
W: sandmillhouse.com

84142

1 Apartment	2 Public Rooms	Sleeps 6

Prices from:	
£750.00-1500.00	**Per week**
£125.00-250.00 per night	**Min 3 nights**

St Andrews, Fife
St Andrews Country Cottages
Map Ref: 2D2

★ UP TO ★★★ SELF TERING

Open: All year
Mr Patrick Wedderburn,
Mountquhanie Estate, by Cupar, Fife KY15 4QJ
T: 01382 330318
E: enquiries@standrews-cottages.com
W: standrews-cottages.com

55709

18 Cottages	2 Public Rooms	Sleeps 4-14
2 Houses	2 Public Rooms	Sleeps 8
3 Apartments	2 Public Rooms	Sleeps 4-8

Prices from:		
Cottage	£195.00-2195.00	per week
	£95.00-150.00	per night
House	£295.00-835.00	per week
	£195.00	per night
Apartment	£195.00-695.00	per week
	£95.00-150.00	per night

St Andrews, Fife
University of St Andrews (David Russell Apartments)
Map Ref: 2D2

Open: June-Mid September
Buchanan Gardens, St Andrews, Fife KY16 9LY
T: 01334 467100
E: drh_reception@st-andrews.ac.uk
W: discoverstandrews.com

70107

46 Apartments	1 Public Room	Sleeps 6

Prices from:	
£535.00	**Per week**
£289.00	**Per 3 nights**

---

nr St Andrews, Fife
Cambo House
Map Ref: 2D2

★ UP TO ★★★ SELF ERING

Open: All year

Cambo House, Kingsbarns,
nr St Andrews, Fife KY16 8QD
T: 01333 450054
E: cambo@camboestate.com
W: camboestate.com

17700

Magnificent apartments in Victorian family mansion, cottages in grounds of wooded estate with walks to sea and Kingsbarns golf course. Renowned walled garden and acres of snowdrops. Close to university and golf courses of St Andrews and picturesque Fife fishing villages.

2 Cottages	1 Public Room	Sleeps 2-4
5 Apartments	1 Public Room	Sleeps 4-8

Prices from:		
Cottage	£355.00-1015.00	Per week
	£45.00	Per night (mid week, min 4 nights)
Apartment	£385.00-1495.00	Per week
	£48.00	Per night (mid week, min 4 nights)

For a full listing of quality assured non-serviced establishments please see pages 229-385.

151

Upper Largo, nr St Andrews
Monturpie Caravan Park

Map Ref: 2D2

★★★
TOURING
PARK

Open: All year
Monturpie Caravan Park,
Monturpie, Upper Largo, Leven, Fife KY8 5QS
T: 01333 360254
E: enquiries@monturpie.co.uk
W: caravancampingsites.co.uk
☉ ♦ 🚐 📶 ⑨ Ⓡ ⛎ ♨ ⛺ 🚐 ♿

Adjacent to A915 Upper Largo to St Andrews road, ¼ mile from village of Upper Largo

68973

Park accommodates 24 pitches
Total Touring Pitches: 24

Prices from:

🚐 £14.00   🚐 £14.00

☉ ♦ 🚐 📶 ⛎ ♿ 🐕 E WC

Walking along the pier beside the harbour at St Andrews, Fife

IMPORTANT: Prices stated are estimates and may be subject to change. Awards correct as of beginning of October 2008.

The village of Dysart, near Kirkcaldy, Fife

For a full listing of quality assured non-serviced establishments please see pages 229-385.

153

Fyvie Castle, Aberdeenshire

ABERDEEN CITY AND SHIRE

Aberdeen City and Shire is an area of contrasts. From the mountains and forests to the towering cliffs, rocky inlets, endless sandy beaches and captivating harbour towns.

Aberdeen is a thriving and cosmopolitan city with magnificent architecture and a host of cultural opportunities, from museums and art galleries to theatres and concert halls.

The 'Granite City' is also famous for its award winning floral displays. With 45 parks in the city and a celebrated Winter Garden at Duthie Park, Aberdeen is always in bloom and every season brings new floral flights of fancy.

It has a busy central shopping area yet just a short distance away there's a brilliant beach complete with an all-year funfair.

The many fascinations of the Aberdeenshire coastline extend beyond the city however. Along the coast you'll find captivating harbour towns like Stonehaven, Peterhead, Fraserburgh and Banff, as well as quaint little places like the stunning Pennan, a former smuggler's town at the foot of a cliff.

Castles and whisky galore

Aberdeen City and Shire is renowned for its castles which come in all shapes and sizes from fairytale castles to crumbling ruins and even royal holiday homes. Some great trails have been laid out for visitors to follow, including the intriguing Castle Trail.

The Deeside towns of Banchory, Ballater and Braemar have all enjoyed many decades of royal patronage, the annual highlight of which is the Braemar Gathering in September.

Alongside the whisky, there are other delights that will soon have you raising your glass – music, song and, of course, fine food. Beautiful Aberdeen Angus beef, sumptuous seafood, fabulous fruit and vegetables – all come fresh to the table, prepared by the finest chefs. The Taste of Grampian, held annually in June at Inverurie, is a must for foodies.

What's more, 2009 is a big year for Scotland – we're celebrating the 250th anniversary of the birth of Robert Burns. There's over 200 special events taking place throughout the year, all over Scotland. Go to homecomingscotland2009.com to find out about events in this area.

So what do you want from your holiday home in Aberdeen and the Grampian Highlands? There's a lot of choice – from seaside cottages to luxury lodges in five star holiday resorts. There a good selection of holiday and touring parks. And yes, perhaps not surprisingly for this part of the world, you can even stay in a castle!

Dunnottar Castle, Aberdeenshire

What's On?

Word 09 – University of Aberdeen Writers Festival
13 – 17 May 2009
A packed programme of readings, lectures and debates as well as musical events, art exhibitions and film screenings showcasing how the Scottish word has changed the world!
abdn.ac.uk/word

Taste of Grampian, Inverurie
6 June 2009
Discover and sample a wide range of quality food and drink products.
tasteofgrampian.co.uk

The Scottish Traditional Boat Festival
2 – 5 July 2009
A colourful celebration of Scotland's great maritime heritage, with events throughout Portsoy and Banff.
stbf.bizland.com/2009

Lonach Gathering & Highland Games
22 August 2009
lonach.org

Braemar Gathering
5 September 2009
Traditional highland games.
braemargathering.org

Stonehaven Fireball Festival
31 December 2009
A spectacular winter festival to bring in the New Year.

DON'T MISS

1   The restored Victorian **Old Royal Station**, Ballater now houses a museum focusing very much
    on Queen Victoria's journeys here, when heading to Balmoral, including a recreated waiting room and
    a replica of a carriage used by Queen Victoria when travelling from Windsor to Ballater. In its heyday,
    many famous people, including the Tsar of Russia, used Ballater Station.

2   **Balmoral Castle**, Scottish home of the Royal Family since the mid 19th century is set amid
    spectacular scenery. See why Queen Victoria described Balmoral as "my dear paradise in the Highlands".
    Visit the largest room in the castle, the ballroom, and learn the history of the castle through an audio-
    visual presentation.

3   From its days as a lively fishing port to its current status as Europe's North Sea oil capital, Aberdeen's
    historic relationship with the sea unfolds at the five-star **Aberdeen Maritime Museum**
    through exciting displays and exhibitions.

4   **Duff House**, a magnificent Baroque mansion designed by William Adam, is now a treasure house
    and cultural arts centre operated by a unique partnership of Historic Scotland, the National Galleries
    of Scotland and Aberdeenshire Council. Storytellers, musicians and artists are at home here and Duff
    House organises a regular artistic programme of exhibitions, music and lectures.

5   Held on the first Saturday of September, one of Scotland's oldest and biggest Highland Gatherings,
    The Braemar Gathering is notable not only for its size, but also for their unique chieftain,
    Her Majesty the Queen. Royalty is always in attendance, presiding over a programme of events that
    includes Highland dancing, tossing the caber, tug of war and piping.

6   Take a stroll along 2 miles of sandy beach at **Aberdeen's beachfront** and discover a range of
    attractions for all the family. The beach itself is famous for its golden sand and its long curved length
    between the harbour and the mouth of the River Don. The beach is a favourite for walkers, surfers and
    windsurfers and has a popular amusement area along the famous Beach Esplanade where there are
    restaurants, a cinema and the city's amusement park.

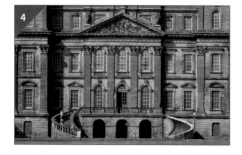

HERITAGE

7   Built in the 16th century, **Crathes Castle** is a splendid example of a tower house, retaining many original interior features, and a stunning walled garden complete with herbaceous borders and an array of unusual plants.

8   The charming **Braemar Castle**, now run by the community of Braemar, re-opened to the public in May 2008, and is undergoing an ambitious restoration programme to ensure a memorable experience for visitors.

9   Wander around the extensive buildings of **Dunnottar Castle**, set in a dramatic cliff top location with the sound of waves crashing on the rocks below and discover the significance of this impenetrable castle which holds many secrets of Scotland's colourful past.

10 With so many stunning castles in the region, it's no surprise that there is a **Castle Trail** taking in thirteen of the most unique examples, from fairytale castles, through rugged ruins to the elegant grandeur of country houses set in some of the most spectacular grounds.

WALKS

11 The walk around **Loch Muick**, in the shadow of Lochnagar, is mainly on fairly flat ground, following a route close to the loch side, with good views of the hills around. Look out for red deer. A short wooded section follows after reaching a Royal lodge, and then continues round the loch, passing a sandy beach, rising slightly before returning to the start point.

12 Scottish Wildlife Trust reserve at **Gight Woods**, north of Aberdeen, offers walks of up to 3 miles. The route follows the forestry track through Badiebath Woods towards the ruined Gight Castle (Byron's ancestral home) passing a number of interesting ruins, and with the opportunity to spot red squirrels.

13 The 5 mile route from **Duff House to Bridge of Alvah** is full of variety, starting through a mature deciduous wood, near the banks of the River Deveron, where you may spot kingfisher and goldeneye. The path then crosses the river, at **Bridge of Alvah**, along tracks and minor roads lined with shrubs, returning via the grounds of MacDuff Distillery back over the river, to Duff House affording great views of Banff.

14 **Ballater Royal Deeside Walking Festival** takes place each year in May, and provides a programme of walks for walkers of all capabilities from 'Munro-baggers' to those who prefer a gentle stroll, all set in magnificent walking country surrounded by breathtaking scenery.

FOOD & DRINK

15 **The Milton Restaurant & Conservatory**, situated opposite Crathes Castle on Royal Deeside, offers exquisite food in picturesque surroundings. The Milton's kitchen team of award winners, including **Grampian Chef of the Year 2008**, is renowned not only for the flavour, but also the stunning presentation of the dishes.

16 Scotch Beef can be found on the menus of top restaurants throughout Europe and the reputation of this high-class product remains undiminished. **Aberdeen Angus** is arguably the best known breed, renowned for the rich and tasty flavour of the meat.

17 On a farm near Inverurie in Aberdeenshire, **Mackie's award winning ice cream** is made using milk from their own Jersey and Holstein herds. Over 20 flavours of ice cream are created using renewable energy: the farm has three wind turbines which produce all the energy required to make this delicious ice cream.

18 **Dean's of Huntly** bake traditional Scottish all-butter shortbread, and at the visitor centre you can learn about its history and watch how the delicious shortbread is made in the viewing gallery, before visiting the café for a tasting.

ACTIVITIES

19 The fairways of Aberdeen City and Shire provide a variety of golfing experiences, from the historic links **Royal Aberdeen** with its towering dunes to the splendid inland and parkland courses which offer new challenges.

20 If you want to take part in an activity, head for **Deeside Activity Park**, where you will be amazed by the number and variety of activities on offer, from fly fishing, rock climbing, archery, kart racing, quad bike trekking to digger manoeuvres. There's a restaurant and farm shop too.

21 Aberdeen City and Shire has miles of unspoilt and often rugged coastline, so why not try **water sports** here? Yachting, canoeing, scuba diving, surfing, and water skiing are all available, but if big waves are your thing, visit Fraserburgh, former host to rounds of Scottish Wavesailing Championships. Or why not team up with Surf and Watersport Club, Banff for some expert tuition?

To find out more, call 0845 22 55 121 or go to visitscotland.com

MAP

©Collins Bartholomew Ltd 2008

VISITOR INFORMATION CENTRES

Visitor Information Centres are staffed by people 'in the know' offering friendly advice, helping to make your stay in Scotland the most enjoyable ever ... whatever your needs!

Aberdeen City and Shire		
Aberdeen	23 Union Street, Aberdeen, AB11 5BP	Tel: 01224 288828
Ballater	The Old Royal Station, Station Square, Ballater, AB35 5QB	Tel: 01339 755306
Braemar	Unti 3, The Mews, Mar Road, Braemar, AB35 5YL	Tel: 01339 741600

LOCAL KNOWLEDGE • WHERE TO STAY • ACCOMMODATION BOOKING • PLACES TO VISIT • THINGS TO DO • MAPS AND GUIDES TRAVEL ADVICE • ROUTE PLANNING • WHERE TO SHOP AND EAT LOCAL CRAFTS AND PRODUCE • EVENT INFORMATION • TICKETS

For information and ideas about exploring Scotland in advance of your trip, call our booking and information service **0845 22 55 121** or go to **visitscotland.com**

If calling from outside the UK and Ireland **+44 1506 832 121**   From Ireland **1800 932 510**

A £4 booking fee applies for accommodation bookings made via a Visitor Information Centre and through our booking and information service.

Live it. Visit *Scotland.*
visitscotland.com/wheretofindus

Aberdeen
Deeside Holiday Park
Map Ref: 4G10

★★★★
HOLIDAY
PARK

Open: All year
South Deeside Road, Mary Culter
Aberdeen AB12 5FX
T: 01224 733860
E: deeside@holiday-parks.co.uk
W: holiday-parks.co.uk

Nestling in the Deeside Valley, this popular family run holiday park is at the gateway to Royal Deeside, only a few minutes drive from the vibrant city of Aberdeen. We welcome touring caravans/tents. Pine lodges and caravans are available for hire.

Leisure facilities: ❋ ✪

☺ ◑ ⋔ ☂ ◫ ⚡ ⊡ ✿ TV ⊨ ⊕ ◫ WC ⊁❋ ⊙ ⌂ ⚑ ⊡ ⎚

On A90 northbound take a left at the Bridge of Dee roundabout approaching Aberdeen. Follow B9077 signposted Maryculter for 5 miles. The park is on the right 100yds past the Old Mill Inn.

Park accommodates 56 pitches

Total Touring Pitches: 50
Prices from:
🚐 (40) £15.00-18.00 ▲ (10) £14.00-16.00 🚚 (5) £15.00-18.00

🛖 (6) £185.00-450.00 per week. Sleeps 2-6.
☺ ◑ ⋔ ☂ ⚑ ⊡ ⚡ ⊡ ✿ TV ⊨ E WC ⊁❋ P ⊙ ⚑   *Thistle*

Aberdeen
Hayfield House
Map Ref: 4G10

AWAITING
GRADING

Open: All year
Equiworld Club,
Hazlehead Park, Aberdeen AB15 8BB
T: 01224 315703
E: info@hayfield.com
W: hayfield.com/house

◎ ⋔ ⊨ ⋔ ⚑ ⊡ ⚡ ⎚ ✿ ⊨ ☂ ⊕ ⊉ ⌶ P C ⛢ ◫ ⊡ ⊡ T SP ⚗ ⊕

1 House	3 Public Rooms	Sleeps 4-6
Prices from:		
£950.00		**Per week**
£550.00		**Per 4 nights**

Aboyne, Aberdeenshire
Royal Deeside Holiday Cottages
Map Ref: 4F11

★★ UP TO
★★★
SELF
CATERING

Open: Mid March-October
Estate Offices, Dinnet, Aboyne, Aberdeenshire, AB34 5LL
T: 013398 85341
E: office@dinnet-estate.co.uk
W: royaldeesideholidaycottages.co.uk

TV ⚗ ☎ ⊞ ◫ ⊡ ⊡ ⚑ ◫ ⊡ ⊞ ◫ ⊞ † ⋔ ⚑ ⊡ ⚡ ⎚ ❋ ⚗ ⋔ ⛢

1 Cottage	1 Public Room	Sleeps 4
3 Houses	1-2 Public Rooms	Sleeps 6
Prices from:		
Cottage:	£340.00	**Per week**
House:	£390.00	**Per week**

By Aboyne, Aberdeenshire
Mrs A Craigmile
Map Ref: 4F11

★★★
SELF
CATERING

Open: All year
40 The Chase, Marshalls Park, Romford, Essex, RM1 4BE
T: 01708 782324
E: alison@holmhead-cottage.co.uk
W: holmhead-cottage.co.uk

TV ⚗ ⊡ ⊡ ⊡ ⚑ ♫ ⊡ ▦ M ⊕ ⋔ ⚑ ⊡ ⚡ ❋ ⚗ ⋔ P ⛢

1 Cottage	2 Public Rooms	Sleeps 4
Prices from:		
£300.00		**Per week**

IMPORTANT: Prices stated are estimates and may be subject to change. Awards correct as of beginning of October 2008.

y Aboyne, Aberdeenshire
arland Camping & Caravaning Club Site
Map Ref: 4F11

★★★
URING
PARK

Open: 2 April-2 November 2009

Tarland, by Aboyne, Aberdeenshire AB34 4UP

T: 0845 130 7633

E: vb@thefriendlyclub.co.uk

W: campingandcaravanningclub.co.uk/tarland

Tarland by Deeside has been favoured by royalty for many years. Queen Victoria chose the area for her home at Balmoral in the 1850s and it is still a favourite with our royal family today.

57689

☉♠☕🚿♨🍴🏇🚻🅿☐🧺☕🏓🎣❄

From Aberdeen on A93, turn right in Aboyne at Struan Hotel onto B9094. After 6 miles take next right and then fork left before bridge, continue for 600 yds, site on left.

Park accommodates	52

Total Touring Pitches: 52
Prices are From:
£17.90-23.30 per couple per night per pitch

---

lford, Aberdeenshire
raich Cottage
Map Ref: 4F10

★★
ELF
ERING

Open: All year

Craich, Tough, Alford, Aberdeenshire, AB33 8EN

T: 01975 562584

E: john.f.wright237@btinternet.com

W: craichcottage.co.uk

Craich Cottage is a renovated and extended cottage on a small working farm in rural Aberdeenshire. Set in a quiet location it is an ideal base to visit the Grampians, the Aberdeenshire Coast and areas in between.

20826

📺🗃🖥🛏📠🖥📼🍴☉◎🚗🐾🛋🗄🏠❄🅿🛁🚲

1 Cottage	2 Public Rooms	Sleeps 6

Prices from:	
£325.00-425.00	**Per week**
£63.00-83.00	**Per night**

---

allater, Aberdeenshire
ruach Mhor
Map Ref: 4E11

★★
ELF
ERING

Open: All year

Mr & Mrs Middleton

26 Seafield Drive West, Aberdeen, AB15 7XA

T: 01224 323506

E: bruach-mhor@mail.com

W: cottageguide.co.uk/bruachmhor

📺🗃🖥🛏📠🖥🎵📼🛏🕑🅿

16643

1 Cottage	2 Public Rooms	Sleeps 2-6

Prices from:	
£350.00-500.00	**Per week**

For a full listing of quality assured non-serviced establishments please see pages 229-385.

Aberdeen City and Shire

Ballater, Aberdeenshire
Invercauld Lodges
Map Ref: 4E11

SELF CATERING ★★★★

79176

Open: All year
Invercauld Road, Ballater AB35 5RP
T: 01339 755015
E: info@invercauldlodges.com
W: invercauldlodges.com

Amidst beautiful pine trees, in a very quiet and safe location 400m from the centre of Ballater, Invercauld Lodges provide peace and relaxation in a lovely garden setting.

6 Lodges	1 Public Room	Sleep 3-5
Prices from:		
£180.00		**Per week**
£60.00		**Per night**

Ballater, Aberdeenshire
3 Knocks Cottages
Map Ref: 4E11

SELF CATERING ★★★★

47529

Open: All year
Catbells, Orestan Lane,
Effingham, Leatherhead, Surrey KT24 5SN
T: 01372 459123
E: cliff.gosden@btinternet.com
W: cliff.gosden.btinternet.co.uk

1 Cottage	1 Public Room	Sleeps 6
Prices from:		
£400.00-650.00		**Per week**

Near Ballater, Aberdeenshire
Royal Deeside Woodland Lodges
Map Ref: 4E11

SELF CATERING ★★★

77039

Open: All year
Dinnet, Near Ballater,
Royal Deeside, Aberdeenshire, AB34 5LW
T: 013398 85229
E: stay@woodland-lodges.com
W: woodland-lodges.com

Set in the heart of Royal Deeside at the Eastern Gateway to the Cairngorm National Park. Our lodges make an ideal base to explore the many tourist and sporting activities available. All lodges have decked seating area and modern facilities.

3 Cabins	1 Public Room	Sleeps 4
Prices from:		
£350.00		**Per week**
£150.00		**Per night**

Banchory, Aberdeenshire
Woodend Chalet Holidays
Map Ref: 4F11

★★★ UP TO ★★★★
SELF CATERING

64499

Open: All year
Glassel, Banchory, Aberdeenshire AB31 4DB
T: 01339 882562
E: info@woodendchalets.co.uk
W: woodendchalets.co.uk

7 Chalets	1 Public Room	Sleeps 2-4
2 Lodges	1 Public Room	Sleeps 2-6
Prices from:		
Chalet:	£160.00	**Per week**
	£40.00	**Per night**
Lodge:	£460.00	**Per week**
	£120.00	**Per night**

IMPORTANT: Prices stated are estimates and may be subject to change. Awards correct as of beginning of October 2008.

Braemar, Aberdeenshire
Mrs S Anderson   Map Ref: 4D11

Open: All year

Birchwood, Chapel Brae,
Braemar, Aberdeenshire, AB35 5YT
T: 013397 41599
E: anderson.birchwood@btinternet.com

15182

1 Cottage	2 Public Rooms	Sleeps 4-5
Prices from:		
£250.00		**Per week**
£40.00		**Per night**

Braemar, Aberdeenshire
Mrs F Moore   Map Ref: 4D11

★★★
SELF
CATERING

Open: All year

Glenshee Road, Braemar, Royal Deeside AB35 5YQ
T: 01339 741627
E: mail@braemarlodge.co.uk
W: braemarlodge.co.uk

69343

8 Cabins	1 Public Room	Sleeps 2-6
1 Bunkhouse		Sleeps 1-12
Prices from:		
Cabin:	£250.00-750.00	**Per week**
	£40.00-180.00	**Per night**
Bunkhouse:	£13.00-18.00	**Per person per night**

Bucksburn, Aberdeen
Scottish Agricultural College   Map Ref: 4G10

★★
CAMPUS

Open: 23 March-12 April & 1 July-25 September

Facilities Office, Hunter Annexe,
Craibstone Estate, Bucksburn, Aberdeen AB21 9TR
T: 01224 711012
E: gwen.bruce@sac.co.uk
W: sac.ac.uk/holidayletsaberdeen

Set in an 800 acre estate with glorious surroundings away from the hustle and bustle of city life, free from busy roads. Craibstone is the ideal setting for a truly relaxing holiday and the perfect base for touring north east Scotland.

53468

Campus Accommodation	60 Ensuite Rooms
Sleeps 1-2	
Prices from:	
£125.00	**Per week**

Crovie, Pennan
Mr H Mitchell   Map Ref: 4G7

★★★
SELF
CATERING

Open: All year

12 Dean Road, Kilmarnock, Ayrshire KA3 1RP
T: 01563 535790
E: 13crovie@freescotland.com
W: freescotland.com/crovie

Traditional cottage at water's edge. Ideal for rest and contemplation. Sunsets a speciality. Fireside with seaview. Parking close, waves closer. Euros accepted. Free Wi-Fi.

40728

trading in euros

1 Cottage	3 Bedrooms	Sleeps 6
Prices from:		
£250.00-460.00/€340.00-520.00		**Per week**
£60.00/€80.00		**Per night**

Cullen, Banffshire
Cullen Bay Holiday Park
Map Ref: 4E7

21676

★★★★
HOLIDAY PARK

Open: April-October
Logie Drive, Cullen, Buckie, Banffshire AB56 4TW
T: 01542 840766   **E:** enquiries@cullenbay.co.uk
W: cullenbayholidaypark.co.uk

From the east on A98 at Cullen turn 1st right onto Seafield Place. Follow to the end. From the west on A98, at Cullen take the 4th left, onto Seafield Place and follow to the end.

Park accommodates 15 pitches

Total Touring Pitches: 12

Prices from:
(12) £14.20-17.50   (12) £14.20-17.50

(3) £195.00-390.00 per week. Sleeps 1-6.

Fordoun, by Laurencekirk
Brownmuir Caravan Park
Map Ref: 4F12

39452

★★★
HOLIDAY PARK

Open: April-October
Fordoun, Laurencekirk, Aberdeenshire AB30 1SJ
T: 01561 320786   **E:** brownmuircaravanpark@talk21.com
W: brownmuircaravanpark.co.uk

From south on A90, 4 miles north of Laurencekirk turn left at junction Fordoun-Auchenblae, then 300 yds turn left over bridge. Park 1 mile on right from north. Turn right on B966 marked Fettercairn then pick up caravan signs.

Park accommodates 25 pitches

Total Touring Pitches: 11

Prices from:
(11) £12.00   (11) £7.00   (11) £12.00

(3) £230.00-250.00 per week.

Huntly, Aberdeenshire
Huntly Castle Caravan Park
Map Ref: 4F9

31214

★★★★★
HOLIDAY PARK

Open: April-October
The Meadow, Huntly, Aberdeenshire AB54 4UJ
T: 01466 794999
E: enquiries@huntlycastle.co.uk
W: huntlycastle.co.uk

Take a break at one of the finest award winning caravan parks in Grampian. Excellent touring base for castle, whisky and coastal trails. 15 golf courses within ½ hour drive. Only a five minute walk to the numerous attractions of Huntly town.

From Aberdeen on A96 (Huntly Bypass) at roundabout on outskirts of Huntly cont on A96 (sign posted Inverness). In approx ¾ mile turn right. Past Tesco turn 2nd left Riverside Drive. Park entrance at bottom of drive. From Inverness turn left at Tesco and continue as above.

Park accommodates 99 pitches

Total Touring Pitches: 66

Prices from:
(66)£15.25-18.90   (30) £8.00-16.90   (66)15.25-18.9

(3) £235.00-510.00 per week.

Inverurie, Aberdeenshire
Mrs R Wiseman
Map Ref: 4G9

67854

★★★
SELF CATERING

Open: All year
St Andrews House, St Andrews Gardens, Inverurie, Aberdeenshire, AB51 3XT
T: 01467 628950
E: rachel@jasmine-pm.demon.co.uk
W: jasmine-pm.demon.co.uk

1 Cottage	2 Public Rooms	Sleeps 1-5
Prices from:		
£300.00-500.00		**Per week**
£50.00-70.00		**Per night**

Johnshaven, Aberdeenshire
Brawliemuir Holiday Cottages
Map Ref: 4G12

16126

★★★★
SELF CATERING

Open: All year
Brawliemuir Farm, Johnshaven, Montrose, Angus, DD10 0HY
T: 01561 362453
E: carole@the-duvalls.com
W: brawliemuircottages.co.uk

2 Cottages	1-2 Public Rooms	Sleeps 2-6
Prices from:		
£225.00-425.00		**Per week**
£100.00		**Per 2 nights**

IMPORTANT: Prices stated are estimates and may be subject to change. Awards correct as of beginning of October 2008.

Kintore, Inverurie

Mrs J Lumsden
Map Ref: 4G10

★★★
SELF
CATERING

Open: All year
Kingsfield House, Kingsfield Road,
Kintore, Aberdeenshire AB51 0UD
T: 01467 632366
E: info@holidayhomesaberdeen.com
W: holidayhomesaberdeen.com

34069

1 Cottage	2 Public Rooms	Sleeps 2-6
Prices from:		
£425.00-625.00		**Per week**

Laurencekirk, Kincardineshire

Dovecot Caravan Park
Map Ref: 4F12

★★★
HOLIDAY
PARK

Open: April-mid October
Northwaterbridge, Laurencekirk, Kincardineshire AB30 1QL
T: 01674 840630   **E:** adele@dovecotcaravanpark.co.uk
W: dovecotcaravanpark.co.uk
Leisure facilities: ✆

From Laurencekirk (A90) 5 miles south at Northwaterbridge, turn right to Edzell woods. Site 300m on left. Signposted.

23038

Park accommodates 46 pitches
Total Touring Pitches: 25
Prices from:
🚐 (25) £12.50   ⛺ (10) £11.00   🚍 (10) £12.50

(1) £250.00 per week. Sleeps 6.

Portsoy, Aberdeenshire

Mr G Christie
Map Ref: 4F7

★★★
SELF
CATERING

Open: All year
Doson, 6 Seafield Terrace,
Portsoy, Aberdeenshire, AB45 2QB
T: 01261 843680   **M:** 07875 101257
E: gjc19963@yahoo.co.uk
W: boyne-cottage.co.uk

40646

1 Cottage	1 Public Room	Sleeps 2-5
Prices from:		
£250.00-350.00		**Per week**

Sandend, Portsoy

Mrs J Winfield
Map Ref: 4F7

★★
SELF
CATERING

Open: All year
Old School House, Sandend,
Portsoy, Banffshire, AB45 2UA
T: 01261 842660
E: sandendholidays@aol.com
W: sandendcaravanpark.co.uk

52958

1 Cottage	1 Public Room	Sleeps 2-4
Prices from:		
£290.00		**Per week**

For a full listing of quality assured non-serviced establishments please see pages 229-385.

165

Glen Coe, Highlands

THE HIGHLANDS AND MORAY

If you're searching for tranquillity, you'll find that life in the Highlands moves at a refreshingly relaxed pace.

Exciting, dramatic and romantic, it's hard not to be moved by the rugged majesty of the mountainous north. It's the stuff of picture postcards, with views that will be etched in your memory forever.

Unspoiled beauty

There are so many places you have to experience: the eerie silence of Glen Coe; the arctic wilderness of the Cairngorms; the deep mysteries of Loch Ness; the wild flatlands of the Flow Country; the astonishing beauty of Glen Affric; and the golden beaches of the west and north coast where you can gaze out to the Atlantic and never meet a soul all day. In this unspoiled natural environment, wildlife flourishes. You'll see red squirrels and tiny goldcrests in the trees, otters chasing fish in fast flowing rivers, deer coming down from the hills to the forest edge, dolphins and whales off the coast, ospreys and eagles soaring overhead.

A natural playground

And this natural playground is yours to share. Climbers, walkers, mountain bikers and hunters take to the hills. Surfers, sailors, canoeists and fishermen enjoy the beaches, rivers and lochs. For the more adventurous there's skiing, canyoning and white water rafting. Whatever outdoor activity you like to pursue, you'll find experienced, professional experts on hand to ensure you enjoy it to the full.

Highland hospitality

Once you've had enough exercise and fresh air, you can be assured of some fine Highland hospitality - whether you're staying in a tiny village, a pretty

To find out more, call 0845 22 55 121 or go to visitscotland.com

town, a thriving activity centre like Aviemore or in the rapidly expanding city of Inverness. In the pubs and hotels, restaurants and other venues around the community, you'll find music and laughter. Perhaps a riotous ceilidh in full fling and unforgettable nights of eating and drinking into the wee small hours.

Back to your roots

Highlanders know how to enjoy life and they're always keen to welcome visitors – especially those who are tracing their Scottish roots. Every year people come to discover the traditional homeland of their clan, learn about their history and walk in their ancestors' footsteps over battlefields like Culloden where the Jacobite army made its last stand. You could follow Bonnie Prince Charlie over the sea to Skye, whether it's by boat or by bridge. You can even take a glass bottom boat trip around the island and watch the sea life below.

What's more, 2009 is a big year for Scotland – we're celebrating the 250th anniversary of the birth of Robert Burns. There's over 200 special events taking place throughout the year, all over Scotland. Go to homecomingscotland2009.com to find out about events in this area.

Wherever you decide to go, the Highlands, Skye and Moray will cast a spell on you and it will be a holiday you will remember for as long as you live.

Belladrum Tartan Heart Festival

What's On?

O'Neill Highland Open, Thurso
29 April – 7 May 2009
One of the most progressive events in competitive surfing.
oneilleurope.com/highlandopen

UCI Mountain Bike World Cup, Fort William
6 - 7 June 2009
Voted best event on the tour two years running.
fortwilliamworldcup.co.uk

Rock Ness, Dores, Loch Ness
13 - 14 June 2009
The only dance event with its own monster.
rockness.co.uk

Tulloch Inverness Highland Games
18 - 19 July 2009
Clan gathering and heavyweight competition in Inverness. The Highland Clans are hosting the Masters World Championships.
invernesshighlandgames.com

Inverness Highland Tattoo
21 July - 1 August 2009
Previewing artists from the Edinburgh International Tattoo.
tattooinverness.org.uk

Belladrum Tartan Heart Festival, Beauly
7 - 8 August 2009
Open air, family-friendly traditional music festival.
tartanheartfestival.co.uk

Highland Feast
September – various dates
A series of unique culinary and gastronomic events.
highlandfeast.co.uk

Blas Festival – Celebrating the Highlands
4 - 12 September 2009
A vast programme of traditional music and events, staged in some of Scotland's most spectacular and iconic landscapes.
blas-festival.com

MAP

VISITOR INFORMATION CENTRES

Visitor Information Centres are staffed by people 'in the know' offering friendly advice, helping to make your stay in Scotland the most enjoyable ever . . . whatever your needs!

Northern Highlands, Inverness, Loch Ness and Nairn

Inverness	Castle Wynd, Inverness, IV2 3BJ	Tel: 01463 252401
Drumnadrochit	The Car Park, Drumnadrochit, Inverness-shire, IV63 6TX	Tel: 01456 459086

Fort William and Lochaber, Skye and Lochalsh

Fort William	15 High Street, Fort William, PH33 6DH	Tel: 01397 701801
Portree	Bayfield Road, Portree, Isle of Skye, IV51 9EL	Tel: 01478 614906
Dunvegan	2 Lochside, Dunvegan, Isle of Skye, IV55 8WB	Tel: 01343 542666

Moray, Aviemore and the Cairngorms

Aviemore	Grampian Road, Aviemore, PH22 1PP	Tel: 01479 810930
Elgin	17 High Street, Elgin, IV30 1EG	Tel: 01343 542666

LOCAL KNOWLEDGE • WHERE TO STAY • ACCOMMODATION BOOKING • PLACES TO VISIT • THINGS TO DO • MAPS AND GUIDES TRAVEL ADVICE • ROUTE PLANNING • WHERE TO SHOP AND EAT LOCAL CRAFTS AND PRODUCE • EVENT INFORMATION • TICKETS

For information and ideas about exploring Scotland in advance of your trip, call our booking and information service **0845 22 55 121** or go to **visitscotland.com**

If calling from outside the UK and Ireland **+44 1506 832 121**   From Ireland **1800 932 510**

A £4 booking fee applies for accommodation bookings made via a Visitor Information Centre and through our booking and information service.

Live it. Visit Scotland.
visitscotland.com/wheretofindus

Looking over to the Summer Isles, Highlands

Northern Highlands, Inverness, Loch Ness and Nairn

Scotland's most northerly mainland territory is characterised by its dramatic mountains, vast wilderness and spectacular coastline.

Take in the west coast, where views of Quinag from near Kylesku are unmissable. Equally essential on the itinerary of any Highland visitor is Loch Ness, Britain's deepest and most mysterious freshwater expanse.

Don't miss the opportunity to see the Moray Firth dolphins from Chanonry Point on the Black Isle or up close from one of many wildlife cruises.

There are many fine towns and villages to visit - Ullapool, Lochcarron, Lochinver and Kinlochbervie to the west, Thurso, John O'Groats, Wick, Dornoch, Strathpeffer and Nairn on the eastern side. You should also take some time to explore the rapidly growing city of Inverness. Capital of the Highlands, it's a thriving, modern city with lots to see and do.

Fireworks set off from the Kessock Bridge, Inverness

To find out more, call 0845 22 55 121 or go to visitscotland.com

1   **Assynt** is stunningly beautiful and is home to a variety of attractions. Chief among them are; the Assynt Visitor Centre, Hydroponicum at Achiltubuie and Kerracher Gardens, Highland Stoneware, Inverpolly Nature Reserve and Ardvreck Castle.

2   **Culloden Battlefield** is the site of the last major battle fought on mainland Britain in 1746. Bonnie Prince Charlie's Jacobite troops were defeated here by the Duke of Cumberland and the Hanoverian government forces. The new visitor centre – opened in 2007 – features a battle immersion cinema and handheld multi-lingual audio devices to bring the battle to life.

3   No visit to this part of Scotland would be complete without taking time to visit **John o'Groats** and the famous signpost pointing towards Lands End – a mere 874 miles away! From here there are also regular summer sailings to Orkney so you can hop on one of the John o'Groats day tours which incorporate the ferry and a coach tour of the main island.

4   Perhaps the most spectacularly scenic of all Scottish lochs, **Loch Maree** greets unsuspecting visitors travelling north-west on the A832 between Inverness and Gairloch. Bounded by the imposing masses of Beinn Eighe to the west and Slioch to the east, the loch's shores play host to a wealth of wildlife, as well as fragments of ancient Caledonian pinewood.

5   One of the largest castles in Scotland, the ruins of **Urquhart Castle** lie on the banks of Loch Ness, near Drumnadrochit. Blown up in 1692 to prevent Jacobite occupation, this 5-star visitor attraction has a fascinating interactive visitor centre which depicts the story of the castle's turbulent history. Explore the ruins of the castle, before visiting the on-site café where you will be rewarded with breathtaking views of Loch Ness.

6   At **Golspie Highland Wildcat Trails** an adrenaline filled mix of testing uphills and challenging fast downhill sections make for an exhilarating day's mountain biking on Ben Bhraggie. After you've reached the top, views west across Sutherland and south across the Dornoch Firth make the uphill all worth it.

FOOD AND DRINK

eatscotland.com

7 Only the freshest of fish straight from the daily catch make it to the table in the **Captain's Galley**. Set in a tastefully renovated old ice house in Scrabster, near Thurso, the award winning restaurant serves up to 10 different species of fish every night. Booking is recommended.

8 **Highland Feast**, an annual food and drink festival held in September, is a celebration of the fantastic produce and culinary skills present in the local area and beyond.

9 Fresh, local ingredients are combined to make the **Falls of Shin Visitor Centre** the ultimate place to stop for lunch. See salmon leap on the magnificent waterfall as you tuck in. There is also a children's playground so you can fill up while the kids are kept entertained.

10 As with many restaurants across the Highlands, **Sutor Creek** prides itself on the use of fresh, local produce, but few produce 'real pizza' like this place. Cooked in their specially built wood-fired oven this friendly bistro in Cromarty also slow-roasts the perfect Sunday meal with local meats infused with home grown herbs and garlic.

GOLF

visitscotland.com/golf

11 **Gairloch Golf Course** is superbly situated above a sandy bay beside the road into Gairloch. This 9-hole links course is one of the Highland's best kept secrets. Take your time soaking up the views towards Skye. Arrange tee times in advance to guarantee a round.

12 **Durness Golf Course**, surrounded by stunning coastal scenery, is notorious for its 9th hole, which requires players to clear the Atlantic Ocean! Check with the secretary in advance to ensure a round is possible.

13 Considered one of the finest links courses in the world, **Royal Dornoch Golf Course** is situated on public land in its namesake royal burgh, 45 miles north of Inverness. Play on the course about which Tom Watson famously remarked 'the most fun I've ever had on a golf course'.

14 A traditional Scottish links course, **Nairn West Golf Club** offers a challenge for all abilities. 20 minutes drive from Inverness, this 18-hole favourite is perfect for the discerning golfer looking to experience a course steeped in tradition.

To find out more, call 0845 22 55 121 or go to visitscotland.com

OUTSTANDING VIEWS

15 A classic view of **Loch Ness** is to be savoured from the beach at the village of Dores (B862 from Inverness), at the quieter side of the loch to the south. Look out for Nessie, or at the very least, the resident Nessie spotter!

16 Round the bay from **Lochinver**, a minor road allows fantastic views back towards the community and the incredible sugar loaf of Suilven rising up in the background.

17 Near John o'Groats see a dramatic coastline where thousands of seabirds nest in vast colonies. A walk across the clifftop fields will reward you with a stunning view south to Thirle Door and the **Stacks of Duncansby**. The first is a rocky arch, the second a group of large jagged sea stacks. This is a spot you will want to savour, with a view that varies as you move along the clifftop path and bring into play different alignments of the stacks and arch.

18 The **Corrieshalloch Gorge** National Nature Reserve, south-east of Ullapool, comprises a box canyon dropping 200ft to the river below. Adding to the drama are the spectacular **Falls of Measach**, best seen from the viewing platform further down the footpath.

WALKS   visitscotland.com/walking

19 **Reelig Glen** is a short walk through spectacular old conifer and broad-leaved trees on easy paths with short gentle gradients, making it a suitable walk for almost anyone. Approximately 10 minutes from Inverness, take the A862 west towards Beauly and after 8 miles, turn left onto the minor road signposted to Reelig and Moniack and continue for 1 mile – follow the Forestry Commission of Scotland sign and look out for Britain's tallest tree named Dughall Mor.

20 Although within the city of Inverness, the **Ness Islands** walk could be a million miles from it. The islands, linked by several old bridges, offer a quiet, scenic walk through tall, native and imported trees. It offers plenty of photo opportunities and an enjoyable family walk which accommodates wheelchairs.

21 Take the minor B869 road to Stoer lighthouse, from which a 3-hour circular walk leads to a spectacular rock-stack – the **Old Man of Stoer** - surrounded by jaw-dropping cliff scenery. The path is clear throughout, and offers views to the Assynt mountains in the south, and to the islands of Lewis and Harris many miles to the west.

22 The **Caithness and Sutherland Walking Festival**, held in May, consists of themed walks led by local guides. These interesting walks explore archaeology, history and wildlife and are a great way to learn more about the surrounding area.

Northern Highlands, Inverness, Loch Ness, Nairn

Altnaharra, Sutherland
Invermudale Annexe
Map Ref: 4A4

★★★★
SELF
CATERING

Open: April- October
Altnaharra, by Lairg, Sutherland, IV27 4UE
T: 01549 411250
E: invermudale@btopenworld.com
W: invermudale.co.uk

32029

1 Cottage	1 Public Room	Sleeps 2
Prices from:		
£325.00-350.00		**Per week**

Applecross, Wester Ross
Caroline and John Wales
Map Ref: 3F9

★★★★
SELF
CATERING

Open: All year
Peggs Lane Cottage,
Queniborough, Leicester LE7 3DF
T: 0116 2605726
E: wales@waitrose.com
W: tighruaraidh.co.uk
Spacious, luxurious house. Stunning location on coast, 7 miles north of Applecross with exceptional views across Inner Sound to Skye and Outer Hebrides. Four bedrooms extremely well equipped. For further information please visit www.tighruaraidh.co.uk or phone 0116 2605726.

72959

1 House	2 Public Rooms	Sleeps 1-7
Prices from:		
£495.00-850.00		**Per week**
£125.00		**Per night**

Ardross, Ross-shire
Lower Inchlumpie
Map Ref: 4B7

★★★★
SELF
CATERING

Open: All year
118 Offington Avenue, Worthing,
West Sussex BN14 9PR
T: 01903 260334   E: margaret@lowerinchlumpie.co.uk
W: lowerinchlumpie.co.uk

83023

1 House	3 Public Rooms	Sleeps 2-8
Prices from:		
£650.00-1250.00		**Per week**

Aultbea, Ross-shire
Ewe View Holidays
Map Ref: 3F6

★★★
SELF
CATERING

Open: All year
Ewe View, Drumchork, Aultbea, Ross-shire IV22 2HU
T: 01445 731394
E: relax@eweview.com
W: eweview.com

25321

2 Apartments	1 Public Room	Sleeps 2-3
Prices from:		
£130.00		**Per week**
£90.00		**Per 3 nights**

IMPORTANT: Prices stated are estimates and may be subject to change. Awards correct as of beginning of October 2008.

Aultbea, Ross-shire
Willow Cottage
Map Ref: 3F6

Open: All year

Mrs Alma Ella, Willow Cottage, Ormiscaig, Aultbea, Ross-shire IV22 2JJ
T: 01445 731263
W: willow-cottage-aultbea.co.uk

64297

1 Apartment	1 Public Room	Sleeps 4-5
Prices from:		
£225.00-370.00		**Per week**
£40.00-62.00		**Per night**

Beauly, Inverness-shire
Aigas Holiday Cottages
Map Ref: 4A8

Open: Febuary-November

Mains of Aigas, Beauly, Inverness-shire IV4 7AD
T: 01463 782423/782942
E: info@aigas-holidays.co.uk
W: aigas-holidays.co.uk

Nestling in the hills overlooking the delightful Beauly Valley 2 courtyard cottages, 1 hillside cottage. Absorb the peace, observe the wildlife, visit the Highland beauty spots, play Aigas golf course and discover the magic that draws visitors back to the Aigas.

37138

3 Cottages	1-2 Public Rooms	Sleeps 4-5
Prices from:		
£235.00-580.00		**Per week**
£50.00-120.00		**Per night**

Beauly, Inverness-shire
Dunsmore Lodge
Map Ref: 4A8

Open: All year

Beauly, Inverness-shire, IV4 7EY
T: 01463 782424
E: inghammar@dunsmorelodges.co.uk
W: dunsmorelodges.co.uk

23855

3 Chalets	1 Public Room	Sleeps 4
Prices from:		
£315.00		**Per week**
£73.00		**Per night**

Beauly, Inverness-shire
Mrs Catherine Guthrie
Map Ref: 4A8

Open: April-October

41 Barrow Point Avenue, Pinner, Middlesex HA5 3HD
T: 0208 866 5026

Croft cottage situated high above sea level and surrounded by hill farming country. Magnificent views of Glen Affric and Strathglass. Four miles from Beauly. Hilltop position with rough road access. Ideal for getting away from city life. Ideally situated for touring.

38725

1 Cottage	2 Public Rooms	Sleeps 4
Prices from:		
£200.00-300.00		**Per week**

For a full listing of quality assured non-serviced establishments please see pages 229-385.

175

Bettyhill, Sutherland
Mrs A Todd
Map Ref: 4B3

★★★★
SELF
CATERING

Open: All year
6 Hoy Farm, Halkirk, Caithness, KW12 6UU
T: 01847 831544
W: visitscotland.com

44774

1 House	2 Public Rooms	Sleeps 6
Prices from:		
£400.00		**Per week**

Black Isle, Ross-shire
Wester Brae Highland Lodges
Map Ref: 4B8

★★★★
SELF
CATERING

Open: All year
Culbokie, by Dingwall, Ross-shire, IV7 8JU
T: 01349 877609
E: westerbrae@btconnect.com
W: westerbraehighlandlodges.co.uk

Four lodges on a small privately owned site with
superb views over Cromarty Firth and Ben Wyvis.
Approx 5 miles (8km) from Culbokie.

63804

4 Lodges	1 Public Room	Sleeps 1-5
Prices from:		
£270.00-475.00		**Per week**
POA		**Per night**

Black Isle, Ross-shire
Mr W MacKay
Map Ref: 4B8

★★★
SELF
CATERING

Open: April to October
Fernvilla, Halebank Road, Widnes, Cheshire, WA8 8NP
T: 0151 425 2129/07795 202718
E: billandalisonmackay@yahoo.co.uk

50019

1 Cottage	2 Public Rooms	Sleeps 2-5
Prices from:		
£350.00		**Per week**

Braes, Ullapool
The Chalet & The Cottage
Map Ref: 3H6

★★
SELF
CATERING

Open: All year
A & M Maclennan, Invercorrie, Braes, Ullapool,
Wester Ross IV26 2TB
T: 01854 612272
E: mlas@globalnet.co.uk
W: invercorrie.co.uk

Comfortable and well-equipped, our traditional croft
cottage and chalet are sited in the peaceful area of
Braes, about a mile south of Ullapool, with lovely
views to the hills across Lochbroom. Ideal centre
for exploring the beautiful N. W. Highlands. Private
Parking.

31966

1 Cottage	2 Public Rooms	Sleeps 6
1 Cabin	1 Public Room	Sleeps 4
Prices from:		
Cottage:	£265.00	**Per week**
	£45.00	**Per night**
Chalet:	£255.00	**Per week**
	£40.00	**Per night**

IMPORTANT: Prices stated are estimates and may be subject to change. Awards correct as of beginning of October 2008.

r Cannich, Glen Affric
omich Holidays
Map Ref: 3H9

★ UP TO
★★★
SELF
TERING

48242

Open: All year

Tomich, Cannich, Inverness-shire, IV4 7LY
T: 01456 415332
E: admin@tomich-holidays.co.uk
W: tomich-holidays.co.uk

| 6 Cottages | 1 Public Room | Sleeps 4-5 |
| 6 Chalets | 1 Public Room | Sleeps 6-8 |

Prices from:		
Cottage:	£260.00	Per week
	£70.00	Per night
Cabin:	£290.00	Per week
	£65.00	Per night

---

lachtoll Bay, nr Lochinver
lachtoll Cottage
Map Ref: 3G5

★★★
SELF
TERING

11841

Open: All year

Contact: Bill Smith
T: 01358 720163
W: clachtollcottage.co.uk

One of the most stunningly beautiful house sites in
the UK. High quality four star accommodation with
panoramic views south to the mountains of Wester
Ross. Enclosed large garden area within 30 acre
coastal site. The cottage is just yards from the beach.

| 1 Cottage | 1 Public Room | Sleeps 6 |

Prices from:	
£500.00-800.00	Per week

---

ulbokie, Black Isle
rs Jane Hughson
Map Ref: 4B8

★★★
ELF
ERING

70464

Open: April to October

Ben Wyvis Views, Bydand, Culbokie, Ross-shire IV7 8JH
T: 01349 877430
E: jane@culbokie.net
W: culbokie.net

| 1 Villa | 2 Public Rooms | Sleeps 8 |

Prices from:	
£550.00-950.00	Per week
£125.00-150.00	Per night

---

ornoch, Sutherland
ornoch Caravan Park
Map Ref: 4B6

★★★
LIDAY
RK

22963

Open: 1st April - 26th October

The Links, River Street, Dornoch, Sutherland IV25 3LX
T: 01862 810423   E: info@dornochcaravans.co.uk
W: dornochcaravans.co.uk   *Leisure park:*

*6 miles north of Tain, turn right for 2 miles to Dornoch. At
bottom of square turn right for 450 yds.*

Park accommodates 138 pitches
Total Touring Pitches: 120

Prices from:		
£9.50	£9.50	£9.50
(18) £140.00-360.00		

---

rumbeg, Lochinver
he Shieling
Map Ref: 3G4

★★
ELF
ERING

49844

Open: April to October

Mr J MacLeod, Pinewood, Scotsburn Rd,
Kildary, Invergordon, Ross-shire, IV18 0NX
T: 01862 842665

| 1 Chalet | 2 Public Rooms | Sleeps 4-5 |

Prices from:	
£200.00-250.00	Per week

For a full listing of quality assured non-serviced establishments please see pages 229-385.

177

Drumnadrochit, Inverness-shire
Balnalurigin
Map Ref: 4A9

SELF CATERING ★★★★

68222

Open: March-October + Xmas and New Year

Mrs D J Beattie, Appleton House,
Errol, Perth, Perthshire PH2 7QE
T: 01821 642412
E: idbeattie@ukonline.co.uk
W: accommodationlochness.co.uk

Overlooking Loch Mieklie and with views of the mountains beyond, this charming well equipped hillside cottage provides a comfortable base from which to explore this beautiful Highland area. Many visitor attractions and outdoor pursuits are within easy reach.

1 Cottage	2 Public Rooms	Sleeps 7

Prices from:
£375.00-580.00   **Per week**

Drumnadrochit, by Loch Ness
Drumnadrochit Lodges
Map Ref: 4A9

★★★ UP TO ★★★★
SELF CATERING

23328

Open: All year

Upper Achmony,
Drumnadrochit, Inverness-shire IV63 6UX
T: 01456 450467
E: drumnadrochit-lodges@tiscali.co.uk
W: drumnadrochit-lodges.com

Spacious quality three bedroom, two bathroom holiday lodges set high on the scenic hillside above Drumnadrochit and Loch Ness. Providing very comfortable accommodation for a refuge of peace and tranquility or a convenient touring centre for the Highlands of Scotland.

4 Lodges	1 Public Room	Sleeps 1-6

Prices from:
£300.00-650.00   **Per week**
£60.00   **Per night**

Dundonnell, Ross-shire
Badrallach Cottage, Campsite and Bothy
Map Ref: 3G6

CAMPING PARK ★★★★

SELF CATERING ★★★★

18007

Open: All year

Croft 9 , Badrallach, Dundonnell, Ross-shire IV23 2QP
T: 01854 633281
E: mail@badrallach.com   W: badrallach.com

Lochshore site overlooking Anteallach on Scoraig Peninsular. Explore, walk, fish, (kayaks, boats, bike hire) or relax and watch otters, porpoises, eagles, orchids, saxifrages. Free hot showers and cosy stone bothy with peat stove and gas lights. Small, family run. Clean. Bliss.

7 miles along winding single track road off A832. 1 mile east of the Dundonnell Hotel.

Park accommodates 19 pitches		
Prices from:		
Cottage		£175.00/long weekend
Bothy (sleeps 12)		£5.00-60.00 per night
🚐 (3) £12.00	⛺ (17) £10.00	🚍 £12.00
🚐 (1) from £40.00/night.		

Durness, Sutherland
Norsehaven Cottages
Map Ref: 4A3

Open: All year
Oldbury House, Ightham, Sevenoaks, Kent, TN15 9DE
T: 01732 882320
E: info@norsehaven.com
W: norsehaven.com

47617

3 Cottages	1 Public Room	Sleeps 2-8

Prices from:
£295.00-595.00 **Per week**

Fort Augustus
Morag's Lodge
Map Ref: 4A10

Open: All year
Bunoich Brae, Fort Augustus PH32 4DG
T: 01320 366289
E: info@moragslodge.com
W: moragslodge.com

38950

1 Hostel	Sleeps 80

Prices from:
£119.00 **Per week**
£17.00 **Per night**

Gairloch, Ross-shire
Family Holiday Houses
Map Ref: 3F7

Open: Easter-New Year
Bunoich Brae, Fort Augustus PH32 4DG
T: 01320 366289
E: barbara.reese@ntlworld.com
W: gairlochholidays.co.uk

25602

6 Houses	1-2 Public Rooms	Sleeps 4-7

Prices from:
£190.00-505.00 **Per week**

Gairloch, Ross-shire
Mr Roderick MacKenzie
Map Ref: 3F7

Open: March-October
16 Strath, Gairloch, Ross-shire, IV21 2BX
T: 01445 712230
E: lyndsey.mackenzie@virgin.net

41784

1 Cottage	2 Public Rooms	Sleeps 7
1 Bungalow	1 Public Room	Sleeps 2

Prices from:

Cottage:	£240.00-320.00	**Per week**
Bungalow:	£220.00-260.00	**Per week**

Glen Strathfarrar, nr Beauly
Culligran Cottages
Map Ref: 3H9

Open: Mid March-Mid November

Glen Strathfarrar, Struy, Beauly, Inverness-shire IV4 7JX
T: 01463 761285
M: 07917 166539
E: info@culligrancottages.co.uk
W: culligrancottages.co.uk

Pure magic! Come for a spell and this Glen will cast one over you. Nature reserve. Fifteen miles of private road. Bikes for hire. Salmon and trout fishing on River Farrar. Tours of the deer farm. Beauly 11 miles. Brochure.

21682

1 Cottage	2 Public Room	Sleeps 1-7
4 Chalets	1 Public Room	Sleeps 1-7

Prices from:

Cottage:	£289.00-529.00	**Per week**
Chalets:	£199.00-499.00	**Per week**

Short break prices on application.

For a full listing of quality assured non-serviced establishments please see pages 229-385.

179

Golspie, Sutherland
Big Barns Self Catering
Map Ref: 4B6

AWAITING GRADING

**Open: March-December
(Open on request January/February)**

Big Barns, Dunrobin, KW10 6SF
T: 01408 633332
E: info@bigbarnscottage.co.uk
W: bigbarnscottage.co.uk

83674

1 Cottage	2 Public Rooms	Sleeps 4
Prices from:		
£400.00-600.00		**Per week**
£200.00-350.00		**Per 3 nights**

Golspie, Sutherland
Mr M Scott
Map Ref: 4B6

★★
SELF CATERING

Open: March-November

The Old School, Ann Street, Gatehouse of Fleet, Castle Douglas, Kirkcudbrightshire DG7 2HU
T: 01557 814058

Very comfortable, well furnished bungalow built from locally grown timber. Woodland setting. High ground. 1½ miles from Golspie Village. Wonderful views over the hills and sea. Fully equipped, all electric kitchen, bath with shower. Bed linen provided. Open log/coal fire.

59556

1 Log Cabin	1 Public Room	Sleeps 5
Prices from:		
£200.00-400.00		**Per week**

Inverness
Blackpark Farm
Map Ref: 3B8

★★★★
SELF CATERING

Open: All year

Westhill, Inverness IV2 5BP
T: 01463 790620
E: l.alexander@blackpark.co.uk
W: blackpark.co.uk

Our self-catering houses are in a perfect position for touring the Highlands. Only three miles from the A9, we are easily found next to the Culloden Battlefield. Skye, John O'Groats can all be explored within a days travelling.

15292

1 Bungalow	4 Public Rooms	Sleeps 6
Prices from:		
£350.00-800.00		**Per week**

IMPORTANT: Prices stated are estimates and may be subject to change. Awards correct as of beginning of October 2008.

Inverness
Bluebell Apartment   Map Ref: 4B8

Open: All year

★★
SELF
CATERING

Swallowcroft, Achindarroch Road, Duror PA38 4BS
T: 0808 1787564
E: reservations@highland-vacation.co.uk
W: highland-vacation.co.uk
Bluebell Apartment located near Loch Ness, and
just two miles from Inverness City, benefiting from
magnificent views over the city and the Moray Firth.
It sleeps four adults comfortably, lovingly furnished
and equipped.

83608

1 Apartment	1 Public Room	Sleeps 1-4

Prices from:
£185.00-500.00   **Per week**

Inverness
Connel Court City Centre Flats   Map Ref: 4B8

Open: All year

★★★
SELF
CATERING

Revd & Mrs A M Roff, Rowan Glen, Culbokie,
Dingwall, Ross-shire, IV7 8GY
T: 01349 877762   E: martin@roff-rowanglen.co.uk
W: highlands-selfcatering.co.uk

51506

2 Apartments	1-2 Public Rooms	Sleeps 4

Prices from:
£280.00   **Per week**
£75.00 per night   **Min 2 nights**

Inverness
Larchview   Map Ref: 4B8

Open: All year

★★
SELF
CATERING

6a Green Drive, Inverness, Inverness-shire, IV2 4EX
T: 01463 236763
E: mackenzie@inverness9.freeserve.co.uk
W: visithighlands.com

42498

1 Bungalow	1 Public Room	Sleeps 5

Prices from:
£180.00-380.00   **Per week**

By Inverness
Mrs Pottie- Easter Dalziel Cottages   Map Ref: 4B8

Open: All year

★ UP TO
★★
SELF
CATERING

Easter Dalziel Farm, Dalcross, Inverness-shire IV2 7JL
T: 01667 462213
E: wts@easterdalzielfarm.co.uk
W: easterdalzielfarm.co.uk
Traditional stone cottages, set amidst farmland
with its abundant wildlife, provide a superb base.
Panoramic views. Central location for castle and
whisky trails, golfing, touring and family holidays.
Mostly ground floor accommodation. Long or short
breaks? You're welcome all year.

69716

3 Cottages	1 Public Room	Sleeps 4-6

Prices from:
£160.00-510.00   **Per week**
£32.00-102.00   **Per night**

Nr Inverness
The Dairy at Daviot

Map Ref: 4B8

★★★★
SELF
CATERING

Open: All year

House of Daviot, Daviot Estate, IV2 5ER
T: 01463 772975
E: info@dairyatdaviot.co.uk
W: dairyatdaviot.co.uk

A converted 19th century farm steading on a private estate, The Dairy at Daviot houses luxury apartments, comfortable lounging area, all-day cafe, and a sheltered courtyard - all within a stone's throw of the spectacular lochs and landscapes world renowned in the Highlands.

6 Apartments	1-2 Public Rooms	Sleeps 2-5

Prices from:

Apartment:	£450.00	**Per week**
	£100.00	**Per night**

John O'Groats, Caithness
John O'Groats Caravan and Camping Site

Map Ref: 4E2

★★★
TOURING
PARK

Open: April-September

Caravan Site, John O'Groats, Caithness KW1 4YR
T: 01955 611329/744   E: info@johnogroatscampsite.co.uk
W: johnogroatscampsite.co.uk

At end of A99, beside 'Last House in Scotland'.

Park accommodates 90 pitches
Total Touring Pitches: 90

Prices from:

£13.00	£11.00	£13.00

Kinlochewe, Ross-shire
Mr M Madden

Map Ref: 3G8

★★★
SELF
CATERING

Open: All year

4 Elm Road, Irby, Wirral, Merseyside, CH61 3UP
T: 0151 648 2454
E: mansefield.madden@virgin.net

1 Bungalow	2 Public Rooms	Sleeps 2-4

Prices from:

£170.00	**Per week**

Kirkhill, by Inverness
Mr E H A Fraser

Map Ref: 4A8

★★★
SELF
CATERING

Open: April-September

Kingillie House, Kirkhill,
Inverness, Inverness-shire IV5 7PU
T: 01463 831275
E: euan-fraser@kingillie.freeserve.co.uk
W: kingillie.co.uk

Relax in a comfortable Highland cottage in beautiful surroundings: secluded but not isolated. Restaurants and shops are within easy reach, but so are spectacular lochs and glens. There is a sheltered garden for sitting out or children's play.

1 Cottage	1 Public Room	Sleeps 4

Prices from:

£285.00-440.00	**Per week**

Kylesku, Sutherland
Mr and Mrs L Cherry
Map Ref: 3H4

Open: All year

Unapool House Cottages,
Kylesku, Sutherland IV27 4HW
T: 01971 502344
E: mail@unapoolhouse.co.uk
W: unapoolhouse.co.uk

Located within three acres of beautiful gardens and woodland fronting Loch Glencoul, our cottages offer stunning views over the loch and the mountains beyond. We are ideally situated for exploring Assynt and North West Sutherland.

80575

3 Cottages	1 Public Room	Sleeps 2-4
Prices from:		
£185.00		**Per week**

Laide, Ross-shire
Rocklea, Little Gruinard
Map Ref: 3G6

Open: All year

Mr & Mrs Gilchrist, 12 Woodhall Road,
Colinton, Edinburgh, EH13 0DX
T: 0131 441 6053
E: aandagilchrist@blueyonder.co.uk
W: heimdall-scot.co.uk/laide

39436

1 Log Cottage	1 Public Room	Sleeps 5
Prices from:		
£220.00-510.00		**Per week**

Lairg, Sutherland
Brown Villa
Map Ref: 4A6

Open: April-October

Mrs Johan Reid, Upper Grange Farm,
Peterhead, Aberdeenshire AB42 1HX
T: 01779 473 116   M: 07732 545123
E: shona.reid@hotmail.co.uk
W: visithighlands.com

16619

1 House	1 Public Room	Sleeps 6
Prices from:		
£280.00-380.00		**Per week**

Lairg, Sutherland
Mrs Tracey Smith
Map Ref: 4A6

Open: All year

Plovers, Sarson Lane, Andover, Hants, SP11 8DY
T: 01264 773319
E: ashsmith65@btinternet.com
W: invercassleycottage.co.uk

31944

1 Cottage	2 Public Rooms	Sleeps 1-6
Prices from:		
£270.00-570.00		**Per week**
Short breaks available on request		

For a full listing of quality assured non-serviced establishments please see pages 229-385.

183

Lochinver, Sutherland
Cathair Dhubh Estate
Map Ref: 3G5

★★★★ SELF CATERING

Open: All year

Achmelvich, Lochinver, Sutherland, IV27 4JB
T: 01571 855277
E: cathairdhubh@btinternet.com
W: cathairdhubh.co.uk

Enjoy superb coastal and mountain views from our luxury fully equipped holiday cottages set in 80 acres of this remote and beautiful part of the Scottish Highlands. A paradise for walking, climbing, white sandy beaches, trout fishing and wildlife.

18551

5 Cottages	1 Public Room	Sleeps 4-6

Prices from:		
£275.00-890.00		**Per week**
£30.00-115.00		**Per night**

[icons]

Lochinver, Sutherland
Glendarroch House
Map Ref: 3G5

★★★★ SELF CATERING

Open: All year

Colin MacKenzie, Braeside, Helmsdale, KW8 6JS
T: 01431 821207
E: colin@glendarroch.net
W: glendarroch.net

Nestling in a secluded glen with glorious views of the mountains this is the perfect setting for a relaxing holiday. Alone in 15 acre grounds with nature all around yet convenient for shops. A tastefully modernised traditional house, exceptionally comfortable and well-equipped.

16042

1 House	2 Public Rooms	Sleeps 1-6

Prices from:	
£425.00-855.00	**Per week**

[icons]

Lochinver, Sutherland
Heather Cottage
Map Ref: 3G5

★★★★ SELF CATERING

Open: All year

Willowbrae, 73 Baddidarroch, Lochinver, IV27 4LP
T: 01571 844383
E: heather@clanranaldholidays.co.uk
W: clanranaldholidays.co.uk

69702

Set in private gardens with amazing views including Lochinver pier, Suilven and Canisp. Excellent appointed traditional cottage is equipped and furnished to a very high standard. Ideal for all outdoor pursuits, fabulous restaurants and more. Pefect holiday base.

1 Cottage	1 Public Room	Sleeps 4

Prices from:		
£250.00-420.00		**Per week**
£50.00		**Per night**

[icons]

IMPORTANT: Prices stated are estimates and may be subject to change. Awards correct as of beginning of October 2008.

Lochinver, Sutherland
Mr & Mrs Lloyd-Jenkins
Map Ref: 3G5

Open: All year
Creigard, Badnaban, Lochinver, Sutherland, IV27 4LR
T: 01571 844448
E: neil@creigard.demon.co.uk
W: creigardholidays.co.uk

41490

1 Cottage	2 Public Rooms	Sleeps 2-3
1 Bungalow	2 Public Rooms	Sleeps 2-4

Prices from:
Cottage:	£205.00-425.00	Per week
	£35.00	Per night (min 3 nts)
Bungalow:	£225.00-465.00	Per week
	£40.00	Per night (min 3 nts)

Lochinver, Sutherland
Mountview Self Catering
Map Ref: 3G5

Open: All year
70 Baddidarrach, Lochinver, Sutherland, IV27 4LP
T: 01571 844648
E: stay@mountview-lochinver.co.uk
W: mountview-lochinver.co.uk

45057

1 Cottage	1 Public Room	Sleeps 2-4
2 Cabins	1 Public Room	Sleeps 2-4

Prices from:
Cottage:	£340.00-720.00	Per week
	£70.00	Per night
Cabin:	£340.00-720.00	Per week
	£80.00	Per night

Lochinver, Sutherland
Spring Cottage
Map Ref: 3G5

Open: All year
Salters House, 10 Thornybank, Dalkeith
Midlothian EH22 3NQ
T: 0131 663 2172
E: helenmwallace@sky.com

Set in lovely gardens with stunning sea views. Spring Cottage benefits from all the village amenities whilst being ideally situated to access the wonderful area of Assynt and beyond. ideal for all holiday types. Pets very welcome.

23137

1 Cottage	1 Public Room	Sleeps 6

Prices from:
£200.00-425.00	Per week

Melvich, Sutherland
Halladale Inn Caravan and Chalet Park
Map Ref: 4C3

Open: Beginning April-end Oct
Melvich, Sutherland KW14 7YJ
T: 01641 531282   E: mazfling@tinyworld.co.uk
W: halladaleinn.co.uk

16 miles west of Thurso on A836

29400

Park accommodates 19 pitches
Total Touring Pitches: 10
Prices from:
🚐 (10) £12.50 ⛺ (9) £5.00 (pp)   🚛 (0)

Melvich, Sutherland
Halladale Inn Caravan and Chalet Park
Map Ref: 4C3

Open: All year
Melvich, Sutherland KW14 7YJ
T: 01641 531282
E: mazfling@tinyworld.co.uk
W: halladaleinn.co.uk

29400

3 Chalets	1 Public Room	Sleeps 4

Prices from:
£190.00-240.00	Per week
£45.00	Per night

nr Melvich, Sutherland
Strath Halladale Partnership
Map Ref: 4C3

★★★ UP TO ★★★★ SELF CATERING

Open: All year
Estate Office, Forsinard, Sutherland KW13 6YT
T: 01641 571271
E: info@strathhalladale.com
W: strathhalladale.com

60534

1 Cottage	3 Public Rooms	Sleeps 4
1 House	4 Public Rooms	Sleeps 6-8
1 Bungalow	3 Public Rooms	Sleeps 4

Prices from:		
Cottage:	£300.00-540.00	**Per week**
House:	£810.00-1300.00	**Per week**
Bungalow:	£250.00-440.00	**Per week**

Nairn, Inverness-shire
Boath Stables
Map Ref: 4C8

★★★★ SELF CATERING

Open: All year
Boath Steading, Auldearn, Nairn, IV12 5TE
T: 01667 451300
E: maxwell_ellen@hotmail.com
W: boathstables.co.uk

15550

| 2 Cottages | 2 Public Rooms | Sleeps 2-6 |

Prices from:	
£450.00-950.00	**Per week**
£100.00	**Per night**

Nairn, Inverness-shire
Mrs Debbie Hardiman
Map Ref: 4C8

★★★ SELF CATERING

Open: All year
Scealladh Scear, Meadowfield, Auldearn IV12 5JZ
T: 01667 451464
M: 07873 210212
E: thesheiling@live.co.uk

The 'Sheiling' is a modern fully equipped bungalow with a bright sunny conservatory set in the village of Auldearn. It can sleep a maximum of six people. It is fully equipped and furnished to a high standard to ensure a comfortable stay.

75159

| 1 Bungalow | 2 Public Rooms | Sleeps 2-6 |

Prices from:	
£330.00-450.00	**Per week**
£47.15-65.00	**Per night**

Nairn, Inverness-shire
Marina View
Map Ref: 4C8

★★★ SELF CATERING

Open: All year
Gary and Jenny Stokel, 48 River Park, Nairn Highlands, IV12 5SR
T: 01667 454464
E: garystokel@hotmail.com
W: harbourviewnairn.co.uk

77894

| 1 Apartment | 1 Public Room | Sleeps 4-5 |

Prices from:	
£275.00	**Per week**
£50.00	**Per night (low season)**

Nairn, Inverness-shire
No 6 The Moorings
Map Ref: 4C8

★★★ SELF CATERING

Open: All year
Mr E S Walker, 1 Findhorn Road, Kinloss, Forres, Moray, IV36 3TX
T: 01309 691266
E: rick.walker1@virgin.net
W: walker712.freeserve.co.uk

40537

| 1 House | 2 Public Rooms | Sleeps 1-5 |

Prices from:	
£200.00	**Per week**
£60.00	**Per night**

Poolewe, Ross-shire
Mr Mitchell
Map Ref: 3F7

★★★ SELF CATERING

Open: All year
14 Croft, Poolewe, Ross-shire, IV22 2JY
T: 01445 781231
E: kbell14@aol.com
W: riverewe.co.uk

41238

1 Cottage	1 Public Room	Sleeps 4

Prices on application

Portmahomack, Ross-shire
Mo-Dhachaidh
Map Ref: 4C7

★★★ SELF CATERING

Open: All year excl Xmas and New Year
Mrs Shirley Duff, 5 Latch Gardens, Brechin DD9 6LN
T: 07977 485026
E: shirleyduff@tiscali.co.uk
W: portmahomackbeachhouse.co.uk

70743

1 Cottage	2 Public Rooms	Sleeps 6

Prices from:
£500.00 — **Per week**

Scourie, Sutherland
An Tigh Earna
Map Ref: 3H4

★★★ SELF CATERING

Open: All year
Mr W. J. O. Nicoll, 3 The Logan,
Liff, by Dundee, Angus DD2 5PJ
T: 01382 580358 E: william.nicoll@virgin.net
W: scourie-selfcatering.co.uk

42032

1 House	2 Public Rooms	Sleeps 2-6

Prices from:
£250.00-450.00 — **Per week**

Scourie, Sutherland
Cnoclochan
Map Ref: 3H4

★★ SELF CATERING

Open: Easter-End of October
9 Nanhurst Park, Elmbridge Road,
Cranleigh, Surrey, GU6 8JX
T: 01483 274846
E: jmwqc@dial.pipex.com

40930

1 Cottage	2 Public Rooms	Sleeps 6

Prices from:
£275.00-400.00 — **Per week**

near Shieldaig, Ross-shire
Mrs M Calcott
Map Ref: 3F8

★★★ SELF CATERING

Open: All year
Tigh Fada, 117 Doire-Aonar, near Shieldaig,
by Strathcarron, Ross-shire, IV54 8XH
T: 01520 755248
E: dougcalcott@btinternet.com

44522

1 Cabin	1 Public Room	Sleeps 4

Prices from:
£320.00 — **Per week**

Skerray, by Tongue
Mr and Mrs Thompson
Map Ref: 4B3

★★ SELF CATERING

Open: All year
32 Parkland Drive, Oadby, Leicester LE2 4DG
T: 0116 2717667
E: RazorApexClean@aol.com
W: visitscotland.com

83536

1 Cottage	2 Public Rooms	Sleeps 1-6

Prices from:
£280.00 — **Per week**
£75.00 — **Per night**

For a full listing of quality assured non-serviced establishments please see pages 229-385.

Strathpeffer, Ross-shire
Ross Holiday Homes
Map Ref: 4A8

★★★
SELF CATERING

Open: March-October
57 Airyhall Crescent, Aberdeen AB15 7QS
T: 01224 318520
E: info@rossholidayhomes.co.uk
W: rossholidayhomes.co.uk

39704

2 Lodges	1 Public Room	Sleeps 4
Prices from:		
£250.00-450.00		**Per week**
£40.00-80.00		**Per night**

Talmine, Sutherland
Mrs Annie Gunn
Map Ref: 4A3

★★★
SELF CATERING

Open: May-October
97 Kenneth Street, Inverness, IV3 5QQ
T: 01463 234420
E: annie@gunn8466.freeserve.co.uk

68223

1 Bungalow	2 Public Rooms	Sleeps 2-5
Prices from:		
£260.00-425.00		**Per week**

Thurso, Caithness
Curlew Cottage
Map Ref: 4D3

★★★★
SELF CATERING

Open: All year
Hilliclay Mains, Weydale,
Thurso,Caithness, KW14 8YN
T: 01847 895638
E: macgregor@curlewcottage.com
W: curlewcottage.com

21775

1 Cottage	2 Public Rooms	Sleeps 1-4
Prices from:		
£300.00-485.00		**Per week**

---

by Thurso, Caithness
The Croft, Dunnet Head
Map Ref: 4D3

★★★★
SELF CATERING

Open: All year
Caithness Self Catering, Clairruah,
Westside, Dunnet, Thurso, Caithness KW14 8YD
T: 01847 851889/07795 230574
E: imogen@caithness-self-catering.co.uk
W: caithness-self-catering.co.uk
Nestled in an unspoiled sea-side and rural location
in the Scottish Highlands, The Croft is surrounded
by countryside, beaches, lochs, spectacular sea
views and an abundance of wildlife. Furnished and
equipped to a very high standard. Relax and enjoy.

83531

1 Cottage	2-3 Public Rooms	Sleeps 2-6
Prices from:		
£345.00-870.00		**Per week**
£45.00		**Per night per person**

IMPORTANT: Prices stated are estimates and may be subject to change. Awards correct as of beginning of October 2008.

Torridon. Ross-shire
Alt Na Criche
Map Ref: 3G8

★★★
SELF
CATERING

Open: All year

Alma House, 12 William Street,
Torphins, Kincardineshire AB31 4FR
T: 07725 636894/07885 363001
E: altnacriche@yahoo.co.uk

A fully modernised cottage offering comfort and
tranquility in a location of exceptional beauty on
the shore of Loch Torridon. Newly fitted kitchen and
bathrooms, one ensuite. Open fire and large picture
window in lounge. Ideal touring base.

69036

1 Cottage	2 Public Rooms	Sleeps 6
Prices from:		
£500.00		**Per week**

Torridon, Ross-shire
Caladh
Map Ref: 3G8

52321

★★★
SELF
CATERING

Open: All year

Rev & Mrs A.M. Roff, Rowan Glen,
Culbokie, Dingwall, Ross-shire, IV7 8GY
T: 01349 877762
E: martin@roff-rowanglen.co.uk
W: highlands-selfcatering.co.uk

1 Bungalow	2 Public Rooms	Sleeps 6
Prices from:		
£360.00		**Per week**

Ullapool, Ross-shire
Mr B Hicks
Map Ref: 3G6

61191

★★
SELF
CATERING

Open: All year

23 Copper Beech View, Tonbridge, Kent TN9 2HF
T: 01732 367827
E: bhbhicks@aol.com

1 House	2-3 Public Rooms	Sleeps 8
Prices from:		
£200.00-450.00		**Per week**

Ullapool, Ross-shire
Newton House
Map Ref: 3G6

69102

★★★
SELF
CATERING

Open: March-October

Newton House, Braes, Ullapool IV26 2SW
T: 01971 502221/01971 502355
E: newtonlge@aol.com
W: newtonhouse-ullapool.co.uk

1 Bungalow	2 Public Rooms	Sleeps 6
Prices from:		
£450.00		**Per week**

For a full listing of quality assured non-serviced establishments please see pages 229-385.

189

Elgol, Loch Scavaig, Isle of Skye

Fort William, Lochaber, Skye and Lochalsh

Fort William is known as the 'Outdoor Capital of the UK' – and little wonder. The area annually hosts the Mountain Bike World Cup and is next door to Scotland's highest mountain, Ben Nevis. The surrounding area provides a huge range of opportunities to enjoy the great outdoors.

The local scenery is quite stunning and there are hundreds of amazing places to visit. From the dramatic beauty of Glen Coe to the breathtaking views across Loch Duich, not forgetting the wild isolation of Knoydart and Ardnamurchan Point.

Take in some of the finest coastal and hill scenery on what is considered one of the great railway journeys of the world. Travel the length of the legendary Road to the Isles on the Jacobite Steam Train from Fort William to Mallaig. Take in the iconic Neptune's Staircase, Glenfinnan Viaduct and glorious coastline of Arisaig and Morar, and when you reach Mallaig you'll be able to see the jagged peaks of the Cuillin mountains on the Isle of Skye.

The turbulent history and majestic scenery of Skye and Lochalsh make the area one of Scotland's most romantic destinations. From the delightfully situated Eilean Donan Castle and the picture-postcard village of Plockton to the soaring craggy heights of the Cuillin and the eerie pinnacles of Trotternish, the area is sure to leave an imprint on your heart.

To find out more, call 0845 22 55 121 or go to visitscotland.com

DON'T MISS

1. One of the most picturesque – and most photographed – castles in Scotland, Eilean Donan Castle, sits on Loch Duich, beside the tiny village of Dornie. Stroll across the causeway that links it to the shore and explore it for yourself. For a panoramic view, follow the path from the village which leads up to the Carr Brae viewpoint.

2. Take a boat trip from Elgol (B8083 from Broadford) to isolated and inspiring Loch Coruisk. You will get up close to Britain's most dramatic landscapes, while your local guide will make sure you don't miss out on seeing the abundant wildlife – including the famous seal colony on the banks of the loch.

3. Accessible only by boat from Mallaig or via a very long walk from Kinlochhourn, Knoydart is recognised as the remotest part of mainland Britain and is perfect for adventurous families. One of the best hiking spots in the country, there are also options for wildlife watching, canoeing and fishing. The scenery is outstanding and will leave a lasting impression.

4. Camusdarach, Traigh and the Silver Sands of Morar are just a selection of exquisite beaches along the shoreline between Arisaig and Mallaig. While away a few hours picnicking with the breathtaking backdrop of the Small Isles of Eigg and Rum rising sheer out of the sea in front of you and admire the changing light on the sea catching the numerous skerries that pepper the coast.

5. To travel the whole length of the Road to the Isles, hop aboard the Jacobite Steam Train. This steam engine runs between Fort William and Mallaig throughout the summer months and takes in some truly impressive sites such as Neptune's Staircase, the Glenfinnan Viaduct and the glorious coastline of Arisaig and Morar. Regarded as one of the Great Railway Journeys of the World, this is a must while in the area, especially for Harry Potter fans who will recognise it from the films.

6. The biggest indoor ice climbing facility in the world, The Ice Factor, is situated in a former aluminium works in Kinlochleven. With rock climbing walls, a gym, sauna, and plunge pool, this is a great day out for the activity enthusiast or indeed, the whole family. As the National Centre for Indoor Ice Climbing, experts can try out new techniques whilst novices can get to grips with the basics in a safe and secure environment.

FOOD AND DRINK

eatscotland.com

7   The **Three Chimneys** restaurant on Skye is known far and wide as one of the most romantic eateries in the land. The candlelit crofter's cottage on the shores of Loch Dunvegan, voted 28th in Restaurant Magazine's 'definitive list' of the World's Top 50 Restaurants, is an idyllic setting for a proposal, a honeymoon or any special occasion. Book ahead to ensure your table.

8   Among the host of west coast seafood restaurants, the EatScotland approved **Holly Tree** in Kentallen stands out. The catch comes into their own pier on the shore of Loch Linnhe and is served up with magnificent views across to the Morven hills.

9   **Crannog** at the Waterfront in Fort William serves the very best in seafood. Be sure to give their speciality a try – the langoustine fresh from Loch Linnhe!

10 For an AA rosette dinner, seek out **Russell's Restaurant**, Smiddy House in Spean Bridge. Innovation and flair are deftly applied to a fine range of local produce.

WALKS

visitscotland.com/walking

11 **Glen Finnan** - From the Glenfinnan Visitor Centre car park, follow the Mallaig road across a bridge and then look out for a sign pointing towards Glenfinnan Lodge. From here continue up the glen where kids will be impressed by the famous viaduct, featured in the Harry Potter films. An easy 5½ mile route, taking in most of this scenic glen, can be completed in roughly 2 hours.

12 **Morar to Loch Morar and Mallaig** - A relatively easy walk you can enjoy without the hassle of taking the car. The starting and finishing points are both adjacent to train stations, so check out scotrail.co.uk to ensure you're onboard! Set off from Morar station and walk south, taking a left turn onto the minor road along Loch Morar's north shore. Kids should keep a look out for Nessie's cousin 'Morag' who supposedly occupies this loch. Continue along, as the road becomes a path, before arriving in Tarbet. Here, a boat departs daily at 3.30 pm throughout the summer to take you back via Loch Nevis to the connecting train at Mallaig. Allow 6 hours for the walk.

13 **Glen Coe** is one of the most popular hiking destinations in Scotland with the likes of Allt Coire for more experienced hikers and, for the less experienced walker, places like the Lost Valley to seek out. From the car parks on the A82, the path takes you across the bridge over the River Coe towards the triple buttresses known as the Three Sisters. Turn right after the bridge and follow the trail upwards. After a couple of miles you'll reach the false summit marking the edge of the hidden basin where the MacDonald clan used to hide their cattle in times of attack.

14 For a longer more challenging walk, drive 6 miles north from Portree on the Isle of Skye (A855), where you will find a car park. A path leads through woodland onto a steep climb to an area of geological formations. There are then a number of paths that can be followed to the base of the **Old Man of Storr**. Along the way you can enjoy good views across the Sound of Raasay. This walk should take in excess of 3 hours.

To find out more, call 0845 22 55 121 or go to visitscotland.com

OUTSTANDING VIEWS

15   As you drive south on the A828, Castle Stalker appears before you against a beautiful backdrop. Stop at the View Café and Gift Shop for stunning vistas across Loch Linnhe to the Morvern Hills. Such a panorama has inspired many artists and here you can really appreciate their motivation.

16   From Rannoch Moor on the A82, the twin peaks of Buachaille Etive Mor and Buachaille Etive Beag spectacularly mark the entrance to Glen Coe. Appearing like steep-sided pyramids they stand sentinel on the moor, offering a glimpse of the wild landscape just around the corner.

17   There are many classic views of the Cuillin Ridge. However, for sheer drama, few views in all of Scotland compare with the sight of Sgurr Nan Gillean rearing up behind Sligachan bridge, or the full mountain range rising almost sheer from Loch Scavaig, opposite the tiny village of Elgol, west of Broadford on Skye.

18   To see the Five Sisters of Kintail from Ratagan Pass, take the Glenelg road from Shiel Bridge on the A87. As you rise up towards Mam Ratagan, about a mile along, take a look back over Loch Duich, framed by the majestic peaks of Kintail. Simply stunning.

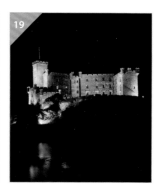

HERITAGE

19   Dunvegan Castle (follow the A850 from Portree), the stronghold of the MacLeod chiefs for nearly 800 years, remains their home today. Highland Cattle roam around the estate, making you feel that you've well and truly reached the Scottish Highlands!

20   Skye's only distillery, Talisker Distillery, is set on the shores of Loch Harport with dramatic views of the Cuillin hills. Enjoy a tipple of this alluring, sweet, full-bodied single malt on the distillery tour.

21   For a full interpretation of this amazing setting, head to the Glencoe Visitor Centre on the A82, 17 miles south of Fort William. Particularly eco-friendly, this centre provides a great viewing platform, as well as an interactive exhibit for kids of all ages where you can find out how it feels to climb on ice!

22   The West Highland Museum is to be found in Fort William and houses an historic collection that dates from Mesolithic times to the modern day. All elements of society are included, from crofters to soldiers and princes to clergy.

Acharacle, Argyll
Mrs Gregson
Map Ref: 3F12

22039

AWAITING GRADING

Open: All year

Rainwalker House,
Wearhead, Bishop Auckland, DL13 1PR
T: 01388 537728
E: maplegarden.services@fsmail.net
W: dalileabungalow.co.uk

Beautiful bungalow and 2x 30ft caravans set in stunning 2½ acre grounds with fine views to Ben Resipole and Loch Shiel. Bungalow and caravans very well equipped - freesat/dvd etc. Close to beautiful beaches and abundant wildlife. Shops and amenities 4 miles.

| 1 Bungalow | 1-2 Public Rooms | Sleeps 6-7 |
| 2 Caravans | | Sleeps 4-5 |

Prices from:		
Bungalow:	£180.00	per week
Caravan:	£135.00	per week

Arisaig, Inverness-shire
Camusdarach Enterprises
Map Ref: 3F11

17863

★★★
SELF
CATERING

Open: All year

Camusdarach, Arisaig, Inverness-shire, PH39 4NT
T: 01687 450221
E: camdarach@aol.com
W: camusdarach.com

| 1 Cottage | 2 Public Rooms | Sleeps 1-8 |
| 2 Apartments | 1-2 Public Rooms | Sleeps 1-6 |

Prices from:		
Cottage:	£375.00	Per week
Apartment:	£325.00	Per week

Arisaig, Inverness-shire
Mr M Kingswood
Map Ref: 3F11

10998

★★★ UP TO
★★★★
SELF
CATERING

Open: All year

Ach na skia Croft, Arisaig, Inverness-shire, PH39 4NS
T: 01687 450606
E: enquiries@achnaskiacroft.co.uk
W: achnaskiacroft.co.uk

Ach na skia Croft lodges and cottage have dramatic views across the sea to the islands of Skye, Eigg and Rum. Sauna, pool-table, table-tennis, volleyball, play area. Close to beaches and golf course. Mallaig 11km for ferries to Skye and Islands.

| 1 Cottage | 2 Public Rooms | Sleeps 2-4+ baby |
| 3 Chalets | 2 Public Rooms | Sleeps 2-5+ baby |

Prices from:		
Cottage:	£300.00-560.00	per week
Chalet:	£325.00-620.00	per week

IMPORTANT: Prices stated are estimates and may be subject to change. Awards correct as of beginning of October 2008.

Ballachulish, Glencoe
Cherry Cottage
Map Ref: 1F1

SELF CATERING

Open: All year

Swallowcroft, Achindarroch Road, Duror, PA38 4BS
T: 0808 178 7564
E: reservations@highland-vacation.co.uk
W: highland-vacation.co.uk

Cherry Cottage, located near Glencoe, benefits from magnficent views over Loch Leven and the surrounding mountain range. It is spread over two floors, featuring disabled facilities, sleeping six adults comfortably. Lovingly furnished and equipped to a luxurious standard.

71378

1 Cottage	2 Public Rooms	Sleeps 1-6
Prices from:		
£225.00-650.00		**Per week**

Ballachulish, nr Glencoe
Dorcha Cottage
Map Ref: 1F1

★★
SELF CATERING

Open: All year

Ms M Muir, Flat 1, Scott's Land,
Main Street, Inverkip, Renfrewshire, PA16 0AU
T: 07751105345
E: scottisholidays@yahoo.co.uk
W: scottisholidays.co.uk

74744

1 Bungalow	1 Public Room	Sleeps 2-6
Prices from:		
£250.00-500.00		**Per week**
£60.00-80.00		**Per night**

Balmacara, Ross-shire
Reraig Caravan Site
Map Ref: 3F9

★★★
TOURING PARK

Open: May-September

Balmacara, Kyle, Ross-shire, IV40 8DH
T: 01599 566215
E: warden@reraig.com   W: reraig.com

On A87 two miles west of junction with A890, by Balmacara Hotel.

51469

Park accommodates 45 pitches
Total Touring Pitches: 40
Prices from:
⛟(40) £12.50   ⛺ (5) £12.00   🚐(40) £12.50

Fort William, Inverness-shire
Blyth, 34 Lochaber Road
Map Ref: 3H12

★★
SELF CATERING

Open: All year

West Highland Hotel, Mallaig,
Inverness-shire, PH41 4QZ
T: 01687 462210/ 01687 460015
E: ann@westhighlandhotel.wanadoo.co.uk
westhighland.hotel@virgin.net

42489

1 House	2 Public Rooms	Sleeps 1-6
Prices from:		
£235.00-345.00		**Per week**
Short breaks available on request		

Fort William, Inverness-shire
Mrs E. K. Clark
Map Ref: 3H12

★★★
SELF CATERING

Open: All year

14 Perth Place, Fort William, Inverness-shire PH33 6UL
T: 01397 702444
E: neil.m.clark@hotmail.co.uk
W: taighnanchleirich.website.orange.co.uk

43091

1 Apartment	1 Public Room	Sleeps 2-4
Prices from:		
£135.00-195.00		**Per week**
£30.00		**Per night**

For a full listing of quality assured non-serviced establishments please see pages 229-385.

195

Fort William, Inverness-shire
Mrs Gillies
Map Ref: 3H12

★★★
SELF
CATERING

Open: All year
Ealasaid, Victoria Road, Fort William,
Inverness-shire, PH33 6BH
T: 01397 704005
E: family.gillies@btinternet.com

24036

Studio apartment 1 Public Room	Sleeps 2
Prices from:	
£190.00-240.00	**Per week**

Fort William, Inverness-shire
Glen Nevis Holidays
Map Ref: 3H12

★★★★★
HOLIDAY
PARK

★★★ UP TO
★★★★
SELF
CATERING

27935

Open: March-October (all accommodation)
December-January (lodges/cottages)
Glen Nevis, Fort William PH33 6SX
T: 01397 702191
F: 01397 703904
W: glen-nevis.co.uk

Spectacular location for self catering, set amidst
beautiful Highland scenery at the foot of Ben Nevis

★ Inclusive of electricity
★ Restaurant and lounge bar
★ All units non-smoking
★ All linen provided
★ Shop on site
★ Pet free

3 Lodges	13 Cottages	22 Caravans
Properties sleep2-6		
Prices from:		
£370.00-935.00 per week		**Lodges/Cottages**
£315.00-540.00 per week		**Caravans**

Fort William, Inverness-shire
The Logs
Map Ref: 3H12

★★★★
SELF
CATERING

59558

Open: All year
24 Zetland Avenue,
Fort William, Inverness-shire PH33 6LL
T: 01397 702532 E: thelogs@scotland-info.co.uk
W: scotland-info.co.uk/thelogs

1 House	3 Public Rooms	Sleeps 2-10
Prices from:		
£550.00-1350.00		**Per week**
£450.00		**Per 4 nights**

Fort William, Inverness-shire
Mount Alexander
Map Ref: 3H12

★★★
SELF
CATERING

39172

Open: May-September
Banavie, Fort William, Inverness-shire PH33 7NF
T: 01397 704466
E: christine@donnachie5987.freeserve.co.uk
W: benneviscottage.co.uk

Three bedroom bungalow three miles from Fort
William. Quiet rural setting. Living and dining room
and kitchen to front. Wonderful views of Ben Nevis
and surrounding hills. Oil heating and coal fire. Large
patio and garden. Fully equipped. Very comfortable.

1 Bungalow	2 Public Rooms	Sleeps 6
Prices from:		
£320.00-520.00		**Per week**

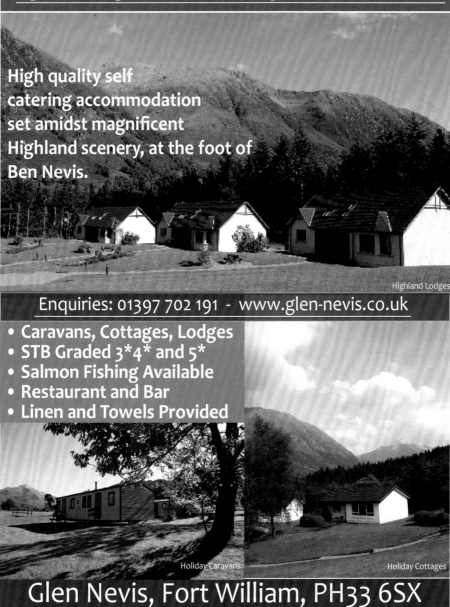
For a full listing of quality assured non-serviced establishments please see pages 229-385.

197

Linnhe
LOCHSIDE HOLIDAYS

Almost a botanical garden, Linnhe is recognised as one of the best and most beautful Lochside parks in Britain. Magnificent gardens contrast with the wild, dramatic scenery of Loch Eil and the mountains beyond. Superb amenities, launderette, shop & bakery, and free fishing on private shoreline with its own jetty all help give Linnhe its Five Star grading.

Linnhe Lochside Holidays is ideally situated for day trips with Oban, Skye, Mull, Inverness and the Cairngorms all within easy driving distance.

We have an extensive five star touring and camping area that boasts a modern water/waste station for Motorhomes and top notch toilet and shower facilities complete with baths.
Please see our website for current prices.

Linnhe
LOCHSIDE HOLIDAYS

www.linnhe-lochside-holidays.co.uk/brochure
Tel: 01397 772 376 to check availability

Glencoe, Argyll
Carefree Holidays Glencoe
Map Ref: 1F1

Open: All year

Carefree Holidays Glencoe,
Clachaig Inn, Glencoe, Argyll PH49 4HX
T: 01855 811252
E: info@glencoeholidays.com
W: glencoeholidays.com

Situated in and around Glencoe, the most scenic glen in the Highlands, all our self catering properties provide the very best of holiday accommodation. They are conveniently placed for pubs, shops, local amenities and easy access to the surrounding countryside.

11 Cottages	1-2 Public Rooms	Sleeps1- 6

Prices from:		
£280.00		Per week
£220.00		Per 3 nights

Glencoe, Argyll
Glencoe Mountain Cottages
Map Ref: 1F1

Open: All year

Glean Leac Na Muidhe, Glencoe, Argyll, PH49 4LA
T: 01855 811598
E: root@glencoemountaincottages.co.uk
W: glencoemountaincottages.co.uk

2 Cottages	1 Public Room	Sleeps 6

Prices from:		
£365.00-638.00		Per week
£100.00-150.00		Per night

Glencoe, Argyll
Invercoe Caravan and Camping Park
Map Ref: 1F1

Open: All year

Invercoe, Glencoe PH49 4HP
T: 01855 811210
E: holidays@invercoe.co.uk
W: invercoe.co.uk

Situated on the shores of the loch our park enjoys magnificent views of loch, mountains and forest. Bring your own tourer tent or hire one of our mobile homes. New slipway access to loch. Open all year. Wi-Fi on park.

At Gleaner Petrol Station turn right on to Kinlochleven Road (B863) for 500 yards. Park on lochside.

Park accommodates 64 pitches		
Total Touring Pitches: 60		
Prices from:		
£19.00	£19.00	£19.00
(4) £375.00		

For a full listing of quality assured non-serviced establishments please see pages 229-385.

199

Glencoe, Argyll
Invercoe Highland Holidays
Map Ref: 1F1

★★★★
SELF
CATERING

Open: All year

Invercoe, Glencoe PH49 4HP
T: 01855 811210
E: holidays@invercoe.co.uk
W: invercoe.co.uk

Set amongst spectacular scenery our lodges
and cottages offer a very high standard of
accommodation. With every modern convenience.
An excellent base to explore the west Highlands.
Plenty to see and do including access to local hotel's
leisure facilities. Wi-Fi also available.

31965

| 3 Cottages | 1 Public Room | Sleeps 1-4 |
| 3 Lodges | 1 Public Room | Sleeps 1-6 |

Prices from:		
Cottage:	£400.00-700.00	**Per week**
Lodge:	£470.00-800.00	**Per week**

Inverinate, by Kyle of Lochalsh
John Fisher's Cottage
Map Ref: 3G10

★★★
SELF
CATERING

Open: All year

28 High Street, Dawlish, EX7 9HP
T: 01626 889098
E: cottage@kintail.info
W: kintail.info

Traditional stone built croft cottage, tastefully
modernised to keep original features; fully equipped
kitchen; free heating, telephone, internet and local
guidebook. On shore of Loch Duich beneath Five
Sisters of Kintail. Ideal for walking, climbing, touring,
water activities and relaxing.

33011

| 1 Cottage | 2 Public Rooms | Sleeps 6 |

| Prices from: | |
| £160.00 | **Per week** |

Knoydart, Inverness-shire
Creag Eiridh
Map Ref:3F11

★★★
SELF
CATERING

Open: All year

Mrs V. Hayward, Blynfield, Stour Row,
Shaftesbury, Dorset SP7 0QW
T: 01747 852289
E: creageiridh@virginiahayward.com
W: creageiridh.co.uk

Situated loch side, this lovely house has spacious
accommodation, equipped and furnished to a
high standard, offering a very comfortable holiday
home for large families or small groups wanting an
unforgettable holiday amid the hills and rivers of this
fantastic area.

15522

| 1 House | 2 Public Rooms | Sleeps 10 |

Prices from:	
£1000.00-1500.00	**Per week**
£230.00	**Per night**

IMPORTANT: Prices stated are estimates and may be subject to change. Awards correct as of beginning of October 2008.

Knoydart, Inverness-shire
Kilchoan Estate
Map Ref: 3F11

★★ UP TO ★★★★ SELF CATERING

76515

VISIT KILCHOAN KNOYDART

Open: All year

Kilchoan Estate Ltd, Inverie,
Knoydart, Mallaig, Inverness-shire PH41 4PL
T: 01687 462724/462133
E: kilchoanestate@btinternet.com
W: kilchoan-knoydart.com

Located on the beautiful Knoydart Peninsula, a haven for walkers, Munro baggers, Kayakers, cyclists and wildlife enthusiasts. Both properties are equipped and furnished to a very high standard. Kilchoan Estate is an ideal base for a relaxing holiday.

| 1 Cottage | 1 Public Room | Sleeps 6-8 |
| 1 Farmhouse | 2 Public Rooms | Sleeps 6-8 |

Prices from:		
Cottage:	£720.00	Per week
	£180.00	Per night
Farmhouse:	£1200.00	Per week
	£240.00	Per night

Knoydart, Inverness-shire
The Old Byre
Map Ref: 3F11

 ★★★★ GROUP ACCOMMODATION

83004

Open: April-New Year

Inverie Village, Knoydart PH41 4PL
T: 01687 460099 (office)/460146
E: info@theoldbyreknoydart.com
W: theoldbyreknoydart.com

| 1 Cottage | 1 Public Room | Sleeps 16 |

| Prices: | |
| £25.00 | Per person per night (min 2 nights) |

Kyle of Lochalsh, Ross-shire
Mr & Mrs Wright
Map Ref: 3F9

★★★ SELF CATERING

20836

Open: April-October

16 Duntrune Terrace, West Ferry, Dundee, DD5 1LF
T: 01382 477462
E: mrw@tabitha.fsnet.co.uk

| 1 Bungalow | 1 Public Room | Sleeps 6 |

| Prices from: | |
| £360.00-435.00 | Per week |

Lochaber, Inverness-shire
Graham Nairn
Map Ref: 3H12

★★★ SELF CATERING

78777

Open: All year

Fersit Log Cottage, Fersit,
Roy Bridge, Inverness-shire PH31 4AR
T: 01397 732323   M: 07900514036
E: booking@fersitlogcottage.co.uk
W: fersitlogcottage.free-online.co.uk

| 1 Cottage | 1 Public Room | Sleeps 4 |

| Prices from: | |
| £305.00-600.00 | Per week |

For a full listing of quality assured non-serviced establishments please see pages 229-385.

201

Lochaber, Fort William
Inverskilavulin Lodges
Map Ref:3H12

★★★★
SELF CATERING

79588

Open: All year

Glenloy, Banavie, Fort William, PH33 7PD
T: 01855 811475
E: glenloyholidays@hotmail.com
W: glenloy.com

Spectacular views over Aoanach Mor in a magical setting. Luxury accommodation with open fire, modern facilities, private grounds next to Caledonian Canal, only fifteen minutes from Fort William, forest walks and cycle path. Ideal base for touring the area.

2 Houses	1 Public Room	Sleeps 6

Prices from:

£450.00-780.00		**Per week**

Lochaber, Glencoe
Glencoe Hideaway/Lochview
Map Ref: 1F1

★★★
SELF CATERING

28045

Open: All year

23 Southcote Rise, Ruislip, Middlesex, HA4 7LN
T: 01895 675662
E: stay@glencoe-hideaway.co.uk
W: glencoe-hideaway.co.uk

1 Cottage	2 Public Rooms	Sleeps 2-6

Prices from:

£300.00-550.00		**Per week**

Lochailort Moidart, Inverness-shire
Roshven Holidays
Map Ref: 3F12

★★★
SELF CATERING

52176

Open: All year

Roshven Farm, Lochailort, Inverness-shire PH38 4NB
T: 01687 470221
E: chalets@roshven.com
W: roshven.com

5 Chalets	1 Public Room	Sleeps 2-4

Prices from:

£250.00-520.00		**Per week**
£60.00		**Per night**

Onich, Fort William
Bunree Holiday Cottages
Map Ref: 3G12

★★★
SELF CATERING

32769

Open: All year

Janika, Bunree, Onich,
Fort William, Inverness-shire, PH33 6SE
T: 01855 821359
E: janika@btinternet.com
W: holiday-homes.org

2 Cottages	1 Public Room	Sleeps 4
2 Apartments	1 Public Room	Sleeps 4

Prices from:

Cottage:	£275.00-465.00	**Per week**
Apartment:	£275.00-465.00	**Per week**

Plockton, Inverness-shire
Mrs Lesley Burrell
Map Ref: 3F9

★★ UP TO ★★★★
SELF CATERING

50008

Open: All year

43a Castle Street, Dumfries,
Dumfries & Galloway, DG1 1DU
T: 01387 269762
E: lesley.burrell@btinternet.com
W: plockton.com also plocktonholidays.com

1 Cottage	2 Public Rooms	Sleeps 6
1 House	2 Public Rooms	Sleeps 8

Prices from:

Cottage:	£500.00-1200.00	**Per week**
House:	£380.00-600.00	**Per week**

IMPORTANT: Prices stated are estimates and may be subject to change. Awards correct as of beginning of October 2008.

Plockton, Ross-shire
Duirinish Lodge and Gardens — Map Ref: 3F9

Open: All year
3A Northumberland Street, Edinburgh EH3 6LL
T: 07771 930880
E: william@duirinish.com
W: aboutscotland.com

23421

1 House	2 Public Rooms	Sleeps 4
Prices from:		
£450.00-650.00		**Per week**

Roy Bridge, Inverness-shire
Bunroy Camping and Caravanning Site — Map Ref: 3H12

Open: March-October
Roy Bridge, Inverness-shire PH31 4AG
T: 01397 712332   E: info@bunroycamping.co.uk
W: bunroycamping.co.uk

From A86 through Roy Bridge, turn opposite Stronlissit Inn. Go over railway bridge and follow lane to the end.

16854

Park accommodates 25 pitches
Total Touring Pitches: 25
Prices from:
(25) £14.00-16.00   (25) £10.00-12.00
(25) £14.00-16.00

Armadale, Isle of Skye
Armadale Castle Cottages — Map Ref: 3E11

Open: All year
Armadale Castle Gardens & Museum of the Isles,
Sleat, Isle of Skye, IV45 8RS
T: 01471 844305
E: office@clandonald.com
W: clandonald.com

Six purpose built cottages situated on the hillside above Armadale, opposite Knoydart with views over the Sound of Sleat. We have also the Forresters cottage that nestles in a clearing and the Flora McDonald Suite situated within the Stables Building.

19449

6 Cottages	1 Public Room	Sleeps 4-6
1 House	1 Public Room	Sleeps 4
1 Apartment	1 Public Room	Sleeps 4
Prices from:		
Cottage:	£310.00-585.00	Per week
	£132.00	Per 2 nights
House:	£310.00-550.00	Per week
	£124.00	Per 2 nights
Apartment:	£410.00-670.00	Per week
	£164.00	Per 2 nights

Carbost, Isle of Skye
Loch View — Map Ref: 3D9

Open: May- September
Mrs Janet Brown, 11 Laggan Road, Inverness IV2 4EH
T: 01463 235793
E: j.brown793@btinternet.com

35966

1 Bungalow	1 Public Room	Sleeps 4-6
Prices from:		
£220.00-350.00		**Per week**
£60.00		**Per night**

Dunvegan, Isle of Skye
Dunvegan Castle Cottages — Map Ref: 3D9

Open: All year
MacLeod Estates, Dunvegan House,
Dunvegan, Isle of Skye IV55 8WF
T: 01470 521206   E: info@dunvegancastle.com
W: dunvegancastle.com

23873

3 Cottages	1-2 Public Rooms	Sleeps 6
Prices from:		
£325.00-640.00		**Per week**
POA		**Min 3 nights**

For a full listing of quality assured non-serviced establishments please see pages 229-385.

203

Portree, Isle of Skye
Portree Garden Cottages

Map Ref: 3E9

50226

★★★
SELF CATERING

Open: All year

1 Portree Garden Cottage,
Home Farm Road, Portree, Isle of Skye, IV51 9LX

T: 01478 613713
E: gardencottages@selfcateringskye.co.uk
W: selfcateringskye.co.uk

This family accommodation equipped to a high standard is available for any length of stay. Set in extensive grounds just five minutes walk from the main centre, restaurants and bars. The cottages are ideally located for exploring this beautiful island.

4 Cottages	1 Public Room	Sleeps 2-4

Prices from:	
£350.00-500.00	**Per week**
£80.00-100.00	**Per night**

TV 🖥️📺💻🚗🛁🔥M ☺ ◎ ➡️ 🐾 🛋️📺 ✂️ ♨️ ❄️ 🐕 ① 🅿️ 🅿️ 🚭 SP

Portree, Isle of Skye
Mrs Rohwer

Map Ref: 3E9

28215

★★★★
SELF CATERING

Open: All year

Cedar Mount, 5 Waterend,
Brompton, Northallerton DL6 2RN

T: 01478 612048
E: rohwersafaris@hotmail.com
W: selfcatering-isleofskye-scotland.com

Magnificent seafront location with wonderful views over harbour and to the Isle of Raasay. Three storey Georgian house, very well equipped and comfortable. Lots of personal touches. Private parking. Two minutes walk to Portree centre. Pets welcome.

1 House	3 Public Rooms	Sleeps 2-6

Prices from:	
£350.00-600.00	**Per week**
POA	**Per night**

TV 🖥️📺💻🚗🛁🔥 🎵 📺 📻 ☺ ➡️ 🐾 🛋️📺 ✂️ ♨️ 🐾 ❄️ 🐕 ① 🛁 ✂️
🅿️ SP 🚭

By Portree, Isle of Skye
Mrs C Lamont

Map Ref: 3E9

20497

★★★★
SELF CATERING

1 Cottage	1 Public Room	Sleeps 4

Prices from:	
£300.00-325.00	**Per week**

Open: All year

Corran Guest House, Eyre,
Portree, Isle of Skye, IV51 9XE

T: 01470 532311

TV 🖥️📺💻🚗🛁🔥 🎵 📺 M ☺ ◎ 🐾 🛋️ ❄️ 🅿️

IMPORTANT: Prices stated are estimates and may be subject to change. Awards correct as of beginning of October 2008.

nr Portree, Isle of Skye
Teeny's Cottage
Map Ref: 3E9

Open: All year

Fasgadh, near Edinbane, Portree,
Isle of Skye, IV51 9PX

T: 01470 582777
E: denis@teenyscottage.com
W: teenyscottage.com

Set in a quiet and rural location with beautiful views
out to sea and the hills around. Ideally suited for
exploring Skye and its many attractions. Equipped to
a high standard and ideal for a couple or family.

1 Cottage	1 Public Room	Sleeps 1-4
Prices from:		
£175.00-450.00		**Per week**

---

kinidin, Isle of Skye
Mr A MacFarlane
Map Ref: 3D9

Open: All year

11 Elm Road, Hale, Altrincham, Cheshire, WA15 9QW
T: 0161 941 3440
E: aa_sa@mcfarlane7789.freeserve.co.uk

1 Bungalow	2 Public Rooms	Sleeps 5
Prices from:		
£280.00-560.00		**Per week**

Ullinish, nr Struan, Isle of Skye
Tarnershiel
Map Ref: 3D9

Open: All year

Ullinish SC Ltd, PO Box 2000,
Oxford Road, Aylesbury, Bucks HP21 8SZ
T: 07767337696
E: mail@ullinish.info
W: ullinish.info

Tarnershiel commands outstanding views in the
Western Isles - The Cuillin Mountains, Portnalong
Lighthouse, the great cliffs of Loch Bracadale and
McLeods Table are clearly visible from the house.
Magnificent sunsets plus local walking: Ullinish is
ideal for exploring Skye.

1 House	3 Public Rooms	Sleeps 8
Prices from:		
£500.00-725.00		**Per week**

Waternish, Isle of Skye
Ardmore Holiday Cottage
Map Ref: 3D8

Open: All year

3 Ardmore, Waternish, Isle of Skye, IV55 8GW
T: 01470 592305
E: info@ardmorecottage.co.uk
W: ardmorecottage.co.uk

1 Bungalow	1 Public Room	Sleeps 4
Prices from:		
£180.00		**Per week**
£50.00		**Per night**

For a full listing of quality assured non-serviced establishments please see pages 229-385.

205

Waternish, Isle of Skye
La Bergerie
Map Ref: 3D8

42700

★★★★
SELF CATERING

Open: All year
Mrs C MacLeod, 33 Lochbay,
Waternish, Isle of Skye, IV55 8GD
T: 01470 592282
E: enquiries@la-bergerie-skye.co.uk
W: la-bergerie.skye.co.uk

1 Cottage	1 Public Room	Sleeps 8
Prices from:		
£500.00-960.00		**Per week**
Special price for occupancy of 2 people.		

Spean Bridge, Inverness-shire
Corrieview Lodges
Map Ref: 3H12

29091

★★★★
SELF CATERING

Open: All year
Grey Corries, Spean Bridge, Inverness-shire PH34 4DX
T: 01397 712395
E: fantasticviews@corrieviewlodges.com
W: corrieviewlodges.com

Fully equipped lodges with two downstairs
bedrooms and upstairs living area. Patio doors
lead from the lounge to a small wooden balcony
with panoramic views across the glen to the Nevis
Mountain Range. Village shops and pubs within a few
minutes walk.

2 Lodges	1 Public Rooms	Sleeps 2-5
Prices from:		
£295.00-550.00		**Per week**
£27.50		**Per night**

Spean Bridge, Inverness-shire
Gairlochy Holiday Park
Map Ref: 3H12

69782

★★★★
SELF CATERING

Open: December-October
Gairlochy Holiday Park,
Spean Bridge, Inverness-shire PH34 4EQ
T: 01397 712711
E: theghp@talk21.com
W: theghp.co.uk

Caravans and lodges for hire situated south end Loch
Lochy on B8004, Great Glen Way and Nevis Range
close by. Free fishing on Loch Lochy, boat launching
available. Linen provided, discount for two persons,
laundrette, play area. All charges inclusive.

3 Lodges	2 Public Rooms	Sleeps 4
4 Caravans	1 Public Room	Sleeps 4
Prices from:		
Lodge:	£200.00-585.00	**Per week**
	£60.00-85.00	**Per night**
Caravan:	£225.00-435.00	**Per week**
	£50.00-70.00	**Per night**

Spean Bridge, Inverness-shire
Highland Lodges
Map Ref: 3H12

30273

★★★
SELF CATERING

Open: All year
Kilfinnan, near Invergarry, Spean Bridge
Inverness-shire PH34 4EB
T: 01809 501225
E: enquiries@highlandlodges.org.uk
W: highlandlodges.org.uk

2 Cabins	1 Public Room	Sleeps 5
Prices from:		
£190.00-510.00		**Per week**
£45.00-80.00		**Per night**

IMPORTANT: Prices stated are estimates and may be subject to change. Awards correct as of beginning of October 2008.

By Spean Bridge, Inverness-shire
Mrs Marilyn Dennis
Map Ref: 3H12

★★★★
SELF CATERING

Open: All year

Riverside Lodges, Invergloy, by Spean Bridge PH34 4DY
T: 01397 712684
E: enquiries@riversidelodge.org.uk
W: riversidelodge.org.uk

The ultimate Highland location. Three unique chalets set in 12 acres mature woodland gardens, waterfalls with private beach on Loch Lochy. Free fishing, BBQ, bird watcher and gardeners paradise! Centrally located for touring and outdoor activities. Pets welcome. Member Outdoor Capital (UK).

70348

3 Chalets	1 Public Room	Sleeps up to 6
Prices from:		
£420.00-750.00		**Per week**
£85.00-110.00		**Per night**

The harbour's edge at Portree, Skye, Inner Hebrides

For a full listing of quality assured non-serviced establishments please see pages 229-385.

207

Loch Morlich at Glenmore

Moray, Aviemore and the Cairngorms

From the active lifestyle of Aviemore and the majestic beauty of the Caringorms; to the lure of Malt Whisky Country and the golden beaches of the Moray coast this is an area as contrasting as it is captivating.

There's inspiring landscape and diverse wildlife to spot so join ranger guided walks in the Cairngorms National Park or on the Moray Coast or spend an evening looking for pine marten and deer in a nature hide.

For watersports, including canoeing, sailing and windsurfing, head for Loch Insh or Loch Morlich. Hillwalkers will find the Cairngorm range is always a challenge while the more leisurely can wander to their heart's content in Rothiemurchus Estate, Culbin Forest, Craigellachie National Nature Reserve,

Glenlivet Estate and many other hidden gems.

For exciting mountain bike action try cycling at Moray Monster Trails or Laggan Wolftrax and ski in the winter at CairnGorm Mountain and The Lecht. There are also lots of opportunities for golfing and fishing. You can even take a steam train trip from Aviemore to Boat of Garten and Broomhill or you can ascend Cairn Gorm on the funicular railway.

Laggan Wolftrax mountain bike trails, near Laggan, Strathspey

To find out more, call 0845 22 55 121 or go to visitscotland.com

DON'T MISS

1   The **Cairngorms National Park** offers many events and activities throughout the year which are suitable for all ages and abilities. Visitor centres and ranger bases have leaflets, guides and trail maps to help you make the most of your time in the Park, and Visitor Information Centres throughout the area will be able to provide you with local information on events, attractions and activities.

2   At the heart of the beautiful Cairngorms National Park is the **CairnGorm Mountain Railway**. It takes 8 minutes from bottom to top, where an interactive exhibition tells the history and ecology of the surrounding area and you can see some stunning panoramic views of the National Park. Have a bite to eat and take in the view stretching from the Cairngorm plateau to the Monadliath Mountains and beyond.

3   **The Malt Whisky Trail** invites you to enjoy the wide-ranging flavour of eight malts as you wind your way through Speyside. Also on the trail is the family owned Speyside Cooperage where you can watch oak whisky barrels being constructed using traditional methods (see number 20).

4   Step back in time to the **Highland Folk Museum** with sites in Kingussie and Newtonmore, where you can experience over 400 years of Highland life. Re-constructions of an 18th century Highland township and 20th century working croft can be seen at Newtonmore. Both locations have programmes of live demonstrations and activities where you can see traditional skills and crafts in action.

5   **Johnstons** is the only Scottish mill to transform cashmere from fibre to garment and its story is told in their visitor centre and interactive exhibition in Elgin. They also have an engaging tour, tempting food hall and courtyard shop.

6   When **ospreys** returned to breed in Scotland the ancient Caledonian pinewood of Loch Garten was their first choice. Watch these magnificent birds bring fish to their chicks from the RSPB hide or on non-invasive CCTV. The reserve also has some excellent walks where you can spot red squirrels, crested tits and dragonflies. The ospreys are in residence from April till August but birds like capercaillie, redstart and goldeneye fill the calendar.

FOOD AND DRINK

eatscotland.com

7   At **The Old Bridge Inn**, on the outskirts of Aviemore, the staff are friendly and the service is excellent. A selection of meat, game and fish awaits and all dishes are cooked simply and with flair. The dining room adjacent to the bar area allows more formal and romantic dining with its open fire, and the puddings are all home-made and vary from day to day.

8   At the Speyside Heather Centre, near Dulnain Bridge, **The Clootie Dumpling** is the perfect opportunity to sample its namesake, a Scottish delicacy. This traditional and versatile pudding can be enjoyed in a variety of different ways from sweet to savoury. The recipe has a mixture of spices, carrots, apple, raisins and more, all mixed together in a 'cloot' (muslin cloth), steamed for hours and served with accompaniments.

9   Dine at **Craggan Mill** in the picturesque water mill near Grantown-on-Spey. Fine dining in a relaxed environment offers you the choice of bistro lunch or à la carte evening meal – all prepared from local, seasonal produce. Local artists exhibit paintings for view and sale within the restaurant and gallery.

10 **Minmore House Hotel** is an EatScotland Silver awarded restaurant set amid the spectacular scenery of the Glenlivet estate in Speyside. Their restaurant specialises in fine Scottish produce using only fresh, local ingredients, including some from their own kitchen garden.

ACTIVITIES

11 Up to 30km of fun-packed mountain biking awaits at the **Moray Monster Trails**. They work as three independent sites all linked to each other. So for those with a truly monster appetite and stamina to match, try all three sites end to end, from Fochabers to Craigellachie. For the more leisurely, the green-graded trail is at Quarrelwood, by Elgin.

12 **Inch Marshes Bird Reserve** is a birdwatching paradise! Around half of all British goldeneyes nest at Inch Marshes in spring. You're also likely to see lapwings, redshanks and curlews, as well as oystercatchers, snipe and wigeon. In winter, the marshes host flocks of whooper swans and greylag geese. Roe deer, wildcats, otters and foxes may all be seen along the edges of the marshes.

13 Enjoy year-round outdoor fun and action at the **Lecht Multi-Activity Centre**. With summer action on quad bikes, fun karts, dévalkarts and chairlift rides, winter is covered by skiing, snowboarding and tubing.

14 Take a step back in time and travel by steam engine. The **Strathspey Railway** runs from Aviemore to Broomhill (also known as Glenbogle from the TV series Monarch of the Glen) and affords beautiful views of the Cairngorms from the carriage window. To make the trip really special, you can even have afternoon tea on board.

WALKS

visitscotland.com/walking

15 **Glenmore Forest Park** has a range of walks from all-ability trails suitable for pushchairs, to longer walks through beautiful woodland which open out to give fantastic views of the Cairngorm Mountains. The Visitor Centre provides an audio-visual presentation plus café, toilets and shop.

16 Walking from **Hopeman to Lossiemouth** as part of the **Moray Coastal Trail** follows a route along the top of cliffs, giving privileged views into sandy coves and rocky headlands. There are lots of opportunities to venture onto beaches where you can relax and take in extensive views across the Moray Firth to the Black Isle and Helmsdale about 50 miles away.

17 There are a variety of waymarked trails throughout the **Rothiemurchus Estate**, with maps available from the visitor centre. The estate is teeming with Highland wildlife, including the red squirrel and the rare capercaillie, with guided tours available courtesy of Scottish Natural Heritage. Free tours on Tuesdays.

18 **Culbin Forest** meets the Moray coast between Nairn and Forres and offers cycling and walking on gentle paths with junction markers so you can make it up as you go along. Bird-watching and even the opportunity to spot otters is on offer as is a magnificent view from the 20m viewing tower at Hill 99 – a 99ft sand dune.

ATTRACTIONS

19 The **Cairngorm Reindeer Centre** is home to the only reindeer herd in the country and you can encounter the animals grazing in their natural environment. During the guided visits you can wander freely among the reindeer, stroking and feeding them. These friendly deer are a delight to all ages and, if you feel especially fond of one, you might be able to adopt it!

20 In the heart of Malt Whisky Country lies the **Speyside Cooperage**; the only working cooperage in the UK where you can experience the ancient art of producing whisky barrels.Based in Craigellachie the family owned company produces the finest casks and you can see the workers using traditional methods and tools.

Aberlour, Banffshire
Speyside Camping & Caravanning Club Site   Map Ref: 4D8

★★★★
TOURING
PARK

Open: 13 March-3 November

Archiestown, Aberlour, Moray AB38 9SL

T: 0845 130 7633
E: vb@thefriendlyclub.co.uk
W: campingandcaravanningclub.co.uk/speyside

Well known distilleries of Speyside using the area's famous springs are only a stone's throw from the site. Set on a gentle south-facing slope, it is lightly wooded giving shade but preserving its open feel.

17836

Park accommodates: 75
Total Touring Pitches: 75
Prices from:
£17.90-£23.30 per couple per night per pitch.

From Inverness take the A96 to Elgin then turn right onto the A941 heading to Rothes. The site is on the B9012.

Archiestown, Moray
Mrs M Mansfield   Map Ref: 4D8

★★
SELF
CATERING

Open: All year

3a Resaurie, Smithton, Inverness, IV2 7NH
T: 01463 791714
E: mbmansfield@uk2.net
W: mansfieldhighlandholidays.com

32377

1 Cottage	1 Public Room	Sleeps 1-4
Prices from:		
£100.00		**Per week**

Aviemore, Inverness-shire
Birchwood/The Scott's House   Map Ref: 4C10

★★★
SELF
CATERING

Open: All year

Ashfield, 31 Nash Road,
Great Horwood,Bucks, MK17 0RA
T: 01296 713849
E: scottatdownhill@aol.com
W: downhill-from-here.com

Set in great locations close to Aviemore, Golf and Country Club, shops and restaurants. Birchwood, sleeping up to seven and the The Scott's House, a bungalow sleeping up to eight, are well equipped, stylish and provide flexible family accommodation. Ideal for family holidays.

60353

1 Bungalow	1 Public Room	Sleeps up to 8
1 House	1 Public Room	Sleeps up to 7
Prices from:		
£300.00		**Per week**

Aviemore, Inverness-shire
A & J Burns-Smith   Map Ref:4C10

★★★ UP TO
★★★★
SELF
CATERING

Open: All year

Pine Bank Chalets, Dalfaber Road,
Aviemore, Inverness-shire PH22 1PX
T: 01479 810000
E: pinebankchalets@btopenworld.com
W: pinebankchalets.co.uk

49818

5 Log Cabins	1-2 Public Rooms	Sleeps 2-6
2 Apartments	2 Public Rooms	Sleeps 2-6
6 Chalets	2 Public Rooms	Sleeps 2-6
Prices from:		
£385.00-725.00		**Per week**

IMPORTANT: Prices stated are estimates and may be subject to change. Awards correct as of beginning of October 2008.

Aviemore, Inverness-shire
Cairngorm Highland Bungalows
Map Ref: 4C10

27905

Open: All year

Glen Einich, 29 Grampian View,
Aviemore, Inverness-shire, PH22 1TF

T: 01479 810653
E: linda.murray@virgin.net
W: cairngorm-bungalows.co.uk

Beautifully furnished and well equipped bungalows ranging from 1-4 bedrooms sleeping 2-8, all have tv/dvd, fridge, cooker, microwave, washer/dryer, some have log fires. All have mountain views and are 10 minutes walk from Aviemore. Golf, leisure club, walking, skiing nearby. Pets welcome.

| 1 House | 2 Public Rooms | Sleeps 8 |
| 2 Bungalows | 1-2 Public Rooms | Sleeps 7 |

Prices from:	
£240.00	**Per week**
£25.00	**Per person per night**

Aviemore, Inverness-shire
Mr D Charnley
Map Ref: 4C10

67772

Open: All year

3 Witcutt Way, Wishaw, Lanarkshire, ML2 0AP
T: 01698 360823 M: 07973444519
E: david3@fsmail.net
W: selfcatering-aviemore.co.uk

| 1 Bungalow | 1 Public Room | Sleeps 2-6 |

Prices from:	
£460.00-560.00	**Per week**
£195.00-220.00	**Per night**

Aviemore, Inverness-shire
Craigellachie View
Map Ref: 4C10

62076

Open: All year

Tremayne, Dalfaber Road,
Aviemore, Inverness-shire PH22 1PU
T: 01479 810694
E: neilhighmore@btinternet.com
W: aviemoreholidayhomes.co.uk

This comfortable detached bungalow lies on the outskirts of Aviemore. There is a wide range of activities available locally including hill walking, mountain biking, skiing, fishing and golf. Nearby there is a restaurant and bar with entertainment.

| 1 Bungalow | 1 Public Room | Sleeps 5 |

Prices from:	
£220.00	**Per week**
£70.00	**Per night**

For a full listing of quality assured non-serviced establishments please see pages 229-385.

213

Aviemore, Inverness-shire
High Range Holiday Lodges
Map Ref: 4C10

★★★ UP TO
★★★★
SELF
CATERING

Open: All year

Grampian Road, Aviemore, Inverness-shire PH22 1PT
T: 01479 810636
E: info@highrange.co.uk
W: highrange.co.uk

Eight well appointed chalets in Birch woodland with one to three bedrooms, 500 metres from shopping centre. Linen supplied free of charge. Newly opened 20 bedroom hotel and Ristorante Pizzeria Bar onsite. Renowned for its friendly atmosphere excellent Italian and local cuisine.

30240

| 8 Chalets | 1 Public Room | Sleeps 2-6 |

Prices from:	
£200.00-680.00	**Per week**
£40.00-100.00	**Per night**

Aviemore, Inverness-shire
Meikle House
Map Ref: 4C10

★★★★
SELF
CATERING

Open: All year

Dalfaber Road, Tremayne,
Aviemore, Inverness-shire, PH22 1PU
T: 01479 810694
E: neilhighmore@btinternet.com
W: aviemoreholidayhomes.co.uk

Situated in the heart of the Highlands, a perfect base to explore the Spey Valley and the Cairngorm Mountains. Superior accommodation, furnished to a high standard to ensure a comfortable stay, located approx 3 miles north of Aviemore.

62076

| 1 House | 2 Public Rooms | Sleeps 9 |

Prices from:	
£350.00	**Per week**
£120.00	**Per night**

Aviemore, Inverness-shire
Peaks and Pines Holidays
Map Ref: 4C10

★★★
SELF
CATERING

Open: All year

Mrs J Green, 47 Commonside,
Selston, Nottingham, NG16 6FN
T: 01773 510041
E: peaksandpinesholidays@btinternet.com
W: peaksandpinesholidays.com

In a quiet residential area within walking distance of local amenities, this delightful spacious holiday home is a well equipped three bedroom bungalow, which sleeps up to six people. An enclosed rear garden overlooks birch woodland and the Cairngorm Mountains.

45850

| 1 Bungalow | 2 Public Rooms | Sleeps 6 |

Prices from:	
£420.00-525.00	**Per week**
Short breaks priced on application	

IMPORTANT: Prices stated are estimates and may be subject to change. Awards correct as of beginning of October 2008.

Aviemore, Inverness-shire
Speyside Leisure Park
Map Ref: 4C10

★★★
SELF
CATERING

Open: All year

Dalfaber Road, Tremayne,
Aviemore, Inverness-shire PH22 1PU
T: 01479 810694
E: neilhighmore@btinternet.com
W: aviemoreholidayhomes.co.uk

The chalet is situated on Speyside Leisure Park at the south end of Aviemore. The park has a play area and a small indoor swimming pool.

1 Chalet	1 Public Room	Sleeps 6

Prices from:

£300.00	Per week
£75.00	Per night

Boat of Garten, Inverness-shire
Beechgrove Mountain Lodges
Map Ref: 4C10

★★★
SELF
CATERING

Open: All year

Mr W Grant, Beechgrove Mountain Lodges
Mains of Garten Farmhouse, Boat of Garten
Inverness-shire PH24 3BY
T: 01479 831551
E: dimar123@btinternet.com
W: beechgrovemountainlodges.co.uk

Set amidst national park with stunning views of Spey Valley this comfortable lodge is ideally situated for most outdoor pursuits, touring and many other spectacular visitor attractions. Close by ospreys. The property is well appointed, perfect for your ideal Scottish holiday.

6 Lodges	1 Public Room	Sleeps 1-6

Prices from:

£200.00-495.00	Per week
£45.00-70.00	Per night

Boat of Garten, Inverness-shire
Mr G Keir
Map Ref: 4C10

★★
SELF
CATERING

Open: March-October

4 High Terrace, Boat of Garten,
Inverness-shire, PH24 3BW
T: 01479 831262
E: dodo.keir@btinternet.com

1 Ground floor flat	1 Public Room	Sleeps 1-4

Prices from:

£155.00-200.00	Per week

Boat of Garten, Inverness-shire
Dyndrum
Map Ref: 4C10

★★
SELF
CATERING

Open: All year

Mrs N C Clark, Dochlaggie,
Boat of Garten, Inverness-shire, PH24 3BU
T: 01479 831242
E: dochlaggie@aol.com

1 House	2 Public Rooms	Sleeps 5

Prices from:

£350.00-500.00	Per week
£60.00	Per night

For a full listing of quality assured non-serviced establishments please see pages 229-385.

215

Drumguish, Kingussie
Mr & Mrs J Robertson — Map Ref: 4B11

★★★
SELF
CATERING

Open: All year
Rubislaw, Newtonmore Road,
Kingussie, Inverness-shire PH21 1HD
T: 01540 661636
E: mail@aonach.ukf.net
W: aonach.ukf.net

52610

1 Bungalow	1-2 Public Rooms	Sleeps 2-6
Prices from:		
£250.00		**Per week**

Grantown-on-Spey, Moray
Clanranald — Map Ref: 4C9

★★★★
SELF
CATERING

Open: All year
Willowbrae, 73 Baddidarroch,
Lochinver, Sutherland, IV27 4LP
T: 01571 844383
E: heather@clanranaldholidays.co.uk
W: clanranaldholidays.co.uk

Ideal central location, minutes walk from High
Street. Very well appointed and furnished to a very
high standard. Fully equipped to ensure a wonderful
holiday. Perfect base for all outdoor pursuits. Private
gardens. Open hearth fire. Three bedrooms.
Great house.

19475

1 House	1 Public Room	Sleeps 7
Prices from:		
£250.00-370.00		**Per week**
£50.00		**Per night**

Grantown-on-Spey, Moray
Grantown-on-Spey Caravan Park — Map Ref: 4C9

★★★★★
HOLIDAY
PARK

Open: All year excl 1 November- 14 December
Seafield Avenue, Grantown-on-Spey, Highland, PH26 3JQ
T: 01479 872474 **E:** team@caravansscotland.com
W: caravansscotland.com

*Turn off A9 two miles north of Aviemore onto A95 for Grantown on Spey, once in
town go straight through traffic lights and take first left by Bank of Scotland. Park
seen in ¼ mile. If coming from the east, follow signs to Grantown on Spey
and once in town at traffic lights turn right and then first left at Bank of
Scotland. Park is straight ahead in ¼ mile.*

28874

Park accommodates 120 pitches		
Total Touring Pitches: 100		
Prices from:		
(100) £15.00	(20) £15.00	

Grantown-on-Spey, Moray
Grianan — Map Ref: 4C9

★★★
SELF
CATERING

Open: All year
Balliefurth Farm, Grantown-on-Spey, PH26 3NH
T: 01479 821636
E: a.maclennan@totalise.co.uk
W: scottishholidayhomes.co.uk

Set on a family run farm on the banks of the River
Spey and at the foot of the Cairngorm Mountains.
Ideal for walking, fishing, climbing, bird watching,
watersports etc. Evening meal available in adjoining
B&B.

71022

1 Apartment	2 Public Rooms	Sleeps 2
Prices from:		
£250.00		**Per week**
£40.00		**Per night**

IMPORTANT: Prices stated are estimates and may be subject to change. Awards correct as of beginning of October 2008.

nsh, Inverness-shire
Kullbery Chalet

Map Ref: 4C10

★★★ SELF CATERING

Open: All year

Annandale, Gordon Hall,
Kingussie, Inverness-shire, PH21 1NR
T: 01540 661560

Situated on the edge of Insh Marshes Bird Reserve of all year interest, amongst beautiful Highland scenery of mountains, lochs and rivers. Climbing, walking and many more attractions. Kullbery is well equipped, carpeted, double glazed, comfortable and cosy with safe parking.

1 Chalet	1 Public Room	Sleeps 4-6
Prices from:		
£180.00-320.00		**Per week**
£45.00		**Per night**

Kincraig, Inverness-shire
Mrs C MacGregor

Map Ref: 4C10

★★★ SELF CATERING

Open: March-December

The Dairy House, Corton Denham,
Sherborne, Dorset, DT9 4LX
T: 01963 220250
E: camacg@talk21.com
W: balbeag.co.uk

1 Bungalow	1 Public Room	Sleeps 8
Prices from:		
£450.00-695.00		**Per week**
£339.00		**3 night short break**

Kincraig, by Kingussie
Alvie Holiday Cottages

Map Ref: 4C10

★★★ SELF CATERING

Open: All year

Alvie Holiday Cottages, Alvie Estate Office,
Kincraig, Kingussie, Inverness-shire, PH21 1NE
T: 01540 651255
E: info@alvie-estate.co.uk
W: alvie-estate.co.uk

Secluded, beautiful Highland Estate, within the Cairngorm National Park, with cottages set amongst farm fields and woodlands. Alvie's breathtaking scenery provides peace and quiet; an unrivalled opportunity for recreation and entertainment. All cottages decorated and furnished to a high standard.

3 Cottages	1-2 Public Rooms	Sleeps 4-6
Prices from:		
£310.00-665.00		**Per week**
£62.00 per night		**Min 2 nights**

Kincraig, Inverness-shire
Fraser and Telford Cottages

Map Ref: 4C10

★★ SELF CATERING

Open: All year

Insh House, Kincraig,
Kingussie, Inverness-shire, PH21 1NU
T: 01540 651377
E: inshhouse@btinternet.com
W: kincraig.com/inshhouse

2 Cottages	1 Public Room	Sleeps 4
Prices from:		
£250.00-400.00		**Per week**

For a full listing of quality assured non-serviced establishments please see pages 229-385.

Moray, Aviemore and the Cairngorms

Laggan, Newtonmore
Cluny Mains
Map Ref: 4B11

Open: All year
Mrs Earp, 6 Willian Way, Letchworth, Hertfordshire
SG6 2HG
T: 01462 673410
W: clunymains.com

1 House	3 Public Rooms	Sleeps 11
Prices from:		
£550.00-1200.00		Per week
£100-150.00		Per night

19747

Lossiemouth, Moray
Beachview Holiday Flat
Map Ref: 4D7

14546

Open: April-October
Mrs A. Reedie, 62 Fernlea,
Bearsden, Glasgow G61 1NB
T: 0141 942 4135
E: info@beachviewholidayflats.co.uk
W: beachviewholidayflats.co.uk

Completely refurbished, spacious 3 bedroom flat.
Outstanding panoramic views over Moray Firth, golf
course and West beach. Ideal for golfing holiday and
as a tourist base.

1 Apartment	1 Public Room	Sleeps 6
Prices from:		
£480.00-550.00		Per week

Nethy Bridge, Inverness-shire
Cairngorm Executive Ltd.
Map Ref: 4C10

17431

Open: All year
Funach View, Crossroads, Durris, Banchory, AB31 6BX
T: 01330 844344
E: info@cairngorm-executive.com
W: cairngorm-executive.com

Superbly furnished and equipped houses in
beautiful forest setting. Osprey has 4 bedrooms, 2
ensuite, one on ground floor. Red Kite has 3 ensuite
bedrooms, one on ground floor. These houses are
five star in all aspects. Pets by arrangement.

2 Houses	2 Public Rooms	Sleeps 2-10
Prices from:		
£525.00-895.00	Per week (Excl festive period)	
Short breaks priced on application		

Nethy Bridge, Inverness-shire
Mrs F M Grant per Innis Bhroc
Map Ref: 4C10

31696

Open: All year
Creagan Gorm, Tulloch, Nethybridge, PH25 3EF
T: 01479 831711
E: jandfgrant@btconnect.com

1 Cottage	1 Public Room	Sleeps 2-6
Prices from:		
£300.00-570.00		Per week
£57.00		Per night

IMPORTANT: Prices stated are estimates and may be subject to change. Awards correct as of beginning of October 2008.

Nethy Bridge, Inverness-shire
Woodbridge   **Map Ref: 4C10**

★★★
SELF CATERING

Open: March-November

Miss K M Grant, Tombae, West Cullachie,
Boat of Garten, Inverness-shire, PH24 3BY
T: 01479 821226

61445

1 Bungalow	1 Public Room	Sleeps 5
Prices from:		
£250.00-400.00		**Per week**

Newtonmore, Inverness-shire
Gaskbeg Cottages   **Map Ref: 4B11**

★★ UP TO ★★★★
SELF CATERING

Open: All year

Gaskbeg Farm, Laggan, Newtonmore PH20 1BS
T: 01528 544336
E: gaskbeg@btinternet.com
W: gaskbeg.co.uk

At the gateway to Cairngorms National Park these
two completely renovated cottages sit in a peaceful
elevated position overlooking a working hill farm
with lovely views to the hills which provided the
backdrop to the hit TV series 'Monarch of the Glen'.

27369

2 Cottages	3 Public Rooms	Sleeps 1-4
Prices from:		
£220.00		**Per week**

Looking from the dunes, along the west beach to Covesea Lighthouse, at Lossiemouth

For a full listing of quality assured non-serviced establishments please see pages 229-385.

219

Warebeth Beach, Stromness, Orkney

THE OUTER ISLANDS
Outer Hebrides, Orkney, Shetland

There's something very special about island holidays and Scotland has so many wonderful islands to explore.

On an island holiday, you can leave all the stresses of mainland life far behind. You don't have to settle for just one destination either – try a bit of island hopping, there's a lot of choice.

A different pace

At Scotland's western edge, the Outer Hebrides look out to the Atlantic swell and life moves at a relaxed pace. In this last Gaelic stronghold, a warm welcome awaits.

You can get there by ferry from Oban or from Uig on Skye – ferry prices to the Outer Hebrides have been reduced for 2009. Or travel by plane - fly to Barra and you'll land on the beach at low tide!

Lewis is the largest of the Outer Hebrides with a busy town at Stornoway and historical sites like the standing stones at Calanais stretching back over 3,000 years. It's distinctly different from the more mountainous Harris. Don't forget to visit the traditional weavers making wonderful Harris Tweed.

North and South Uist, Benbecula, Eriskay and Barra are all well worth a visit too and each has its own attractions.

Life at the crossroads

Island life can also be experienced in Scotland's two great northern archipelagos. Some 70 islands make up Orkney with 21 inhabited. Shetland, at the crossroads where the Atlantic meets the North Sea, has over 100 islands and is home to around 22,000 people and well over a million seabirds.

In Orkney, you can see the oldest houses in northern Europe at Papa Westray, dating back to 3800 BC.

To find out more, call 0845 22 55 121 or go to visitscotland.com

The influence of the Vikings in these parts is everywhere. Orcadians spoke Old Norse until the mid 1700s and the ancient Viking Parliament used to meet at Scalloway in Shetland.

These islands enjoy long summer days and at midsummer it never really gets dark. You can even play midnight golf in the 'Simmer Dim'.

In winter, the nights are long but the islanders have perfected the art of indoor life. Musicians fill the bars and community halls and there always seems to be something to celebrate.

Two great unmissable events are the winter fire festival of Up Helly Aa in Lerwick, Shetland and the Ba' in Kirkwall, Orkney, where up to 400 players take to the streets for a game of rough and tumble that is somewhere between football, rugby and all-out war.

Have a wild time

Orkney and Shetland are a joy for wildlife watchers. There are millions of birds to observe as well as otters, seals, dolphins and whales. Being surrounded by sea, angling, yachting, sea kayaking, cruising and diving are readily available.

Wherever you decide to experience island life, remember that island holidays are a popular choice and while there is a reasonable range of self catering accommodation and island-based camping and caravan sites, it does make sense to book well in advance.

The impressive cliffs of Esha Ness, north west coast of mainland, Shetland

What's On?

Orkney Jazz Weekend
24 – 26 April 2009
A weekend of jazz with local and visiting performers.
stromnesshotel.com

Shetland Folk Festival
30 April – 3 May 2009
The UK's most northerly folk festival is regarded a prestigious event for performers, locals and visitors alike.
shetlandfolkfestival.com

Orkney Folk Festival
21 – 24 May 2009
The best in modern and traditional folk music.
orkneyfolkfestival

Johnsmas Foy
18 – 28 June 2009
Recently revived festival that used to mark the arrival of the Dutch herring fleet in Shetland.
johnsmasfoy.com

St Magnus Festival
19 – 24 June 2009, Kirkwall
Midsummer celebration of the Arts.
stmagnusfestival.co.uk

Lewis Golf Week
July 2009, Stornoway
A week of golf at Stornoway Golf Club.

Taransay Fiddle Week
July 2009
Learn new skills from leading fiddlers.

Creative Connections
3 - 9 August 2009
Learn arts and crafts, traditional fiddle playing and the art of storytelling.

Harris Arts Festival
August 2009 – various dates
Celebrate arts and crafts on the island.

DON'T MISS

1 The combination of peace and tranquillity that can be found throughout the Outer Hebrides, blended with the vibrant nature of the people and their language, has been a true inspiration to many. This is demonstrated in the islands' crafts, music and culture. Arts venues such as An Lanntair in Stornoway and Taigh Chearsabhagh in Uist often attract internationally renowned performers.

2 The 5,000 year old Calanais Standing Stones on the west side of Lewis are one of the most famous landmarks in the Outer Hebrides. Second only to Stonehenge, these mystical stones are unique in their cross-shaped layout which has caused endless fascinating debate. Check out the visitor centre to form your own opinion!

3 Seallam! Visitor Centre in Northton at the southern end of the beautiful Isle of Harris provides a variety of exhibitions for both first-time and returning visitors. Browse among exhibits about the history and natural environment of the Hebrides, and find out what has influenced the development of the various island communities. Whether you wish to spend an hour or a whole day, there is plenty to occupy your attention. There is even a tea and coffee bar and a small craft-shop.

4 The area around Loch Druidibeg on South Uist is a National Nature Reserve with many different habitats including freshwater, brackish lagoon, dune, machair, peatland and scrub woodland. The loch itself is shallow but very large, with many islands: one of which is home to a resident colony of herons. The greylag geese which breed around the loch contribute to the resident population that remain in the Uists all year. Birds of prey include golden eagle, hen harriers, kestrel, peregrine and merlin.

5 Kisimul Castle is a sight to behold, situated in the bay of Castlebay Village on Barra. The stronghold of the MacNeils of Barra, this is the only surviving medieval castle in the Hebrides. Day tickets to visit the castle can be obtained at the local Visitor Information Centre.

ACTIVITIES

7 There are five official golf courses in the Hebrides: in Barra, Uist, Benbecula, Harris and Lewis. The 9-hole course at Scarista on Harris, in particular, is legendary for its stunning setting and challenging situation. You may think it's an easy option but the small greens, massive sand dunes and ever-present Atlantic winds combine for an enjoyable round!

8 The surf around the Hebrides is so good that the area is now on the map for international lovers of the sport. With over 70 beaches from white shell sands to pebble shores and almost always empty, it really is a surfer's paradise. The Isle of Lewis is positioned so it receives swells from almost every direction and is classed as having the most consistent surf in Europe.

9 With some of the most beautiful coastline in Britain and warmer water temperatures, the Hebrides is the perfect wilderness to explore by kayak. See otters, dolphins and puffins as you glide through the crystal clear waters around the islands. The coastline is a labyrinth of complex bays, inlets, dramatic cliffs, secret coves, sandy beaches and offshore islands.... a sea paddler's paradise.

10 The Outer Hebrides is a game angler's dream location and will fill you with all the emotions and pleasures associated with this wonderful and rewarding sport. Whether you are a solitary angler, form part of a larger group or simply looking for a tranquil family vacation, the Outer Hebrides has it all - namely, some of the best summer salmon and trout fishing in Europe set amidst spectacular scenery.

To find out more, call 0845 22 55 121 or go to visitscotland.com

DON'T MISS

1 Skara Brae (B9056, 19 miles from Kirkwall) is an unrivalled example of life in Stone Age Orkney. Without doubt the best preserved village in western Europe, the houses contain stone beds, dressers, hearths and drains, giving a fantastic insight into how life was 5,000 years ago. Together with several other historical sites, it is part of a designated World Heritage Site.

2 Discovered in 1958, the Tomb of the Eagles is a 5,000 year old tomb containing ceremonial tools, beds, talons and other bones of the white-tailed eagle, pottery and working tools.

3 In the heart of Orkney's main town, Kirkwall, lies St Magnus Cathedral. It was built in 1137 by Earl Rognvald, in memory of his cousin Magnus who was earlier murdered by another cousin, Haakon, co-ruler at that time. Today the beautiful sandstone building continues to be a place of worship for the local people.

4 The Pier Arts Centre was reopened in 2007 and houses a remarkable collection of 20th century British art. The Collection charts the development of modern art in Britain and includes key work by Barbara Hepworth, Ben Nicholson and Naum Gabo amongst others.

5 Orkney is blessed with an abundance of birds and marine wildlife. Late spring sees the arrival of thousands of breeding seabirds including everybody's favourite – the colourful puffin. Grey seals breed in huge numbers around the coast in late autumn, while whales, dolphins and porpoises are regularly sighted off-shore throughout the summer. Wildlife is everywhere, and with a diverse range of professional guiding services there is something to suit everyone.

HISTORY AND HERITAGE

6 The Ring of Brodgar and the Standing Stones of Stenness (both just off the B9055) are also included within the World Heritage Site. Undeniably mystical, these spiritual places reward visitors with a real sense of ancient times.

7 Maeshowe is a central feature of the Neolithic Orkney World Heritage Site. A chambered cairn (off the A965), it is considered to be one of the finest architectural achievements of its time, around 5,000 years ago. Timed ticketing is in operation, allowing the informative guides to point out all the interesting aspects of the site, including Viking graffiti.

8 The Broch of Gurness at Aikerness (A966) is a well-organised Iron Age village, giving fascinating insight into community life 2,000 years ago.

9 Travel across the first of the Churchill Barriers to see an artistic phenomenon at the Italian Chapel. Built by Italian POWs in WWII, using only the most modest of materials, the intricate interior is all the more impressive.

DON'T MISS

1 Whatever your interests, there is something to suit every taste in Shetland. Our beautiful landscape is perfect for **walkers** – offering everything from coastal treks to energetic hikes. There are over 300 lochs holding brown trout and sea fishing is superb.

2 **Midsummer** is an especially magical time in Shetland when there are almost 19 hours of daylight to enjoy. It never really gets dark at this time of year – the other five hours between sunrise and sunset are filled with an eerie lingering twilight that's known locally as the "Simmer Dim".

3 Ever since **bird watching** became a popular British leisure pursuit in the late 19th century, Shetland's been famous, among those in the know, as the place to enjoy sensational seabird colonies and amazing rarities. If you want a close-up view of tens of thousands of breeding gannets, alongside guillemots, puffins, razorbills, kittiwakes and fulmars, then head for Sumburgh Head, Noss or Hermaness Nature Reserves.

4 Built on the historic site of Hay's Dock, is the impressive new **Shetland Museum and Archives** offers a rich insight into the development of Shetland from its geological beginnings to present day. See the museum's outstanding collection of historic boats hanging in the dramatic three-storey boat hall.

5 The accessibility of Shetland's coastline is ideal for **sea kayakers**. There are hundreds of miles of cliffs and deserted beaches as well as some of Europe's finest sea caves. Enjoy stunning cliff scenery, stack, arches and sheltered inlets. There are large colonies of seals and seabirds, most of them easily reachable by sea.

ATTRACTIONS

6 One of the best places to enjoy the cliff scenery by road is **Eshaness Lighthouse**, perched above a precipice of volcanic lava. A short walk away is an impressive collapsed cave, Da Hols o' Scraada ('the Devil's Caves'). Nearby is Da Grind o' da Navir ('Gate of the Borer'), a huge gateway in the cliffs where the sea has ripped out a huge chunk of rock and hurled it inland.

7 **Shetland Crofthouse**, Boddam, is a typical thatched crofthouse of the 19th century restored with traditional materials. The layout of the house is similar to Norse houses from 1,000 years earlier. The sweet smell of peat smoke, thick walls and cramped living space will instantly take you back to life in 1870s.

8 The broch, or fortified Iron Age tower, on the little island of Mousa is the only one in the world to have survived almost complete for more than 2,000 years. Built as a refuge against raiding local tribes, **Mousa Broch** is a wonder of archaeology, not to mention ornithology. Tiny storm petrels nest in its stone, visiting the broch only after dark – a night excursion to hear their eerie calls is an experience not to be missed.

9 A recent archaeological dig at **Old Scatness Broch**, next to Sumburgh Airport, has revealed one of Britain's most exciting Iron Age villages, with many buildings standing at or near roof height and some still even 'decorated' with yellow clay! Buried for nearly 2,000 years, the site is rich in artefacts and remarkably well preserved.

To find out more, call 0845 22 55 121 or go to visitscotland.com

MAP

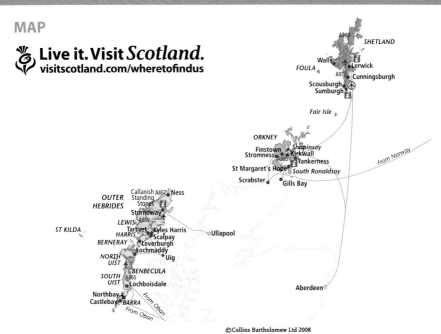

Live it. Visit *Scotland.*
visitscotland.com/wheretofindus

©Collins Bartholomew Ltd 2008

i VISITOR INFORMATION CENTRES

Visitor Information Centres are staffed by people 'in the know' offering friendly advice, helping to make your stay in Scotland the most enjoyable ever . . . whatever your needs!

Outer Hebrides *i*		
Stornoway	26 Cromwell Street, Stornoway, Isle of Lewis, HS1 2DD	Tel: 01851 703088

Orkney *i*		
Kirkwall	The Travel Centre, West Castle Street, Kirkwall, Orkney KW15 1GU	Tel: 01856 872856

Shetland *i*		
Lerwick	Market Cross, Lerwick, Shetland, ZE1 0LU	
Sumburgh (Airport)	Wilsness Terminal, Sumburgh Airport, Shetland ZE3 9JP	Tel: 01595 693434

LOCAL KNOWLEDGE • WHERE TO STAY • ACCOMMODATION BOOKING • PLACES TO VISIT • THINGS TO DO • MAPS AND GUIDES TRAVEL ADVICE • ROUTE PLANNING • WHERE TO SHOP AND EAT LOCAL CRAFTS AND PRODUCE • EVENT INFORMATION • TICKETS

For information and ideas about exploring Scotland in advance of your trip, call our booking and information service **0845 22 55 121** or go to **visitscotland.com**

If calling from outside the UK and Ireland **+44 1506 832 121**   From Ireland **1800 932 510**

A £4 booking fee applies for accommodation bookings made via a Visitor Information Centre and through our booking and information service.

Outer Hebrides

Kyles Harris, Isle of Harris
Taigh Iomhair
Map Ref: 3D6

★★★
SELF
CATERING

Open: All year
1 Carragreich, Isle of Harris HS3 3BP
T: 01859 502225
E: dollag@btinternet.com
W: taighiomhair.co.uk

42893

1 Cottage	1 Public Room	Sleeps 3
Prices from:		
£230.00		**Per week**

Scalpay, Isle of Harris
Hamarsay House
Map Ref: 3D6

★★★★
SELF
CATERING

Open: All year
9 Merlin Crescent, Inverness IV2 3TE
T: 01463 236049
E: norman.macleod@tiscali.co.uk
W: hamarsay-house.com

29426

1 Bungalow	2 Public Rooms	Sleeps 6
Prices from:		
£300.00-400.00		**Per week**
£40.00		**Per night (low season)**

Tarbert, Isle of Harris
Kirklea Cottages
Map Ref: 3C6

★★★★
SELF
CATERING

Open: All year
Manse Road, Tarbert, Isle of Harris, HS3 3DF
T: 01859 502364
E: angus@hotel-hebrides.com
W: hotel-hebrides.com

A charming terrace of four cottages in an elevated position overlooking Tarbert. Faced in Harris stone, they are tastefully furnished and full of character. Decorated to an exacting standard, each offers 900 sq. ft of warmth and comfort, accommodating 4-6 people.

34333

4 Cottages	1 Public Room	Sleeps 4-6
Prices from:		
£350.00-450.00		**Per week**
£65.00-130.00		**Per night**

Tarbert, Isle of Harris
Ullabhal and Cleiseabhal
Map Ref: 3C6

★★★★
SELF
CATERING

Open: All year
Hill Cottage, Tarbert, Isle of Harris HS3 3DL
T: 01859 502063
E: camerontarbert@btinternet.com
W: cameronharrisltd.co.uk

30485

2 Houses	1 Public Room	Sleeps 2
Prices from:		
£100.00-395.00		**Per week**

visitscotland.com/wildlife

WILDLIFE
SCOTLAND
To find out about watching wildlife in Europe's leading wildlife destination log on to
visitscotland.com/wildlife

IMPORTANT: Prices stated are estimates and may be subject to change. Awards correct as of beginning of October 2008.

Finstown, Orkney
Atlantis Lodges
Map Ref: 5B12

★★★ SELF CATERING

Open: All year

Boat House, Finstown, Orkney KW17 2EH
T: 01856 761581
E: info@atlantislodges.com
W: atlantislodges.com

Self contained waterside apartments. Breathtaking sea views from each apartment. Central location for all visitor attractions. Available for one night or longer. Private on-site parking. Bus route close by. One or two bedroom apartments available.

12 Apartments	1 Public Room	Sleeps 2-4

Prices from:		
POA		Per week
POA		Per night

Kirkwall, Orkney
Apartment 76 and 1 Palace Gardens
Map Ref: 5B12

★ UP TO ★★★ SELF CATERING

Open: All year

Mr & Mrs W McEwan,
Oaklea Farm, St Ola, Orkney, KW15 1 SX
T: 01856 877782
E: office@sebaymill.co.uk   W: sebaymill.co.uk

1 Cottage	1 Public Room	Sleeps 2
1 Apartment	1 Public Room	Sleeps 4

Prices from:		
Cottage :	£500.00	Per week
	£75.00	Per night
Apartment :	£465.00	Per week
	£65.00	Per night

South Ronaldsay, Orkney
Mrs C Fletcher
Map Ref: 4E2

★ UP TO ★★★ SELF CATERING

Open: All year

Banks, Cleat, South Ronaldsay, Orkney, KW17 2RW
T: 01856 831605
E: info@banksoforkney.co.uk
W: banksoforkney.co.uk

With panoramic views over Pentland Firth, the traditional stone built cottages are located on 5 acres of coastline. Recently refurbished and well equipped. Ideal for walkers, bird watchers and relaxation. Bistro on location supplying fresh Orkney produce.

3 Cottages	1 Public Room	Sleeps 2-7

Prices from:	
£150.00-450.00	Per week
£20.00 per person	Per night

Inkerness, by Kirkwall, Orkney
Sebay Mill Holiday Apartments
Map Ref: 5B12

★ UP TO ★★★ SELF CATERING

Open: All year
Mr & Mrs W McEwen,
Oaklea Farm, St Ola, Orkney, KW15 1SX
T: 01856 877782
E: office@sebaymill.co.uk   W: sebaymill.co.uk

6 Apartments	1 Public Room	Sleeps 2-4

Prices from:	
£425.00-675.00	Per week
£60.00-90.00	Per night

Shetland

Cunningsburgh, Shetland
Tamara Apartment/Flat

Map Ref: 5F6

★★★
SELF
CATERING

Open: All year excl Xmas and New Year
Tamara, Longwell, Cunningsburgh, Shetland ZE2 9HG
T: 01950 477350
E: info@shetlandholidaylets.co.uk
W: shetlandholidaylets.co.uk

44569

1 Apartment	1 Public Room	Sleeps 1-4
Prices from:		
£230.00-275.00		**Per week**

The Sands of Brecon (an award-winning white sand beach), North Yell, Shetland

IMPORTANT: Prices stated are estimates and may be subject to change. Awards correct as of beginning of October 2008.

Aberdeen

Bimini Flat	69 Constitution Street, Aberdeen AB24 5ET	01224 646912	★★★	Self Catering
Broomhill Apartments	79 Brighton Place, Aberdeen, Aberdeenshire, AB10 6RT	01224 322518	★★★	Self Catering
Chapel Apartments	Chapel Apartments, 28 Gauchhill Road, Kintore, Aberdeenshire, AB51 0SZ	07824 666321	★★★ → ★★★★	Serviced Apartments
City Wharf Apartments	City Wharf Apartments, 19-21 Regent Quay, Aberdeen, Aberdeenshire, AB11 5BE	0845 942424	★★★	Serviced Apartments
Deskford House	Backhill of Fetterrletter, Fyvie, Aberdeenshire, AB53 6RL	01651 891605	★★★	Self Catering
Forest & Albyn Apartments	Forest Albyn Apartments, 42 Thorngrove Ave, Aberdeen AB15 7XR	01224 315992	Awaiting Grading	
Forest Bank Apartment	Forest Bank House, 88 Ashgrove Road West, Aberdeen AB16 5EE	01224 693743	★★★★	Self Catering
Hillhead Halls	Conference & Event Office, University of Aberdeen, Aberdeen AB24 3FX	01224 272660	★★	Self Catering 🦽
Hilton Self Catering	58 Kirk Brae, Cults, Aberdeen, Aberdeenshire, AB15 9QQ	01224 867184	★★★ → ★★★★	Self Catering
Skene House Holburn	Skene House Holburn, 6 Union Grove, Aberdeen, Aberdeenshire, AB10 6SY	01224 580000	★★★★	Serviced Apartments
Skene House Rosemount	Skene House, 96 Rosemount Viaduct, Aberdeen, Aberdeenshire, AB1 1NX	01224 645971	★★★ → ★★★★	Serviced Apartments
Skene House Whitehall	Skene House Whitehall, 2 Whitehall Place, Aberdeen, Aberdeenshire, AB25 2NX	01224 646600	★★★★	Serviced Apartments
Woolmanhill Flats	The Robert Gordon University, Schoolhill, Aberdeen, Aberdeenshire, AB10 1FR	01224 262141	★★	Self Catering 🦽
48 Skene Terrace	Greystones, 118 Victoria Street, Dyce, Aberdeen, AB21 7BE	01224 722243	★★★★	Self Catering

By Aberdeen

The Bothy, Blairs	The Bothy, Wedderhill Farm, Blairs, Aberdeen, AB12 5YX	01224 869960	★★★	Self Catering

Aberdour

The Chaumer	The Chaumer, Barns Farm, Aberdour, Fife, KY3 0RY	01383 823872	★★★	Self Catering
The Farmhouse Flat	Dalachy Farm, Aberdour, Fife, KY3 0RL	01383 860340	★★★	Self Catering
Willow Tree Cottage	Pleasants Farm, Aberdour, Fife, KY3 0RR	01383 860661	★★★	Self Catering

Aberfeldy

Balbeg Farm	Balbeg Farm, Lawers, Aberfeldy, Perthshire, PH15 2NZ	01567 820642	★★★★	Self Catering
Bracken Lodges	Bracken Lodges, Ardtalnaig, Loch Tay, by Kenmore, Aberfeldy, Perthshire, PH15 2HX	01567 820169	★★★★	Self Catering
Briar Croft	16 Glenalmond Terrace, Perth, Perthshire, PH2 0AU	01738 622336	★★	Self Catering
Bridgend Cottage	Little Burn Cottage, Burn Houses, Duns, Berwickshire, TD11 3TT	01361 882895	★★★★	Self Catering
Callwood Smiddy	Callwood Cottage, Comrie Bridge, Aberfeldy, Perthshire, PH15 2ND	01887 830543	★★★★	Self Catering
Capercaillie Cottage	Dovetail Barn, Morchard Bishop, Crediton, Devon, EX17 6RG	01363 877676	★★★★	Self Catering
Castle Menzies Farm Holiday Cottages	Castle Menzies Home Farm, Aberfeldy, Perthshire PH15 2LY	01887 820260	★★★ → ★★★★	Self Catering
Clachmhor	54 Drumby Crescent, Clarkston, Glasgow G76 7HW	0141 6382643	★★★	Self Catering

🦽 Unassisted wheelchair access 🦽 Assisted wheelchair access ♟ Access for visitors with mobility difficulties
⟦🌿⟧ Bronze Green Tourism Award ⟦🌿🌿⟧ Silver Green Tourism Award ⟦🌿🌿🌿⟧ Gold Green Tourism Award
For further information on our Green Tourism Business Scheme please see page 9.

Cruck Cottage	Drumdewan Farmhouse, Dull, Aberfeldy, Perthshire, PH15 2JQ	01887 820071	★★★★	Self Catering
Dunskiag Farmhouse	Dunskiag Farmhouse, Dunskiag, Aberfeldy PH15 2EY	01887 829111	★★★★	Self Catering
Hawthorn Cottage	Clach an Tuirc, Fearnan, Aberfeldy, Perthshire, PH15 2PG	01887 830615	★★★	Self Catering
Hideaway Cottage	14 Bank Street, Aberfeldy, Perthshire, PH15 2BB	01887 829008	★★★★	Self Catering
Hillview House & Cottage	Arbour House, 74 Forest Lane, Kirklevington, Yarm, Stockton on Tees, TS15 9ND	01642 782111	★★★ → ★★★★	Self Catering
Laurelbank Cottage & Lilac Cottage	33 Appin Place, Aberfeldy, Perthshire, PH15 2AH	01887 820478	★★★★	Self Catering
Lavender, Appletree and Tomghuibhais	5 Templars Cramond, Edinburgh EH4 6BY	0131 339 6548	★★★ → ★★★★	Self Catering
Loch Tay Lodges	Remony, Aberfeldy, Perthshire, PH15 2HR	01887 830209	★★★	Self Catering &wheelchair;
Machuim Farm Cottages	Machuim Farm, Lawers, Aberfeldy, Perthshire, PH15 2PA	01567 820670	★★★	Self Catering
Mains of Murthly Cottages	Mains of Murthly House, Aberfeldy, Perthshire, PH15 2EA	01887 820427	★★★★	Self Catering
Moness Country Club	Moness Country Club, Crieff Road, Aberfeldy, Perthshire, PH15 2DY	01887 822100	★★★★	Self Catering
No 3 The Beeches	22 Langdale Rise, Maidstone, Kent, ME16 0EU	01622 764765	★★★★	Self Catering
Novar	Arnsbrae, 10 Connor Street, Peebles EH45 8HD	01721 720292	★★★★	Self Catering
Taronga	Moville, Kinnaird, Pitlochry, Perthshire, PH16 5JL	01796 470100	★★★★	Self Catering
The Cottage	6 The Beeches, Kenmore Road, Aberfeldy, Perthshire, PH15 2BZ	01887 829490	★★★★	Self Catering
The Turret House	The Turret House, C/O Willow Croft, Swindon Bank, Pannal, N. Yorks, HG3 1JD	07739 777117	★★★★	Self Catering
Drumcroy Lodges	Mains of Murthly, Aberfeldy, Perthshire, PH15 2EA	01887 820978	★★★★	Self Catering &wheelchair;
Tomvale	Tomvale, Tom of Cluny Farm, Aberfeldy, Perthshire, PH15 2JT	01887 820171	★★★	Self Catering &wheelchair;

By Aberfeldy

The Cottage, Grandtully	The Cottage, Nether Pitcairn, Aberfeldy, Perthshire, PH15 2EQ	01887 820992	★★★	Self Catering
Innerwick Estate, Glen Lyon	Innerwick House, Glenlyon, Aberfeldy, Perthshire, PH15 2PP	01887 866208	★★★★ → ★★★★★	Self Catering
Grandpa's Cottage	Balnald Farmhouse, Fortingall, Near Aberfeldy, Perthshire, PH15 2LL	01887 830315	★★★★	Self Catering
Mains of Taymouth Country Estate	Mains of Taymouth Country Estate, Mains of Taymouth, Kenmore, Aberfeldy, Perthshire, PH15 2HN	01887 830226	★★★★ → ★★★★★	Self Catering
Pier, Waterfall & Sky Cottages	Rock House, Achianich, Aberfeldy, Perthshire, PH15 2HU	01887 83036	★★★ → ★★★★★	Self Catering
The Ghillies Cottage	Farleyer Field House, By Aberfeldy Perthshire, PH15 2JE	01887 829553	★★★★	Self Catering &mobility;

Aberfoyle

8 Staball 'Ard	Larne Cottage, Fore Road, Kippen, Stirlingshire, FK8 3DT	01786 871197	★★★★	Self Catering
Creag Darach Cottage	Creag Darach, Lochard Road, Aberfoyle, Stirling, FK8 3TD	01877 382476	★★★	Self Catering
Dunardry	27 Osprey Avenue, Westhoughton, Bolton, Lancashire, BL5 2SL	01942 816010	★★★	Self Catering
Inverard Lodge Cabin	Inverard Lodge, Lochard Road, Aberfoyle, Stirling FK8 3TD	01877 389113	★★★	Self Catering

To find out more, call 0845 22 55 121 or go to visitscotland.com.

Loch Dhu Cottage	Loch Dhu House, Kinlochard, Aberfoyle, Stirlingshire, FK8 3TS	01877 387712	★★★	Self Catering	
Lomond View Cottage	Lomond View Cotttage, C/O Corrie Glen, Manse Road, Aberfoyle, Stirlingshire, FK8 3XF	01877 382427	★★★★	Self Catering	
The Hayloft, Forth House	Forth House, Lochard Road, Aberfoyle, Stirling, FK8 3TD	01877 382 696	★★★	Self Catering	
Trossachs Farmhouse Cottages	Trossachs Farmhouse Cottages, Longlands, Gartmore, Stirling, FK8 3SA	01877 382075	★★★★	Self Catering	🍏🍏

By Aberfoyle

| Hillview Holiday Cottage | 12 Mosshead Road, Bearsden, Glasgow G61 3HN | 0141 9428299 | ★★★ | Self Catering | |
| Ben Lomond Lodges | Trossachs Holiday Park, By Aberfoyle, Stirling FK8 3SA | 01877 382732 | ★★★★ | Self Catering | |

Aberlady

| Upper Flat, Sunset View | Quill House, High Street, Aberlady, East Lothian, EH32 0RB | 01875 870405 | ★★★ | Self Catering | |

Aberlour

Allachy House	Seafab Properties Ltd, Wellheads Terrace, Wellheads Ind Estate, Dyce, Aberdeen, AB21 7GF	01224 797946	★★★	Self Catering	
Farm Steading	Newton of Forgie, Keith, Banffshire, AB55 6RN	01542 882218	★★★★	Self Catering	
Rhynagarrie Mill	Ridgebourne, Kington, Herefordshire HR5 3EG	01544 230218	★★★★★	Self Catering	

By Aberlour

| Milton Cottage and Sunnybank | Craighead, Upper Knockando, Nr Aberlour, Banffshire, AB38 7SG | 01340 810389 | Awaiting Grading | | |

Aboyne

East Wing, Dorevay	Dorevay, Birse, Aboyne, Aberdeenshire, AB34 5BT	013398 86232	★★★★	Self Catering	
St Katherine's Cottage	St Katherine's Cottage, Aboyne, Aberdeenshire, AB34 5BR	01339 886551	★★★★	Self Catering	
The Stocket	17 Golf Crescent, Aboyne, Aberdeenshire, AB34 5GP	01339 887370	★★★★	Self Catering	

By Aboyne

Royal Deeside Holiday Cottages, Dinnet	Estate Office, Dinnet, Aboyne, Aberdeenshire, AB34 5LL	01339 85341	★★ → ★★★	Self Catering	
Glen Tanar Estate, Glen Tanar	Glen Tanar Estate, Brooks House, Aboyne, Aberdeenshire, AB34 5EU	013398 86451	★★ → ★★★★	Self Catering	♿ 🍏
Tanar View, Glen Tanar	Dalwhing Mill House, Glen Tanar, Aboyne, Aberdeenshire, AB34 5ET	01339 885764	★★★★	Self Catering	
Holmhead Cottage	40 The Chase, Marshalls Park, Romford, Essex, RM1 4BE	01708 782324	★★★	Self Catering	
West Woodside	9 Viewfield Gardens, Aberdeen AB15 7XN	01224 315008	★★★	Self Catering	

Acharacle

Ben View Hotel Holiday Cottages	Ben View Hotel, Strontian, Argyll, PH36 4HY	01967 402333	★★★	Self Catering	
Burnbank Croft Cottage	Burnbank, Acharacle, Argyll, PH36 4JL	01967 431223	★★★	Self Catering	
Caber Faidh	Western Highland Cottages, Beresford Lodge, Bedgebury Road, Goudhurst, TN17 2QX	01580 212133	★★★	Self Catering	
Garmoran Square	Garmorgan Square, Mingarry, Acharacle, Lochaber, PH36 4JX	01967 431456	★★★★ → ★★★★★	Self Catering	

♿ Unassisted wheelchair access　ᕤ Assisted wheelchair access　🚶 Access for visitors with mobility difficulties
🍏 Bronze Green Tourism Award　🍏🍏 Silver Green Tourism Award　🍏🍏🍏 Gold Green Tourism Award
For further information on our Green Tourism Business Scheme please see page 9.

Honeysuckle Cottage	Western Highlands Cottages, Beresford Lodge, Bedgebury Road, Goudhurst, Cranbrook, Kent, TN17	01580 212133	★★	Self Catering	
Rowanhill	Baile na Coille, Balmoral, Ballater, Aberdeenshire, AB35 5TB	01339 742278	★★★	Self Catering	
Steading Holidays	Steading Holidays, 17 Old Golf Course, Kilchoan, Argyll, PH36 4LH	01972 510262	★ → ★★	Self Catering	

Achiltibuie

Caberfeidh	Dorevay, Birse, Aboyne, Aberdeenshire, AB34 5BT	013398 86232	★★★	Self Catering	
The Haven	Heisgeir, Slackbuie Crescent, Inverness, Inverness-shire, IV2 4QH	01463 234826	★★	Self Catering	
The Old Post Office	Northminster, Tuesley Lane, Godalming, Surrey, GU7 1SN	01483 421524	★★★	Self Catering	
The Steading	Blairbuie, Achiltibuie, Ullapool, Ross-shire, IV26 2YS	01854 622416	★★★★	Self Catering	✦
Achnahaird Farm Cott, Suilven, & Cul Mor	Achnahaird Farm Cottage, Achnahaird, Achiltibuie, Ross-shire, IV26 2YT	01854 622 348	★★★★	Self Catering	
Bothan Na'Tilleadh & Tigh Na'Tilleadh	Tigh na'Tilleadh, Polbain, Achiltibuie, Ullapool, Ross-shire, IV26 2YW	01854 622448	★★ → ★★★	Self Catering	
Cottage	Cottage, 230 Polbain, Achiltibuie, Ullapool IV26 2YW	01854 622361	★★★	Self Catering	
Stac Pollaidh Self Catering	Stac Pollaidh Self Catering, Achnahaird, Achiltibuie, Ullapool, Ross-shire, IV26 2YT	01854 622340	★★★ → ★★★★	Self Catering	

Achnasheen

Brentwood	Poolewe Partnership/ Poolewe Hotel, Poolewe, Achnasheen, Ross-shire, IV22 2JX	01445 781241	★★★	Self Catering	
Cairn Shiel	An Caorann, Melvaig, By Gairloch, Ross-shire, IV21 2EA	01445 771225	★★★★	Self Catering	
Fionn Cottage	Fionn Cottage, Achnasheen, Ross-shire, IV22 2EE	0208 896 0521	★★★	Self Catering	

By Achnasheen

Kildonan	14 Bruce Court, St Andrews Road, Dingwall, Ross-shire, IV15 9LG	01349 864317	★★★	Self Catering	
Caladh	Rowan Glen, Culbokie, Dingwall IV7 8JY	01349 877762	★★★	Self Catering	
Eilean View Bungalow and Apartment	1 Mellon Charles, Aultbea, Ross-shire, IV22 2JN	01445 731546	★★★★	Self Catering	

Airdrie

Acorn Cottage	Easter Glentore Farm, Slamannan Road, Greengairs, Airdrie, Lanarkshire, ML6 7TJ	01236 830243	★★★★	Self Catering	✦ 🍃🍃

Alexandria

Blairhosh Cottage	Blairhosh, by Balloch, Alexandria, Dumbartonshire, G83 8LY	01389 758267	★★	Self Catering	
Cameron House Lodges	Cameron House Lodges, Loch Lomond, Alexandria, Dunbartonshire, G83 8QZ	01389 755625	★★★★★	Self Catering	

Alford

Balfluig Castle	30 Abbey Gardens, London NW8 9AT	020 7624 3200	★★★	Self Catering	
Craich Cottage	Craich, Tough, Alford, Aberdeenshire, AB33 8EN	01975 562584	★★★	Self Catering	✦ 🍃
Haughton Country Park	Landscape Services, Aberdeenshire Council, Harlaw Way, Inverurie, Aberdeenshire, AB51 4SG	01467 627622	★ → ★★	Self Catering	
Kennels Cottage	National Trust for Scotland, 28 Charlotte Square, Edinburgh EH2 4ET	0131 243 9335	★★	Self Catering	

♿ Unassisted wheelchair access   ♿ Assisted wheelchair access   ✦ Access for visitors with mobility difficulties
🍃 Bronze Green Tourism Award   🍃🍃 Silver Green Tourism Award   🍃🍃🍃 Gold Green Tourism Award
For further information on our Green Tourism Business Scheme please see page 9.

| No 12 Station Court | Dockenwell, Sauchen, Inverurie, Aberdeenshire, AB51 7PJ | 01330 833548 | ★★★★ | Self Catering | |
| Steading Cottage | National Trust for Scotland, 28 Charlotte Square, Edinburgh EH2 4ET | 0131 243 9335 | ★★ | Self Catering | |

By Alford
| 5 Glenkindie Steadings | 60 Bowencraig, Largs, Ayrshire, KA30 8TB | 01475 674473 | ★★★★ | Self Catering | |

Alloa
| Orchard Lodge | c/o Gean House, Tullibody Road, Alloa, Clackmannanshire, FK10 2EL | 01259 226400 | ★★★★ | Self Catering | ⵌ |

Alloway
| South Lodge | Brigend House, Doonside Estate, Alloway, Ayr, KA7 4EB | 01292 441313 | ★★★ | Self Catering | ♿ |

Almondbank
| Moulinalmond Cottage | Moulinalmond Cottage, Moulinalmond, Almondbank, Perth, PH1 3NW | 01738 583206 | ★★★ | Self Catering | 🍃🍃 |

Alness
| Lower Inchlumpie | 118 Offington Avenue, Worthing, West Sussex, BN14 9PR | 01903 260334 | ★★★★ | Self Catering | |

Altnaharra
| Invermudale Annexe | Invermudale Annexe, Altnaharra, by Lairg, Sutherland, IV27 4UE | 01549 411250 | ★★★★ | Self Catering | ⵌ |

Alva
Balquharn Farm	Balquharn Farm, Alva, Clackmananshire, FK12 5NZ	01259 762490	★★★★	Self Catering	
Boll Holiday Cottages	Boll Farm, Brook Street, Alva, Clackmannanshire, FK12 5AW	01259 769638	★★★ → ★★★★	Self Catering	ⵌ
Barton of Muiryhill	55 Cecil Road, Lancing, West Sussex, BN15 8HP	01903 767273	★★★★	Self Catering	

Alyth
Cairnleith Cottage	22 Donaldson Avenue, Alloa, Clackmannanshire, FK10 2ET	01259 218408	★★★	Self Catering	
The Reed & The Toftin	Old Stables, Losset Road, Alyth, Perthshire, PH11 8BT	01828 632547	★★★	Self Catering	ⵌ
The Steadings	Upper Case Consultants Ltd, The Steading, Auchteralyth, Alyth, Perthshire, PH11 8JT	01575 530474	★★★★	Self Catering	
Ardormie Farm Cottage	Ardormie Farm, Ardormie, Alyth,Blairgowrie, Perthshire, PH11 8HL	01828 633047	★★★★	Self Catering	🍃🍃
Monument Cottage	Downie Hill House, Monikie, Angus, DD5 3QN	01382 370633	★★★★	Self Catering	
No 8 Shore	Private Dentistry, 61 High Street, Arbroath, Angus, DD11 1AN	01241 879111	★★★	Self Catering	

Annan
3 Woodhall	5 Woodhall, Eastriggs, Annan, Dumfries, DG12 6RH	01461 40814	★★★	Self Catering	
Cormorant & Dunlin Cottages	7 Browhouses, Eastriggs, Annan, Dumfriesshire, DG12 6TG	01461 40873	★★★	Self Catering	
Kinmount Court	Kinmount Leisure Ltd, Kinmount Court, Annan, Dumfriesshire, DG12 5RT	01461 700486	★★★	Self Catering	

Anstruther

6 Chalmers Brae	2312 Stratford Road, Hockley Heath, Solihull, West Midlands, B94 6NY	01564 782428	★★★★	Self Catering	
East and West Barns	Airdrie House, Anstruther, Fife, KY10 3LE	01333 310527	★★★★	Self Catering	
Fifie	Florence Villa, East End, Freuchie, Fife, KY15 7ET	01337 858805	★★★★	Self Catering	
Gardner Properties	Gardner Properties, 21 St Adrians Place, Anstruther, Fife, KY10 3DX	07812 663854	★★★ → ★★★★	Self Catering	
Harbour Views	The Waterfront, 18/20 Shore Street, Anstruther, Fife, KY10 3EA	01333 312200	★★★★	Self Catering	
Lobster Pot Cottage	Inchardie Farmhouse, Kilconquhar, Fife, KY9 1JU	01333 340640	★★★★	Self Catering	♿
Shore Holidays	11/25 Landsend Lane, Jacksonville, Florida 32225	07772 420692	★★★	Self Catering	
Sunny Patch	21 Moffat Ave, Carronshore, Falkirk FK2 8TB	01324 559976	★★★	Self Catering	
The Garden Flat and The Red House	The Great Lodging, 21 High Street, Anstruther Wester, Fife, KY103DJ	01333 312389	★★★ → ★★★★	Self Catering	
The Haven	Grand Productions Limited, 3 Robert Drive, Glasgow G51 3HE	0141 270 7000	★★★	Self Catering	

By Anstruther

The Gatehouse	4 Cluny Terrace, Edinburgh, Lothian, EH10 4SW	0131 4469011	★★★★	Self Catering	

Appin

Appin Holiday Homes	Appin Holiday Homes, Appin, Argyll, PA38 4BQ	01631 730287	★★★	Self Catering		
Appin House Apartments	Appin House Apartments & Lodges, Appin House, Appin, Argyll, PA38 4BN	01631 730207	★★★★	Self Catering	♿	🍃
Ardselma	160 Felsham Road, Putney, London, SW15 1DP	0208 788 2075	★★★	Self Catering		
Kinlochlaich House	Kinlochlaich House, Appin, Argyll, PA38 4BD	01631 730342	★★★ → ★★★★	Self Catering		
Loch Linnhe Lodges	Loch Linnhe Waterside Lodges, Kentallen Pier, Kentallen, Argyll, PA38 4BY	01631 740292	★★★	Self Catering		
The Farmhouse & The Lodge	SAC Advisory Office, Glencruitten Road, Oban, Argyll, PA34 4DW	01631 563093	★★★	Self Catering		

Applecross

Holly's House	Tigh A Phuist, Lonbain Applecross, Ross-shire, IV54 8XY	01520 744 399	★★★★	Self Catering	
Tigh Ruaraidh	Peggs Lane Cottage, Queniborough, Leicester LE7 3DF	01162 605726	★★★★	Self Catering	

Arbroath

Kirkton Mill House	Kirkton Mill Holidays, Inverkeilor, Arbroath, Angus, DDII 4UU	07966 135069	Awaiting Grading		
Saughmont Cottage	1 Firhills, Letham Grange, Arbraoth, Angus, DD11 4QZ	01241 890743	★★★	Self Catering	
The Steading Cottage	West Seaton, Arbroath, Angus, DD11 5SB	01241 873216	★★★	Self Catering	
Woodfield Cottage	Woodfield House, Forfar Road, Arbroath, Angus, DD11 3RB	01241 437456	★★★	Self Catering	

By Arbroath

The Chauffeurs Cottage & The Studio	Firm of P and R Ramsay, West Mains of Kinblethmont, By Arbroath, Angus, DD11 4RW	01241 890204	★★★★	Self Catering	

♿ Unassisted wheelchair access   ♿ Assisted wheelchair access   🚶 Access for visitors with mobility difficulties

🍃 Bronze Green Tourism Award   🍃🍃 Silver Green Tourism Award   🍃🍃🍃 Gold Green Tourism Award

For further information on our Green Tourism Business Scheme please see page 9.

Archiestown

| Ivy Cottage | Stonea, 3a Resaurie, Smithton, Inverness-shire, IV2 7NH | 01463 791714 | ★★ | Self Catering | |

Ardelve, by Kyle

| Tigh na Coille Flat | Conchra Self Catering Cottages, Tigh na Coille, Conchra, Aldelve, by Kyle of Lochalsh, Ross-shire, IV40 8DZ | 01520 722344 | ★★★★ | Self Catering | |
| Conchra Farm Cottages | Tigh-na-Coile, Conchra, Ardelve, Ross-shire, IV40 8DZ | 01520 722344 | ★★ → ★★★ | Self Catering | ᏁᏁ |

Arden

| The Gardener's Cottages | The Gardener's Cottages, Arden House, Arden, Dunbartonshire, G83 8RD | 01389 850601 | ★★★★ | Self Catering | ᏁᏁ |

Ardersier

| Dolphin Bay Suites | Woodside House, Piperhill, Nairn, Nairnshire, IV12 5SD | 01667 404604 | ★★★ | Self Catering | |

Ardgour

| Kingairloch Estate | Kingairloch Estate, Kingairloch, Ardgour, Fort William, PH33 7AE | 01967 411242 | ★★★ → ★★★★★ | Self Catering | |

Ardhasaig

| Clisham Cottage | Ardhasaig House, Ardhasaig, Isle of Harris HS3 3AJ | 01859 502500 | ★★★★ | Self Catering | |
| Seaview | Seaside Cottage, 5 Old Pier Road, Tarbert, Isle of Harris, Western Isles, HS3 3BQ | 01859 502845 | ★★★ | Self Catering | |

Ardlui

| Ardlui Luxury Lodges | Ardlui Holiday Home Park, Ardlui, Loch Lomond, Argyll, G83 7EB | 01301 704243 | ★★★★ | Self Catering | |
| McVey Lodge | Ardlui Holiday Park, Ardlui Hotel, Ardlui, Loch Lomond, Argyll, G83 2EB | 01301 704268 | ★★★ | Self Catering | |

Ardnamurchan

| Glenmore House, Cottage & Otter Lodge | Port an Aiseig, Glenborrodale, Acharacle, Argyll, PH36 4JP | 01972 500263 | ★★★★ → ★★★★★ | Self Catering | |

Ardrishaig

| Brenfield Shores | Brenfield Shores, Ardrishaig, Argyll, PA30 8ER | 01546 603284 | ★★★★ | Self Catering ⋀ | |
| Kilfinan View | Five Oaks, Knowl Wall, Beech, Stoke on Trent, Staffs, ST4 8SE | 01782 659303 | ★★★★ | Self Catering | |

Ardvasar

Loch Hourn	10 Aird, Ardvasar, Isle of Skye, IV45 8RN	01471 844 205	★★★★	Self Catering	
Oak Tree Cottage	Oak Tree Cottage, 233 Stainbeck Lane, Meanwood, Leeds, West Yorks, LS7 2PS	01132 781638	★★★	Self Catering	
The Old Church	Bramble Cottage, Hollins Green, Bradwall, Middlewich, CW10 0LA	01270 759635	★★★	Self Catering	

Argyll

East Kames	8 Undercliffe Rise, Ilkley, West Yorkshire, LS29 8RF	01943 601729	★★★★	Self Catering	
Linnhe Croft Holiday Cottages	Linnhe Croft, Holiday Cottages, Port Appin, Argyll, PA38 4DE	01631 730474	★★★	Self Catering	
No. 6 Feochan Cottages	13 The Glebe, Kilmelford, Argyll, PA34 4XF	01852 200346	★★★	Self Catering	

  ᰀ Unassisted wheelchair access   ᰁ Assisted wheelchair access   ⋀ Access for visitors with mobility difficulties
Ꮑ Bronze Green Tourism Award   ᏁᏁ Silver Green Tourism Award   ᏁᏁᏁ Gold Green Tourism Award
For further information on our Green Tourism Business Scheme please see page 9.

Awards correct as of mid August 2008

Arisaig

Achnaskia Croft	Ach na skia Croft, Arisaig, Inverness-shire, PH39 4NS	01687 450606	★★★ → ★★★★	Self Catering	🍀🍀
Caimbebridge House, Caimbebridge Studio	Invercambie Croft and Caravan site, Arisaig, Inverness-shire, PH39 4NT	07918 872309	★★★ → ★★★★	Self Catering	
Camusdarach Enterprises	Camusdarach Enterprises, Camusdarach, Arisaig, Inverness - shire, PH39 4NT	01687 450221	★★★	Self Catering	
Derryfad House	Derryfad Holiday Home, Back of Keppoch, Arisaig, Inverness-shire, PH39 4NS	01687 450667	★★★	Self Catering	
Kinloid Cottages	Kilmartin Farm Guesthouse, Kinloid Farm, Kilmartin, Arisaig, Inverness-shire, PH39 4NS	01687 450366	★★★	Self Catering	
Kinneddar Lodges	Kinneddar Properties, Kinneddar House, Lossiemouth, Morayshire, IV31 6SA	01343 814845	★★ → ★★★	Self Catering	
Traigh Lodges	Traigh Lodges, Arisaig, Inverness-shire, PH39 4NT	01687 450645	★★ → ★★★	Self Catering	

Armadale

Hughag's House	177 Cheltenham Road, Longlevens, Gloucester, Gloucestershire, GL2 0JJ	01452 525627	★★★	Self Catering

Arncroach

The Old Barn	Alexander Whiteford & Company, Over Kellie Farm, ARNCROACH, Fife, KY10 2RX	01333 720235	★★★★	Self Catering

Aros

Argyll House	Argyll House, Salen, Aros, Isle of Mull, PA72 6JG	01680 300555	★★★	Self Catering
Rowan Cottage	46 Robslee Road, Giffnock, Glasgow, G46 7BX	0141 638 6287	★★★	Self Catering
Seaview Cottage	Ulva, Newlands Road, Jackton, East Kilbride G75 8RS	07802 632273	★★★★	Self Catering
The Bothy	The Old Byre, Dervaig, Isle of Mull, PA75 6QR	01688 400229	★★★	Self Catering
The Old Stables	Creag A' Croman, Salen, Isle of Mull, Argyll, PA72 6JB	01680 300557	★★★	Self Catering
The Square, The Farmhouse & The Dairy	Ivy Cottage, Owslebury, Winchester, Hampshire, SO21 1LN	01680 300371	★★ → ★★★	Self Catering

Arrochar

Argyll View Cottage	Argyle View Cottage, Main Street, Arrochar, Dunbartonshire, G83 7AA	01301 702932	★★★	Self Catering
Mansefield House	Mansefield House, Shore Road, Arrochar, Argyll, G83 7AG	01301 702956	★★★★	Self Catering
Tighairn Cottage	Mansfield House, Arrochar, Argyll & Bute, G83 7AH	01301 702956	★★★	Self Catering

Ascog, Isle of Bute

Balmory Hall	Balmory Hall, Ascog, Isle of Bute, PA20 9LL	01700 500669	★★★★	Self Catering

Ashkirk

Headshaw Farm Holiday Cottage	Headshaw Farm, Ashkirk, Selkirk, TD7 4NT	01750 32233	★★★★	Self Catering
New Woll Estate	New Woll Estate, Ashkirk, Selkirkshire, TD7 4PE	01750 32799	★★★★	Self Catering
Synton Mains Farm	The Davies Partnership, Synton Mains Farm, Ashkirk, Selkirk, TD7 4PA	01750 32388	★★★	Self Catering 🦽

 ♿ Unassisted wheelchair access   🦽 Assisted wheelchair access   🚶 Access for visitors with mobility difficulties
🍀 Bronze Green Tourism Award   🍀🍀 Silver Green Tourism Award   🍀🍀🍀 Gold Green Tourism Award
For further information on our Green Tourism Business Scheme please see page 9.

Askernish, Isle of South Uist

298 Kilpheader	Heatherview, Askernish, Isle Of Uist, HS8 5SY	01878 700204	★★★	Self Catering	

Auchenblae

The Cottage	Cedar House, Kintore, Auchenblane, Aberdeenshire, AB30 1XP	01561 320340	★★	Self Catering	
Drumtochty Stables	1 Bernham Crescent, Stonehaven, Aberdeendhire, AB39 2WQ	01569 760982	★★★★	Self Catering	

Auchencairn

Hazel Cottage	Rascarrel Farm, Auchencairn, Kirkcudbrightshire, DG7 1RJ	01556 640210	★★★★	Self Catering	
Studio Cottage	Carlingwark Cottage, Carlingwark Street, Castle Douglas DG7 1HD	01556 503932	★★	Self Catering	
Craigshall Cottage	Craigshall, Shore Road, Auchencairn, Castle Douglas, Kirkcudbrightshire, DG7 1QY	01556 640028	★★★	Self Catering	

Auchengray

Muirhall Holiday Cottages	Muirhall Holiday Cottages, Muirhall Farm, Auchengray, Lanarkshire, ML11 8LL	01501 785240	★★★★★	Self Catering	

Auchenmalg

Seabank	Dalhabboch Farm, New Luce Newton Stewart, DG8 0AY	01581 600228	★★★	Self Catering	

Auchrannie

Cloy Lodge	58-60 Hamilton Street, Saltcoats, Ayrshire, KA21 5DS	01294 472772	★★★★	Self Catering	

Auchterarder

Duchally Country Estate	Duchally Country Estate, by Gleneagles, Auchterarder, Perthshire, PH3 1PN	01764 663071	★★★★★	Self Catering	&.
Glenearn Country Cottages	Dalfruan Cottage, Orchil Road, Auchterarder, Perth, PH3 1NB	01764 660224	★★★★★	Self Catering	
Glenmhor	Duncairn, Orchil Road, Auchterarder, Perthshire, PH3 1LS	01764 664575	★★★★	Self Catering	
Greenacres	Broadlees Industrial Estate, Carlisle Road, Chapelhall, Airdrie, North Lanarkshire, ML6 8RH	07836 683612	★★★★	Self Catering	
No 17 Guthrie Court	Cliath Holidays, Hillhall, Drummawhandie Road, Crieff, Perthshire, PH7 4DS	07789 692518	★★★★	Self Catering	
No. 28 Dunbar Court	79 Springkell Avenue, Pollokshields, Glasgow G41 4DL	0141 4231480	★★★★	Self Catering	
Panholes Cottages	Mains of Panholes, Blackford, Auchterarder, Perthshire, PH4 1RF	01764 682351	★★★★★	Self Catering	
The Old Dairy Cottage	Ben Lawers, The Old Dairy, Auchterarder, PH3 1AB	01764 662369	★★★	Self Catering	

Auchterhouse

The Hideaway	Balkello Farm, Auchterhouse, Dundee, DD3 0RA	01382 320261	★★★★	Self Catering	

Auchtermuchty

Baincraig Lodge	Baincraig Lodge, Leckiebank Road, Auchtermuchty, Fife, KY14 7EB	01337 828386	★★★★	Self Catering	🍃
Pitcairlie House	Pitcairlie House, Auchtermuchty, Fife, KY14 6EU	01337 828464	★★★★	Self Catering	

&. Unassisted wheelchair access   &. Assisted wheelchair access   ↟ Access for visitors with mobility difficulties
🍃 Bronze Green Tourism Award   🍃🍃 Silver Green Tourism Award   🍃🍃🍃 Gold Green Tourism Award
For further information on our Green Tourism Business Scheme please see page 9.

Auldearn

Boath Stables	Boath Stables, Boath Steading, Auldearn, Nairn, IV12 5TE	01667 451300	★★★★	Self Catering	🍃🍃
Firth View and Larch Cottage	Broomton Farm Cottages, Broomton Farm, Auldearn, Nairnshire, IV12 5LB	01309 641505	★★★★	Self Catering	
The Cottage	Newton of Park Farm, Auldearn, Nairn, IV12 5HY	01667 453261	★★★	Self Catering	
The Sheiling	17 Tenby Road, Chadwell Heath, Romford, Essex, RM6 6NB	020 8597 7280	★★★	Self Catering	

Auldgirth

The Byre	The Byre, Low Kirkbride, Auldgirth, Dumfries, DG2 0SP	01387 820258	★★★★	Self Catering	♿

Aultbea

31 Mellon Charles	8 Ormiscaig, Aultbea, Achnasheen, Ross-shire, IV22 2JJ	01445 731382	★★★★	Self Catering	♿
Aultbea Highland Lodges	c/o 4 Winds, Golf Road, Brora KW9 6QT	01408 621041	★★★★	Self Catering	
Ewe View	Ewe View, Drumchork, Aultbea, Ross-shire, IV22 2HU	01445 731394	★★★	Self Catering	
Mellondale Bungalows	Mellondale, 47 Mellon Charles, Aultbea, Ross-shire, IV22 2JL	01445 731326	★★★★	Self Catering	
Willow Cottage Flat	Willow Cottage, Ormiscaig, Aultbea, Ross-shire, IV22 2JJ	01445 731263	★★★	Self Catering	

Aviemore

10 Spey Avenue	Home Farm, Murchieson Road, Houston, Renfrewshire, PA6 7JU	01505 613665	★★★	Self Catering	
108 Dalnabay	12 Braidpark Drive, Giffnock, Glasgow G46 6NB	0141 633 2656	★★★	Self Catering	
3 Dalfaber Park	18 Millbank, Balerno, Edinburgh EH14 7GA	0131 466 6917	★★★★	Self Catering	
45 Dalnabay	6 Dean Park Gardens, Kirkcaldy, Fife, KY2 6XX	01592 203883	★★★	Self Catering	
7 Morlich Place & 140 Dalnabay	Mossywood House, Mossywood Farm, Cumbernauld G67 4HF	01236 879390	★★★	Self Catering	
81 Dalnabay	1 Kincaid Street, Greenock, Renfrewshire, PA16 7TN	01475 632779	★★★★	Self Catering	
Aberlour	3 Riccartsbar Avenue, Paisley, Renfrewshire, PA2 6BQ	0141 847 1558	★★★★	Self Catering	
Achlean	17 Ashburnham Gardens, South Queensferry, West Lothian, EH30 9LB	0131 331 4941	★★★★	Self Catering	
Appintree Cottage	30C Albany Road, West Ferry, Dundee PH22 1TD	01382 480619	★★★	Self Catering	
Ard Tigh	Aviemore Holiday Lets, 20 Burnside Way, Largs, Aryshire, KA30 DL	01475 673885	★★★★	Self Catering	
Avielochan Farm Holiday Cottages	Avielochan Farm, Aviemore, Inverness-shire, PH22 1QD	01479 810846	★★★	Self Catering	⚡
Aviemore Holiday Homes	Aviemore Holiday Homes, 113 Dalnabay, Aviemore PH22 1TA	01479 810499	★★★ → ★★★★	Self Catering	⚡
Avonglen	Flat 0/2, 2 St Francis Rigg, Gorbals, Glasgow G5 0UF	07999 819762	★★★★	Self Catering	
Badaguish	Badaguish, Cairngorm Outdoor Centre, Aviemore, Inverness-shire, PH22 1QU	01479 861285	★★★	Self Catering	♿
Ben Bheag	83 Ellon Road, Paisley, Renfrewshire, PA3 4BW	0141 587 0451	★★★	Self Catering	
Birch End	47 Commonside, Selston, Notts NG16 6FN	01773 510041	★★★	Self Catering	

♿ Unassisted wheelchair access   ♿ Assisted wheelchair access   ⚡ Access for visitors with mobility difficulties
🍃 Bronze Green Tourism Award   🍃🍃 Silver Green Tourism Award   🍃🍃🍃 Gold Green Tourism Award
For further information on our Green Tourism Business Scheme please see page 9.

Name	Address	Phone	Rating	Type	
Birchwood, 14 Cairn Slowne and The Scott's House	Ashfield, 31 Nash Road, Great Horwood, Bucks, MK17 0RA	01296 714400/01296	★★★	Self Catering	
Braeriach	3 Iain Road, Bearsden, Glasgow G61 4LX	0141 586 5024	★★★★	Self Catering	
Caberfeidh Log Cabin	Ralia, Newtonmore, Inverness-shire, PH20 1BD	01540 673177	★★★	Self Catering	
Cairngorm Highland Bungalows	Glen Einich, 29 Grampian View, Aviemore, Inverness-shire, PH22 1TF	01479 810653	★★★ → ★★★★	Self Catering	
Cairngorm Holiday Bungalows	Glen Einich, 29 Grampian View, Aviemore, Inverness-shire, PH22 1TF	01479 810653	★★★	Self Catering	
Caledonia Holiday & Leisure	7 Carn Dearg, Osprey Grange, Aviemore, Inverness-shire, PH22 1LQ	01479 811326	★★★	Self Catering	
Claymore	8 William Street, Cairnbulg Aberdeenshire, AB43 8WS	01346 582035	★★	Self Catering	
Cooks Cottage	Lynwilg House, Aviemore, Inverness-shire, PH22 1PZ	01479 811685	★★★★	Self Catering	
Craigellachie View	Tremayne, Dalfaber Road, Aviemore, Inverness-shire, PH24 1PU	01479 810694	★★★	Self Catering	
Culduthel	48 Davieland Road, Glasgow, East Renfrewshire, G46 7LX	0141 638 1258	★★★★	Self Catering	
D&K Charnley	3 Witcutt Way, Wishaw, Lanarkshire ML2 OAP	01698 360823	★★★	Self Catering	
Drumchork	Puldohran, G'ryffe Road, Kilmalcolm, Renfrewshire, PA13 4BA	01479 811347	★★★	Self Catering	
Falcon Lodge	Highland Holiday Homes, Station Sq, Grampian Rd, Aviemore, Inverness-shire, PH22 1PD	01479 811463	★★★	Self Catering	
Glenrothay	Mambeag, Lochiepots Road, Miltonduff, Elgin, Moray, IV30 8WL	01343 540608	★★★	Self Catering	
Great North Lodges	The River House Stables, 2A Dalfaber Road, Aviemore PH22 1PU	01479 811400	★★★★ → ★★★★★	Self Catering	
Heiland Hame	Superior Highland Lets, 14 Scott Street, Largs, Ayrshire, KA30 9NU	01475 689921	★★★	Self Catering	
High Range Self Catering Chalets	High Range Holiday Lodges, Grampian Road, Aviemore, Inverness-shire, PH22 1PT	01479 810636	★★★ → ★★★★	Self Catering	♿
Hilton Coylumbridge	Hilton Craigendarroch Resort, Braemar Road, Ballater AB35 5XA	01479 810661	★★★★	Self Catering	🍃
Inchmurrin,claireinch and Keppinch	12 Inch Murrin, East Kilbride G74 2JX	07771 957390	★★★★	Self Catering	
Lairig Vue	Lairig Vue, 5 Dalfaber Park, Aviemore, Inverness-shire, PH22 1QF	01479 810212	★★★	Self Catering	
Locha'an	11 Alltmor, Aviemore, Inverness-shire, PH22 1QQ	01479 810735	★★★	Self Catering	
Lochan Mhor Apartment	6 Rosehaugh High Drive, Avoch, Ross-shire, IV9 8RX	01381 622461	★★★★	Self Catering	
Macdonald Dalfaber Golf & Country Club	MacDonald Dalfaber Golf and Country Club, Dalfaber Drive, Aviemore, Highland, PH22 1ST	01479 811244	★★ → ★★★★	Self Catering	
Macdonald Highland Lodges	Macdonald Highland Lodges, Aviemore, Inverness-shire, PH22 1PJ	01479 815100	★★★★	Serviced Apartments	🍃
Mairi Sine	North Muir of Rettie, Boyndie, Banff, Banffshire, AB45 2LS	01261 842699	★★★★	Self Catering	
McAndrew House	Aviemore Luxury Accommodation, c/o 22 Woodlands Crescent, Aberdeen, Aberdeenshire, AB15 9DH	07725 470765	★★★★	Self Catering	⚡
Pine Bank Chalets	Pine Bank Chalets, Dalfaber Road, Aviemore, Inverness-shire, PH22 1PX	01479 810000	★★★ → ★★★★	Self Catering	⚡
Pityoulish Estate Cottages	Mill of Cantray, Cawdor, Nairn, IV12 5XT	01667 493312	★★	Self Catering	
Silver Birch Cottage	Flat 9, 5 Woodlands Gate, Glasgow G3 6HX	07768 054291	★★★★	Self Catering	
Silverglades Holiday Homes	Silverglades Holiday Homes, Dalnabay, Aviemore, Inverness-shire, PH22 1TD	01479 810165	★★★	Self Catering	♿

& Unassisted wheelchair access   & Assisted wheelchair access   ⚡ Access for visitors with mobility difficulties
🍃 Bronze Green Tourism Award   🍃🍃 Silver Green Tourism Award   🍃🍃🍃 Gold Green Tourism Award
For further information on our Green Tourism Business Scheme please see page 9.

Speyside Leisure Park	Speyside Leisure Park, Dalfaber Road, Aviemore, Inverness-shire, PH22 1PX	01479 810236	★★ → ★★★	Self Catering
Sunbury	6 Hamilton Avenue, Glasgow G41 4JF	07753 622959	★★★★	Self Catering
The Apartment	22 Cromwell Road, Winnington, Northwich, Cheshire, CW8 4BN	01606 782891	★★★	Self Catering
The Highland Council @ Badaguish	The Highland Council at Badaguish, Sluggan, Aviemore, Highland, PH22 1QU	01479 861734	★★★	Self Catering ♿
The Retreat	Strathspey House, Grampian Road, Aviemore, Inverness-shire, PH22 1RP	01479 812453	★★★★	Self Catering

By Aviemore

| Aquila Lodge | Aquila Lodge, c/o The Old Joiners Shed, High Street, Markington, Harrogate, North Yorks, HS3 3NR | 01765 677508 | ★★★★ | Self Catering |
| Meikle House | Tremayne, Dalfaber Road, Aviemore, Inverness-shire, PH24 1PU | 01479 810694 | ★★★★ | Self Catering |

Avoch

| Bay Farm Holiday Cottages | Rosehaugh Estate Office, Avoch, Ross-Shire, IV9 8RF | 01463 811205 | ★★★★ | Self Catering |

Ayr

12 Marlborough Court & Flat D,	Failford House, Mauchline, Ayrshire, KA5 5TA	01290 550483	★★★	Self Catering
5A Park Circus	5 Park Circus, Ayr KA7 2DJ	07968 749945	★★★	Self Catering
Citadel Penthouse	Langley bank, 39 Carrick Road, Ayr, Ayrshire, KA7 2RD	01292 264246	★★★★	Self Catering
Country Courtyard Cottages	Country Courtyard Cottages, Bellsbank Farm, Ayr, Ayrshire, KA6 5JP	01292 570251	★★★★	Self Catering
Craig Tara Holiday Park	Craig Tara Holiday Park, Dunure Road, Ayr, Ayrshire, KA7 4LB	01292 265141	★★★	Self Catering
Orchid House	Ardeer Steading, Stevenson, Ayrshire, KA20 3DD	01294 465438	★★★★	Self Catering
Perryston Farm Cottage	Perryston Farm, Dunure Road, Ayr, Ayrshire, KA7 4LD	01292 441315	★★★	Self Catering
Stewartlea Stables	Dalruwzion, Fort William Road, Newtonmore, Highland, PH20 1DG	01540 673447	★★★	Self Catering
Turnberry House	26 Brodie Road, Woodford, Stockport, Cheshire, SK7 1QJ	07919 174484	★★★	Self Catering
Oakley Property Rentals	Oakley, 17 Ayr Road, Prestwick, Ayrshire, KA9 1SX	01292 474642	★★★ → ★★★★	Self Catering

By Ayr

Auldbyres Bungalow	Auldbyres Farmhouse, by Ayr, Ayrshire, KA6 6HG	01292 570301	★★★	Self Catering
Bothy Cottage	Dunduff Farm, Dunure, Ayr, Ayrshire, KA7 4LH	01292 500225	★★★	Self Catering
Gadgirth Estate Lodges	Gadgirth Cottage, Annbank, by Ayr, Ayrshire, KA6 5AJ	01292 520721	★★★★	Self Catering

Ayton

| Foulden Hill Farm | Foulden Hill Farm, Ayton, Berwickshire, TD15 1UG | 018907 81207 | ★★★ | Self Catering |

Backies, Golspie

| The Log Cabin | The Old School, Ann Street, Gatehouse of Fleet, Kirkcudbrightshire, DG7 2HU | 01557 814058 | ★★ | Self Catering |

♿ Unassisted wheelchair access   ♿ Assisted wheelchair access   ♟ Access for visitors with mobility difficulties
🍃 Bronze Green Tourism Award   🍃🍃 Silver Green Tourism Award   🍃🍃🍃 Gold Green Tourism Award
For further information on our Green Tourism Business Scheme please see page 9.

To find out more, call 0845 22 55 121 or go to visitscotland.com.

Balfron Station

Oldhall Cottages	Oldhall Cottages, Glenside House, Balfron, by Glasgow, G63 0RP	01360 440136	★★★	Self Catering	
Ballat Smithy Cottage	Ballat Smithy Cottage, Ballat Smithy, Balfron Station, Stirlingshire, G63 0SE	01360 440269	★★★★	Self Catering	🍃🍃
Ballochruin Farm Accommodation	Ballochruin Farm, Balfron Station, Stirlingshire, G63 0LE	01360 440496	★★★★	Self Catering	
The Stables & The Ploughmans Cottage	Loch Lomond and Trossachs Farm Cottages, Meikle Camoquhill Farm, Balfron, Glasgow, G63 0QW	01360 440325	★★★★	Self Catering	🚶

Balivanich, Isle of Benbecula

Gramsdale Inn Holiday Home	3 Gramsdale, Balivanich, Benbecula, HS7 5LZ	01870 602432	★★	Self Catering	

Ballachulish

Ben Vheir Cottage	Ben Vheir House, Glenachulish, Ballachulish, Argyll, PH49 4JX	01855 811200	★★★★	Self Catering	
Cherry Cottage	Swallowcroft, Achindarroch, Duror of Appin, Argyll, PA38 4BS	08081 787564	★★★★	Self Catering	
Glencoe Hideaway, Lochview	23 Southcote Rise, Ruislip, Middlesex, HA4 7LN	01895 675662	★★★	Self Catering	
Holly Cottage	13 Croft Road, Ballachulish, Argyll, PH49 4JW	01855 811419	★★★★	Self Catering	
Lia-Fail	4 Windyedge Cottage Crosshouse, Kilmarnock, East Ayrshire, KA2 0BX	07974 330861	Awaiting Grading		
Number 1,2,and 3 Quarry Cottages	Carefree Self Catering Holicays, Clachaig Inn, Glencoe, Aryll, PH49 4HX	01855 811252	★★★★	Self Catering	
Red Peak	Farleigh, Broadway, Fairlight Cove, East Sussex, TN35 4DA	01424 813249	★★★★	Self Catering	
Sorcha	Flat 1 Main Street, Inverkip, Renfrewshire, PA16 0AU	01475 522536	★★★	Self Catering	
Stone Cottage	Stone Cottage, Tigh Phuirt, Ballachulish, Argyll, PH49 4AN	01855 811115	★★★	Self Catering	

Ballantrae

Auchenflower Cottage	Auchenflower Farm House, Auchenflower Farm, Ballantrae, Girvan, Ayrshire, KA26 0LW	01465 831077	★★★	Self Catering	
Balnowlart Lodge	Ardstinchar Cottage, 81 Main Street, Ballantrae, Ayrshire, KA26 0NA	01465 831343	★★★	Self Catering	

Ballater

Arisaig Cottage	36 Victoria Road, Ballater, Aberdeenshire, AB35 5QX	013397 55177	★★★★	Self Catering	
Averill	18 Clydeford Drive, Uddingston, Glasgow, G71 7DJ	01698 811932	★★★	Self Catering	
Ballater Lodge	124 Craighall Road, Glasgow G4 9TR	0141 332 3211	★★★★	Self Catering	
Balmoral Estates	Balmoral Estates, Balmoral, Ballater, Aberdeenshire, AB35 5TB	01339 742534	★★★	Self Catering	
Bonn-na Coille	Bonn-Na Coille, 8 Braemar Road, Ballater, Aberdeenshire, AB35 5RL	01339 755414	★★★★	Self Catering	♿
Bruach Mhor	Holburn Properties Ltd, 26 Seafield Drive West, Aberdeen, Aberdeenshire, AB15 7XA	01224 315607	★★★	Self Catering	
Claybokie	National Trust for Scotland, 28 Charlotte Square, Edinburgh EH2 4ET	0131 243 9335	★★★★★	Self Catering	
Craig Vallich	Jackal Properties, 12 Bayview Road, Aberdeen, Aberdeenshire, AB15 4EY	01224 317713	★★★★	Self Catering	
Hilton Craigendarroch	Hilton Craigendarroch Resort, Braemar Road, Ballater, Aberdeenshire, AB35 5XA	01339 755558	★★★★ → ★★★★★	Self Catering	🍃

& Unassisted wheelchair access   &. Assisted wheelchair access   🚶 Access for visitors with mobility difficulties
🍃 Bronze Green Tourism Award   🍃🍃 Silver Green Tourism Award   🍃🍃🍃 Gold Green Tourism Award
For further information on our Green Tourism Business Scheme please see page 9.

Invercauld Lodges	Invercauld Lodges, Invercauld Road, Ballater, Aberdeenshire, AB35 5RP	01339 755015	★★★★	Self Catering		
Lary Cottage	Shepley Carr House, Shepley, Huddersfield HD8 8BR	01484 606258	★★★★	Self Catering		
Myrtle Cottage	East Steading, South Bandodle, Midmar, Inverurie, AB51 7NN	01224 205819	★★★★	Self Catering		
Rosedale Cottage	Rosedale Cottage, Roscobie,Kirk Drive, Cults, Aberdeenshire, AB15 9RG	01224 867975	★★★	Self Catering		
The Coach House & the Garden House	Balgonie, Braemar Place, Ballater, Aberdeenshire, AB55 5NQ	01339 755482	★★★★	Self Catering		
The Firs	12 Woodburn Avenue, Aberdeen, Aberdeenshire, AB15 8JQ	01224 312069	★★★★	Self Catering		
Tigh-Na-Croabh	21 St Swithin Street, Aberdeen, Aberdeenshire, AB10 6XB	01224 318257	★★★★	Self Catering		
6 Braichlie Buildings	12 Skateraw Road, Newtonhill, Stonehaven, Kincardineshire, AB39 9PT	01569 731831	★★★	Self Catering		
7 Old Stables Courtyard	Tresta, 35A Forbesfield Road, Aberdeen AB15 4NX	01224 316876	★★★	Self Catering		

By Ballater

No 3 Knocks Cottages	Catbells, Orestan Lane, Effingham, Leatherhead, Surrey, KT24 5SN	01372 459123	★★★★	Self Catering		
Royal Deeside Log Cabins	Royal Deeside Woodland Lodges, Dinnet, Nr Ballater, Royal Deeside, Aberdeenshire, AB34 5LW	013398 85229	★★★	Self Catering		

Ballindalloch

Bluefolds Highland Holiday Cottages	Bluefolds Highland Holiday Cottages, Folds Cottage, Glenlivet, Ballindalloch, Banffshire, AB37 9DS	01340 881616	★★★★	Self Catering		⌂
Cragganmore Lodge	Heatherstalks, Avonbridge, Falkirk FK1 2LD	07887 621443	★★★	Self Catering		
Easter Corrie	Easter Corrie, Tomnavoulin, Ballindalloch, Banffshire, AB37 9JB	01807 590241	★★★	Self Catering	⅄	⌂⌂⌂

Ballinluig

Cherry Cottage	Cherry Cottage, Ballinluig, Perthshire, PH9 0LG	01796 482409	★★★★	Self Catering		

Balloch

Laudervale Gardens	1 Drumkinnon Road, Balloch G83 8SX	0791 814 2090	★★★★	Self Catering		
Lomond Fairways	PF 56602, FCO Islamabad, King Charles Street, London SW1A 2AH	07855 769338	★★★★	Self Catering		
Lomond Woods Holiday Park	Lomond Woods Holiday Park, Old Luss Road, Balloch, Dunbartonshire, G83 8QP	01389 755000	★★★★	Self Catering		
Palombos of Balloch	Palombos of Balloch, Loch Lomond, 40-48 Balloch Road, Balloch, Alexandria, West Dunbartonshire, G83 8LE	01389 753501	★★	Self Catering		
Park View Apartment	Kyme House, 3 Upper Carman Road, Renton G82 4LZ	01389 755792	★★★★	Self Catering		
Riverside Court & Drumkinnon Apartment 1/1	2 Endrick Wynd, Helensburgh G84 7SU	01436 676564	★★★ → ★★★★★	Self Catering		
The Old Smiddy	The Old Smiddy, Haldane Terrace, Balloch, Alexandria, G83 8ER	01389 750767	★★★	Self Catering		

Ballygrant, Isle of Islay

Craigard Holiday Accommodation	Craigard Holiday Accommodation, Traigh Cill an Rubha, Bridgend, Isle of Islay, PA44 7NY	01496 810728	★★ → ★★★★★	Self Catering	⅄	⌂⌂

Balmacara

Craggan Cottage	National Trust for Scotland, 28 Charlotte Square, Edinburgh EH2 4ET	0131 243 9335	★★★	Self Catering		

Balmaclellan

West Holmhead Cottage	Craig Farm, Balmaclellan, Castle Douglas DG7 3QS	01644 420636	★★★	Self Catering

Balmaha

Loch Lomond Waterfront	Loch Lomond Waterfront, Main Road, Balmaha, Stirlingshire, G63 0JQ	01360 870446	★★★★★	Self Catering

Balnain

Lochletter Lodges	Lochletter Lodges, Balnain, Drumnadrochit, Inverness-shire, IV63 6TJ	01456 476313	★★★	Self Catering ♿

Balquhidder

Gartnafuaran Farm Cottage	Gartnafuaran Farm, Balquhidder, Perthshire, FK19 8PB	01877 384221	★★★★	Self Catering
Kings House Cottages	Kings House Hotel, Balquhidder, Perthshire, FK19 8NY	01877 384646	★★★	Self Catering
Loch Voil Cottage	Meadhon Monachyle, Monachyle Tuarach, Balquhidder, Perthshire, FK19 8PB	01877 384740	★★★	Self Catering ♀
Lochside Cottages	Muirlaggan, Balquhidder, Lochearnhead, Perthshire, FK19 8PB	01877 384219	★★★★	Self Catering ♿

Balvicar

Kilbride Cottage	Kilbride Croft, Balvicar, Isle of Seil, PA34 4RD	01852 300475	★★ → ★★★	Self Catering
Achnacroish Cottage	7 Shearwater Road, Cheam, Surrey SM1 2AR	020 8661 1834	★★★	Self Catering

Banavie

Inverskilavulin	Hightrees Cottage, West Larrach, Ballachullish PH49 4JQ	01855 811475	★★★★	Self Catering
Seangan Self Catering	3 Verona Avenue, Glasgow G11 5BL	0141 5890014	★★★	Self Catering

Banchory

Birch & Willow Lodges	Craiglea, Inchmarlo Home Farm, Banchory, Aberdeenshire, AB31 4BT	01330 822622	★★★★	Self Catering ♀
Bridge of Bennie Cottage	Bridge of Bennie House, Banchory, Kincardinshire, AB31 5PY	01330 824288	★★★★	Self Catering ♀
Cluny Cottage	Cluny Crichton, Banchory, Aberdeen-shire, AB31 4EB	01330 825555	★★★	Self Catering
East Lodge	National Trust for Scotland, 28 Charlotte Square, Edinburgh EH2 4ET	0131 243 9335	★★★	Self Catering
Greenlands	Ballogie Estate Enterprises, Ballogie Estate Office, Aboyne, Aberdeenshire, AB34 5DS	01339 886497	★★★★	Self Catering
Inchmarlo Golf Club	Inchmarlo, Banchory, Royal Deeside AB31 4BQ	01330 826420	★★★★	Serviced Apartments
Manse Croft	18 Oak Tree Avenue, Banchory, Kincardinshire, AB31 5ZX	07702 269609	★★★★	Self Catering
No. 40 Scolty Place	3 Grant Road, Banchory, Aberdeenshire, AB31 5WA	01330 823143	★★★★	Self Catering
Oakhill Apartments	Oakhill House, Banchory-Devenick, Aberdeen, Aberdeenshire, AB12 5XN	07912 058441	★★★★ → ★★★★★	Serviced Apartments
The Pine Lodge	Greenpark House, Banchory, Aberdeenshire, AB31 4DB	01330 825544	★★★★	Self Catering
Toll Bridge Lodge	Toll House, Bridge of Feugh, Banchory, Kincardinshire, AB31 6NH	01330 822686	★★★★	Self Catering

♿ Unassisted wheelchair access   ♿ Assisted wheelchair access   ♀ Access for visitors with mobility difficulties
🄿 Bronze Green Tourism Award   🄿🄿 Silver Green Tourism Award   🄿🄿🄿 Gold Green Tourism Award
For further information on our Green Tourism Business Scheme please see page 9.

By Banchory

Woodend Chalet Holidays	Laigh Riggs, Kincardine Road, Torphins, Banchory, Aberdeenshire, AB31 4GH	01339 882562	★★★ → ★★★★	Self Catering	♿
The Bothy @ Collonach	Keirn of Collonach, Drumoak, Kincardineshire, AB31 5HL		★★★★	Self Catering	
Drumhead Cottage	Drumhead Cottage, Drumhead, Finzean, by Banchory, Aberdeenshire, AB31 6PB	01330 850771	★★★★	Self Catering	

Banff

57A Denside	18 Victoria Street, Arbroath, Angus, DD11 2BP	01241 874718	★★★★	Self Catering	
6 Turnkeys	Silverwells Farm, Turriff, Aberdeenshire, AB53 8BS	01888 568804	★★★	Self Catering	
Badger Cottage	Wood of Shaws, Alvah, Banff, Banff-shire, AB45 3UL	01261 821223	★★★	Self Catering	
Cowfords Cottage	Culbirnie, Banff, Aberdeenshire, AB45 3AX	01261 843227	★	Self Catering	
Craig Cottage	Banff Country Estate, Craig Alvah Lodge, Bridge of Alvah, Banff, Aberdeenshire, AB45 3TD	01261 821552	★★★★	Self Catering	
Mill of Alvah	Craigewan, 8 Doocot Park, Banff, Aberdeenshire, AB45 1DW	01261 818557	★★	Self Catering	
Mitchell's Cottage	21 Powis Terrace, Aberdeen, Aberdeen-shire, AB45 3YP	07803 503052	★★★★	Self Catering	
St Brandon House Cottages	St Brandon House Cottages, Boyndie, Banff, Aberdeenshire, AB45 2JT	01261 843234	★★★★	Self Catering	
The Lodge	Fife Lodge, Sanyhill Road, Banff, Aberdeenshire, AB45 1BE	01261 812436	★★★	Self Catering	

By Banff

1 & 2 Dallochy Cottages, Boyndie	Dallachy Farm, Boyndie, Banff, AB45 2LA	01261 861206	★★★	Self Catering	
Crovie Cottage (No. 7)	National Trust for Scotland, 28 Charlotte Square, Edinburgh EH2 4ET	0131 243 9335	★★★★	Self Catering	
Antiquity Cottage	Antiquity Cottage, Thorax Farm, Banff, Aberdeenshire, AB45 2HT	01466 751278	★★★★	Self Catering	

Baquhidder Station

Leitters Cottage	Leitters, Balquhidder Station, Perthshire, FK19 8NX	01567 830212	★★★★	Self Catering	

Barcaldine

Lochside Lodges	Lochside Lodges, Creran Moorings, Barcaldine, Oban, Argyll, PA37 1SG	01631 720265	★★★	Self Catering	
Creran Chalets	Barcaldine Home Farm, Barcaldine, Oban, Argyll, PA37 1SG	01631 720 253	★★★	Self Catering	

Barvas, Isle of Lewis

24 Lower Shader	79 Chessfield Park, Little Chalfont, Bucks, HP6 6RX	01494 763074	★★	Self Catering	
Ocean View	1154 Bayview Drive, Woodlawn, Ontario, Canada, K0A 3MO	001 613 832 2244	★★★★	Self Catering	

Bathgate

Ballencrieff Fishery	Ballencrieff Fishery, Ballencrieff Toll, Bathgate, West Lothian, EH48 4LD	01506 630808	★★★★	Self Catering	
The Cottage Self Catering	6 Matthews Crofts, Blackbridge, Bathgate, West Lothian, EH48 3TJ	01501 752301	★★★	Self Catering	

♿ Unassisted wheelchair access   ♿ Assisted wheelchair access   ♟ Access for visitors with mobility difficulties
🅑 Bronze Green Tourism Award   🅢🅢 Silver Green Tourism Award   🅖🅖🅖 Gold Green Tourism Award
For further information on our Green Tourism Business Scheme please see page 9.

244   To find out more, call 0845 22 55 121 or go to visitscotland.com.

Bayhead

13 Knockintorran and Bliochan	Balard, Paiblesgarry, Bayhead, North Uist, HS6 5EF	01876 510 379	★★★	Self Catering

Beauly

Glen Affric Chalet Park	Glen Affric Chalet Park, Cannich, Inverness-shire, IV4 7LT	01456 415369	★★	Self Catering
Old Stable, Old Diary and Cui na Caillach	Mains of Aigas, Beauly, Inverness-shire, IV4 7AD	01463 782423	★★★	Self Catering
Kiltarlity Lodges	Kiltarlity Lodges, Chalet Park, Kiltarlity, Beauly, Inverness-shire, IV4 7HR	01463 741481	★★★	Self Catering

By Beauly

Moalnaceap	41 Barrow Point Avenue, Pinner, Middlesex, HA5 3HD	020 8866 5026	★	Self Catering	
Dunedin	Dunedin, Cannich, By Beauly, Inverness-shire, IV4 7LS	01456 415238	★★★	Self Catering	🕆
Dunsmore Lodges	Dunsmore Lodges, By Beauly, Inverness-shire, IV4 7EY	01463 782424	★★★★	Self Catering	🕆
Invercannich Farm	Invercannich Farm, Cannich, Beauly, Inverness-shire, IV4 7LS	01456 415216	★★★	Self Catering	
Rheindown Farm Chalets	Rheindown Farm, Beauly, Inverness-shire, IV4 7AB	01463 782461	★	Self Catering	
Riverside, Lodges, Fishermans, Stalkers Wing	Kerrow House, Cannich, By Beauly, Inverness-shire, IV4 7NA	01456 415243	★★★	Self Catering	
Shepherds Cottage	Grays, Angel street, Petworth, West Sussex, GU28 0BG	01798 344 500	★★	Self Catering	
Willowburn Cottage	C/O Suilven, Macualway Road, Southend, Argyll, PA28 6RF	01586 830323	★★★★	Self Catering	

Benbecula, Isle of Benbecula

1 Grimsay Island	16 Griminish, Benbecula, Western Isles, HS7 5QA	01870 602591	★★★	Self Catering
9 Torlum	7 Torlum, Benbecula, Outer Hebrides, HS7 5PP	01870 603296	★★★	Self Catering
Am Bothan	Am Buthan, c/o Lionacleit Guest House, Benbecula, Outer Hebridies, HS7 5PY	01870 602176	★★★	Self Catering
Ford House	3 Creagorry, Benbecula, Western Isles, HS7 5PG	01870 602239	★★★	Self Catering

Benderloch

Seabank	Seabank, South Shian, Benderloch, By Oban, Argyll, PA37 1SB	01631 720602	★★★★	Self Catering	
Tralee Bay Holidays	Tralee Bay Purple Thistle Holidays, Benderloch, By Oban, Argyll, PA37 1QR	01631 720255	★★★ → ★★★★	Self Catering	
Tunnag Cottage	Lachan Cottage, South Shian Road, Benderloch, By Oban, Argyll, PA37 1QS	01631 720700	★★★	Self Catering	🕆

Benmore

9 Lamont Lodge	6 Deer Park, Benmore, By Dunoon, Argyll, PA23 8RA	01369 706591	★★★	Self Catering

Bernera, Isle of Lewis

14 Tobson	17 Upper Garrabost, Point, Isle of Lewis, HS2 0PN	01851 870706	★★★	Self Catering

Bettyhill

Dhualton	6 Belper Crescent, Carlton, Nottingham NG4 3RQ	0115 9403352	★★	Self Catering

♿ Unassisted wheelchair access   ♿ Assisted wheelchair access   🕆 Access for visitors with mobility difficulties

🄟 Bronze Green Tourism Award   🄟🄟 Silver Green Tourism Award   🄟🄟🄟 Gold Green Tourism Award

For further information on our Green Tourism Business Scheme please see page 9.

25 Airdneiskich	6 Hoy, Halkirk, Caithness, KW12 6UU	01847 831544	★★★★	Self Catering
Rhivale	191 May Lane, Kings Heath, Birmingham, West Midlands, B14 4AW	0121 4442683	★★★	Self Catering

Biggar

Crossridge Country Cottages	Crossridge Country Cottages, Crossridge House, Carmichael, Biggar, South Lanarkshire, ML12 6NG	01555 880589	★★★★	Self Catering 🕴

By Biggar

Carmichael Country Cottages	Carmichael Estate Office, West Mains, Carmichael, by Biggar, Lanarkshire, ML12 6PG	01899 308336	★★ → ★★★★	Self Catering

Birnam

3A Tower Buildings	Barberswells, Craigton, Kirriemuir, Angus, DD8 5NZ	01575 530248	★★★	Self Catering
Flat 1	The Retreat, Perth Road, Birnam, PERTHSHIRE, PH8 0AA	01350 727005	★★★	Self Catering
Ladyhill Coach House	51 Bennochy Road, Kirkcaldy, Fife, KY2 5QZ	01592 264369	★★★★	Self Catering
Byways Apartment	Byways Bed & Breakfast, Perth Road, Birnam, Dunkeld, Perthshire, PH8 0DH	01350 727542	★★★★	Self Catering

Blackwaterfoot, Isle of Arran

Achagorm	Kilpatrick Farm, Blackwaterfoot, Isle of Arran, KA27 8EP	01770 860203	★★★	Self Catering
Bellevue Farm Cottage	Bellevue Farm Cottage, Bellevue Farm, Blackwaterfoot, Isle of Arran, KA27 8EX	01770 860251	★★★	Self Catering
Clifton Cottage	Crobhlair, Gordon Road, Alford, Aberdeenshire, AB33 8AL	01975 562255	★★	Self Catering
Hope Cottage	7 Torr-righe, Shiskine, Isle of Arran, KA27 8HD	01770 860377	★★★	Self Catering
Mill Cottage	Drumaghinier, Blackwaterfoot, Isle of Arran, KA27 8EX	01770 860308	★★★	Self Catering
Rowanside	Tigh na Druim, Shiskine, Isle of Arran KA27 8ER	01770 860367	★★★	Self Catering

Blair Atholl

Glen Bruar Lodge	Atholl Estates, Estate Offices, Blair Atholl, Perthshire, PH18 5TH	01796 481355	★★★	Self Catering
Kindrochet Lodge	Atholl Estate, Estate Office, Blair Atholl, Perthshire, PH18 5TH	01796 481355	★★★★	Self Catering
Old Blair Lodge	Atholl Estates, Estate office, Blair Atholl, Perthshire, PH18 5TH	01796 481355	★★★	Self Catering
The Firs Lodge	The Firs, St Andrews Crescent, Blair Atholl, Perthshire, PH18 5TA	01796 481256	★★★	Self Catering
Tigh Seonag	The Grain Store, Blair Atholl, Nr Pitlochry, Perthshire, PH18 5SG	01796 481349	★★★	Self Catering
Vale of Atholl Country Cottages	Vale of Atholl Country Co, Blair Atholl, Perthshire, PH18 5TE	01796 481567	★★★	Self Catering

Blairgowrie

Clunskea Farm	Clunskea Farm, Enochdhu, by Blairgowrie, Perthshire, PH10 7PJ	01250881 358	★★★	Self Catering
Ericht Holiday Lodges	Ericht Holiday Lodges, Balmoral Rd, Blairgowrie, Perthshire, PH10 7AH	01250 874686	★★★	Self Catering
Finegand Estate	Newrow, Methven Perthshire, PH1 3RE	01764 683222	★★ → ★★★	Self Catering
Glenbeag Mountain Lodges	Glenbeag Mountain Lodges, Spittal of Glenshee, Perthshire, PH10 7QE	01250 885204	★★★ → ★★★★	Self Catering 🦽

 🦽 Unassisted wheelchair access   🦽 Assisted wheelchair access   🕴 Access for visitors with mobility difficulties

Ⓟ Bronze Green Tourism Award   ⓅⓅ Silver Green Tourism Award   ⓅⓅⓅ Gold Green Tourism Award

For further information on our Green Tourism Business Scheme please see page 9.

Little Doocot 1 & 2	The Dovetails, Bridge of Cally, Blairgowrie, Perthshire, PH10 7JL	01250 886349	★★★★	Self Catering
Miramichi	Goldcrest, Golf Course Road, Blairgowrie, Perthshire, PH10 6LQ	01250 873310	★★★	Self Catering
Neids	Drumknock, Kilry, Blairgowrie, Perthshire, PH11 8HR	01575 560731	★★★	Self Catering
Pine Lodges, Blairgowrie Holiday Park	Blairgowrie Holiday Park, Rattray, Perthshire, PH10 7AL	01250 876666	★★★★	Self Catering
Pondfauld Holidays Ltd	Pondfauld Holidays, Alyth Road, Blairgowrie, Perthshire, PH10 7HF	01250 873284	★★ → ★★★	Self Catering
Rannagulzion Apt.	Rannagulzion House, Blairgowrie, Perthshire, PH10 7JR	01250 886359	★★★	Self Catering
The Bothy	Newmill Of Kinloch, Clunie, by Blairgowrie, Perthshire, PH10 6SG	01250 884263	★★★★	Self Catering
The Old Byre	Balcairn Farm Steading, Kinloch, Blairgowrie, Perthshire, PH10 6SD	01250 884756	★★★★	Self Catering

By Blairgowrie

Auchavan Stables	Leguna, Merthly, Perth, Perthshire, PH1 4HE	01738 710440	★★★	Self Catering
Larch Cottage	East Mill Farms, Hole of Ruthven, Airlie, by Kirriemuir, Angus, DD8 5NZ	01575 530258	★★★	Self Catering
The Whitehouse	23 Elm Bank Gardens, Barnes, London SW13 0NU	0208 878 8635	★★★	Self Catering
Braveheart Cottage	Suite 13/14, 22 Market Place, Ringwood, Hampshire, BH24 1AW	01828 640445	★★★	Self Catering

Blairs

The Bothy	The Bothy, Wedderhill Farm, Blairs, Aberdeen, AB12 5YX	01224 869960	★★★	Self Catering

Boat of Garten

3 High Terrace	4 High Terrace, Boat of Garten, Inverness-shire, PH24 3BW	01479 831262	★★	Self Catering
Chalet Morlich	Moorfield House, Deshar Road, Boat of Garten, Inverness-shire, PH24 3BN	01479 831646	★★	Self Catering
Cherry Cottage	Werain, 4 The Paddocks, Seton Mains, Longniddry, EH32 0PG	01875 853491	★★	Self Catering
Corronich	Corronich, Boat of Garten, Inverness-shire, PH24 3BN	01479 831357	★★★★	Self Catering
Corrour	21 North Close, Medmenham, Marlow, Bucks, SL2 2EL	0049 6371 918897	★★★	Self Catering
Firhill Cottage	Granlea House, Deshar Road, Boat of Garten, Inverness-shire, PH24 3BN	01479 831601	★★★	Self Catering
Flat 3, Craigview	10 Gailes Park, Bothwell, Glasgow G71 8TS	01698 852901	★★	Self Catering
Heath Cottage	Fairknowe, 6 Crosshill Crescent, Strathaven, Lanarkshire, ML10 6DT	01357 520148	★★★	Self Catering
Mountain Lodges	Beechgrove, Mains of Garten Farm, Boat of Garten, Inverness-shire, PH24 3BY	01479 831551	★★★	Self Catering
Tyndrum	Dochlaggie, Boat of Garten, Inverness-shire, PH24 3BU	01479 831242	★★★	Self Catering
Woodland Lodge	5 Northbank Avenue, Kirkintilloch, Glasgow, G66 1HA	07711 909077	★★★★	Self Catering

Bonar Bridge

Achue Croft Cottage	Drumbhan, Airdens, Bonar Bridge, Sutherland, IV24 3AS	01863 766144	★★★	Self Catering
Ceannloch	21 Pinewood Avenue, Lenzie, Glasgow G66 4EB	0141 5789121	★★	Self Catering

♿ Unassisted wheelchair access   ♿ Assisted wheelchair access   🧍 Access for visitors with mobility difficulties
🍃 Bronze Green Tourism Award   🍃🍃 Silver Green Tourism Award   🍃🍃🍃 Gold Green Tourism Award
For further information on our Green Tourism Business Scheme please see page 9.

Bonnybridge

Antonine Wall Cottages	Antonine Wall Cottages, Bonnyside House, Bonnyside Road, Bonnybridge, Stirlingshire, FK4 2AA	01324 811875	★★★★	Self Catering 🕴

Borgue

Allanhead	Pound Cottage, Lapworth Street, Lapworth, Solihull, Warwickshire, B94 5QP	01564 784476	★★★	Self Catering
Brighouse Bay Holiday Park	Central Booking Office, Brighouse Bay, Kirkcudbright, Kirkcudbrightshire, DG6 4TS	01557 870267	★★ → ★★★	Self Catering
Carrick Holiday Cottages	Owl Cote Byre, Carrick, Gatehose of Fleet DG7 2DT	01557 814130	★★★	Self Catering
Cormorant Cottage	Ardgour Cottage, Borgue, Kirkcudbright, Dumfries and Galloway, DG6 4SN	01557 870606	★★★★	Self Catering
Factors House and Grooms Cottage	Knockbrex Self Catering, Croft Cottage, High Street, Elswick, Preston, Lancashire, PR4 3ZB	01995 671909	★★★★	Self Catering
Craig Cottage, Kirkandrews	Roberton, Borgue, Kirkcudbrightshire, DG6 4UB	01557 870217	★★★	Self Catering
Castleview Cottage, Lennox Plunton	Lennox Plunton, Borgue, Kirkcudbrightshire, DG6 4UG	01557 870210	★★	Self Catering

Borve, Isle of Lewis

Sonas	3 Lower Shader, Barvas Isle of Lewis, HS2 0RH	01851 850 489	★★	Self Catering

Bowglass, Isle of Harris

Tigh na Seileach	Tigh na Seileach, Bowglass, Harris, HS3 3AD	01859 502411	★★	Self Catering

Bowmore

Bowmore Distillery	Bowmore Distillery, School Street, Bowmore, Islay, PA43 7JS	01496 810671	★★★★	Self Catering
Clachan Cottage	Clachan Cottages, Bowmore, Isle of Islay, Argyll, PA43 7JF	01496 810440	★★	Self Catering
Corrary Cottage	Island Farm, Bowmore, Isle of Islay, PA43 7JF	01496 810229	★★★	Self Catering
High Street	168 High Street, Bowmore, Isle of Islay, Argyll, PA43 7JE	01496 810524	★★	Self Catering
Lambeth Lodge	72 Jamieson Street, Bowmore, Isle of Islay, PA43 7HL	01496 810792	★★	Self Catering
The Cottage	Kilennan, High Street, Bowmore, Isle of Islay, PA43 7JE	01496 810488	★★	Self Catering
The Old Stables ,Flats 1 & 2	Newton Cottage, Jamieson Street, Bowmore, Isle of Islay, Argyll, PA43 7HL	01496 810414	★★★	Self Catering 🕴
Red Lodge, Ghillie Brae, Laggan Cottage	Red Lodge, Laggan Properties Ltd, Laggan Estate Office, Bowmore, Isle of Islay, PA43 7JF	01496 810235	★★ → ★★★	Self Catering

Boyndie

1 & 2 Dallochy Cottages	Dallachy Farm, Boyndie, Banff, AB45 2LA	01261 861206	★★★	Self Catering
Bankfoot Croft	Bankfoot Croft, Lodgehills,Boyndie, Banff, Aberdeenshire, AB45 2AH	01261 842003	★★★	Self Catering

Braemar

Birchwood	Birchwood, Chapel Brae, Braemar, Aberdeenshire, AB35 5YT	01339 741599	★★★	Self Catering
Braemar Lodge Hotel	Braemar Holiday Lodges, Glenshee Road, Braemar, Aberdeenshire, AB35 5YQ	013397 41627	★★★	Self Catering 🕴
Braeriach	National Trust for Scotland, 28 Charlotte Square, Edinburgh EH2 4ET	0131 243 9335	★★★	Self Catering

  ♿ Unassisted wheelchair access   ♿ Assisted wheelchair access   🕴 Access for visitors with mobility difficulties
🅟 Bronze Green Tourism Award   🅟🅟 Silver Green Tourism Award   🅟🅟🅟 Gold Green Tourism Award
For further information on our Green Tourism Business Scheme please see page 9.

Broom Cottage	36 Cairds Wynd, Banchory, Aberdeenshire, AB31 5XU	01330 820740	★★★	Self Catering
Bynack	National Trust for Scotland, 28 Charlotte Square, Edinburgh EH2 4ET	0131 243 9335	★★★	Self Catering
Creag Bhalg	National Trust for Scotland, 28 Charlotte Square, Edinburgh EH2 4ET	0131 243 9335	★★★★★	Self Catering
Croft Muicken	11 Russel Place, Edinburgh, Midlothian, EH5 3HQ	0131 552 3866	★★★	Self Catering
Dalvorar	National Trust for Scotland, 28 Charlotte Square, Edinburgh EH2 4ET	0131 243 9335	★★★	Self Catering
Derry	National Trust for Scotland, 28 Charlotte Square, Edinburgh EH2 4ET	0131 243 9335	★★★	Self Catering
Elvenstones	87b Hepburn Gardens, St Andrews, Fife, KY16 9LT	01334 476679	★	Self Catering
Havelock	6 Alford Place, Aberdeen, Aberdeenshire, AB10 1YD	01224 649101	★★	Self Catering
Macdui	National Trust for Scotland, 28 Charlotte Square, Edinburgh EH2 4ET	0131 243 9335	★★★	Self Catering

Breakish, Isle of Skye

Tigh Holm Cottages	Tigh Holm Cottages, Scullamus Moss, Breakish, Isle of SKye, IV42 8QB	01471 820077	★★★	Self Catering

By Brechin

Parker's Retreat, Farnell	Greenden Farmhouse, Farnell, Brechin, Angus, DD9 6TS	07831 333333	★★★★★	Self Catering
Mill of Blackhall	Blackhall, Menmuir, By Brechin, Angus, DD9 7RJ	01356 660211	★★★★	Self Catering

Bridge of Allan

3, Allan Water Apartments	Allanbank House, Mill Row, Dunblane FK15 0EL	01786 821255	★★★★	Self Catering
Logie Barn	Logie House, Logie Lane, Bridge of Allan, Stirling, FK9 4SB	01786 833343	Awaiting Grading	

Bridge of Cally

Cromald Cottages	Cromald Cottages - West & East, Whitehouse Farm, Bridge of Cally, Perthshire, PH10 7NG	01250 886 391	★★★★	Self Catering

Bridge of Earn

River Edge Lodges	River Edge Lodges, Back Street, Bridge of Earn, Perthshire, PH2 9AB	01738 812370	★★★	Self Catering 👤

Bridge of Weir

m [DMaple Cottage	Maple Cottage, Quarriers Village, Bridge of Weir, Renfrewshire, PA11 3SX	01505 616044	Awaiting Grading	

Bridgend, Isle of Islay

2 Bola na Traigh	Craigends, Gruinart Isle of Islay, PA43 7LL	01496 850256	★★★	Self Catering
Cnoc Ard	Jamieson Street, Bowmore, Isle of Islay, PA43 7HL	01496 810 547	★★★★	Self Catering
Coullabus Keepers Cottage	Newton House, Bridgend, Isle of Islay, PA44 7PD	01496 810293	★★★	Self Catering
Craigmhor	Flat F, 1 Pollokshields Square, Glasgow G41 4QT	01414 234936	★★★	Self Catering
Neriby Cottage	Neriby Farm, Bridgend, Isle of Islay, Argyll, PA44 7PZ	01496 810274	★★★★	Self Catering
The Old Schoolroom	The Old School Room, Moin-A-Choire, Bridgend, Isle of Islay, Argyll, PA44 7PG	01496 810242	★★★★	Self Catering

  ♿ Unassisted wheelchair access   🦽 Assisted wheelchair access   👤 Access for visitors with mobility difficulties
  🄑 Bronze Green Tourism Award   🄑🄑 Silver Green Tourism Award   🄑🄑🄑 Gold Green Tourism Award
For further information on our Green Tourism Business Scheme please see page 9.

Broadford, Isle of Skye

Ardmore	3 Lime Park, Broadford, Isle of Skye, IV49 9AE	01471 822372	★★★★★	Self Catering	
Corriegorm Beag	Corriegorm, Bayview Crescent, Broadford, Isle of Skye, IV49 9BD	01471 822515	★★★	Self Catering	🕴
Mary's Thatched Cottages	Mary's Thatched Cottages, 26 Elgol, Broadford, Isle of Skye, IV49 9BL	01471 866275	★★★★	Self Catering	🍃
Rowan Cottage	Roskhill Barn, Roskhill, By Dunvegan, Isle of Skye, IV55 8ZD	0789 9660200	★★★	Self Catering	
Tighban	The Old Stables, High Street, Piddlehinton, Dorchester, DT2 7TD	07810 555 643	★★★★	Self Catering	

By Broadford, Isle of Skye

The Schoolhouse	11 Rue Rousselet, Paris 75007 France	0033 1 473 40 358	★★	Self Catering	
1/2 of 2	4 Upper Dean Terrace, Edinburgh, Lothiians EH4 1NU	0131 332 1544	★★★★	Self Catering	
Clover Hill Holiday Cottage	Rowanlea, Torrin, Broadford, Isle of Skye, IV49 9BA	01471 822763	★★★★	Self Catering	
Sea Drift, Ard Dorch	Sea Drift, The Skye Picture House, Ard Dorch, Broadford, Isle of Skye, IV49 9AJ	01471 822531	★★★	Self Catering	🕴

Brodick, Isle of Arran

Shore Cottage	34 Hill Road, Stonehouse, Larkhall, South Lanarkshire, ML9 3EA	01698 792905	★★★	Self Catering	
5 Alma Park	75 Atwood Road, Didsbury, Manchester M20 6TB	0161 4450067	★	Self Catering	
A'chir, Strathwhillan House	A'Chir, Strathwhillan House, Strathwhillan Road, Brodick, Isle of Arran, KA27 8BQ	01770 302331	★★★	Self Catering	
Auchrannie Country House Hotel Lodges	Auchrannie Country House, Brodick, Isle of Arran, KA27 8BZ	01770 302020	★★★★★	Self Catering	🍃
Balmore Cottage	Balmore Cottage, Alma Road, Brodick, Isle of Arran, KA27 8AZ	01770 302881	★★	Self Catering	
Belvedere	Belvedere Guest House, Alma Road, Brodick, Isle of Arran, KA27 8AZ	01770 302397	★★★	Self Catering	🕴
Brandon Lodge	Honey Hill Farm, Quarry Berry Lane, Chilcote, Swadlincote, DE12 8DN	01827 373600	★★★★	Self Catering	
Brodick Castle Kennels,Sannox Garden &	Arran Estate Office, Douglas Park, Brodick, Isle of Arran, KA27 8EJ	01770 810218	★★★ → ★★★★★	Self Catering	
Carwinshoch	20 Seaton Street, Ardrossan, Aryshire, KA22 8JH	01294 608774	★★★	Self Catering	
Cir Mhor & Fuchsia Cottage	Cir Mhor, Glen Rosa Road, Brodick, Isle of Arran, KA27 8DF	01770 302274-	★★★ → ★★★★	Self Catering	
Crosslea	6 Scarrend View, Dewsbury, West Yorkshire, WF13 4NX	01924 469150	★★★	Self Catering	
Evergreen	1 Deanston Gardens, Doune FK16 6AZ	01786 841966	★★★	Self Catering	
Glendale	The Old Manse, 73 Main Street, Dunlop, Ayrshire, KA3 4AG	01560 484898	★★★★	Self Catering	
Grans Cottage & Reaper Weary	Glen Rosa Campsite, Glen Rosa, Brodick, Isle of Arran, KA27 8DF	01770 302380	★★★★★	Self Catering	
Hunters Apartment	Hunters Apartment, Alma Road, Brodick, Isle of Arran, KA27 8BU	01770 302211	★★	Self Catering	
Loudon Cottage	40 Kay Park Crescent, Kilmarnock, Ayrshire KA3 7BA	01563 524263	★★★	Self Catering	
Moss and Banner Cottages	St Helens, Brodick, Isle of Arran, KA27 8BU	01770 302659	★★★★	Self Catering	
No 19 Murray Crescent	9 Taytallon Drive, Paisley, Renfrewshire, PA2 9JT	01505 348260	★★	Self Catering	

♿ Unassisted wheelchair access   👥♿ Assisted wheelchair access   🕴 Access for visitors with mobility difficulties
🍃 Bronze Green Tourism Award   🍃🍃 Silver Green Tourism Award   🍃🍃🍃 Gold Green Tourism Award
For further information on our Green Tourism Business Scheme please see page 9.

250   To find out more, call 0845 22 55 121 or go to visitscotland.com.

Orwin Cottage	Raithmuir Farm, Galston KA4 8PP	01560 700693	★★★	Self Catering
Rowanbank Holiday Cottages	Rowanbank Holiday Cottages, Rowanbank, Brodick, Isle of Arran, KA27 8DW	01770 302447	★★★	Self Catering
Sonas	293 Guardwell Crescent, Edinburgh, Midlothian, EH17 7SL	0131 6646981	★★★	Self Catering
Springbank Farmhouse Apartment	Springbank Farmhouse, Brodick, Isle of Arran, KA27 8BG	01770 302947	★★★	Self Catering
The Flat at Invercloy	Tamarind, 24 Arran Ave, Kilmarnock, Ayrshire, KA3 1TP	01563 571788	★★★	Self Catering
The Shore House	The Shore House, Shore Road, Brodick, Isle of Arran, KA27 8AJ	01770 302377	★★	Self Catering
The Willows	Pendragon Property Management Ltd, 5 Doonview Gardens, Doonfoot, Ayr, Ayrshire, KA7 4HZ	01292 441161	★★★	Self Catering
Tulloch-Ard	18 Victoria Crescent Road, Glasgow G12 9DB	0141 339 4241	★★★	Self Catering
Wellingtonia Cottage	15 Lockharton Gardens, Edinburgh EH14 1AU	0131 4443 557	★★	Self Catering
Coralyn House & Kinnandalloch	28 Bowancraig, Largs KA30 8TB	07771 811 299	★★★ → ★★★★	Self Catering

Brodie

The Laird's Apartment	National Trust for Scotland, 28 Charlotte Square, Edinburgh EH2 4ET	0131 243 9335	★★★★	Self Catering

Brora

The Links Apartments	Highland Escape, Golf Road, Brora, Sutherland, KW9 6QS	01408 621252	★★★ → ★★★★	Self Catering
Tigh Fada Apartment & The Eyrie	Tigh Fada, 18 Golf Road, Brora, Sutherland, KW9 6QS	01408 621 332	★★★	Self Catering 𝑘

Broughton, By Biggar

Merlindale Holiday Apartment	Merlindale Holiday Apartment, Merlindale House,Broughton, By Biggar, Peeblesshire, ML12 6JD	01899 830221		Awaiting Grading
Powsail Cottage	1 Barnton Gardens, Edinburgh EH4 6AF	0131 3364043	★★★	Self Catering

Broughty Ferry

41 Church Street and 8 Bath Street	Broughty Ferry Accommodation, 74B Gray Street, Broughty Ferry, Dundee, DD5 2BP	01382 738631	★★★	Self Catering
Forbes of Kingennie	Omachie Farm, Kingennie, By Dundee, Tayside, DD5 3RE	01382 350777	★★★★	Self Catering ♿

Broxburn

Bankhead Farm	Dechmont, Broxburn, West Lothian, EH52 6NS	01506 811209	★★★★★	Self Catering

Bruichladdich, Isle of Islay

Caberfeidh Cottage	Ardinning, Moor Rd, Strathblane, Glasgow, G63 9EX	01360 770308	★★★	Self Catering
Curlew Cottage	14 Kingsburgh Road, Edinburgh, Lothian, EH12 6DZ	0131 3372561	★★★	Self Catering
Foreland Estate	Denston Hall Estate c/o Sunderland Farm, Bruichladdich, Isle of Islay, Argyll, PA49 7UT	01496 850259	★★	Self Catering
Kilchoman Cottages	Kilchoman Cottages, Kilchoman House, Bruichladdich, Isle of Islay, PA49 7UY	01496 850382	★★★	Self Catering
Coull Farm Holiday Cottage & Flat	Coull Farm, Kilchoman, Bruichladdich, Isle of Islay, PA49 7UT	01496 850317	★★★	Self Catering 𝑘

♿ Unassisted wheelchair access   𝕝ₖ Assisted wheelchair access   𝑘 Access for visitors with mobility difficulties
Ⓡ Bronze Green Tourism Award   ⓇⓇ Silver Green Tourism Award   ⓇⓇⓇ Gold Green Tourism Award
For further information on our Green Tourism Business Scheme please see page 9.

Awards correct as of mid August 2008   251

Brydekirk

Haven Cottage	2 Woodcockair Street, Brydekirk, Annan, DG12 5NA	01461 201612	★★★	Self Catering

Buckie

10 Great Eastern Road	8 Great Eastern Road, Buckie, Banffshire, AB56 1SL	01542 831277	★★★	Self Catering 🏃
Maryhill Log Cabins	Birchfold, Drybridge, Buckie, Morayshire, AB56 5JB	01542 834999	★★	Self Catering
Taigh Na Mara	30 Church Street, Portknockie, Buckie, Moray, AB56 4LN	01542 841145	★★★	Self Catering
The Old Drapery	Maxwell House, 12 Maxwell Street, Fochabers, Moray, IV32 7DE	01343 820304	★★★★	Self Catering

By Buckie

Auchentae Farm House	Auchentae Farm House, Arradoul, By Buckie, Moray, AB56 5BD	01542 834293	★★★	Self Catering

Bunachton

Baile na Creige	45 Cluny Gardens, Edinburgh EH10 6BL	0131 477 4481	★★★	Self Catering
Kilimanjaro	25 Cairn Road, Bieldside, Aberdeen AB15 9AL	01224 865763	★★★★	Self Catering

Bunessan, Isle of Mull

Ardfenaig Farmhouses	Ardness House, Tiraghoil, Bunessan, Isle of Mull, PA67 6DU	01681 700260	★★★★	Self Catering
Ardtun House & Cottages	Ardtun House, Bunessan, Isle of Mull, Argyll, PA67 6DG	01681 700264	★★ → ★★★	Self Catering
Gowanbrae Cottage	Sleekburn Cottage Farm, Barrington Road, Bedlington, Northumberland, NE22 7AP	01670 823063	★★★	Self Catering
Keills Cottage	Waterside, Station Road, Gargunnoch, Stirling, FK8 3DA	01786 860739	★★★	Self Catering
Knockan	21 Montgomery Crescent, Dunblane FK15 9FB	01786 825510	★★★	Self Catering
Salachran	Welwyn, Firpark Terrace, Cambusbarron, Stirling FK7 9ND	01786 472900	★★★	Self Catering 🏃
Saorphin Cottages - Tigh Beag & Tigh Mor	Estate Office, Herriard Park, Herriard, Basingstoke, Hampshire, RG25 2PL	01256 381275	★★	Self Catering
Scoor House	Ploughmans Cottage, Scoor Isle of Mull, PA67 6DW	01681 700105	★★	Self Catering

By Bunessan, Isle of Mull

Ardachy House Apartment	Ardachy House Hotel, Uisken, Bunessan, Isle of Mull, Argyll, PA67 6DS	01681 700505	★★★	Self Catering
Ardfenaig Coach House	Ardfenaig House, By Bunnessan, Isle of Mull, PA67 6DX	01681 700210	★★★★	Self Catering
Iona Cottage	1 Canon Lane, Edinburgh EH3 5HD	0131 556 8794	★★	Self Catering

Burnside

Glebe Cottage	Burnside House, Burnside, Scone, Perthshire, PH2 6LP	01738 551268	★★★★	Self Catering

Burntisland

Cullaloe Lodge Annexe	Cullaloe Lodge, Aberdour, Burntisland, Fife, KY3 0LU	01383 860575		Awaiting Grading

♿ Unassisted wheelchair access   ♿ Assisted wheelchair access   🏃 Access for visitors with mobility difficulties
🍂 Bronze Green Tourism Award   🍂🍂 Silver Green Tourism Award   🍂🍂🍂 Gold Green Tourism Award
For further information on our Green Tourism Business Scheme please see page 9.

252   To find out more, call 0845 22 55 121 or go to visitscotland.com.

Bute

Grand Marine	14 Foster Close, Seaford, East Sussex, BN25 2JL	01323 873688	★★★	Self Catering

Cairndow

Cairndow Cottage	C/O Gurtons, Good Easter, Chelmsford, Essex, CM1 4QH	01245 231657	★★★★	Self Catering
Inverfyne & Bridge Cottage	Achadunan, Cairndow, Argyll, PA26 8BJ	01499 600238	★★★	Self Catering
The Butler's Quarters	Ardkinglas, The Square, Cairndow, Argyll, PA26 8BG	01499 600261	★★	Self Catering

By Cairndow

Upper Croitachonie	c/o Ailey Cottage, North Ailey Road, Cove, Near Helensburgh, G84 0ND	01436 840040	★★★	Self Catering

Calgary, Isle of Mull

Frachadil Farm Steadings	Frachadil Farm, Calgary, Isle of Mull, PA75 6QQ	01688 400265	★★★	Self Catering
Sands Cottage	14 Croxted Road, London SE21 8SW	7799595446	★★★	Self Catering

By Calgary, Isle of Mull

Treshnish & Haunn Cottages	House of Treshnish, Treshnish Point, By Calgary, Isle of Mull, Argyll, PA75 6QX	01688 400249	★★★ → ★★★★	Self Catering	♿ 🍃🍃🍃

Callander

Annfield Cottage	Norlea, Ancaster Road, Callander, Perthshire, FK17 8EL	01877 330234	★★★	Self Catering
Ardchoille Cottage	138 Main Street, Callander, Perthshire, FK17 8BG	01877 330753	★★★	Self Catering
Auld Toll Cottages	Riverview House, Leny Road, Callander, Perthshire, FK17 8AL	01877 330635	★★★ → ★★★★	Self Catering
Brook Linn Cottage	Brook Linn Country House, Leny Feus, Callander, Perthshire, FK17 8AU	01877 330103	★★★★	Self Catering
Craignethan Cottage	3 Tulipan Crescent, Callander, Perthshire, FK17 8AR	01877 330720	★	Self Catering
Highland View	54 Beech Crescent, Denny, Stirlingshire FK6 6LL	01324 891113	★★	Self Catering
Lime Tree Cottage	42 Vorlich Crescent, Callander, Perthshire, FK17 8JE	01877 330289	★★★★	Self Catering
Mid Torrie Farm Cottage	Mid Torrie Farm, Callander, Perthshire, FK17 8JL	01877 330203	★★★★	Self Catering

By Callander

The Lodge, Kilmahog	Drumardoch Farm, Callander, Perthshire, FK17 8LT	01877 330568	★★★★	Self Catering	
Kilravock and Ardnandave	The Knowe, Ancaster Road, Callander, Perthshire, FK17 8EL	01877 330076	★★★★	Self Catering	
Frennich House	Frennich House, Brig O'Turk, Kilmahog, Callander, Perthshire, FK17 8HT	01877 376274	★★★★	Self Catering	🍃

Calvine

Kinaldy Cottage	Kinaldy Cottage, Kinaldy House, Calvine, Pitlochry, PH18 5UE	01796 483310	★★★	Self Catering

Campbeltown

Drumore-Na-Bodach	High Bellochantuy Farm, Bellochantuy, Campbeltown, Argyll, PA28 6QE	01583 421138	★★★	Self Catering

♿ Unassisted wheelchair access   ♿ Assisted wheelchair access   🚶 Access for visitors with mobility difficulties
🍃 Bronze Green Tourism Award   🍃🍃 Silver Green Tourism Award   🍃🍃🍃 Gold Green Tourism Award
For further information on our Green Tourism Business Scheme please see page 9.

| The Dairy, Rhoin Farm | Rhoin Holidays, Rhoin Farm, Campbeltown, Argyll, PA28 6NT | 01856 820220 | ★★★★ | Self Catering | ♿ |
| Shore Cottage West | 32 The Old Yews, New Barn, Longfield, Kent, DA3 7JS | 01474 707616 | ★★★ | Self Catering | |

By Campbeltown

Carraig	20 Victorian Lanterns, Miller Street, Summerseat, Bury, Lancashire, BL9 5PX	07778 036137	★★★★	Self Catering	
Dalriada	Rowan Cottage, 7 Croftside, Aviemore, Highlands, PH22 1QJ	01479 812167	★★★★	Self Catering	
Torrisdale Castle Estate	Torrisdale Castle, Carradale, by Campbeltown, Argyll, PA28 6QT	01583 431233	★★ → ★★★	Self Catering	&#8472;

By Cannich

| Tomich Holidays | Tomich Holidays, Tomich, by Cannich, Inverness-shire, IV4 7LY | 01456 415332 | ★★★ → ★★★★ | Self Catering | |

Carbost, Isle of Skye

21 Fiscavaig	7 Maxwell Drive, Inverness IV3 5EX	01463 224435	★★	Self Catering	
Loch View	11 Laggan Road, Inverness, Inverness-shire, IV2 4EH	01463 235793	★★	Self Catering	
No. 8 crossal	2 West Drip Farm Cottages, Stirling, Stirlingshire, FK9 4UJ	01786 471455	★★★★	Self Catering	
Torgorm Cottage	10 Lawn Drive, Chudleigh, Newton Abbot, Devon, TQ13 0LT	01626 852266	★★★	Self Catering	
Trien Cottage	7 Portnalong, Portnalong, Isle of Skye, IV47 8SL	01478 640254	★★	Self Catering	

By Carbost, Isle of Skye

| Cuillin Lodge | 12 Brook Hill, Oxted, Surrey RH8 9LR | 01883 715301 | ★★★ | Self Catering | |
| 1 Eynort | 10 Newton Street, Stornoway, Isle of Lewis, HS1 2RE | 01851 701790 | ★★★ | Self Catering | |

Cardrona

| Cardrona Breaks | 21 Cardrona Way, Cardrona Way, Tweeddale, EH45 9LD | 01896 830371 | ★★★ → ★★★★ | Self Catering | |

Cargill

| Beech Hedge Chalets | Beech Hedge Caravan Park, Cargill, Perth, Perthshire, PH2 6DU | 01250 883249 | ★★★ | Self Catering | |

Carloway, Isle of Lewis

| 14 Kirivick | Monteray, Bakers Road, Newmarket, Isle of Lewis, HS2 0EA | 01851 703632 | ★★★ | Self Catering | |
| No 3 Gearrannan | 5a Cearrannan, Carloway, Isle of Lewis, HS2 9AL | 01851 643416 | ★★★ → ★★★★ | Self Catering | |

Carnoustie

Balhousie Farm Cottages	John P Gray & Son, Auchrennie Farm, Muirdrum, Carnoustie, Angus, DD7 6LU	01241 856465	Awaiting Grading		
Beachview / Twiga Cottage	10 East Row, Westhaven, Carnoustie, Angus, DD7 6BG	01241 855203	★	Self Catering	
Bruce Court	Brookfield Lodge, 6B High Street, Carnoustie, Angus, DD7 6AQ	01241 856133	★★★★	Self Catering	
Greenside	20 Broadlands, Carnoustie, Angus, DD7 6JY	01241 410025	★★★★	Self Catering	
Semi Detached Villa	Ceiling Decor Ltd, Casa Rosa, 74 Montrose Road, Arbroath, Angus, DD11 5JW	01241 872539	★★★★	Self Catering	

♿ Unassisted wheelchair access   ♿ Assisted wheelchair access   ✉ Access for visitors with mobility difficulties
℘ Bronze Green Tourism Award   ℘℘ Silver Green Tourism Award   ℘℘℘ Gold Green Tourism Award
For further information on our Green Tourism Business Scheme please see page 9.

The Old Manor Cottage	The Old Manor, Panbride, Carnoustie, Angus, DD7 6JP	01241 854804	★★★★	Self Catering	
Golf Cottage	13 Links Parade, Carnoustie, Angus DD7 7JF	01241 853245	★★	Self Catering	

By Carnwath

Wester Walston Lodge	Westerwalston Cottage, Walston, Carnwath, South Lanarkshire, ML11 8NF	01899 810335	★★★★	Self Catering	

Carradale

Ballynacuaig	Carradale House, Carradale Estate, Carradale, Argyll, PA28 6QQ	01583 431234	★★★★	Self Catering	
Mingulay	South Park, Kilkerran Road, Campbeltown, Argyll, PA28 6JN	01586 553108	★★★	Self Catering	
Cliff Cottage	The Steading Grogport, Carradale, Campbelltown, Argyll, PA28 6QL	01583 431399		Awaiting Grading	

Carrbridge

2 Carr Cottage	Carr Cottage, Branahvie, Inchmore by Kirkhill, Highland, IV5 7PX	01463 831479	★★★	Self Catering	
Lochanhully Woodland Club	Lochanhully Woodland Club, Carrbridge, Aviemore PH23 3NA	01479 841234	★★★	Self Catering	
Tormore	Longstowe, Lower Sutherland Crescent, Helensburgh G84 9PG	01436 672335	★★★★	Self Catering	

Carrick

Reid Country Retreats	20 Tudbury Way, Salford, Manchester, Lancs, M3 6TW	01618 325350		Awaiting Grading	

Carrutherstown

Valdheim Holiday Cottage	Valdheim Holiday Cottage, Hetland Garden Nursery, Carrutherstown, Dumfries, DG1 4JX	01387 840632	★★★	Self Catering	

Castle Douglas

45 Academy Street	11 Barnton Park Place, Edinburgh EH4 6ET	0131 336 4779	★★	Self Catering	
Balcary Mews	Balcary Mews, Balcary Bay, Auchencairn, Castle Douglas, DG1 7QZ	01556 640276	★★★★	Self Catering	
Ballantines	Ballantines, The Old Exchange, Castle Douglas, Dumfries & Galloway, DG7 1TR	01556 504 954	★★★	Self Catering	🌱
Barncrosh Farm	Barncrosh Leisure, Barncrosh Farm, Ringford, Castle Douglas, Dumfries and Galloway, DG7 1TX	01556 680216	★★ → ★★★	Self Catering	🦽
Chapelerne Farmhouse	Trowdale, Bridge of Urr, Castle Douglas, Dumfries and Galloway, DG7 3BY	01556 650270	★★★★	Self Catering	🦽
Cloud Cuckoo Lodge	Cuckoostone Cottage, St John's Town of Dalry, Castle Douglas DG7 3UA	01644 430375	★★★★	Self Catering	
Croys Lodge	Croys House, Bridge of Urr, Castle Douglas, Kirkcudbrightshire, DG7 3EX	01556 650237	★★★	Self Catering	
Dildawn Courtyard House & Extension	Dildawn House, Kelton, Castle Douglas DG7 1SE	01556 680 377	★★ → ★★★	Self Catering	
Edenbank Cottage	16 Mere Pool Road, Sutton Coldfield, West Midlands, B75 6ND	0121 308 3371	★★	Self Catering	
Ferryboat Cottage	2 Warwick Farm, Warwick-on-Eden, Carlisle, Cumbria, CA4 8PA	01228 561875	★★★★	Self Catering	
Garden Cottage	White-of-Morn, 23 Enniskellen Road, Mullybritt, Lisbellaw, Co. Fermanagh, BT94 5ER	028 66385854	★★★	Self Catering	
Gate Lodge	National Trust for Scotland, 28 Charlotte Square, Edinburgh EH2 4ET	0131 243 9335	★★★	Self Catering	
Granary Cottage	National Trust for Scotland, 28 Charlotte Square, Edinburgh EH2 4ET	0131 243 9335	★★	Self Catering	

♿ Unassisted wheelchair access   🦽 Assisted wheelchair access   🚶 Access for visitors with mobility difficulties
🌱 Bronze Green Tourism Award   🌱🌱 Silver Green Tourism Award   🌱🌱🌱 Gold Green Tourism Award
For further information on our Green Tourism Business Scheme please see page 9.

Awards correct as of mid August 2008

Ironcannie Mill Cottage	Ironmacannie Mill, Balmaclellan, Castle Douglas DG7 3QS	01644 420889	★★★	Self Catering	🏵🏵
Lochhill Cottages	Lochhill Cottages, Ringford, Castle Douglas, Dumfries, DG7 2AR	01557 820225	★★★	Self Catering	
Millwheel	National Trust for Scotland, 28 Charlotte Square, Edinburgh EH2 4ET	0131 243 9335	★★	Self Catering	
Netheryett Cottage	Netheryett, Haugh of Urr, Castle Douglas, Kirkcudbrightshire, DG7 3JZ	1556660213	★★★	Self Catering	
Queenshill Country Cottages	Fellend, Ringford, Castle Douglas, Dumfries-shire, DG7 2AT	01557 820227	★★★	Self Catering	
Redcastle House & Studios 1 & 2	Redcastle House, Haugh of Urr, Castle Douglas, Kirkcudbrightshire, DG7 3LB	01556 660475	★★★	Self Catering	🧍
Rhone Park Farmhouse	4 Cyprus Terrace, Sheffield, Yorks, S6 3QH	01142 323559	★★	Self Catering	
Rose Cottage	Rose Cottage Guest House, Gelston, Castle Douglas, Kirkcudbrightshire, DG7 1SH	01556 502513	★★★	Self Catering	🧍
Screel Mill and Doach Cottage	Charlotte Bell Ltd, Gelston Lodge, Gelston, Castle Douglas, Dumfries and Galloway, DG7 1SP	01556 502853	★★★★	Self Catering	
The Old Sunday School	The Old Sunday School, Balliol House, Buittle, Castle Douglas, Kirkcudbrightshire, DG7 1NP	01556 610811	★★★★	Self Catering	
The Rache & Glen of Spottes	Spottes, Castle Douglas, Stewartry of Kirkcudbright, DG7 3JX	01556 660202	★★★ → ★★★★	Self Catering	

By Castle Douglas

| Craigadam Lodge | Craigadam, Kirkpatrick Durham, Castle Douglas, Kirkcudbrightshire, DG7 3HU | 01556 650233 | ★★★★ | Self Catering | ♿ |

Castlebay, Isle of Barra

Atlantic View	Kishmuil, Croft Na Creich, North Kessock, Inverness, IV1 3ZE	01463 731331	★★★	Self Catering	
Braeval	Carradale, Castlebay, Isle of Barra HS9 5XN	01871 810387	★★	Self Catering	
Ceum A Bhealaich	Ceum A Bhealaich, 36 Kentangaval, Castlebay, Isle of Barra, Western Isles, HS9 5XL	01871 810644	★★★	Self Catering	

Cathcart

| The Coach House | National Trust for Scotland, 28 Charlotte Square, Edinburgh EH2 4ET | 0131 243 9335 | ★★★ | Self Catering | |

Cawdor

| Cawdor Cottages | Cawdor Estate Office, Cawdor, Nairnshire, IV12 5RE | 01667 402402 | ★★★★ | Self Catering | |
| Number 5 | Sandwood, Wester Galcantray, Cawdor, Nairnshire, IV12 5XX | 01667 493815 | ★★★★ | Self Catering | |

Cellardyke

Puffin Cottage	24 Pickford Crescent, Cellardyke, Anstruther KY10 3AL	01333 310694	★★★	Self Catering	
Second Floor West	Springbank, Kirkton, Dumfries, Dumfries-shire, DG1 1ST	01387 710271	★★★★	Self Catering	
Castle Cliff	9 Millbank, Cupar, Fife, KY15 5DW	01334 655334	★★★	Self Catering	
Seaview	Braeriach, West Huntingtower, by Perth, Perthshire, PH1 3JS	01738 583 705	★★★	Self Catering	
Wor-a-bide	28 Lyngal Avenue, Great Sutton, Ellesmere Port, Cheshire, CH66 2HX	07917 162635	★★★★	Self Catering	

Ceos, Isle of Lewis

| Tigh Na Mara | Beech Cottage, Ceos, Isle of Lewis, HS2 9JT | 01851 830479 | ★★★ | Self Catering | |

♿ Unassisted wheelchair access   ♿ Assisted wheelchair access   🧍 Access for visitors with mobility difficulties
🏵 Bronze Green Tourism Award   🏵🏵 Silver Green Tourism Award   🏵🏵🏵 Gold Green Tourism Award
For further information on our Green Tourism Business Scheme please see page 9.

Chirnside

Edington Fox Covert	Edington Fox Covert, Chirnside, Berwickshire, TD11 3LE	01890 818345	★★★	Self Catering

Clachan, By Tarbert

Airigh An Obain	Cnoc Na Luib, Clachan, Locheport, North Uist, HS6 5HD	01876 580229	★★★★	Self Catering
Stables Cottage	Stables Cottage, The Old Smithy, Clachan, By Tarbert, Argyll, PA29 6XL	01880 740635	★★★	Self Catering

Clackmannanshire

Redcarr Lodge	Redcarr Lodge, Fergusson Group Ltd, Castlecraig Business Park, Stirling FK7 7SH	01786 477210	★★★★	Self Catering

Clashnessie

Old Post Office	5 Finglen Gardens, Milngavie, Glasgow GG2 7RW	0141 956 3753	★★★	Self Catering

Cluer, Isle of Harris

Cnoc A'Chlachain	Northwood, Urquhart, By Conon Bridge, Ross & Cromarty, IV7 8HU	01349 877065	★★★★	Self Catering

Clynder

An Caladh	Annach Mhor, Shore Road, Clynder, Helensburgh, G84 0QD	01436 831312	★★★★	Self Catering

Cockburnspath

Cloverknowe Cottages	Pathhead Farm, Pathhead, Cockburnspath, Berwickshire, TD13 5XB	01368 830318	★★★ → ★★★★	Self Catering	⟦♺♺⟧
Neuk Farm Holiday Cottages	Neuk Farm Holiday Cottages, Neuk Farm, Cockburnspath, Berwickshire, TD13 5YH	01368 830459	★★★★	Self Catering	
Red Gauntlet	Tower Farm Holiday Houses, 3 Gardener Street, Dunbar EH42 1AP	0778 9791667	★★★★	Self Catering	
The Sheiling Cottage	Ashley House, Cockburnspath, Berwickshire, TD13 5XA	07747 174388	★★★	Self Catering	

Coldingham

Crosslaw Farmhouse	Crosslaw Farm Cottage, Coldingham, Eyemouth, Berwickshire, TD14 5UH	01890 771319	★★★	Self Catering	
Muscovy House	Courtburn House, School Road, Coldingham, Berwickshire, TD14 5NS	01890 771266	★★★	Self Catering	
Press Mains Cottages	Press Mains, Coldingham, Berwickshire, TD14 5TS	01890 771310	★★★★	Self Catering	⟦♺♺♺⟧
West Loch House Estate	West Loch House, Coldingham, Berwickshire, TD14 5QE	018907 71270	★★ → ★★★	Self Catering	

Coldstream

Abbey House	36 Rawlings Street, London SW3 2LS	0207 5848996	★★★	Self Catering	
Garden Cottage	2 Swinton Mill Cottage, Coldstream, Berwickshire, TD12 4JS	01890 840421	★★★★	Self Catering	
Little Swinton Cottages, Cotoneaster & Honeysuckle	Leet Villa, Leet Street, Coldstream, Berwickshire, TD12 4BJ	01890 882173	★★★	Self Catering	♿
Lochton Farm Cottages	Lochton Farm, Coldstream, Berwickshire, TD12 4NH	01890 830208	★★★★	Self Catering	
Meg's & Nellie's Cottages	Fireburn Mill, Coldstream, Berwickshire, TD12 4LN	01890 882124	★★★	Self Catering	

♿ Unassisted wheelchair access   ♿ Assisted wheelchair access   ♿ Access for visitors with mobility difficulties
♺ Bronze Green Tourism Award   ♺♺ Silver Green Tourism Award   ♺♺♺ Gold Green Tourism Award
For further information on our Green Tourism Business Scheme please see page 9.

Awards correct as of mid August 2008

257

Colinsburgh

Northfield	Northfield, Colinsburgh, Fife, KY9 1HQ	01333 340214	★★★★	Self Catering

Colintraive

Ardachearnbeg Farmhouse Cottages	Ardachearnbeg Farmhouse and Cottages, Glendarvel, Colintraive, Argyll, PA22 3AE	01369 820272	★★★	Self Catering
The Watermill	The Watermill, Glendaruel, Colintraive, Argyll, PA22 3AB	01369 820203	★★★★	Self Catering
Ormidale House	Auchengrange, Belltrees Road, Lochwinnoch, Renfrewshire, PA12 4JS	01505 843678	★★★★	Self Catering

By Colintraive

Waulkmill Cottage	Waulkmill Cottage, Glendaruel, By Colintraive, Argyll, PA22 3AF	01369 820292	★★	Self Catering

Coll, Isle of Lewis

Potters House	Potters House, Coll Pottery, Coll, Isle of Lewis, HS2 0JP	01851 820219	Awaiting Grading	

Collin

Beechfoot Cottage	Beechfoot Cottage, Wathbridge, Collin, Dumfries, DG1 4PY	01387 830636	★★	Self Catering
West Mains Bungalow	Lakeside Cottage, Three Mile Lane, Whitmore, Newcastle, Staffs, ST5 5HW	01782 680968	★★★	Self Catering

Colvend, by Dalbeattie

Rush Croft & Old Glenstocken	Glenstocken, Colvend, Dalbeattie, Dumfriesshire, DG5 4QE	01556 630224	★★★ → ★★★★	Self Catering
Kirkfield	14 Ratcliffe Lane, Sherry Magur, Atherstone, Warwickshire, CV9 3QY	01827 713601	★★★	Self Catering

Comrie

2 Arnottsfield	18 Moorfoot Ave, Giffnock, Glasgow G46 7BY	07710 549729	★★★	Self Catering
Bobbin Mill	Bobbin Mill, Mill of Ross, Comrie, Perthshire, PH6 2JR	01764 679830	★★★★	Self Catering
Boltachan	21 Campbell Park Crescent, Colinton, Edinburgh, Lothian, EH13 0HT	0131 4413133	★★★★	Self Catering
Comrie Cottage	59 Glendaruel Avenue, Bearsden, Glasgow G61 2PP	0141 942 8211	★★★	Self Catering
Glen Cottage	4 Aros Field East, Comrie, Crieff, Perthshire, PH6 2GA	01764 671003	★★★	Self Catering
Glenbuckie Cottage	Glenbuckie Cottage, 2 Drummond Street, Comrie, Perthshire, PH6 2DX	01764 679413	★★	Self Catering
Glenbuckie House	Lawers Estate Company Ltd, Lawers Estate Office, Lawers House, Comrie, Perthshire, PH6 2LT	017674 670050	★★★★	Self Catering
Highland Heather Lodges	Highland Heather Lodges, South Crieff Road, Comrie, Perthshire, PH6 2JA	01764 670440	★★★★	Self Catering 🦽
Melville House	The Royal Hotel, Melville Square, Comrie, Nr Crieff, Perthshire, PH6 2DN	01764 679200	★★★★	Self Catering
Riverside Log Cabins	, Comrie, Perthshire, PH6 2JZ	01764 685310	★★★	Self Catering
Suilven	52 Station Road, Thankerton, Biggar, South Lanark, ML12 6NZ	01899 308479	★★★	Self Catering
The Bothy	Tullichettle, Comrie, Perthshire, PH6 2HU	01764 670349	★★★	Self Catering
The Old Bakery	Cliath Holidays, Hillhall, Drummawhandie Road, Crieff, Perthshire, PH7 4DS	07789 692518	★★★★	Self Catering

&. Unassisted wheelchair access&. Assisted wheelchair access♁ Access for visitors with mobility difficulties
Ⓟ Bronze Green Tourism AwardⓅⓅ Silver Green Tourism AwardⓊⓊⓊ Gold Green Tourism Award
For further information on our Green Tourism Business Scheme please see page 9.

Towyn House	Stamcarty, Little London, Stroud GL5 5DU	01453 762169	★★★★	Self Catering
Viewfield Self Catering Holidays	8 Gleneagles Gate, Newton Mearns, Glasgow G77 5UN	0141 6162373	★★★★	Self Catering
Wallace Lodge	Lochview Farm, Mill of Fortune, Comrie, Perthshire, PH6 2JE	01764 670677	★★★	Self Catering

Conon Bridge

Balinoe	115 Sussex Road, Petersfield, Hampshire, GU31 4LB	01730 267448	★★★★	Self Catering

By Conon Bridge

Alcaig Cottages, alcaig	Alcaig Cottages, Easter Lodge, Alcaig by Conon Bridge, Ross-shire, IV7 8HS	01349 862031	★★★	Self Catering

Corpach

Caledonian Holiday Apartments	Premier Developments (Locharber), Spean Bridge Garage, Spean Bridge, Inverness-shire, PH34 4DX	07770 533817	★★★★★	Self Catering
Kilmallie Chalet	Kilmallie House, Corpach, Inverness-shire, PH33 7JJ	01397 772459	★★★	Self Catering
Snowgoose Holidays	27 Hillview Drive, Corpach, Fort William, Inverness-shire, PH33 7LS	01397 772467	★★★	Self Catering

Corrie, Isle of Arran

Bluebell Cottage	Skew Cottage, High Street, Yelvertoft, Northampton, NN6 6LA	[D01225 4659	★★	Self Catering
Seawinds, Spindrift & Springtide	Cir Mhor, Sannox, Isle of Arran, KA27 8JD	01770 810248	★★★★	Self Catering
Studio Apartment	25 Entake Lane, Dunnington, York, Yorkshire, YO19 5NX	01904 481336	★★★	Self Catering
The Garden Cottage	Brackenbury Self Catering, 3 Sheshader, Point, Isle of Lewis, HS2 0EW	01851 870576	★★★	Self Catering
The Shieling	The Shieling, Corrie, Isle of Arran, K27 8JB	01770 810 240	★★★	Self Catering
The Steading, The Byre and The Barn	The Steading, Corrie, Arran, KA27 8JB	01770 810668	★★ → ★★★	Self Catering

Corriecravie

Corriecravie Farm Cottage	12 Belhaven Terrace, Dowanhill, Glasgow G12 0TG	0141 339 3455	★★★	Self Catering

Cove

Craigrownie Castle	Craigrownie Castle, Stanley Apartment, 1A South Ailey Road, Cove, Argyll & Bute, G84 0PN	01436 840146	★★★★	Self Catering

By Cove

Bayview Bungalows, Pollewe	Bayview Bungalows, 4 Oraiscaig, Aultbea, Ross-shire, IV22 2JJ	01445 731151	★★★★	Self Catering

Craighouse

Stalkers Cottage	Upper Floor, Bank of Scotland, Shore Street, Bowmore, Islay, PA43 7LB	01496 810023	★	Self Catering

Craigmore

Balmoral	Balmoral, 44 Mount Stuart Road, Craigmore, Rothesay, PA20 9EB	01700 503371	★★	Self Catering

Craignure, Isle of Mull

Coach House	28 Cleveland Road, Barnes, London, SW13 0AB	02088 767549	★★★	Self Catering

 ♿ Unassisted wheelchair access ♿ Assisted wheelchair access ∟ Access for visitors with mobility difficulties

Bronze Green Tourism Award   Silver Green Tourism Award   Gold Green Tourism Award

For further information on our Green Tourism Business Scheme please see page 9.

Craignure Bay House	Beechwood, 3 Bainbridge Road, Sedbergh, Cumbria, LA10 5AU	01539 620343	★★★★	Self Catering
Gardeners Cottage	Torosay Castle and Gardens, Craignure, Isle of Mull, PA65 6AY	01680 812421	★★★	Self Catering
Shieling Holidays Cottage	Shieling Holidays, Craignure, Isle of Mull, Argyll, PA65 6AY	01680 812496	★★★	Self Catering
Shore Cottage	Torosay Castle and Gardens, Craignure, Isle of Mull, PA65 6AY	01680 812421	★★	Self Catering

Craigrothie

Athan Cottage	Shillinghill, Old Mill Road, Craigrothie, Fife, KY15 5PZ	01334 828361	★★★	Self Catering

Crail

16 High Street	2 Castle Street, Crail, Fife, KY10 3SQ	01333 450 538	★★	Self Catering
3 Nethergate North	Sandcastle Holidays (Scotland) Ltd, 24 Craigleith View, Edinburgh EH4 3JZ	0131 476 4011	★★★★	Self Catering
43 Shoregate	15 St Leonard's Bank, Edinburgh EH8 9SQ	0131 667 2175	★★★	Self Catering
9 Westgate North	61 Eastwoodmains Road, Glasgow G76 7HQ	0141 554 5281	★★★	Self Catering
Alton Garden Apartment	Alton, Roome Bay Avenue, Crail, Fife, KY10 3TR	01333 451483	★★	Self Catering
Bishop Cottage	3 Alpin Drive, Dunblane FK15 0FQ	01786 821702	★★★★	Self Catering
Craigary	52 Harelaw Avenue, Glasgow, Strathclyde, G44 3HY	0141 571 9432	★★★	Self Catering
Craighead Farm	27 Collins Crescent, Dalgety Bay Fife, KY11 9FG	01383 820397	★★★★	Self Catering
Crail House	Crail House, Castle Street, Crail, Fife, KY10 3SJ	01333 450270	★★★ → ★★★★	Self Catering
Old Coach House	191 Benfieldside Road, Shortly Bridge, Consett, Co.Durham, DH8 0RB	01207 583612	★★★	Self Catering
Seaview Cottage	35 Rose Street, Dunfermline, Fife, KY12 0QT	01383 723366	★★★★	Self Catering
St. Anne's	367 High Street, Edinburgh, Midlothian, EH1 1PW	0131 226 5227	★★★	Self Catering
The Gables	384 Lanark Road, Edinburgh, Lothian, EH13 0LX	0131 441 2006	★★★	Self Catering

Craobh Haven

Craobh Haven Cottages	Craobh Haven Cottages, 17 Brunton Terrace, Edinburgh EH7 5EH	0131 661 2783	★★★★	Self Catering
Morvern Cottage	3 Glenbrook Road, London NW6 1TW	02074 358900	Awaiting Grading	
The Deckhouse	Schiehallion, Smiddyhill, Alford, Aberdeenshire, AB33 8NA	01975 563502	★★★★	Self Catering
Mullach Dubh	High House, Chapel Yard, Station Road, Ivinghoe, Leighton Buzzard, Buckinghamshire, LU7 9EB	01296 668637	★★★★	Self Catering

Crarae, Inveraray

Linwood Cottage	National Trust for Scotland, 28 Charlotte Square, Edinburgh EH2 4ET	0131 243 9335	★★★	Self Catering

Crathie

Birch Cottage	58 Beaconfield Place, Aberdeen AB35 5TJ	01224 643030	★★★★	Self Catering	
Crathie Opportunity Holidays	Crathie Opportunity Holidays, The Manse Courtyard, Crathie, Ballater, AB35 5UL	01339 742100	★★★★	Self Catering ♿	🌿🌿🌿

♿ Unassisted wheelchair access   🦽 Assisted wheelchair access   🚶 Access for visitors with mobility difficulties
🌿 Bronze Green Tourism Award   🌿🌿 Silver Green Tourism Award   🌿🌿🌿 Gold Green Tourism Award
For further information on our Green Tourism Business Scheme please see page 9.

Crawfordjohn

Stonehill Cottage	Stonehill Cottage, Stonehill Farm, Crawfordjohn, Lanarkshire, ML12 6SU	01864 504217	★★★	Self Catering	🏳🏳

Crianlarich

Glengarry Lodge	Glengarry lodge, Tyndrum, Crianachlarich, Perthshire, FK20 8RY	01838 400224	★★★	Self Catering
Portnellan Highland Lodges	Portnellan Highland Lodge, Glen Dochart, By Crianlarich, Perthshire, FK20 8QS	01838 300284	★★★★ → ★★★★★	Self Catering

Crieff

10A Willoughby Street	4 Mount Pleasant, Yardley Goblon, Nr Towcester, Northants, NN12 7TL	01908 263800	★★★	Self Catering	
Aberturret Cottage	Aberturret House, Crieff, Perthshire, PH7 4HA	01764 650064	★★★★	Self Catering	
Avocet, 80 Queens Road	9 Earnmuir Road, Comrie, Crieff, Perthshire, PH6 2EY	01764 670119	★★★★	Self Catering	
Avonlea	Avonlea, 23 Huntley Ave, Giffnock, Glasgow, G46 6LW	0141 6 203734	★★★★	Self Catering	
Braehead	Cul Beag, Balquhidder, Lochearnhead, Perthshire, FK19 8PB	01877 384271	★★★★	Self Catering	
Crieff Hydro Hotel Chalets	Crieff Hydro Hotel, Crieff, Perthshire, PH7 3LQ	01764 655555	★★★ → ★★★★★	Self Catering	♿
Croftweit & St Ninian's Tower Apartment	Apartment 3, Croftweit, Strathearn Terrace, Crieff, Perthshire, PH7 3AQ	01764 650707	★★★★★	Self Catering	
Hawkshaw House & Merlin Cottage	4E Airlie Gardens, London W8 7AJ	020 72219017	★★★★	Self Catering	
Ladeside	Comrie House, Comrie, Crieff, Perthshire, PH6 2LR	01764 670640	★★★★	Self Catering	
Loch Monzievaird	Loch Monzievaird, Ochtertyre, Crieff, Perthshire, PH7 4JR	01764 652586	★★★★	Self Catering	🏳🏳🏳
Millhouse Garden Flat	Millhouse Garden Flat, Millhouse, South Bridgend, Crieff, Perthshire, PH7 4NH	01764 650443	★★★★	Self Catering	♁
Old St Michaels	Old St Michaels, Broich Terrace, Crieff, Perthshire, PH7 3BD	01764 654059	★★★★	Self Catering	
The Strathearn and The Penthouse	Mansio Properties, Qakwood, 13 Marcosty Gardens, Crieff, Perthshire, PH7 4LP	07967 679787	★★★★★	Self Catering	
Westlodge	Westlodge, Westacre, New Fowlis, by Crieff, Perthshire, PH7 3NH	01764 683365	★★★★	Self Catering	

Crocketford, Nr Dumfries

Burnbrae Mill	Burnside Self Catering Holidays,Horseclose, Burnbrae Farm, Milton, Crocketford,nr Dumfries, Dumfries and	01556 690505	★★★★	Self Catering

Croftamie

Lomond Luxury Lodges	Oakwoods, Crofthamie, Alexandria, G63 0EX	01360 660054	★★★★ → ★★★★★	Self Catering	🏳🏳

Croftinloan, Pitlochry

Courtyard Cottage	Courtyard Cottage, Croftinloan Farm, Croftinloan, Pitlochry, Perthshire, PH16 5TA	01796 474433	★★★★	Self Catering

Cromarty

Lydia Cottage	National Trust for Scotland, 28 Charlotte Square, Edinburgh EH2 4ET	0131 243 9335	★★★	Self Catering

Crosbie Mains, West Kilbride

The Ploughman's Rest	John F Parker & Co, Crosbie Mains, West Kilbride, Ayrshire, KA23 9PH	01294 822281	★★★★	Self Catering

♿ Unassisted wheelchair access   ♿ Assisted wheelchair access   ♁ Access for visitors with mobility difficulties
🏳 Bronze Green Tourism Award   🏳🏳 Silver Green Tourism Award   🏳🏳🏳 Gold Green Tourism Award
For further information on our Green Tourism Business Scheme please see page 9.

Awards correct as of mid August 2008

Crossmichael

Airdside	Airds Farmhouse, Crossmichael, Castle Douglas, Kirkcudbrightshire, DG7 3BG	01556 670418	★★★	Self Catering	

Crovie Village

13 Crovie	12 Dean Road, Kilmarnock, Ayrshire, KA3 1RP	01563 535790	★★★	Self Catering	

Croy

Balblair	Balblair, Croy, Inverness, IV2 5PH	01667 493407	★★★	Self Catering	𝝅	🄿
The Coach House and Gate Lodge	Dalcross Estate, c/o 19 Pembridge Square, London W2 4EJ	07748 873699	★★★★	Self Catering		

Crulivig, Isle of Lewis

4 Earsharder	31 Danes Drive, Glasgow, Renfrewshire, G14 9HY	0141 569 8007	★★	Self Catering	
Hollyburn	Dachaidh Ur, Lower Bayble Point, Isle of Lewis, HS2 0QB	01851 870483	★★★	Self Catering	

Culbokie

Achbuie	Achbuie, Breachloch, Culbokie, Ross-shire, IV7 8GY	01349 877770	★★★	Self Catering	
Dunvournie Farm Cottage	Dunvournie Farm, Culbokie, By Dingwall, Ross-shire, IV7 8JB	01349 877246	★★	Self Catering	
Wester Brae Highland Lodges and Chalets	Westerbrae Lodges/Chalets, Westerbrae, Culbokie, by Dingwall, Ross-shire, IV7 8JU	01349 877609	★★★★	Self Catering	𝝅

Cullen

16 Albert Terrace	East Hillochs, Tullynessie, Alford, Aberdeenshire, AB33 8QR	01975 562214	★★★	Self Catering	
236 Seatown	Hill of Blackford, Rothienorman, Inverurie, Aberdeenshire AB51 8YC	01651 821229	★★★	Self Catering	
78 Seatown	Lesina, Kennethmont, Huntly, Aberdeenshire, AB54 4NN	01464 831696	★★★	Self Catering	
88 Seatown	Buschweide, Pitkeathly Wells Road, Bridge of Earn, Perthshire, PH2 9HA	01738 812862	★★★	Self Catering	
Seatown Cottage	61 Abergeldie Road, Aberdeen AB10 6ED	01224 590676	★★★	Self Catering	

Culloden

Culloden Stables	Douglas and MacKay Holiday Lets, 1B Slackbuie Avenue, Inverness, Inverness-shire, IV2 4QL	01463 709816	★★★	Self Catering	
Clava Lodge Holiday Homes	Clava Lodge Holiday Homes, Culloden Moor, Inverness-shire, IV2 5EJ	01463 790228	★★ → ★★★	Self Catering	

Culsalmond, Insch

Snipie's Bothy	Snipefield, Culsalmond, Insch, Aberdeenshire, AB52 6TU	01464 841394	★★★★	Self Catering	🄿🄿🄿

Cupar

Garden Cottage	Kinloss House, Cupar, Fife, KY15 4ND	01334 654169	★★★★	Self Catering	
Middle Cottage	National Trust for Scotland, 28 Charlotte Square, Edinburgh EH2 4ET	0131 243 9335	★★	Self Catering	
St Andrews Country Cottages	St Andrews Country Cottages, Mountquhanie Estate, By Cupar, Fife, KY15 4QJ	01382 330318	★★★ → ★★★★	Self Catering	𝝅
St Andrew's House	National Trust for Scotland, 28 Charlotte Square, Edinburgh EH2 4ET	0131 243 9335	★★★	Self Catering	

     🪑 Unassisted wheelchair access   🪑 Assisted wheelchair access   𝝅 Access for visitors with mobility difficulties
     🄿 Bronze Green Tourism Award   🄿🄿 Silver Green Tourism Award   🄿🄿🄿 Gold Green Tourism Award
For further information on our Green Tourism Business Scheme please see page 9.

Upper West Wing Flat	National Trust for Scotland, 28 Charlotte Square, Edinburgh EH2 4ET	0131 243 9335 ★★	Self Catering	
West Cottage	National Trust for Scotland, 28 Charlotte Square, Edinburgh EH2 4ET	0131 243 9335 ★★	Self Catering	

By Cupar

Bishop Cottage, Ceres	Way Side, 6 Castle Road, Longforgan, Perthshire, DD2 5HA	01382 360294 ★★★★	Self Catering	

Dalbeattie

26&70 Barend Holiday Village	Barend Holiday Village, Sandyhills, Dalbeattie, Dumfries & Galloway, DG5 4NU	★★	Self Catering	
Barclosh Farm, Stable, Mill & Barn Cottages	G&S Cook, Barclosh Farm, Dalbeattie, Kirkcudbrightshire, DG5 4PL	01556 610380 ★★★ → ★★★★	Self Catering	𝓟𝓟
Bracken Cottage	Bracken Cottage, Fairgirth Farm, Dalbeattie, Dumfries & Galloway, DG5 4NS	01387 780221 ★★★★	Self Catering	
Craigbittern Cottage	Craigbittern House, Sandyhills, By Dalbeattie, Kirkcudbrightshire, DG5 4NZ	01387 780247 ★★★	Self Catering	
Drumbeg	The Sycamores, Bradford Road, Tingley, Wakefield, West Yorkshire, WF3 1QU	01132 528234 ★★★	Self Catering	
Kippford Holiday Park	Kippford Holiday Park, Dalbeattie, Kirkcudbrightshire, DG5 4LF	01556 620636 ★★★	Self Catering ✦	
Rockyknowe	Rockyknowe, Croft Corner, Meikle Richorn, Dalbeattie, Dumfries and Galloway, DG5 4QT	01556 611549	Awaiting Grading	
The Mount	8 Lovers Walk, Dumfries DG1 1LP	01387 264212 ★★★★	Self Catering	
Thistle Lodge	Thistle Lodges Ltd, Monkhouse Hill, Sebergham Nr Caldbeck, Cumbria, CA5 7HW	016974 76254 ★★★	Self Catering	
Wood End	Lampacre, Stoke Lane, Stoke Lacy, Bromyard, Herefordshire, HR7 4HD	01885 490286 ★★	Self Catering	

By Dalbeattie

Allbony Cottage	4 Quinton Place, Codford St Peter, Wiltshire, BA12 OJU	01985 850134 ★★★	Self Catering	
Kirkfield	14 Ratcliffe Lane, Sherry Magur, Atherstone, Warwickshire, CV9 3QY	01827 713601 ★★★	Self Catering	
Magnet Cottage	634 Clarkston Road, Netherlee, Glasgow KA27 8QH	0141 585 7076 ★★★	Self Catering	
Rush Croft & Old Glenstocken	Glenstocken, Colvend, Dalbeattie, Dumfriesshire, DG5 4QE	01556 630224 ★★★ → ★★★★	Self Catering	
Watersedge	Lochend, Colvend, By Dalbeattie DG5 4QD	01556 630382 ★★★	Self Catering	

Dalcross

East Dalziel Cottages	Easter Dalziel Farm, Dalcross, Inverness-shire, IV2 7JL	01667 462213 ★★★ → ★★★★	Self Catering	

Dalfaber

Cairngorm Lodge	4 Creag A'Ghrensaiche, Dalfaber, Aviemore, Highland, PH22 1LD	07774 401639 ★★★	Self Catering	

Dalgety Bay

Seaview Apartment	Shadha, 5 Nagle Road, Kingseat, Fife, KY12 0UN	01383 620942 ★★★★	Self Catering	
The Courtyard	8 East Bay, North Queensferry, Fife, KY11 1JX	01383 413242 ★★★★	Self Catering	

Dalkeith

The Garden Apartment	AEM Holiday Apartment, 45 Eskbank Road, Dalkeith By Edinburgh, Mid Lothian, EH22 3BH	0131 663 3291 ★★★★	Self Catering	

      ♿ Unassisted wheelchair access   ♿ Assisted wheelchair access   ✦ Access for visitors with mobility difficulties
      𝓟 Bronze Green Tourism Award   𝓟𝓟 Silver Green Tourism Award   𝓟𝓟𝓟 Gold Green Tourism Award
      For further information on our Green Tourism Business Scheme please see page 9.

By Dalkeith

Cornes Cottage	47 Hadfast Road, Cousland, by Dalkeith, Midlothian, EH22 2NZ	0131 663 0084	★★★★	Self Catering

Dalmally

Blarghour Farm	Blarghour Farm, Dalmally, Argyll, PA33 1BW	01866 833246	★★★★	Self Catering
Creagan	26 Achlonan, Taynuilt, Argyll, PA35 1JJ	01866 822334	★★★	Self Catering

By Dalmally

Ardbrecknish House	Ardbrecknish House, South Lochaweside, By Dalmally, Argyll, PA33 1BH	01866 833223	★★	Self Catering
Kintyre Apartments, Inveraray Lodge, Harrier	Argyll Chalets, Sonachan House, Portsonachan, By Dalmally, Argyll, PA33 1BN	01866 833240	Awaiting Grading	
Millside & Garden Cottages	Inistrynich, by Dalmally, Argyll, PA33 1BQ	01838 200256	Awaiting Grading	

Dalry

Baidland Mill	2 Oldstede, Chestnut Street, Borden, Sittingbourne, Kent, ME9 8DA	01795 843844	★★★	Self Catering
Blair, The Stable Flat	Blair, The Stable Flat, The Carriage House, Dalry, Ayrshire, KA24 4ER	01294 833100	★★★★	Self Catering
Dukieston Cottage	Dukieston Cottage, Forrest Estate, Dalry, Castle Douglas, Dumfries & Galloway, DG7 3XS	01644 430230	★★★	Self Catering

Dalrymple

Springwater Chalets Ltd	Springwater Chalets Ltd, Springwater Fishery, Dalrymple, By Ayr, Ayrshire, KA6 6AW	07792 499957	★★★	Self Catering	⋀

Darnick, Melrose

Harleyburn Cottages, Stables and Saddlery	The Coach House, Chiefswood Road, Darnick,Melrose, Roxburghshire, TD6 9BA	01896 822300	★★★★	Self Catering

Daviot

The Dairy at Daviot	House of Daviot, Daviot Estate, Inverness IV2 5ER	01463 772110	★★★★	Self Catering

Denny

Wellsfield Farm Holiday Lodges	Wellsfield Farm Holiday Lodges, Stirling Road, Denny, Stirlingshire, FK6 6QZ	01324 825044	★★★★	Self Catering

Dervaig, Isle of Mull

Ardrioch Farm	Ardrioch Farm, Dervaig, Isle Of Mull, PA75 6QR	01688 400415	★★★	Self Catering	
Clachan Cottage	The Clachan, Dervaig, Isle of Mull, Argyll, PA75 6QR	01688 400303	★★★	Self Catering	
Coille Grianach	57 Orchard Road, Tewin, Welwyn, Hertfordshire, AL6 0HL	01438 798700	★★★	Self Catering	
Corrieyairack & Fas Na Cloich	Cocklaw Farm, Biggar, Lanarkshire, ML12 6RD	01899 220473	★★★★	Self Catering	⋀
Croig	Croig, Dervaig, Isle of Mull, PA75 6QS	01688 400219	★★★	Self Catering	
Glenview	Glenview, Dervaig, Isle of Mull, Argyll, PA75 6QJ	01688 400239	★★★	Self Catering	
The Old Mill	The Old Mill, Penmore, Dervaig, Isle of Mull, PA75 6QS	01688 400242	★★★★	Self Catering	𝄢𝄢
Torr a'Clachan	Kengharair Farm, Dervaig, Isle of Mull, PA75 6QR	01688 400251	★★★	Self Catering	

   ♿ Unassisted wheelchair access   ♿ Assisted wheelchair access   ⋀ Access for visitors with mobility difficulties
   𝄢 Bronze Green Tourism Award   𝄢𝄢 Silver Green Tourism Award   𝄢𝄢𝄢 Gold Green Tourism Award
For further information on our Green Tourism Business Scheme please see page 9.

To find out more, call 0845 22 55 121 or go to visitscotland.com.

Half-Moon House	110 Boundary Lane, Congleton, Cheshire CW12 3JF	01260 298512	★★★★	Self Catering
Achadh A'Mhullaich	20 West Lorne Street, Chester, Cheshire, CH1 4AF	01244 373862	★★★	Self Catering

Dingwall

Ballyskelly Lodge	Ballyskelly House, Poyntzfield, Dingwall, Black Isle, IV7 8LX	01381 610253	★★★	Self Catering

By Dingwall

Magnelia House	Ben Wyvis Views, Bydand, Culbokie, Ross-shire, IV7 8JH	01349 877430	★★★★	Self Catering
Seaforth Highland Country Estate	Seaforth Highland Estate, Brahan, Dingwall, Ross-shire, IV7 8EE	01349 861150	★★ → ★★★★	Self Catering
Fodderty Lodge	Fodderty Lodge, Fodderty, by Dingwall, ROSS-SHIRE, IV15 9UE	01997 421393	★★★ → ★★★★	Self Catering
Rose Cottage	Inchvannie, Strathpeffer, Ross-shire, IV14 9AD	01997 421436	★★★	Self Catering

Dippen, Isle of Arran

Woodlea Cottage	Woodlea House, Dippen, Isle of Arran, KA27 8RN	01770 820298	★★★	Self Catering

Dollar

Arndean Cottages	Arndean Cottages, Arndean, Dollar, Clackmannanshire, FK14 7NH	01259 743525	★★★★	Self Catering 🦽
Campbell Cottage	Campbell Cottage, 13 Campbell Street, Dollar, Clackmannanshire, FK14 7EX	01259 743765	★★★★	Self Catering
Tigh-Na-Mairi	The Stables, Burnfoot, Glendevon, Dollar, Clackmannanshire, FK14 7JY	01259 781270	★★★★	Self Catering

Dores

Loch Ness Log Cabins	Loch Ness Log Cabins, Drummond, Dores, Inverness-shire, IV2 6TX	01463 751251	★★	Self Catering

Dornie

Birchwood Holiday Cottage	Birchwood Holiday Cottage, Mo Dhachaidh, Badicaul, Kyle, Ross-shire, IV40 8BB	01599 534823	★★★★	Self Catering

By Dornie

Tighe Mo Cridhe, carnduby	20 Hermand Gardens, West Calder, West Lothian, EH55 8BT	01506 872063	★★★★	Self Catering

Dornoch

1 Church Street	Easdale, Carnaig Street, Dornoch, Sutherland, IV25 3LT	01862 810484	★★★	Self Catering
5 Dornoch Square East	Spinwell Cottage, Nursery Walk, Spinfield Lane, Marlow, Buckinghamshire, SL7 2LL	01628 486801	★★★★	Self Catering
East Dune	2 Temperance Street, St Albans, Herts, AL3 4QA	01727 840805	★★★★	Self Catering
Fairways	14 Ardlui Gardens, Milngavie, Glasgow G62 7RL	0141 9550644	★★★	Self Catering
Glenmuir Cottage	Highfield House, 62 Old Edinburgh Rd, Inverness IV2 3PG	01463 238892	★★★★	Self Catering
Kenmore	5 Acredales, Linlithgow, West Lothian, EH49 6HY	01506 842494	★★	Self Catering
Links Cottage	Balbain House, Rosebery Avenue, Dornoch, Sutherland, IV25 3SZ	01862 811192	★★★	Self Catering
Miltown of Evelix Cottage	Cyderhall, Dornoch, Sutherland, IV25 3RW	01862 810414	★★★	Self Catering

♿ Unassisted wheelchair access   🦽 Assisted wheelchair access   🚶 Access for visitors with mobility difficulties
🌿 Bronze Green Tourism Award   🌿🌿 Silver Green Tourism Award   🌿🌿🌿 Gold Green Tourism Award
For further information on our Green Tourism Business Scheme please see page 9.

| Oatfield | 3 Stevenson Drive, Abingdon, Oxon OX14 1SN | 01235 529940 | ★★★ | Self Catering | |

Doune, Stirling

| Gled Cottage, 92 Cooperage Quay & 17 Bridgend Court | Mackeanston House, Doune, Perthshire FK16 6AX | 01786 850213 | ★★★★ | Self Catering | ⬈ |

Dowanhill

| Glasgow Gem | 134 Brownside Road, Cambuslang, Glasgow G72 8AH | 0141 6413239 | ★★★★ | Self Catering | |

Drem

| The Byre Cottage | The Byres Cottage, 2 Newmains Farm Steading, Drem, East Lothian, EH39 5BL | 01620 880300 | ★★★ → ★★★★ | Self Catering | |

Drumbeg

| The Sheiling | Pinewood, Scotsburn Road, Kildary, Invergordon, Ross-shire, IV18 0NX | 01862 842665 | ★★ | Self Catering | |

Drummore

| Harbour Row | 10 Mill St, Drummore DG9 9PS | 01776 840631 | ★★★ → ★★★★ | Self Catering | ⬈ |
| Old Diary Cottage | 2 Low Currochtrie, Drummore, Stranraer, Wigtownshire, DG9 9QS | 01776 840242 | ★★★★ | Self Catering | ⬈ |

By Drummore

Kittiwake House	National Trust for Scotland, 28 Charlotte Square, Edinburgh EH2 4ET	0131 243 9335	★★★	Self Catering	
Old Lighthouse Keepers' Cottage	National Trust for Scotland, 28 Charlotte Square, Edinburgh EH2 4ET	0131 243 9335	★★★	Self Catering	
Puffin House	National Trust for Scotland, 28 Charlotte Square, Edinburgh EH2 4ET	0131 243 9335	★★★	Self Catering	

Drumnadrochit

Achmony Holidays	Achmony Holidays, Achmony, Drumnadrochit, By Loch Ness, IV63 6UX	01456 450357	★★★★	Self Catering	
Ancarraig Lodges	Ancarraig Lodges, Bunloit, Drumnadrochit, Inverness-shire, IV63 6XG	01456 450377	★★★	Self Catering	
Cherry Trees, Milton	Glaichmor, Milton, Drumnadrochit, Inverness-shire, IV63 6TZ	01456 450257	★★★	Self Catering	
Drumnadrochit Lodges	Upper Achmony, Drumnadrochit, By Loch Ness, IV63 6UX	01456 450467	★★★★	Self Catering	
Glenurquhart Lodges	Glenurquhart Lodges, Drumnadrochit, Inverness-shire, IV63 6TJ	01456 476234	★★ → ★★★	Self Catering	
Kilmartin Chalet Park	Kilmartin Chalet Park, Glenurquhart, Drumnadrochit, Inverness-shire, IV63 6TN	01456 476799	★★ → ★★★	Self Catering	
McNeill's, Larch, Marnies & Iolaire	Borlum Farm, Drumnadrochit, Inverness-shire, IV63 6XN	01456 450358	★★★ → ★★★★	Self Catering	
Rillan	The Conifers,87 High Road, Leavesden, Watford, Herts, WD25 7AL	01923 674525	★★★	Self Catering	

Drymen

Drymen Holiday Apartment	Drymen Holiday Apartment, Flat 4, 23 Stirling Road, Drymen, Stirlingshire, G63 0BW	01360 660105	★★★★	Self Catering	
Elmbank	Fraser Associates, 10b Stirling Road, Drymen G63 0BN	01360 661016	★★	Self Catering	
Flat 2	Flat 3/2, 150 Wilton Street, Glasgow G20 6DG	07724 428810	★★★★	Self Catering	
Foxglove Cottages	Foxglove Cottages, Gartness Road, Drymen, Loch Lomond, Glasgow, G63 0DW	01360 661128	★★★★★	Self Catering	♿ 𝓟𝓟𝓟

          ♿ Unassisted wheelchair access   ♿ Assisted wheelchair access   ⬈ Access for visitors with mobility difficulties
       𝓟 Bronze Green Tourism Award   𝓟𝓟 Silver Green Tourism Award   𝓟𝓟𝓟 Gold Green Tourism Award
For further information on our Green Tourism Business Scheme please see page 9.

266   To find out more, call 0845 22 55 121 or go to visitscotland.com.

Inches	Inches, 25 Balmaha Road, Drymen, Stirlingshire, G63 0BX	01360 660141	★★★★	Self Catering	
Loaninghead Farm Bothy	Loaninghead Farm, Balfron Station, Loch Lomond, Glasgow, G63 0SE	01360 440432	★★★★	Self Catering	℗℗
Templelea Farm Cottage	Ballochearn, Wester Ballochearn Farm, Balfron, by Glasgow, G63 0QE	01360 860357	★★★	Self Catering	
The Annex	The Annex, 64 Main Street, Drymen, Stirlingshire, G63 0BG	01360 660008	★★★	Self Catering	
Tullycross Cottage	Tullycross Cottage, Croftamine, Drymen, Stirlingshire, G63 OHG	01360 661124	★★★	Self Catering	

By Drymen

Chalet 30	14 Ballencriess Mill, Balmurr Road, Bathgate EH48 4LL	01506 650725	★★★★	Self Catering	
Dalhougal House Apartment, Croftamie	Dalhougal House, Croftamie, Glasgow G63 0EU	01360 660558	★★★★	Self Catering	

Drynachan

Banchor Cottage	Cawdor Castle, Nairn IV12 5RD	01667 404401	★★★★	Self Catering	

Dufftown

Moray Cottages	Moray Cottages, Auchinhandoch, Dufftown, Banffshire, AB55 4DR	01340 820007	★★★★	Self Catering	
Hillview	Stonefolds, Fyvie, Turriff, Aberdeenshire, AB53 8NN	01651 891267	★★★★	Self Catering	
Parkmore Farm Holiday Cottages	Parkmore Farm, Dufftown, Keith, Moray, AB55 4DN	01340 820072	★★★ → ★★★★	Self Catering	♿

Duirinish

Duirinish Lodge East Wing	3 Northumberland Street, Edinburgh, Lothian, EH3 6LL	0131 556 0101	★★★★★	Self Catering	
Granny's Croft House & Quiraing	Seann Bhruthach, Duirinish, by Plockton, Ross-shire, IV40 8BE	01599 544204	★★★★	Self Catering	♁
Rowan Bank	West Muirton, Sauchen, Inverurie, Aberdeenshire, AB51 7QQ	01330 833310	★★★	Self Catering	

Dulnain Bridge

Fiathail House	4 Comely Bank, Perth, Perthshire, PH2 7HU	01738 624788	★★★★	Self Catering	
Lanson	Lanson, Broomhill, Dulnain Bridge, Inverness-shire, PH26 3LX	01479 851314	★★★	Self Catering	
The Cabrach & Corrimony	The Cabrach, Skye of Curr, Dulnain Bridge, Inverness-shire, PH26 3PA	01479 851229	★★★★	Self Catering	
Thistle Cottage & Dulnain House	Speyside Heather Centre, Skye of Curr, Dulnain Bridge, Inverness-shire, PH26 3PA	01479 851359	★★★★	Self Catering	

Dumbarton

Albion House	Elstow House, Benington, Herts, SG2 7DE	01438 869554	★★★	Self Catering	
Barnhill House	Barnhill, Milton, Dumbartonshire, G82 2TD	01389 761401	★★★	Self Catering	

Dumfries

Alder and Acorn	The Cedars, Clarencefield, Dumfries, Dumfries-shire, DG1 4NF	01387 870608	★★★★	Self Catering	♿
Arden Holiday Cottages	Arden Holiday Cottages, Irongray, Dumfries, Dumfriesshire, DG2 9SQ	01387 730309	★★★★	Self Catering	
Armandii Cottage	The Lodge, Newtonairds, Dumfries DG2 0JL	01387 820203	★★★	Self Catering	

♿ Unassisted wheelchair access   ♿ Assisted wheelchair access   ♁ Access for visitors with mobility difficulties
℗ Bronze Green Tourism Award   ℗℗ Silver Green Tourism Award   ℗℗℗ Gold Green Tourism Award
For further information on our Green Tourism Business Scheme please see page 9.

Ashwell Holiday Home	Ashwell, Lockerbie Road, Dumfries, Dumfriesshire, DG1 3PG	01387 255 469	★★★	Self Catering
Cairnyard Holiday Lodges	Nether Cairnyard, Beeswing, Dumfries, Dumfriesshire, DG2 8JE	01387 730218	★★★	Self Catering ☺
Conheath Gatelodge	Conheath, Glencaple, Dumfries, Dumfriesshire, DG1 4UB	01387 770205	★★★ → ★★★★	Self Catering ♿
Dalswinton Mill	Dalswinton Mill, Dalswinton, Dumfries, Dumfries & Galloway, DG2 0XY	01387 740421	★★	Self Catering
Friars Carse Hotel (Self-Catering)	Friars Carse Hotel, Auldgirth Dumfries and Galloway, DG2 0SA	01387 740388	★★★	Self Catering
Greenhead Lodge	Greenhead Lodge, Dunscore, Dumfries, Dumfriesshire, DG2 0JT	01387 820396	★★★	Self Catering
Gubhill Farm	Gubhill Farm, Ae, Dumfries, Dumfriesshire, DG1 1RL	01387 860648	★★ → ★★★	Self Catering ♿
Mews Flat	Dalswinton House, Dalswinton, Dumfries DG2 0XZ	01387 740220	★★★★	Self Catering
Mill Cottage	Old Mill House, Near Shawhead, Irongay, Dumfries, Dumfries & Galloway, DG2 9SQ	01387 730417	★★★★	Self Catering
Nunland Country Holidays	Nunland Country Holidays, by Lochfoot, Dumfries DG2 8PZ	01387 730214	★★★ → ★★★★	Self Catering ♿
Park of Brandedleys	Park of Brandedleys, Crocketford, Dumfries DG2 8RG	01387 266 700	★★	Self Catering
Pleasance Holiday Letting	Pleasance Holiday letting, Pleasance of Cargen, Islesteps, Dumfries, Dumfriesshire, DG2 8EU	01387 253908	★★★	Self Catering

Dunbar

10B Beachmont Place	67A Parsonage Gardens, Enfield, Middlesex, EN2 6JR	020 8366 6165	★★★	Self Catering
Brunt House	Aromanock Forestry Ltd, Nr Spott, Dunbar, East Lothian, EH42 1RL	01368 862100	★★★★	Self Catering
Goldenoak Chalet	West Meikle Pinkerton, Dunbar, East Lothian, EH42 1RX	01368 840669	★★★	Self Catering
The Harbour House	1 High Street, Bellhaven, Dunbar, East Lothian, EH42 1NP	01368 862427	★★★★	Self Catering

By Dunbar

Belhaven Gardens	1 Stevens Way, Amersham, Bucks, HT7 0HE	07789 693381	★★★	Self Catering
Nirvana Cottage	32 Tenison Avenue, Cambridge, Cambridgeshire, CB1 2DY	01223 356038	★★★	Self Catering
Surfsplash	Surfsplash, 3 Fiddlers Yard, Woodbush, Dunbar, East lothian, EH42 1HB	01620 860374	★★★★	Self Catering

Dunbeath

Strathallan	Corrigall' Main Road Watten, Wick, Caithness, KW1 5XG	01955 621955	★★★★	Self Catering

Dunblane

Beggshill Bothy	Beggshill Bothy, Little Beggshill, Dunblade, Huntly, Aberdeenshire, AB54 6AN	01466 740325	★★★	Self Catering
Cauldhame Cottages	Cauldhame Cottage, Sheriffmuir, Dunblane, Perthshire, FK15 0LN	01786 823138	★★★	Self Catering
Craighead Farm	Craighead Farm, Braco, Dunblane, Perthshire, FK15 9LP	01786 880321	★★★★★	Self Catering
Stable Cottage	Stable Cottage, Row House, Dunblane, Perthshire, FK15 9NZ	01786 841200	★★★	Self Catering ☺

Dundee

Balmuirfield House	Balmuirfild House, Harestane Road, Dundee DD3 0NU	01382 818444	★★★★	Self Catering

♿ Unassisted wheelchair access   ♿ Assisted wheelchair access   ☺ Access for visitors with mobility difficulties
✏ Bronze Green Tourism Award   ✏✏ Silver Green Tourism Award   ✏✏✏ Gold Green Tourism Award
For further information on our Green Tourism Business Scheme please see page 9.

To find out more, call 0845 22 55 121 or go to visitscotland.com.

Redmyre Farmhouse	Redmyre Farm, Tarrylan, Balbeggie, Perth, Perthshire, PH2 6HL	01821 640234	★★★★	Self Catering
Seabraes Self Catering Flats	Sanctuary Management Services, Heathfield Office, 75 Old Hawkhill, Dundee, Angus, DD1 5EN	01382 573111	★★	Self Catering ⛶

By Dundee

East Mains House	East Mains House, Auchterhouse, by Dundee, Angus, DD3 0QN	01382 320206	★★★	Self Catering
Piperdam	Piperdam, Fowlis, by Dundee, Angus, DD2 5LP	01382 581374	★★★★	Self Catering

Dundonnell

Heathmount	23 Wych Elm Road, Oadby, Leicester LE2 4EF	0116 271 0353	★★★★	Self Catering	
Pottery Croft Cottage	Croft 9, Badrallach, Dundonnell, Ross-shire, IV23 2QP	01854 633281	★★★★	Self Catering	⫶
Tigh-na-Mara & Ceol-na-Mara	4 Camusnagaul, Dundonnell, Ross-shire, IV23 2QT	01854 633237	★★★	Self Catering	

Dunfermline

Bowleys Farm Self Catering	Bowleys Farm Self Catering, Dunfermline, Fife, KY12 0SG	01383 721056	★★★	Self Catering
North Dhuloch Cottage	North Dhuloch House, Dunfermline KY11 8HW	01383 419163	★★★★	Self Catering
The Garden Town House	The Garden Town House, 7 Park Avenue, Dunfermline, Fife, KY12 7HX	01383 739539	★★★	Self Catering

Dunkeld

City Hall Apartments	Auchlou, Inver, Dunkeld, Perthshire, PH8 0JR	01350 727569	★★★★	Self Catering	
Erigmore Estate Leisure Park	President Leisure Ltd, The Yacht Harbour, Inverkip, Renfrewshire, PA16 0AS	01350 727236	★★★	Self Catering ⛶	⫶⫶
Farmhouse Cottage	Meikle Logie Farmhouse, Trocary, Dunkeld, Perthshire, PH8 0BP	01350 723282	Awaiting Grading		
Laighwood Self Catering	Laighwood Self Catering, Dunkeld, Perthshire, PH8 OHB	01350 724241	★★★ → ★★★★	Self Catering	
Laird's Inn	Blackhill, Dunkeld Perthshire, PH8 0HQ	01738 710446	★★★	Self Catering	
Little Puddockwells	Puddockwells, Dunkeld, Perthshire, PH8 0HQ	01738 710536	★★★	Self Catering	
The Ell House	National Trust for Scotland, 28 Charlotte Square, Edinburgh EH2 4ET	0131 243 9335	★★★	Self Catering	
Tomnagairn Cottage	Tomnagrew, Dunkeld, Perthshire, PH8 OBX	01350 723228	★★★	Self Catering	

By Dunkeld

Inch Cottage	35 Chester Street, Edinburgh, Midlothian, EH3 7EN	0131 225 5235	★★★	Self Catering
Log Cabin	135 Grahamsdyke Street, Laurieston, Falkirk, Stirlingshire, FK2 9LP	01324 625019	★★	Self Catering
Kinnaird Estate	Kinnaird Estate, Kinnaird, by Dunkeld, Perthshire, PH9 0LB	01796 482440	★★★ → ★★★★★	Self Catering

Dunnet

The Croft	Clairruah, West Side, Dunnet, Thurso, Caithness	01847 851889	Awaiting Grading

Dunning

Duncrub Holidays Ltd	Duncrub Holidays Ltd, Dalreoch, Dunning, Perthshire, PH2 0QJ	01764 684368	★★★★ → ★★★★★	Self Catering ♿

     ♿ Unassisted wheelchair access   ♿ Assisted wheelchair access   ⛶ Access for visitors with mobility difficulties
    ⫶ Bronze Green Tourism Award   ⫶⫶ Silver Green Tourism Award   ⫶⫶⫶ Gold Green Tourism Award
    For further information on our Green Tourism Business Scheme please see page 9.

Dunoon

Name	Address	Phone	Rating	Type	
17 Fairhaven	The Close, Mill Lane, Cloughton, near Scarborough, N Yorkshire, YO13 0AB	01723 870455	★★★	Self Catering	
2 Lamont Lodges	Oriel Cottage, East Links Road, Dunbar, East Lothian, EH42 1LT	01368 863920	★	Self Catering	
4 Deercroft Hafton	15 Deercroft Hafton, Dunoon, Argyll, PA23 8HP	01369 703586	★★★	Self Catering	
71 Fairhaven	Serendipity, Blythewood Place, Port Elphinstone, Inverurie, Aberdeenshire, AB51 3XE	01467 626071	★★★	Self Catering	
Chase The Wild Goose	River Cottage, Rashfield, Dunoon, Argyll, PA23 8QT	01369 840672	★★★	Self Catering	
Clyde Cottage	Ri Cruin, Kilmartin, By Lochgilphead, Argyll, PA31 8QF	01546 510316	★★★★	Self Catering	
Hunters Quay Holiday Village	Hunters Quay Holiday Village, Hunters Quay, Dunoon, Argyll, PA23 8HP	01369 707772	★★★	Self Catering	
Lyall Cliff	Lyall Cliff, 141 Alexandra Parade, East Bay, Dunoon, Argyll, PA23 8AW	01369 702041	★★★	Self Catering	
North Lodge	North Lodge Kilmun, The Anchorage, South Fergus Place, Kirkcaldy, Fife, KY1 1YA	01595 202564	★★	Self Catering	
Sebright	14 SA Alexandra Parade, Dunoon, Argyll, PA23 8AN	01369 704860	★★★	Self Catering	
Strathspey	Mallards, Potton End, Elisley, St Neots, Cambridgeshire, PE19 6TH	01480 880395	★★★	Self Catering	

By Dunoon

Name	Address	Phone	Rating	Type	
Stewart's Lodge	4 Rose Crescent, Gourock PA19 1TA	01475 638080	★★★	Self Catering	
Duncreggan House	70 Grange Road, Erdington, Birmingham B24 0DF	07973 129490	★★★	Self Catering	
Fintry	1 Myrtle Avenue, Lenzie, Kirkintilloch, Glasgow, G66 4HW	0141 776 3158	★★★	Self Catering	
Glenstriven and Knockdow Estate	The Lodge, Glenstriven Estate, Toward, by Dunoon, PA23 7UN	01369 870007	★★★ → ★★★★	Self Catering	
Stronchullin Holiday Cottages	Stronchullin Holiday Cottages, Blairmore, by Dunoon, Argyll, PA23 8TP	01369 810246	★★★	Self Catering	𝕏
Hafton Lodge	Invincible Property Services, Invincible House, Harbour Place, Ardrossan, Ayrshire, KA22 8BU	01294 474040		Awaiting Grading	
Innellan Farmhouse	Innellan Farmhouse, South Campbell Road, Innella, by Dunoon, Argyll, PA33 7SL	0141 357 5080	★★★	Self Catering	
Fasgadh	Scougal, Sandbank, Dunoon, Argyll, PA23 8PD	01369 701146	★★★	Self Catering	
Eilan Donan	15 Whin Avenue, Barrhead, Glasgow G78 1JQ	0141 589 6811	★★★	Self Catering	
Argyll Lodge	89 Edward Street, Dunoon, Argyll, PA23 7AS	01369 703022	★★★	Self Catering	
Argyll Lodge	89 Edward Street, Dunoon, Argyll, PA23 7AS	01369 703022	★★★	Self Catering	
Fasgadh	Scougal, Sandbank, Dunoon, Argyll, PA23 8PD	01369 701146	★★★	Self Catering	
Eilan Donan	15 Whin Avenue, Barrhead, Glasgow G78 1JQ	0141 589 6811	★★★	Self Catering	
Egmont	25 Larchfield Avenue, Newton Mearns, Glasgow G77 5PW	0141 639 3129	★★★★	Self Catering	𝕏
Culzean House	Culzean Properties Ltd, Glen Finnart Hotel, Glen Finart, Ardentinny, By Dunoon, Argyll and Bute, PA23 8TT	01369 810331	★★★★	Self Catering	
Fern, Glencairn and Coach House	Garrachrhune, Kilmun, Dunoon, Argyll, PA23 8SD	01369 840206	★★★	Self Catering	
Dalcamond House, Innellan	Dalcalmond House, Shore Road, Innellan, Argyll, PA23 7TR	01369 830309	★★★★	Self Catering	

⌕ Unassisted wheelchair access　ᾔ Assisted wheelchair access　𝕏 Access for visitors with mobility difficulties
𝒫 Bronze Green Tourism Award　𝒫𝒫 Silver Green Tourism Award　𝒫𝒫𝒫 Gold Green Tourism Award
For further information on our Green Tourism Business Scheme please see page 9.

270

To find out more, call 0845 22 55 121 or go to visitscotland.com.

Duns

2 Kimmerghame Mains Cottages	176 Coniscliffe Road, Darlington, County Durham, DL3 8PA	01325 358725	★★★	Self Catering	
Courtyard Cottage	Fogo Mains, Duns, Berwickshire, TD11 3RA	01890 840259	★★★★	Self Catering	
Green Hope	Green Hope, Ellemford, Duns, Berwickshire, TD11 3SG	01361 890242	★★★	Self Catering	🚪
Cumledge Mill Holiday let, Preston	Coromandel, The Avenue, Eyemouth, Berwickshire, TD14 5EA	01890 752142	★★★	Self Catering	

Dunscore

The Tower House	The Tower House, 20 Alnwick Drive, Eaglesham, Glasgow, Renfrewshire, G76 0AZ	01355 303078	★★★	Self Catering	

Dunvegan, Isle of Skye

7 Geary	2 Upper Halistera, Waternish, Dunvegan, Isle of Skye, IV55 8GN	01470 592276	★	Self Catering	
Beinn an Fhraoich	11 Elm Road, Hale, Altrincham, Cheshire, WA15 9QW	0161 9413440	★★★	Self Catering	
MacLeod Estates	MacLeod Estates, Dunvegan Castle, Dunvegan, Isle of Skye, IV51 8WF	01470 521 206	★★	Self Catering	
Osdale Farmhouse	Cnoc Uaine, Mount Eagle Road, Culbokie, By Dingwall, Ross-shire, IV7 8JY	01349 877039	★★★★	Self Catering	

By Dunvegan, Isle of Skye

Roskhill Barn	Roskhill Barn, Roskhill, by Dunvegan, Isle of Skye, IV55 82D	01470 521755	★★★	Self Catering	

Durnamuck

Sail Mhor View	16 Aston Hill, Wilmcote, Stratford on Avon, Warwickshire, CV37 9XS	01789 204355	★★★	Self Catering	

Durness

Ceannabeinne, Cranstackie, Craigmor	Oldbury House, Ightham, Sevenoaks, Kent, TN15 9DE	01732 882320	★★★	Self Catering	
Churchend Chalets	Churchend Chalets, Sangomore, Durness, by Lairg, Sutherland, IV27 4PZ	01971 511350	★★	Self Catering	

Duror, Lochaber

Lorien	34 Madeira Drive, Liverpool, Merseyside, L25 2NY	0151 7098598	★★★	Self Catering	

Earlston

Sorrowlessfield Cottage	Sorrowlessfield Cottage, Sorrowless Farm, Earlston, Berwickshire, TD4 6AG	01896 849906	★★★	Self Catering	

East Bennan, Isle of Arran

Craigdhu Farm Cottages (Stable Cottage & Bushmill)	Craigdhu, East Bennan, Isle of Arran KA27 8SH	01770 820225	★★★ → ★★★★	Self Catering	🍃🍃

East Kilbride

East Rogerton Cottages	East Rogerton Lodge, Markethill Road, East Kilbride, South Lanarkshire, G74 4NZ	01355 263176	★★★ → ★★★★	Self Catering	

East Linton

Castlepark Cottage and Cotslaw Cottage	Sunnyside Farm, East Linton, East Lothian, KY16 8PN	07793 804587	★★★ → ★★★★	Self Catering	
Grieve's Cottage/The Bothy	Grieves Cottage/The Bothy, Stonelaws Farm, East Linton East Lothian EH40 3DX	01620 870606	★★★ → ★★★★	Self Catering	

♿ Unassisted wheelchair access   🚪 Assisted wheelchair access   ♸ Access for visitors with mobility difficulties
🍃 Bronze Green Tourism Award   🍃🍃 Silver Green Tourism Award   🍃🍃🍃 Gold Green Tourism Award
For further information on our Green Tourism Business Scheme please see page 9.

Awards correct as of mid August 2008

Newbyth Garden Cottage	Newbyth House, East Linton, East Lothian, EH40 3DU	01620 870 646	★★★★★	Self Catering
The Stable	8 Browns Place, East Linton, East Lothian, EH40 3BG	01620 861041	★★★	Self Catering

East Lothian

12 Lawson Court	Monkswalk Cottage, 58B High Street, Dunbar, East Lothian, EH42 1JH	07879 025492	★★★	Self Catering

East Tarbert

Dalhanna	Dalhanna Self Catering, 19 Kyles, Tarbert, Isle of Harris, HS3 3BS	01859 502099	★★★★	Self Catering

Edinbane

Colgrain	Bramble Cottage, Hollinsgreen, Bradwall, Middlewich, Cheshire, CW10 0LA	07799 512679	★★★★	Self Catering
Edinbane Holiday Homes	Rhu-Vanish, 15 Edinbane, Edinbane, Isle of Skye, IV51 9PR	01470 582270	★★★	Self Catering

By Edinbane

Steading Cottage & The Boathouse	Beauthorne, 4 Young Street, Nairn, Invernesshire, IV12 4ET	01667 451578	Awaiting Grading	

Edinburgh

1 Parliament Square & 1A Black Ford Grange	Nutrend Ltd, Mitchell House, 5 Mitchell Street, Edinburgh, Midlothian, EH6 7BD	0131 554 7564	Awaiting Grading	
1/6, 2 St Leonard's Crag	Parkside, Buccleuch Road, Hawick TD9 0EL	01450 374150	★★★	Self Catering
10 Glenfinlas Street	10 Glenfinlas Street, Edinburgh EH3 6AQ	0131 225 8695	★★★★★	Serviced Apartments
11 Morrison Circus	Dalrunzion, Fort William Road, Newtonmore, Highland, PH20 1DG	01540 673447	★★★	Self Catering
11/15 Huntingdon Place	Colzie House, Easter Balgedie, Perth & Kinross, KY13 9HQ	01592 840729	★★★★	Self Catering
11/2 Learmonth Terrace	71 Daiches Braes, Edinburgh, Lothian, EH15 2RD	0131 6575210	★★★★	Self Catering
126/3 High Street and Old Tolbooth Wynd	26 Maplewood Park, Livingston, West Lothian, EH45 8BB	01506 463536	★★★ → ★★★★	Self Catering
13 Frederick Street	Headshaw Farm, Ashkirk, Selkirk, TD7 4NT	01750 32233	★★★★	Self Catering
13 Stanley Street	13 Stanley Street, Portobello, Edinburgh EH15 1JJ	0131 669 1998	★★★	Self Catering
17/4 Cornwall Street	17/4 Cornwall Street, Edinburgh EH1 2EQ	07714 206654	★★★	Self Catering
2 Rossie Place	11 Paisley Gardens, Edinburgh EH8 7JN	0131 661 1934	★★★	Self Catering
21 (2F2) Heriot Row	18 Denham Green Terrace, Edinburgh EH5 3PD	0131 5525183	★★★★★	Self Catering
21/10 Blair Street	7 Durward Drive, Glenrothes, Fife, KY6 2LB	0131 2255729	★★★	Self Catering
21/2 21/3 Hanover Street	Flat 1, 29 Devonshire Place, London WIG 6TQ	020 7224 4677	★★★★★	Self Catering
24 Warrender Park Crescent	Edinburgh First, University of Edinburgh, Pollock Halls, Edinburgh, Lothian, EH16 5AY	0131 651 2011	★	Self Catering
25 Saxe - Coburg Place	Farmhall Farm, Fordandenny, Perth PH2 9HR	01738 812764	★★★★★	Self Catering
29/5 & 33/5 Drummond House	21 Abbots Lea, Tweedbank, Galashiels TD1 3RZ	07804 187402	★★★	Self Catering
3/6forrest Hill, Flat 14 8Jeffrey St, 11 Kings stables	44 Rosslyn Crescent, Edinburgh EH6 5AX	0131 5552596	★★★	Self Catering

♿ Unassisted wheelchair access   ♿ Assisted wheelchair access   ♿ Access for visitors with mobility difficulties

🅟 Bronze Green Tourism Award   🅟🅟 Silver Green Tourism Award   🅟🅟🅟 Gold Green Tourism Award

For further information on our Green Tourism Business Scheme please see page 9.

272   To find out more, call 0845 22 55 121 or go to visitscotland.com.

Name	Address	Phone	Rating	Type	
30/3 Abbey Lane	7 Castleton Avenue, Newton Mearns G77 5NF	0141 639 7721	★★★★	Self Catering	
32 Terrars Croft & Lady Wynd	City Nights, 97 Market Street, Musselburgh, East Lothian, EH21 6PY	0131 6657140	★★★	Self Catering	
45 Cumberland Street	Blairshinnoch, Kirkgunzeon, Dumfries, Dumfries and Galloway, DG2 8JJ	01387 760230	★★★★★	Self Catering	
48/1 Candlemaker Row	630 Lanark Road, Edinburgh, Lothian, EH14 5EW	0131 538 0352	★★★★	Self Catering	🌳🌳
4A Regent Terrace	4 Regent Terrace, Edinburgh, Lothian, EH7 5BN	0131 558 9536	★★★★	Self Catering	
5/4 & 5/6 Tower Street	Seton Mains Farm, Longniddry, East Lothian EH32 0PG	01875 852881	★★★★	Self Catering	
77 Hanover St, 33/2 Queen St,97 Rose St	27 Queen Street, Edinburgh EH2 1JX	07973 345559	★★★ → ★★★★★	Self Catering	
8 Woodhall Road, 4 York Place & 5 Coates Place	11 Spylaw Street, Colinton, Edinburgh EH13 0JS	0131 441 2373	★★★ → ★★★★	Self Catering	
9 Hart Street	29 Regent Terrace, Edinburgh EH7 5BS	0131 5588381	★★★★	Self Catering	
94/1 Inchview Terrace	94/7 Inchview Terrace, Edinburgh EH7 6TF	07711 297521	★★★★	Self Catering	
Aarajura Apartments	Aarajura Guest House, 14 Granvale Terrace, Edinburgh EH10 4PQ	0131 2296565	★★ → ★★★	Self Catering	
AJEM 142 Easter Road	AJEM Self Catering Edinburgh, 132/4 Easter Road, Edinburgh EH7 5RJ	0131 466 8443	★★	Self Catering	
Alba Executive	21-23 Church Hill Place, Edinburgh, Lothian, EH10 4BE	0131 447 9994	★★★★★	Serviced Apartments	
Albern Morningside Apartment	10/2 Ettrick Road, Edinburgh, Mid Lothian, EH10 5BJ	0131 228 3232	★★★★	Self Catering	
Anderson Apartment	Anderson Apartment, 4/1 Dundonald Street, Edinburgh, Midlothian, EH3 6RY	01896 830999	★★★	Self Catering	
Annandale Street Apartments	24 East Claremount Street, Edinburgh EH7 4JP	0131 557 4676	★★★★	Self Catering	
Anne House Apartments	128 Blackford Avenue, Edinburgh, Midlothian, EH9 3HH	0131 667 3843	★★★	Self Catering	
Apartment By Castle	65 Durham Square, Edinburgh, Midlothian EH15 1PP	0131 6695662	★★★★	Self Catering	
Apartment by Royal Mile	Smithfield Garden Cottage, Peebles, Borders, EH45 8QG	01721 729992	★★★★	Self Catering	🌳🌳
Apartments Edinburgh	179 High Street, Edinburgh EH1 1PD	0131 2258023	★★★★	Self Catering	
Apartments Royal	58 Cammo Grove, Edinburgh EH4 8EZ	07806 387846	★★★★	Serviced Apartments	
Apt 39 Lothian House & 21 Cordiner's Land	Apartment 39, Lothian House, 124 Lothian Road, Edinburgh EH3 9DD	0780 1064820	★★★★	Self Catering	
Apts 68 & 85 Lothian House	10 Glenfinlas Street, Charlotte Square, Edinburgh EH3 6AQ	0131 225 8695	★★★★	Self Catering	
Atholl Brae	Atholl Brae, C/O 20 Bellfield Crescent, Eddleston, Peebles, Peebleshire, EH45 8RQ	01721 730679	★★★★	Self Catering	♿
Atria 22 Apartment	Atria 22 Apartment, 56 Glasgow Road, Edinburgh, Lothian, EH12 8HN	7775791740	★★★★	Self Catering	
Auld Reekie Properties	27 Letham Mains, Haddington, East Lothian EH41 4NW	01620 823294	★★★	Self Catering	
Aurora Flat	23 Pitcairn Road, Dundee DD3 9EE	01382 810526	★★★	Self Catering	
Ballantrae Apartments	Ballantrae Apartments, 12 York Place, Edinburgh, Midlothian, EH1 3EP	0131 4784748	★★★★	Serviced Apartments	
Botanic Garden Apartment	46/1 Inverleith Row, Edinburgh, Lothians, EH3 5PY	07770 732576	★★★	Self Catering	
Broughton Apartments	3 Willowbrae Avenue, Willowbrae, Edinburgh, East Lothian, EH8 7HB	0131 556 6083	★★★★★	Self Catering	

♿ Unassisted wheelchair access   ♿ Assisted wheelchair access   🧍 Access for visitors with mobility difficulties
🌳 Bronze Green Tourism Award   🌳🌳 Silver Green Tourism Award   🌳🌳🌳 Gold Green Tourism Award
For further information on our Green Tourism Business Scheme please see page 9.

Calton Apartments	Calton Apartments, C/o Greenside Hotel, 9 Royal Terrace, Edinburgh, Midlothian, EH7 5AB	0131 556 3221	★★★★	Self Catering
Cambridge Street Apartment	City Trust Properties, 26/3 Ferry Road Avenue, Edinburgh, Mid Lothian, EH4 4BL	07828691181/0	★★★★	Self Catering
Canon Court	Canon Court, 20 Canonmills, Edinburgh, Lothian, EH3 5LH	0131 474 7000	★★★★	Serviced Apartments ⫩
Carduus Morrison	44 St Martins Gate, Haddington, East Lothian, EH41 4BA	01620 826133	★★★	Self Catering
Carmichael Cottages	Carmichael Estate Office, West Mains, Carmichael, by Biggar, Lanarkshire, ML12 6PG	01899 308336	★★★★	Self Catering
Castle Apartment	5/1 Blackfriars Street, Edinburgh EH1 1NB	0131 5574570	★★★	Self Catering
Castle Court Apartments	6 Queen Street, Edinburgh EH2 1JE	0131 240 0080	★★ → ★★★	Serviced Apartments
Castle View	Begbie Farmhouse, Begbie, Haddington, East Lothian, EH41 4HQ	01620 829487	★★★★	Self Catering
Castleview Appartments, Lawnmarket	Medhurst, Hazelwood Road, Sneyd Park, Bristol BS9 1PS	0117 9681962	★★★	Self Catering
Clarendon Crescent	12a Claredon Crescent, Edinburgh, Lothian, EH4 1PU	0131 315 3061	★★★★	Self Catering
Craiglieth Apartment	Kilmorie House, Rectory Road, Whepstead, Bury St Edmunds, Suffolk, IP29 4TB	01284 735848	★★★	Self Catering
Craigmoss Apartment	62 Pilrig Street, Edinburgh, Scotland, EH6 5AS	0131 554 3885	★★★★	Self Catering
Craigwell Cottage	Sandcastle Holidats (Scotland) Ltd, 24 Craigleith View, Edinburgh, Mid Lothian, EH4 3JZ	0131 476 4011	★★★★	Self Catering
Dalry Church Flat 15/1 & 17/4	Candusso Property, Bankton House Hotel, Muireston, Livingston, West Lothian, EH54 9AQ	01506 434176	★★★★	Self Catering
Dean Street Mews	26-28 Dean Street, Edinburgh EH4 1LW	0131 3436747	★★★★	Self Catering
Dean Village Apartment	Redsox Developments, The Smithy, 7-9 Bells Place, Edinburgh, Lothians, EH4 3BJ	07855 824955	Awaiting Grading	
Dunalton	Dunalton, 43 Braid Farm Road, Edinburgh, Midlothian, EH10 6LE	0131 447 3065	★★★★	Self Catering
Dunstaffnage Flat	Dunstaffnage House, 12 Regent Terrace, Edinburgh, Mid Lothian, EH7 5BN	0131 556 8309	★★★★	Self Catering
Duthus Apartments	Duthus Apartments, 15/14 Roseburn Maltings, Edinburgh, Midlothian, EH12 5JG	0131 337 6876	★★★★	Serviced Apartments
Edinburgh Apartments City Central	3 Old Priory Park, Old London Road, St Albans, Herts, AL1 1QF	07950 018865	★★★	Self Catering ⫩
Edinburgh Axis Apartments	Treetops Development Compant (TEL) Ltd, 19 Dublin Street Lane South, Edinburgh, Mid Lothian, EH1 3PX	0131 623 7777	Awaiting Grading	
Edinburgh Blair Street Apartment	Edinburgh Blair Street Apartment, 21/9 Blair Street, Edinburgh EH1 1QR	0131 669 8535	★★★★	Self Catering
Edinburgh Castle view, Play House Flat, Rose St Flat	Edinburgh Flats partnership, 12 Inverleith Place, Edinburgh, Midlothian, EH3 5PZ	0131 467 4726	★★★	Self Catering
Edinburgh Castle Wynd	5 Hillside Farm, Dunblane, Perthshire, FK15 9NT	01786 822214	★★★	Self Catering
Edinburgh Central Apartments	20 West Relugas Road, Edinburgh, Midlothian, EH9 2PL	0131 6676362	★★★	Self Catering
Edinburgh City Centre Apartments	69 Old Edinburgh Road, Inverness IV2 3PG	01463 239134	★★★★	Self Catering
Edinburgh New Town Apartment	1 Duddingston Grove West, Edinburgh, Mid Lothian, EH15 1RT	07989 982032	★★★★	Self Catering
Edinburgh Pearl Apartments	73 Dalry Road, Haymarket, Edinburgh, Scotland, EH11 2AU	0131 664 9292	★★★★	Self Catering
Edinburgh Self Catering	Edinburgh Self-Catering, 161/18 Easter Road, Edinburgh EH7 5QB	0131 553 6641	★★★ → ★★★★	Self Catering
Edinburgh Self Catering	Edinburgh Self-Catering, C/O 35/1 Lower London Road, Edinburgh, Lothian, EH7 5TE	0131 661 1479	★★★ → ★★★★	Self Catering

To find out more, call 0845 22 55 121 or go to visitscotland.com.

Fairnington Apartments	Fairnington Properties, 152/154 Dalkeith Road, Edinburgh, Midlothian, EH16 5DX	0131 6677042	★★★ → ★★★★	Self Catering
Featherhall Garden Court	92 Corstorphine Road, Murrayfield, Edinburgh, Midlothian, EH12 7TG	0845 430143/0	★★★	Self Catering ☂
Flat 1/5 Borthwick's Close	24 Deans Way, Edgware, Middlesex HA8 9NL	020 8959 4256	★★★★	Self Catering
Flat 12	Quartermile Serviced Apartments, 21 Queen Street, Edinburgh, Midlothian, EH4 2DG	0131 343 2239	★★★★	Serviced Apartments
Flat 2	Kirkbanny Farm, Foulden, Berwick on Tweed, TD15 1UH	01289 386565	★★★★	Self Catering
Flat 2F1 Baillie Fyfes Close	62 Bullsmoor Lane, Enfield, Middlesex, EN3 6TN	020 8885 8585	★★★★	Self Catering
Flat 2F3	Scottish Holiday Retreats, 39 East Trinity Road, Edinburgh, Mid lothian, EH5 3DL	0131 552 3084	★★★★	Self Catering
Flat 3	1 McDonald Road, Longforgan, By Dundee, Perthshire, DD2 5BW	01738 626672	★★★★	Self Catering
Flat 6/14 Bethlehem Way	9 Aylesford Street, Pimlico, London SW1V 3RY	07973 629459	★★★	Self Catering
Flat 70, Lothian House	2 Regent Court, 31 Green St Willingham, Cambridge CB4 5JA	01954 261721	★★★	Self Catering
Fountain Court Apartments	115 Lauriston Place, Edinburgh EH3 9JG	0131 622 6677	★★★★	Serviced Apartments
Fountain Court Edinburgh Quay Serviced Apartments	123 Grove Street, Edinburgh EH3 8AA	0131 622 6677	★★★★★	Serviced Apartments
Gairnshiel	45 Hillview Road, Edinburgh EH12 8QH	0131 3346473	★★★★	Self Catering
Ground Floor Georgian Drawing Room Flat	Walltower, Howgate, Penicuik, Midlothian, EH26 8PY	01968 674686	★★★	Self Catering
Ground Floor Georgian Drawing Room Flat, New	Walltower, Howgate, Penicuik, Midlothian, EH26 8PY	01968 674686	★★★	Self Catering
Holyrood Aparthotel	Holyrood Aparthotel, 1 Nether Bakehouse, Holyrood, Edinburgh, EH8 8PE	0131 524 3200	★★★★	Serviced Apartments ☂
Hot-el Apartments	9 Breakwater, Western Harbour, Edinburgh, Midlothian, EH6 6PZ	0131 553 6051	Awaiting Grading	
Inner City Lettings	74/3 Thistle Street, Edinburgh, Midlothian, EH2 1EN	07776 184455	★★★	Self Catering
Irvine Apartments	24 Hillpark Brae, Edinburgh, Lothian, EH4 7TD	0131 312 6843	★★★★	Self Catering
James Square	47 North Castle Street, Edinburgh EH2 3BG	0131 2257808	★★★★	Self Catering
Kew Apartments	Kew House, 1 Kew Terrace, Edinburgh, Lothian, EH12 5JE	0131 313 0700	★★★★ → ★★★★★	Serviced Apartments
Leith Apartment	5/8 Dock Street, Edinburgh, Midlothian, EH6 6HU	7900255881	★★★★	Serviced Apartments
Lochend Serviced Apartments	Lochend Serviced Apartments, 147/1 Lochend Road, Edinburgh EH7 6ET	0131 561 4000	★★★★	Self Catering
Luxury Capital Apartments	Luxury Capital Apartments, 56D London Road, Kilmarnock, East Ayrshire, KA3 7AJ	01563 544034	★★★★	Self Catering
Merchiston Apartment	Invermark, 60 Polwarth Terrace, Edinburgh EH11 1NJ	0131 337 1066	★★	Self Catering
Mews Apartment	Dovecot House, 6 Dovecot Road, Edinburgh, Lothians, EH12 7LE	0131 467 7467	★★★★	Self Catering
Napier University	Napier University, Sightill Campus, 9 Sighthill Court, Edinburgh EH11 4BN	0131 455 3738	★★	Self Catering ♿
No 10, The Arc	Stonehouse, Blackburn Road, Ribchester, Preston, Lancashire, PR3 3ZP	07811 127920	★★★★	Self Catering
No 15 & 15a Dundas Street	Braemore Estates, Gamefield, Auchtertyre Estate, By Crieff, PH7 4JR	01764 650303	★★★★★	Self Catering
No 22 Dalry Road	Edinburgh Apartments Ltd, 22 Dalry Road, Edinburgh, Midlothian, EH11 2BA	0131 313 5313	★★★	Self Catering

Name	Address	Phone	Grading	Type
No 22/7 Murano Place	16 Ravenscraig Street, Kirkcaldy, Fife, KY1 2AL	01592 592538	★★★	Self Catering
No 3 Raeburn Mews	Williamstone House, North Berwick, East Lothian, EH39 5DG	01620 894374	★★★	Self Catering
No 32 & No 19 The Apartment	The Cross House, The Cross, Ceres, Fife, KY15 5NE	01334 828697	★★★★	Self Catering
No 37 William Street	49 Nelson Road, Wimbledon, London SW19 1HS	07939 113299	★★★★	Self Catering
No 4/2 Cowgatehead	48 Bruntsfield Crescent, Dunbar, East Lothian, EH42 1QZ	01368 862697	★★★★	Self Catering
No 4/4 Craigcrook Place	Edinburgh Quarters, 8 Hillpark Avenue, Edinburgh EH4 7AT	0131 4760858	★★★	Self Catering
No 457/4 Lawnmarket	Pillowstops, 12 Charterhall Road, Edinburgh, Lothian, EH9 3HP	0131 229 3771	★★★★	Self Catering
No 5 Abercorn Terrace	No 5 Apartments, 5 Abercorn Terrace, Portobello, Edinburgh, EH15 2DD	0131 669 1044	★★★	Self Catering
No 5/3 Hopetoun Crescent	40/5 Annandale Street, Edinburgh, Mid Lothian, EH7 4AZ	07791 453102	★★★★	Self Catering
No 5/9 Dean Bank Lane	93 Queensferry Raod, Edinburgh, Midlothian, EH4 3TN	07956 542166	★★★★	Self Catering
No 56/15 Belford Road	14/1 Carlton Terrace, Edinburgh, Midlothian, EH7 5DD	0131 558 8812	★★★★	Self Catering
No 5A Bellevue Crescent	The Walton, 79 Dundas Street, Edinburgh, Lothian, EH3 6SD	0131 556 1137	★★★	Self Catering
No. 30/3 William Street	Inchallan House, Stirling Road, Dunblane FK15 9EX	01786 825067	★★★★	Self Catering
North lane Apartments	Nine, 15 Charlotte Lane, Edinburgh, Lothian, EH2 4QZ	0131 225 606	Awaiting Grading	
Number Ten	Amadeus Leisure Ltd, 6 Gloucester Place, Edinburgh, Midlothian, EH3 6EF	0131 225 2720	★★★★★	Serviced Apartments
Oakfield Apartment	Kildonan Lodge Hotel, 27 Craigmillar Park, Edinburgh, Mid Lothian, ED16 5PE	0131 667 2793	★★★ → ★★★★	Self Catering
Oceanside Apartments	34 McAuley Drive, Craigiebutler, Aberdeen, Grampian, AB15 8FL	01224 321681	★★★★	Self Catering
Paradise Penthouse	Durham House, 33A Old Elvet, Durham, Co Durham, DH1 3HN	0191 384 3904	★★★★★	Self Catering
Penthouse Flat	Courtburn House, School Road, Coldingham, Berwickshire, TD14 5NS	01890 771266	★★★★	Self Catering
Pentland, Cheviot, Ochil, Grampian	Oak Property Letting, 23 Main Street, Kelty, Fife, KY4 0AA	01383 830077	Awaiting Grading	
Pilrig House	Pilrig House, 30/3 Pilrig House Close, Edinburgh EH6 5RF	0131 5544794	★★★★	Self Catering
Portland Apartment, Leith	Portlands Apartments, 18 Boreland Park, Inverkeithing, Fife, KY11 1ES	01383 616070	★★★★	Self Catering
Portsburgh Court & Lady Nicolson Court	Portshaugh Court, 56 Lady Lawson Street, Edinburgh, Lothian, EH3 9DH	0131 656 0798	★★★	Self Catering
Queenshill	Silverdale, The Stell, Kirkcudbright, Dumfries & Galloway, DG6 4SA	01557 332337	★★★★	Self Catering
Royal Garden Apartments	Mayfair Suites, Royal Garden Apartments, 2 York Buildings, Queen Street, Edinburgh, EH2 1HY	0131 625 2345	★★★★	Serviced Apartments ♁
Royal Mile Apartment - Dunbars Close	25/3 Saxe Coburg Place, Edinburgh, Lothians, EH3 5BP	07879 408800	★★★★	Self Catering
Royal Mile Apartments	Ploughlands, Maxton, Melrose, Roxburghshire, TD6 ORP	01835 823 248	★★★★	Self Catering
Royal Mile Residence	65 Cockburn Street, Edinburgh, Midlothian, EH1 1BU	0131 2265155	★★★★★	Serviced Apartments
Royal Scots Mews	The Royal Scots Club, 29 Abercromby Place, Edinburgh, Lothian, EH3 6QE	0131 556 4270	★★★★	Self Catering
Silvermills	118 Victoria Street, Dyce, Aberdeen AB21 7BE	01224 722243	★★★★	Self Catering

♿ Unassisted wheelchair access   ♿ Assisted wheelchair access   ♁ Access for visitors with mobility difficulties
🅟 Bronze Green Tourism Award   🅟🅟 Silver Green Tourism Award   🅟🅟🅟 Gold Green Tourism Award
For further information on our Green Tourism Business Scheme please see page 9.

Name	Address	Phone	Grading	Type	
Southside Apartments	Destination Edinburgh Apartments, 48 Eastfield, Edinburgh, Midliothian, EH15 1PN	0131 669 4499	★★★★	Self Catering	
Spring Gardens	Woodcroft, 23 Midton Road, Ayr, Ayrshire, KA7 2SF	01292 264383	★★★★	Self Catering	
St Stephen Street Flat	28 Springfield Terrace, South Queensferry, Edinburgh, Lothian, EH30 9XF	7758272284	★★★	Self Catering	
Swanston Farm Cottages	Swanston Farm Ltd, 109/3a Swanston Road, Edinburgh EH10 7DS	0131 4455744	★★★★	Self Catering	
The Anchorage	8 Newbattle Gardens, Eskbank, Midlothian, EH22 3DR	07950 706626	Awaiting Grading		
The Apartment	4 Regent Terrace, Edinburgh, Lothians, EH7 5BN	07739 638913	★★★★	Self Catering	
The Artist's Studio	236 Cannongate, Royal Mile, Edinburgh, Midlothian, EH8 8AB	07968 208892	★★★	Self Catering	
The Boat House	Dundas Castle, South Queensferry, Edinburgh, Lothians, EH30 9SP	0131 319 3801	★★★★	Self Catering	
The Bond	23 Prestonfield Road, Edinburgh, East Lothian, EH16 5EL	0131 554 5985	★★★	Self Catering	
The Causewayside Apartment	The Causewayside Apartment, 20/1 Steads Place, Edinburgh, Lothian, EH6 5DS	07789 907335	★★★ → ★★★★	Self Catering	🍃
The Chester Residence	The Chester Residence Ltd, 9 Chester Street, Edinburgh, Lothian, EH3 7RF	0131 2262075	★★★★★	Serviced Apartments	
The Georgian Retreat	Fidra, 36 Regent Street, Edinburgh, Midlothian, EH15 2AX	0131 669 5394	★★★	Self Catering	
The Gladstone Flat	National Trust for Scotland, 28 Charlotte Square, Edinburgh EH2 4ET	0131 243 9335	★★★	Self Catering	
The Harrison Flat	National Trust for Scotland, 28 Charlotte Square, Edinburgh EH2 4ET	0131 243 9335	★★★	Self Catering	
The Knight Residence	12 Lauriston Street, Edinburgh, Midlothian, EH3 9DJ	0131 622 8120	★★★★★	Serviced Apartments	
The Moorings	12 Wallaceneuk, Kelso, Roxburghshire, TD5 6BF	01573 224171	★★★★	Self Catering	
The Parkgate Apartment	The Parkgate Apartment, 65/6 Holyrood Road, Edinburgh EH8 8AU	07900 447713	★★★★	Self Catering	
The Penthouse	Sandhaven, 33 Cults Avenue, Aberdeen, Aberdeen-shire, AB15 9RS	01224 869459	★★★★★	Self Catering	
The Town House Apartment	The Town House, 65 Gilmore Place, Edinburgh EH3 9NU	0131 229 1985	★★★★	Self Catering	
The Upper Villa	The Upper villa, 3 Dean Park Cresent, Edinburgh EH4 1PN	0131 477 9645	★★★★	Self Catering	
The West End Rothesay Apartment	7/2 Calder Grove, Edinburgh EH11 4NB	07739 099257	★★★	Self Catering	🍃
The Wright Place	73 Easter Drylaw Place, Edinburgh EH4 2QH	0131 467 9844	★★★★	Self Catering	
West End Apartments	2 Learmonth Terrace, Edinburgh EH4 1PQ	0131 3320717	★★★★	Self Catering	

Edington, Chirnside

Name	Address	Phone	Grading	Type
Edington Mill	243 Colinton Mains Drive, Edinburgh, Midlothian, EH13 9AY	0131 441 6698	★★★★	Self Catering

Ednam

Name	Address	Phone	Grading	Type	
Plumbrae's Barn	Cliftonhill, Ednam, Kelso, Roxburghshire, TD5 7QE	01573 225028	★★★ → ★★★★	Self Catering	🏃
Houndridge Holiday Cottage	Houndridge Holiday Homes, Houndridge,Ednam, Kelso, Roxburghshire, TD5 7QN	01573 470604	★★★	Self Catering	

Edzell

Name	Address	Phone	Grading	Type
Netherton	Kiloran, No 8 The Glebe, Edzell, Angus, DD9 7SZ	01356 648426	★★★	Self Catering

♿ Unassisted wheelchair access   ♿ Assisted wheelchair access   🏃 Access for visitors with mobility difficulties
🍃 Bronze Green Tourism Award   🍃🍃 Silver Green Tourism Award   🍃🍃🍃 Gold Green Tourism Award
For further information on our Green Tourism Business Scheme please see page 9.

Oakbank	6 Castle Gardens, Edzell, Angus, DD9 7SY	01356 648615	★★★★	Self Catering	
Rose Cottage	Northesk Lodge, 18A High Street, Edzell, Angus, DD9 7TJ	01356 647409	★★★	Self Catering	
Cottage at Mill of Lethnot	Engelstedsgade 58, Copenhagen, Denmark2100		★★★	Self Catering	🍃🍃

Elgin

Blackhills Estate Houses	Blackhills Estate, Elgin, Moray, IV30 8QU	01343 842223	★★ → ★★★	Self Catering	
Limuru	Ardgye House, Elgin, Morayshire, IV30 8UP	01343 850616	★★★★	Self Catering	
Parkneuk	Little Buinach Farm, Kellas, Elgin, Morayshire, IV30 8TS	01343 890233	★★★	Self Catering	
Springburn Log Cabins	Springburn Log Cabin, Miltonduff, Elgin, Moray, IV30 8TL	01343 541939	★★★ → ★★★★	Self Catering	
Westmuir	Riverside Cottage, Mill Road, Nairn IV12 5EP	01667 451739	★★	Self Catering	

By Elgin

Curlew Cottage, Burghead	10 Seaview Road, Cummingston, Elgin, Moray, IV30 5YU	01343 831114	★★★★	Self Catering	⍭
Carden Self-Catering	Carden Self-catering, Old Steading, Carden, Alves, Elgin, Moray, IV30 8UP	01343 850222	★★★ → ★★★★	Self Catering	⍭ 🍃

Elie

Devon Cottage	8 Tibbermore Gardens, Perth, Tayside, PH1 2BX	01738 632252	★★	Self Catering	
Elie Letting	The Stable, The Park, Bank Street, Elie, Fife, KY9 1BW	01333 330219	★★★★	Self Catering	⍭
Stenton Cottage	42 Fairies Road, Perth, Perthshire, PH1 1LZ	01738 442953	★★★	Self Catering	
The Granary	Flat 6, 18 Cassland Road, London E9 7AN	07946 535314	★★★★	Self Catering	
Viewforth Cottage, Earlsferry	35 Seafield Crescent, Aberdeen, Aberdeenshire, AB15 7UT	01224 209151	★★★	Self Catering	

Ellenabeich, Isle of Seil

The Bolt-hole	4 Leyfield Close, Strensall, York, North Yorkshire, YO32 5XE	01904 492111	★★★★	Self Catering	

Ellon

Stables Flat	National Trust for Scotland, 28 Charlotte Square, Edinburgh EH2 4ET	0131 243 9335	★★	Self Catering	

By Ellon

Beechgrove Cottage	National Trust for Scotland, 28 Charlotte Square, Edinburgh EH2 4ET	0131 243 9335	★★★	Self Catering	

Elphin

Fir Chlis	Fir Chlis, 399 Elphin, By Lairg, Sutherland, IV27 4HH	01854 666218	★★★	Self Catering	

Evanton

The Pavilion & The Bakehouse	The Foulis Castle Trust, Storehouse of Foulis, Foulis Ferry, Evanton, Dingwall, Ross-Shire, IV16 9UX	01349 830204	★★★ → ★★★★	Self Catering	

Eyemouth

51 High Street	Near Meres, Welsh Frankton, Oswestry, Shropshire, SY11 4NX	01691 622360	★★★	Self Catering	

👨‍🦽 Unassisted wheelchair access   👨‍🦽 Assisted wheelchair access   ⍭ Access for visitors with mobility difficulties
🍃 Bronze Green Tourism Award   🍃🍃 Silver Green Tourism Award   🍃🍃🍃 Gold Green Tourism Award
For further information on our Green Tourism Business Scheme please see page 9.

Albannach	13 Market Place, Eyemouth, Berwickshire, TD14 5HE	01890 752456	★★★	Self Catering
Nisbet's Tower	Gunsgreen House Trust, The Garden House, Netherbyres, Eyemouth, Berwickshire, TD14 5SE	01890 750337	★★★	Self Catering
Puffin House	24 Chalmers Street, Dunfermline, Fife, KY12 8DF	01383 622109	★★★	Self Catering
Seagull Cottage	14 Eslington Terrace, Jesmond, Newcastle Upon Tyne, England, NE2 4RL	01912 121211	★★★	Self Catering

Fairlie

Bayview	93 Mossgiel Road, Newlands, Glasgow G43 2BY	0141 570 1258	★★★	Self Catering
Fencefoot Farm	Fencefoot Farm, Fairlie, Ayrshire, KA29 0EG	01475 568918	★★★	Self Catering

Falkirk

24 Creteil Court	23 Gartcows Drive, Falkirk, Stirlingshire, FK1 5QQ	07740 502083	★★★	Self Catering
Lawford Lodge	R Denholm & Son, Westerlochdrum Farm, Bonnybridge, Stirlingshire, FK4 2HA	01324 813090	★★★★	Self Catering ⚡

Falkland

Braehead	21 Belvidere Crescent, Aberdeen AB25 2NH	01224 638738	★★★★	Self Catering

Farnell, By Brechin

Parker's Retreat	Greenden Farmhouse, Farnell, Brechin, Angus, DD9 6TS	07831 333333	★★★★★	Self Catering

Farr

Dalvourn Holidays	Inverarnie House, Inverarnie, Inverness, IV2 6XA	01808 521467	★★★★	Self Catering ♿ 🍃🍃🍃

Fearn

Mounteagle Estate Holidays	Mounteagle Estate Holidays, Mounteagle, Fearn, Easter Ross, IV20 1RP	01862 832720	★★★★	Self Catering

Fearnan

Tigh Na Clachan	Stanton House, Stanton, Morpeth, Northumberland, NE65 8PS	01670 772234	★★★★	Self Catering

Feddinch, St Andrews

Rose Studio	Rose Studio, 2 The Walled Garden, Feddinch, St Andrews, Fife, KY16 8NR	01334 479078	★★★★	Self Catering

Fife

140 North Street	12 Howard Place, St Andrews, Fife, KY16 9HL	01334 472684	★★★★	Self Catering
17 Queens Gardens	Shakespeare-Scotland, Greenways,Waterlane, Enton, Surrey, GU8 5AG	01483 424743	★★★	Self Catering
2 Chamberlain Street	55 Ullswater, Ivy Farm estate, Macclesfield, Cheshire, SK11 7YW	01625 611975	★★	Self Catering
247 Lamond Drive	89 Foxhouse Lane, Liverpool, Merseyside, L31 6EE	0151 5262116	★★★	Self Catering
4 School View & Lavender Cottage	48 Laird Street, Dundee DD3 9PY	01382 457869	★★★ → ★★★★	Self Catering
54 Haig Avenue	4 Erica Avenue, Woodlands Park, Bedworth, Warwickshire, CV12 0AU	02476 491448	★★★	Self Catering

Findhorn

100 Findhorn	Heath House, Findhorn, Moray, IV36 3WN	01309 691082	★★★	Self Catering
Findhorn Bay Holiday Park	Findhorn Bay Holiday Park, Findhorn, Moray, IV36 3TU	01309 690203	★★★	Self Catering

Finsbay, Isle of Harris

Cnoc Na Ba	Cnoc Na Ba, Finsbay, Isle of Harris, Western Isles, HS3 3JD	01859 530232	★★★★	Self Catering

Fionnphort, Isle of Mull

Ach Na Brae Cottages	Ach na Brae Cottages, Monachuich, Fionnphort, Isle of Mull, PA66 6BW	01681 700260	★★★★	Self Catering	🅟
Caol-Ithe Self Catering	Caol-Ithe, Fionnphort, Isle of Mull, Argyll, PA66 6BL	01681 700375	★★★	Self Catering	
Taigh Foise	Dail an Inshire, Kintra, Finnophort, Isle of Mull, PA66 6BT	01681 700509	★★★★	Self Catering	🕴

Fochabers

Collie Farmhouse	Collie Farmhouse, Orton, Fochabers, Morayshire, IV32 7QF	01343 880330	★★★★	Self Catering

Fordyce

Stable Cottage	Stable Cottage, Glassaugh Lodge, Fordyce, Aberdeenshire, AB45 2UL	01261 843434	★★★	Self Catering

Forfar

Chapelpark House	21 Academy Street, Forfar, Angus, DD8 2HA	01307 463972	★★★★	Self Catering

By Forfar

Cookston Stables	Cookston Farm, Eassie, By Forfar, Angus, DD8 1SH	01307 840332	★★★★	Self Catering
Baldardo Steading Cottage	Rowanlee, Rescobie, Forfar, Angus, DD8 2TE	01307 830466	★★★★	Self Catering
Hunters Cabins	Hunters Cabins, Justinhaugh, Forfar, Angus, DD8 3SB	01307 860305	★★★	Self Catering
Bank Cottage	Hatton of Ogilvy, Glamis, by Forfar, Angus, DD8 1UH	01307 840229	★★★	Self Catering
Finavon Castle	C/O Attention to Detail, 5 Park Grove, Edinburgh, Midlothian, EH16 6JE	0131 4787003	★★★★	Self Catering
Broom Cottage	Brok Farm, Tannadice, Forfar, Angus, DD83SJ	01307 850267	★★★	Self Catering
No 2 Cottage	Cotterbank, Balglassie, Aberlemno, by Forfar, Angus, DD8 3PH	01307 830208	★★	Self Catering

Forgandenny

Redbraes & Whitecraigs	Pond Cottage, Ardargie, Fordangenny, Perthshire, PH2 9DQ	01738 445588	Awaiting Grading

Forres

America Cottage	America Cottage, Rafford, Forres, Moray, IV36 0RU	01343 890454	★★★★	Self Catering
Cormack's Lodge	National Trust for Scotland, 28 Charlotte Square, Edinburgh EH2 4ET	0131 243 9395	★★★	Self Catering
Daltullich Cottage	14 Saxe Coburg Place, Edinburgh EH3 5BR	0131 315 2775	★★★★	Self Catering
Fisherman's Bothies	Fisherman's Bothies, The Main of Sluie, Dunphail, Forres, Moray, IV36 2QG	01309 611263	★★★	Self Catering

🚹 Unassisted wheelchair access   ♿ Assisted wheelchair access   🕴 Access for visitors with mobility difficulties
🅟 Bronze Green Tourism Award   🅟🅟 Silver Green Tourism Award   🅟🅟🅟 Gold Green Tourism Award
For further information on our Green Tourism Business Scheme please see page 9.

To find out more, call 0845 22 55 121 or go to visitscotland.com.

Lochindorb Lodge and Bothy Cottage	Logie House, Forres, Moray, IV36 2QN	01309 611278	★★ → ★★★	Self Catering
Manse Cottage	Kirkton, Dallas, Forres, Moray, IV36 2RZ	01343 890421	★★★	Self Catering
South Lodge	National Trust for Scotland, 28 Charlotte Square, Edinburgh EH2 4ET	0131 243 9335	★★★	Self Catering

By Forres

Cottage No1, Dyke	Wellhill Farm, Dyke, Forres, Moray, IV36 2TG	01309 641205	★	Self Catering
Thornhall Chalet	Thornhall, Dyke, by Forres, Moray, IV36 2TL	01309 641283	★★★★	Self Catering

Fort Augustus

Flat 17, The Raven Wing	The Willows, Dalchreichart, Glenmoriston, Inverness-shire, IV63 7YJ	01320 340371	★★★★	Self Catering
Mount Pleasant	2 Balmaglaster, By Spean Bridge, Inverness-shire, PH34 4EB	01809 501289	★★	Self Catering
Old School 11 (Eleven)	Island Cottage, Inverfarigaig, Inverness, Inverness-shire, IV2 6XR	01456 486631	★★★★	Self Catering

Fort William

16 Perth Place	16 Perth Place, Fort William, Inverness-shire, PH33 6UL	01397 704392	★★	Self Catering
Achintee Cottage	Achintee Farm, Achintee, Fort William, Inverness-shire, PH33 6TE	01397 702240	★★★	Self Catering
Alyth, 34 Lochaber Road	West Highland Hotel, Mallaig, Inverness-shire, PH41 4QZ	01687 462210	★★★	Self Catering
Ard Na Faire	Ard Na Faire, The Gantocks, Achintore Road, Fort William, Highland, PH33 6RN	01397 702050	Awaiting Grading	
Ardvullin	Hopscotch Children's Charity, 42 Silverknowes Road, Edinburgh, Midlothian, EH4 5LF	0131 336 5554	★	Self Catering
Balcarres	Balcarres, Seafield Gardens, Fort William, Inverness-shire, PH33 6RJ	01397 704444	★★★★	Self Catering
Bank Cottage	33 Kirkwall Road, Cathcart, Glasgow G44 5UN	0141 6378591	★★	Self Catering
Ben View Self Catering	Ben View Guest House, Belford Road, Fort William PH33 6ER	01397 772017	★★★	Self Catering
Ben-View Lodges, Lochyside	Benview Holidays, Alveston, Lochyside, Fort William, Inverness-shire, PH33 7NX	01397 704124	★★★★	Self Catering
Berkeley House	Berkeley House, Belford Road, Fort William, Inverness-shire, PH33 6BT	01397 701185	★★★	Self Catering
Brae Mhor Cottage	Coire Vullin, Blarmafoldach, Fort William, Inverness-shire, PH33 6SZ	01397 700415	★★★★	Self Catering	🍂
Cedar Breaks	Woodside, Tomacharich, Fort William, Inverness-shire, PH33 6SW		★★★	Self Catering
Coruanan Farhouse	57 Napier Avenue, London SW6 3PS	0207 736 4684	★★★ → ★★★★	Self Catering
Dalaraban	Strone Farmhouse, Banavie, Inverness-shire, PH33 7PB	01397 712773	★★★	Self Catering
Ealasaid	Ealasaid, Victoria Road, Fort William, Inverness-shire, PH33 6BH	01397 704 005	★★★	Self Catering
Fordon	Fordon, Badabrie, Fort William, Inverness-shire, PH33 7LX	01397 772737	★★★	Self Catering
Glasphein	10 Hatch Close, Chapel Row, Berkshire, RG7 6NZ	01189 714330	★★★	Self Catering
Glen Nevis Holiday Cottages	Glen Nevis Holiday Cottages, Glen Nevis, Fort William, Inverness-shire, PH33 6SX	01397 702191	★★★ → ★★★★★	Self Catering
Glengyle Holiday Home	Glengyle Holiday Home, Glen Nevis, Fort William, Inverness-shire, PH33 6PF	01397 708622	★★★★	Self Catering

    ♿ Unassisted wheelchair access   ♿ Assisted wheelchair access   ♀ Access for visitors with mobility difficulties
    🍂 Bronze Green Tourism Award   🍂🍂 Silver Green Tourism Award   🍂🍂🍂 Gold Green Tourism Award
    For further information on our Green Tourism Business Scheme please see page 9.

Hawthorn	57 Kilmallie Road, Caol, Fort William, Inverness-shire, PH33 7DA	01397 700267	★★★	Self Catering	
Linnhe Lochside Holidays	Linnhe Lochside Holidays, Corpach, Fort William, Inverness-shire, PH33 7NL	01397 772376	★★★ → ★★★★	Self Catering	𝒫𝒫
Loch Leven Chalets	Loch Leven Chalets, North Ballachulish, Fort William, Inverness-shire, PH33 6SA	01855 821272	★★★	Self Catering	
Loch View	Loch View, Dolalans7 Blaich, Fort William Inverness-shire, PH33 7AN	01397 772808	★★★★	Self Catering	
Lochview	Lochview House, Heathercroft, off Argyll Terrace, Fort William, Inverness-shire, PH33 6RE	01397 703149	★★★	Self Catering	
Lonavla	Lonavla, Lochy-Side, Fort William, Inverness-shire, PH33 7NX	01397 702600	★★★★	Self Catering	
Mount Alexander	Mount Alexander, Banavie, Fort William, Inverness-shire, PH33 7NF	01397 704466	★★★	Self Catering	
Old Blar Cottages	Old Blar Cottages, Old Blar House, Banavie, Fort William, Inverness-shire, PH33 7NG	01397 708998	★★★★	Self Catering	
Smirisary	Smirisary, Achintore Road, Fort William, Inverness-shire, PH33 6RW	01397 702918	★	Self Catering	
Springwell Holiday Homes	Springwell Holiday Homes, Waterside House, Strathcathro, Brechin, Angus, DD9 7QF	07977 981370	★★ → ★★★★	Self Catering	
Taigh Nan Chleirich	14 Perth Place, Fort William, Inverness-shire, PH33 6UL	01397 702444	★★★	Self Catering	
The Old Schoolhouse	The Old Schoolhouse, Lochybridge, Fort William, Inverness-shire, PH33 7NE	01397 703690	★★★	Self Catering	
The Snuggle Bug & Wanderer's End	Aberfoyle House, Argyll Road, Fort William, Inverness-Shire, PH33 6LE	01397 704813	★★★ → ★★★★	Self Catering	
Tigh-A-Phuirt Holiday Cottages	Tigh-A-Phuirt Holiday Cottages, Lochyside, Fort William, Inverness-shire, PH33 7NX	01397 704610	★★★★	Self Catering	
Torosay	3 Ryefield Close, Solihull, West Midlands, B91 1PP	0121 7045100	★★★	Self Catering	
Whinbrae Cottage	Whinbrae, 6 Perth Place, Fort William, Inverness-shire, PH33 6UL	01397 703743	★★★	Self Catering	
Whinburn Self Catering	Whinburn Self Catering, Lundavra Road, Fort William, Inverness-shire, PH33 6RF	01397 701104	★★★	Self Catering	
Whinknowe Holiday Cottages	Whinknowe, Banavie, Fort William, Inverness-shire, PH33 7PB	01397 772227	★★★ → ★★★★	Self Catering	

Fortingall

Stablefield	6 Wyvern Park, Edinburgh, Midlothian, EH9 2JY	0131 662 4528	★★★★	Self Catering
Keepers Cottage	Garth Lodge, Fortingall, Aberfeldy, Perthshire, PH15 2NF	01887 830689	★★★★★	Self Catering

Fortrose

Flowerburn House Holiday Homes	Flowerburn Holiday Homes, Flowerburn House, Fortrose, Ross-shire, IV10 8SL	01381 621069	★★★	Self Catering
Fuchsia Cottage	19 Sandhurst Road, Four Oaks, Sutton Coldfield, West Midlands, B74 4UE	0121 353 7750	★★★	Self Catering
The Byre	Fasgadh, Ness Road, Fortrose, Ross-shire, IV10 8SD	01381 620367	★★★	Self Catering

Fossoway

Gateside Farm Cottage	Gateside Farm Cottage, Gateside Farm, Fossoway, Kinross, KY13 0QL	01577 840223	★★	Self Catering

Foulden

The Paddock	Foulden Hagg, Foulden, Berwickshire, TD15 1UH	01289 386339	Awaiting Grading

      ♿ Unassisted wheelchair access   ♿ Assisted wheelchair access   ✻ Access for visitors with mobility difficulties

𝒫 Bronze Green Tourism Award   𝒫𝒫 Silver Green Tourism Award   𝒫𝒫𝒫 Gold Green Tourism Award
For further information on our Green Tourism Business Scheme please see page 9.

Fraserburgh

Newseat & Kirklea	Kirktown, Tyrie, Fraserburgh, Aberdeenshire, AB43 7DQ	01346 541231	★ → ★★★	Self Catering
Fisherman's Cottage	157 Foxcroft Drive, Rastrick, Brighouse, West Yorkshire, HD6 3UP	01484 716979	★★★★	Self Catering

By Fraserburgh

Cortes House, Lonmay	3 Lyndhurst, London NW3 5NS	0207 7948114	★★★★	Self Catering

Freuchie

Creg-Ny-Baa	Abercorn Cottage, Abercorn, Hopetown, South Queensferry, West Lothian, EH30 9SL	0131 331 4753	★★★	Self Catering

Fyvie

Tehillah Farm Cottage (The Bothy)	The Bothy, Mosside of Gight, Fyvie, Aberdeenshire, AB53 8LY	01651 806376	★★★★	Self Catering

Gairloch

16 Strath	16 Strath, Gairloch, Ross-shire, IV21 2BX	01445 712230	★★★	Self Catering
30 Strath	8 Eildon View, Tweedmouth, Berwick upon Tweed, Northumberland, TD15 2FQ	01289 303197	★★★	Self Catering
Apronhill House	Primrose Cottage, Badachro, Gairloch, Ross-shire, IV21 2AB	01445 741317	★★	Self Catering
Ard Sheen	Ard Sheen, Badachro, Gairloch, Wester Ross, IV21 2AA	01445 741711	★★	Self Catering
Ardgrianach	1 Achadesdale, Gairloch, Ross-shire, IV21 2BY	01445 712417	★★	Self Catering
Cairns Cottage	Torriesley, Kirkton of Oyne, Insch, Aberdeenshire, AB52 6QU	01464 851396	★★★	Self Catering
Creag Mhor Chalets	Heatherdale, Charleston, Gairloch, Rossshire, IV21 2AH	01445 712388	★★★	Self Catering
Family Holiday Houses, Gairloch	Gillymere, Horseshoe Lane, Ash Vale, Aldershot, Hants, GU12 5LJ	01252 325119	★★★ → ★★★★	Self Catering
Glendale House	Glendale House, 20 South Erradale, Gairloch, Ross-shire, IV21 2AU	01445 741755	★★★	Self Catering
Heather Croft	Heather Croft, 20 Big Sand, Gairloch, Ross-shire, IV21 2DD	01445 712084	★★★	Self Catering
Millcroft Hotel Apartments	Millcroft Hotel, Strath, Gairloch, Ross-shire, IV21 2BT	01445 712376	★★	Self Catering
The Bothy	Kumargram, Longmore, Gairloch, Ross-shire, IV21 2DB	01445 712468	★★★★	Self Catering
The Croft, Sea Croft and Staffa	18 Rossther Road, North Lancing, West Sussex, BN15 0NP	01903 767803	★★★	Self Catering
Tigh-na-Mhuillean	70 St.Andrews Drive, Bridge of Weir, Renfrewshire, PA11 3HY	01505 614343	★★★	Self Catering
Willow Croft	40 Big Sand, Gairloch, Ross-shire, IV21 2DD	01445 712448	★★★	Self Catering 🦽

By Gairloch

Douglas Cottage, Achtercairn	The Croft, 11 Balvaird, Muir of Ord, Ross-shire, IV6 7RQ	01463 871661	★★★	Self Catering
Freyja	An Caorann, Melvaig, By Gairloch, Ross-shire, IV21 2EA	01445 771225	★★★	Self Catering
Rhona & Raasay	An Caorann, Melvaig, By Gairloch, Ross-shire, IV21 2EA	01445 771225	★★★★	Self Catering

&. Unassisted wheelchair access &. Assisted wheelchair access 🏃 Access for visitors with mobility difficulties
🅟 Bronze Green Tourism Award 🅟🅟 Silver Green Tourism Award 🅟🅟🅟 Gold Green Tourism Award
For further information on our Green Tourism Business Scheme please see page 9.

Galashiels

The Coach House	The Hawthorns, Galashiels, Selkirkshire, TD1 3NS	01896 753426	★★★★★	Self Catering

By Galashiels

No 9 Galabank Cottages	10 Galabank Cottages, Stow, Galashiels, Selkirk shire, TD1 2RP	01578 730289	★★★★	Self Catering

Gardenstown

73 Denside	Buchan House, Strichen AB43 6TP	01771 637367	★★★★	Self Catering
Eva's Cottage	511 Brook Street, Broughty Ferry, Dundee, Angus, DD5 2EA	01382 779818	★★★	Self Catering
No. 131 Harbour Road	131 Harbour Road, Gardenstown, Aberdeenshire, AB45 3YS	07879 604980	★★★	Self Catering
Seilie Cottage	Seilie Cottage, 81 Braeheads, Macduff, Aberdeenshire, AB44 1SF	01261 831503	★★★★	Self Catering
Two Bears Cottage	23 Highgate, Goosnargh, Preston, PR3 2BX	01772 863214	★★★★	Self Catering

Garlieston

15 Cowgate	Top Flat Left, 29 Camphill Avenue, Langside, Glasgow, G41 3AU	0141 632 8379	★★★★	Self Catering

Gartocharn

Greystonelea Lodge	Greystonelea, Gartocharn, Alexandria, Loch Lomond, G83 8SD	01389 830419	★★★★	Self Catering 🦽 📁📁
The Lorn Mill Cottages	The Lorn Mill Cottages, The Lorn, Gartocharn, Dunbartonshire, G83 8LX	01389 753074	★★★★	Self Catering

Garve

Drovers Rest	Bridgefield House, Little Garve, Garve, Ross-shire, IV23 2PU	01997 414384	★★★★	Self Catering

Gatehead,Kilmarnock

Old Rome Mews	Old Rome Farmhouse B & B, Gatehead, Kilmarnock, Ayrshire, KA2 9AJ	01563 850265	★★★★	Self Catering

Gatehouse of Fleet

1 Tannery Brae	Corbieton Farmhouse, Haugh of Urr, Castle Douglas, DG7 3JJ	01556 660312	★★★	Self Catering
1 Tannery Wynd	12 Waulkmill Drive, Penicuik, Midlothian, EH26 8LA	01968 674129	★★★	Self Catering
5 Tannery Wynd	103 Golf Drive, Nuneaton, Warwickshire, CV12 8JT	02476 347919	★★★	Self Catering
7 Tannery Brae	Niddamoor, Old Lees Road, Hedden Bridge, West Yorks, HX7 8HW	01422 843762	★★★	Self Catering
Clachan Cottage	Anwoth, Old Schoolhouse, Gatehouse of Fleet DG7 2EF	01557 814444	★★★★	Self Catering
Clachanside	Alton Cottages, Moffat Dumfries & Galloway, DG10 9LB	01683 220870	★★★★	Self Catering
Craiglure	41 Hotspur Street, Tynouth, Tyne & Wear NE30 4SN	0191 2965041	★★	Self Catering
Driftwood	Morton Cottages, Low Hesket, Carlisle, Cumbria, CA4 0ET	01697 473 578	★★★★	Self Catering
Galloway Cottage	4 Twizell Place, Ponteland, Newcastle upon Tyne, Northumberland, NE20 9QH	0845 644 6547	★★★★	Self Catering
Galloway Hideaways	Drumruck, Gatehouse of Fleet, Kirkcudbrighsthire, DG7 2BN	01557 814672	★★ → ★★★	Self Catering

🦽 Unassisted wheelchair access   🦽 Assisted wheelchair access   🚶 Access for visitors with mobility difficulties
📁 Bronze Green Tourism Award   📁📁 Silver Green Tourism Award   📁📁📁 Gold Green Tourism Award
For further information on our Green Tourism Business Scheme please see page 9.

284   To find out more, call 0845 22 55 121 or go to visitscotland.com.

Garden Cottage	Rusko Holidays, Gatehouse of Fleet, Castle Douglas, Dumfries & Galloway, DG7 2BS	01557 814215	★★★	Self Catering 🛉	
Gilfillan	4 Woodhouse Close, Woodhouse Road, Hove, East Sussex, BN3 5LS	01273 413655	★★★	Self Catering	
Marvic Cottage	5 Robin Close, Tamworth, Staffordshire, B77 1GS	01827 250515	★★★★	Self Catering	
Rusko Holidays	Rusko Holidays, Gatehouse of Fleet, Castle Douglas, Dumfries & Galloway, DG7 2BS	01557 814215	★★ → ★★★★	Self Catering 🦽	🔲
Shilfa	The Old Manse, Borgue, Kirkcudbrightshire DG6 4SH	01557 870356	★★★	Self Catering	
Vital Spark	Meikle Sypland, Kirkcudbright, Kirkcudbrightshire, DG6 4XW	01557 331303	★★★	Self Catering	
Leath Lobhair	8 Holkham AVenue, Beeston, Nottingham NG9 5EQ	0115 9227830	★★★★	Self Catering	

Gateside

Edenshead Cottage	Edenshead Cottage, Edenshead, Gateside, Fife, KY14 7ST	01337 868210	★★★★	Self Catering 🛉	

Gattonside, Melrose

Drumblair	Camberley, Abbotsford Road, Darnick, Melrose, Roxburghshire, TD6 9AJ	01896 823648	★★★★	Self Catering

Gifford

The Woodturner's Cottage	The Lodge, Yestermains, Gifford, East Lothian, EH41 4JG	01620 810131	★★★★	Self Catering
Tyrone Cottage	Yestermains, Gifford, East Lothian, EH41 4JG	01620 810378	★★★	Self Catering

Girvan

7D Wilson Street	Troloss Farm, ElvanFoot, Biggar, Lanarkshire, ML12 6TH	01848 500268	★★★	Self Catering	
Bank Cottage	7 Longlands Way, Heatherside, Camberley, Surrey, GU15 1RH	07901 551887	★★	Self Catering	
Carlenrig Cottage	19 Main Street, Colmonell, Girvan, Ayrshire, KA26 0RY	01465 881265	★★★ → ★★★★	Self Catering	
Dalreoch Cottage	The Estate Office, Stratfield Saye, nr Reading, Berkshire, RG7 2BT	01256 882694	★★★	Self Catering	
Downanhill Cottage	Langdale Farm, Ballantrae, Girvan, Ayrshire, KA26 0PB	01465 831368	★★★	Self Catering 🛉	

By Girvan, Barr

Changue House	Changue House, Barr, South Ayrshire, KA26 9TN	01465 861149	★★★★	Self Catering
Gladneuk Cottage	Gladneuk Cottage, Glenginnet Road, Barr, by Girvan, South Ayrshire, KA26 9TU	01465 861275	★★★	Self Catering
Glengennet & Upper Barr Cottages	Glengennet Farm, Barr, Girvan, Ayrshire, KA26 9TY	01465 861220	★★ → ★★★★	Self Catering

Glasgow

11 Falkland Street	Manor Farm, Charlcombe Lane, Bath BA1 8DS	07798 695764	★★★★	Self Catering
319 Sheriff Court	Morland Hall, Morland, Penrith, Cumbria, CA10 3BB	01931 714715	★★★	Self Catering
9 Kirklee Circus, 8 Sydenham Rd and Georgian	8 Sydenham Road, Dowanhill, Glasgow G12 9NP	0141 339 0008	★★★	Self Catering
964 Sauchiehall St	Argyll Hotel, 973 Sauchiehall Street, Glasgow G3 7TQ	0141 3347802	★★★★	Self Catering
Art Apartment Glasgow	Art Apartment Glasgow, 5 Park Quadrant, Glasgow G3 6BS	07880 602623	★★★	Self Catering

🦽 Unassisted wheelchair access   🦽 Assisted wheelchair access   🛉 Access for visitors with mobility difficulties
🔲 Bronze Green Tourism Award   🔲 Silver Green Tourism Award   🔲 Gold Green Tourism Award
For further information on our Green Tourism Business Scheme please see page 9.

Benview Holiday Lodges	Benview Holiday Lodges, Balfron Station, Glasgow, Lanarkshire, G63 0QY	01360 850001	Awaiting Grading	
City Apartments - Glasgow	City Apartments Hotel Ltd, Craigie Hall6 Rowan Road Glasgow, G41 5BS	0141 419 1919 ★★★★	Serviced Apartments	
City Apartments - Glasgow South	City Apartments Glasgoe South, 32 Balvicar Street, Glasgow G42 8QW	0141 423 1152 ★★★	Serviced Apartments	
City Apartments & Embassy Suites	1 Mount Harriet Avenue, Stepps, Glasgow G33 6DH	0141 779 5868 ★★★★	Self Catering	
City Slicker Apartment	3/1 54 Hughenden Lane, Glasgow, Lanarkshire, G12 9XJ	0141 579 2360 ★★★★	Self Catering	
City Slicker Apartments	Glasgow City Flats, Flat 31, 54 Hughenden Lane, Glasgow, Lanarkshire, G12 9XJ	0141 579 236	Awaiting Grading	
Flat 0/2 & Flat 0/1, 3A & 5 Sherbrook Drive	17 Kirkview Crescent, Newton Mearns, Glasgow, East Renfrewshire, G77 5DB	0141 5854310 ★★★	Self Catering	
Flat 101/119/201	My Place in Glasgow (Omminal Ltd), Hollygrove, Borrowfield, Station Road, Cardross, Argyll & Bute, G82	01389 841583 ★★★★	Self Catering	
Flat 2	Lethamhill, 20 West Dhuhill Drive, Helensburgh, Dunbartonshire, G84 9AW	01436 676016 ★★★	Self Catering	
Flat 2A Millbrae Upper & Lower Flats	28 Merrylee Road, Newlands, Glasgow G43 2SN	0141 637 2415 ★★★★	Self Catering	
Flat On The Green	26 Harelaw Avenue, Glasgow, Lanarkshire, G44 3HZ	07703 314428 ★★★	Self Catering	
Forbes & Garnett Hall	University of Strathclyde, 50 Richmond Street, Glasgow G1 1XP	0141 552 4400 ★	Self Catering	
Fraser Suites Glasgow	Fraser Suites Glasgow, 1-19 Albion Street, Glasgow G1 1NY	0141 553 4288 ★★★★	Serviced Apartments	♿
Glasgow Central Apartments	9 Western Harbour, Breakwater, Edinburgh, Lothian, EH6 6PZ	0131 553 6051	Awaiting Grading	
Glasgow Centrale Serviced Apartments	Glasgow Centrale Serviced Apartments, 219 St Vincent Street, Glasgow G2 5QY	0141 248 3010 ★★★	Serviced Apartments	
Glasgow Lofts	Glasgow Lofts, Fleming House, 134 Renfrew Street, Glasgow G3 6ST	0141 332 1976 ★★★★★	Serviced Apartments	
Hamilton Drive	Kilburn Holiday Home, 1 Hamilton Drive, Cambuslang, Glasgow, South Lanarkshire, G72 8JG	0141 641 8046 ★★★	Self Catering	
Italian Centre Apartments	Italian Centre Apartments Ltd, 4 Park Circus Place, Glasgow G3 6AN	08700 858100 ★★★★	Serviced Apartments	
Kelvin Apartment	The Kelvin, 15 Buckingham Terrace, Glasgow G12 8EB	0141 339 7143 ★★★★	Self Catering	
Lomond Mews	The Firm of Gilchrist & Murray, 20 Lynedoch Crescent, Glasgow G3 6EQ	0141 341 1155 ★★ → ★★★	Self Catering	
Merchant City Virginia Apartment	Merchant City Virginia Apartments, 3 Clarendon Road, Kings Park, Stirling, FK8 2RN	07967 206164 ★★★	Self Catering	
No 190 West George Street	190 West Geroge Street, Glasgow G2 2NR	0141 331 0295	Awaiting Grading	
No 38 Bath Street	TCS Freehold Investments, Town Centre House, The Merron Centre, Leeds, W. Yorkshire, LS2 8LY	01132 221234 ★★★★	Serviced Apartments	
Queen's Gate Apartments	33 Queen's Gate, 107 Downhill Street, Glasgow G12 9EQ	0141 3391615 ★★★ → ★★★★	Self Catering	
Regency Apartments	8 Ochil Road, Stirling, Stirlingshire, FK9 5JF	01786 475973 ★★★	Self Catering	
Saco House	The Serviced Apartment Company, 40 Whiteladies Road, Bristol BS8 2LG	0117 9745931 ★★★★	Serviced Apartments	
Streets Ahead Self Catering	Streets Ahead, 252A Castlemilk Road, Kingspark, Glasgow G44 4LB	0141 644 1066 ★★★	Self Catering	
The Knowes	The Knowes, 32 Riddrie Knowes, Glasgow G33 2QH	0141 770 5213 ★★★	Self Catering	♟
The Spires	531 Great Western Road, Aberdeen AB10 6PE	0845 2700090 ★★★	Serviced Apartments	
White House Apartments	White House Apartments, 11-13 Cleveden Crescent, Glasgow G12 0PB	0141 339 9375 ★★★ → ★★★★	Self Catering	

♿ Unassisted wheelchair access   ♿ Assisted wheelchair access   ♟ Access for visitors with mobility difficulties

🌿 Bronze Green Tourism Award   🌿🌿 Silver Green Tourism Award   🌿🌿🌿 Gold Green Tourism Award
For further information on our Green Tourism Business Scheme please see page 9.

| Wilton Mansions | Suite 3/2, 156 Wilton Street, Glasgow, Lanarkshire, G20 6BS | 0141 9463937 | ★★★ | Self Catering | |

By Glasgow

Bankell Farm Cottage, Milngavie	Bankell Farm Cottage, Strathblane Road, Milngavie, Glasgow G62 8LE	0141 956 4643	★★★	Self Catering	
The Coach House, Cathcart	National Trust for Scotland, 28 Charlotte Square, Edinburgh EH2 4ET	0131 243 9335	★★★	Self Catering	
Firfield, Killearn	Firfield, Gartness Road, Killearn, Glasgow, G63 9NT	01360 550 508	★★★	Self Catering	

Glen Cloy, Brodick, Isle of Arran

| Bluebird, Peacock & Finch Cottage | Kilmichael Country House, Brodick, Isle of Arran, KA27 8BY | 01770 302219 | ★★★★★ | Self Catering | ☂ |

Glen Orchy

| The Old House | The New House, Arichastlich, Glen Orchy, Argyll, PA33 1BD | 01838 200399 | ★★★★ | Self Catering | |

Glenashdale

| Strathconon | Suilven, Macharioch Road, Southend, Argyll, PA28 6RF | 01586 830323 | ★★★★ | Self Catering | ☂ |

Glenborrodale, By Acharacle

| Glenbay Cottages and The Tower And Ruin | Greenwood, Ardslignish, By Acharacle, Argyll, PH36 4JG | 01972 500201 | ★★★★ | Self Catering | |
| Shoreline Cottages | Feorag House, Glenborrodale, Acharacle, Argyll, PH36 4JP | 01972 500248 | ★★★★★ | Self Catering | |

Glencoe

Callart View Cottage	4 Elm Road, Irby, Wirral, CH61 3UP	01516 482454	Awaiting Grading		
Camus Bhan	Callart View, Invercoe, Glencoe, Argyll, PH49 4HP	01855 811259	★★★★	Self Catering	
Carefree Self Catering Holidays	Clachaig Inn, Glencoe, Argyll, PH49 4HX	01855 811252	★★★★ → ★★★★★	Self Catering	
Ceol Mara	3 Enderby Dr, Highford Pk, Hexham, Northumberland, NE46 2PA	01434 606512	★★★	Self Catering	
Craigavon House & Cottages	Dalcraig, Ballachulish, Argyll, PH49 4JQ	01855 811608	★★★★ → ★★★★★	Self Catering	
Glencoe Cottages	Glencoe Cottages, Torren, Glencoe, Argyll, PH49 4HX	01855 811207	★★★	Self Catering	☂ 🏅🏅🏅
Glencoe Mountain Cottages	Glencoe Mountain Cottages, Glean Leac Na Muidhe, Glencoe, Argyll, PH49 4LA	01855 811598	★★★★	Self Catering	

Glendale

| Denekin | Po Box 37, Isle of Skye IV55 8WZ | 07957 752001 | ★★ | Self Catering | |
| Seagull's Rest | Carters Rest, 8/9 Upper Milovaig, Glendale, Isle of Skye, IV55 8WY | 01470 511272 | ★★★★ | Self Catering | |

Glendaruel

| Maymore | Ardacheranmor, Glendaruel, Argyll, PA22 3AE | 01369 820209 | ★★ | Self Catering | |

Glendevon

| Glendevon Park | Glendevon Park, Glendevon, Perthshire, FK14 7JY | 01259 781569 | ★★★ | Self Catering | |
| Rosslyn Cottage | Rosslyn House, Glendevon, Perthshire, FK14 7JY | 01259 781360 | ★★★ | Self Catering | |

♿ Unassisted wheelchair access   ♿ Assisted wheelchair access   ☂ Access for visitors with mobility difficulties
🍃 Bronze Green Tourism Award   🍃🍃 Silver Green Tourism Award   🍃🍃🍃 Gold Green Tourism Award
For further information on our Green Tourism Business Scheme please see page 9.

Gleneagles, Auchterarder

Gleneagles Windsor Glen	41 Frogston Road West, Edinburgh, Lothian, EH10 7AH	0131 445 4543	★★★★	Self Catering

Glenelg

Holly Cottage	Southmoor, 11 Dean Park Road, Bournemouth, Dorset, BH1 1HU	01202 298775	★★★★	Self Catering

Glenfarg

Duncreavie Log Cabins	4 Salisbury Place, Arbroath, Scotland, DD11 2AD	01241 430730	★★★★ → ★★★★★	Self Catering	🍃🍃🍃
Lavender Cottage & The Old Cottage	Colliston, Glenfarg, Perthshire, PH2 9PE	01577 830434	★★★ → ★★★★	Self Catering	
Newhill Granary	Newhill Granary, Newhill Farm, Glenfarg, Perth, PH2 9QN	01577 830245	★★★★★	Self Catering	
Steading Cottage	West Newton Of Balcanquhal, Glenfarg, Perthshire, PH2 9QD	01577 830268	★★★★	Self Catering	

By Glenfarg

The Millers Cottage	The Millers Cottage, Glendy, By Glenfarg, Perthshire, PH2 9QL	01577 830445	★★★★	Self Catering	🍃

Glenfinnan

Glenfinnan Cottages	Glenfinnan Cottages, The Colt House, Glenfinnan, Inverness-shire, PH37 4LT	01397 722 234	★★	Self Catering

Glenforsa, By Salen, Isle of Mull

Tigh Bhan	Callachally Farm, Salen, Isle of Mull, PA72 6JN	01680 300424	★★★	Self Catering

Glengap

The Shieling	Trostrie Cottage, Glengap, Twynholm, by Kirkcudbright, DG6 4PS	01557 860349	★★★★	Self Catering

Glenhinnisdal

Garybuie	Garybuie, 4 Balmeanach, Glenhinnisdal, Isle of Skye, IV51 9UX	01470 542310	★★★	Self Catering

Glenisla, By Kirriemuir

Tipperwhig & Brankam	Purgavie Farm, Lintrathen, Kirriemuir, Angus, DD8 5HZ	01575 560364	★★★ → ★★★★	Self Catering	♀

Glenlivet

Beechgrove, Kirkton and Aspen	Beechgrove Post Office, Tomnavoulin, Banffshire, AB37 9JA	01807 590220	★★	Self Catering
Deskie Cottage	Deskie Farm, Glenlivet, Ballindalloch, AB37 9BX	01807 590207	★★★	Self Catering
Enoch Dhu	Deepdale, Auchbreck, Glenlivet, Banffshire, AB37 9EJ	01807 590364	★★★	Self Catering
Lochranza	10 Sandfield Lane, Hartford, Northwich, Cheshire, CW8 1PU	01606 75208	★★★★	Self Catering

By Glenlochar

Livingstone House & Cottage	Discover Scotland (Agency), 27 King Street, Castle Douglas, Kirkcudbrightshire, DG7 1AB	01556 504030	★ → ★★	Self Catering

Glenluce

Craw's Nest Bungalow	45 West View Road, Sutton Coldfield, West Midlands, B75 6AZ	0121 378 1844	★★★	Self Catering

 & Unassisted wheelchair access && Assisted wheelchair access ♀ Access for visitors with mobility difficulties
🍃 Bronze Green Tourism Award 🍃🍃 Silver Green Tourism Award 🍃🍃🍃 Gold Green Tourism Award
For further information on our Green Tourism Business Scheme please see page 9.

Whitecairn - Island Lodge	Whitecairn Holiday Park Lodge, Whitecairn, Glenluce, Wigtownshire, DG8 0NZ	01581 300267	★★★★	Self Catering
Glenalmar	24 St John Street, Whithorn, Newtown Stewart, Wigtownshire, DG8 8PF	01988 500203	★★★	Self Catering

Glenmoriston

Binnilidh Mhor	Keeper's Cottage, Dundreggan Estate, Glenmoriston, Inverness-shire, IV63 7YJ	01320 340258	★★★★★	Self Catering 🏃

Glenshee

Holly Tree Lodge	K Construction (Scotland) Ltd, 15 Marionville Road, Edinburgh EH7 5TY	07947 585975	Awaiting Grading	
New Steading Cottage/Old Steading Cottage	Dalnoid Holiday Cottages, Dalnoid Farmhouse, Glenshee, Blairgowrie, Perthshire, PH10 7LR	01250 882200	★★★★	Self Catering 🏃

Glenshiel

Brook Cottage	Aird View, Dornie, Kyle of Lochalsh, IV40 8EH	01599 555201	★★★	Self Catering

Glenurquhart

Balnalurigin	Appleton House, Errol, Perth, Perthshire, PH2 7QE	01821 642412	★★★★	Self Catering
Old Stables	The Grange, Corrimony, Glenurquhart, Inverness-Shire, IV63 6TW	01456 476367	★★★★	Self Catering 🏃 🄿
Torcroft Lodges	Braefield Croft, Glenurquhart, Inverness-shire, IV63 6TJ	01456 459424	★★★ → ★★★★	Self Catering
Buntait Farm Cottage	Buntait Farm Cottage, Buntait Farm, Glenurquhart, By Drumnadrochit, Inverness-shire, IV63 6TN	01456 476256	★★★★	Self Catering 🄿

Gramsdale, Isle of Benbecula

Tigh Curstaig	2 Kyles Flodda, Gramsdale, Benbecula, Western Isles, HS7 5QR	01870 602536	★★★★	Self Catering

Grantown-on-Spey

6 Wood Park	The Neuk, Grant Road, Grantown on Spey, Highlands, PH26 3LA	07834 355491	★★★	Self Catering
Auchernack	Auchernack, Grantown on Spey, Morayshire, PH26 3NH	01479 872093	★★★	Self Catering
Auchnagonalin House	LHH LTD, Poyntzfield House, Poyntzfield, By Dingwall, Ross-shire, IV7 8LX	01381 610496	★★★★	Self Catering
Birchbank	Auchernack, Grantown on Spey, Morayshire, PH26 3NH	01479 872093	★★★★	Self Catering
Clanranald	Willowbrae, 73 Buddidarroch, Lochinver, By Lairg, Sutherland, IV27 4LP	01571 844383	★★★★	Self Catering
Craignay	Baile na Coille, Balmoral, Ballater, Aberdeenshire, AB35 5TB	01339 742278	★★★	Self Catering
Grianan	Scottish Holiday Homes, Balliefurth Farm, Grantown on Spey PH26 3NH	01479 821636	★★★	Self Catering 🄿🄿
Cedar Cottage	14 McPherson Drive, Gourock, Renfrewshire, PA19 1LJ	01475 632 830	★★★	Self Catering
Easter Duiar Cottage	Begbie Farmhouse, Begbie, Nr Haddington, East Lothian, EH41 4HQ	01620 829 488	★★★★	Self Catering
Failte & Kangei	41 Mid Liberton, Edinburgh EH16 5QT	0131 478 3539	★★ → ★★★	Self Catering
Lower Lynemore Croft	West-Anagach, Grantown on Spey, Morayshire, PH26 3NQ	01479 872898	★★★	Self Catering
Muckrach Castle	Savills, 55 York Place, Perth PH2 8EH	01738 445588	★★★★	Self Catering
West Gorton	Craggan, Grantown-on-Spey, Morayshire, PH26 3NT	01479 872120	★★★	Self Catering

   ♿ Unassisted wheelchair access   ♿ Assisted wheelchair access   🏃 Access for visitors with mobility difficulties
🄿 Bronze Green Tourism Award   🄿🄿 Silver Green Tourism Award   🄿🄿🄿 Gold Green Tourism Award
For further information on our Green Tourism Business Scheme please see page 9.

By Grantown-on-Spey

Top Cottage	Muir of Blebo, Blebo Craigs, Cupar, Fife, KY15 5UG	01334 850781	★★★	Self Catering

Great Bernera, Isle of Lewis

25 Valasay	25 Valasay, Great Bernera, Isle of Lewis, Western Isles, HS2 9NB	01851 612288	★★★★	Self Catering
5 Hacklete	5 Hacklete, Great Bernera, Isle of Lewis, HS2 9ND	01851 612269	★	Self Catering
Harsgeir View Cottage	9 Kiln Ridge, Stornoway HS1 2TY	01851 703612	★★★★	Self Catering
Lochanview Cottage	15 Riverview Crescent, Cardross, Argyll & Bute, G82 5LT	01389 841509	★★★★	Self Catering

Greenock

James Watt College	James Watt College, Finnart Street, Greenock, Renfrewshire, PA16 8HF	01475 731360	★★	Self Catering

Grimsay, Isle of North Uist

Glendale	Glendale, 7 Kallin, Grimsay, North Uist, HS6 5HY	01870 602029	★★★	Self Catering
Rona View	100 Ollershaw Lane, Marstow, Northwich CW9 6ER	01606 44422	★★★	Self Catering

Gruinart, Isle of Islay

Byre Cottage & Farmhouse Cottage	Drumlanrig, Carnduncan, Gruinart, Isle of Islay, PA44 7PS	01496 850503	★★★★	Self Catering
Benmore Estate	Strutt & Parker, 28 Melville Street, Edinburgh EH3 7HA	0131 2262500	★★ → ★★★★	Self Catering

Gulberwick, Shetland

Fairview	Cotswold House, Hassobury, Farnham, Bishop Stortford, CM23 1JR	07770 955830	★★★★	Self Catering

Gullane

10 Muirfield Apartments	129 High Street, North Berwick, East Lothian, EH39 4HM	01620 893204	★★★★	Self Catering
9 Lammerview Terrace	Mallard Hotel, East Links Road, Gullane, East Lothian, EH31 2AF	01620 843288	★★	Self Catering
Tern Cottage	129 High Street, North Berwick, East Lothian, EH39 4HM	01620 893204	★★★★	Self Catering
The Bield & Wellbank	Bryce Houstoun Properties Ltd, 5 Stenhouse Mill Lane, Edinburgh EH11 3LR	0131 4440405	★★★ → ★★★★	Self Catering

Haddington

No 1 Goodalls Place	Williamstone House, North Berwick, East Lothian, EH39 5DG	01620 894374	★★★★	Self Catering

Halkirk

Achalone	North Achalone, Halkirk, Caithness, KW12 6XA	01847 831326	★★★★	Self Catering

Halleattis, Lochmaben

Courtyard Cottage	Courtyard Lettings, 1 The Stables, Halleaths, Lochmaben, Dumfries and Galloway, DG11 1LS	01387 810369	★★★★	Self Catering

Hamilton

Flat & 20 Pillans Court	36 Russell Street, Burnbank, Hamilton ML3 0PQ	07768 932496	★★★	Self Catering

♿ Unassisted wheelchair access   ♿ Assisted wheelchair access   🕴 Access for visitors with mobility difficulties
🍃 Bronze Green Tourism Award   🍃🍃 Silver Green Tourism Award   🍃🍃🍃 Gold Green Tourism Award
For further information on our Green Tourism Business Scheme please see page 9.

290   To find out more, call 0845 22 55 121 or go to visitscotland.com.

Hamnavoe, Shetland

Fishers Croft Hamnavoe	The Rectory, Fishers Lane, Oswell, Royston, Herts, SG8 5QX	01223 208437	★★★★	Self Catering	

Harris

Crowlin	Avalon, 64 Abbotshall Drive, Cults, Aberdeen, AB15 9JN	01224 867392	★★★★	Self Catering	
Fraser Cottage	Point House, 8 Grosebay, Harris, Western Isles, HS3 3ER	01859 530 251	★★★ → ★★★★	Self Catering	🌿

Haugh of Urr

Drumpellier	12 Highfield Road, Scone, Perth, Perthshire, PH2 6RE	01738 551348	★★★	Self Catering	
Glenfinart Cottage	Hillhouse, Sandy Lane, Locharbriggs, Dumfries, Dumfries & Galloway, DG1 1SA	01387 710409	★★★	Self Catering	
The Sheilin	Milton Park Farm, Haugh of Urr, Castle Douglas, Kirkcudbrightshire, DG7 3JJ	01556 660212	★★★	Self Catering	

Hawick

10 Mansfield Mills House	10 Roberton Place, Hawick TD9 0DB	01450 373237	★★★★	Self Catering	🚶
Jo's Cottage	Billerwell Farm, Bonchester Bridge, Hawick, Roxburghshire, TD9 8JF	01450 860656	★★★	Self Catering	🚶 🌿
Willowherb Cottage	Wiltonburn Farm, Hawick, Roxburghshire, TD9 7LL	01450 372414	★	Self Catering	

By Hawick

The Steadings, Chesters	The Steadings, Roundabout Farm, Chester, Hawick, Roxburghshire, TD9 8TH	01450 860730	★★★	Self Catering	

Helensburgh

Flat 1, Sinclair House	Sinclair House, 91/93 Sinclair Street, Helensburgh, Argyll & Bute, G84 8TR	01436 676301	★★★★	Self Catering	
Garden Cottage	Rosebank Cottage, 28a Campbell Street, Helensburgh, Argyll & Bute, G84 8BQ	01436 675372	★★★	Self Catering	
Pier View	Arran View, 32 Barclay Drive, Helensburgh G84 9RA	01436 673713	★★★	Self Catering	
The Coach House	185 East Clyde Street, Helensburgh, Argyle & Bute, G84 7AG	01436 672865	★★★★	Self Catering	
The Flat, Rhu Lodge	Rhu Lodge, Rhu, Helensburgh G84 8NF	01436 821315	★★★★	Self Catering	
Tolsta	Tolsta, 8 Middleton Drive, Helensburgh, Argyll & Bute, G84 7BE	01436 678538	★★★	Self Catering	

By Helensburgh

Cove Park, Peaton Hill	Cove Park, Peaton Hill, Near Helensburgh, Argyll & Bute, G84 0PE	01436 850123	★★ → ★★★	Self Catering	
Crosskeys	Crosskeys, Glen Fruin, By Helensburgh, Argyll, G84 9EE	01389 850595	★★★	Self Catering	
Garemount Lodge	Garemount Lodge, Shandon, By Helensburgh, Argyll, G84 8NP	01436 820780	★★★★	Self Catering	
Gareside Lodge	Gareside Cottage, Shandon, By Helensburgh, Argyll & Bute, G84 8NW	01436 820745	★★★★	Self Catering	

Helmsdale

Valhalla	28 Auchenmaid Drive, Largs, Ayrshire, KA30 9JJ	01475 673136	★★★	Self Catering	

♿ Unassisted wheelchair access   ♿ Assisted wheelchair access   🚶 Access for visitors with mobility difficulties
🌿 Bronze Green Tourism Award   🌿🌿 Silver Green Tourism Award   🌿🌿🌿 Gold Green Tourism Award
For further information on our Green Tourism Business Scheme please see page 9.

By Helmsdale

Balvallioch	Hinwick Lodge, Nr Wellingborough, Northamptonshire, NN29 7JQ	01234 782578	★★★	Self Catering

Hopeman

Mossyards	Mossyards, Roseisle, Elgin, Moray, IV30 5YD	01343 830250	★★	Self Catering
Hopeman Lodge Flats	Hopeman Lodge, Hopeman, Elgin, Moray, IV30 5YA	01343 830245	★★	Self Catering

By Hopeman

Gamekeepers Cottage	Inverugie, By Hopeman, Moray, IV30 5YB	01343 830253	★★★	Self Catering

Houston

Heather Cottage & Garden Cottage	The Old School, Barochan Road, Houston, Renfrewshire, PA6 7HT	01505 690628	★★★	Self Catering

Huntingtower

Garden Flat	Garden Flat, Clocktower House, 2 The Clocktower, Huntingtower, Perth, Perthshire, PH13UB	01738 583882	★★★★	Self Catering
Huntingtower Lodges	Huntingtower Lodges, Huntingtower, Perth, Perthshire, PH1 3JT	01738 582444	★★★	Self Catering

Huntly

Deveron Valley Cottages	Mains of Auchingoul, Bridge of Marnoch, Huntly AB54 7XE	01466 780180	★★★ → ★★★★	Self Catering
Drumdelgie house	Drumdelgie House, Cairnie, Huntly, Aberdeenshire, AB54 4TH	01466 760346	★★	Self Catering ♿
Easterton	21 Deveron Road, Turriff, Aberdeenshire, AB53 5BB	01888 568327	★★★	Self Catering
West Lodge	National Trust for Scotland, 28 Charlotte Square, Edinburgh EH2 4ET	0131 243 9335	★★	Self Catering

By Huntly

The Factors House, Cairnie	Smallburn Enterprises, Smallburn, Cairnie, by Huntly, Aberdeenshire, AB54 4UE	01466 760 219	★★★★	Self Catering
Glenside, Cairnie	Glenside, Glen of Coachford, Cairnie, Huntly, Aberdeenshire, AB54 4TU	01466 760750	★★★	Self Catering
Aswanley Cottages, Glass	Aswanley Cottages, Glass, Huntly, Aberdeenshire, AB54 4XJ	01466 700262	★★★ → ★★★★	Self Catering

Hutton

Broadmeadows	Broadmeadows House, Hutton, Berwickshire, TD15 1TN	01289 386834	★★★★	Self Catering

Inner Hebrides

The Bothy	National Trust for Scotland, 28 Charlotte Square, Edinburgh EH2 4ET	0131 243 9335	★★	Self Catering

Innerleithen

Caddon View Lodge	Caddon Lodge, 14 Pirn Road, Innerleithen, Peebleshire, EH44 6HH	01896 830208	★★★★	Self Catering
The Bothy at Orchard Walls	The Bothy at Orchard Walls, By Traquair, Innerleithen, Peeblesshire, EH44 6PU	01896 831227	★★★★★	Self Catering
The Bothy	Traquair Mill House, Tranquair, Inverleithen, Peeblesshire, EH44 6PT	01896 833182	★★★	Self Catering

♿ Unassisted wheelchair access   ♿ Assisted wheelchair access   ☥ Access for visitors with mobility difficulties
🍂 Bronze Green Tourism Award   🍂🍂 Silver Green Tourism Award   🍂🍂🍂 Gold Green Tourism Award
For further information on our Green Tourism Business Scheme please see page 9.

Insh

Green Slate Cottage	Green Slate Cottage, 22 Rannes Street, Inch, Aberdeenshire, AB52 6JJ	01464 820015	★★★★	Self Catering
Kullbery	Annandale, Gordon Hall, Kingussie, Inverness-shire, PH21 1NR	01540 661560	★★★	Self Catering
Kate's Cabins	Little Birch Cabin & The Old Log Shed, Insh, by Kingussie, Inverness-shire, PH21 1NU	01540 661829	★★★	Self Catering

Inveraray

Arkland Self Catering	Arkland B&B, 15 Arkland, Inveraray, Argyll, PA32 8UD	01499 302361	★★	Self Catering
Braleckan House	Brenchoille Farm, Inveraray, Argyll, PA32 8XN	01499 500662	★★★	Self Catering
St Malieu Hall	148 Newhaven Road, Edinburgh EH6 4PZ	0131 5544257	★★★★	Self Catering
The Paymaster's House	Treetops, Gowhouse Road, Kilmacolm, Renfrewshire, PA13 4DJ	01505 871305	★★★★	Self Catering

Invergarry

Ardochy House Cottages	Ardochy House Cottages, Glengarry, Invergarry, Inverness-shire, PH35 4HR	01809 511292	Awaiting Grading	
Faichemard Farm Chalets	Faichemard Farm Chalets, Faichemard Farm, Invergarry, Inverness-shire, PH35 4HG	01809 501314	★★	Self Catering
Highgarry Lodges & Cottage	Highgarry Lodges & Cottage, Ardgarry Farm, Faichem, Invergarry, Inverness-shire, PH35 4HG	01809 501226	★★★ → ★★★★	Self Catering
Old Ground Invergarry	Lann Dearg, Dalcataig, Invermoriston, Inverness-shire, IV63 7YG	01456 459092	★★★★	Self Catering
Poulary	30 The Lane, Tebworth, Leighton Buzzard, Bedfordshire, LU7 9QG	01525 874166	★★★	Self Catering
Tangusdale	Ardfriseal, Mandally Road, Invergarry, Inverness-shire, PH35 4HP	01809 501281	★★★★	Self Catering

Inverbeg

Inverbeg Holiday Park	Inverbeg Holiday Park, Inverbeg, Luss, Argyll & Bute, G83 8DP	01436 860267	★★★★ → ★★★★★	Self Catering

Invercoe

Invercoe Highland Holidays	Invercoe Highland Holidays, Invercoe, Glencoe PH49 4HP	01855 811210	★★★★	Self Catering

Inverfarigaig

Hazelgrove	Evergreen, Inverfarigaig, Inverness-shire, IV2 6XR	01456 486717	★★★★	Self Catering	🍃🍃🍃

Invergordon

Larchwood	Tullich Muir, Delny, Invergordon, Ross-shire, IV18 0LJ	01862 842384	★★★★	Self Catering	🍃🍃

Inverinate

John Fishers Cottage	28 High Street, Dawlish EX7 9HP	01626 889098	★★★	Self Catering	🍃
Shoreside	Shoreside, Mullardoch, Inverinate, Ross-shire, IV40 8HB	01599 511227	★★★★	Self Catering	

Inverkeilor

Grieve's Cottage	Priestfield Farm, Inverkeilor, Arbroath, Angus, DD11 5SW	01241 830202	★★★	Self Catering
Flat 1, 2, 3 Chance Inn	Chance Inn, 32 Main Street, Inverkeilor, Arbroath, Angus, DD11 5RN	01241 830562	★★	Self Catering

♿ Unassisted wheelchair access   ♿ Assisted wheelchair access   🚶 Access for visitors with mobility difficulties
🍃 Bronze Green Tourism Award   🍃🍃 Silver Green Tourism Award   🍃🍃🍃 Gold Green Tourism Award
For further information on our Green Tourism Business Scheme please see page 9.

Awards correct as of mid August 2008

293

Inverkip

Glen Brae House	3 Crawford Lane, Inverkip, Inverclyde, PA16 0BW	01475 529713	★★★	Self Catering

Invermoriston

Invermoriston Holiday Chalets	Invermoriston Holiday Chalets, Invermoriston, Inverness-shire, IV63 7YF	01320 351254	★★★ → ★★★★	Self Catering	🧑‍🦽	𝑃𝑃
Lann Dearg Studios	Lann Dearg Studios, Lann Dearg, Dalcataig, Invermoriston, IV63 7YG	01320 351353	★★★★	Self Catering		

Inverness

16 Wellingtonia Court	13 Beverley Close, Newtownards, Co Down BT23 7FN	02891 816744	★★★★	Self Catering	
2 Hedgefil [Deld Cottage	Muirfield House, Muirfield Road, Inverness, Inverness-shire, IV2 4AY	01463 222134	★★★★	Self Catering	
28H The Courtyard	Kellydown, Glaickbea, Kiltarlity, by Beauly, Inverness-shire, IV4 7HR	01463 741797	★★★★	Self Catering	
38 Glenburn Drive	Laerchen Strasse 694336 Hunderdorf Germany	0049 9422 348	★★★	Self Catering	
4 & 10 Connel Court	Rowan Glen, Culbokie, Dingwall IV7 8JY	01349 877762	★★★★	Self Catering	
6 Connel Court	Cedar Lodge, Green Drive, Inverness IV2 4EX	01463 237086	★★★★	Self Catering	
Aspenwood Cottage	Lower Birchwood House, Inverfarigaig, Inverness IV2 6XR	01456 486415	★★★★	Self Catering	
Bearnock Cottages	Bearnock Country Centre, Glanurquhart, Inverness-shire, IV63 6TN	01463 230218	★★★★★	Self Catering	
Bell Tower	Douglas Lodge, 18 Crown Drive, Invrerness IV2 3NL	01463 234547	★★★	Self Catering	
Brodie Cottage	9 Hatch Close, Chapel Row, Buckleburgh, Berkshire, RG7 6NZ	01189 712374	★★★	Self Catering	
Easdale	Shamal, Upper Cullernie, Balloch, Inverness, IV2 7HU	01463 790446	★★★	Self Catering	
Garden Flat & Hill Street Apt	Garden Flat, 34 Ardconnel Street, Inverness, Inverness-shire, IV2 3EX	01463 717568	★★★★	Serviced Apartments	
Glen View Apartment	Inverness Apartments, 6 Druid Temple Crescent, Inverness IV2 6UT	01463 236060	★★★	Serviced Apartments	
Hilton Crescent	1 Nunholm Place, Dumfries, Dumfries & Galloway, DG1 1JR	01387 268065	★★★★	Self Catering	
Home Farm Cottages	Home Farm Cottages, Oldtown Of Leys Farm, Inverness, Inverness-shire, IV1 6AE	01463 238238	★★★ → ★★★★	Self Catering	
Holiday Lets in Inverness	5 Culcabock Road, Inverness, Inverness-shire, IV2 3XW	01463 223030	★★★	Self Catering	
Inverness Apartments & Cottages	Inverness Apartments, 6 Druid Temple Crescent, Inverness IV2 6UT	01463 236060	★★★ → ★★★★	Self Catering	
Inverness Riverside	Lonnie Farm, Dalcross, Invernesshire, IV27JH	01463 794405	★★★★	Self Catering	
Inverness Riverside Apartment	8 Cawdor Road, Inverness IV2 3NR	01463 237477	★★★	Self Catering	
Larchview	6a Green Drive, Inverness, Inverness-shire, IV2 4EX	01463 236763	★★★	Self Catering	
Loch Ness Cottages	Brachla, Loch Ness Side, Inverness IV3 8LA	01456 459469	★★★★★	Self Catering	𝑃
Ness Castle Lodges	Ness Castle Lodges Limited, Stoneyfield House, Stoneyfield Business Park, Inverness, Inverness-Shire,	01463 229342	★★★★ → ★★★★★	Self Catering	
Ness Cottage	Ness Cottage, Dores, Inverness, Inverness-shire, IV2 6TR	01463 751298	★★★	Self Catering	
Ness Cottage & Courtyard Cottage	East Dene, 6 Ballifeary Road, Inverness IV3 5PJ	01463 232976	★★★★	Self Catering	𝑃

& Unassisted wheelchair access   𝑘 Assisted wheelchair access   𝑘 Access for visitors with mobility difficulties

𝑃 Bronze Green Tourism Award   𝑃𝑃 Silver Green Tourism Award   𝑃𝑃𝑃 Gold Green Tourism Award

For further information on our Green Tourism Business Scheme please see page 9.

294   To find out more, call 0845 22 55 121 or go to visitscotland.com.

Ness-side Cottage	2 Heather Court, Muir of Ord, Ross-shire, IV6 7PW	01463 871166	★★★★	Self Catering	
Rivana House & Cottage	Rivana, Culloden Road, Westhill, Inverness IV2 5BP	01463 792780	★★★	Self Catering	
River Ness Apartment	12 Priory Way, Beauly, Inverness-shire, IV4 7GF	01463 782878	★★★★	Self Catering	
Riverside City Apartment	Castle Hotel, Huntly, Aberdeenshire, AB54 4SH	01466 792696	★★★	Self Catering	
Rookery Nook	54 Culcabock Avenue, Inverness, Inverness-shire, IV2 3RQ	01463 237085	★★★	Self Catering ♿	
Stanford House	Stanford House, 2 Friars Place, Inverness IV3 8EY	0777 4087512	★★★	Self Catering	
The Garden Flat	The Garden Flat, 42A Broadstone Park, Inverness, Inverness-shire, IV2 3LA	01463 222615	★★★★	Self Catering	
Wilderness Cottages	Wilderness Cottages, Roebuck Cottage, Errogie, Stratherrick, Inverness-shire, IV2 6UH	01456 486358	★★★★	Self Catering	⌐⌐⌐

Inverness-shire

Dochgarroch Cottage	National Trust for Scotland, 28 Charlotte Square, Edinburgh, Midlothian, EH2 4ET	0131 243 9335	★★★	Self Catering	
No. 6 Lynstock Park	50 Viewforth Terrace, Edinburgh Midlothian, EH10 4LJ	0131 220 9212	★★★	Self Catering	

Inverurie

Aquhorthies Cottage	J S Reid Partnership, West Aquhorthies, Fetternear, Inverurie, Aberdeenshire, AB51 5JY	01467 642321	★★★★	Self Catering ♟	
Muirtown Cottage	Muirtown Steading, Chapel of Garioch, Inverurie, Aberdeenshire, AB51 5HX	01467 681321	★★★	Self Catering	
Shieldon Cottage	Shieldon Steading, Bourtie, Inverurie AB51 0JT	01651 873199	★★★	Self Catering	
St Andrews Cottage	St Andrews House, St Andrews Gardens, Inverurie, Aberdeenshire, AB51 3XT	01467 628 950	★★★	Self Catering	

By Inverurie

Millbank Cottage	Millbank Cottage, Sauchen, by Inverurie, Aberdeenshire, AB51 7RX	01330 833379	★★	Self Catering	

Irvine

Donegal Self Catering	Middleton Farm, Irvine, Ayrshire, KA11 2AJ	01294 211676	★★★	Self Catering ♟	

Island of Rona

Dry Harbour Cottages	Rona Lodge, Isle Of Rona, Portree, Isle Of Skye, IV51 9RA	07831 293963	★★★ →★★★★	Self Catering	

Islay

Ballimony Cottage	Le Ressec, Sere', Tarascon-sur Ariege, Ariege, France9400	33561651921	★★★	Self Catering	⌐⌐⌐
Lyndon Cottage	53C Millersneuk Drive, Lenzie, Glasgow G66 5JE	0141 777 6675	★★★	Self Catering	
Outback Accommodation	Outback Accommodation, Sanaigmore, Gruinart, Bridgend, Isle of Islay, PA44 7PT	01496 850259	★★★★	Self Catering	

Isle of Arran

Bayview Cottage and Castle View Apartment	52 Eaglesham Road, Newton Mearns, Glasgow, East Renfrewshire, G27 5BU	0141 639 9175	★★ →★★★	Self Catering	
Birchgrove	Caledonia, Goirtean Alisdair, Lamlash, Isle of Arran, KA27 8NL	01770 600400	★★★	Self Catering	
Bracklinn	8 Milngavie Road, Bearsden, Glasgow, Strathclyde, G61 2HX	0141 5779418	★★★	Self Catering	

♿ Unassisted wheelchair access   ♿ Assisted wheelchair access   ♟ Access for visitors with mobility difficulties
⌐ Bronze Green Tourism Award   ⌐⌐ Silver Green Tourism Award   ⌐⌐⌐ Gold Green Tourism Award
For further information on our Green Tourism Business Scheme please see page 9.

Butt Lodge Country House	Jingumae, 3-33-17-101, Shibuya-Ku 150-0001	03 5772 2672	★★★★	Self Catering
Flaxmill Cottage	Flaxmill cottage, Kilmory House, Lagg, Isle of Arran, KA27 8PQ	01770 870342	★★★	Self Catering
Greenways Cottage	21 Bailie Drive, Bearsden, Glasgow G61 3AL	0141 9428017	★★★	Self Catering
Hazelbank	Manely Dunford, St Veep, Lostwithiel, Cornwall, PL22 0NS	01208 873420	★★★	Self Catering
Heathfield House & Main Cottage	House 1, Casa Verde, 64F Sheung SZe Wan Road, Clear Water Bay, New Territories, Hong Kong	+852 28190697	★★★★	Self Catering
Invercloy House Apartments	Arran Hideways, Invercloy House, Brodick, Isle of Arran, KA27 8AJ	01770 302303	★★★	Self Catering
Kilbride Farmhouse	Sannox House, Sannox, Isle of Arran, KA27 8JD	01770 810230	★★★★	Self Catering
No 2 Alma Terrace	7 Kent Drive, Burnside, Glasgow G73 5AP	0141 5624155	★★★	Self Catering
Otterburn	4 Manse Crescent, Brodick, Isle of Arran, KA27 8AS	01770 302334	★★★★	Self Catering
Point House Cottage & Summer Cottage	Glenashdale Properties, Brodick, Isle of Arran, KA27 8AX	01770 302121	★★ → ★★★	Self Catering
Shannochie Cottages & Kilbride Cottage	Shannochie Cottages, Shannochie, Isle of Arran KA27 8SJ	01770 820291	★★★ → ★★★★	Self Catering
St Columbas	Flat 1, 35 Jackson Lane, Highgate, London, N6 5SR	02083 406069	★★★	Self Catering
The Grange, Peacock, & Alt Ardoch	The Grange, Shore Road, Whiting Bay, Isle of Arran, KA27 8QH	07850 189747	★★★	Self Catering
The Millhouse	105 St Alban's Road, Edinburgh EH9 2PQ	0131 6672267	★★★	Self Catering
Wee Meadow Cottage and Poppies	Meadow Cottage, Pirnmill, Isle of Arran KA27 8HP	01770 850236	★★★★	Self Catering
Croft Cottage	Ocean View, 78 Borve, Castlebay, Isle of Barra, HS9 5XR	01871 810590	★★	Self Catering
Harbour Cottage	30 Stonehouse Road, Sandford, South Lanarkshire, ML10 6PD	01357 528810	★	Self Catering

Isle of Canna

Lag nam Boitean	National Trust for Scotland, 28 Charlotte Square, Edinburgh EH2 4ET	0131 243 9335	★★	Self Catering

Isle of Colonsay

Colonsay Estate Cottages	Bookings Office, Colonsay Estate Office, Isle of Colonsay PA61 7YR	01951 200312	★ → ★★★	Self Catering	🍃
Creag Mhor	Fairnielaw House, Athelstaneford, North Berwick, EH39 5BE	01620 880282	★★★★	Self Catering	
Isle Colonsay Holiday Chalets	Isle of Colonsay Holiday Chalets, Isle of Colonsay, Argyll, PA61 7YR	01951 200320	★ → ★★★★	Self Catering	
Seaview	Seaview, Isle of Colonsay, Argyll, PA61 7YR	01951 200315	★★ → ★★★	Self Catering	

Isle of Eriskay

Eriskay Self-Catering	Manor Park Hotel, 28 Balshagray Drive, Glasgow G11 7DD	0141 339 2143	★★★★	Self Catering	🚶

Isle of Gigha

Gigha Hotel Cottages	Gigha Hotel, Isle of Gigha, Argyll, PA41 7AD	01583 505254	★ → ★★★	Self Catering	🍃

 ♿ Unassisted wheelchair access ♿ Assisted wheelchair access ▲ Access for visitors with mobility difficulties
 🍃 Bronze Green Tourism Award 🍃🍃 Silver Green Tourism Award 🍃🍃🍃 Gold Green Tourism Award
For further information on our Green Tourism Business Scheme please see page 9.

To find out more, call 0845 22 55 121 or go to visitscotland.com.

Isle of Harris

1 Rhenigdale, Seaforth Cottage	1A Scaladale, Isle of Harris, Western Isles, HS3 3AA	01859 502447	★★	Self Catering
5 Urgha	5 Urgha, Isle of Harris, Western Isles, HS3 3BW	01859 502114	★★★	Self Catering
Bayhead	9a Aignish Point, Isle of Lewis HS2 0PB	01851 870810	★★★	Self Catering
Beannachd	The Old School House, 17B Lower bank Road, Fulwood, Preston, PR2 8NS	01772 787939	★★★★	Self Catering
Beul-Na-Mara Cottages	Beul Na Mara12 Seilebost Isle of Harris, HS3 3HP	01859 550205	★★★★	Self Catering
Caberfeidh	Glen View, Jagger Green, Holywell Green, Halifax, West Yorkshire, HX4 9DE	01422 378983	★★★★★	Self Catering
Croft Cottage	3 Diracleit, Isle of Harris, Western Isles, HS3 3DP	01859 502338	★★★★★	Self Catering ᵻ⬦ ▱▱
Gasker House	Gasker House Self Catering Holiday, 10 Scaristavore, Leverburgh, Isle of Harris, Western Isles, HS5 3HX	01859 520265	★★★★	Self Catering
Rowan Cottage	16 Kyles, Isle of Harris, Western Isles, HS3 3BS	01859 502204	★★★★	Self Catering
Seaside Cottage	Leachin House, Leachin, Tarbert, Isle of Harris, HS3 3AH	01859 502157	★★★★★	Self Catering
Seaside House	Old Wharf, Wharf Road, Shillingford, Oxfordshire, OX10 7EW	01235 850246	★	Self Catering
Seaview Chalet	Seaview, Bunavoneader, Isle of Harris HS3 3AL	01859 502482	★★★★	Self Catering
Shore Cottage & Atlantic Cottage	5 Luskentyre, Isle of Harris, Western Isles, HS3 3HL	01859 550219	★★★★ → ★★★★★	Self Catering

Isle of Islay

An Sabhal Cottages	7 Shore Street, Portnahaven, Isle of Islay, PA47 7SH	01496 860293	★★★★	Self Catering
Carnain Cottage	4 Ormidale Terrace, Edinburgh EH12 6EQ	0131 347 8853	★★★★	Self Catering
Claggan Farmhouse	Ivy Lodge, Radway, Warwick CV35 0UE	01295 670371	★★	Self Catering
Cross House West	Manor Farm, Charlcombe Lane, Bath BA1 8DS	07798 695764	★★★★	Self Catering
Cuil Sith	Glenmachrie, Port Ellen, Isle of Islay, Argyll, PA42 7AW	01496 302560	★★★★	Self Catering
Easter Ellister	Woodhead Farm, Blackwood Estate, Lesmahagow ML11 0JG	01555 892785	★★★★	Self Catering
Glenmachrie	Glenmachrie, Port Ellen, Isle of Islay, Argyll, PA42 7AW	01496 302560	★★★★	Self Catering
Glen-na-airidh & Blackpark Croft	Blackpark, Bridgend, Isle of Islay, PA44 7PL	01496 810376	★★★	Self Catering ᵻ⬦ ▱▱
Islay Beach Cottage	13 Danbury Street, London N1 8LD	07713 264032	★★★	Self Catering ⸸
Octovullin Farmhouse & Eallabus Cottage	Islay Estates Co, Bridgend, Isle of Islay, Argyll, PA44 7PB	01496 810221	★★ → ★★★	Self Catering
Tigh Na Coille	Woodhouses, Blore, Nr Ashbourne, Derbyshire, DE6 2BS	01335 350214	★	Self Catering

Isle of Jura

Ardlussa House	Ardlussa House, Ardlussa Estate, Isle of Jura, Argyll, PA60 7XW	01496 820323	★	Self Catering
Braeside	5 Kelvin Drive, Glasgow G20 8QG	0141 9464361	★★	Self Catering
Heather Cottage	Easter Lennieston, Thornhill, by Stirling FK8 3QP	01786 850274	★	Self Catering

     ♿ Unassisted wheelchair access   ᵻ⬦ Assisted wheelchair access   ⸸ Access for visitors with mobility difficulties
    ▱ Bronze Green Tourism Award   ▱▱ Silver Green Tourism Award   ▱▱▱ Gold Green Tourism Award
    For further information on our Green Tourism Business Scheme please see page 9.

Tarbert Lodge	76 Overhaugh Street, Galashiels, Selkirkshire, TD1 1DP	01896 751300	★	Self Catering

Isle of Lewis

10 Tolsta Chaolais	10 Tolsta Chaolais, Isle of Lewis HS2 9DW	01851 621722	★★★	Self Catering
25 South Shawbost	25 South Shawbost, Isle of Lewis HS2 9BJ	01851 710461	★★★★	Self Catering
6 Tolsta Chaolais	8 Tolsta Chaolais, Isle of Lewis, Western Isles, HS2 9DW	01851 621260	★★★	Self Catering
Aultbeithe	Glen View, Jagger Green, Holywell Green, Halifax. West Yorkshire, HX4 9DE	01422 378983	★★★★★	Self Catering
Callan Maran	Callan Maran, 7 Callanish Isle of Lewis, HS2 9DY	01851 621706	★★★	Self Catering
Craigard House	10 Sherwood Terrace, Glen Osmond, South Australia 5064	0061 84837913	★★★	Self Catering
The Mollans	4 Crossbost, Isle of Lewis HS2 9NP	01851 860577	★★★★	Self Catering
Westside	3 Linsiadar, Isle of Lewis, Western Isles, HS2 9DR	01851 621311	★★★	Self Catering

Isle of Luing

Creagard Country House	9B Netherton Court, Ayr Road, Newtonmearns, Glasgow, G77 6EN	0141 6394592	★★★★	Self Catering

Isle of Mull

Achnacraig	Achnacraig, Dervaig, Isle of Mull, PA75 6QW	01688 400309	★★★★	Self Catering
Aros Mains	Aros Mains, Aros, Isle of Mull, PA72 6JP	01680 300307	★★★ → ★★★★	Self Catering
Burnside	6 Alverstone Avenue, Wimbledon Park, London SW19 8BE	020 8947 3181	★★	Self Catering
Craig Ben Cottage	115 Ashfield Street, London E1 3EX	0207 790 4304	★★★★	Self Catering
Druimgigha Farm	Druimgigha, Dervaig, Isle of Mull, PA75 6QR	01688 400228	★★★★	Self Catering
Druimnacroish	Druimnacroish, Dervaig, Isle of Mull, Argyll, PA75 6QW	01688 400274	Awaiting Grading	
Heather Cottage	Clachan House, Lochdon Isle of Mull, PA64 6AB	01680 812439	★★★	Self Catering
Hideaway Lodges	Hideaway Lodges, Gruline, Isle of Mull, Argyll, PA71 6HR	01680 300567	★★★★	Self Catering
Pennygown Farmhouse & Cottage	Knockalla, Garmony Farm, Craignure, Isle of Mull, Argyll, PA65 6BA	01680 812193	★★★	Self Catering
The Old Schoolhouse	Durden Lodge, Beauworth, Alresford, Hants, PA63 6AH	01962 771557	★★ → ★★★	Self Catering
The Smithy	Piercey's, Northend Commons, Henley on Thames, Oxfordshire, RG9 6LJ	01491 639299	★★★	Self Catering
The Steading	The Steading, Tiroran, Isle of Mull, Argyll, PA69 6ES	01681 705217	★★★★	Self Catering
Tigh Na Caora	16 Court Street, Nayland, Colchester, Essex, CO6 4JL	01206 272780	★★	Self Catering
Twelve Oaks	Twelve Oaks, Lochdon, Isle of Mull, Argyll, PA64 6AP	01680 812187	★★★	Self Catering
Gruline Estate	Gruline Estate, Gruline House, Isle of Mull PA71 6HS	01680 300332	★★★	Self Catering

Isle of North Uist

Kintail Cottage	Goulaby, Clachan Farm, Isle of North Uist, Western Isles, HS6 5AY	01876 500899	★★★★	Self Catering

Unassisted wheelchair access   Assisted wheelchair access   Access for visitors with mobility difficulties
Bronze Green Tourism Award   Silver Green Tourism Award   Gold Green Tourism Award
For further information on our Green Tourism Business Scheme please see page 9.

The Boathouse	Duncree House, King Street, Newton Stewart, Wigtonshire	01671 402554	★★★★	Self Catering

Isle of Scalpay

Stac Pollaidh	Hirta House, Isle of Scalpay, Harris, Western Isles, HS4 3XZ	01859 540394	★★★★	Self Catering

Isle of Seil

Insh Cottage	18 Ellenabeich, Isle of Seil, By Oban, Argyll, PA34 4RQ	01852 300573	★★★	Self Catering
No 7 Tramway	7 Tramway Cottages, Ellenabeich, Isle od Seil, Argyll, PA34 4RQ	07810 710494	★★★★	Self Catering
Oban Seil Farm	Oban Seil Farm, Isle of Seil, by Oban, Argyll, PA34 4TN	01852 300 245	★★★★	Self Catering
Oban Seil Croft Cottages	Oban Seil Croft Cottages, Oban Seil Croft, Isle of Seil, Oban, Argyll, PA34 4TN	01852 300457	★★★★	Self Catering 🏃

Isle of Skye

Dun Flashader	National Trust for Scotland, 28 Charlotte Square, Edinburgh EH2 4ET	0131 243 9335	★★★	Self Catering
The Old School House & Allt Dearg	Glendrynoch Lodge, Carbost, Isle Of Skye, IV47 8SX	01478 640218	★★ → ★★★	Self Catering

Isle of South Uist

Corncrake Cottage	364 South Boisdale, Isle of South Uist, Western Isles, HS8 5TE	01878 700371	★★★★	Self Catering
The Old School House	Burnside, Daliburgh, Isle of South Uist, HS8 5SS	01878 700295	★★★★	Self Catering

Isle of Tiree

Airighbeg	60 Manchester Drive, Glasgow G12 0NQ	0141 3347563	★	Self Catering
Cottage at Port A Mhuillin	Baugh, Isle of Tiree, Argyll, PA77 6UN	01879 220538	★★★	Self Catering
Kenoreef	Heylipol Farm, Heylipol, Isle of Tiree, Argyll, PA77 6TY	01879 220321	★★★★	Self Catering

Isle of Uist

Heisker	Viewlands, Osborne Avenue, Hexham, Northumberland, NE46 3SN	01434 603401	★★★★	Self Catering

Isle of Whithorn

Morrach Holiday Cottages	Cutreoch Farm, Isle of Whithorn, Wigtownshire, DG8 8JD	01988 500428	★★★★	Self Catering
Steinview, Ronsat 9A and 9B	121a Psalter Lane, Sheffield, S. Yorks S11 8YR	0114 280 2902	★★ → ★★★★	Self Catering

Jedburgh

14 Tweed Cottages	1/10 Ocean Way, Edinburgh EH6 7DG	07980 865028	★★★★	Self Catering
Log Lodge	Lothian Estates, Bonjedward, Jedburgh, Roxburghshire, TD8 6UF	01835 862201	★★★	Self Catering
Overwells Country Cottages	Overwells, Jedburgh, Roxburghshire, TD8 6LT	01835 863020	★★★★	Self Catering
The Spinney Self-catering Chalets	The Spinney Guest House, Langlee, Jedburgh, Roxburghshire, TD8 6PB	01835 863525	★★★★	Self Catering
Wild Rose & Owl Cottages	Stewards Cottage, The Bairnkine, Jedburgh, Roxburghshire, TD8 6PH	01835 840389	★★★	Self Catering
1A Old Bridge End	69 High Street, Innerleithen, Peebleshire, EH44 6HD	01896 831544	★★★	Self Catering

  ♿ Unassisted wheelchair access   Assisted wheelchair access   🏃 Access for visitors with mobility difficulties

Ⓟ Bronze Green Tourism Award   ⒫⒫ Silver Green Tourism Award   ⒫⒫⒫ Gold Green Tourism Award

For further information on our Green Tourism Business Scheme please see page 9.

John O'Groats

Horseman's Cottage	Mill House, John O' Groats, Wick, Caithness, KW1 4YR	01955 611239	★★★	Self Catering	

Keith

Anvil Cottage	Maxwell House, 12 Maxwell Street, Fochabers, Moray, IV32 7DE	01343 820304	★★★★	Self Catering	

Kelso

4 Barony Knoll	3 Barony Knoll, Jedburgh Road, Kelso, Scottish Borders, TD5 8JE	01573 223240	★★	Self Catering	
Craggs Cottage & Jocks Cottage	5 Smailholm Mains, by Kelso, Roxburghshire, TD5 7RT	01573 460318	★★★★	Self Catering	
Hendersyde Farm Cottages	Hendersyde Farm, Kelso, Roxburghshire, TD5 7QA	01573 223495	★★★★	Self Catering	🍃🍃
Holiday Cottages	Roxburgh Barns, Kelso, Roxburghshire, TD5 8LU	01573 450 257	★★★★	Self Catering	🍃🍃
No 4 Havannah Court S/C Apartment	Brimham House, Girrick, Kelso, Scottish Borders, TD5 7SA	01573 460647	★★★	Self Catering	
Old Threshing Mill	Old Threshing Mill, Millfield, Makerstoun, Kelso, Roxburghshire, TD5 7PD	01573 460349	★★★★	Self Catering	
Roxburgh Newtown Farm	Roxburgh Newtown Farm, Kelso, Roxburghshire, TD5 8NN	01573 450250	★★★★	Self Catering 🕆	
Sydenham House	12 India Street, Edinburgh, Lothian, EH3 6EZ	07774 775008	★★★★	Self Catering	

By Kelso

Edenmouth Farm Holiday Cottages	The Granary, Edenmouth, Kelso, Roxburghshire, TD5 7QB	01890 830391	★★★ → ★★★★	Self Catering 🕆	
Glebe House	Bellenden House, Walkerburn, Tweeddale, EH43 6BA	01896 870762	★★★	Self Catering	

By Kenmore

The White Tower	White Gables, Wester Larse, Aberfeldy, Perthshire, PH15 2JJ	01887 830723	★★★★★	Self Catering	

Kentallen

The Cottage	The Cottage, Kentallen House, Kentallen, Argyll, PA38 4BU	01631 740318	★★★	Self Catering	

Kessock

The Old Herdsman's Cottage	Tigh-Na-Innis, Bogallan Croft, Kessock, Inverness, IV1 3XE	01463 731869	★★★★★	Self Catering	🍃

Kettleholm

Kilnpotlees	Kilnpotlees, Kettleholm, Nr Lockerbie, DG11 1DD	01576 510249	★★★	Self Catering	

Kilchattan Bay, Isle of Bute

Dykenamar	Mayhill, Shaftesbury Road, Woking, Surrey, GU22 7DU	01483 772506	★★★★	Self Catering	

Kilchoan

Glashven & Strathconon	2 The Planters, Greasby, Wirral, Merseyside, CH49 2QY		★★ → ★★★	Self Catering	
Ian's A Lodge	12 Bear Street, Nayland, Suffolk, CO6 4HX	01206 262064	★★	Self Catering	
Ockle Holidays	3 Pier Road, Kilchoan, Argyll, PH36 4LJ	01972 510321	★★ → ★★★	Self Catering	

      ☺ Unassisted wheelchair access   ☺ Assisted wheelchair access   🕆 Access for visitors with mobility difficulties
    🍃 Bronze Green Tourism Award   🍃🍃 Silver Green Tourism Award   🍃🍃🍃 Gold Green Tourism Award
For further information on our Green Tourism Business Scheme please see page 9.

Kilchrenan

Ardabhaigh	Dundorran, Kilbride, Inveraray, Argyll, PA32 8XT	01499 302736	★★★★	Self Catering	
Kilconquhar Castle Estate	Kilconquhar Castle Estate, Kilconquhar, Fife, KY9 1EZ	01333 340501	★★★★ → ★★★★★	Self Catering	🍃🍃

Kildary

Marybank Lodge	Balnagowan Castle Properties Ltd, Balnagowan Estate, Kildary, by Invergordon, IV18 0NU	01862 843601	★★★★★	Self Catering	

Kildonan

Auchenhew Holiday Cottages	Auchenhew Holiday Cotts, Kildonan, Isle of Arran, KA27 8SG	01770 820 243	★★★	Self Catering	
Craigend	Cnoc Farm, Kildonan, Isle of Arran, KA27 8SE	07748 787069	★★★	Self Catering	
Creagenroin & The Granary	Lenamhor Farm, Kilmory, Arran, KA27 8PH	01770 870263	★★★	Self Catering	
Grianan House and Grianan Cottage	Grianan, Fern Cottage, Shannochie, Isle of Arran, KA27 8SJ	01770 820236	★★★★	Self Catering	🚶
Island Properties	Miodar Mor House, Shore Road, Kildonan, Isle of Arran, KA27 8SE	01770 820624	★★★★	Self Catering	♿
Kildonan School & Schoolhouse	Egmond Estates, Egmond, Torwoodhill Road, Rhu, Helensburgh, Argyll & Bute, G84 8LE	01436 820956	★★★	Self Catering	♿
Kirk Kildonan	Kirk Kildonan, Church Brae, Kildonan, Isle of Arran, KA27 8SE	01770 820624	★★★★	Self Catering	
Seacliffe Cottages	Seacliffe Cottages, Dippin, Kildonan, Isle of Arran, KA27 8RN	01770 820323	★★★	Self Catering	
Seacrest	Burn Brae, Upperwell, Carwood, Biggar, Lanarkshire, ML12 6LX	01899 221678	★★★	Self Catering	
The Beach House	33 Hoyle Crescent, Cumnock, Ayrshire, KA18 1RX	01290 421412	★★★★	Self Catering	♿
The Whins, Willow & Beech Apartments	Drumla Farm, Kildonan, Isle of Arran, KA27 8RP	01770 820256	★★★ → ★★★★	Self Catering	

By Kildonan

Burnside House	563 Shields Road, Pollokshields, Glasgow G41 2RW	0141 423 7939	★★★	Self Catering	

Killiecrankie

Atholl Cottage	Dalnasgadh, Killiecrankie, by Pitlochry, Perthshire, PH16 5LN	01796 470017	★★★★	Self Catering	
Holiday Lodges @ Old Faskally	Holiday Lodges at Old Faskally, The Lodge, Old Faskally, Killiecrankie, Perthshire, PH16 5LR	01796 473436	★★★	Self Catering	
The Old Mill	Westerhawes, Clathy, Gask, Perthshire, PH7 3PH	01738 730336	★★★★	Self Catering	

Killin

Acharn Courtyard Cottages	Acharn Highland Lodges, Killin, Perthshire, FK21 8RA	01567 820139	★★★★	Self Catering	
Bridge Park Cottage	Shaft House, Shaft Road, Monkton Combe, Bath, BA2 7HN	01225 837545	★★	Self Catering	
Craiglea	Craiglea, Main Street, Killin, Perthshire, FK21 8TE	01567 820475	★★★	Self Catering	
Gracedieu	RowanBank, Dochart Road, Killin, Perthshire, FK21 8SN	01567 820396	★★★	Self Catering	
Greenbank	Greenbank, Main Street, Killin FK21 8UT	01567 820462	★★	Self Catering	
Killin Highland Lodges	, Comrie, Perthshire, PH6 2JZ	01764 685310	★★★ → ★★★★	Self Catering	🚶

♿ Unassisted wheelchair access   ♿ Assisted wheelchair access   🚶 Access for visitors with mobility difficulties
🍃 Bronze Green Tourism Award   🍃🍃 Silver Green Tourism Award   🍃🍃🍃 Gold Green Tourism Award
For further information on our Green Tourism Business Scheme please see page 9.

Kinnell Farm Cottage	Kinnell Estate, Killin, Perthshire, FK21 8SR	01567 820590	★★	Self Catering	
Lawers & Tarmachan	Auchmore Apartments, 4 Auchmore, Killin, Perthshire, FK21 8ST	01567 820646	★★★	Self Catering	
Tigh an Eilean and Wee Dalerb	Dalerb, Craignavie Road, Killin, Perthshire, FK21 8SH	01567 820961	★★★★	Self Catering	☀

By Killin

Ballinloan	Kennels Cottage, Boreland, by Killin, Perthshire, FK21 8UA	01567 820562	★★★	Self Catering	
Fiddlers Bay Lodge	The Firs, Oxnam Road, Jedburgh, Roxburghshire, TD8 6QL	01835 863250	★★★★	Self Catering	
Morenish Mews	Morenish Mews, by Killin, Perthshire, FK21 8TX	01567 820527	★★★★	Self Catering	🍃🍃
Loch Tay Highland Lodges, Milton Morenish	Loch Tay Highland Lodges Ltd, Milton Morenish, Killin, Perthshire, FK21 8TY	01567 820323	★★★ → ★★★★	Self Catering	

Kilmacolm

| Hillside Cottage | Greenhill Cottage, by Hillside Farm, Kilmalcolm, Renfrewshire, PA13 4TH | 01505 872077 | ★★★ | Self Catering | |
| Beggar Ha | Kelk Cottage, Crosshouse, Kilmarnock, Ayrshire, KA2 0BG | 01563 525269 | ★★★ | Self Catering | |

Kilmartin

| Duntrune Cottages | Duntrune Castle, Kilmartin, Argyll, PA31 8QQ | 01546 510283 | ★★★ | Self Catering | |
| The Bullock Shed & The Stable | Ri Cruin, Kilmartin, By Lochgilphead, Argyll, PA31 8QF | 01546 510316 | ★★★★ | Self Catering | |

Kilmelford

Garden Cottage	Maolachy House, Lochavich, by Taynuilt, Argyll, PA35 1HJ	01866 844212	★★★	Self Catering	
The Steadings	6 Scotch Street, Whitehaven, Cumbria CA28 2BJ	01946 692847	★★	Self Catering	
Ardenstur Cottages	Woodside, Park Avenue, Hartlepool, Cleveland, TS26 0EA	01429 267266	★★ → ★★★★	Self Catering	
Old Dairy Cottage	Fearnach House, Kilmelford, Oban, Argyll, PA34 4XD	01852 200208	★★★	Self Catering	

By Kilmory

| Laggwood Cottage | 1/2 86 Marlborough Avenue, Broomhill, Glasgow G11 7BJ | 0141 3341673 | ★★★ | Self Catering | |

Kilmuir

| Buaile Nan Carn | 8 Hungladder, Kilmuir, Isle of Skye, IV51 9YT | 01470 552279 | ★★★ | Self Catering | |

Kilmun

| Old Kilmun House | Auchengrange, Bellfrees Road, Lochwinnoch, Renfrewshire, PA12 4JS | 01505 843678 | ★★★★ | Self Catering | |

Kilninian, Ulvaferry, Isle of Mull

| Tostary Cottage | 16 Highworth Avenue, Cambridge CB4 2BG | 01223 352860 | ★★★ | Self Catering | |

Kilwinning

| Ailsa Craig View | High Smithstone Farm B&B, High Smithstone, Kilwinning, Ayrshire, KA13 6PG | 01294 552361 | ★★★★ | Self Catering | ♿ |

♿ Unassisted wheelchair access   ♿ Assisted wheelchair access   ☀ Access for visitors with mobility difficulties
🍃 Bronze Green Tourism Award   🍃🍃 Silver Green Tourism Award   🍃🍃🍃 Gold Green Tourism Award
For further information on our Green Tourism Business Scheme please see page 9.

Kincraig

Alvie Trust Holiday Cottages	Alvie Trust Holiday Cottages, Alvie Estate, Kincraig, Inverness-shire, PH21 1NE	01540 651255	★★★	Self Catering		
Aspen	6 Ancrum Bank, Dalkeith, Midlothian, EH22 3AY	0131 654 2291	★★★★	Self Catering		
Balbeag	The Dairy House, Corton Denham, Sherborne, Dorset, DT9 4LX	01963 220250	★★★	Self Catering		
Blackmill House	Fair-A-Far, Rowan Park, Carrbridge, Inverness-shire, PH23 3BE	01479 841262	★★★	Self Catering		
Fraser & Telford Cottages	Insh House, Kincraig, by Kingussie, Inverness-shire, PH21 1NU	01540 651377	★★★	Self Catering		𝒫𝒫
Loch Insh Chalets	Insh Hall Lodge, Kincraig, Inverness-shire, PH21 1NU	01540 651272	★★ → ★★★	Self Catering	♿	
March House	March House, Feshiebridge, Kincraig, Inverness-shire, PH21 1NG	01540 651388	Awaiting Grading			

By Kincraig

Glenfeshie House	East Muirend House, 33 Gillespie Road, Edinburgh EH13 0NW	0131 4411431	★★★★	Self Catering		

Kinghorn

Hideaway Beach House	Hideaway Beach House, 107 Pettycur Road, Kinghorn, Fife, KY3 9RW	01592 892535	★★★★	Self Catering		
Salmon Cottage	50 Great Moor Street, Great Moor, Stockport, Cheshire, SK2 7PQ	07817120384/0	★★★★	Self Catering		
The Wee House	9 Carlin Craig, Kinghorn, Fife KY3 9RX	01592 890320	★★★	Self Catering		

Kingsbarns

Sweethope Cottage	Croft Butts, Smiddy Burn, Kingsbarns, Fife, KY16 8SN	01334 880 247	★★	Self Catering		
Daisybank & The Smithy	Clyde Associated Engineers Ltd, Block 5, 76 Beardmore Way, Clydebank Ind. Estate, Clydebank, Dunbartonshire,	0141 951 1331	★★★★	Self Catering		

Kingussie

Aonach	Rubislaw, Newtownmore Road, Kingussie, Inverness-shire, PH21 1HD	01540 661220	★★★	Self Catering		
Calum's Cottage	Calum's Lodge, Acres Road, Kingussie, Inverness-shire, PH21 1LA	01540 661442	★★★★	Self Catering		
Carrick House,Landseer House	The Old Oven, Banbury Street, Kineton, Warwickshire, CV35 0JS	01926 640560	★★★	Self Catering		
Feshieway Cottage	Greenfields, Back Lane,Preston, Hitchin, Herts, SG4 7UJ	01462 423198	★★	Self Catering		
Ruthven House Cottages	Ruthven House, Kingussie, Inverness-shire, PH21 1NR	01540 661226	★★ → ★★★	Self Catering		
Sonas	24 Skye Drive, Cumbernauld, Glasgow, G67 1NZ	01236 730615	★★★	Self Catering		
Spindrift Cottage	Spindrift Cottage, The Steadings at Ruthven, Kingussie, Inverness-shire, PH21 1NR	01540 662328	★★★★	Self Catering		
Suidhe Cottage	Suie Guest House, Kincraig, Kingussie, Inverness-shire, PH21 1NA	01540 651344	★★★	Self Catering		

Kinloch Rannoch

Cnoc Eoghainn	26/3 Kirk Street, Edinburgh, Midlothian, EH6 5EZ	07799 232700	★★★	Self Catering		𝒫𝒫
Craigvar	112 Harvey Road, Cairns, Old Australia 4570	07 4039 0487	★★★	Self Catering		
Dunalastair Holiday Houses	Lochgarry House, Kinloch Rannoch, Perthshire, PH16 5PD	01882 632314	★★★ → ★★★★	Self Catering	♿	𝒫

    ♿ Unassisted wheelchair access   ♿ Assisted wheelchair access   🕴 Access for visitors with mobility difficulties
    𝒫 Bronze Green Tourism Award   𝒫𝒫 Silver Green Tourism Award   𝒫𝒫𝒫 Gold Green Tourism Award
    For further information on our Green Tourism Business Scheme please see page 9.

| Dall Mill | 7 Colbridge Terrace, Edinburgh EH12 6AB | 0131 337 5780 | ★★★ | Self Catering | |

Kinlochard

| Forest Hills Lochside Resort | MacDonald Dalfaber Golf and Country Club, Dalfaber Drive, Aviemore, Highland, PH22 1ST | 01479 811244 | ★★★★ | Self Catering | |
| Lochside Cottages | A&S Properties (Glasgow), 27 Moor Road, Balfron, Glasgow, G13 0PB | 01360 449060 | ★★★★ | Self Catering | ⚹ |

Kinlochbervie

| Bracken Cottage | Fir Chlis, 399 Elphin, By Lairg, Sutherland, IV27 4HH | 01854 666218 | ★★★ | Self Catering | |
| Horseshoe & Anvil Cottage | Smithy House, Oldshoremore, Kinlochbervie, Sutherland, IV27 4RS | 01971 521729 | ★★★ → ★★★★ | Self Catering | ⚹ |

Kinlocheil, by Fort William

| Altdarroch Farm | Essan House, Morar, Mallaig, Inverness-shire, PH40 4PA | 01687 460014 | ★★★ → ★★★★ | Self Catering | |

Kinlochewe

Beinn Eighe and Slioch	The Vicarage, Millans Park, Ambleside, Cumbria, LA22 9AD	01539 433205	★★★	Self Catering	
Mansfield	4 Elm Road, Irby, Wirral, Merseyside, CH61 3UP	0151 648 2454	★★★	Self Catering	
The Old Nurses Cottage	12 Hailes Gardens, Edinburgh, Lothian, EH13 0JL	0131 441 9318	★★	Self Catering	

Kinlochlaggan

| Ardverikie Estate Houses | The Estate Office, Ardverikie Estate, Kinlochlaggan, Inverness-shire, PH20 1BY | 01528 544300 | ★★ → ★★★ | Self Catering | |

Kinlochleven

| Bonnie Bheinn House | 66 Queensberry Street, Dumfries, Dumfries and Galloway, DG1 1BG | 07742 087839 | ★★★ | Self Catering | |

Kinlochspelve

| Barrachandroman Farmhouse | The Barn, Barrachandroman, Lochbuie, Isle of Mull, PA62 6AA | 01680 814220 | ★★★★ | Self Catering | |

Kinross

Roselea Guest House	Roselea Guest House, Drummond Place, Main Street, Kinnesswod, Perthshire, KY13 9HN	01592 840167	★★★	Self Catering	
Escape To Scotland	West Wing Apartment Suite, Hatchbank House, Kinross, Kinross-shire, KY13 0LF	01577 850214	★★★★	Self Catering	
The Lodge	8 Bishop Terrace, Kinnesswood, Tayside, KY13 9JW	01592 840403	★★★	Self Catering	

Kintore

| The Greenknowe | Kingsfield House, Kingsfield Road, Kintore, Aberdeenshire, AB51 0UD | 01467 632366 | ★★★★ | Self Catering | ⚹ | 🄿 |

Kintra

| Maple Cottage | 17 Crosshill Drive, Rutherglen, Glasgow G73 3QT | 0141 6477288 | ★★★ | Self Catering | |
| The Long House | Cardew Farm, Dalston, Carlisle, CA5 7JQ | 01228 710661 | ★ | Self Catering | |

Kintra Beach, Isle of Islay

| Kintra Beach Cottages | Kintra Farm, Kintra Beach, Port Ellen, Islay, PA42 7AT | 01496 302051 | ★★★ | Self Catering | |

ᕕ Unassisted wheelchair access   ᕗ Assisted wheelchair access   ⚹ Access for visitors with mobility difficulties
🄿 Bronze Green Tourism Award   🄿🄿 Silver Green Tourism Award   🄿🄿🄿 Gold Green Tourism Award
For further information on our Green Tourism Business Scheme please see page 9.

Kippen

Bellview	Nethercarse Farm, Kippen, Stirling, FK8 3JJ	01786 860543	★★★★	Self Catering	🛉
Fordhead Cottage	Fordhead, Kippen, Stirling FK8 3SQ	01786 870329	★★★★	Self Catering	
Larne Coach House & Brucehill	Larne Coach House, Fore Road, Kippen, Stirlingshire, FK8 3DT	01786 871197	★★★★	Self Catering	

By Kippen

Thorntree Barn	Thorntree, Fintry Road, Arnprior, Stirling, FK8 3EY	01786 870710	★★★	Self Catering	🍃

Kippford

Kildorran	Kildorran, Jubilee Path, Kippford, Dalbeattie, Kirkcudbrightshire, DG5 4LW	01556 620288	★★★	Self Catering
Lochanview	Dougnou, Kirkmahoe, Dumfries, Dumfries & Galloway, DG1 1RE	01387 710126	★★★★	Self Catering
Kippford Holiday Lodges	Kippford Forest Lodges, C/O Walker Property Management23 Patrick Street Greenock, PA16 8NB	01475 787251	★★★★	Self Catering
Elm Cottage	Barncleugh, Irongray, Dumfries DG2 9SE	01387 730210	★★★	Self Catering
Birchlea Lodge	Percy Bros (Dumfries), Karail, River View Park, Kippford, Dalbeattie, Dumfries and Galloway, DG8 4LG	01556 620125	★★★★	Self Catering
Fonthill	24 Main Street, Thorner, Leeds, West Yorkshire, LS14 3DX	0113 2893460	★★★	Self Catering
Welburn	Dyke Nook, Bassenthwaite, Keswick, Cumbria, CA12 4QG	01768 776263	★★★	Self Catering

Kirk Yetholm

The Gypsy Palace	Goodwood, The Green, East Ord, Berwick upon Tweed, Northumberland, TD15 2NS	01789 305735	★★★★	Self Catering
Chelsea Cottage	Orchard Lodge, Little Kinloch, Ladybank, Fife, KY15 7UT	01337 831477		Awaiting Grading

Kirkcaldy

Kilrie Granary	John M Drysdale & Co, Kilrie Farm, Kilrie, Kirkcaldy, Fife, KY2 5UW	01592 269035	★★★★	Self Catering
The Kyle atop Ravenscraig	286 Richmond Road, Oakville, Ontario, L6H 3B5, CANADA	01 905 845 59	★★★★	Self Catering

By Kirkcaldy

East Wing Lawers and 13 The Maltings	Lawers, Newbigging, Auchtertool, Fife, KY2 5XJ	01592 781656	★★★	Self Catering

Kirkcudbright

1,2,3 High Kirkland	Cannee Farm, Kirkcudbright, Kirkcudbrightshire, DG6 4XD	01557 330684	★★★	Self Catering
13A High Street	Niddamoor, Old Lees Road, Hebden Bridge, West Yorkshire, HX7 8HW	01422 843762	★★★	Self Catering
19 & 32 St Cuthbert Street	9 Brown Road, Kirkcudbright, Dumfries & Galloway, DG6 4HP	01557 330579	★★★ → ★★★★	Self Catering
24a Millburn Street	3 Hinckley Road, Stoke Golding, Nuneaton, Warks, CV13 6DU	01455 212955	★★★	Self Catering
57 High Street	59 High Street, Kirkcudbright, Kirkcudbrightshire, DG6 4JZ	01557 330583	★★★	Self Catering
3 Gladstone Place	34 Rubislaw Drive, Bearsden, East Dunbartons G61 1PS	0141 942 3022	★★★	Self Catering
Baytree House Garden Studio	Baytree House Garden Studio, 110 High Street, Kirkcudbright, Dumfries & Galloway, DG6 4JQ	01557 330824	★★★	Self Catering

♿ Unassisted wheelchair access   ♿ Assisted wheelchair access   🛉 Access for visitors with mobility difficulties
🍃 Bronze Green Tourism Award   🍃🍃 Silver Green Tourism Award   🍃🍃🍃 Gold Green Tourism Award
For further information on our Green Tourism Business Scheme please see page 9.

Blue Door	National Trust for Scotland, 28 Charlotte Square, Edinburgh EH2 4ET	0131 243 9335	★★★★	Self Catering
Canee Cottages	Canee Cottages, Orchard Cottage, Kirkudbright, Dumfries & Galloway, DG6 4XD	01557 330245	★★★★	Self Catering
Cottage Above	Stockarton, Kirkcudbright DG6 4XS	01557 330430	★★★	Self Catering
Croig	Croig Self Catering, 95 St Mary Street, Kirkcudbright, Dumfries and Galloway, DG6 4EL	01557 330197	★★★	Self Catering
Cutlars, Orroland & Abbotsway	Auchengashell, Dundrennan, Kirkcudbright, Kirkcudbrighshire, DG6 4QS	01557 500697	★★★ → ★★★★	Self Catering
Glenauld Cottage	Glenauld, Tongland, Kirkcudbright, DG6 4NF	01557 330656	★★★	Self Catering
Haven Cottage	118 High Street, Kirkcudbright Dumfries and Galloway, DG6 4JQ	01557 331960	★★★	Self Catering
Kirkland Mill	Galloway Smokehouse, Carsluith, Newton Stewart DG8 7DN	01671 820354	★★★★	Self Catering
Low Newton	The Hawthorn, Hodgehill Lane Lower, Withington, Cheshire SK11 9LU	01260 224160	★★★	Self Catering
Mews Lane Cottage	Mews Lane Cottage, 4 Mews Lane, Kirkcudbright, Galloway, DG6 4HE	01557 331673	★★★	Self Catering
Milk House and Honey House	Barcloy Cottage, Barcloy Farm, Kirkcudbright, Dumfries & Galloway, DG6 4XR	01557 500588	★★★★	Self Catering
Millstones	18 Carmelaws, Linlithgow, Lothians, EH49 6BU	01506 847535	★★★	Self Catering
Mint Cottage	Silverdale, The Stell, Kirkcudbright, Dumfriesshire, DG6 4SA	01557 332337	★★★	Self Catering
No. 4 Meikle Sypland Cottage	Meikle Sypland, Kirkcudbright, Kirkcudbrightshire, DG6 4XW	01557 331303	★★	Self Catering
Senwick Glebe	Senwick Glebe, Borgue, Kirkcudbright DG6 4TR	01557 870137	★★★	Self Catering
The Dhoon & Tigh-Na-Mara	21 Inglewood Road, Rainford, St Helens, Merseyside, WA11 7QL	01744 889855	★★★	Self Catering
The Waterhouse	The Waterhouse, 1 Stockarton Cottage, Kirkcudbright, Galloway, DG6 4XS	01557 331266	Awaiting Grading	

Kirkhill

Kingillie	Kingillie House, Kirkhill, Inverness-shire, IV5 7PU	01463 831275	★★★	Self Catering

Kirkibost

Tigh-na-Mara	16 Galston Avenue, Newton Mearns G77 5SF	07930 164013	★★★★★	Self Catering

Kirkmichael

Blair Bratach	18 The Glen, Endcliffe Vale Road, Sheffield, South Yorkshire, S10 3FN	01142 663188	★★★★	Self Catering
Cloncaird Castle Estate	Cloncaird Castle Estate, Kirkmichael, Aryshire, KA19 7LU	01655 750345	Awaiting Grading	
Riverview	Riverview, Kirkmichael Perthshire, PH10 7NU	07850 745872	★★★★	Self Catering
Rocksite	13 Pittbauchie, Dumfermline, Fife, KY11 8DP	01383 729618	★★★	Self Catering ⫟

Kirkton Manor, Peebles

Castlehill	23,Silver Street, Stony Stratford, Bucks, MK11 1JS	01908 565467	★★★	Self Catering
Glenrath Farms Ltd	Glenrath Farm, Kirkton Manor, Peebles, Peeblesshire, EH45 9JH	01721 740221	★★★ → ★★★★	Self Catering

To find out more, call 0845 22 55 121 or go to visitscotland.com.

Kirriemuir

Ascreavie Cottages	Ascreavie House, Kirriemuir, Angus, DD8 5HA	01575 574718	★★★	Self Catering	
Glenprosen Cottages	Glenprosen Cottages, Balnaboth, Glenprosen, Angus, DD8 4SA	01575 540302	★ → ★★★	Self Catering	🛦 Ⓟ
Pathhead Cottage	Pathhead Cottage, Forfar Road, Kirriemuir, Angus, DD8 5BY	01575 572173	★★	Self Catering	
Pearsie Lodge	Pearsie Estate Co Ltd, West Kinwhirrie, Kirriemuir, Angus, DD8 4QA	01575 540234	★★★★	Self Catering	🛦
The Crowe's Nest	The Crowe's Nest 'Annfield' 16 Woodend Drive Kirriemuir, Angus, DD8 4TF	01575 573604	★★	Self Catering	
Thrums Cottage	National Trust for Scotland, 28 Charlotte Square, Edinburgh EH2 4ET	0131 243 9335	★★	Self Catering	
Weaver's Cottage	92 Glamis Road, Kirriemuir, Angus, DD8 5DF	01575 572085	★★★	Self Catering	
Winters Cottage	Camperdown House, Darlingscott, Shipson on Stour, Warwickshire, CV36 4PN	01608 682570	★★★	Self Catering	

By Kirriemuir

Littleton of Airlie Farm Cottages	Littleton of Airlie Farm Cottages, by Kirriemuir, Angus, DD8 5NS	01575 530422	★★★	Self Catering	⒫⒫
Kenny Farm Cottages	Little Kenny, Lintrathen, By Kirriemuir, Angus, DD8 5JD	01575 560292	★★★	Self Catering	
Tipperwhig & Brankam	Purgavie Farm, Lintrathen, Kirriemuir, Angus, DD8 5HZ	01575 560364	★★★ → ★★★★	Self Catering	🛉

Kishorn

Ceol-Na-Mara	52 Argyll Street, Inverness, Inverness-shire, IV2 3BB	01463 220858	★★★	Self Catering	
Woodside Cottage & Pine Lodge	Beehive Cottage, Achintraid, Kishorn, Ross-shire, IV54 8XB	01520 733256	★★★	Self Catering	

Knoydart, Mallaig

Kilchoan Farmhouse & Grieves Cottage	Kilchoan Estate Ltd, Inverie, Knoydart, Mallaig, Inverness-shire, PH41 4PL	01687 462724	★★★ → ★★★★	Self Catering	

Kyle of Lochalsh

Ferry Cottage	National Trust for Scotland, 28 Charlotte Square, Edinburgh EH2 4ET	0131 243 9335	★★★	Self Catering	
1 Station Cottages	21 Inkerman Road, Kentish Town, London NW5 3BT	0207 2676548	★★★	Self Catering	
Craig Cottage	16 Duntrune Terrace, West Ferry, Dundee, Tayside, DD5 1LF	01382 477462	★★★	Self Catering	
Tigh-A-Chnuic	102 Church Road, Wick, Bristol, South Glos, BS30 5PD	01179 372816	★★★★	Self Catering	
Whitefalls Retreats	Whitefalls, 1 Camusluinie, Killilan, Kyle of Lochalsh, IV40 8EA	01599 588205	★ → ★★	Self Catering	

By Kyle of Lochalsh

Seadrift Chalet, Avernigh	Seadrift Bed & Breakfast & Holiday Lets, Seadrift, Avernish, By Kyle, Ross-Shire, IV40 8EQ	01599 555415	★★★	Self Catering	
Lamont Bungalow	Creagmhor, Glenelg, Kyle of Lochalsh, Ross-shire, IV40 8JZ	01599 522231	★★★	Self Catering	
Rosdail	Mo Dhachaidh, Inverinate, By Kyle, Ross-shire, IV40 8HB	01599 511351	★★★	Self Catering	
The Lodge - Tigh Na Creag	The Lodge - Tigh Na Creag, Glenelg, by Kyle of Lochalsh, Ross-shire, IV40 8JT	01599 522226	★★★★	Self Catering	

      ♿ Unassisted wheelchair access   🛦 Assisted wheelchair access   🛉 Access for visitors with mobility difficulties
      Ⓟ Bronze Green Tourism Award   ⒫⒫ Silver Green Tourism Award   ⒫⒫⒫ Gold Green Tourism Award
      For further information on our Green Tourism Business Scheme please see page 9.

Kyleakin

Inver Rose	8 Moor Crescent, Gilesgate, Durham City DH1 1PD	07867 800423	★★★★	Self Catering

Kyles, Isle of Harris

Tigh Iomhair	1 Carragreich, Kyles Harris, Isle of Harris, Westen Isles, HS3 3BP	01859 502225	★★★	Self Catering

Kylesku

An Caladh	15 Blackthorne Road, GT Bookham, Surrey, KT23 4BN	01372 451406	★★★★	Self Catering
Unapool House Cottages	Unapool House, Unapool, Kylesku, Sutherland, IV27 4HW	01971 502344	Awaiting Grading	

Ladybank

Eden Cottage	New Kirk Manse, 25 Ballinard Gardens, Broughty Ferry, Dundee, DD5 1BZ	01382 778874	★★★	Self Catering

Laggan, By Newtonmore

Bailnan Cnoc, Allt na Criche, Allt Bronach	Gaskbeg Farm, Laggan, by Newtonmore, Inverness-shire, PH20 1BS	01528 544336	★★★ → ★★★★	Self Catering

Laide

Fraoch Eilean Beag	1 Second Coast, Laide, Ross-shire, IV22 2NF	01445 731228	★★★★	Self Catering
Rocklea, Little Gruinard	Grassvalley Cottage, 12 Woodhall Road, Edinburgh EH13 0DX	0131 441 6053	★★★★	Self Catering ♿
The Sheiling	The Sheiling, Achgarve, Laide, Ross-shire, IV22 2NS	01445 731487	★★★★	Self Catering

Lairg

Arkle	13 Weld Close, Staple Hurst, Tonbridge, Kent, TN12 0SJ	01580 892750	★★★	Self Catering
Ben More	Ben More Cottage, 13 Rosebay Glade,Adambrae, Livingston, West Lothian, EH54 9JU	01906 409939	★★★	Self Catering
Brown Villa	Upper Grange Farm, Peterhead, Aberdeenshire, AB42 1HX	01779 473116	★★★	Self Catering
Cnoclochan	9 Nanhurst Park, Elmbridge Road, Cranleigh, Surrey, GU6 8JX	01483 274846	★★	Self Catering
Lagbuie	24 Achfrish, Shinness, Lairg, Sutherland, IV27 4DN	01549 402223	★★★	Self Catering
Milnclarin Holiday Homes	Woodside, Station Road, Golspie, Sutherland, KW10 6SR	01408 634300	★★★★	Self Catering
Reid's Cottage	Old Park, Parklane, Maplehurst, Horsham, West Sussex, RH13 6LL	01403 891989	★★★★	Self Catering

By Lairg

Duchally Lodge	Balnagowan Castle Properties Ltd, Balnagowan Estate, Kildary, by Invergordon, IV18 0NU	01862 843601	★★★★	Self Catering
Invercassley Cottage	Plovers, Sarson Lane, Amport, Andover, Hampshire, SP11 8AA	01264 773319	★★★	Self Catering
Knockan Crag Holidays	Knockan Crag Holidays, Elphin, By Lairg, Sutherland, IV27 4HH	01628 628474	★★	Self Catering
no. 143 Skinnet	Via Cassia 1170, Rome, Italy 1170	0039 0630 360861	★★★	Self Catering
The Old Library	Ashintully, 143 Main Street, Townhill, Dumfernline KY12 0HB	01383 737954	★★★	Self Catering
Tuinne-Na-Mara	97 Kenneth Street, Inverness IV3 5QQ	01463 234420	★★★	Self Catering

♿ Unassisted wheelchair access   ♿ Assisted wheelchair access   ♿ Access for visitors with mobility difficulties
Ⓟ Bronze Green Tourism Award   ⓅⓅ Silver Green Tourism Award   ⓅⓅⓅ Gold Green Tourism Award
For further information on our Green Tourism Business Scheme please see page 9.

Badnabay and Kinloch Cottages	Reay Forest Estate, Achfary, by Lairg, Sutherland, IV27 4PQ	01971 500221	★★★	Self Catering

Lamlash, Isle of Arran

10A Murray Place	29 Argyle Road, Saltcoats, Ayrshire, KA21 5NS	01294 471901	★★★	Self Catering
23 Hamilton Terrace	Lakeland Gates, Low Road, Brigham, Cockermouth, Cumbria, CA13 0XH	01900 825627	★★★	Self Catering
Braehead Cottage	Braehead, c/o Bass,10 Corstorphine House Ave, Edinburgh, Midlothian, EH12 7AD	01770 303111	★★★★	Self Catering
Cherrytrees	18 Mount Avenue, Kilmarnock, Ayrshire, KA1 1UF	01563 521667	★★★★	Self Catering
Clauchlands View Holiday Cottage	Clauchlands View Holiday Cottage, Clauchlands Farm, Lamlash, Isle of Arran, KA27 8LH	01770 600317	★★★★	Self Catering 🕇
Craig Dhu Cottage	Craig Dhu Cottage, Shore Road, Lamlash, Isle of Arran, KA27 8LH	01770 600276	★★★	Self Catering
Craigbank	Craigbank, 4 Lochview Crescent,Hogganfield, Glasgow G33 1QW	0141 770 6805	★★★★	Self Catering
Croftside Cottage	Cairnkinna, Irongray, Dumfries, DG2 9TN	01387 720161	★★★	Self Catering
Douglas Villa Cottage	14 White Dales, Edinburgh, Mid Lothian, EH10 7JQ	0131 4455586	★★★★	Self Catering
Drive Houses	Mid West Bungalow, Lamlash, Isle of Arran, KA27 8JG	01770 600795	★★★	Self Catering
Dyemill Lodges	Dyemill House, Monamhor Glen, Lamlash, Isle of Arran, KA27 8NU	01770 600419	★★★	Self Catering
Greenfinch	10 Abbotsmoss, Falkirk, Central Region, FK1 5UA	01324 476963	★★★	Self Catering
Island Bank Cottage	Island Bank Cottage, Lamlash Isle of Arran, KA27 8LG	01770 600279	★★	Self Catering
Jubilee Cottage	Rathgar, 2 Romany Road, Oulton Broad, Lowestoft, Suffolk, NR32 3PJ	01502 582011	★★★★	Self Catering
Kinneil	Kinneil Self catering Apartments, Kinneil,Shore Road, Lamlash, Isle of Arran, KA27 8JT	01770 600307	★★★	Self Catering
Liosmor	Edgehill, The Avenues, Lamlash, Isle of Arran, KA27 8JU	01770 600752	★★★★	Self Catering
Meall Buidhe	Laigh Letter Farm limited, 1 Zetland Road, Hillington Park, Glasgow, G52 4BW	0141 8109900	★★★★	Self Catering
Oakbank Farm	Oakbank Farm, Lamlash, Isle of Arran, KA27 8LH	01770 600404	★★★	Self Catering 🕇
Oakwood Cottage	Ferenze Lodge, Shore Road, Lamlash, Isle of Arran, KA27 8LH	01770 600790	★★★★	Self Catering
Prospect Hill House and Prospect Hill Studio	1 Spey Place, Carseford, Johnstone PA5 0PT	01505 702746	★★★	Self Catering
Sandcliffe	15 Boclair Road, Bearsden, Glasgow G61 2AF	0141 9421128	★★★	Self Catering
Seabank	St Catherine's House, Forres IV36 1LS	01309 671846	★	Self Catering
Spion Kop Cottage	Spion Kop Cottage, Spion Kop, Lamlash, Isle of Arran, KA27 8NL	01770 600474	★★★	Self Catering
Sunnybank	Hazeldean, 38 Spring Hill Road, Sheffield, South Yorkshire, S10 1ES	0114 2680019	★★★	Self Catering
The Anchorage	95 Mountcastle Crescent, Edinburgh EH8 7SE	0131 477 7033	★★★	Self Catering
The Chimney	1 Craigdhu Avenue, Milngavie, Glasgow G62 6DX	0141 5637156	★★★	Self Catering
The Shore	The Shore, Shore Road, Lamlash, Isle of Arran, KA27 8JY	01770 303111	★★★	Self Catering
Tigh an Eilean	5 Bruce Gate, Airth, Falkirk FK2 8GN	01324 832738	★★★★	Self Catering

  🦽 Unassisted wheelchair access   🦽 Assisted wheelchair access   🕇 Access for visitors with mobility difficulties
🍁 Bronze Green Tourism Award   🍁🍁 Silver Green Tourism Award   🍁🍁🍁 Gold Green Tourism Award
For further information on our Green Tourism Business Scheme please see page 9.

| Tigh Na Traigh | Taylor Bowls Ltd, 217 Bernard Street Glasgow, G40 3NB | 0141 554 5255 | ★★★★ | Self Catering | |
| Ghillie's and Drovers | Glenkiln, Lamlash, Isle of Arran, KA27 8NT | 01770 600291 | ★★★★ | Self Catering | 🚶 🅿🅿 |

Lanark

Bankhead Accommodation	Bankhead Accommodation, Bankhead Farm, Braxfield Road, Lanark ML11 9BU	01555 666560	★★★ → ★★★★	Self Catering
Corehouse Farm	Corehouse Farm, Kirkfieldbank, Lanark ML11 9TQ	01555 661377	Awaiting Grading	
Kilnhills Farm	Kilnhills Farm, Hawksland, Lesmahagow, Lanark, Lanarkshire, ML11 9PZ	01555 892235	★★★★	Self Catering
Town House	1 Roman Court, Cleghorn, Lanark, ML11 7RU	01555 665283	★★★	Self Catering

Langholm

| Georgefield & Copperfield Cottages | Georgefield, Westerkirk, Langholm, Dumfriesshire, DG13 0NJ | 01387 370227 | ★★★ | Self Catering |
| Jamestown Cottage | The Kerr, Canonbie, Dumfriesshire, DG14 0XP | 01387 371420 | ★★★★ | Self Catering |

Largs

1A, 4C and 5D Sandringham	2 Sandringham, Largs, Ayrshire, KA30 8BT	01475 673387	★	Self Catering	
3 Scott Street	3 Scott Street, Largs, Ayrshire, KA30 9NP	01475 674898	★★	Self Catering	
3c Kirklands	Corra Bheinn, 35 Greenock Road, Largs, Ayrshire, KA30 8PJ	01475 673873	★★★	Self Catering	
Douglas House	Douglas Street, Largs, Ayrshire, KA30 8PT	01475 673992	★★★★	Self Catering	
Seger Property Mgnt	Seger Property Mgnt, 55 Greenock Road, Largs, Ayrshire, KA30 8PL	01475 686369	★★★★	Self Catering	🚶
Zion House	Haus Saron, 106 Greenock Road, Largs, Ayrshire, KA30 8PG	01475 673162	★★★	Self Catering	
Largs Holiday Apartments	35 Ryan Road, Wemyss Bay, Inverclyde PA18 6DH	01475 521916	★★★	Self Catering	
East Wing, Brisbane Glen	Noddsdale Cottage, Brisbane Glen, Largs, Ayrshire, KA30 8SL	01475 673757	★★★	Self Catering	

By Larkhall

| Clyde Valley Cottages, Dalserf | Clyde Valley Cottages, Cornsilloch Farm, Dalserf, Larkhall, ML9 2UA | 01698 889021 | ★★★ → ★★★★ | Self Catering |
| The Studio, Ashgill | 10 Bartie Gardens, Ashgill, Larkhall, Lanarkshire, ML9 3FB | 01698 884060 | ★★★ | Self Catering |

Lasswade

| Gorton House | Gorton House, Gorton, Lasswade, Midlothian, EH18 1EH | 0131 440 4332 | ★★ → ★★★ | Self Catering |
| Pine Cottage | Pine Cottage, Kings Acre Golf Course, Lasswade, Midlothian, EH18 1AU | 0131 663 3456 | ★★★★ | Self Catering |

Latheron

| Studio Apartment | Studio Apartment, Old Manse, Latheron, Caithness, KW5 6DJ | 01593 741740 | ★★★ | Self Catering |

Latheronwheel

| Craiglea | 168 Granville Road, London NW2 2LD | 020 87317771 | ★★★★ | Self Catering |

♿ Unassisted wheelchair access ♿ Assisted wheelchair access 🚶 Access for visitors with mobility difficulties
🅿 Bronze Green Tourism Award 🅿🅿 Silver Green Tourism Award 🅿🅿🅿 Gold Green Tourism Award
For further information on our Green Tourism Business Scheme please see page 9.

310   To find out more, call 0845 22 55 121 or go to visitscotland.com.

Lauder

Airhouses	Airhouses, Oxton, Lauder, Borders, TD2 6PX	01578 750642	★★★★ → ★★★★★	Self Catering	⅘ 🄿🄿
Larkhill Cottage	Larkhill, Lauder, Berwickshire, TD2 6RS	01578 718778	★★★★	Self Catering	🄿
Thirlestane Castle Trust	Thirlestane Castle Trust, Thirlestane Castle, Lauder, Berwickshire, TD2 6RD	01578 722430	★★★★★	Serviced Apartments	
Thirlestane Farm Cottages	Thirlestane Farm, Lauder, Berwickshire, TD2 6SF	01578 722216	★★★	Self Catering	

Laurencekirk

| Arbuthnott Holiday Lets | Estate Office, Arbuthnott, Laurencekirk, Kincardineshire, AB30 1PA | 01561 320417 | ★★★ | Self Catering | |

Lentran

| Pine Chalets | Pine Chalets, Stockdarroch, 24 Commissioner Street, Crieff, Perthshire, PH7 3AY | 01764 654537 | ★★★ | Self Catering | |
| Courtyard Cottages | Pitglassie Farm, Dingwalll, Ross-shire, IV15 9TR | 01349 862004 | ★★★★ | Self Catering | |

Lerags, by Oban

| Lagnakeil | Lag-na-Keil Chalets, Lerags, By Oban, Argyll, PA34 4SE | 01631 562746 | ★★★ → ★★★★ | Self Catering | |
| The Cottage | Kilbride Farm, Lerags, by Oban, Argyll, PA34 4SE | 01631 562878 | ★★ | Self Catering | |

Leven

| Kerrera Cottage | 6587 Windsong Ave, Otawa, Ontario, Canada, KIC- 6NZ | 001613 830384 | ★★★ | Self Catering | |

Leverburgh

Blacksheep House	Blacksheep House, 12 Borrisdale, Isle of Harris, Western Isles, HS5 3UE	01859 520306	★★★★	Self Catering	
Shalom Self Catering	Shalom Self Catering, 12 Strond, Leverburgh, Isle of Harris, HS5 3UD	01859 520 259	★★★★★	Self Catering	⋔
Taransay	Monadh Liath, Main Street, Newtonmore, Inverness-shire, PH20 1DD	01540 673531	★★	Self Catering	

Lewis

| 33 North Shawbost | 22 North Shawbost, Shawbost, Isle of Lewis, HS2 9BQ | 01851 710591 | ★★★ | Self Catering | |

Linlithgow

11 Dawson Court	144 Avontoun Park, Linlithgow, West Lothian, EH49 6QH	01506 847104	★★★★	Self Catering	
Craigs Lodges	Craigs Lodges Ltd, Williamcraigs, Linlithgow, West Lothian, EH49 6QF	01506 845025	★★ → ★★★	Self Catering	
Linlithgow Cottages	1 Bonsyde Terrace, Bonsyde, Linlithgow, West Lothian, EH49 7NZ	01506 840793	★★★★	Self Catering	
Avon Glen Lodges	Avon Glen Lodges, Melons Place, Maddiston, Falkirk, FK2 0BT	01324 861166	★★★	Self Catering	⅘

Livingston

| Loch Lomond Chalet | 19 Murieston Green, Livingston, West Lothian, EH54 9EQ | 01506 203433 | ★★★★ | Self Catering | |

Loanhead

| Aaron Glen Apartments | Aaron Glen Apartments, 7 Nivensknowe Road, Loanhead, Midlothian, EH20 9AU | 0131 440 1293 | ★★★★ | Self Catering | |

🦽 Unassisted wheelchair access   🦽 Assisted wheelchair access   ⋔ Access for visitors with mobility difficulties
🄿 Bronze Green Tourism Award   🄿🄿 Silver Green Tourism Award   🄿🄿🄿 Gold Green Tourism Award
For further information on our Green Tourism Business Scheme please see page 9.

Awards correct as of mid August 2008

311

Loch Broom

Braemore Square Country House	Braemore Square, Braemore, Lochbroom, Wester Ross, IV23 2RX	01854 655357	★★★★	Self Catering 🍃🍃

Loch Carron

Rose Cottage & Woodside Cottage	5 Hargate Close, Bury, Lancashire, BL9 5NU	01706 826590	★★★★	Self Catering

Loch Creran, Appin

Inver Boathouse & Boathouse Cottage	28 Rhondda Grove, London E3 5AP	0163173421	★★★ → ★★★★	Self Catering

Loch Lomond

Inchmurrin Island Self-catering	Inchmurrin Hotel, Inchmurrin Island, Loch Lomond G63 0JY	01389 850245	★★★	Self Catering

By Loch Ness

Millness Croft Luxury Cottages	Millness Croft Luxury Cottages, Glen Urquharat, Nr Loch Ness, Inverness-shire, IV63 6TW	01456 476761	★★★★★	Self Catering 🚶 🍃🍃

Loch Rannoch

Croiscrag	St Jude's Lodge, Old London Road, Mickleham, Surrey, RH5 6BY	01883 714039	★★	Self Catering

Lochailort

Roshven Farm Chalets	Roshven Farm, Lochailort, Inverness-shire, PH38 4NB	01687 470221	★★★	Self Catering

Lochan Mor

Tigh na Lochan	85 Stockiemuir Avenue, Bearsden, Glasgow G61 3LL	0141 248 5051	★★★★	Self Catering

Lochans

Braeside Cottage	East Cottage, Lochans Mill, Stranraer, Dumfries and Galloway, DG9 9BA	01776 820684	★★★	Self Catering

Lochboisdale, Isle of South Uist

Ocean View	409 Smerclate, Lochboisdale, South Uist, HS8 5TU	01878 700383	★★★★	Self Catering

Lochbroom

Broomview and Sunset	Spindrift, Keppoch Farm, Dundonnell, Ross-shire, IV23 2QR	01854 633269	★★★★	Self Catering
Taigh a'Braoin	1 Hillhouse Place, Stewarton, Ayrshire, KA3 3HT	01560 484 003	★★★★	Self Catering 🚶

Lochbuie

Kathleen & Mabel Cottages	Lochbuie House, Lochbuie, Isle of Mull, Argyll, PA62 6AA	1680814214	★★	Self Catering

Lochcarron

Seabank, Tor Fionn & Shellach Cottage	Craig Cottage, Achnashellach, by Strathcarron, Ross-shire, IV54 8YU	01520 766288	★★★ → ★★★★	Self Catering
Struan Cottage	113 Morriston Road, Bishopmill, Elgin, Morayshire, IV30 4WB	01520 722494	★★★	Self Catering

Lochearnhead

Ballimore Farm Cottage	Ballimore, Balquhidder, Lochearnhead, Perthshire, FK19 8PE	01877 384287	★★★★	Self Catering

♿ Unassisted wheelchair access   ♿ Assisted wheelchair access   🚶 Access for visitors with mobility difficulties
🍃 Bronze Green Tourism Award   🍃🍃 Silver Green Tourism Award   🍃🍃🍃 Gold Green Tourism Award
For further information on our Green Tourism Business Scheme please see page 9.

To find out more, call 0845 22 55 121 or go to visitscotland.com.

Cnoc Famh	Cnoc Famh, Balquhidder, Lochearnhead, Perthshire, FK19 8PB	07946 740404	★★★	Self Catering 🍃
Corriebeg	27 Ashburnham Loan, South Queensferry, Edinburgh, Mid Lothian, EH30 9LE	0131 331 5440	★★★	Self Catering
Earnknowe	Earnknowe, Lochearnhead, Perthshire, FK19 8PY	01567 830238	★★★	Self Catering 🕇
Lochearnhead Lochside Chalets	Lochside Cottages, Lochearhead, Perthshire, FK19 8PT	01567 830268	★★★	Self Catering

Locheport, Isle of North Uist

18 Illeray	18 Illeray, Clachan, Locheport, North Uist, Western Isles, HS6 5HD	01876 580672	★★★	Self Catering
The Moorings	23 Cormorant Avenue, Craigends, Houston, Renfrewshire, HS6 7LG	01505 614660	★★★	Self Catering

Lochgelly

Balbedie Farm Cottage	Balbedie Farm Cottage, Kinglassie, Lochgelly, Fife, KY5 0UE	01592 882242	★★	Self Catering

Lochgilphead

Barnlongart House & Ormsary Lodges	Ormsary Estate, Ormsary, Lochgilphead, Argyll, PA31 8PE	01880 770222	★ → ★★★	Self Catering 🕇
Clachandush,South Lodge and Finchairn	Lime Farm, Sutton-Cum-Granby, Notts, NG13 9QA	01949 850372	★★★	Self Catering
Crinan House	Obergasse 28a, Thaining, Germany D86943	49 08194 8263	★★★★	Self Catering
Ellary Estate	Ellary Estate, Ellary, Lochgilphead, Argyll, PA31 8PA	01880 770209	★★ → ★★★★	Self Catering

By Lochgilphead

Craigdhu Farmhouse	Barbreck Trust, Landmark, Carrbridge, Inverness-shire, PH23 3AJ	01479 841613	★★★	Self Catering
Dairy Cottage & Byre Cottage	Achnashelloch Farm, By Lochgilphead, Argyll, PA31 8RE	01546 605273	★★★	Self Catering
Gallanach cottage	40-42 South Street, Perth, Perthshire, PH2 8PD	01738 626644	★★	Self Catering
Lerigoligan	31 Banavie Road, Glasgow G11 5AW	0141 3393064	★★★	Self Catering
Drumalban	c/o K Richardson, Millhouse, Ardfern, By Lochgilphead, Argyll, PA31 8QN		★★★★	Self Catering
Aird House	Aird Farm, Ardfern, Lochgilphead, Argyll, PA31 8QS	01852 500224	★★★★ → ★★★★★	Self Catering
Kilmahumaig Barn Flats	Kilmahumaig Barn Flats, Kilmahumaig, Crinan, by Lochgilphead, Argyll, PA31 8SW	01546 830238	★★	Self Catering
Tigha Charnain	Stroneskar Farm, Ford, by Lochgilphead, Argyll, PA31 8RJ	01546 810286	★★★	Self Catering

Lochgoil

Darroch Mhor Chalets	Darroch Mhor, Carrick Castle, Lochgoil, Argyll, PA24 8AF	01301 703249	★★	Self Catering

Lochinver

Ardvar Cottage	Glendarroch Wood, Lochinver, Sutherland, IV27 4LP	01571 844756	★★★★	Self Catering
Clachtoll Cottage	120 Esslemont Circle, Ellon, Aberdeenshire, AB41 9XG	01358 720163	★★★★	Self Catering
Creigard	Creigard, Badnaban, Lochinver, Sutherland, IV27 4LR	01571 844448	★★★★	Self Catering
Heather Cottage	52 Dumgoyne Drive, Bearsden, Glasgow, G61 3AW	0141 931 5775	★★★★	Self Catering

♿ Unassisted wheelchair access   ♿ Assisted wheelchair access   🕇 Access for visitors with mobility difficulties
🍃 Bronze Green Tourism Award   🍃🍃 Silver Green Tourism Award   🍃🍃🍃 Gold Green Tourism Award
For further information on our Green Tourism Business Scheme please see page 9.

Kirkaig Chalets	Firm of Clachtoll Beach Campsite, 134 Clachtoll, Nr Lochinver, Sutherland, IV27 4JD	01571 855343	★★★	Self Catering
Lochinver Holiday Lodges	Inver Lodge, 30 Main Street, Lochinver, Sutherland, IV27 4JY	01571 844318	★★★★	Self Catering
Mountview Self-catering	70 Mountview, Baddidarroch, Lochinver, Sutherland, IV27 4LP	01571 844648	★★★★	Self Catering 🦽
Spring Cottage	12 Craigleith Gardens, Edinburgh EH4 3JW	0131 332 1100	★★★	Self Catering
Taigh Na Fraoch	Somewhere Special Ltd, Balwill Cottage, Balfron Station, Glasgow, G63 0QY	01360 850130	★★★★	Self Catering
Tigh Beag	Ardrisnich, 111/115 Achmelvich, Lochinver, Sutherland, IV27 4JB	01571 844414	★★★	Self Catering
Tigh na Mara	Tigh-mo-Chridhe, Baddidarrach, Lochinver, Sutherland, IV27 4LP	01571 844377	★★★	Self Catering
Unst	Oakleigh, West Torrington, Market Rasen, Lincolnshire, LN8 5SQ	07909 726585	★★	Self Catering
Cathair Dhubh Estate	Cathair Dhubh Estate, Lochinver, Sutherland, IV27 4JB	01571 855277	★★★★	Self Catering 🧍
252 Culkein	28 Laggan Road, Inverness, Inverness-shire, IV2 4EH	01463 230985	★★	Self Catering
The Lower Apartment	National Trust for Scotland, 28 Charlotte Square, Edinburgh EH2 4ET	0131 243 9335	★★★	Self Catering
The Upper Apartment	National Trust for Scotland, 28 Charlotte Square, Edinburgh EH2 4ET	0131 243 9335	★★★	Self Catering
Tigh Na Craig	Witchwells, Woodriffe Road, Newburgh, Fife, KY14 6DW	01337 840178	★★★★	Self Catering
Strathan, Midtown and Assynt	Caisteal Liath Chalets, 74 Baddidarroch, Lochinver, Sutherland, IV27 4LP	01571 844457	★★★★	Self Catering

By Lochinver

Buailard House	1-127 Walmer Road, Toronto, Ontario, CANADA, M5R 2X8		★★★	Self Catering
Glendarroch House	Braeside, Navidale Road, Helmsdale, Sutherland, KW8 6JS	01431 821207	★★★★	Self Catering 🧍
Sealladh Na Mara	Fat Ox Farm, Houlsyke, Whitby, North Yorkshire, YO21 2LH	01287 660076	★★★★	Self Catering

Lochmaddy

17 Kersavagh	7 Martineau Close, Esher, Surrey, KT10 9PW	01372 469340	★★★	Self Catering
An T-Seann Dachaidh	7 Hay Place, Elgin, Moray, IV30 1LZ	01343 550805	★★★	Self Catering
Clachan	Smeorach, Claddach, Lochmaddy, North Uist, HS6 5HE	01876 580644	★★	Self Catering
Loch Portain House	Trinity Factors, 209 Bruntsfield Place, Edinburgh EH10 4DH	0131 447 9911	★★★	Self Catering
Torran Gorm	Smithy Croft, Lochmaddy, North Uist HS6 5AA	01876 500391	★★★★	Self Catering

Lochranza, Isle of Arran

Cnoc Cottage	18 Rowallan Gardens, Glasgow G11 7LJ	0141 334 6998	★★	Self Catering
Ornsay Cottage	Ornsay, Lochranza, Isle of Arran, KA27 8HJ	01770 830304	★★★	Self Catering
The Shieling	The Shieling, Lochranza, Isle of Arran, KA27 8HL	01770 830349	★★★	Self Catering

Lochs, Isle of Lewis

13 Glen Gravir	18 St Vincent Street, Edinburgh EH3 6SJ	0131 557 4938	★★★★	Self Catering

🦽 Unassisted wheelchair access   🦽 Assisted wheelchair access   🧍 Access for visitors with mobility difficulties
🌿 Bronze Green Tourism Award   🌿🌿 Silver Green Tourism Award   🌿🌿🌿 Gold Green Tourism Award
For further information on our Green Tourism Business Scheme please see page 9.

Achmore Self Catering	29 Lewis Street, Stornoway, Isle of Lewis, HS1 2JW	01851 700310	★★★★	Self Catering	
The Stack	Handa, 18 Keose Glebe, Keose Glebe, Isle of Lewis, HS2 9JX	01851 830334	★★★★	Self Catering	
Thule Cottage	1 School Hill, Ranish, Lochs, Isle of Lewis, HS2 9NW	01851 700216	★★★	Self Catering	
Shiantview	2 Cnoc Iomhair, Stornoway, Isle of Lewis, HS1 2UL	01851 705283	★★★★	Self Catering	

Lochwinnoch

East Lochhead Cottages	East Lochhead, Largs Road, Lochwinnoch, Renfrewshire, PA12 4DX	01505 842610	★★★★	Self Catering	♿ 🍃🍃🍃

Lockerbie

Bonshawbrae	59 St Andrews Drive, Bridge of Weir, Renfrewshire, PA11 3HY	01505 690202	★★★	Self Catering	
Kirkwood Cottages	Kirkwood, Lockerbie, Dumfries-shire, DG11 1DH	01576 510200	★★ → ★★★	Self Catering	

By Lockerbie

Bruce Suite and Johnstone Suite	Cove Estate, Kirkpatrick Fleming, By Lockerbie, Dunfriesshire, DG11 3AT	01461 800323	★★★★	Self Catering	
Dalton Pottery Art Cafe	Dalton Pottery, Meikle Dyke, Dalton, Nr Lockerbie, Dumfriesshire, DG11 1DU	01387 840236	★★★ → ★★★★	Self Catering	

Lossiemouth

17 Marine Court	2 Darklass Place, Dyke, Forres, Moray, IV36 2GX	01309 641334	★★★★	Self Catering	
Beachview Apartment	Links Lodge, Stotfield Road, Lossiemouth, Moray, IV31 6QS	01343 813815	★★★	Self Catering	
Beachview Holiday Flats	62 Fernlea, Bearsden, Glasgow G61 1NB	0141 942 4135	★★★★	Self Catering	
No. 1 Pitgaveny Court	Scaraben, 1 Paradise Lane, Lossiemouth, Moray, IV31 6QW	01343 813495	★★★	Self Catering	

By Lossiemouth

Covesea Skerry	National Trust for Scotland, 28 Charlotte Square, Edinburgh EH2 4ET	0131 243 9335	★★★	Self Catering	
Halliman	National Trust for Scotland, 28 Charlotte Square, Edinburgh EH2 4ET	0131 243 9335	★★★	Self Catering	

Lower Burnmouth

Seal Cottage	Coast & Country Cottages Ltd, Riverbank Road, Alnmouth, Northumberland, NE66 2RH	01665 830783	★★	Self Catering	
Rockpool Cottage	Birch Cottage, 3 Largo Road, Lundin Links, Fife, KY8 6DG	01333 320844	Awaiting Grading		

Lumphanan

Boghead Cottage	Boghead Cottage, Dalliebity Croft, Baillieswells Road, Beildside, Aberdeen, Aberdeenshire, AB15 9BQ	01224 868372	★★★★	Self Catering	
The Flat	The Flat, Cairnview, Lumphanan, Aberdeenshire, AB31 4QJ	01339 883557	★★★	Self Catering	

Lundin Links

Emsdorf Place	Gleniffer, 15 Main Street, Upper Largo, Fife, KY8 6EL	01333 360403	★★★	Self Catering	
No 18 Links Road	18 Links Road, Lundin Links, Fife, KY8 6AU	01333 320497	★★★	Self Catering	🍃
Tweedbank	Kirklea, Durie Street, Leven, Fife, KY8 4HA	07917 224033	★★★	Self Catering	

♿ Unassisted wheelchair access   ♿ Assisted wheelchair access   🚶 Access for visitors with mobility difficulties
🍃 Bronze Green Tourism Award   🍃🍃 Silver Green Tourism Award   🍃🍃🍃 Gold Green Tourism Award
For further information on our Green Tourism Business Scheme please see page 9.

White Pillars Apartment	White Pillats, 8 Hillhead Lane, Lundin Links, Fife, KY8 6DE	01333 329536	★★★★	Self Catering

Luss

Loch Lomond Haven	Broomfield Cottage, School Road, Luss, Argyll & Bute, G83 8PA	01436 860252	★★★★	Self Catering
Loch Lomond Hideaways	Inverbeg Holiday Park, Inverbeg, Luss, Argyll & Bute, G83 8DP	01436 860267	★★★★ → ★★★★★	Self Catering ⟨ᵬ⟩
No. 14 Lomond Castle	14 Lomond Castle, Luss, Argyll, G83 8EE	01389 850711	★★★★	Self Catering
Shegarton Farm Cottages	Shegarton Farm, Luss, Loch Lomond, Argyll, G83 8RH	01389 850269	★★★★	Self Catering
Shemore Farm Cottage	Shantron Farm, Luss, Alexandria, Dunbartonshire, G83 8RH	01389 850231	★★★	Self Catering 🍃

Lybster

Taigh an Clachair	South Riding, Roachill, South Molton, Devon, EX36 4EB	01398 341692	★★★	Self Catering

Macduff

Mariner's Cottage	Creel Cottage, High Shore, Macduff, Banffshire, AB44 1SN	01261 832414	★★★★	Self Catering

Machrie, Isle of Arran

Balnagore, Cairnfield & Rowanbank	Jackson's Cottage, Rudgwick, Sussex, RH12 3AB	0140 3822364	★★★ → ★★★★	Self Catering
Druid Farmhouse	8 Mount Charles Crescent, Ayr, Ayrshire, KA7 4NY	01292 443769	★★★	Self Catering
Machrie House	Machrie House, Machrie, Isle of Arran, KA27 8DZ	01770 840223	★★★	Self Catering
Sandmartin Cottage	Auchencar Farm, Machrie, Isle of Arran, KA27 8EB	01770 840338	★★★★	Self Catering
Whitefield Cottage	39 Alexandra Street, Kirkintilloch, Dumbartonshire, G66 1HE	0141 776 3838	★★★	Self Catering

Machrihanish

Bayvoyach	The Garth, Tynron, Thornhill, Dumfriesshire, DG3 4JY	01848 200364	★★	Self Catering

Maidens

Ailsa View	Hunters Contracts (Scotland) Ltd, 11 Cambuslang Road, Glasgow G32 8NB	0141 646 1551	★★★★	Self Catering
1 Seabank View	16 Braidpark Drive, Giffnock, Glasgow, Lanarkshire, G46 6NB	0141 6379704	★★★★	Self Catering

Mainsriddle

Little Solway	The Old Manse, Mainsriddle, Dumfries and Galloway, DG2 8AG	01387 780262	★★★	Self Catering

Mallaig

Ceithir Raithean	4 Willow Mead, Romiley, Stockport, Cheshire, SK6 4GA	0161 406 6010	★★★★	Self Catering
Creag-Eiridh	Blynfield, Stour Row, Shaftesbury, Dorset, SP7 0QW	01747 852289	★★★	Self Catering
Essan Cottage	Essan House, Morar, Mallaig, Inverness-shire, PH40 4PA	01687 460014	★★★	Self Catering

Marwick

Corks	14 Regent Terrace, Edinburgh EH7 5BN	0131 5567051	★★★★	Self Catering

ᚷ Unassisted wheelchair access ᚸ Assisted wheelchair access ᚩ Access for visitors with mobility difficulties
🍃 Bronze Green Tourism Award 🍃🍃 Silver Green Tourism Award 🍃🍃🍃 Gold Green Tourism Award
For further information on our Green Tourism Business Scheme please see page 9.

To find out more, call 0845 22 55 121 or go to visitscotland.com.

Mauchline

Darnhay Cottage Holidays	Darnhay Farmhouse, Mauchline, East Ayrshire, KA5 6HG	01290 559428	★★★★	Self Catering
Overtoun Farm Cottage	Overtoun Farm, Mauchline, Ayrshire, KA5 5SY	01290 550337	★★★	Self Catering

Maybole

Brewhouse Flat	National Trust for Scotland, 28 Charlotte Square, Edinburgh EH2 4ET	0131 243 9335	★	Self Catering
Dove and Rainbow Cottages	Burnmouth Farm, Cassillis, Maybole, Ayrshire, KA19 7JN	01292 560 426	★★★★★	Self Catering
Hoolity Ha	National Trust for Scotland, 28 Charlotte Square, Edinburgh EH2 4ET	0131 243 9335	★	Self Catering
Kileekie Cottage	Kileekie, Crosshill, Maybole, Ayrshire, KA19 7PY	01655 740236	★★★	Self Catering
Loch Ayim Cottage	4 Arrol Drive, Ayr KA7 4AF	01292 264022	★★★	Self Catering
North Segganwell	National Trust for Scotland, 28 Charlotte Square, Edinburgh EH2 4ET	0131 243 9335	★★	Self Catering
Royal Artillery Cottage	National Trust for Scotland, 28 Charlotte Square, Edinburgh EH2 4ET	0131 243 9335	★	Self Catering ᐊ
South Segganwell	National Trust for Scotland, 28 Charlotte Square, Edinburgh EH2 4ET	0131 243 9335	★★	Self Catering

Meavaig

Riverside	Riverside, Meavaig, South Harris, HS3 3DY	01859 502156	★★★★	Self Catering

Mellon Charles

Shore Croft	23 North Road, Grassendale Park, Liverpool, Merseyside, L19 0LP	0151 494 1488	★★★★★	Self Catering

Melrose

12 Glentress	46 Lindfield Gardens, Guildford, Surrey, GU1 1TS	01483 534877	★★★	Self Catering
Courtyard Cottage	Kirklands, Melrose TD6 9DL	01896 822183	★★★	Self Catering
Dimpleknowe Mill & Cottage	Dimpleknowe, Lilliesleaf, Melrose, Roxburghshire, TD6 9JU	01835 870333	★★★ → ★★★★	Self Catering ᐊ [PP]
Eildon Holiday Cottages	Eildon Holiday Cottages, Dingleton Mains, Melrose, Roxburghshire, TD6 9HS	01896 823258	★★★ → ★★★★	Self Catering ♿
Fishermans Flat & Stable Cottage	The Holmes, St Boswells, Melrose, Roxburghshire, TD6 0EL	01835 822356	★★★	Self Catering
Glendevon	Melrose Self Catering Cottages, 7 Townhead Way, Newstead, Melrose, Scottish Borders, TD6 9BU	01896 820388	★★★	Self Catering
Harmony Cottage	National Trust for Scotland, 28 Charlotte Square, Edinburgh EH2 4ET	0131 243 9335	★★	Self Catering
Harmony House	National Trust for Scotland, 28 Charlotte Square, Edinburgh EH2 4ET	0131 243 9335	★★★	Self Catering
Newstead Mill	Melrose Self Catering Cottages, 7 Townhead Way, Newstead, Melrose, Scottish Borders, TD6 9BU	01896 820388	★★★★	Self Catering
Pavilion Cottage	Melrose Self Catering Cottages, 7 Townhead Way, Newstead, Melrose, Scottish Borders, TD6 9BU	01896 820388	★★★★	Self Catering
Swallow Cottage	Cotgreen, Melrose, Roxburghshire, TD6 9BE	0189682 2608	★★	Self Catering
Swallow Cottage	Swallow Cottage, 8 Townhead Way, Newstead, Melrose, Roxburghshire, TD6 9BU	01896 820388	★★★★	Self Catering
The Cloister House	The Vivat Trust, 70 Cowcross Street, London EC1M 6EJ	0845 0900194	★★★★	Self Catering

♿ Unassisted wheelchair access   ᐊ Assisted wheelchair access   ☏ Access for visitors with mobility difficulties
[P] Bronze Green Tourism Award   [PP] Silver Green Tourism Award   [PPP] Gold Green Tourism Award
For further information on our Green Tourism Business Scheme please see page 9.

The Old Dairy	Treetops, Hall Lane, Tathwell, Lonth, Lincolnshire, LN11 9SR	01507 606757	★★★★	Self Catering	
Tweedmount	Kippilaw House, Melrose, Roxburghshire, TD6 9ST	01835 822790	★★★	Self Catering	

Melvich

Halladale Inn Chalet Park	Halladale Inn, Melvich, Sutherland, KW14 7JY	01641 531282	★★	Self Catering	
Netstore & Fishery Cottage	The Strath Halladale & Sainn Partnership, The Estate Office, The Kennels, Forsinard, Strath Halladale,	01641 571271	★★★ → ★★★★	Self Catering	

Menstrie

Menstrie Castle	21 Ochil Street, Alloa, Clackmannanshire, FK10 2DS	01259 212478	★★★	Self Catering	

Methven

Cloag Farm Cottages	Cloag Farm, Methven, Perthshire, PH1 3RR	01738 840239	★★★	Self Catering	🌱
Strathearn Holidays Ltd	Reservations Department, Strathearn Holidays Ltd, Kilda Way, North Muirton Ind Est, Perth, Perthshire, PH1 3XS	01738 633322	★★★★	Self Catering	

Millport, Isle of Cumbrae

1 Guildford Street	Muirhall Farm, Larbert, Stirlingshire, FK5 4EW	01324 554430	★★ → ★★★★	Self Catering	
Cumbrae Holiday Apartments Ltd	Cumbrae Holiday Apartments, 12 Stuart Street, Millport, Isle of Cumbrae, KA28 0AN	01475 530094	★★	Self Catering	
Lochknowe	Lochknowe, 9 Kames Bay, Millport, Isle of Cumbrae, KA28 0EA	01475 530630	★	Self Catering	

Milton of Campsie

Campsie Outdoors	Campsie Outdoors, Antermony Loch, Milton of Campsie, East Dunbartonshire, G66 8AB	01360 311811	★★★★	Self Catering	
The Lodge	Upper Woodburn, Milton of Campsie G66 8AN	01236 823249	★★★ → ★★★★	Self Catering	

Minard

Minard Castle	Minard Castle, Minard, Argyll, PA32 8YB	01546 886272	★★★	Self Catering	
Brondeg Lodge	Inverae, Minard, Inveraray, Argyll, PA32 8YF	01546 886655	★★★	Self Catering	
The Anchorage	Flat 1, Scott's Land, Main Street, Inverkip, Greenock, Renfrewshire, PA16 0AU	01475 522536	★★★	Self Catering	

Minto

Townhead Steading	Townhead Steading, Minto, Roxburghshire, TD9 8SG	01450 870422	★★★★	Self Catering	

Moffat

6 The Glebe	20 Avenue Road, Brentford, Middlesex, TW8 9NS	020 85608820	★★★	Self Catering	
Dye Mill Cottage	The Dye Mill, Sidmount Avenue, Moffat, Dumfriesshire, DG10 9BS	01683 220681	★★	Self Catering	
Heatheryhaugh Lodges	Heatheryhaugh Lodges, Heatheryhaugh, Moffat, Dumfriesshire, DG10 9LD	01683 220107	★★★	Self Catering	
Hillview	9 Beechgrove, Moffat, Dumfriesshire, DG10 9RS	01683 221021	★★	Self Catering	
Holmedale	8 Kensington Gardens, North Shields, North Shields, Tyne & Wear, NE30 2AL	0191 2901461	★★★	Self Catering	
Kirsty Cottage	75 Jersey Close, Redditch, Worcestershire, B98 9LT	01527 585585	★★★	Self Catering	

♿ Unassisted wheelchair access   ♿ Assisted wheelchair access   ♿ Access for visitors with mobility difficulties
🌱 Bronze Green Tourism Award   🌱🌱 Silver Green Tourism Award   🌱🌱🌱 Gold Green Tourism Award
For further information on our Green Tourism Business Scheme please see page 9.

318   To find out more, call 0845 22 55 121 or go to visitscotland.com.

Lochhouse Farm Retreat Centre	Lochhouse Farm Retreat Centre, Beattock, Moffat, Dumfriesshire, DG10 9SG	01683 300451	★★★	Self Catering	🦽
The Villa, Holm Park	2 Timsway, Staines, Middlesex, TW18 3JY	01784 740892	★★★★	Self Catering	

Montrose

21 King Street	10 Inchinnan Road, Renfrew, Renfrewshire, PA4 8ND	0141 569 5275	★★★	Self Catering	
Brawliemuir Farm	Brawliemuir Farm, Johnshaven, Montrose, Angus, DD10 0HY	01561 362453	★★★★	Self Catering	☆
North Flat	National Trust for Scotland, 28 Charlotte Square, Edinburgh EH2 4ET	0131 243 9335	★★	Self Catering	
South Flat	National Trust for Scotland, 28 Charlotte Square, Edinburgh EH2 4ET	0131 243 9335	★★	Self Catering	
Westerton Cottage	Westerton Cottage, Westerton & Rossie, Montrose, Angus, DD10 9TN	01674 820238	★★★	Self Catering	
Lilybank Cottage	The School House, Corgarff, Strathdon, Aberdeenshire, AB36 8YL	01975 651474	★★★	Self Catering	

By Montrose

The Green House, Ferryden	Crosslea, 12 Marchbank Rd, Bieldside, Aberdeen, AB15 9DJ	01224 864458	★★★	Self Catering	

Morar

Sandholm Cottages	Sandholm, Morar, Mallaig, Inverness-shire, PH40 4PA	01687 462592	★★★	Self Catering	

Morayshire

Millburn Cottage	Brickhouse, 7 Barnsley Road, Ackworth Pontefract, West Yorkshire, WF7 7BS	01977 612525	★★★★	Self Catering	

Morebattle

Caddy Cottage	The Firs, Oxnam Road, Jedburgh, Roxburghshire, TD8 0QL	01835 863250	★★★	Self Catering	

Moulin

The White House	1 Springhill, Eastington, Stonehouse, Gloucestershire, GL10 3AT	01453 823992	★★	Self Catering	
Old Post Office Cottage	Jetrigg, Cavelstone, Kinross, Kinross-shire, KY13 9JT	01577 863245	★★★	Self Catering	

Muir Of Ord

Benview	Daduse, Tower Brae North, Inverness IV2 5FE	07706 134891	★★★★	Self Catering	
Honeysuckle Cottage	16 Balvaird, Muir of Ord, Ross-shire, IV6 7RP	01463 871060	★★★	Self Catering	

Mull of Kintyre

Harvey's House	National Trust for Scotland, 28 Charlotte Square, Edinburgh EH2 4ET	0131 243 9335	★★★	Self Catering	
Hector's House	National Trust for Scotland, 28 Charlotte Square, Edinburgh EH2 4ET	0131 243 9335	★★★	Self Catering	

Mull-of-Galloway, Stranraer

Glen Auchie Cottage	East Muntloch Croft,Cairngaan Road, Drummore, Mull of Galloway, Stranraer, Dumfries and Galloway, DG9 9HN	01776 840264	★★★	Self Catering	

Musselburgh

45A Dalrymple Loan	45 Dalrymple Loan, Musselburgh, East Lothian, EH21 7DJ	0131 6658050	★★★	Self Catering	

🦽 Unassisted wheelchair access   🦽 Assisted wheelchair access   ☆ Access for visitors with mobility difficulties

🍂 Bronze Green Tourism Award   🍂🍂 Silver Green Tourism Award   🍂🍂🍂 Gold Green Tourism Award

For further information on our Green Tourism Business Scheme please see page 9.

Musselburgh Apartment	15 Champigny Court, Musselburgh, East Lothian, EH21 7HW	07730 410437	★★★	Self Catering	

Muthill

The Wee House At The Loaning	The Wee House at The Loaning, The Loaning, Peat Road, Muthill, Perthshire, PH5 2DR	01764 681383	★★★★	Self Catering	

Nairn

6 The Moorings	1 Findhorn Road, Kinloss, Forres, Moray, IV36 3TX	01309 691266	★★★	Self Catering	
Altonburn Cottage	Assich Steading, Cawdor, Nairn IV12 5XU	01667 493305	★★★★	Self Catering	
Ceolmara Garden Flat	Ceolmara Garden Flat, Links Place, Nairn, Nairnshire, IV12 4NH	01667 452495	★★★★	Self Catering	
Cottar House	Cottar House, 2 Manse Road, Nairn, Highland Region, IV12 4RN	01667 455137	★★★★	Self Catering	
Flora's Cottage	3 St James Walk, London EC1R 0AP	7877354564	★★★	Self Catering	
Hidden Glen Holidays	Laikenbuie Holidays, Grantown Road, Nairn IV12 5QN	01667 454630	★★ → ★★★★	Self Catering	♿
Inverwick Cottage,	Inverwick House, Albert Street, Nairn, Inverness-shire, IV12 4HE	01667 455050	★★★★	Self Catering	
Marina View	48 River Park, Nairn Highland, IV12 5SR	01667 454464	★★★	Self Catering	
Mill Lodge & Burnside Lodge	Raitloan, Geddes, Nairn, Inverness-shire, IV12 5SA	01667 454635	★★★★	Self Catering	♿
The Bungalow	Easter Dalziel Farm, Dalcross, Inverness, Highland, IV2 7JL	01667 462213	★★★★	Self Catering	
The Pine Tree House	12 Waverley Road, Nairn IV12 4RQ	01667 456930	★	Self Catering	

Nenthorn, Kelso

Burnbrae Holidays	Burnbrae Holidays, Burnbrae, Nenthorn, Kelso, Roxburghshire, TD5 7RY	01573 225570	★★★★	Self Catering	♿ 🍃🍃🍃

Nethy Bridge

Cluny-Mhore	Rhuarden, Seafield Avenue, Grantown-on-Spey, Morayshire, PH26 3JF	01479 872675	★★★★	Self Catering	♿ 🍃
Fern Cottage	Longfield, Aylesbury Road, Princes Risbrough, Bucks, MP27 0JW	7767846474	★★★	Self Catering	
Lorien	3 Albert Drive, Bearsden, East Dunbartonshire, G61 2NT		★★★	Self Catering	
Mountain Bear Lodge	C/O Great North Lodges, River House Stables2A Dalfaber Road, Aviemore Inverness-shire, PH22 1PY	01479 812266	★★★★★	Self Catering	
The Cottage & The Lodge	Inchdryne Croft, Tulloch Moor, Nethy Bridge, Inverness-shire, PH25 3EF	01479 831384	★★★★	Self Catering	🍃🍃
Aultmore	Aultmore, Nethybridge, Inverness-shire, PH25 3ED	01479 821 473	★★★★ → ★★★★★	Self Catering	
Balnagowan Mill & Woodlark	33 Argyle Grove, Dunblane, Perthshire, FK15 9DT	01786 824957	★★★★	Self Catering	
Birchfield Cottages	Birchfield, Nethybridge, Inverness-shire, PH25 3DD	01479 821613	★★★ → ★★★★	Self Catering	🍃🍃
Corner Cottage	6 Warriston Crescent, Edinburgh EH3 5LA	0131 2269180	★★★★	Self Catering	
Dell of Abernethy Cottages	Dell of Abernethy, Nethybridge, Inverness-shire, PH25 3DL	01479 821643	★★ → ★★★	Self Catering	♿
Fhuarain Forest Cottages	Badanfhuarain, Nethybridge, Inverness-shire, PH25 3ED	01479 821642	★★★★	Self Catering	♿ 🍃🍃
Gowanlea	5 Blinkbonny Grove West, Edinburgh EH4 3HJ	0131 539 5078	★★★	Self Catering	

To find out more, call 0845 22 55 121 or go to visitscotland.com.

Innis Bhroc	Creagan Gorm, Tulloch, Nethybridge PH25 3EF	01479 831711	★★★★	Self Catering	
Osprey House & Red Kite House	Funach View, Crossroads, Durris, Banchory, AB31 6BX	01330 844344	★★★★★	Self Catering 🕇	
Ryvoan Lodge	56 East Trinity Road, Edinburgh, Midlothian, EH5 3EN	0131 5520198	★★★★	Self Catering	🌳🌳
Woodbridge	Tombae, West Cullachie Farm, Boat of Garten, Inverness-shire, PH24 3BY	01479 821 226	★★★	Self Catering	

New Abbey, Dumfries

| Auchenfad Cottage | Auchenfad Farm, New Abbey, Dumfries DG2 8EG | 01387 850267 | ★★★ | Self Catering |

New Cumnock

Overcairn Farm Cottage	Overcairn Farm Cottage, Overcairn, New Cumnock, Ayrshire, KA18 4NW	01290 338273	★★★	Self Catering	
Annabells, Connel village	Hillside, Connel, Argyll, PA37 1PH	01631 710737	★★★★	Self Catering	
Ashmark Farm Cottage, Glen Afton	Ashmark Farm, Glen Afton, New Cumnock, Ayrshire, KA18 4PR	01290 338830	★★★★	Self Catering 🕇	

New Galloway

| Glenlee Holiday Houses | Glenlee Holiday Houses, New Galloway, Castle Douglas, Kirkcudbrightshire, DG7 3SF | 01644 430212 | ★★★ | Self Catering |

New Lanark

| The Water Houses | New Lanark Mill Hotel, New Lanark, Lanarkshire, ML11 9DB | 01555 667200 | ★★★★ | Self Catering | 🌳🌳🌳 |

Newburgh

| Abbotshill | Ardlinn, Mount Pleasant, Newburgh, Fife, KY14 6AA | 01337 840175 | ★★★★ | Self Catering |
| The Thatched Cottage | The Thatched Cottage, 167 Main Street, Newburgh, Cupar, Fife, KY14 6DY | 01337 842760 | ★★★ | Self Catering |

Newington

| Coachman's Gate | Dawe Properties Ltd, 3 Hillcrest Street, Milngavie, Glasgow, G62 8AH | 0141 956 6527 | ★★★ | Self Catering |

Newmachar

| Middle Hill | Woodstock, Highlands, Newmachar, Aberdeenshire, AB21 0QA | 01651 862241 | ★★★★ | Self Catering |
| The Newmachar Hotel | The Newmachar Hotel, Old Meldrum Road, Aberdeen, Aberdeenshire, AB21 0QD | 01651 862636 | ★★ | Self Catering |

Newmarket, Isle of Lewis

| Benside Cottage | 15 A Benside, Newmarket, Stornoway, Isle of Lewis, HS2 0DZ | 01851 700369 | ★★★★ | Self Catering |

Newport-on-Tay

Fernbrae House Apartment	Fernbrae House Apartments, 21-23 Wellgate Street, Newport on Tay, Fife, DD6 8HS	01382 542088	★★★	Self Catering
The Ice Barn	The Old Rectory, Everleigh, Marlborough, Wiltshire, SN8 3EY	01264 850 344	★★★★	Self Catering
The Haven and Little Haven	Balwill Cottage, Balfron Station, Glasgow G63 0QY	01360 850130	★★★★	Self Catering
Thorndene	Balmore, 3 West Road, Newport-On-Tay, Fife, DD6 8HH	01382 542274	★★★	Self Catering

                      ♿ Unassisted wheelchair access   ♿ Assisted wheelchair access   🕇 Access for visitors with mobility difficulties
                            🌳 Bronze Green Tourism Award   🌳🌳 Silver Green Tourism Award   🌳🌳🌳 Gold Green Tourism Award
                                  For further information on our Green Tourism Business Scheme please see page 9.

Newtomore

Netherwood	7 Rattray Way, Edinburgh EH10 5TU	0777 1981229	★★★	Self Catering

Newton Mearns

Maple Cottage	Star & Garter Estate, Newton Mearns, Glasgow, G77 6RS	01355 500214	★★★	Self Catering

Newton Stewart

3 Penkiln Mews	4 Mere Road, Weston, Crewe, Cheshire, CW2 5LN	01270 583892	★★	Self Catering
42 Laigh Isle	58 Sunderton Lane, Clanfield, Waterlooville, Hampshire, PO8 0NT	023 9259 3468	★★	Self Catering
5 Laigh Isle	Wigmore House, 10 Ballydevitt Road, Aghadowey, Coleraine, Londonderry, N Ireland, BT51 4DR	028 70868396	★★	Self Catering
Amisfield	Meikle Killantrae, Whauphill, Newton Stewart, Wigtownshire, DG8 9PW	01988 700284	★★★★	Self Catering
Barholm Croft	Barholm Croft, Creetown, Newton Stewart, Wigtownshire, DG8 7EN	01671 820440	★★	Self Catering
Brigton Farm	Brigton Farm, Bargrennan, Newton Stewart, Wigtownshire, DG8 6SR	01671 840278	★★★	Self Catering
Cairnhouse Farm	Cairnhouse Farm, Newton Stewart, Wigtownshire, DG8 9TH	01988 403217	★★★★	Self Catering
Clugston Farm	Clugston Farm, Kirkcowan, Newton Stewart, Wigtownshire, DG8 9BH	0167183 0338	★★ → ★★★	Self Catering
Conifers Leisure Park	Conifers Leisure Parks, Kirroughtree, Newton Stewart, Wigtownshire, DG8 6AN	01671 402107	★★★	Self Catering
Cree & Sienna Cottage	Penninghame House, Penninghame, Newton Stewart, Wigtownshire, DG8 6RD	01671 403341	★★★★	Self Catering
Dirnow Schoolhouse	Dirnow Schoolhouse, Kirkcowan, Newton Stewart, Wigtownshire, DG8 0ET	01671 830297	★★★★	Self Catering
Glencaird Farmhouse	2 Bunkers Hill, Wildwood Road, London NW11 6XA	0208 4557124	★★★★	Self Catering
Low Cordorcan Cottage	Low Cordorcan, Wood of Cree Reserve, Newton Stewart, Wigtownshire, DG8 6SP	01671 840311	★★★★	Self Catering
Myrtle Cottage	12 Deers Farm Close, Wisley, Woking, Surrey, GU23 6QX	01932 336767	★	Self Catering
Spittal Cottages	Spittal Cottages, Spittal Farm, Creetown, Newton Stewart, Wigtownshire, DG8 7DE	01671 820224	★★★	Self Catering
The Nether Barr Steading	The Nether Barr Steading, Nether Barr Farm, Newton Stewart, Wigtownshire, DG8 6AU	01671 404326	★★★	Self Catering
Tighe Na Rosan	62 Sutton Lane, Adlington, Chorley, Lancs, PR6 9SP	01257 474319	★★★	Self Catering

By Newton Stewart

Bridge & Heron Crofts	10 Monduff Road, Muchalls, Aberdeenshire, AB39 3XR	01569 731623	★★★★	Self Catering
Holmpark Cottages, Minnigaff	Holmpark Farm, Creebridge, Minnigaff, Newton Stewart, Wigtownshire, DG8 6NR	01671 402499	★★★★	Self Catering
Stable Cottage, Palnure	Cosy Cottages, Silverdale, The Stell, Kirkcudbrightshire, Dumfries and Galloway, DG6 4SA	01557 330578	★★★	Self Catering

Newtonmore

Biallid House	West Bradfield House, Bradfield, Devon EX15 2QY	07974 226862	★★★	Self Catering	
Blaragie Cottage	Blaragie, Laggan, Newtonmore, Inverness-shire, PH20 1AJ	01528 544229	★★★	Self Catering	⌂
Cluny Mains	6 Willian Way, Letchworth, Hertfordshire, SG6 2HG	01462 673410	★★★★	Self Catering	

♿ Unassisted wheelchair access   ♿ Assisted wheelchair access   ♁ Access for visitors with mobility difficulties
⌂ Bronze Green Tourism Award   ⌂⌂ Silver Green Tourism Award   ⌂⌂⌂ Gold Green Tourism Award
For further information on our Green Tourism Business Scheme please see page 9.

322   To find out more, call 0845 22 55 121 or go to visitscotland.com.

Crubenbeg Holiday Cottages	Crubenbeg Holiday Cottages, Newtonmore, Inverness-shire, PH20 1BE	01540 673 566	★★★★	Self Catering	🍃🍃🍃
Steading 5, Balvatin Cottages	5 Baneberry Path, East Kilbride, Glasgow, G74 4UZ	01355 260498	★★★	Self Catering	
Tigh Na Bruach & The Beehive	Tigh Na Bruach, Station Road, Newtonmore, Inverness-shire, PH20 1AR	01540 670191	★★★	Self Catering	
Treetops	Tree Tops Holidays, 130 Psalter Lane, Sheffield, South Yorkshire, S11 8YU	0114 2668626	★★★	Self Catering	
Woodlands	Woodlands, 16 King Malcolm Close, Edinburgh, Lothians, EH10 7JB	0131 445 2070	★★★	Self Catering	

Newtyle

| Kinpurnie | Kinpurnie Estate, North Street, Newtyle PH12 8TT | 01828 650500 | ★★★★ → ★★★★★ | Self Catering | 🚶 |

North Berwick

1 Church Road	129 High Street, North Berwick, East Lothian, EH39 4HM	01620 893204	★★	Self Catering	
11 Lorne Lane	The White House, 24 Dirleton Avenue, North Berwick, East Lothian, EH39 4BQ	01620 890555	★★★	Self Catering	
14 Cromwell Road	129 High Street, North Berwick, East Lothian, EH39 4HM	01620 893204	★★★★	Self Catering	
1A Market Place	8 Penrith Avenue, Giffnock, Glasgow, East Renfrewshire, G46 6LU	0141 620 0083	★★★★	Self Catering	
25G Melbourne Place	129 High Street, North Berwick, East Lothian, EH39 4HM	01620 893204	★★	Self Catering	
31 Westgate	129 High Street, North Berwick, East Lothian, EH39 4HM	01620 893204	★★★★	Self Catering	
4 Milsey Court	15 Dundas Avenue, North Berwick, East Lothian, EH39 4PS	01620 892 638	★★★	Self Catering	
45 Westgate	28 Goodwell Lea, Brancepath, Durham DH7 8EN	0191 3781097	★★★	Self Catering	
4E Market Place	2 Hillview Road, Edinburgh EH12 8QN	0131 334 5951	★	Self Catering	
5 Lorne Lane	6 Lorne Square, North Berwick, East Lothian, EH39 4HU	01620 893435	★★★	Self Catering	
8 West Bay Road	Blake Holt, Brownsea View Ave, Lillieput, Poole, Dorset, BH14 8LQ	01202 707894	★★★	Self Catering	
90 High Street	129 High Street, North Berwick, East Lothian, EH39 4HM	01620 893204	★★★	Self Catering	
Aaran Apartment	Leigh Developments, 6 Inveresk Gate, Inveresk, East Lothian, EH21 7TB	0131 665 4608	★★★★★	Self Catering	
Aviemore	Appletree Cottage, GARVALD, East Lothian, EH41 4LN	01620 830206	★★★	Self Catering	
Beach Haven	NB Flats, 129 High Street, North Berwick, East Lothian, EH39 4HB	07914 809152	★★★	Self Catering	
By The Sea	NB Flats, 129 High Street, North Berwick, East Lothian, EH39 4HB	01620 893204	★★★	Self Catering	
Cairnsmore - Top Flat	Cairnsmore, 14 Marine Parade, North Berwick, East Lothian, EH39 4LD	01620 894554	★★★	Self Catering	
Chelmsford	51 Braefoot Avenue, Milngavie, Glasgow G62 6JS	0141 5849608	★★★	Self Catering	
Cottage Garden	Grove Coach Lodge, London Road, Retford, Notts, DN22 7HY	01777 719107	★★★★	Self Catering	
Fishermens Hall	The Banks, Hopetoun, South Queensferry, West Lothian, EH30 9SL	0131 331 3878	★★★★	Self Catering	
Flat 2	165 Knighton Road, Leicester LE2 3TS	0116 2335557	★★	Self Catering	
Flat 3	129 High Street, North Berwick, East Lothian, EH39 4HM	01620 893204	★★★	Self Catering	

    ♿ Unassisted wheelchair access   ♿ Assisted wheelchair access   🚶 Access for visitors with mobility difficulties
🍃 Bronze Green Tourism Award   🍃🍃 Silver Green Tourism Award   🍃🍃🍃 Gold Green Tourism Award
For further information on our Green Tourism Business Scheme please see page 9.

Flat 3,	NB Flats, 129 High Street, North Berwick EH39 4HB	01620 893204	★★★★	Self Catering
Flat 6, Hyndford House	129 High Street, North Berwick, East Lothian, EH39 4HM	01620 893204	★★★	Self Catering
Glenconner Cottage	Crathorne House, Crathorne Yarm, North Yorkshire, TSL5 0AT	01642 700431	★★★	Self Catering
Glentruim Self-Catering Cottage	Glentruim, 53 Dirleton Avenue, North Berwick, East Lothian, EH39 4BL	01620 890064	★★★★	Self Catering
Ithaca House	12 Succoth Gardens, Edinburgh EH12 6BS	0131 337 3617	★★★	Self Catering
Kirkview	NB Flats, 129 High Streeet, North Berwick, East Lothian, EH39 4HB	01620 893204	★★★	Self Catering
M G Villa	90E High Street, North Berwick EH39 4HE	01620 894295	★★	Self Catering
Mews Cottage	Mews Cottage, 6 Quarry Court,Abbotsford Road, North Berwick, East Lothian, EH39 5DB	01620 892030	★★★★★	Self Catering
Nia Roo	13 Craigleith Hill Crescent, Edinburgh, Midlothian, EH4 2LA	0131 332 4320	★★★	Self Catering
No 8 Marine Parade	NB flats, 129 High Street, North Berwick, East Lothian, EH39 4HB	01620 893204	★★★★	Self Catering
No 8 Melbourne Place	NB Flats, 129 High Street, North Berwick, East Lothian, EH39 4HB	01620 893204	★★	Self Catering
North Berwick Golf Lodge	Lorimers House, 18 Fidra Road, North Berwick, East Lothian, EH39 4NG	01620 892457	★★★★★	Self Catering
Puffins	NB Flats, 129 High Street, North Berwick, East Lothian, EH39 4HB	01620 893204	★★★★	Self Catering
Scougall Farm Cottages	Scoughall Farm, North Berwick, East Lothian, EH39 5PP	01620 870210	★★	Self Catering
Seafield	NB Flats, 129 High Street, North Berwick, East Lothian, EH39 4HB	01620 893204	★★	Self Catering
Seaview	Cumberland Street Flat, 12a Cumberland Street, Edinburgh, Lothians, EH3 6SA	0131 5565445	★★★	Self Catering
Stewart Lodge	NB Flats, 129 High Street, North Berwick, East Lothian, EH39 4HB	01620 893204	★★★	Self Catering
The Hideaway	NB Flats, 129 High Street, North Berwick, East Lothian, EH39 4HB	01620 893204	★★	Self Catering
The House at the Beach	20 Camperdown Street, Broughty Ferry, Dundee DD5 3AB	01382 778928	★★★	Self Catering
The Neuk	Coast Properties, 38 Main Street, Gullane, East Lothian, EH39 4NU	01620 671966	★★★	Self Catering
The Retreat Cottage	The Retreat, 5 Nungate Road, North Berwick, East Lothian, EH39 4PD	01620 892429	★★★	Self Catering
Vale End	4 Upper Dean Terrace, Edinburgh, Lothians, EH4 1NU	0131 3321544	★★★★	Self Catering
West Fenton Court Cottages	West Fenton Court Cottages, West Fenton Farm, North Berwick, East Lothian, EH39 5AL	01620 842154(	★★★★	Self Catering
112 High Street	129 High Street, North Berwick, East Lothian, EH39 4HB	01620 893204	★★★	Self Catering
30 Royal Apartments	NB Flats, 129 High Street, North Berwick, East Lothian, EH39 4HB	01620 893204	★★★★	Self Catering

By North Berwick

Denis Duncan House, Dirleton	Eastgate House, Upper East Street, Sudbury, Suffolk, CO10 1UB	01787 37234	★★★★	Self Catering	♿

North Connel

An Cladach	Carr House, High Stittenham, Sheriff Hutton, York, YO60 7TW	01347 878418	★★★	Self Catering
Ardshellach	Frith Hill Farm, Great Missenden, Bucks., HP16 9QF	01494 866424	★★★★	Self Catering

♿ Unassisted wheelchair access   ♿ Assisted wheelchair access   ♿ Access for visitors with mobility difficulties
🄟 Bronze Green Tourism Award   🄟🄟 Silver Green Tourism Award   🄟🄟🄟 Gold Green Tourism Award
For further information on our Green Tourism Business Scheme please see page 9.

324   To find out more, call 0845 22 55 121 or go to visitscotland.com.

Staffa Annex	Staffa Annex, Achnacreebeag, North Connel, Argyll, PA37 1RD	01631 710681	★★★	Self Catering

North Kessock

Little Woodside	Rose Cottage, Kilmuir, North Kessock, Inverness-shire, IV1 3ZG	01463 731739	★★★★	Self Catering
Plover Cottage	Fernvilla, Halebank Road, Widnes, Cheshire, WA8 8NP	0151 425 2129	★★★	Self Catering

North Muir

Crawford Cottages	Crawford Cottages, Mid Road, Northmuir, Angus, DD8 4PJ	01575 572655	★★★★	Self Catering

North Queensferry

MacKenzies Roost	11 Park Lane, Aberdour Fife, KY3 0TN	01383 860271	★★★	Self Catering
Northcliff	1 Inverkeithing Road, Crossgates, Cowdenbeath, Fife, KY4 8AL	01383 510666	★★ → ★★★	Self Catering
Shoreland Studio	Shoreland Studio, Main Road, North Queensferry, Fife, KY11 1HA	01383 413126	★★★	Self Catering

North Tolsta

Slios Na Beinne	Slios Na Beinne, 3 Hill Street, North Tolsta, Isle of Lewis, HS2 0NG	01851 890259	★★★	Self Catering

North Uist

12 Balemore	Druimard, Balemore, North Uist, HS6 5EB	01876 510342	★★	Self Catering
Tigh Alasdair	285 Hill Park Drive, Glasgow G43 2SD	0141 585 3155	★★★	Self Catering
Tigh Na Boireach & Boreray	4 Clachan Sands, Lochmaddy, North Uist, Western Isles, HS6 5AY	01876 560403	★★★★★	Self Catering

Oban

12 High Street	Glenaros, Drummore Road, Oban Argyll, PA34 4JL	01631 565368	★★	Self Catering
15 Albany Apartments	Greencourt Guest House, Benvoullin Road, Oban, Argyll, PA34 5EF	01631 563987	★★★★	Self Catering
19 Albany Apts	Broomhill, Fereneze Road, By Neilston, Glasgow, G78 3AE	0141 8806707	★★★	Self Catering
23 Albany Apartments	Duriehill Self Catering, Duriehill, Connel, by Oban, Argyll, PA31 1PQ	01631 710569	★★★	Self Catering
27 Creag An Airm	4 Whitelees Drive, Lanark, South Lanarkshire, ML11 7SX	01555 660229	★★★	Self Catering
29 Albany Apartments	Glenburnie Hotel, Esplanade, Oban, Argyll, PA34 5AQ	01631 562089	★★★★	Self Catering
3 Oban Times Buildings	Driftwood, Polvinister Road, Oban, Argyll, PA34 5TN	01631 562815	★★★	Self Catering
Albany Apartments 3	Morven, Benvoullin Road, Oban, Argyll, PA34 5EF	01631 566909	★★★★	Self Catering
Anvil Edgemmont Annexe	Edgemont, Rockfield Road, Oban, Argyll, PA34 5DH	01631 569499	★★★	Self Catering
Ardara	2 R Services, Ardara, Clachan Seil, By Oban, Argyllshire, PA34 4TL	01852 300379	★★	Self Catering
Ardoran Marine Chalet	Ardoran Marine Ltd, Lerags, Oban, Argyll, PA34 4SE	01631 566123	★★★	Self Catering
Ardura Flat	Ardura, Duncraggan Road, Oban, Argyll, PA34 5DU	01631 562380	★★★	Self Catering
Baravullin Cottage	Duriehill Self Catering, Duriehill, Connel, by Oban, Argyll, PA31 1PQ	01631 710569	★★★	Self Catering

♿ Unassisted wheelchair access   ♿ Assisted wheelchair access   ♟ Access for visitors with mobility difficulties
🍃 Bronze Green Tourism Award   🍃🍃 Silver Green Tourism Award   🍃🍃🍃 Gold Green Tourism Award
For further information on our Green Tourism Business Scheme please see page 9.

Name	Address	Phone	Rating	Type	
Cawdor Terrace Apartment	48 Whitelea Road, Kilmacolm, Inverclyde PA13 4HH	day:0141 885	★★★★	Self Catering	
Cedars Chalet	Cedars Chalet, Connel Road, Oban, Argyll, PA34 5JG	01631 565829	★★	Self Catering	
Esplanade Court Apartments	Esplanade Court Apartments, Corran Esplanade, Oban, Argyll, PA34 5PW	01631 562067	★★★ → ★★★★	Self Catering	
Flats 2 & 6	Belvoir Cottage, Bells Drove, Welney, Wisbech PE14 9TG	01354 610435	★★★★	Self Catering	
Glen Cottage	Glen Cottage, Longsdale Road, Oban, Argyll, PA34 5JU	01631 563420	★★★	Self Catering	
Harbour View	Kerrydale, Creagbhan Village, Glengallan Road, Oban, Argyll, PA34 4GZ	01631 567271	★★	Self Catering	
Katie's Flat	Eileriaig, 17 Coe Gardens, Oban, Argyll, PA34 4JT	01631 562272	★★★	Self Catering	
Kings Arms Apartments	McDougalls of Oban Ltd, 32 Combie Street, Oban, Argyll, PA34 4HT	01631 562304	★★★	Self Catering	
Lismore House (Flat 3/6)	Kimberly Hotel, Dalriach Road, Oban, Argyll, PA34 5JE	01631 562041	★★★★	Self Catering	
Lochnagar, Ben Nevis	Innesdale, 4 Etive Gardens, Oban, Argyll, PA34 4JF	01631 564653	★★★	Self Catering	
Melfort Village	Melfort Village, Kilmelford, Oban, Argyll, PA34 4XD	01852 200257	★★★★	Self Catering	⌐⌐⌐
Rockmount Cottage	Rockmount Cottage, Glencruitten Road, Oban, Argyll, PA34 4PU	01631 564647	★★	Self Catering	
The Barn at Scammadale Farm	Scammadale Farm, Kilinver, By Oban, Argyll, PA34 4UU	01852 316282	★★★★	Self Catering	⚡
The Gallery Flat	12 Longcroft, Braithwaite, Keswick, Cumbria, CA12 5TE	01768 778518	★★★	Self Catering	
The Harbour	Stevenson Terrace Flats, Kinlochleven PH50 4RP	07814 051853	★★★	Self Catering	
Ulva Cottage	Ulva Villa, Soroba Road, Oban, Argyll, PA34 4JF	01631 563 042	★★★	Self Catering	

By Oban

Name	Address	Phone	Rating	Type	
No 1 & 2 Tramway Cottages, Easdale	42 Ellenabeich, Easdale, Oban, Argyll, PA34 4RQ	01852 300112	★★★★	Self Catering	
Bracken Cottage, Kilmore	Bracken Cottage, c/o Lochnell View Cottage, Kilmore, By Oban, Argyll, PA34 4QP	01631 770283	★★★★	Self Catering	
Clan Cottages, Kilmore	Clan Cottages, Dalnabreac, Kilmore, Oban, Argyll, PA34 4XU	01631 770372	★★★★	Self Catering	⌐⌐
Lagnakeil, Lerags	Lag-na-Keil Chalets, Lerags, By Oban, Argyll, PA34 4SE	01631 562746	★★★ → ★★★★	Self Catering	
The Cottage, Lerags	Kilbride Farm, Lerags, by Oban, Argyll, PA34 4SE	01631 562878	★★	Self Catering	
Blaran	21 Lindisfarne Road, Newcastle-upon-Tyne NE2 2HE	0191 281 1695	★★★★	Self Catering	
Brae House	Kilchurn, Killin, Perthshire, FK21 8TN	01567 820298	★★★	Self Catering	
Cologin Country Chalets	Cologin Farmhouse, Lerags Glen, by Oban, Argyll, PA34 4SE	01631 564501	★★★ → ★★★★	Self Catering	♿
Eleraig Highland Lodges	Eleraig Highland Lodges, Kilninver, by Oban, Argyll, PA34 4UX	01852 200225	★★	Self Catering	
Moorcroft	Moorcroft, North Connel, By Oban, Argyll, PA37 1QZ	01631 710403	★★★	Self Catering	
The Haven	Strathendrick, Kilbryde Crescent, Dunblane, Stirling, FK15 9BB	01786 825582	★★★★	Self Catering	
Tigh Grianach	Achnacree Bay, North Connel, by Oban, Argyll, PA37 1QZ	01631 710288	★★★ → ★★★★	Self Catering	⚡
Ardmaddy Castle Holiday Cottages, Ardmaddy	Castle Holiday Cottages, Ardmaddy Castle, by Oban, Argyll, PA34 4QY	01852 300353	★★★★	Self Catering	♿

♿ Unassisted wheelchair access   ♿ Assisted wheelchair access   ⚡ Access for visitors with mobility difficulties
⌐ Bronze Green Tourism Award   ⌐⌐ Silver Green Tourism Award   ⌐⌐⌐ Gold Green Tourism Award
For further information on our Green Tourism Business Scheme please see page 9.

To find out more, call 0845 22 55 121 or go to visitscotland.com.

By Ochiltree

Barlosh Court	Barlosh Court, Barlosh House, By ochiltree, Ayrshire, KA18 2QS	01290 700996	★★★★★	Self Catering	

Old Deer, Peterhead

Aonach Eagach	Aonach Eagach, Kirkgate, Old Deer, Peterhead, Aberdeenshire, AB42 5LJ	01771 624447	★★★	Self Catering	
4 Mount Pleasant Drive	4 Mount Pleasant Drive, Old Kirkpatrick, Dunbartonshire, G60 5HJ	01389 8706903	★★	Self Catering	

Onich

Creag Mhor Boathouse	Creag Mhor Boathouse, Onich, Fort William, Inverness-shire, PH33 6RY	01855 821319	★★★	Self Catering	
Langall Cottage	Langhall Cottages, 27 North Ballachulish, Onich, Fort William, PH33 6SA	01855 821534	★★★★	Self Catering	🍃🍃🍃
Inchree Chalets	The Inchree Centre, Inchree, Onich PH33 6SD	01855 821287	★★★	Self Catering	
Bunree Holiday Cottages	Janika, Bunree, Onich, Fort William, Inverness-shire, PH33 6GE	01855 821359	★★★	Self Catering	
South Ferry View	5 Tait Drive, Southbroomage, Larbert, FK5 3EU	01324 554455	★★★★	Self Catering	

Orkney

1 & 2 Netherbutton	Scarhven, Holm, Orkney KW17 2RZ	01856 781312	★★★★	Self Catering	
12 Scapa Court	Westbrae, 7 Grainbank Road, Kirkwall, St Ola, Orkney, KW15 1RD	01856 872517	★★★	Self Catering	
14 Buttquoy Park	New Voy, Toab, Orkney KW17 2QG	01856 861267	★★★	Self Catering	♿
Mill O' Cara	Cott O' Paplay, Holm, Orkney, KW17 2SD		★★★★	Self Catering	
New Lighthouse	New Lighthouse, Deerness, Orkney, KW17 2QH	01856 741326	★★★★	Self Catering	
Seaquoys	Cranfield, Cannigall Road, Kirkwall, Orkney, KW15 1SX	01856 871169	★★★★	Self Catering	
Snelsetter	Snelsetter Partnership, Snelsetter Farm, Longhope, Orkney, KW16 3PA	01856 701244	★★★★	Self Catering	
Corkaquina, Birsay	Upper Scapa, St Ola, Orkney, KW15 1SD	01856 874100	★★★★	Self Catering	
Forst, Birsay	Ness, Twatt, Birsay, Orkney, KW17 2LZ	01856 721323	★	Self Catering	
Langskaill Cottage, Birsay	Langskaill Cottage, Marwick, Birsay, Orkney, KW17 2ND	01856 721428	★★	Self Catering	
Loons Cottage, Birsay	Netherdale, Birsay, Orkney, KW17 2NA	011856 721386	★★★	Self Catering	
Mid-Comloquoy Cottage, Birsay	Mid Comloquoy, Marwick, Birsay, Orkney, KW17 2ND	01856 721218	★★	Self Catering	
Palace Cottage, Birsay	Kellyan, Birsay, Orkney Isles, KW17 2LX	01856 721418	★★★	Self Catering	
Poppy's Place, Birsay	Poppy's Place, Ourigaire, Burray, Orkney, KW17 2SS	01856 731349	★★★	Self Catering	
Skesquoy, Birsay	Orkney Self Catering, The Boat House, Finstown, Orkney, KW17 2EH	01856 761581	★★★	Self Catering	
Wattle House, Birsay	Wattle Farm, Birsay Orkney, KW17 2LS	01856 721206	★★★	Self Catering	
Braemill, Deerness	Staye, Deerness, Orkney, KW17 2QH	01856 741240	★★★	Self Catering	
Deersound Cottage, Deerness	Mossquoy, Deerness, Orkney, KW17 2QL	01856 741331	★★★★	Self Catering	♿

♿ Unassisted wheelchair access   ♿ Assisted wheelchair access   🚶 Access for visitors with mobility difficulties
🍃 Bronze Green Tourism Award   🍃🍃 Silver Green Tourism Award   🍃🍃🍃 Gold Green Tourism Award
For further information on our Green Tourism Business Scheme please see page 9.

Lochland Chalets, Dounby	Bigging, Dounby, Orkney, KW17 2HR	01856 771340	★★★ → ★★★★	Self Catering	♟
Mallard Cottage, Dounby	2 Meaford Avenue, Stone, Staffs, ST15 8LT	01785 812290	★★★★	Self Catering	
Norton Cottage, Dounby	Saither, Dounby Orkney, KW17 2HS	01856 771284	★★★★	Self Catering	
Nurses Cottage, Dounby	Nurses Cottage, Kelton, Dounby, Orkney, KW17 2JA	01856 771865	★★★	Self Catering	
Shady Neuk, Dounby	Inshallah, Dounby, Orkney, KW17 2HS	01856 771405	★★	Self Catering	
The Peedie Hoose, Dounby	The Peedie Hoose, New Vola, Dounby, Orkney, KW17 2JQ	01856 841724	★★★★	Self Catering	
The Old St Nicholas Manse, East Holm	Big House on the Bay, The Old St Nichloas Manse, East Holm, Orkney, KW17 2SD	01856 781758	★★	Self Catering	
Sties, Eday	69 Ormond Crescent, Hampton, Middlesex, TW12 2TQ	020 8941 5291	★★★	Self Catering	
Craigview, Evie	40 Holme Road, West Bridgford, Nottingham, England, NE2 5AA	01159 825014	★★★	Self Catering	
Eviedale Centre, Evie	Eviedale Centre, Evie, Orkney, KW17 2PJ	01856 751254	★★★	Self Catering	
Upper Quoys, Evie	Nigley, Evie, Orkney, KW17 2PH	01856 751 298	★★★	Self Catering	
Brekkan, By Evie	The Longhouse, Hundland, Swannay by Evie, Orkney, KW17 2LP	01856 721407	★★★	Self Catering	
Atlantis Lodges, Finstown	Orkney Self Catering, The Boat House, Finstown, Orkney, KW17 2EH	01856 761581	★★★★	Self Catering	
Auldkirk Apartments, Finstown	5 Clumly Avenue, Kirkwall, Orkney, KW15 1YU	01856 575498	★★★★	Self Catering	♿
Buan House, Finstown	Burness, Firth, Finstown, Orkney, KW17 2ET	1856761442	★★★★	Self Catering	
Orkney Self Catering, Finstown	Orkney Self Catering, The Boat House, Finstown, Orkney, KW17 2EH	01856 761581	★★★★	Self Catering	
Rowan Cottage, Finstown	C/O Rowandale, Finstown, Orkney, KW17 2EJ	01856 761551	★★★★	Self Catering	
Byre at Heddle, Firth	Orkneycrofts.com, Hall of Heddle, Firth, Orkney Isles, KW15 2JX	01856 761437	★★★★★	Self Catering	
Nabban House, Firth	Rosekandi, Eastquay Road, Kirkwall, Orkney, KW15 1LT	01856 873404	★★★★	Self Catering	
North Wald Cottage, Firth	North Wald Cottage, Burness Road, Firth, Orkney, KW17 2ET	01856 761599	★★★	Self Catering	
South Heddle, Firth	Virginia, Stenness, Orkney, KW16 3HG	01856 761282	★★★	Self Catering	
Breckan, Harray	Karona, Stoneyhill Road, Harray, Orkney, KW17 2JS	01856 771442	★★★	Self Catering	
Furso, Harray	Lynnbrekk, The Meadows, Kirkwall, Orkney, KW15 1DE	01856 875135	★★★	Self Catering	
New Breckan Flat, Harray	New Breckan, Harray, Orkney, KW17 2JR	01856 771233	★★★	Self Catering	
Rickla, Harray	Rickla, Grimeston Road, Harray, Orkney, KW17 2JT	01856 761575	★★★★★	Self Catering	
Yeldavale, Harray	Netherburn, Harray, Orkney, KW17 2LE	01856 771303	★★	Self Catering	
Howe Cottage, Harray	Brough Farm, South Ronaldsay, Orkney, KW17 2RW	01856 831324	★★★	Self Catering	
Commodore Chalets, Holm	Commodore Chalets, St Mary's, Holm, Orkney, KW17 2RU	01856 781319	★★★	Self Catering	
Craebreck House, Holm	Craebreck House, Holm, Orkney, KW17 2RX	01856 781220	★★★	Self Catering	
Crearhowe, Holm	The Old Post Office, Blebo Craigs, Cupar, Fife, KY15 5UF	01334 850310	★★★★	Self Catering	

♿ Unassisted wheelchair access   ♿ Assisted wheelchair access   ♟ Access for visitors with mobility difficulties
🅟 Bronze Green Tourism Award   🅟🅟 Silver Green Tourism Award   🅟🅟🅟 Gold Green Tourism Award
For further information on our Green Tourism Business Scheme please see page 9.

Erracht, Holm	Kynshera, Holm, Orkney KW17 2RZ	01856 781368	★★★★	Self Catering
Midhouse, Holm	Midhouse, Holm, Orkney, KW17 2RY	01856 781327	★★★	Self Catering
Park Cottage, Holm	Burnbank, Burray, Orkney, KW17 2SS	01856 731246	★★★	Self Catering
Burnhouse, Hoy	Melfea, Cannigall Road, St Ola, Orkney, KW15 1SX	01856 870058	★★★	Self Catering
New House, Hoy	21 Hillside Road, Stromness, Orkney, KW16 3HR	01856 850253	★★★★	Self Catering
Pools, Hoy	Salwick, Longhope, Hoy, Orkney, KW16 3NZ	01856 701211	★★★★	Self Catering
West Linksness, Hoy	90 Dundas Street, Stromness, Orkney, KW16 3DA	01856 851116	★★★	Self Catering
Cantick Head Lighthouse, Island of Hoy	Cantickhead Lighthouse, South Walls, Longhope, Orkney, KW16 3PQ	01856 701255	★★★★	Self Catering
10 & 12 Clay Loan, Kirkwall	10 Dundas Crescent, Kirkwall Orkney, KW15 1JQ	01856 875556	★★★	Self Catering
8 West Tankerness Lane, Kirkwall	Westness, Lynn Park, Kirkwall, Orkney, KW15 1SL	01856 878594	★★★★	Self Catering
Auld Smokehoose & Scapa Lodge, Kirkwall	Resolution, Tankerness, Orkney, KW17 2QT	01856 861385	★★★★	Self Catering
Broadsands Self-Catering, Kirkwall	2 Broadsands Road, Kirkwall Orkney, KW15 1BP	01856 876038	★★★★	Self Catering
Dornie, Kirkwall	Dornie Self Catering, Brigend, The Bu, Orphir, Orkney, KW17 2RD	01856 811375	★★★	Self Catering
Eastbank Cottages, Kirkwall	Bank House, East Road, Kirkwall, Orkney, KW151LX	01856 873561	★★★	Self Catering
Eastmount Apartment, Kirkwall	Eastmount, East Road, Kirkwall, Orkney, KW15 1LX	01856 874391	★★★	Self Catering
Grain Park Apartments, Kirkwall	Grain House, Junction Road, Kirkwall, Orkney, KW15 1AX	01856 874404	★★★★	Self Catering
High Park Lodges, Kirkwall	High Park Properties Orkney LTD, 1 Dundas Crescent, Kirkwall, Orkney, KW15 1JQ	01856 873541	★★★★	Self Catering
Holiday Apartment, Kirkwall	Haughead, St Ola, Orkney, KW15 1TR	01856 875265	★★ → ★★★	Self Catering
Inganess Lodge, Kirkwall	Arncorrie, Linklater Drive, Kirkwall, Orkney, KW15 1SP	01856 870646	★★★★	Self Catering
Kingston Self Catering, Kirkwall	Flat 1, 60 Victoria Street, Kirkwall, Orkney, KW15 1DN	01856 870984	Awaiting Grading	
Kjarstad, Kirkwall	Flat 8/3, 505 Stobcross Street, Glasgow, Renfrewshire, G3 8GJ	0141 222 2098	★★★★	Self Catering
Laingbrae Cottage, Kirkwall	Laingbrae Cottage, 6 Bignold Park Road, Kirkwall, Orkney, KW15 1PT	01856 877573	★★★★	Self Catering 🦽
Lynn View Self Catering, Kirkwall	Ben -Doll, Holm Road, Kirkwall, Orkney, KW15 1RX	0779 6498068	★★★★★	Self Catering
No. 5 Highbury Villas, Kirkwall	Oakleigh, Westray, Orkney, KW17 2DW	01857 677394	★★★	Self Catering
Pharos, Kirkwall	Eskadale, Finstown, Orkney, KW17 2ER	01856 761116	★★★	Self Catering
Scapa Flow Chalets, Kirkwall	Verona, Holm Branch Road, Kirkwall, Orkney, KW15 1RY	01856 874106	★★★★	Self Catering
Seaview and Berstane House, Kirkwall	Berstane House, Kirkwall, Orkney, KW15 1SZ	01856 876277	★★★	Self Catering
Soulisquoy Barn, Kirkwall	Carradale, Weyland Bay, Kirkwall, Orkney, KW15 1TD	01856 874725	★★★★	Self Catering
Sunrise Apartment, Kirkwall	Sunrise Apartment, 28A Albert Street, Kirkwall, Orkney, KW15 1HL	01856 873759	★★★	Self Catering
The Courtyard Apt. & Bay View Apt., Kirkwall	Craigiefield House, Craigiefield Road, St Ola, Orkney, KW15 1UJ	01856 878477	★★★ → ★★★★	Self Catering

    ♿ Unassisted wheelchair access   ♿ Assisted wheelchair access   ↯ Access for visitors with mobility difficulties

    ☯ Bronze Green Tourism Award   ☯☯ Silver Green Tourism Award   ☯☯☯ Gold Green Tourism Award

For further information on our Green Tourism Business Scheme please see page 9.

Crantit House, Kirkwall	Crantit House, St Ola, Kirkwall, Orkney, KW15 1RZ	01856 872899	★★★ → ★★★★	Self Catering
Grimbister Farm Cottage, Kirkwall	Grimbister Farm, By Kirkwall, Orkney, KW15 1TT	01856 761318	★★★	Self Catering
Dennishill, North Ronalsay	6 Burnside, Kirkwall, Orkney Isles, KW15 1TF	01856 874486	★★★	Self Catering
Bachylis Self Catering, Orphir	Bachylis Self-catering, Bachylis, Orphir, Orkney, KW16 3HD	01856 811363	★★★	Self Catering
Buxa Farm Chalets, Orphir	Westrow Lodge, Orphir, Orkney, KW17 2RD	01856 811360	★★★★	Self Catering ⫯
Cottage of Oback, Orphir	Evie Surgery, Greystones, Evie, Orkney, KW17 2PQ	01856 751283	★★★	Self Catering
Creel Cottage, Orphir	Creel Cottage, Breck, Orphir, Orkney, KW17 2RD	01856 811739	★★★	Self Catering
Cullya-Quoy, Orphir	The Bungalow, Orquil, St Ola, Orkney, KW15 1SA	01856 872265	★★★★	Self Catering ⫯
Findlays Cottage, Orphir	Chances House, Church Street, Clun, Shropshire, SY7 8JW	01588 640941	★★★	Self Catering
Gray's Inn, Orphir	Roadside Cottage, Smoogro, Orphir, Orkney, KW17 2RB	01856 811393	★★	Self Catering
Hall of Clestrain, Orphir	Hall of Clestrain, Orphir, Stromness, Orkney, KW16 3HB	01856 850365	★★★	Self Catering
Heatherlea Self Catering, Orphir	Heatherlea Self Catering, Houton, Orphir, Orkney, KW17 2RE	01856 811251	★★★	Self Catering
Lash, Orphir	Littleworth, Surrey Gardens, Effingham, Leatherhead, Surrey, KT24 5HF	01483 282461	★★	Self Catering
Little Bu, Orphir	Windbreck, Butchers Lane, Boughton, Northampton, NN2 8SL	01604 843275	★★★	Self Catering
Orkney Shore Cottage, Orphir	Old Point, Smoogro Road, Orphir, Orkney, KW17 2RB	01856 811772	★★★	Self Catering
Owlswood Lodge, Orphir	South Greenigoe, Orphir Orkney, KW17 2RA	01856 873596	★★★★	Self Catering ♿
Scapa Flow Lodges, Orphir	Scorralee, Scorraleee Road, Orphir, Orkney, KW17 2RF	01856 811268	★★★★	Self Catering
The Bothy, Orphir	Swanbister House, Swanbister, Orphir, Orkney, KW17 2RB	01856 811212	★★★	Self Catering
The Noust, Orphir	The Noust, Orphir, Orkney, KW17 2RB	01856 811348	★★★★	Self Catering
Summerdale Self Catering, Orphir	Summerdale, Orphir, Stromness, Orkney, KW16 3HD	01856 811285	★★★	Self Catering
Smoogro Estates Ltd, Rendall	Parkhill House, Princess Street, Durham, Co Durham, DH1 4RD	0191 3865555	★★★★	Self Catering
Widefirth Cottages, Rendall	The Riff Cottage, Rendall, Orkney KW17 2PB	01856 761028	★★★★	Self Catering ♿ 🍀🍀🍀
Banks, South Ronaldsay	Banks, Cleat, South Ronaldsay Orkney, KW17 2RW	01856 831605	★★★ → ★★★★	Self Catering
West Shaird House, South Ronaldsay	Hools, St Margaret's Hope, Orkney, KW17 2RH	01856 831265	★★★	Self Catering
Cauldhame, St Margarets Hope	Farewell Farm, St Margaret's Hope, Orkney, KW17 2TW	01856 831266	★★★★	Self Catering 🍀🍀
Garleton, St Margarets Hope	The Priory, Beccles Road, St Olaves, Great Yarmouth, Norfolk, NR31 9HE	01493 488609	★★★	Self Catering
Leith's, St Margarets Hope	45 Nursery Road, Bishops's Stortford, Herts, KW17 2SL	01279 505621	★★★	Self Catering
The Peedie House, grimness, St Margaret's	The Peedie House, Gerraquoy Organic Farm, Grimness, St Margaret's Hope, Orkney, KW17 2TH	01856 831240	★★★★	Self Catering 🍀🍀
10 Graham Place & 88 Victoria Street, Stromness	Lyness House, 8 Graham Place, Stromness, Orkney, KW16 3BY	01856 850581	★★ → ★★★	Self Catering
16 Graham Place, Stromness	51 John Street, Stromness, Orkney KW16 3AD	01856 850818	★★★	Self Catering

♿ Unassisted wheelchair access   ♿ Assisted wheelchair access   ⫯ Access for visitors with mobility difficulties
🍀 Bronze Green Tourism Award   🍀🍀 Silver Green Tourism Award   🍀🍀🍀 Gold Green Tourism Award
For further information on our Green Tourism Business Scheme please see page 9.

2 Victoria House, Stromness	Carnethy, Firth, Orkney, KW17 2ES	01856 761543	★★★	Self Catering
25 Southend, Stromness	15 Grieveship Terrace, Stromness, Orkney, KW16 3AY	01856 851314	★★	Self Catering
30 Hillside Road, Stromness	Hestigeo, Hillside Road, Stromness, Orkney, KW16 3HS	01856 850042	★★★	Self Catering
41 & 43 John Street, Stromness	25 John Street, Stromness, Orkney, KW16 3AD	01856 850469	★★★	Self Catering
52 Dundas Street & Marina Apts, Stromness	54 Dundas Street, Stromness, Orkney, KW16 3DA	01856 850255	★★★★	Self Catering
Braehead Farm, Stromness	Braehead Farm, Stromness, Orkney, KW16 3JH	01856 851313	★★★★	Self Catering
Camusbeag, Stromness	Bea House, Back Road, Stromness, Orkney, KW16 3AW	01856 851043	★★★	Self Catering
Garden Cottage, Stromness	Kierfiold House, Sandwick, Stromness, Orkney, KW16 3JE	01856 841583	★★★	Self Catering
Hamnavoe Apartments, Stromness	Hoygar, Innertown, Stromness, Orkney, KW16 3JR	01856 851202	★★★★	Self Catering
Harbourlee House, Stromness	Browns Self Catering Accommodation, Parklane House,45/47 Victoria Street, Stromness, Orkney, KW16	01856 850661	★★★	Self Catering
Howe Holiday Homes, Stromness	Howe Holiday Homes, Stromness, Orkney, KW16 3JU	01856 850302	★★★	Self Catering
Ingasquoy Lets, Stromness	Cott of Howe, Cariston, Stromness, Orkney, KW16 3JU	01856 851139	★★★	Self Catering
Lindisfarne, Stromness	Lindisfarne, Stromness, Orkney, KW16 3LL	01856 850828	★★★	Self Catering
No 37 Graham Place, Stromness	Kardale, Sandwick, Stromness, Orkney, KW16 3HY	01856 841733	★★★	Self Catering
Norheim, Stromness	Dounby House, Dounby Orkney, KW17 2HN	01856 771935	★★★	Self Catering 🖒
Old Hall Cottage, Stromness	Old Hall Cottage, Longhope, Stromness, Orkney, KW16 3PQ	01856 701213	★★★	Self Catering 🖒
Outbrecks Cottages, Stromness	Outbrecks Cottages, Stenness, Stromness, Orkney, KW16 3EY	01856 851223	★★★ → ★★★★	Self Catering
Peedie Cottage & Peedie Flat, Stromness	Stenigar, Ness Road, Stromness, Orkney, KW16 3DW	01856 850438	★★★	Self Catering
Pier House, Stromness	34 Dundas Street, Stromness, Orkney, KW16 3BZ	01856 850415	★★★★	Self Catering
Quildon Apartment 1, Quildon Apartment 2,	Toomal, Back Road, Stromness, Orkney, KW16 3JW	01856 850849	★★★★	Self Catering
Quoydale Cottage, Stromness	Quoydale, Stromness, Hoy, Orkney, KW16 3NJ	01856 791315	★★★	Self Catering
Springfield, Stromness	15 Garson Drive, Stromness, Orkney, KW16 3JG	01856 850776	★★★★	Self Catering
Stevand, Stromness	Stackaldbrae, Downie's Lane, Stromness, Orkney, KW16 3EP	01856 851305	★★★★	Self Catering
The Cottage, Stromness	Stairwaddie Croft, Stromness, Orkney, KW16 3HT	01856 851032	★★★	Self Catering
The Flat, Stromness	13 John Street, Stromness, Orkney, KW16 3AD	01856 851969	★★★	Self Catering
The Holms of Stromness, Stromness	The Holms of Stromness, Stromness, Orkney, KW16 3JU	01856 850889	★★	Self Catering
The Peedie Hoose, Stromness	Burnbrae, 21 Burnside, Kirkwall, Orkney, KW15 1TF	01856 876933	★★★★	Self Catering
Blinkbonny Holiday Homes, St Ola	Blinkbonny Holiday Homes, St Ola, Orkney, KW15 1SF	01856 870208	★★★ → ★★★★	Self Catering
Greenfield Cottage & Stables, St Ola	Greenfield, Carness Road, St Ola, Orkney, KW15 1TB	01856 873235	★★★ → ★★★★	Self Catering
Holm View, Papa Westray	Bayview, Papa Westray, Orkney, KW17 2BU	01857 644211	★★★★	Self Catering 🖒

🖒 Unassisted wheelchair access   🖒 Assisted wheelchair access   🖐 Access for visitors with mobility difficulties
⌂ Bronze Green Tourism Award   ⌂⌂ Silver Green Tourism Award   ⌂⌂⌂ Gold Green Tourism Award
For further information on our Green Tourism Business Scheme please see page 9.

Ben End, Stenness	Loch an Eilein, New Macher Aberdeenshire, AB21 0UQ	01651 862234	★★★★	Self Catering
Lochend, Stenness	Lochend, Stenness, Orkney Isles, KW16 3JY	01856 851003	★★★	Self Catering
Odin, Stenness	56b Riverside Drive, Aberedeen, Aberdeenshire, AB10 7LE	01224 593029	★★★★	Self Catering
Overbigging, Stenness	Kiruna, Stenness, Orkney KW16 3HQ	01856 761485	★★★★	Self Catering
Sebay Mill Holiday Apartments & Apartment 76,	76 Junction Road, Kirkwall, Orkney, KW15 1AR	01856 872281	★★★★ → ★★★★★	Self Catering ⚹ 🍃
Bis Geos Self Catering, Westray	4a Shore Street, Shandwick, Tain, Ross-shire, IV20 1UU	01857 667420	★★★ → ★★★★	Self Catering
Daisy Cottage, Westray	Daisy Cottage, Pierowall, Westray, Orkney, KW17 2DD	01857 677398	★★★	Self Catering
Daybreak, Westray	Hegra, Lynn Park, Kirkwall, Orkney, KW15 1SL	01856 876579	★★★	Self Catering
House, Westray	Sand o' Gill, Westray, Orkney, KW17 2DN	011857 677374	★★★	Self Catering
Orcadee, Westray	The Lodge, Shirlett, Nr Broseley, Shropshire, TF12 5BH	01952 727814	★★★	Self Catering
Skaill Cottage, Westray	Skaill Farm, Westray, Orkney, KW17 2DN	011857 677226	★★★	Self Catering

Orton
East St Mary's, Bruntlands Farmhouse	Estate Office, Orton, by Fochabers, Moray, IV32 7QE	01343 880240	★ → ★★★	Self Catering

Pairc, South Lochs
Gravir	89 Newmarket, Stornoway, Isle of Lewis, HS2 0EA	01851 704279	★★★	Self Catering

Paisley
Flat 4 Brough Hall	Dunvalanree, Port Righ, Carradale, Campbeltown, PA28 6SE	01538 431226	★★★	Self Catering

Palnure, Newton Stewart
Stable Cottage	Cosy Cottages, Silverdale, The Stell, Kirkcudbrightshire, Dumfries and Galloway, DG6 4SA	01557 330578	★★★	Self Catering

Paxton
The Lodge, Rose Cottage & Stable Cottage	Spital House, Paxton, Berwickshire, TD15 1TD	01289 386139	★★★ → ★★★★	Self Catering

Peebles
6 Northgate Vennel	Liddisdale, Millfield Road, Riding Mill, Northumberland, NE44 6DL	01434 682220	★★★★	Self Catering
7 Rosetta Road	6 Ash Grove, Norwich NR3 4BE	01603 301 702	★★★	Self Catering
Chapelhill Farm Cottages	Chapelhill Farm, Peebles, Peeblesshire, EH45 8PQ	01721 720188	★★ → ★★★	Self Catering
Coachman's Cottage	Kailzie Gardens, Peebles, Peeblesshire, EH45 9HT	01721 720007	★★	Self Catering
Courtyard Cottages	Winkston Farmhouse, Edinburgh Road, Peebles, Peeblesshire, EH45 8PH	01721 721264	★★★★	Self Catering ⚹
Kerfield Coach House	Kerfield Cottage, Innerleithen Road, Peebles, Peeblesshire, EH45 8BG	01721 720264	★★★★	Self Catering
Lyne Cottage	Lyne Farmhouse, Peebles EH45 8NR	01721 740255	★★★	Self Catering
No 2 Mains Farm Steading	Glentress Holidays, 7 St Leonard's Way, Cardrona, Peebles, Peeblesshire, EH45 9LE	07745 969833	★★★★	Self Catering

♿ Unassisted wheelchair access   ♿ Assisted wheelchair access   ⚹ Access for visitors with mobility difficulties
🍃 Bronze Green Tourism Award   🍃🍃 Silver Green Tourism Award   🍃🍃🍃 Gold Green Tourism Award
For further information on our Green Tourism Business Scheme please see page 9.

332   To find out more, call 0845 22 55 121 or go to visitscotland.com.

| No 57 Rosetta Road | The Old Post Office, Stobo Village Peebleshire, EH45 8NX | 07789 543703 | ★★★ | Self Catering | |

Pencaitland

| Wintonhill Farmhouse & Winton Cottage | Winton Trust, Winton House, Pencaitland, East Lothian, EH34 5AT | 01875 340222 | ★★★★ → ★★★★★ | Self Catering | ♟ |

Penicuik

| Eastside Farm Holiday Cottages | Eastside Steading, Eastside Farm, Penicuik, Midlothian, EH26 9LN | 01968 677842 | ★★★★ | Self Catering | |
| New House | Execulets, Cornbank House, 59 Carlops Road, Penicuik, Edinburgh, EH26 9HR | 01968 670136 | ★★★★ | Self Catering | |

By Penicuik

| Flotterstone Cottage, Milton Bridge | The Flotterstone Inn, A702 Biggar Road, Milton Bridge, Near Penicuik, Midlothian, EH26 0PP | 01968 673717 | ★★★ | Self Catering | |

Perth

12 Affric Avenue	132 Perth Road, Scone, Perth, Perthshire, PH2 6JL	01738 570079	★★★★	Self Catering	
Alexander Residence	Algo Business Centre, Glenearn Road, Perth, Perthshire, PH2 0NJ	01738 450455	★★★★★	Self Catering	
Inchtuthill Coachhouse	Inchtuthill, Spittalfield, Murthly, Perth, PH1 4LA	01738 710332	★★★	Self Catering	
Orchard Cottage	The Hirsel, Huntingtower, Perth, Perthshire, PH1 3JL	01738 620783	★★★★	Self Catering	♟
Perth Holiday Apartments	Perth Holiday Apartments, 17 Rose Terrace, Perth, Perth & Kinross, PH1 5HA	01738 587899	★★★★	Self Catering	
Summerfield View	Summerfield View, Summerfield, Rait Road, Balbeggie, Perth, Perthshire, PH2 7PP	01821 640760	★★★★	Self Catering	♟
Tower View Coach Houses	G S Brown Construction, The Nurseries, St Madoes, Perth, PH2 7NF	01738 446577	★★★★	Self Catering	♟
Stjohnsuk	Huntingtower House, Crieff Road, Perth, Perthshire, PH1 3JJ	01738 447933	★★★ → ★★★★	Self Catering	
Pear Tree	Easter Tarsappie Farmhouse, Rhynd Road, Perth, Perthshire, PH2 8QL	01738 621342	★★★	Self Catering	
The Coach House	Forteviot House, Forteviot, Perth, Perthshire, PH2 9BS	01764 684250	★★★★	Self Catering	

By Perth

| Buchanan's Bothy, Inchyra | Tayside, Inchyra Perthshire, PH2 7LT | 01738 860765 | ★★★★ | Self Catering | |

Perthshire

Fingask Cottages, Rait	Fingask Cottages, Fingask Castle, Rait, Perthshire, PH2 7SA	01821 670777	★★★	Self Catering	
Moulinalmond Cottage, Almondbank	Moulinalmond Cottage, Moulinalmond, Almondbank, Perth, PH1 3NW	01738 583206	★★★	Self Catering	PP
22 Galvelmore Street	Southcroft, Connaught Tce, Crieff, Perthshire, PH7 3DJ	07718 737128	★★★★	Self Catering	
2B South Inch Court	46 Muirs, Kinross, Perth & Kinross KY13 8AU	01577 863367	★★★★	Self Catering	
64 Commissioner Street	44 Kettilstoun Mains, Linlithgow, West Liothian, EH49 6SL	01506 671549	★★★	Self Catering	
6B Cathedral Street & N & S Mill (Meikle Trochry)	Meikle Trochry, By Dunkeld, Perthshire, PH8 0DY	01350 723200	★★★★	Self Catering	
No 38 Riverside Park	334 Hilldale Drive, Ann Arbor, Michigan 48105, United States of America48105	+734 6625831	★★★	Self Catering	
Raith Farmhouse	Raith Farmhouse, Crieff, Perthshire, PH7 3RJ	01764 683468	★★★★	Self Catering	

Awards correct as of mid August 2008

| The Doocot | St Andrews Cottage, Dunning, Perthshire, PH2 0RH | 01764 684358 | ★★★★ | Self Catering |

Peterculter

| Gordon House Self Catering Apartment | East Court, 47 North Deeside Road, Peterculter, Aberdeen AB14 0QL | 01224 732284 | ★★★★ | Self Catering |

Peterhead

| Berryhill Cottage | Berryhill House, Longside Road, Peterhead, Aberdeenshire, AB42 3JY | 01779 472225 | ★★★ | Self Catering |

Pirnmill, Isle of Arran

Sealladh Na Mara	22 Hagbourne Road, Didcot, Oxon, OX11 8DR	01235 511532	★★	Self Catering
The Back House	Bayview House, Pirnmill, Isle of Arran, KA27 8HP	01770 850230	★★★	Self Catering
The Wee Rig	The Learig, Pirnmill Isle of Arran, KA27 8HP	01770 850228	★★★	Self Catering
Willow Cottage	16 Merrylee Road, Glasgow G43 2SH	0141 637 2945	★★★	Self Catering

Pitlochry

1A Robertson Crescent	12 Robertson Crescent, Pitlochry, Perthshire, PH16 5HD	01796 473353	★★★★	Self Catering
3B Robertson Crescent	3 Knockard Avenue, Pitlochry, Perthshire, PH16 5JE	01796 472157	★★★	Self Catering
An Treasaite	Macdonalds Restaurant & Guest House, 140 Atholl Road, Pitlochry, Perthshire, PH16 5AG	01796 472170	★★★	Self Catering
Ardenlea & The Retreat	Clunebeg Farm, By Pitlochry, Perthshire, PH16 5LS	01796 472758	★★★ → ★★★★	Self Catering
Ardvane	Ardvane, 8 Lower Oakfield, Pitlochry, Perthshire, PH16 5DS	01796 472683	★★★★	Self Catering
Atholl Palace Holiday Accommodation	Atholl Palace Holiday Accommodation, Atholl Palace Hotel, Pitlochry, Perthshire, PH16 5LY	01796 472400	★★★ → ★★★★	Self Catering
Atholl Villa	Atholl Villa Guest House, 29/31 Atholl Road, Pitlochry, Perthshire, PH16 5BX	01796 473820	★★★	Self Catering
Atom Crow Cottage	25 Eliot Place, Blackkheath, London SE3 0QL	01796 473444	★★★	Self Catering 🚶
Blithe Nook	336 Clepington Road, Dundee, Angus, DD3 8RZ	01382 826680	★★★★	Self Catering
Carie	Carie, Rannoch, Pitlochry, Perthshire, PH17 2QJ	01882 632341	★★★★★	Self Catering
Cnoc Aluinn	55 Bailielands, Linlithgow EH49 7SX	01506 848104	★★★	Self Catering
Convalloch Lodge	Atholl Estates, Estate Offices, Blair Atholl, Perthshire, PH18 5TH	01796 481355	★★★	Self Catering
Corrie Beag Self Catering	Corrie Beag Self Catering, Gayfield, Perth Road, Pitlochry, Perthshire, PH16 5LY	01796 473003	★★★	Self Catering
Craigard	Craigard, Strathview Terrace, Pitlochry, Perthshire, PH16 5AT	01796 473695	★★ → ★★★	Self Catering
Craigroyston Lodge	Craigroyston Guest House, 2 Lower Oakfield, Pitlochry, Perthshire, PH16 5HQ	01796 472053	★★★	Self Catering
Dail Na Coille & Courtyard Studio	21 West Moulin Road, Pitlochry, Perthshire, PH16 5EA	01796 473449	★★★	Self Catering
Dall Estate	Dall House, Rannoch, Pitlochry, Perthshire, PH17 2QQ	01882 632397	★★★	Self Catering
Dalshian Chalets	Dalshian Chalets, Old Perth Road, Pitlochry, Perthshire, PH16 5TD	01796 473080	★★★★	Self Catering ♿
Dawn Cottage	11 Mt. Charles Crescent, Alloway, Ayr, Ayrshire, KA7 4NY	01292 443979	★★★★	Self Catering

♿ Unassisted wheelchair access   ♿ Assisted wheelchair access   🚶 Access for visitors with mobility difficulties
🏵 Bronze Green Tourism Award   🏵🏵 Silver Green Tourism Award   🏵🏵🏵 Gold Green Tourism Award
For further information on our Green Tourism Business Scheme please see page 9.

334   To find out more, call 0845 22 55 121 or go to visitscotland.com.

Elnagar Cottage	Elnagar Cottage, 2 Knockard Road, Pitlochry, Perthshire, PH16 5HJ	01796 472871	★★★	Self Catering
Esk Cottage	Jandaia, Lettoch Terrace, Pitlochry, Perthshire, PH16 5BA	01796 472322	★★★	Self Catering
Flat 12 Dean Court	PAUL BABBAR (business), 49 Seaford Close, Ruislip, Middlesex, HA4 7HN	1895676519	★★★	Self Catering
Ivy Cottage	Carra Beag Guest House, 16 Toberargan Road, Pitlochry, Perthshire, PH16 5HG	1796472835	★★★	Self Catering
Ivy Cottage	112 Braid Road, Edinburgh, Midlothian, EH10 6AS	0131 4477494	★★★★	Self Catering
Kinnaird Woodland Lodges	Kinnaird House, Kirkmichael Road, Pitlochry, Perthshire, PH16 5JL	01796 472843	★★★★	Self Catering
Lassintullich Lodge	Lassintullich Lodge, Kinloch Rannoch, Pitlochry, Perthshire, PH16 5QE	01882 632330	★★★★	Self Catering
Markova	Lavalette, Manse Road, Moulin, Pitlochry, Perthshire, PH16 5EP	01796 472364	★★★	Self Catering
No. 7 Dean Court	Tomnabrachd, Pitlochry, Perthshire, PH16 5JT	01796 482278	★★★	Self Catering
Oak Cottage	Afton Bank, Cuilc Brae, Pitlochry PH16 5QS	01796 472046	★★★★	Self Catering
The Coach House (Almond Lee)	Almond Lee, East Moulin Road, Pitlochry, Perthshire, PH16 5HU	01796 474048	★★★	Self Catering
Tummel Valley Holiday Park	Parkdean Holidays plc, 2nd floor, One Gosforth Park Way, Gosforth Bus Park, Newcastle Upon Tyne, Tyne & Wear,	0191 2560710	★★★★	Self Catering
Woodside	71 Bay Road, Wormit, Newport on Tay, Fife, DD6 8LX	01382 541024	★★★★	Self Catering
4 Viewbank Gardens	Westendstr 25, D-63329 Egelsbach, Germany	0049 6103 432	★★★	Self Catering

By Pitlochry

10 Braeside Road	Edintian Farm, Pitlochry, Perthshire, PH16 5RJ	01796 473277	★★★	Self Catering
River Cottage	River Cotttage, Enochdhu, Perthshire, PH10 7PF	01250 881377	★★★	Self Catering
Stable Cottage	The Grieve's house, Moulinarn, Pitlochry, Perthshire, PH8 0ET	01796 482770	★★★	Self Catering

Pittenweem

2 The Gyles	The Clachan, 12 East Shore, Pittenweem, Fife, KY10 2NH	01333 310695	★★★★	Self Catering
8 and 9 East Shore	Harbourside Holidays, 30 Pickford Crescent, Anstruther, Fife, KY10 3AL	01333 310421	★★★★	Self Catering
Abermharra	54 Hunter Grove, Bathgate EH48 1NW	07736 871769	★★★	Self Catering
East Haven	Glenlusset, 21 Redwood Crescent, Bishopton, Renfrewshire, PA7 5DJ	01505 862398	★★★	Self Catering
Gyles House	54A St Annes Crescent, Lewes, East Sussex, BN7 1SD	01273 473484	★★★	Self Catering
Kilheugh Cottage	4 Meadowbank Avenue, Strathaven, South Lanarkshire, ML10 6JS	01357 520463	★★	Self Catering
Puffin's Neuk	Puffins Neuk, 582 Lanark Road West, Balerno, Edinburgh, EH14 7BN	0131 451 5888	★★★	Self Catering
The Coach House	The Manse, 2 Milton Place, Pittenweem, Fife, KY10 2LR	01333 311255	★★★★	Self Catering
Tigh Na Mara	Abbey Lodge, 1 Abbey Wall Road, Pittenweem, Fife, KY10 2NB	01333 310307	★★★	Self Catering
Spindle Cottage	C/O 18 Cecil Avenue, Queens Park, Bournemouth, Dorset, BH8 9EH	01202 257914	★★★★★	Self Catering

♿ Unassisted wheelchair access   ♿ Assisted wheelchair access   ⚷ Access for visitors with mobility difficulties
⍟ Bronze Green Tourism Award   ⍟⍟ Silver Green Tourism Award   ⍟⍟⍟ Gold Green Tourism Award
For further information on our Green Tourism Business Scheme please see page 9.

Awards correct as of mid August 2008

335

Plockton

30a Harbour Street	24 North Street, Sandwick, Isle of Lewis, HS2 0AD	01851 702085	★★	Self Catering
7 & 19 Harbour Street	43A Castle Street, Dumfries, Dumfries & Galloway, DG1 1DU	01387 269762	★★ → ★★★★	Self Catering
Plockton Cottages	Plockton Cottages, Frithard Road, Plockton, Ross-shire, IV52 8TQ	1599544255	★★★	Self Catering

Point

Aite Beathag	Garnieside, Station Road, Buchlyvie, Stirlingshire, FK8 3NE	01360 850766	★★★★	Self Catering
Hebridean Cottages	Braighe House, 20 Braighe Road, Stornoway, Isle of Lewis, HS2 0BQ	01851 705287	★★★★	Self Catering

Poolewe

Crofter's Cottages	Torwood Croft, Poolewe, Ross-shire, IV22 2JY	01445 781268	★★	Self Catering
Innes Maree Bungalows	Innes Maree Bungalows, Poolewe, Ross-shire, IV22 2JU	01445 781454	★★★	Self Catering
The Narrows	14 Croft, Poolewe, Ross-shire, IV22 2JY	01445 781231	★★★★	Self Catering

Port Appin

Bothan Darach	78 Gower Street, Glasgow G41 5PU	0141 4270814	★★★★	Self Catering

Port Askaig, Isle of Islay

Persabus Farm Cottage & Mill House	Persabus Farm Cottage, Persabus Farm, Port Askaig, Isle of Islay, Argyll, PA46 7RB	01496 840243	★★★ → ★★★★	Self Catering

Port Charlotte, Isle of Islay

9 Shore Street	47 Drumlin Drive, Milngavie, Glasgow G62 6NF	0141 9565743	★★★★	Self Catering
Cala Seimh	Strada Guardia 64, 10040 Cumiana, Torino ITALY	7508887779	★★★	Self Catering
Cala Sith	Dunollie, Bruach Dubh, Port Charlotte, Isle of Islay, PA48 7TY	01496 850159	★★★	Self Catering
Kilchiaran Cottage	Kilchiaran Cottage, Port Charlotte, Isle of Islay, Argyll, PA48 7UB	01496 850248	Awaiting Grading	
Octomore & Distillery Cottage	Octomore Farm, Port Charlotte, Isle of Islay, PA48 7UD	01496 850235	★★★ → ★★★★	Self Catering
Saddlers Brae	80 Douglas Park Crescent, Bearsden, Glasgow G61 3DN	0141 943 1858	★★★★	Self Catering
Tigh Beag	The Old Granary, Dallicott Farm, Bridgenorth, Shropshire, WV15 5PL	01746 716350	★★★	Self Catering
Lorgba Holiday Cottages	Lorgba Holiday Cottages, Port Charlotte, Isle of Islay, Argyll, PA48 7UD	01496 850208	★★★★	Self Catering
Saligo, Kilchoman and Ardnave	Port Charlotte Homes Ltd, 27 Southview Drive, Bearsden, Glasgow, G61 4HQ	0141 9432529	★★★★	Self Catering
Sgioba Cottage	Sgioba Cottage, Port Charlotte, Isle of Islay, PA48 7UD	011496 850334	★★★	Self Catering

Port Ellon, Isle of Islay

Ballivicar Farm	Ballivicar Farm, Port Ellen, Isle of Islay, Argyll, PA42 7AW	01496 302251	★★	Self Catering
Laggan View	Linnhe, Eastmill Farm, Abbey Road, Auchterarder, Perthshire, PH3 1DN	01764 663316	★★★	Self Catering 🧍
Lili-Nan-Gleann	15 Secaurin Ave, Stonehouse, Larkhall, Lanarkshire, ML9 3NZ	01698 791553	★★★	Self Catering

⅃ Unassisted wheelchair access　 ⅃⅃ Assisted wheelchair access　 🧍 Access for visitors with mobility difficulties
🄿 Bronze Green Tourism Award　 🄿🄿 Silver Green Tourism Award　 🄿🄿🄿 Gold Green Tourism Award
For further information on our Green Tourism Business Scheme please see page 9.

Machrie Hotel	The Machrie Hotel, Port Ellen, Isle of Islay, PA42 7AN	01496 302310	★ → ★★	Self Catering
Middle Cracabus Cottage	C/O Suzy Smith, Middle Cracabus, Port Ellen, Argyll, PA42 7AX	0031 541 5187	★★	Self Catering
Ardtalla Farmhouse	6 Ardview, Port Ellen, Isle of Islay, PA42 7BP	01496 302430	★★ → ★★★★★	Self Catering

Port Logan, Stranraer

Dundrum Cottage	Kirkbride Farm, Port Logan, Stranraer, Wigtownshire, DG9 9NP	01776 840260	★★★★★	Self Catering

Port of Menteith

Cardross Holiday Homes	Cardross Holiday Homes, Cardross House, Port of Menteith, Perthshire, FK8 3JY	01877 385223	★★★	Self Catering
Glenny Cottages	Nether Glenny, Port of Menteith, Kippen, Stirlingshire, FK8 3RD	01877 385229	★★★	Self Catering
Lochend Chalets	Lochend Chalets, Port of Menteith, Stirlingshire, FK8 3JZ	01877 385268	★★★ → ★★★★	Self Catering	🍃

Port of Ness, Isle of Lewis

Bayview House	Scott Cottage, Britwell Salome, Watlington, Oxon, OX49 5LG	01491 612559	★★★	Self Catering
Ceol-Na-Mara	9B Port of Ness Isle of Lewis, HS2 0XA	01851 810429	★★★★	Self Catering

By Portpatrick

Morroch Bay Beach Cottages	Hilltop House, Glossop, Derbyshire SK13 7QJ	07887 868889	★★★ → ★★★★	Self Catering

Port Righ

Port Righ Cottage	Dunvalanree, Port Righ, Carradale, Campbeltown, Argyll, PA28 6SE	01583 431226	★★★	Self Catering

Port William

41 Main Street	184 Spring Grove Road, Isleworth, Middlesex TW7 4BG	0208 560 6820	★	Self Catering
Garheugh Cottages	Sweethaws Farm, Crowborough, East Sussex, TN6 3SS	01892 655045	★★★	Self Catering
High Killantrae Cottage	17 Dingle Terrace, Park Bridge, Ashton-U- Lyne OL6 8AH	07968 032741	★★★	Self Catering
West Barr Cottage	West Barr Holiday Park, Port William DG8 9QS		★★★	Self Catering

Port-Ellen

Coillabus Cottage	35 Madeira Street, Edinburgh, Midlotian, EH6 4AJ	0131 553 1911	★★★	Self Catering	🍃

Portknockie

Lismore	Prospect House, Hayton, Aspatria, Wigton, Cumbria, CA5 2PD	016973 20481	★★★	Self Catering
Scott Holiday Homes	Scott Holiday Homes, 29 Viewfield Avenue, Aberdeen, Aberdeenshire, AB15 7XJ	01224 323218	★★★	Self Catering	♀

Portmahomack

Dolphin View Holiday Properties	Sandbank Cottage, Portmahomack, Ross-shire, IV20 1YH	01862 871576	★★★★	Self Catering
Killearn Cottage	Po Box 144228, Spokane USA, WA99214	15098925895	★★★	Self Catering
Mo Dhachaidh	5 Latch Gardens, Brechin, Angus DD9 6LN	01356 623543	★★★★	Self Catering

👟 Unassisted wheelchair access   👟 Assisted wheelchair access   ♀ Access for visitors with mobility difficulties
🍃 Bronze Green Tourism Award   🍃🍃 Silver Green Tourism Award   🍃🍃🍃 Gold Green Tourism Award
For further information on our Green Tourism Business Scheme please see page 9.

Awards correct as of mid August 2008

337

By Portmahomack

No 3 Tarrel Farm Cottages	41 Hillside Gardens, Barnet, Herts, EN5 2NQ	020 8440 2826	★★★	Self Catering

Portnahaven, Isle of Islay

Arichalloch	Kelsay Farm, Portnahaven, Islay, Argyll, PA47 7SZ	01496 860274	★★★★	Self Catering
Cladville Dairy	Cladville, Portnahaven, Isle of Islay, PA47 7SZ	01496 860243	★★★★	Self Catering

Portpatrick

No 3D Hill Street	19 Glenfield Gardens, Paisley, Renfrewshire, PA2 8BF	0141 5809113	★★★	Self Catering
Portpatrick Holiday	Port Patrick Holiday, 47 Main Street, Portpatrick, Dumfries & Galloway, DG9 8JW	01776 810555	★★★★	Self Catering
Port-side Cottage	9 Ballyhamage, Doagh, Ballyclare, Co Antrim, Northern Ireland, BT39 0PZ	02893 341733	★★	Self Catering
Sandeel House	3 Saxon Road, Middle Wallop, Stockbridge, Hants, SO20 8GG	01473 829419	★★★	Self Catering
The Knowe	Balbeg House, Straiton, Maybole, Ayrshire, KA19 7NN	01655 770343	★★★★	Self Catering
The Port House	Seabank House, 65 Sheuchan Street, Stranraer, Galloway, DG9 0EE	01776 704127	★★★★	Self Catering
Dunskey Estate Cottages	Dunskey Estate Cottages, Dunskey, Portpatrick,Stranraer, Wigtownshire, DG9 8TJ	01776 810211	★★	Self Catering

Portree

1 Grealin	Lilacs, High Street, Coddenham, Ipswich, Suffolk, IP6 9PN	01449 760428	★★★★	Self Catering	
Aird View	Roskhill Barn, Roskhill, By Dunvegan, Isle of Skye, IV55 8ZD	7899660200	★★★	Self Catering	
Ard Dearg & Summerhouse	Ard Dearg, Budhmor, Portree, Isle of Skye, IV51 9DJ	01478 612749	★★★	Self Catering	
Brescalan Cottage	3 Borve, Portree Isle of Skye, IV51 9PE	01470 532425	★★★	Self Catering	&#9855;
Brook Cottage	Brook Cottage, Viewfield Road, Portree, Isle of Skye, IV51 9EU	01478 612980	★★★★	Self Catering	
Creagalain Cottage	The Cottage, 24 Borve, Portree, Isle of Skye, IV51 9PE	01470 532391	★★★	Self Catering	
Cruachan View	5 Ardroil, Uig, Isle of Lewis, Western Isles, HS2 9EU	01851 672255	★★★	Self Catering	
Dalrigh	48 Carbeth Road, Milngavie, Glasgow, East Dunbartonshire, G62 7AX	0141 9565056	★★★★	Self Catering	
Fisherfield Self Catering	Fisherfield Self Catering, Viewfield Road, Portree, Isle of Skye, IV51 9EU	01478 612696	★★★★★	Self Catering	
Flat 1, Bayfield House	29 Queensberry Avenue, Bearsden, Glasgow G61 3LP	01419 426531	★★★★	Self Catering	
Gleniffer House	Cedar Mount, 5 Waterend, Brompton, Northallerton, North Yorkshire, DL6 2RN	01478 612048	★★★★	Self Catering	
Harbour View	3 Tokavaig, Teangue, Sleat, Isle of Skye, IV44 8QL	01471 855253	★★★	Self Catering	
Hosta	Kersivay, Viewfield Road, Portree, Isle of Skye, IV51 9EU	01478 611061	★★★	Self Catering	
Loch Snizort View	3 Dalrymple Crescent, Musselburgh, Midlothian, EH21 6DT	0131 653 2635	★★★	Self Catering	
Number 6	Maligan, Achachork, Portree, Isle of Skye, IV51 9HT	01478 613167	★★★	Self Catering	♿ 𝓟𝓟
Park Cottage	136 Culduthel Park, Inverness IV2 4RZ	01463 221526	★★★	Self Catering	

♿ Unassisted wheelchair access   ♿ Assisted wheelchair access   ♂ Access for visitors with mobility difficulties
𝓟 Bronze Green Tourism Award   𝓟𝓟 Silver Green Tourism Award   𝓟𝓟𝓟 Gold Green Tourism Award
For further information on our Green Tourism Business Scheme please see page 9.

To find out more, call 0845 22 55 121 or go to visitscotland.com.

Portree Bay Cottage	Fuaran, Viewfield Road, Portree, Isle Of Skye, IV51 9ES	07917 628982	★★★	Self Catering
Portree Garden Cottages	1 Portree Garden Cottage, Home Farm Road, Portree, Isle of Skye, Inverness-shire, IV51 9LX	01478 613713	★★★	Self Catering
Seafield House	2 Fisherfield, Portree, Isle of Skye, IV51 9EU	01478 612269	★★★★	Self Catering
Tarven Cottage	Tarven Cottage, Staffin Road, Portree, Isle of Skye, IV51 9HS	01478 612679	★★★★	Self Catering
Teeny's Cottage	Teeny's Cottage, Fasgadh, Nr Edinbane, Portree, Isle of Skye, IV51 9PX	01470 582777	★★★★	Self Catering
The Cedar	233 Stainbeck Lane, Leeds, West Yorkshire, LS7 2PS	0113 2781638	★★★★	Self Catering
The Cottage	Viewfield House Hotel, Portree, Isle of Skye, IV51 9EU	01478 612217	★★★	Self Catering

By Portree

6 Knott	19 Warnborough Road, Oxford OX2 6JA	7779422497	★★★★	Self Catering		
Aite Taimh	19 Chesterfield Avenue, Glasgow G12 0BN	0141 3392676	★★★★	Self Catering		
Bayview Croft	Bracadale House, Albert Street, Nairn IV12 4HF	01667 452547	★★★★	Self Catering		
Dunsgiath	1 Quay Street, Portree, Isle of Skye, IV51 9HX	7720051212	★★★★	Serviced Apartments		
Edinbane Self Catering	Nuig House, 3 Edinbane, Portree, Isle of Skye, IV51 9PR	01470 582221	★★★	Self Catering	🕴	𝄙𝄙
Gardeners Cottage	Peinmore House, By Portree, Isle Of Skye, IV51 9LG	01478 612574	★★★★	Self Catering		
Kirsty's Cottage	Kirsty's Cottage, 2 Peinachorran, Braes, by Portree IV51 9LL	01478 650349	★★★	Self Catering		
Lawries Thatched Cottage	2 Totescore, Kilmuir, By Portree, Isle of Skye, IV51 9YW	01470 542409	★★★	Self Catering		𝄙𝄙
Seacroft Cottage	64 Upper Road, Poole, Dorset BH12 3EW	01202 708847	★★★★	Self Catering		
Storr Lochs Lodge	23 Langside Avenue, London SW15 5QT	0208 876 5777	★★★	Self Catering		
The Cottage	2 Tote, Skeabost, by Portree, Isle of Skye, IV51 9PQ	01470 532382	★★★	Self Catering		
Almondbank	Almondbank, 26 Main, Bernisdale, Portree, Isle of Skye, IV51 9NS	01470 532326	★★★	Self Catering		
Corran Holiday Home	Corran Guest House, Eyre, Kensaleyre, Portree, Isle of Skye, IV51 9XE	01470 532311	★★★★	Self Catering		
Beatons Cottage, Bornesketaig	National Trust for Scotland, 28 Charlotte Square, Edinburgh EH2 4ET	0131 243 9335	★★	Self Catering		

Portsoy

1 North High Street	6 Seafield Terrace, Portsoy, Banffshire, AB45 2QB	01261 843680	★★★★	Self Catering
6 & 7 Shorehead	Portsoy Marble, Shorehead, Portsoy, Banffshire, AB45 2PB	01261 842404	★★★	Self Catering
Amhersy Cottage	Aldour, Union Terrace, Buckie, Banffshire, AB56 1QN	01542 833049	★★★	Self Catering
Sandhaven Cottage	Old School House, Sandend, Portsoy, Banffshire, AB45 2UA	01261 842660	★★★	Self Catering
Stella Maris	11 Murray Terrace, Aberdeen AB11 7SA	01224 584814	★★★	Self Catering
Tigh-na-Drochaid	36 Prospect Road, Sevenoaks, Kent, TN13 3UA	01732 456442	★★★	Self Catering

     🚹 Unassisted wheelchair access   🚹 Assisted wheelchair access   🕴 Access for visitors with mobility difficulties
     𝄙 Bronze Green Tourism Award   𝄙𝄙 Silver Green Tourism Award   𝄙𝄙𝄙 Gold Green Tourism Award
For further information on our Green Tourism Business Scheme please see page 9.

Potterton

The Byre	Butterywells, Potterton, Aberdeen AB23 8UY	01358 742673	★★★	Self Catering	⚹

Prestwick

44 Links Road	Willow Lodge, Fownhope Court, Fownhope, Herefordshire, HR1 4 PB	01432 860221	★★★	Self Catering
Oakley Property Rentals	Oakley, 17 Ayr Road, Prestwick, Ayrshire, KA9 1SX	01292 474642	★★★ → ★★★★	Self Catering
Woodcroft, Church and Garden Cottage	Woodcroft, 23 Midton Road, Ayr, Ayrshire, KA7 2SF	01292 264383	★★★	Self Catering

Rait, By Perth

Fingask Cottages	Fingask Cottages, Fingask Castle, Rait, Perthshire, PH2 7SA	01821 670777	★★★	Self Catering

Rannoch

Liarn Farm Holiday Cottages	Liarn Farm Holiday Cottages, Rannoch, Pitlochry, Perthshire, PH17 2QW	01882 633264	★★★★	Self Catering
Rannoch Lodge Estate	Rannoch Lodge Estate, Bridge of Gaur, Rannoch Station Perthshire, PH17 2QD	01882 633278	★★★	Self Catering

Ratagan, Kyle of Lochalsh

Kintail	Middle Barrows Green, Kendal, Cumbria, LA8 0JG	01539 560242	★★★★	Self Catering

Rattray, Blairgowrie

Glenshieling Lodge	Glenshieling House, Hatton Road, Blairgowrie, Perthshire, PH10 7HZ	01250 874605	★★★	Self Catering
The Bothy	South Littleton Farm, Alyth Road, Rattray, Blairgowrie, Perthshire, PH10 7 HF	01250 870611	★★★	Self Catering

Ravenstruther, By Lanark

The Annexe	The Annexe Cottage, Newhouse Farm, Ravenstruther, by Lanark, Lanarkshire, ML11 8NP	01555 870906	★★★★	Self Catering

Reddingmuirhead

Lower Doune	Lower Doune, 9 Wallacestone Brae, Reddingmuirhead, Stirlingshire, FK2 0DQ	01324 715597	★★★	Self Catering

Rhenigidale

The School House	Burnside, Rhenigidale, Harris, Western Isles, HS3 3BD	01859 502177	★★★	Self Catering

Rhiconich

Gull Cottage (The Barn)	Gull Cottage (The Barn), Achriesgill, Rhiconich, Sutherland, IV27 4RJ	01971 521717	★★★	Self Catering

Roberton

Willowbank & Allangarth	Bonnybank, Branxholme Park, Hawick, Roxburghshire, TD9 0JT	01450 377754	★★	Self Catering

Rockcliffe

Badgers Cottage	Wavecrest, Cresswell, Morpeth, Northumberland, NE61 5LA	01670 860882	★★★	Self Catering
Corner Cottage	11 Mill Lane, Blackpill, Swansea, SA3 5BD	01792 405466	★★★	Self Catering
Millbrae Studio	Millbrae House, Rockcliffe, By Dalbeattie, Dumfries and Galloway, DG5 4QG	01556 630217	★★★	Self Catering

⚹ Unassisted wheelchair access   ⚹ Assisted wheelchair access   ⚹ Access for visitors with mobility difficulties

🄑 Bronze Green Tourism Award   🄑🄑 Silver Green Tourism Award   🄑🄑🄑 Gold Green Tourism Award
For further information on our Green Tourism Business Scheme please see page 9.

| Port Donnel Cottage | National Trust for Scotland, 28 Charlotte Square, Edinburgh EH2 4ET | 0131 243 9335 | ★★★ | Self Catering | |
| Pittullie, Barcloy Mill | The Grammar House, Langport, Somerset, TA10 9PU | 01458 250868 | ★★★★ | Self Catering | |

Rodel

Harris White Cottage	14 Cornwall Gardens, London SW7 4AN	07787 851155	★★★★	Self Catering	
Rodel Valley Log Cabins	Rodel Valley Log Cabins, Rodel, Isle of Harris, Western Isles, HS5 3TW	01859 520465	★★★★	Self Catering	
St Clement's Croft	65 Hawthorn Drive, Inverness, Invernesshire, IV3 5RQ	01463 240788	★★★	Self Catering	

Rogart

Aultibea	Lynmhor Backies, Golspie Sutherland, KW10 6SE	01408 633512	★★★	Self Catering	
Elcaila	Sciberscross, Rogart, Sutherland, IV28 3XN	01408 641361	★★★	Self Catering	
Glebe House	St Callans Manse, Rogart, Sutherland, IV28 3XE	01408 641363	★★	Self Catering	

Rosehall

| Milton Cottage & Inveroykel Lodge | Balnagowan Castle Properties Ltd, Balnagowan Estate, Kildary, by Invergordon, IV18 0NU | 01862 843601 | ★★★★ → ★★★★★ | Self Catering | |

Rosemarkie

| East & West Whinstone Cottages | Flowerburn Mains, Rosemarkie, Ross-shire, IV10 8SJ | 01381 620946 | ★★★ → ★★★★ | Self Catering | |
| Hillockhead Holiday Cottages | Hillockhead Farm, Eathie Road, Rosemarkie, Ross-shire, IV10 8SL | 01381 621184 | ★★★ → ★★★★ | Self Catering | |

Rosewell

Hunter Holiday Cottages	Thornton Farm, Rosewell Midlothian, EH24 9EF	0131 440 2082	★★★	Self Catering	௹
Pantiles	Orchard House B&B, The Walled Garden, Whitehill Road, Rosewell, Midlothian, EH24 9EQ	0131 440 4515	★★★	Self Catering	𝒫𝒫𝒫
Park Neuk	Kinnen Dell, Westfield, Bathgate, West Lothian, EH48 4NJ	01506 653095	★★★	Self Catering	⋔

Roslin

| Lea Farm Holiday Cottage | Lea Farm, Roslin, Midlothian EH25 9PY | 0131 440 2196 | ★★★ | Self Catering | |

Ross-shire

| Kinettas Cottage | The Gables, Highfield, Muir of Ord, Ross-shire, IV6 7XN | 01463 870141 | ★★★ | Self Catering | |
| Russell House | National Trust for Scotland, 28 Charlotte Square, Edinburgh EH2 4ET | 0131 243 9335 | ★★★★ | Self Catering | |

Rothesay, Isle of Bute

Arranview @ Stewart Hall	Arranview, Stewart Hall, Rothesay, Isle of Bute, PA20 0QE	01700 500006	★★★★★	Self Catering	
Flat 9 & Flat 13, Grand Marine Court	1 North Biggar Road, Airdrie, North Lanarkshire, PA20 0AX	01236 755051	★★★	Self Catering	
Harbourside Apartments	Harbourside Apartments, Guildford Court, 3 Watergate, Rothesay, Isle of Bute, PA20 9AB	01700 503770	★★	Self Catering	
Morningside	10 Craignethan, Rothesay Isle of Bute, PA20 0QX	01700 504237	★★★	Self Catering	
Prospect House	21 Battery Place, Rothesay, Isle of Bute, PA20 9DU	01700 503526	★★★	Self Catering	

௹ Unassisted wheelchair access   ௹ Assisted wheelchair access   ⋔ Access for visitors with mobility difficulties
𝒫 Bronze Green Tourism Award   𝒫𝒫 Silver Green Tourism Award   𝒫𝒫𝒫 Gold Green Tourism Award
For further information on our Green Tourism Business Scheme please see page 9.

Rothesay Apartments	Suite 3/2, 156 Wilton Street, Glasgow, Lanarkshire, G20 6BS	0141 9463937	Awaiting Grading	
The Commodore	The Commodore, 12 Battery PLace, Rothesay, Isle of Bute, PA20 9DP	01700 502178	★★★	Self Catering
Ardencraig House	Ardnacraig House Apartments, Highcraigmore, Rothesay, Isle of Bute, PA20 9EP	01200 505077	★★★★	Self Catering
West St. Colmac Farm	East St. Colmac Farm, Rothesay, Isle of Bute, PA2 0QT	01700 502144	★★★	Self Catering
Westview	76 Switchback Road, Glasgow, Lanarkshire, G61 1AF	0141 5779091	★★★★	Self Catering

Rowardennan

Dubh Loch Cottage	111 Avalon Gardens, Linlithgow, West Lothian, EH49 7PL	01506 845353	★★★★	Self Catering
Loch Lomond Lodge	11 Courthill, Bearsden, Glasgow G61 3SN	07974 427380	★★★★	Self Catering
Rowardennan Lodges	Rowardennan Lodges (Loch Lomond), Eadie House, 74 Kirkintilloch Road, Bishopbriggs, Glasgow, G64 2AH	0141 762 4828	★★★ → ★★★★	Self Catering
Rowardennan Lodges	6 Crawley Gardens, Whickham, Newcastle, NE16 4HA	0191 4229581	★★★	Self Catering
Sandwood Lodge	15 Corrennie Drive, Edinburgh EH10 6EG	0131 4469181	Awaiting Grading	
Lodges 25 & 26	No.7 Montrose Way, Drymen, Stirlingshire, G63 0DR	01360 660265	★★★★	Self Catering

Roy Bridge

Bunroy Holiday Lodges	Bunroy Holiday Lodges, Bunroy Park, Roy Bridge, Inverness-shire, PH31 4AG	01397 712332	★★★	Self Catering
Fersit Log Cottage	Fersit Log Cottage, Fersit, Roybridge, Inverness-Shire, PH31 4AR	01397 732323	★★★★	Self Catering	🌿

Ruthwell

Radcliffe Cottage	9 Runic Place, Ruthwell, Dumfriesshire, DG1 4NW	01387 870 213	★★★	Self Catering

Salen, Isle of Mull

Ard Shellach	3 Pinfold Close, Repton, Derbyshire, DE65 6FR	01283 702982	★★★	Self Catering
Faoileann Ghlas	Camas-An-Fheidh, Lochdon, Isle of Mull, Argyll, PA64 6AP	01769 581677	★★★★	Self Catering
Glenaros Farm Cottages	Kilmore House, Kilmore, By Oban, PA34 4XT	01631 770369	★★	Self Catering
Puffer Aground	Puffer Aground, Aros, Salen, Isle of Mull, PA72 6JB	01680 300389	★★★★	Self Catering
Resipole Farm	Resipole Farm, Loch Sunart, Acharacle, Argyll, PH36 4HX	01967 431235	★★★	Self Catering

By Salen, Isle of Mull

Gruline Home Farm Cottages	Gruline Home Farm, Gruline, Nr Salen, Isle of Mull, PA71 6HR	01680 300581	★★★★	Self Catering

Saline

Balgonar	Balgonar, Saline, Fife, KY12 9TA	01383 852286	★★★	Self Catering

Saltcoats

Lochwood Farm Steading	Lochwood Farm, Saltcoats, Ayrshire, KA21 6NG	01294 552529	★★★★	Self Catering

To find out more, call 0845 22 55 121 or go to visitscotland.com.

Sandhead, Stranraer

Ginger Tom's	Ginger Tom's, 57 Main Street, Sandhead, Dumfries & Galloway, DG9 9JF	01776 830371	★★★	Self Catering
Old School House	Auchness Farm, Ardwell, Stranraer, Wigtownshire, DG9 9NA	01776 860 228	★★★★	Self Catering

Sandness

Crawton	Spiggie Hotel, Scousburgh, Shetland ZE2 9JE	01950 460409	★★★	Self Catering

Sandyhills

Glen Rhuad Lodge	Barnhourie Farm, Sandyhills, Dumfries & Galloway, DG5 4PN	01387 780693	★★★	Self Catering
Galloway Country Cottages	The Old Schoolhouse, Ringford, By Castle Douglas, Kirkcudbrightshire, DG7 2AL	01557 820250	★★★ → ★★★★	Self Catering
Cumstoun Lodge	The Green, Rampton, Cambridgeshire, CB4 8QB	01954 200345	★★★	Self Catering

Sannox, Isle of Arran

Sannaig	Sannaig, Shore Road, Sannox, Isle of Arran, KA27 8JD	01770 860376	★★★	Self Catering
Woodside Cottage	106 (Flat 2F), Portobello High Street, Edinburgh, Lothian, EH15 1AL	0131 468 0615	★★★	Self Catering

Sanquhar

Bogg Cottage	15 Church Rd, Sanquhar, Dumfries-shire, DG4 6DF	01659 50561	★★	Self Catering
Nith Riverside Lodges	Blackaddie House Hotel, Blackaddie Road, Sanquhar, Dumfriesshire, DG4 6JJ	01659 50270	★★★	Self Catering ♿

Sauchen, Inverurie

The John Bell Flat	National Trust for Scotland, 28 Charlotte Square, Edinburgh EH2 4ET	0131 243 9335	★★★	Self Catering
West Wing	Gightfarmhouse, Gight Farmhouse, Suuchen, Inverurie, Aberdeenshire, AB31 7LP	01330 833647	★★★★	Self Catering

Sauchie, Alloa

Devon Valley Drive	Rainbow Letts, 2 Coningsby Place, Alloa, Clackmananshire, FK10 1DR	01259 725986	★★★	Self Catering

Scalpay

Hamarsay	9 Merlin Crescent, Inverness, Inverness-shire, IV2 3TE	01463 236049	★★★★	Self Catering

Scarfskerry

Midskerry Cottage	South Leckaway Farm, by Forfar, Angus DD8 1XF	01307 463324	★★	Self Catering
Starbank	108 Belton Lane, Grantham, Lincolnshire, NG31 9PR	01476 561239	★★★	Self Catering

Scarista

Blue Reef Cottages	5 Scaristavore, Scarista, Isle of Harris HS3 3HX	01859 550370	★★★★★	Self Catering PPP

Scourie, By Lairg

Hill Cottage	Mid Cambushinnie Farm, Dunblane, Perthshire, FK15 9JU	01786 880631	★★★	Self Catering
An Tigh Earna	3 The Logan, Liff, By Dundee, Angus, DD2 5PJ	01382 580358	★★★★	Self Catering

♿ Unassisted wheelchair access ♿ Assisted wheelchair access ♿ Access for visitors with mobility difficulties
℗ Bronze Green Tourism Award ℗℗ Silver Green Tourism Award ℗℗℗ Gold Green Tourism Award
For further information on our Green Tourism Business Scheme please see page 9.

Awards correct as of mid August 2008

343

Selkirk

Aikwood Tower	Aik Wood Tower, Ettrick Valley, Selkirk, Scottish Borders, TD7 5HJ	01750 52253	★★★	Self Catering
Crook Cottage and Elspinhope	Ettrick Holidays, Cossarshill Farm, Ettrick Valley, Selkirk TD7 5JB	01750 62259	★★★★	Self Catering ♿ 🌿🌿🌿
Nether Whitlaw Farm Cottage	Nether Whitlaw, Selkirk, Selkirkshire, TD7 4QN	01750 21217	★★★★	Self Catering
Whitmuir Hall	Whitmuir Hall, Whitmuir, Selkirk, Selkirkshire, TD7 4PZ	01750 20118	★★★ → ★★★★	Self Catering

Shandon

Shandonbank Cottage	Inverallt, Shandon, Helensburgh, Argyll & Bute, G84 8NR	01463 820314	★★★★	Self Catering

Shannochie

The Old Farmhouse	1 Horsburgh Gardens, Balerno, Edinburgh, Midlothian, EH14 7BY	0131 4663124	★★★★	Self Catering

Shetland

8 Thorfinn Street	13 Ronald Street, Lerwick, Shetland, ZE1 0BQ	01595 692317	★★★	Self Catering
Faa	Toam, North Roe Shetland, ZE2 9RY	01806 533217	★★★	Self Catering
Kinlea	South Burland, Trundra, Scalloway, Shetland, ZE1 0XL	01595 880961	★★★★	Self Catering
Langbiggin	Langbiggin, Bixter, Shetland, ZE2 9NA	01595 810361	★★★	Self Catering ♿
Tresta	Tresta, Fetlar, Shetland ZE2 9DS	01957 733231	★★★★	Self Catering
16 Monthooly Street	Tamara, Longwell, Cunningsburgh, Shetland, ZE2 9HG	01950 477350	★★★	Self Catering
Lower Cottage, Aith	Lower Cottage, Vementry, Aith, Shetland, ZE2 9ND	01595 810439	★★	Self Catering
Havra Cottage, Bigton	Claver Cottage, Longhill, Maywick, Bigton, Shetland, ZE2 9JF	01950 422214	★★★★	Self Catering
Ronan Cottage, Bigton	1 North Heights, Quarff, Shetland, ZE2 9EY	01950 477552	★★★	Self Catering ♿
Bevlah, Bixter	Bevlah, West Skeld, Bixter, Shetland, ZE2 9NL	01595 860361	★★★	Self Catering
Culswick Crofthouse Apartments, Bixter	Gilbraes Chalets, Twatt, Bixter, Shetland, ZE2 9LX	01595 810222	★★★★	Self Catering
Gilbraes Chalets, Bixter	Gilbraes Chalets, Twatt, Bixter, Shetland, ZE2 9LX	01595 810222	★★	Self Catering
Queans, Bixter	Kwenjali, Tumblin, Bixter, Shetland, ZE2 9LS	01595 810231	★★★★	Self Catering
Scarvataing, Bixter	Keldara, Aith, Bixter, Shetland, ZE2 9NE	01595 810421	★★★★	Self Catering
The Lodge, Bixter	Seaview, Sandsound, Bixter, Shetland, ZE2 9LU	01595 810280	★★★	Self Catering
Bressay Lighthouse, Bresssay	Shetland Amenity Trust, Lerwick, Shetland, ZE1 0NY	01595 694688	★★★	Self Catering
The Croft House, Bresssay	The Croft House, Garth Of Ham, Bressay, Shetland, ZE2 9ER	01595 820332	★★★	Self Catering
Briar Cottage, Burra	Bay Cottage, Hamnavoe, Burra, Shetland, ZE2 9JY	01595 859419	★★★	Self Catering
Lurnea, Burra	Brekka, Bridge End, Burra, Shetland, ZE2 9LD	01595 859413	★★★	Self Catering
Highmount, Burra	Burland, Trondra, Shetland ZE1 0XL	01595 880647	★★★	Self Catering

♿ Unassisted wheelchair access   ♿ Assisted wheelchair access   ♀ Access for visitors with mobility difficulties
🌿 Bronze Green Tourism Award   🌿🌿 Silver Green Tourism Award   🌿🌿🌿 Gold Green Tourism Award
For further information on our Green Tourism Business Scheme please see page 9.

Highmount, Burra Isle	Burland, Trondra, Shetland ZE1 0XL	01595 880647	★★★	Self Catering
Glover Chalets, Cunningsburgh	Glover Chalets, Ocraquoy, Cunningsburgh, Shetland, ZE2 9HA	01950 477596	★★★★	Self Catering
Longwell Cottage, Cunningsburgh	Seashells, Cunningsburgh, Shetland, ZE2 9HG	01950 477204	★★★	Self Catering
Apartment @ Ovrevagen, Cunningsburgh	Ovrevagen, Cunningsburgh, Shetland, ZE2 9HG	01950 477633	★★★	Self Catering
Irvine, Effirth	Nia-Roo, Effirth, Bixter, Shetland, ZE2 9LY	01595 810325	★★★★	Self Catering
Almara Chalet, Hillswick	Almara, Upper Urafirth, Hillswick, Shetland, ZE2 9RH	01806 503261	★★★★	Self Catering
Stobrek In Shetland, Hillswick	Economic Partnerships, Ouseburn Farm, Ouseburn Road, Newcastle upon Tyne NE1 2PA	07958 356990	★★★	Self Catering
Swarthoull, Hillswick	Swarthoul Self Catering, Swarthoul, Heylor, Hillswick, Shetland, ZE2 9RH	01806 503397	★★★	Self Catering
Braewick, Eshaness	4 Queeness Road, Vidlin, Shetland, ZE2 9QB	01806 577269	★★★	Self Catering
Eshaness Lighthouse, eshaness	Shetland Amenity Trust, Lerwick, Shetland, ZE1 0NY	01595 694688	★★★	Self Catering
Fishers Croft, Hamnavoe	The Rectory, Fishers Lane, Oswell, Royston, Herts, SG8 5QX	01223 208437	★★★★	Self Catering
19c St Magnus Street, Lerwick	Cairnlea, Sandwick, Shetland, ZE2 9HW	01950 431496	★★★	Self Catering
25 Westerloch Drive, Lerwick	25 Westerloch Drive, Lerwick, Shetland, ZE1 0GD	01595 695649	★★★★	Self Catering
4 Greenfield Square, Lerwick	2 Hillcrest, Lerwick, Shetland, ZE1 0ST	01595 696056	★★★	Self Catering
4-6 Burns Lane, Lerwick	14 Scalloway Road, Lerwick, Shetland, ZE1 0LD	01595 695922	★★★★	Self Catering
59A King Harald Street, Lerwick	59 King Harald Street, Lerwick, Shetland, ZE1 0ER	01595 693054	★★★	Self Catering
6 Water Lane, Lerwick	Upper Leogh, Fair Isle, Shetland, ZE2 9JU	01595 760248	★★★	Self Catering
63 Burgh Road & Decca, Lerwick	Inches, Bells Road, Lerwick, Shetland, ZE1 0QB	01595 695354	★★★	Self Catering ♿
9 Navy Lane, Lerwick	7 Navy Lane, Lerwick, Shetland, ZE1 0BS	01595 694152	★★	Self Catering
Flat 55 King Harald Street, Lerwick	55 King Harald Street, Lerwick, Shetland, ZE1 0ER	01595 695758	★★★	Self Catering
King Harald Apartments, Lerwick	Norwood, Lower Sound, Lerwick, Shetland, ZE1 0GF	01595 694014	★★★	Self Catering
No 5 Queens Place, Lerwick	Romda Taff, Isbister, Whalsay, Shetland, ZE2 9AJ	01806 566577	★★	Self Catering
No 7A Hillhead, Lerwick	7 Hillhead, Lerwick, Shetland, ZE1 0EJ	01595 696774	★★★	Self Catering
No. 9 Chapel House, Lerwick	117 Union Grove, Aberdeen AB10 6SL	07899 990580	★★★	Self Catering
Office Lodge, Lerwick	PO Box 11682, Lerwick, Shetland, ZE1 0XS	08707 708881	★★★	Serviced Apartments
The Cottage, Lerwick	49 King Harald Street, Lerwick, Shetland, ZE1 0EQ	01595 693782	★★	Self Catering
Top Floor Flat, Lerwick	7 West Hillcrest, Lerwick, Shetland, ZE1 0JZ	01595 697137	Awaiting Grading	
Valeind, Lerwick	Leagarth, Weisdale Shetland, ZE29LQ	01595 830219	★★★	Self Catering
Coel Na Mara, Mid Yell	Schoolhouse, Mid Yell, Shetland ZE29BJ	01957 702102	★★★	Self Catering
Gremister, Mid Yell	1 New Road, Scalloway, Shetland ZE1 0TS	01595 880117	★★★★	Self Catering

♿ Unassisted wheelchair access   ♿ Assisted wheelchair access   ♿ Access for visitors with mobility difficulties
🌿 Bronze Green Tourism Award   🌿🌿 Silver Green Tourism Award   🌿🌿🌿 Gold Green Tourism Award
For further information on our Green Tourism Business Scheme please see page 9.

Voeview Cottage, Mid Yell	Voeview, Hillend, Mid-Yell, Shetland, ZE2 9BJ	01957 702307	★★	Self Catering
Sandibanks, Mossbank	4 Lochside, Lerwick, Shetland, ZE1 0RB	01595 692701	★★★★	Self Catering
The Cottage, North Mavine	Busta, Brae, Shetland, ZE2 9QN	01806 522589	★★★	Self Catering
South House, North Mavine	The Old Manse, Hillswick, Shetland, ZE2 3RW	1806 503277	★★★	Self Catering
Langaskaill Flat, Sandwick	Binscarth House, Firth, Orkney, KW17 2JZ	01856 761200	★★★	Self Catering
Roadside Cottage and Tamara, Sandwick	Tamara, Longwell, Cunningsburgh, Shetland, ZE2 9HG	01950 477350	★★★	Self Catering
Netherstove, Sandwick	Netherstove, Quoyloo, Sandwick, Orkney, KW16 3LS	01856 841625	★★	Self Catering
Islehavn Chalet, Skellister	Vardasta, Gletness, Skellister, Shetland, ZE2 9PS	01595 890342	★★★	Self Catering
Spiggie House, Scousburg	Spiggie House, Scousburgh, Shetland, ZE2 9JE	01950 460152	★★★	Self Catering
Wildrig, Scousbury	Thurdistoft, Scousburgh, Shetland, ZE2 9JE	01950 460373	★★★★	Self Catering
Sumburgh Lighthouse, Sumburgh	Shetland Amenity Trust, Garthspool, Lerwick, Shetland, ZE1 0NY	01595 694688	★★	Self Catering
Gaza, Sullom	Northerhouse, Sullom, Shetland, ZE2 9RD	01806 522239	★★★	Self Catering
Midfield Cottage & Askalong, Ollaberry	Sunnyside, Ollaberry, Shetland, ZE2 9RT	011806 544277	★★★ → ★★★★	Self Catering
Da Barn, Unst	Da Barn, Westing, Unst, Shetland, ZE2 9DW	01957 755255	★★	Self Catering
Dale Cottage, Unst	Buness Country House, Baltasound, Unst, Shetland, ZE2 9DS	01957 711315	★★★★	Self Catering
North Booth, Unst	Cockmuir House, Longmorn, By Elgin, Morayshire, IV30 3SL	01343 860227	★★	Self Catering
North Dale & 3 Voesgarth Crescent, Unst	Clingera Guest House, Baltasound, Unst, Shetland, ZE2 9DT	01957 711579	★★ → ★★★	Self Catering
Saxa Vord, Unst	Saxa Vord, Haroldswick, Unst, Shetland, ZE2 9TJ	01957 711711	★★★	Self Catering
Aesthus, Vidlin	Aesthus, Sandyburn, Vidlin, Shetland, ZE2 9QB	01806 577274	★★★★	Self Catering
Croft Cottage, Vidlin	North House, Swining, Vidlin, Shetland, ZE2 9QE	01806 577224	★★★	Self Catering
Upper Garden, Vidlin	Ulvik, Skelberry, Vidlin, Shetland, ZE2 9QD	01806 577215	★★★★	Self Catering
Nordagerdi, Vidlin	Sunnydell, Virkie, Shetland, ZE3 9JS	01950 461929	★★	Self Catering
Anderlea, Wadbister, Girlsta	Voehead, Wadbister, Girlsta, Shetland, ZE2 9QS	01595 840484	★★	Self Catering
Burnside Cottage, Walls	Burnside Cottage, Walls Shetland Isles, ZE2 9PG	01595 809366	★★	Self Catering
2 Bothies, Whalsay	1 Bothies, Symbister, Whalsay, Shetland Isles, ZE2 9AQ	01806 566 429	★★	Self Catering

Shieldaig

Flora's House	Beeches Barn, Ranmoor Hill, Hathersage, Sheffield, Yorkshire, S30 1BU	01433 650361	★★★	Self Catering	
Tortola Log Cabin	Tigh Fada, 117 Doireaonar, Shieldaig, by Strathcarron, Ross-shire, IV54 8XH	01520 755 248	★★★★	Self Catering	🖉
Campbell House	14 Liddell Avenue, Melling, Merseyside L31 1BT	0151 2902330	★★★	Self Catering	

♿ Unassisted wheelchair access   ♿ Assisted wheelchair access   ✝ Access for visitors with mobility difficulties
🖉 Bronze Green Tourism Award   🖉🖉 Silver Green Tourism Award   🖉🖉🖉 Gold Green Tourism Award
For further information on our Green Tourism Business Scheme please see page 9.

346   To find out more, call 0845 22 55 121 or go to visitscotland.com.

Shiskine, Isle of Arran

An Caladh	Rhubaan, Toward, Dunoon, Argyll, PA23 7UA	01369 870388	★★★★	Self Catering
Aros Beag	Craigview Cottage, Sliddery, Isle of Arran, KA27 8PB	01770 870367	★★★	Self Catering
Old Smiddy Cottage	Shedock Farm, Shiskine, Isle of Arran, KA27 8EW	01770 860261	★★★	Self Catering
Sealladh Breagh	Sanda, Blackwaterfoot, Isle of Arran KA27 8EU	01770 860530	★★★★	Self Catering
Strathdoon	17 St Vincent Crescent, Ayr, Ayrshire, KA7 4QW	01292 442512	★★★★	Self Catering

Skeabost Bridge

Crepigill & The Bothy	7 Achachork, Portree, Isle of Skye, IV51 9HT	01478 613104	★★★ → ★★★★★	Self Catering
Crepigill Lodge	Half of 2-3 Glengrasco Woodend, Portree, Isle of Skye, IV51 9LH	01478 611894	★★★★★	Self Catering
Taigh Na H-Aibhne	12 Seaforth Drive, Edinburgh EH4 2BT	0131 332 6622	★★★★	Self Catering 🧍

Skerray by Tongue

126 Skerray Mains	Razorclean, 32 Parkland Drive, Oadby, Leicester, LE2 4DG	01162 717667	★★★	Self Catering

Skigersta, Ness

The Sheiling	The Cottage, High Street, Skigersta, Ness, Isle of Lewis, HS2 0TS	01851 810131	★★★	Self Catering

Slackbuie

Bluebell Apartment	Swallowcroft, Achindarroch Road, Duror of Appin, Argyll, PA38 4BS	08081 787564	★★★	Self Catering

Sleat

Armadale Castle Cottages	Armadale, Sleat, Isle of Skye, IV45 8RS	01471 844305	★★★ → ★★★★	Self Catering

Sliddery

2 Burnside Cottage	6 Pembroke Road, Framlingham, Woodbridge, Suffolk, IP13 9HA	01728 723629	★★	Self Catering
Hayshed & Ploughman's Bothy	Hayshed, Ivy Cottage, Sliddery, Isle of Arran, KA27 8PB	01770 870295	★★★	Self Catering
Stewart Cottage	Meadowview, 2 Ridgeway, Papworth Everard, Cambs, CB3 8RW	01480 831407	★★★★	Self Catering
Whin Cottage	Broomley, Osborne Avenue, Hexham, Northumberland, NE46 3JN	01434 604673	★★★	Self Catering

Sollas

Larkfield House	Springburn, Sollas, North Uist, HS6 5BS	01876 560 238	★★★	Self Catering

South Alloa, Falkirk

Plumtree Cottage	Bridgend Farm, Moss Road, Nr Airth, Falkirk, Stirlingshire, FK2 8RT	01324 832060	★★★★	Self Catering

South Lochs

10 Glen Gravir	8 Maryhill, Stornoway, Isle of Lewis, HS2 0DJ	01851 703575	★★★	Self Catering
8B Calbost	Lukhaya, Back, Isle of Lewis, HS2 0NA	01851 820969	★★★	Self Catering

♿ Unassisted wheelchair access   ♿ Assisted wheelchair access   🧍 Access for visitors with mobility difficulties
🄿 Bronze Green Tourism Award   🄿🄿 Silver Green Tourism Award   🄿🄿🄿 Gold Green Tourism Award
For further information on our Green Tourism Business Scheme please see page 9.

Awards correct as of mid August 2008

347

South Shawbost

27 South Shawbost	49 York Road, Middlesbrough TS7 0EZ	01642 313282	★★★	Self Catering

South Uist

2 Sandwick	194 Old Woosehill Lane, Wokingham, Berks, RG41 3HQ	01189 782587	★★★	Self Catering
Benview	32 Glengavel Crescent, Robroyston, Glasgow G33 1HJ	0141 557 5058	★★★	Self Catering

Southend

Allt Mor	Ormsary Farm, Southend, by Campbeltown, Argyll, PA28 6RN	01586 830665	★★★	Self Catering
Glenmanuilt	High Butterby Farm, Shincliffe, Durham, Durham, DH1 2TJ	01913 843626	★★	Self Catering
Meadow View	9 Stormont Road, Scone, Perth, Perthshire, PH2 6RH	01738 552553	★★★	Self Catering

Southerness

Craig Na Mara Cottage	48 Broompark Drive, Newtonmearns, Clarkston, Glasgow G77 5DZ	01387 880689	★★	Self Catering
Lennox	68 Kermoor Avenue, Bolton, Lancs, BL1 9HN	01204 593132	★	Self Catering
West Cottage	26 Vine Street, Kersal, Salford, Lancashire, M7 3PG	0161 792 3877	★★	Self Catering

Southwick

Clifton Farm	Clifton Farm, Southwick, Dumfries, DG2 8AR	01387 780206	★★★★	Self Catering	🕴

Spean Bridge

Achaneich Chalet & Stable	Achaneich, Spean Bridge, Inverness-shire, PH34 4EU	01397 712715	★★★★	Self Catering	
Burnbank Lodges	Burnbank Lodges, Burnbank House, Spean Bridge, Inverness-shire, PH34 4EU	01397 712520	★★★	Self Catering	[PP]
Corrieview Lodges	Corrieview Lodges, Grey Corries, Spean Bridge, Inverness-shire, PH34 4DX	01397 712395	★★★★	Self Catering	
Gairlochy Holiday Park	Gairlochy Holiday Park, Spean Bridge, Inverness-shire, PH34 4EQ	01397 712711	★★★★	Self Catering	
Highland Lodges	Highland Lodges, Kilfinnan, Near Invergary, Inverness-shire, PH34 4EB	01809 501225	★★★	Self Catering	
Spean Cottage & River House	Spean Lodge, Spean Bridge, Inverness-shire, PH34 4EP	01397 712004	★★★ → ★★★★	Self Catering	
Springburn Self Catering	Springburn, 3 Stronaba, Spean Bridge, Inverness-shire, PH34 4DX	01397 712707	★★★★	Self Catering	
The Old Smiddy	Smiddy House, Roy Bridge Road, Spean Bridge, Inverness-shire, PH34 4EU	01397 712335	★★★★	Self Catering	
Tirindrish Steading	Lake Cottage, Beccles Road, Fritton, Great Yarmouth, Norfolk, NR31 9EU	01493 488320	★★★★	Self Catering	
The Heathers (Fraoch Cottage)	The Heathers, Invergloy Halt, Spean Bridge, Inverness-shire, PH34 4DY	01397 712077	★★★★	Self Catering	
Riverside Lodges	Riverside Lodges, Invergloy, by Spean Bridge, Inverness-shire, PH34 4DY	01397 712684	★★★★	Self Catering	

Spittal of Glenshee

Dalmunzie Highland Cottages	Dalmunzie Ltd, Spittal of Glenshee, Perthshire, PH10 7QE	01250 885 226	★★ → ★★★	Self Catering

St Andrews

1 Greenside Court	5 Glasgow Road, Milngavie, Glasgow G62 6AQ	0141 956 2532	★★★	Self Catering	
12 Golf Place	East Fife Letting Company, Craigforth Cottage, Earlsferry, Elie, Fife, KY9 1AD	01333 330241	★★★★	Self Catering	
143 Market Street	17 The Lawns, Shenley, Hertfordshire, WD7 9EZ	0207 9176233	★★★	Self Catering	
15 Greyfriars Gardens & 17a Queens Gardens	27 Windsor Avenue, Newton Mearns, Glasgow G77 5NX	0141 571 8965	★★★	Self Catering	
150A North Street	2 Chesterhill Steadings, Boarhills, Fife, KY16 8PP	01334 880684	★★★★	Self Catering	
16 Kilrymont Road	11 Gadloch View, Lenzie, Glasgow, G66 5NS	0141 5780614	★★★	Self Catering	
18 The Scores	10 Lansdown Crescent, Bath BA1 5EX	01248 6442577	★★★★	Self Catering	
185 South Street	41 Westgate, Weatherby West Yorkshire, LS22 6NH	07798 806801	★★★	Self Catering	
20 College Street	42 Rhodes Park, North Berwick, East Lothian, EH39 5NA	01620 895520	★★★	Self Catering	
25 City Road	1 Marlborough Close, Devizes, Wiltshire, SN10 2JN	07909 521082	★★★★	Self Catering	
25 Sloan Street	Greystones, 118 Victoria Street, Dyce, Aberdeen, AB21 7BE	01224 722243	★★★	Self Catering	
29 North Street	20 Belgrave Crescent, Edinburgh, Midlothian, EH4 3AJ	0131 3329499	★★★★	Self Catering	
3C Gillespie Terrace	Eastview, Brookside Lane, Badby, Daventry, NN11 3AU	01327 704797	★★★	Self Catering	
4 & 5 Abbotsford Place	St Andrews Country Cottages, Mountquhanie Estate, By Cupar, Fife, KY15 4QJ	01382 330318	★★★★	Self Catering	
58 Argyle Street	Birchdale, Market Lane, Crimplesham, King's Lynn, Norfolk, PE33 9DZ	01366 382455	★★★	Self Catering	
6 Livingstone Place	10 Western Road, Insch, Aberdeenshire, AB52 6JR	01464 820871	★★★	Self Catering	
6 Queens Gardens	PO Box 10496, Grand Cayman, IslandsCayman, Western Caribbean, KY1-1005	01334 870013	★★★★	Self Catering	
90 Scooniehill Road	45 Swanspring Avenue, Edinburgh, Lothian, EH10 6NA	0131 445 3235	★★★	Self Catering	
Albany Apartments	2 Easter Belmont Road, Edinburgh, Lothian, EH12 6EX	0131 3464327	★★★★★	Self Catering	
Burnside	Daphne Cottage, Park Road, Chipping Campden, Gloucestershire, GL55 6EA	01386 848864	★★★	Self Catering	
Cambo Cottage & Flats & 116H Market St	Cambo House, Kingsbarns, Nr St Andrews, Fife, KY16 8QD	01333 450313	★★★ → ★★★★	Self Catering	
Craigtoun Meadows Holiday Park	Craigtown Meadows Holiday Park, Mount Melville, St Andrews, Fife, KY16 8PQ	01334 475959	★★★★	Self Catering	
David Russell Hall	Conference & Group Services, 79 North Street, St Andrews, Fife, KY16 9AD	01334 463000	★★★	Self Catering	🍀🍀🍀
Droncourt Holidays	Droncourt Holidays, 8 Dunure Place, Newton Mearns, Glasgow, G77 5TZ	0141 616 3491	★★★ → ★★★★	Self Catering	
Flat B & C, Gerrards Cross	Flat A, Gerrards Cross, 91 Hepburn Gardens, St Andrews, Fife, KY16 9LT	01334 473989	★★★ → ★★★★	Self Catering	
Flat No 1	5 Blacklaws Steading, Blacklaws, Anstruther, Fife, KY10 3GZ	01333 312613	★★★	Self Catering	
Flowers of May Cottage	Flowers of May Cottage, By Boarhills, St Andrews KY16 8PN	01334 880616	★★★★	Self Catering	
Garden Flat & The Coach House	Rockview, The Scores, St Andrews, Fife, KY16 9AR	01334 475844	★★ → ★★★	Self Catering	
Inchdairnie Properties	Inchdairnie Properties, 50 Argyle Street, St Andrews, Fife, KY16 9BU	01334 477011	★★★ → ★★★★	Self Catering	

    ♿ Unassisted wheelchair access   ♿ Assisted wheelchair access   ♿ Access for visitors with mobility difficulties

🍀 Bronze Green Tourism Award   🍀🍀 Silver Green Tourism Award   🍀🍀🍀 Gold Green Tourism Award

For further information on our Green Tourism Business Scheme please see page 9.

Ivybank	39 Vernon Drive, Blythewood, Ascot, Berwickshire, SL5 8TN	01344 626431	★★★	Self Catering	
Kildonan House	4B Links Crescent, St Andrews, Fife, KY16 9HP	01334 473446	★★★	Self Catering	
Kingask Country Cottages	Kingask, St Andrews, Fife, KY16 8PN	01334 472011	★★★	Self Catering	
Kinglassie House	St Helens, St Andrews Road, Ceres, Cupar, Fife, KY15 5NQ	01334 828862	★★★★	Self Catering	
Kinness Lodge	Rufflets Country House, Strathkinness Low Road, St Andrews, Fife, KY16 9TX		★★★★	Self Catering	
Ladybrand	147 Oak Tree Lane, Bournville, Birmingham, West Midlands, B30 1TT	0121 472 7404	★★★	Self Catering	
Linskill House	2 Sinclair Avenue, Bearsden, Glasgow G61 3BT	0141 942 7498	★★★	Self Catering	
Morton of Pitmilly	Morton of Pitmilly, Kingsbarns, St Andrews, Fife, KY16 8QF	01334 880466	★★★★	Self Catering	₽₽₽
No 24 Chamberlain Street	45 Highbevendge Well, Dunfermline, Fife, KY12 9ER	01383 723069	★★★	Self Catering	
No 6	43 Fishpool Street, St Albans, Herts, AL3 4RU	01727 832065	★★★★	Self Catering	
No 8 Sandyhill Crescent	16 Torquay Drive, Luton, Beds, LU4 9UN	01582 575625	★★★	Self Catering	
No. 3 Canongate	37 Spottiswoode Gardens, St Andrews, Fife, KY16 8SA	01334 473406	★★★	Self Catering	
Rigg's End	56 South Street, St Andrews, Fife, KY16 9JT	01334 473310	★★★★★	Self Catering	
Royal George	Baidland, 19 Lade Braes, St Andrews, Fife, KY16 9ES	01334 473365	★★★★	Self Catering	
Sandmill House	The Priory, Crail, Fife, KY10 3JY	01333 450549	★★★★	Self Catering	
Scribbles & Cobwebs	Fortrenn, St Fillans, Perthshire, PH6 2NG	01764 685485	★★★	Self Catering	
South Cassingray Cottage	South Cassingray Farm, Largoward, St Andrews, Fife, KY9 1JD	01334 840254	★★★	Self Catering	
St Andrews Golfing Lodge	St Andrews Golfing Lodge, 15 Queens Terrace, St Andrews, Fife, KY16 9QF	01334 477676	★★★★★	Self Catering	
St Marys	2 Castlemount Ave, Newton Mearns, Glasgow G77 5LQ	0141 639 3860	★★★	Self Catering	
St. Andrews Coach Houses	St Andrews Coach Houses, Priorletham, St Andrews, Fife, KY16 8NP	01334 477593	★★★★	Self Catering	
Swilken View	Middlebank, Errol, Perthshire, PH2 7SX	01828 686261	★★★★	Self Catering	
Templars	6 Park Street, St Andrews, Fife, KY16 8AQ	01334 478589	★★★★	Self Catering	
The Auld Hoose	13 Naysmyth Avenue, Bearsden, Glasgow, East Dunbartonshire, G61 4SQ	07748 700458	★★★★	Self Catering	
The Bothy	1 The Walled Garden, Feddinch, St Andrews, Fife, KY16 8NR	01334 479127	★★★★	Self Catering	
The Dunes, The Keep and The Haven	Hillview House, South St, Falkland, Fife, KY15 7AT	07889 722488	★★★★	Self Catering	
The Hirsel Cottage	The Hirsel, 50 The Scores, St Andrews, Fife, KY16 9AS	01334 472578	★★★	Self Catering	
The Residence	The Residence, No 9 The links, St Andrews, Fife, KY16 9JB	01334 461307	★★★★★	Self Catering	
The Whins, 1 Chambers Place	10 Pinegrove Gardens, Edinburgh EH4 8DA	0131 339 0098	★★★★	Self Catering	
Vardon House	Vardon House, 22 Murray Park, St Andrews, Fife, KY16 9AW	01334 475787	★★★	Self Catering	
Willow Cottage @ The Flaghouse	The Flaghouse, Dura Den, St Andrews, Fife, KY15 5TJ	01334 653862	★★★	Self Catering	

♿ Unassisted wheelchair access   ♿ Assisted wheelchair access   ♿ Access for visitors with mobility difficulties

₽ Bronze Green Tourism Award   ₽₽ Silver Green Tourism Award   ₽₽₽ Gold Green Tourism Award

For further information on our Green Tourism Business Scheme please see page 9.

To find out more, call 0845 22 55 121 or go to visitscotland.com.

41 Auldburn Park	11 Riccartsbar Avenue, Paisley, Renfrewshire, PA2 6BQ	0141 889 6327	★★	Self Catering

By St Andrews

Rose Studio, Feddinch	Rose Studio, 2 The Walled Garden, Feddinch, St Andrews, Fife, KY16 8NR	01334 479078	★★★★	Self Catering
Balmashie Holiday Cottages	Balmashie Holiday Cottages, by St Andrews, Fife, KY16 8PN	01334 880666	★★★★	Self Catering ϗ
Park Mill Cottage	Millens House, Parkmill, Boarhills, St Andrews, Fife, KY16 8PS	01334 880254	★★	Self Catering
The Smithy	The Smithy, Anvil Cottage, Radernie, By St Andrews, Fife, KY15 5LN	01334 840824	★★★	Self Catering

St Boswells

Barnhill	Roxburgh Newton, Kelso TD5 8NN	01573 450250	★★★★	Self Catering
The Estate of Maxton	The Estate of Maxton, Maxton House, St Boswells, Roxburghshire, TD6 0EX	01835 824400	★★★★	Self Catering
Clint Lodge Cottage	Clint Lodge Country House, Clinthill, St Boswells, Melrose, TD6 0DZ	01835 822027	★★★★	Self Catering
Halftown Cottages	Croft Kennels, Croitachonie, Cairndow, Argyll, PA26 8BH	01499 600239	★★★★	Self Catering

St Fillans

Ancala and Ardcraig	Achray House Hotel, St Fillans, Perthshire, PH6 2NF	01764 685231	★★★	Self Catering
The Old Church	36 College Road North, Blundellsands, Liverpool, L23 8UT	0151 9312843	★★★★	Self Catering

St John's Town of Dalry

Lochinvar Cottage	95 Ayr Road, Newton Mearns, Glasgow, East Renfrewshire, G77 6QR	0141 639 6680	★★★	Self Catering

St Madoes

Tower View and Tayview	Atholl House, Main Street, Bridge of Earn, Perth, PH2 9PJ	01738 813045	★★★★	Self Catering

St Monans

Periwinkle	16 Inglis Road, Colchester, Essex, CO3 3HU	01206 547835	★★★	Self Catering
The Cooperage	10 Queen Elizabeth Road, Pittenweem, Fife, KY10 2PU	01333 310864	★★★★	Self Catering
1 Midshore	Coastal Life, 7-13 Dublin Street Lane South, Edinburgh EH1 3PX	0131 5388300	★★★★ → ★★★★★	Self Catering

Staffin

The Cottage	Burnside, Culnacnoc, By Portree, Isle of Skye, IV51 9JH	01470 562235	★★★	Self Catering
Carn Ban	12 Church Street, Clitheroe, Lancashire, BB7 2DG	07971 950 126	★★★	Self Catering

Stanley

Strathmore View Cottage & Beech Lee	Lomond View, Airntully Village, Stanley, Perthshire, PH1 4PH	01738 828463	★★★ → ★★★★	Self Catering

By Stanley

The Old Smiddy	The Old Smiddy, Kinclaven, by Stanley, Perthshire, PH1 4QJ	01250 883236	★★★	Self Catering

ϗ Unassisted wheelchair access   ϗ Assisted wheelchair access   Υ Access for visitors with mobility difficulties
ϙ Bronze Green Tourism Award   ϙϙ Silver Green Tourism Award   ϙϙϙ Gold Green Tourism Award
For further information on our Green Tourism Business Scheme please see page 9.

Stein, Waternish

Henderson House and The Old Post Office	End House, Stein, Waternish, Isle of Skye, Inverness-shire, IV55 8GA	01470 592 235	★★★★	Self Catering

Stirling

14a Melville Terrace	14 Melville Terrace, Stirling, Stirlingshire, FK8 2NE	01786 475361	★★	Self Catering
15/01 Lower Bridge Street	3 Duchlage Terrace, Crieff, Perthshire, PH7 3AS	01764 652211	★★★	Self Catering
Broom Farm	Broom Farm, Causewayhead, Stirling FK9 5PL	01786 474329	★★★	Self Catering 🏃
Cotkerse House	West Lodge, Blairlogie, Stirling FK9 5QE	01259 761423	★★★★	Self Catering
Glendale	2 Small Holdings, Sauchenford, Stirling FK7 8AP	01786 811162	★★★	Self Catering
Hawthorn Cottage	West Drip Farm, Stirling FK9 4UJ	01786 472523	★★★★	Self Catering 🦽
New Holme	New Holme, 19 Birkhill Road, Stirling FK7 9LA	01786 442001	★★★★	Self Catering
No 12 Queen Street	Tormhor, Buchanan Castle Estate, Drymen, Stirlingshire, G63 0HX	01360 660268	★★★	Self Catering
No 20 Victoria Square	Laurel Properties (Scotland) Ltd, 4 Clarendon Place, Stirling, Stirling-shire, FK8 2QW	01786 445676	★★★★	Self Catering
Old Town Apartment	17 Castlevillage Rise, Celbridge, Co. Kildare, Ireland, IE	353 16274466	★★★★	Self Catering
Pendreich Way Chalets	Commercial Manager, University of Stirling, Department of Commercial Operations, Stirling, Stirlingshire, FK9 4LA	01786 467145	★★★	Self Catering
The Courtyard	1 Gladstone Place, Stirling, Stirlingshire, FK8 2NN	01786 469433	Awaiting Grading	
Watergate	Blairlogie Cottage, Blairlogie, Stirling FK9 5PX	01259 761667	★★★	Self Catering

By Stirling

1 Gartcarron	8 Undercliffe Rise, Ilkley, West Yorkshire, LS29 8RF	01943 601729	★★★	Self Catering
Gillies Cottage, cambusbarron	Gillies Cottage, 39 Main Street, Cambusbarron, Stirling, Stirlingshire, FK7 9NN	01786 470616	★★★	Self Catering

Stoer

Tigh Nan Shian & Stoer Smithy	The Smithy House, Stoer, Sutherland, IV27 4JE	01571 855363	★★★	Self Catering
Clashmore Holiday Cottages	216 Clashmore, Stoer, by Lairg, Sutherland, IV27 4JQ	01571 855226	★★★	Self Catering
Achnacarnin Chalets and Nedd Lodge	Caladh, Stoer, By Lairg, Sutherland, IV27 4JE	01571 855240	★★	Self Catering

Stonehaven

3 Rodney Terrace	1 Charleston Crescent, Love Bay, Aberdeen, Aberdeenshire, AB12 3DZ	01224 873275	★★★	Self Catering
95 Barclay Street	24 David Street, Stonehaven, Kindcardineshire, AB39 2AL	01569 765985	★★★	Self Catering
Arduthie Garden Flat	1 Willow Row, Stonehaven, Kincardineshire, A [DAB39 2GH	01569 766241	★★★	Self Catering
Ellerslie House	Ellerslie House Accommodation, 15a Robert Street, Stonehaven, Kincardineshire, AB39 2DS	01569 764504	★★★★	Self Catering
Hollyburn Lodge	Hollyburn Lodge, Elrick Farm, Stonehaven AB39 3RU	01569 730210	★★★★	Self Catering

♿ Unassisted wheelchair access   🦽 Assisted wheelchair access   🏃 Access for visitors with mobility difficulties

🄿 Bronze Green Tourism Award   🄿🄿 Silver Green Tourism Award   🄿🄿🄿 Gold Green Tourism Award

For further information on our Green Tourism Business Scheme please see page 9.

352   To find out more, call 0845 22 55 121 or go to visitscotland.com.

Stoneybridge

An Seann Tigh	209 Stoneybridge, Isle of South Uist, Western Isles, HS8 5SD	01870 620322	★★★	Self Catering

Stornoway, Isle of Lewis

22 Braighe Road	21 Braighe Road, Stornoway, Isle of Lewis, HS2 0BQ	01851 702304	★★★	Self Catering
3A Branahuie	Macrae House, 3A Branahuie, Stornoway, Isle of Lewis, HS2 0BB	01851 706205	★★★★	Self Catering
6 Laxdale Lane	Woodside, Laxdale Lane, Stornoway, Isle of Lewis, HS2 0DR	01851 706966	★★★★	Self Catering
Braighe Lodge	Hal o The Wynd Guest House, Newton Street, Stornoway, Isle of Lewis, HS1 2RE	01851 706073	★★★★	Self Catering
Chalet Cottages	Chalet Cottages, 54 Newvalley, Stornoway, Isle of Lewis, HS2 0DN	01851 705771	★★	Self Catering
Creagan	Creagan, Callanish, Stornoway, Isle of Lewis, HS2 9DY	01851 621200	★★★	Self Catering
Dunard	31 Urquhart Gardens, Stornoway, Isle of Lewis, HS1 2TX	01851 702458	★★★★	Self Catering
Herbridean Self Catering	Hebrides Self Catering, 29 Kenneth Street, Stornoway, Isle of Lewis, HS1 2DR	01851 700100	★★★★ → ★★★★★	Self Catering 🦽 𝄞𝄞
Kirklea Chalet	Kirklea Chalet, 8 School Road, Vatisker, Stornoway, Isle of Lewis, HS2 0JY	01851 820379	★★★	Self Catering
Park House	Lukhaya, Back, Isle of Lewis, HS2 0NA	01851 820969	★★★★	Self Catering
Plasterfield Cottage	Glamis, 10a Tong, Stornoway, Western Isles, HS2 0HS	01851 701038	★★★★	Self Catering
Vancouver	17 Tobson, Great Bernera, Isle of Lewis, HS2 9NA	01851 612347	★★★	Self Catering
Wemyss House	Tower Guest House, 32 James Street, Stornoway, Isle of Lewis, HS1 2QN	01851 703150	★★★	Self Catering
Gladstone House	14 Adabrock Ness, Stornaway, Isle of Lewis, HS2 0TW	01851 810269	★★★★	Self Catering
Newvalley Cottage	2 Bayview Crescent, Broadford, Isle of Skye, Inverness-shire, IV49 9BD	01471 822750	★★★★	Self Catering

Strachur

March Cottage	26 St Mary's Paddock, Wellingborough, Northamptonshire, NN8 1HJ	07722 532630	★★★	Self Catering

Straiton

Balbeg House	Balbeg House, Balbeg, Straiton, Ayrshire, KA19 7NN	01655 770665	★★★ → ★★★★	Self Catering 🦽
Blairquhan Castle Holiday Cottages	Blairquhan Estate Office, Straiton, Maybole, Ayrshire, KA19 7LZ	01655 770239	★★ → ★★★	Self Catering

Stranraer

Culmore Bridge	West Cottage, Culgroat, Stoneykirk, Stranraer, Wigtownshire, DG9 9DZ	01776 830539	★★★★	Self Catering ♿
High Drummore Cottage	Cardryne Farm, Drummore, Stranraer, Dumfries and Galloway, DG9 9HL	01776 840326	★★★★	Self Catering
Keek Afar	Dalhabboch Farm, New Luce Newton Stewart, DG8 0AY	01581 600228	★★★	Self Catering
Mains of Airies Holiday Cottages	Mains of Airies Holiday Cottages, Mains of Airies, Kirkcolm, Stranraer, Dumfries & Galloway, DG9 0RD	01776 854226	Awaiting Grading	
Mid Curghie	The Old Smiddy, Kirkmaiden, Drummore, Stranraer, Wigtownshire, DG9 9QR	01776 840676	★★★★	Self Catering
Mid Muntloch Farm	Mid Muntloch Farm, Drummore, Stranraer, Wigtownshire, DG9 9HL	01776 840225	★★	Self Catering

& Unassisted wheelchair access   🦽 Assisted wheelchair access   ♿ Access for visitors with mobility difficulties
𝄞 Bronze Green Tourism Award   𝄞𝄞 Silver Green Tourism Award   𝄞𝄞𝄞 Gold Green Tourism Award
For further information on our Green Tourism Business Scheme please see page 9.

Port-O-Spittal Bungalow	Port-O-Spittal Farmhouse, Portpatrick, Stranraer, Wigtownshire, DG9 9AD	01776 810412	★★★★	Self Catering	
The Loft	Whiteleys Farm, Stranraer Wigtownshire, DG9 3LY	01776 702994	★★★★	Self Catering	
The Stable & The Hayloft	Spoutwells, Stranraer Wigtownshire, DG9 8LX	01776 704086	★★★	Self Catering	
Dairy Cottage,East Challoch Farmhouse	East Challoch Farmhouse, Dunragit, Nr Stranraer, Dumfries and Galloway, DG9 8PY	01581 400391	★★★	Self Catering	

Strathaven
Drumboy Lodge	Springholm, Drumclog, Strathaven ML10 6QJ	01357 440544	★★★★	Self Catering	⋔

Strathcarron
Rowan Cottage	Rowan Cottage, 1 The Yews, Chippenhall Street, Crondall, Farnham, Surrey, SU10 5NX	01252 852382	★★★	Self Catering

Strathconon
Caberfeidh	Inverchoran, Strathconon, Muir Of Ord, Ross-shire, IV6 7QQ	01997 477252	★★★	Self Catering

Strathdon
Buchaam Farm	Buchaam Farm, Strathdon, Aberdeenshire, AB36 8TN	01975 651238	★★★	Self Catering

Strathkinness
4 Mount Melville	7 Elmbank Road, Langbank, Renfrewshire, PA14 6YT	01475 540441	★★★	Self Catering
Strathkinness House	Strathkinnes House, Sunnyside, by St Andrews, Fife, KY16 9XP	01334 850506	★★★★	Self Catering

Strathpeffer
Ben Wyvis Lodges	57 Airyhall Crescent, Aberdeen AB15 7QS	01224 318520	★★★	Self Catering
Birch Cottage	Kinellan Farmhouse, Strathpeffer, By Dingwall, Ross-shire, IV14 9ET	01997 421075	★★★	Self Catering
Nutwood House	Nutwood House, Nutwood, Strathpeffer, Ross-shire, IV14 9DT	01997 421344	★★★★	Self Catering
White Cottage	White Cottage, The Square, Strathpeffer, Ross-Shire, IV14 9AL	01997 421730	★★★	Self Catering

Strathtay
Dundarave Cottage	Dundarave Cottage, Strathtay, Perthshire, PH9 0PG	01887 840277	★★★	Self Catering

Strathyre
Ardoch Lodge	Ardoch Lodge, Strathyre, Perthshire, FK18 8NF	01877 384666	★★★ → ★★★★	Self Catering	🖉
Riverview	23 Starbank Road, Edinburgh EH5 3B7	0131 5512732	★★★★	Self Catering	

Strichen
Buchan House Cottage	Buchan House Cottage, Strichen AB43 6TP	01771 637367	★★★	Self Catering

Stromeferry
Portachullin Holidays	Portachullin Holidays, 167 Portachullin, Stromeferry, Ross-shire, IV53 8UW	01599 577267	★★★★	Self Catering

& Unassisted wheelchair access &. Assisted wheelchair access ⋔ Access for visitors with mobility difficulties
🖉 Bronze Green Tourism Award 🖉🖉 Silver Green Tourism Award 🖉🖉🖉 Gold Green Tourism Award
For further information on our Green Tourism Business Scheme please see page 9.

To find out more, call 0845 22 55 121 or go to visitscotland.com.

Strone

Angel Cottage	Riverside Quarter, Flat 211 Milliness House, London SW18 1LP	0208 871 9646	Awaiting Grading	

Stronmilchan

Celtic Cottages/Craig Lora	C/O Gurtons, Good Easter, Chelmsford, Essex, CM1 4QH	01245 231657	★★★★	Self Catering

Strontian, By Acharacle

Bluebell Croft	Bluebell Croft, 15 Anaheilt, Strontian, Highlands, PH36 4JA	01967 402226	★★★★★	Self Catering ♿ 🍃🍃🍃
Bruadar Iain	Dunwood House Farm, Dunwood Lane, Endon, Stoke on Trent, Staffs, ST9 9AP	01538 385853	★★★★	Self Catering
The Bield	14 St Quintin Park, Bathpool, Taunton, Somerset, TA2 8TB	01823 413840	★★★	Self Catering
Tom Fraoich	Cnoc Nam Fiadh, Longrigg Road, Strontian, By Acharacue, Argyll, PH36 4HY	01967 402470	★★★	Self Catering

Struan

Bracadale Holiday Cottages	The Sycamores, 2 Balgown, Struan, Isle of Skye, IV56 8FA	01470 572231	★★★	Self Catering
Meadale Cottage	Meadale Farm, Struan, Isle of Skye, IV56 8FY	01470 572216	★★★	Self Catering
Tarnershiel	Ashfield House, St Leonards, Tring, Hertfordshire, HB23 6NP	01494 758348	★★	Self Catering

Struy, by Beauly

Culligran Cottages	Culligran Cottages, Glen Strathfarrar, Struy, by Beauly, Inverness-shire, IV4 7JX	01463 761285	★★ → ★★★	Self Catering

Sutherland

Cambusmore Lodge	Cambusmore Lodge, Dornoch, Sutherland, IV25 3JD	01408 633187	★★ → ★★★	Self Catering
Riverside Cottage	Estate Office, The Kennels, Forsinard, Strath Halladale, Sutherland, KW13 6YT	01641 571271	★★★	Self Catering

Symington

Lily Cottage	Greenaway Scottish Holidays, 4 Woodland Street, Prestwick, Ayrshire, KA9 1RE	01292 473594	★★★★	Self Catering

By Tain

5/6 Geanies Farm Cottages	47 Kings Road, Tonbridge, Kent, TN9 2HB	01732 368 338	★★★	Self Catering

Talmine

Post Office Flat	Post Office Flat, Skinnet, Talmine, Sutherland, IV27 4YT	01847 601250	★★	Self Catering 🧍

Tannadice

Kalulu House	Kalulu House, East Murthill, Tannadice, Forfar, Angus, DD8 3SF	01307 860205	★★★ → ★★★★	Self Catering

Tarbert, Argyll

Afton Lodge	8 Canniesburn Quadrant, Bearsden, Glasgow G61 1RW	0141 942 2792	★★★	Self Catering
Ardyne	Flat 2/1, 397 Great Western Road, Glasgow G4 9HY	07940 564192	★★★★	Self Catering
Barr Na Criche Cottage	Barr Na Criche Cottage, Tarbert, Argyll, PA29 6YA	01880 820833	★★★	Self Catering

♿ Unassisted wheelchair access   ♿ Assisted wheelchair access   🧍 Access for visitors with mobility difficulties
🍃 Bronze Green Tourism Award   🍃🍃 Silver Green Tourism Award   🍃🍃🍃 Gold Green Tourism Award
For further information on our Green Tourism Business Scheme please see page 9.

Crubasdale Lodge Chalet	Crubasdale Lodge Chalet, Muasdale, Tarbert, Argyll, PA29 6XD	01583 421358	★★	Self Catering
Dunmore Court	Dunmore Court, Kilberry Road, Tarbert, Argyll, PA29 6XZ	01880 820654	★★	Self Catering
Killean Estate	Ruttle Plant Lancaster House, Common Bank Ind Estate, Chorley, Lancs, PR7 1NH	12570266511	★★★ → ★★★★	Self Catering
Laundry Cottage	Kilberry Castle, Kilberry, Tarbert, Loch Fyne, Argyll, PA29 6YD	01880 770217	★★★	Self Catering
Petersville	152 Weymouth Drive, Kelvindale, Glasgow G12 0ET	0141 334 3935	★★★	Self Catering
Skipness Holiday Cottages	Skipness Castle, Tarbert, Argyll, PA29 6XU	01880 760 207	★★ → ★★★	Self Catering
Tigh-Na-Creage	Tigh-Na-Creage, Muasdale, Tarbert, Argyll, PA29 6XD	01583 421270	★	Self Catering
West Loch Tarbert Holiday Park	West Loch Shores Tarbert, West Loch, Tarbert, Argyll, PA29 6YF	01880 820873	★★★★	Self Catering
Eriskay	The Croft, 43 High Street, Dollar, Clackmannanshire, FK14 7BJ	01259 742237	★★★★	Self Catering
Jura Apartments	Jura Apartments, Muasdale, Tarbert, Argyll, PA29 6XD	01583 421207	★★★	Self Catering
Loch Lomond Holiday Park	Loch Lomond Holiday Park, Inveruglas, by Tarbet, Argyll & Bute, G83 7DW	0141 956 1126	★★★★ → ★★★★★	Self Catering
Wee Dunultach	Dunultach, Clachan, by Tarbert, Argyll, PA29 6XW	01880 740650	★★★★	Self Catering

Tarbert, Isle of Harris

5 Caw	35 Nevis Park, Inverness, Inverness-shire, IV3 8RX	01463 223621	★★★	Self Catering
Fasgadh Studio	Fasgadh Studio, Main Street, Tarbert, Isle of Harris, HS3 3DJ	01859 502 060	★★★★	Self Catering
Kinnoull	7 Woodmarket, Kelso TD5 7AT	01573 224751	★★★	Self Catering
Kirklea Cottages	MacLeod Motel, Pier Road, Tarbert, Isle of Harris, Western Isles, HS3 3DJ	01859 502364	★★★★	Self Catering
Seaforth Cottage	Leuchair Cottage, Tarbert, Isle of Harris, HS3 3DB	01859 502473	★★★★	Self Catering
Tamh	82 Merrylee Road, Glasgow G43 2QZ	0141 6333744	★★★★	Self Catering
Ullabhal & Cleiseabhal	Hill Cottage, Tarbert, Isle of Harris, HS3 3DL	01859 502063	★★★★	Self Catering

Tarbet

Taobh an Allt	Kirstian House, 16 Stillingfleet Road, London SW13 9AE	0208 563 7535	★★★	Self Catering
The Smiddy	Stepping Stones, 5A Bellevue Road, Kirkintilloch, Glasgow G66 1AL	0141 578 1039	★★★	Self Catering

Tarland

9 Strachan Cottages	Mill Cottage, Logie Coldstone, Aboyne AB34 5PQ	01339 881401	★★	Self Catering

Taynuilt

Achadacallan	Tigh Na Haibhne, Taynuilt, Argyll, PA35 1JW		★★★	Self Catering
Airdeny Chalets	Airdeny Chalets, Glen Lonan, Taynuilt, Argyll, PA35 1HY	01866 822648	★★★ → ★★★★	Self Catering 𝒌
Airds Cottage	Airds Cottage, Taynuilt, Argyll, PA35 1JW	01866 822349	★★★	Self Catering
Ballimore House, Cottage and Lodge	Churchhouse Studios, Hudnall Lane, Little Gaddesden, Herts, HP4 1QE	07775 802050	★★★ → ★★★★	Self Catering

Bonawe House	Bonawe House, Taynuilt, by Oban, Argyll, PA35 1JQ	01866 822309	★★★ → ★★★★	Self Catering	🟊🟊
Kirkton Cottage & Mountain View	Dalry, Kirkton, Taynuilt, Argyll, PA35 1HW	01866 822657	★★★ → ★★★★	Self Catering	
Pine Lodge	Pine Lodge, Dalavaich, Taynuilt, Argyll, PA35 1HN	01866 844065	★★	Self Catering	
Sithean	Bunanta, Barguillean, Taynuilt, Argyll, PA35 1HY	01866 822110	★★★★	Self Catering 🦽	🟊🟊🟊
Tigh an Daraich	Tigh an Daraich, Bridge of Awe, Taynuilt, Argyll, PA35 1HR	01866 822693	★★★★ → ★★★★★	Self Catering 🦽	

By Taynuilt
Druimdarroch Cottage	5 Richmond Grove, Rutherglen, Glasgow G73 3LD	0141 6479016	★★★	Self Catering

Tayvallich
The Steading No 3	Inchjura, Carsaig Bay, Tayvallich, Argyll, PA31 8PN	01546 870294	★★★★	Self Catering

Thornhill
Clonwood	Sykes Farm, Scorton, Nr Preston, Lancashire, PR3 1DA	01524 791283	★★★	Self Catering
Hope Cottage	Carronhill, Thornhill, Dumfriesshire, DG3 5AZ	01848 331510	★★★★	Self Catering
Norrieston	Norrieston, Thornhill, Stirling, FK8 3QE	01786 850234	★★★	Self Catering
Old Tannery Cottage	95 South Drumlanrig Street, Thornhill, Dumfriesshire DG3 5LU	01848 330116	★★★★	Self Catering
Scaurbank Cottage	Scaurbank, Keir, Thornhill, Dumfries-shire, DG3 4DD	1848330933	★★★★	Self Catering
Templand Cottages	Templand Cottages, Templand Mains, Thornhill, Dumfriesshire, DG3 5AB	01848 330775	★★★	Self Catering 🦽
Hillcrest Barn	Hillcrest, Burnhead, Thornhill, Dumfriesshire, DG3 4AD	01848 331557	★★★	Self Catering

By Thornhill
Morton Mains Cottage	Oat Furlong, Winson, Cirencester, Glos, GL7 5ES	01285 720705	★	Self Catering

Thurso
Ash Cottage	West Greenland Farm, Castletown, Caithness KW14 8SX	01847 821633	★★★	Self Catering
No 2 Millbank Mews	Bridge House, Millbank Road, Thurso, Caithness, KW14 8PS	01847 891118	★★★	Self Catering
Shormary Cottage	Brier Cottage, Scarfskerry, Thurso, Caithness, KW14 8XN	01847 851357	★★★	Self Catering
Upper Clayock Cottage	56 Bravallen Road, Ballymoney, Antrim BT53 7DT	02827 666163	★★★	Self Catering

By Thurso
Curlew Cottage	Curlew Cottage, Hilliclay Mains, Weydale, Thurso, Caithness, KW14 8YN	01847 895638	★★★★	Self Catering 🚶

Tighnabruaich
Connas Cottage	Glen Maree, Millhouse, Tighnabruaich, Argyll & Bute, PA21 2DA	01700 811346	★★	Self Catering
Cuilbeag	3 Ledcameroch Road, Bearsden, Glasgow G61 4AA	0141 9427170	★★	Self Catering

🦽 Unassisted wheelchair access   🦽 Assisted wheelchair access   🚶 Access for visitors with mobility difficulties
🟊 Bronze Green Tourism Award   🟊🟊 Silver Green Tourism Award   🟊🟊🟊 Gold Green Tourism Award
For further information on our Green Tourism Business Scheme please see page 9.

By Tighnabruaich

Acharossan House	Old Schoolhouse, Strathlachlan, Strachur, Argyll, PA27 8BU	01369 860377	★★★★★	Self Catering
Largiemore Holiday Estate	Largiemore Holiday Estate, Otter Ferry, by Tighnabruaich, Argyll, PA21 2DH	01700 821235	★★ → ★★★★	Self Catering

Tillicoultry

West Wing- Westbourne House	Westbourne House, 10 Dollar Road, Tillicoultry, Clackmannanshire, FK13 6PA	01259 750314	★★★★	Self Catering

Timsgarry

Tigh A Bheannaich	Ocean View, Aird, Timsgarry, Isle of Lewis, HS2 9JA	01851 672360	★★★	Self Catering

Timsgearraidh

7a Eader Dha Fhadhail	1 Rosebery Mews, Mentmore, Leighton Buzzard, Bedfordshire, LU7 0UE	01296 668118	★★★★	Self Catering

Tobermory

Ach-Na-Clauran	Ling Mell, West End, Long Preston, Skipton, North Yorkshire, BD23 4QL	01729 840328	★★★	Self Catering
Assynt	Pendle House Farm, Barley, Nelson, Lancashire, BB9 6LG	01282 692816	★★★★	Self Catering
Bealach an Dreathan- Donn Cottage	Bealach An Dreathan Donn Cottage, Salen Road, Tobermory, Isle of Mull, PA75 6QB	01688 302517	★★★★	Self Catering
Beech & Willow, Cill-Mhoire	Cill-Mhoire, Dervaig, Tobermory, Isle of Mull, PA75 6QN	01688 400445	★★★	Self Catering ♿
Braeside House	c/o The Cottage, 48 Lichfield Lane, Mansfield, Nottinghamshire, NG18 4RE	01623 477670	★★★★	Self Catering
Bruach Roineach	Geat Nan Croisean, Calgary, Tobermory, Isle of Mull, Argyllshire, PA75 6QT	01688 400213	★★★★	Self Catering
Burnside Cottage	Baliscate House, Tobermory, Isle of Mull, PA75 6QA	01668 302048	★★★★	Self Catering
Calve and Aros	Caol Muile, Breadalbane Street, Tobermory, Isle of Mull, PA75 6PE	01688 302193	★★★	Self Catering
Crosslake	40 Crawford Drive, Glasgow G15 6TN	0141 944 4473	★★★	Self Catering
Dunard Cottage	Dunard House, Tobermory, Isle of Mull, Argyll, PA75 6PX	01688 302114	★★★	Self Catering
Fisherman's Cottage	AM Krautgarten 22-7, 1220 WIEN, Vienna, Austria1220	0043 1280 914	★★★	Self Catering
Glenfuran	12 Short Lane, Long Itchington, Southam, Warwickshire, CV47 9PB	01926 815744	★★★★	Self Catering
No 2 Royal Buildings	The Old Mill, Achleck, Torloisk, Isle of Mull, PA74 6NH	01688 500259	★★	Self Catering
No 6	5 Trent Place, Broadmeadows, East Kilbride, South Lanarkshire, G75 8RU	01355 236317	★★	Self Catering
Oakfield Cottage	77 Woodfield Park, Edinburgh, Lothian, EH13 0RA	0131 441 1259	★★★	Self Catering
Oxlip Cottage	Gordondale Cottage, 16 Kendal Road, Kemnay, Inverurie, Aberdeenshire, AB51 5RN	01467 641584	★★★	Self Catering
Penmore Beg	New Barns, Ravensthorpe, Northampton, NN6 8EH	01604 770868	★★	Self Catering
Raraig House	Raraig House, Raeric Road, Tobermory, Isle of Mull, PA75 6PU	01688 302390	★★★	Self Catering
Rockcliffe	Rockcliffe, Main Street, Tobermory, Isle of Mull, PA75 6NU	01688 302537	★★	Self Catering
Rowan Cottage	Wellpark Cottage, 10 wellpark Lane, Neilston, Renfrewshire, G78 3LF	0141 880 5208	★★★	Self Catering

♿ Unassisted wheelchair access   ♿ Assisted wheelchair access   ♿ Access for visitors with mobility difficulties
🅿 Bronze Green Tourism Award   🅿🅿 Silver Green Tourism Award   🅿🅿🅿 Gold Green Tourism Award
For further information on our Green Tourism Business Scheme please see page 9.

Name	Address	Phone	Rating	Type	
Spey Cottage	12 Knightsridge Road, Dechmont EH52 6LT	01506 811488	★★★	Self Catering	
Sunart, Morvern	Ledaig Holidays, Caladh, 5 Craigspuir Lane, Tobermory, Isle of Mull, Argyll, PA75 6RD	01688 302629	★★★	Self Catering	
The Lodge, Tigh Faire, Garden & Beadoun Cottages	Beadoun Cottage, Tobermory, Isle of Mull, PA75 6QA	01688 302075	★★★ → ★★★★	Self Catering	𝒫𝒫𝒫
The Rowans	19112 Bloomfield Road, Olney MD 20832, USA	001 301 92405	★★★	Self Catering	
Tigh Failte	33 Rushfords, Lingfield, Surrey, RH7 6EG	01342 834191	★★	Self Catering	
Tigh Na Acha	59 Church Road, Epsom, Surrey, KT17 4DN	01372 728525	★★★	Self Catering	
Torness	25 Munro Gate, Bridge of Allan FK9 4DJ		★★★★	Self Catering	
Tralee	19 Orwell Road, Walsall, West Midlands, WS1 2PJ	01922 624091	★★★★	Self Catering	
Ulva House Cottage	Ulva House, Tobermory, Isle of Mull, PA75 6PR	01688 302044	★★★★ → ★★★★★	Self Catering	
Victoria Cottage	Stoke Cottage, Mill Pool Lane, Barbridge, Nantwich, Cheshire, CW5 6AU	01270 528045	★★★	Self Catering	

By Tobermory

Name	Address	Phone	Rating	Type
Achnadrish House	Achnadrish House, Dervaig Road, by Tobermory, Isle of Mull, PA75 6QF	01688 400388	★★★	Self Catering
Glengorm Castle	Glengorm Castle, by Tobermory, Isle of Mull, PA75 6QE	01688 302321	★★★ → ★★★★★	Self Catering

Tolsta Chaolais, Isle of Lewis

Name	Address	Phone	Rating	Type
Tigh Bhisa Blackhouse	Loch Roag, 3 Tolsta Chaolais, Isle of Lewis, Western Isles, HS2 9DW	07884 310772	★★★★	Self Catering

Tomintoul

Name	Address	Phone	Rating	Type
Altnavoir	Altnavoir, Main Street, Tomintoul, Banffshire, AB37 9EX	01807 580336	★★★	Self Catering
Benavon	Benavon, 33 Main Street, Tomintoul, Ballindalloch, AB37 9EX	01807 580221	★★★	Self Catering
Croughly Cottage	Feochan, 11 Fisherfield, Viewfield Road, Portree, Isle of Skye, IV51 9EU	01478 613508	★★★	Self Catering
Livet Cottage Holidays	Livet Cottage Holidays, Livet House, 34 Main Street, Tomintoul, Banffshire, AB37 9EX	01807 580727	★★★	Self Catering

Tomnacharich

Name	Address	Phone	Rating	Type
The Logs	24 Zetland Avenue, Fort William, Inverness shire, PH33 6LL	01397 702532	★★★★	Self Catering

Tong, Isle of Lewis

Name	Address	Phone	Rating	Type
Beechland Self Catering Annexe	Beechland, Milkinghill, Tong, Isle of Lewis, HS2 0HU	01851 701533	★★★	Self Catering

Tore

Name	Address	Phone	Rating	Type
Kilcoy Chalets	Kellydown, Glaickbea, Kiltarlity, by Beauly, IV4 7HR	01463 741797	★★★	Self Catering

Torloisk

Name	Address	Phone	Rating	Type
Tostarie House	20 Braid Crescent, Edinburgh, Midlothian, EH10 6AU	0131 477 2130	★★	Self Catering
Bac Mor	Port Ranich Cottage, Torloisk, Ulvaferry, Isle of Mull, PA74 6NH	01688 500224	★★★	Self Catering

& Unassisted wheelchair access   𝒦 Assisted wheelchair access   𝑓 Access for visitors with mobility difficulties

𝒫 Bronze Green Tourism Award   𝒫𝒫 Silver Green Tourism Award   𝒫𝒫𝒫 Gold Green Tourism Award

For further information on our Green Tourism Business Scheme please see page 9.

Torphichen

Silver Mines	Wester Tartraven, by Cairnpapple Hill, Torphichen, West Lothian, EH48 4NP	01506 630836	★★★	Self Catering

Torridon

Badarroch	Badarroch Retreat, Croft 25, Diabaig, Torridon, Ross-shire, IV2 2HE	01445 790257	★★★★	Self Catering
Stalkers Cottage	National Trust for Scotland, 28 Charlotte Square, Edinburgh EH2 4ET	0131 243 9335	★★★	Self Catering
Wavecrest	Woodley Cottage, Goose St, Southwick, Trowbridge, Wilts, BA14 9RQ	01225 766379	★★★	Self Catering
Criche Cottage	Alma House, 12 William Street, Torphins, Banchory, Kincardineshire, AB31 4FR	01339 882711	★★★	Self Catering
The New Lodge, The Thrail House	Ben Damph Estates, Ethie Mains, Inverkeilor, Arbroath, Angus, DD11 5SN	01241 830258	★ → ★★★	Self Catering

By Torridon

Annat Lodge	46 Plewlands Gardens, Edinburgh, Mid Lothian, EH10 5JR	0131 447 5276	★★★★	Self Catering

Tranent

Woodside and Gateside	Faside Castle, Tranent, East Lothian, EH33 2LE	0131 665 7654	★★★★	Self Catering

Troon

124a Bentinck Drive	Little Heath House Cottage, Little Heath Lane, Berkhamsted, Herts, HP4 2RT	020 7637 3225	★★★	Self Catering
24H Bradan Road	11 Buford Street, Hoddesdon, Hertfordshire, EN11 8HP	07770 220840	★★★	Self Catering
Hillcrest	Southside Farm, Corriath Road, Troon, Ayrshire, KA10 7ET	01292 312534	★★★	Self Catering
Portland Villa	Portland Villa, 120 West Road, Congleton, Cheshire, CW12 4EU	07773 297674	★★★★	Self Catering
South Beach Cottage	14 Douglas Drive, Glasgow G77 6HR	0141 5770376	★★★★	Self Catering

Tullibody

7 McAlpine Court	3 Duchliage Terrace, Crieff, Perthshire, PH7 3AS	01764 652211	★★★	Self Catering

Turnberry

No. 1B, 1C, 1J	120 Eastwoodmains Road, Glasgow G76 7HH	0141 638 5760	★★★★★	Self Catering

Turrif

Preston Tower Apartment	National Trust for Scotland, 28 Charlotte Square, Edinburgh EH2 4ET	0131 243 9335	★★★	Self Catering	
Ardmiddle Mains	Ardmiddle Enterprises, Ardmiddle Mains, Turriff, Aberdeenshire, AB53 8AG	01888 562443	★★★★	Self Catering	🍃
Delgatie Castle	Delgatie Castle, Turriff, Aberdeenshire, AB53 5TD	01888 563479	★★★	Self Catering	♿
Garden Cottage	Byth House, New Byth AB53 5XN	01888 544230	★★★★	Self Catering	🦽
Penelopefield House	Penelopefield, Forglen, Turriff, Aberdeenshire, AB53 4LD	01888 562486	★★	Self Catering	
Stonefolds Farm Cottage	Stonefolds Farm Cottage, Fyvie, Turriff, Aberdeenshire, AB53 8NN	01651 891267	★★★★	Self Catering	🧍
The Cottage	South Brownhill Farm, Turriff, Aberdeenshire, AB53 4GZ	01466 781032	★★★★	Self Catering	

♿ Unassisted wheelchair access   🦽 Assisted wheelchair access   🧍 Access for visitors with mobility difficulties
🍃 Bronze Green Tourism Award   🍃🍃 Silver Green Tourism Award   🍃🍃🍃 Gold Green Tourism Award
For further information on our Green Tourism Business Scheme please see page 9.

To find out more, call 0845 22 55 121 or go to visitscotland.com.

By Turriff

Garden Cottage	National Trust for Scotland, 28 Charlotte Square, Edinburgh EH2 4ET	0131 243 9335	★★★★	Self Catering
Nettle Cottages, Auchterless	Nettle Cottages, Bogs Of Seggat, Auchterless, By Turriff, Aberdeenshire, AB53 8DL	01888 511168	★★★★	Self Catering

Twynholm

Doon Cottage	26 Queen Square, Strathbungo, Glasgow G41 2AZ	0141 423 9024	★★★★	Self Catering
Buie	High Borgue, Borgue, Kirkcudbright, DG6 4SX	01557 870226	★★★	Self Catering

Tyndrum

4 Clifton	16 Whitechapel Close, Oakwood, Leeds, West Yorkshire, LS8 2PT	0113 2329360	★★	Self Catering
Burnbrae Cottage	East Cottage, Auchtertyre, Tyndrum, Perthshire, FK20 8RU	01838 400251	★★★	Self Catering

Tynron

The Bothy at the Garth	The Garth, Tynron, Thornhill, Dumfriesshire, DG3 4JY	01848 200364	★★★	Self Catering
Millhouse Cotage	1 Brian Court, Sydney Road, London N1O 2LU	07765 252760	★★★	Self Catering

Uig, Isle of Skye

11B Riof	69A Upper Tollington Park, London N4 4DD	02072 634174	★★★	Self Catering		
23 Valtos	The Batch, Chesterblade, Shepton Mallet, Somerset, BA4 4QU	01749 880380	★★	Self Catering		
Barnellan	Lorien House, Station Road, Fort Augustus, Inverness-shire, PH32 4AY	01320 366736	★★★★	Self Catering		
Hawthorn Cottage	5 Linshader, Isle of Lewis HS2 9DR	01851 621419	★★★★	Self Catering		
Ocean View	19 Assaye Place, Stornoway, Isle of Lewis, HS1 2HA	01851 704751	★★★★	Self Catering		
Primrose Cottage Apartments	Cuil Lodge, Cuil, Uig, Isle of Skye, IV51 9YB	01470 542216	★★★	Self Catering		
Riof Ocean Cottage	Tigh a Mhuil, 7A Reef, Miavaig, Uig, Isle of Lewis, HS2 9HU	01851 672732	★★★★	Self Catering	♿	🍃
Scaliscro Lodge	Scaliscro Lodge, Scaliscro, Uig, Isle of Lewis, HS2 9EL	01851 672325	★	Self Catering		
Tigh-a-Ghoba & Tigh-nan-Eilean	17 Uigen, Uig, Stornoway, Isle of Lewis, HS2 9HX	1851672377	★★★ → ★★★★	Self Catering	♿	
Valtos Cottage	Valtos Cottage, 6 Long Lang, Stornoway, Isle of Lewis, HS1 2UA	01851 703957	★★★★★	Self Catering	♿	

Ullapool

Ailleag	Ullapool Holidays, Northfield, Beechcroft, Chislehurst, Kent, BR7 5DB	0208 4687086	★★★★	Self Catering
Ardmair House	13 Upper Bourtree Drive, Burnside, Glasgow, Lanarkshire, G73 4EJ	0141 634 1681	★★★	Self Catering
Ardvreck	13 Carmel Drive, Springside, Irvine, Ayrshire, KA11 3AG	01294 216991	★★★	Self Catering
Arkle House	Arkle Holidays, Skiba Lodge, Garve Road, Ullapool, Wester Ross, IV26 2SX	01854 612368	★★★	Self Catering
Beinn Ghobhlach & Carnfune Cottages	The Willows, Elphin, by Lairg, Sutherland, IV27 4HH	01854 666 217	★★★	Self Catering
Dolphin (House & Flat)	White's Farm House, Letcombe Bassett, Wantage, Oxfordshire, OX12 9LW	01235 763139	★★ → ★★★	Self Catering

♿ Unassisted wheelchair access   ♿ Assisted wheelchair access   🚶 Access for visitors with mobility difficulties
🍃 Bronze Green Tourism Award   🍃🍃 Silver Green Tourism Award   🍃🍃🍃 Gold Green Tourism Award
For further information on our Green Tourism Business Scheme please see page 9.

Hallival	24 West Shore Street, Ullapool, Ross-shire, IV26 2UR	01854 612680	★★★★	Self Catering	
Highveld	The Sheiling, Garve Road, Ullapool, Wester Ross, IV26 2SX	01854 612947	★★★	Self Catering	
Kilbrannan	Achmore, Moss Road, Ullapool IV26 2TF	01854 612236	★★★★	Self Catering	
Leckmelm Holiday Cottages	Leckmelm Holiday Cottages, Lochbroom, Ullapool, Ross-shire, IV23 2RL	01854 612471	★ → ★★★	Self Catering	🍃🍃🍃
Newton	Scourie Stores, Scourie, Sutherland IV27 4SX	01971 502221	★★★★	Self Catering	
No 3 Broom Cottages & Crofton House	Loch Broom Self Catering, West House, West Argyll Street, Ullapool, Ross-shire, IV26 2TY	01854 613126	Awaiting Grading		
Rubha Mor Self Catering	Rubha Mor Self Catering, Peacock House, Garve Road, Ullapool, Ross-shire, IV26 2SX	01854 612323	★★★★	Self Catering	🧍♿
Seagulls	Seagulls Ullapool, 80 Graeme Road, Enfield, Middlesex, EN1 3UT	02083 660843	★★★★	Self Catering	
The Chalet & The Cottage	Invercorrie, Braes, Ullapool, Wester Ross, IV26 2TB	01854 612272	★★	Self Catering	
Tigh Na Reultan	Jacob House Braes, Ullapool, Ross-shire, IV26 2SZ	01854 612775	★★★★	Self Catering	
Tigh Na Sith	23 Copper Beech View, Tonbridge, Kent, TN9 2HF	01732 367827	★★	Self Catering	
Waterfront Cottage	Waterfront Cottage, 27 West Shore Street, Ullapool, Ross-shire, IV26 2NR	01854 613454	★★★	Self Catering	
Clachan Garden Lodge	5 Allarburn Park, Kiltarlity, Inverness-shire, IV4 7HD	01463 741315	★★★★	Self Catering	

By Ullapool

Rhiroy Holiday Bungalow	1A Rhiroy, Lochbroom, Ullapool, Ross-shire, IV23 2SF	01854 655229	★★★★	Self Catering	

Ulva Ferry

Kilninian Schoolhouse	Birkscairn, 4 Venlaw Quarry Road, Peebles EH45 8RJ	01721 724428	★★★	Self Catering	

Upper Kilchattan

Colnatarun Cottage	Colnatarun Cottage, Upper Kilchattan, Isle of Colonsay, PA61	01951 200355	★★★	Self Catering	

Upper Largo

Holly Tree Cottage	2 Church Place, Upper Largo, Fife, KY8 6EH	01333 360297	★★★★	Self Catering	

Uyeasound

Hannigarth	Yarleton Oak, Yarleton Lane, May Hill, Longhope, Glos., GL19 0RF	01452 831881	★★★	Self Catering	

Walkerburn

57 Galashiels Road	48 Edinburgh Road, Penicuik, Midlothian, EH26 8NR	01968 672045	★★	Self Catering	

By Walkerburn

Eliburn Cottage	Elibank House, Nr Walkerburn, Peeblesshire, EH43 6DA	01896 870218	★★★★	Self Catering	

Wanlockhead

2 Mitchell Place	Silver Rake, Brynford, Holywell, Flintshire, CH8 8LS	01352 714992	★★★	Self Catering	

♿ Unassisted wheelchair access   ♿ Assisted wheelchair access   🧍 Access for visitors with mobility difficulties
🍃 Bronze Green Tourism Award   🍃🍃 Silver Green Tourism Award   🍃🍃🍃 Gold Green Tourism Award
For further information on our Green Tourism Business Scheme please see page 9.

To find out more, call 0845 22 55 121 or go to visitscotland.com.

Waternish, Isle of Skye

11 Hallin Park	23 Langside Avenue, London SW15 5QT	020 8876 3054	★★★	Self Catering
Ardmore Holiday Cottage	3 Ardmore, Waternish, Isle of Skye, IV55 8GW	01470 592305	★★★	Self Catering
Auld Orwell Cottage	Auld Orwell Cottage, 17 Lochbay, Waternish, Isle of Skye, IV55 8GD	01470 592363	★★★★	Self Catering ♿
Clachan View	Leachkin Lodge, Inverness, Inverness-shire, IV3 8PN	01463 713199	★★★	Self Catering
Eilean Isay	6 Lowther Avenue, Bearsden, Glasgow G61 4RE	0141 222 3410	★★	Self Catering
La Bergerie	La Bergerie, 33 Lochbay, Waternish, Isle of Skye, IV55 8GD	01470 592282	★★★★	Self Catering ♿
Lochbay Boathouse	Barr Cottage, Auchencairn, Castle Douglas, Dumfriesshire, DG7 1QL	01556 640245	★★★★	Self Catering
Stein Inn Apartment	Stein Inn, MacLeods Terrace, Waternish, Isle of Skye, IV55 8GA	01470 592362	★★★	Self Catering
The Old Mission Hall	285 Hill Park Drive, Glasgow G43 2SD	0141 585 3155	★★★	Self Catering
Tigh Na Mara	9 Moy Terrace, Inverness Highlands, IV2 4EL	01463 715939	★★★	Self Catering
Gesto Cottage	20 Lochbay, Waternish, Isle of Skye, Inverness-shire, IV55 8GD	01470 592 281	★★★	Self Catering

Waterside

The Wee Byre	Hareshaw Farm, Waterside, Kilmarnock, Ayrshire, KA3 6JA	01560 600360	★★★	Self Catering

West Dunbartonshire

The Cat's Whiskers	The Cat's Whiskers, Cat's Castle, Cardross Road, W Dunbartonshire, G82 5EN	01309 762710	★★★★	Self Catering

By West Calder

Crosswoodhill Farm	Crosswoodhill Farm, By West Calder, West Lothian, EH55 8LP	01501 785205	★★★ → ★★★★★	Self Catering ♿

West Fishwick

Bunnahabhain,Strathisla,and Tomatin	Strathmore, West Fishwick, Berwick Upon Tweed TD15 1XQ	01289 386279	★★★★★	Self Catering ♿

West Linton

Anne's Cottage & Roberton Mains Lodge	Roberton Mains Farm, Dolphinton, Peeblesshire, EH46 7AB	01968 682256	★★★	Self Catering
Croft Loft	Croft Loft, Croft Road, West Linton, Peebles-shire, EH46 7DZ	01968 661333	★★★★	Self Catering
Loch & America Cottages	Slipperfield House, West Linton, Peeblesshire, EH46 7AA	01968 660401	★★★ → ★★★★	Self Catering

By West Linton

Mill Cottage, Romanno Bridge	Damside, Romanno Bridge, West Linton, Peeblesshire, EH46 7BY	01968-660887	★★★★	Self Catering ✝
Steading Cottage, Dolphinton	Ferniehaugh, Dolphinton, Peebleshire, EH46 7HJ	01986 682257	★★★	Self Catering

West Wemyss

Dorothy Cottage	160 Hall Lane, Horsforth, Leeds, West Yorkshire, LS18 5EG	07831 869663	★★★★	Self Catering

♿ Unassisted wheelchair access   ♿ Assisted wheelchair access   ✝ Access for visitors with mobility difficulties
🏵 Bronze Green Tourism Award   🏵🏵 Silver Green Tourism Award   🏵🏵🏵 Gold Green Tourism Award
For further information on our Green Tourism Business Scheme please see page 9.

Westhill

Firthview House, Links View & The Gatehouse	Blackpark Farm, Westhill, Inverness IV2 5BP	01463 790620	★★★★	Self Catering	🦽	🍃🍃🍃
Pond Cottage	Broomfold, Kingswells, Aberdeen, Aberdeenshire, AB15 8SS	01224 743033	★★★★	Self Catering		

Westmuir

Westmuir Holiday	5 High Street, Alyth, Perthshire, PH11 8DW	01828 632568	★★★	Self Catering	🚶

Whitebridge

Wildside Highland Lodges	Wildside Highland Lodges, Whitebridge, Inverness IV2 6UN	01456 486373	★★★★	Self Catering

Whitecairns

Ardo Mains House & Garden Cottage	Ardo House, Whitecairns, Aberdeenshire, AB23 8XN	01358 742276	★★★	Self Catering

Whitehills

Belvedere	Keithen, Cuminestown, Turriff, Aberdeenshire, AB53 8JD	01888 544359	★★★	Self Catering

Whiteinch

Manor Apartments	Manor Park Hotel, 28 Balshagray Drive, Glasgow G11 7DD	0141 339 2143	★★★	Self Catering

Whithorn

Mid Bishopton Bungalow	Old Bishopton, Whithorn, Wigtownshire, DG8 8DE	01988 500754	★★	Self Catering
Pend and Precint House	3 George Street, Whithorn, Wigtownshire, DG8 8NS	01988 500475	★★★★	Self Catering
Ravenstone Mains Cottage	Ravenstone Stables, Ravenstone, Whithorn, Newton Stewart, Dumfries and Galloway, DG8 8DS	01988 850377	★★★	Self Catering

Whiting Bay, Isle of Arran

Ardbeag	Adrbeag Properties, McLarens Nurseries,Lochlibo Road, Uplawnmoor,Barrhead, Glasgow, G78 4DN	01505 850666	★★★	Self Catering	
Arnhall Cottage	Arnhall, Shore Road, Whiting bay, Arran, KA27 8PX	01770 700054	★★★	Self Catering	
Benview Cottage	Benview, Golf Course Road, Whiting Bay, Isle of Arran, KA27 8QT	01770 700275	★★★	Self Catering	
Birchbrae	Birchbrae, Silver Hill, Whiting Bay, Isle of Arran, KA27 8QR	01770 700436	Awaiting Grading		
Braehead Cottage	Tower House, Milliken Park Road, Kilbarchan, Renfrewshire, PA10 2DB	01505 703299	★★★	Self Catering	
Bramble Cottage	50 Bellahouston Drive, Glasgow G52 1HQ	0141 882 2094	★★★	Self Catering	
Cairnsaieh	22 Whittingehame Drive, Glasgow G12 0XX	01770 302303	★★★	Self Catering	
Carraig Dhubh Nos 1,2 & 3	Rowarden, Lamlash, Isle of Arran, KA27 8NB	01770 600 324	★★★	Self Catering	
Dunollie	18 Thorncliffe Gardens, Glasgow G41 2DE	0141 636 0542	★★★	Self Catering	
Fiodh Ban	Fiodh Ban, Golf Course Road, Whiting Bay, Isle of Arran, KA27 8QJ	7771907575	★★★	Self Catering	
Grenrof	37 Mount Charles Crescent, Ayr, Ayrshire, KA7 4PA	01292 443267	★★★	Self Catering	🚶
Kebars	2 Crawfurds View, Lochwinnoch, Renfrewshire, PA12 4EJ	01505 842120	★★	Self Catering	

🦽 Unassisted wheelchair access   🦽 Assisted wheelchair access   🚶 Access for visitors with mobility difficulties
🍃 Bronze Green Tourism Award   🍃🍃 Silver Green Tourism Award   🍃🍃🍃 Gold Green Tourism Award
For further information on our Green Tourism Business Scheme please see page 9.

Nirvana	166 Carscadden Road, Glasgow G15 8SY	0141 944 4479	Awaiting Grading	
Norwood Cottage & The Smiddy	Norwood and The Smiddy, Smiddy Brae, Whiting Bay, Isle of Arran, KA27 8PR	017707 00 536	★★★★	Self Catering
Runrig	1 Borden Road, Glasgow G13 1RB	0141 9548068	★★★	Self Catering
Sandbraes Lodge	Sandbraes Villa, Whiting Bay, Isle of Arran, KA27 8RE	01770 700235	★★★	Self Catering 🕆
Seaview Croft & Seahaven Cottage	Glenburn, Whiting Bay, Isle of Arran, KA27 8PZ	01770 700680	★★★★	Self Catering
The Coach-House	The Coach-House, Whiting Bay, Isle of Arran, KA27 8QH	01770 303111	★★★	Self Catering
The Summer House	Knockankelly Farm, Whiting Bay, Isle of Arran, KA27 8RQ	01770 700649	★★★	Self Catering 🌿🌿
Trafalgar & Garret Cottage	Flat 2/2, 31 Garry Street, Cathcart, Glasgow G44 4AZ	0141 6332322	★★★	Self Catering

Wick

| Bilbster Mains | Bilbster Mains, Wick, Caithness, KW1 4TA | 01955 621226 | ★★★★ | Self Catering |
| Corner House | 37-38 Bank Row, Wick, Caithness, KW1 5EY | 01955 603500 | ★★★★ | Self Catering |

Wigtown

| Maidland Lodge | Maidland Lodge, Maidland Farm, Wigtown, Newton Stewart, DG8 9AA | 01988 403270 | ★★★ | Self Catering |
| The Barn At Glenturk | The Firm Of Glenturk Pedigree Herds, Glenturk, Wigtown, Newton Stewart, Dumfries & Galloway, DG8 9TF | 01988 402281 | ★★★★ | Self Catering |

Wilsontown, Forth

| Cleugh Farm | Cleugh Farm, Wilsontown Forth, Lanark, ML11 8ES | 01555 811932 | ★★★★ | Self Catering |

Yarrowford

| Broadmeadows House | Yarrow House, Yarrowford, Selkirk, TD7 5LZ | 01750 725014 | ★★★★ | Self Catering |

Yell, Shetland

| Overby | Manfield Park, Bowling Green Lane, Manfield, Darlington, North Yorkshire, DL2 2RL | 01325 710143 | ★★★ | Self Catering |

Yetholm

| 3 Lambing Field Cottage | Cliftoncote Farm, Yetholm, Roxburghshire, TD5 8PU | 01573 420241 | ★★ | Self Catering |
| Cherrytrees Cottage | 10 Hillpark Crescent, Edinburgh, Midlothian, EH4 7BG | 0131 336 5329 | ★★★★ | Self Catering |

 Unassisted wheelchair access   Assisted wheelchair access 🕆 Access for visitors with mobility difficulties
🌿 Bronze Green Tourism Award 🌿🌿 Silver Green Tourism Award 🌿🌿🌿 Gold Green Tourism Award
For further information on our Green Tourism Business Scheme please see page 9.

Awards correct as of mid August 2008

365

Aberfeldy

Aberfeldy Caravan Park	Dunkeld Road, Aberfeldy, Perthshire, PH15 2AQ	01887 820662	★★★★	Touring Park

Aberfoyle

Cobleland Caravan and Campsite	Aberfoyle, Stirling, FK8 3RR	01877 382392	★★★	Touring Park	
Trossachs Holiday Park	Aberfoyle, Stirling, FK8 3SA	01877 382614	★★★★★	Holiday Park	₽₽₽

Aberlady

Aberlady Station Caravan Park	Aberlady, East Lothian, EH32 0PZ	01875 870666	★★★	Touring Park

Aberlour

Speyside Camping & Caravanning Club Site	Archiestown, Aberlour, Morayshire, AB38 9SL	0845 1307633	★★★★	Touring Park
Aberlour Gardens	Caravan & Camping Park, Aberlour, Morayshire, AB38 9LD	01340 871586	★★★★★	Holiday Park

Abington

Mount View Caravan Park	Station Road, Abington, South Lanarkshire, ML12 6RW	01864 502808	★★★★	Holiday Park

Aboyne

Tarland Camping & Caravanning Club Site	Drummie Hill, Tarland, Aboyne, Aberdeenshire, AB34 4UP	0845 1307633	★★★★★	Touring Park
Royal Deeside Log Cabins	By Loch Kinord, Dinnet, Aboyne, Aberdeenshire, AB34 5LW	013398 85229	Holiday Caravan	

Acharacle

Branault Croft Caravans	Achateny, Acharacle, Argyll, PH36 4LG	01972 510284	Holiday Caravan	
Burnbank	Acharacle, Argyll, PH36 4JL	01967 431223	Holiday Caravan	

By Acharacle

Resipole Farm Caravan Park	Loch Sunart, By Acharacle, Argyll, PH36 4HX	01967 431235	★★★★	Holiday Park

Achnasheen

Kinlochewe Caravan Club Site	Kinlochewe, Achnasheen, Highland, IV22 2PA	01445 760239	★★★★★	Touring Park

Alford

Haughton Caravan Park	Montgarrie Road, Alford, Aberdeenshire, AB33 8NA	01975 562107	★★★★	Holiday Park

Annan

Galabank Caravan & Camping Site	North Street, Annan, Dumfriesshire, DG12 5DQ	01556 503806	★★	Touring Park
Queensberry Bay Caravan Park	Powfoot, Annan, Dumfriesshire, DG12 5PU	01461 700205	★★★★	Holiday Park

Appin

Appin Holiday Homes	Appin, Argyll, PA38 4BQ	01631 730287	★★★★	Holiday Park

♧ Unassisted wheelchair access   ♧ Assisted wheelchair access   ☰ Access for visitors with mobility difficulties
₽ Bronze Green Tourism Award   ₽₽ Silver Green Tourism Award   ₽₽₽ Gold Green Tourism Award
For further information on our Green Tourism Business Scheme please see page 9.

366   To find out more, call 0845 22 55 121 or go to visitscotland.com.

Ardlui

Beinglas Farm Campsite	Inverarnan, Ardlui, Dumbartonshire, G83 7DX	01301 704281	★★★★	Camping Park

Arisaig

Camusdarach	Camusdarach Lodge, Arisaig, Inverness-shire, PH39 4NT	01687 450221	★★★★	Touring Park	🍃🍃🍃
Kinloid Caravans	Arisaig, Inverness-shire, PH39 4NS	01687 450366		Holiday Caravan	

Armadale

Poulouriscaig	169 West End, Armadale, Caithness, KW14 7SA	01641 541269	Holiday Caravan

Aros, Isle of Mull

Crannich Holiday Caravans	Crannich Farm, Aros, Isle of Mull PA72 6JP	01680 300495	Holiday Caravan
Pennygown Farm	Aros, Isle of Mull PA72 6JN	01680 300335	Holiday Caravan
Rock Cottage	Aros, Isle of Mull PA72 6JB	01680 300506	Holiday Caravan
Torr Gorm	Salen, Aros, Isle of Mull PA72 6JB	01680 300501	Holiday Caravan

Arrochar

Ardgartan Camping & Caravanning Club Site	Coilessan Road, Arrochar, Dunbartonshire, G83 7AR	0845 1307633	★★★	Touring Park
Ardgarten Caravan & Campsite	Arrochar, Dunbartonshire, G83 7AR	01301 702293	★★★	Touring Park

Aviemore

Dalraddy Holiday Park	Aviemore, Inverness-shire, PH22 1QB	01479 810330	★★★★	Holiday Park
Glenmore Caravan & Campsite	Glenmore, Aviemore, Inverness-shire, PH22 1QU	01479 861271	★★★★	Touring Park
Speyside Highland Leisure Park	Aviemore, Inverness-shire, PH22 1PX	01479 810694		Holiday Caravan
Speyside Leisure Park	Dalfaber Road, Aviemore, Inverness-shire, PH22 1PX	01479 810236	★★★★	Holiday Park

Ayr

Craig Tara	Dunure Road, Ayr, Ayrshire, KA7 4LB	01292 265141	★★★★	Holiday Park
Craigie Gardens Caravan Club Site	Craigie Road, Ayr, Ayrshire, KA8 0SS	01292 264909	★★★★★	Touring Park
Heads of Ayr Caravan Park	Dunure Road, Ayr, Ayrshire, KA7 4LD	01292 442269	★★★★	Holiday Park

By Ayr

Middlemuir Park	Tarbolton, By Ayr, Ayrshire, KA5 5NR	01292 541647	★★★★	Holiday Park
Croft Head Caravan Park	By Ayr, Ayrshire, KA6 6EN	01292 263516	★★★★	Holiday Park
Sundrum Castle Holiday Park	Coylton, By Ayr, Ayrshire, KA6 6HX	01292 570057	★★★★★	Holiday Park

Ballachulish

Glencoe Camping & Caravanning Club Site	Ballachulish, Argyll, PH49 4LA	0845 1307633	★★★★	Touring Park

  ♿ Unassisted wheelchair access   ♿ Assisted wheelchair access   🕴 Access for visitors with mobility difficulties
🍃 Bronze Green Tourism Award   🍃🍃 Silver Green Tourism Award   🍃🍃🍃 Gold Green Tourism Award
For further information on our Green Tourism Business Scheme please see page 9.

Ballater

Ballater Caravan Park	Anderson Road, Ballater, Kincardineshire, AB35 5QR	01339 855727	★★★	Holiday Park

Banchory

Feughside Caravan Park	Strachan, Banchory, Aberdeenshire, AB31 6NT	01330 850669	★★★★	Holiday Park

Banff

Banff Links Caravan Park	Banff Links, Banff, Grampian, AB45 2JJ	01261 812228	★★★★	Holiday Park

Beauly

Rheindown Farm	Beauly, Inverness-shire, IV4 7AB	01463 782461	Holiday Caravan
The Croft House	9 Ruilick, Beauly, Inverness-shire, IV4 7AB	01463 782381	Holiday Caravan

By Beauly

Dunedin	Cannich, By Beauly, Inverness-shire, IV4 7LS	01456 415238		Holiday Caravan
Cannich Caravan & Camping Park	Cannich, By Beauly, Inverness-shire, IV4 7LN	01456 415364	★★★★	Holiday Park

Blackburn

Mosshall Farm Caravan Park	Blackburn, West Lothian, EH47 7DB	01501 762318	★★	Touring Park	
Blair Castle Caravan Park	Blair Atholl, Perthshire, PH18 5SR	01796 481263	★★★★★	Holiday Park	🌿🌿

Blairgowrie

Blairgowrie Holiday Park	Rattray, Blairgowrie, Perthshire, PH10 7AL	01250 876666	★★★★★	Holiday Park
Five Roads Caravan Park	by Alyth, Blairgowrie, Perthshire, PH11 8NB	01828 632255	★★★★	Holiday Park

By Blairgowrie

Corriefodly Holiday Park	Bridge of Cally, By Blairgowrie, Perthshire, PH10 7JG	01250 886236	★★★★★	Holiday Park

Blairlogie

Witches Craig Caravan Park	Blairlogie, Stirling, FK9 5PX	01786 474947	★★★★★	Touring Park

Boat of Garten

Boat of Garten Holiday Park	Desmar Road, Boat of Garten, Inverness-shire, PH24 3BN	01479 831652	★★★★	Holiday Park
Loch Garten Caravan Park	Loch Garten Road, Boat of Garten, Inverness-shire, PH24 3BY	01479 831769	★★★★	Holiday Park

Braemar

The Invercauld Caravan Club Site	Glenshee Road, Braemar, Aberdeenshire, AB35 5YQ	01339 741373	★★★★	Touring Park

Brechin

Glenesk Caravan Park	by Edzell, Brechin, Angus, DD9 7YP	01356 648565	★★★★	Holiday Park

♿ Unassisted wheelchair access   ♿ Assisted wheelchair access   ⛹ Access for visitors with mobility difficulties
🌿 Bronze Green Tourism Award   🌿🌿 Silver Green Tourism Award   🌿🌿🌿 Gold Green Tourism Award
For further information on our Green Tourism Business Scheme please see page 9.

368   To find out more, call 0845 22 55 121 or go to visitscotland.com.

Brora

Dalchalm Caravan Club Site	Dalchalm, Brora, Sutherland, KW9 6LP	01408 621479	★★★★★	Touring Park

Buckie

Strathlene Caravan Park	Portessie, Buckie, Banffshire, AB56 4DJ	01542 834851	★★★★	Holiday Park

Bunessan, Isle of Mull

Newcrofts	6 Uisken Road, Bunessan, Isle of Mull PA67 6PS	01681 700471		Holiday Caravan

Cairnryan

Cairnryan Caravan Park	Cairnryan, Wigtownshire, DG9 8QX	01581 200231	★★★★	Holiday Park

Callander

Keltie Bridge Caravan Park	Callander, Perthshire, FK17 8LQ	01877 330606	★★★★	Touring Park
Gart Caravan Park	Stirling Road, Callander, Perthshire, FK17 8LE	01877 330002	★★★★★	Holiday Park

By Campbeltown

Peninver Sands Holiday Park	Craig View, Peninver, By Campbeltown, Argyll, PA28 6QP	01586 552262	★★★★	Holiday Park
Peniver Beach	By Campbeltown, Argyll, PA28 6PW	01586 810210		Holiday Caravan
Seaviews at Pennyseorach Farm	Southend, By Campbeltown, Argyll, PA28 6RF	01586 830217		Holiday Caravan

Carnoustie

Woodlands Caravan Park	Newton Road, Carnoustie, Angus, DD7 7SR	01241 854430	★★★★	Touring Park

Castle Douglas

Loch Ken Holiday Park	Parton, Castle Douglas, Kirkcudbrightshire, DG7 3NE	01644 470282	★★★★	Holiday Park
Lochside Caravan & Camping Site	Lochside Park, by Carlingwark Loch, Castle Douglas, Kirkcudbrightshire, DG7 1EZ	01556 503806	★★★★	Touring Park
Netheryett Caravan	Netheryett, Castle Douglas, Kirkcudbrightshire, DG7 3JZ	01556 660213		Holiday Caravan

By Castle Douglas

Barlochan Caravan Park	Palnackie, By Castle Douglas, Kirkcudbrightshire, DG7 1PF	01556 600256	★★★★	Holiday Park

Cocksburnpath

Pease Bay Caravan Park	Cocksburnpath, Berwickshire, TD13 5YP	01368 830206	★★★★★	Holiday Park	♿

Coldingham

Crosslaw Caravan Park	Coldingham, Berwickshire, TD14 5NS	01890 771316	★★★★★	Holiday Park	♿
Scoutscroft Holiday Centre	St Abbs Road, Coldingham, Berwickshire, TD14 5NB	01890 771338	★★★★★	Holiday Park	

Comrie

West Lodge Caravan Park	West Lodge, Comrie, Perthshire, PH6 2LS	01764 670354	★★★★	Holiday Park

& Unassisted wheelchair access   & Assisted wheelchair access   ♈ Access for visitors with mobility difficulties
Bronze Green Tourism Award   Silver Green Tourism Award   Gold Green Tourism Award
For further information on our Green Tourism Business Scheme please see page 9.

Connel

| Cluaran House | Ardconnel Farm, Connel, Argyll, PA37 1RN | 01631 710051 | | Holiday Caravan |

By Connel

| Oban Camping & Caravanning Club Site | Barcaldine, By Connel, Arygll, PA37 1SG | 0845 1307633 | ★★★★ | Touring Park |

Contin

| Riverside Chalets & Caravan Park | Contin, Ross-shire, IV14 9ES | 0800 074 4843 | ★★ | Touring Park |

Corpach

| Cruachan | 19 Badabrie, Corpach, Fort William, PH33 7JG | 01397 772573 | | Holiday Caravan |

Craignure, Isle of Mull

| Shieling Holidays | Craignure, Isle of Mull PA65 6AY | 01680 812496 | ★★★★★ | Camping Park |

By Craignure, Isle of Mull

| Inverlussa | By Craignure, Isle of Mull PA65 6BD | 01680 812436 | | Holiday Caravan |

Crail

| Sauchope Links Caravan Park | Crail, Fife, KY10 3XJ | 01333 870446 | ★★★★★ | Holiday Park |

Crianlarich

| Glendochart Caravan Park | Luib, Crianlarich, Perthshire, FK20 8QT | 01567 820637 | ★★★★ | Holiday Park |

Crieff

| Braidhaugh Park | South Bridgend, Crieff, Perthshire, PH7 4HP | 01764 652951 | ★★★★ | Holiday Park |

By Crieff

| Comrie Croft | A85, By Crieff, Perthshire, PH7 4JZ | 01764 670140 | | Awaiting Grading |

Crocketford

| Park of Brandedleys | Crocketford, Dumfriesshire, DG2 8RG | 01387 266700 | ★★★★ | Holiday Park |

Cullen

| Cullen Bay Holiday Park | Logie Drive, Cullen, Banffshire, AB56 4TW | 01542 840766 | ★★★★ | Holiday Park |

Culloden Moor

| Culloden Moor Caravan Club Site | Newlands, Culloden Moor, Inverness-shire, IV2 5EF | 01463 790625 | ★★★★★ | Touring Park |

Dalbeattie

| Glenearly Caravan Park | Park Farm, Dalbeattie, Kirkcudbrightshire, DG5 4NE | 01556 611393 | ★★★★ | Holiday Park |

By Dalbeattie

| Sandyhills Bay Leisure Park | Sandyhills, By Dalbeattie, Kirkcudbrightshire, DG5 4NY | 01387 780257 | ★★★★ | Holiday Park |

Dalkeith

Lothian Bridge Caravan Park	Lothian Bridge, Newton Grange, Dalkeith, Midlothian, EH22 4TP	0131 663 6120	★★★★	Touring Park

Daviot East

Auchnahillin Caravan & Camping Park	Daviot East, Inverness-shire, IV2 5XQ	01463 772286	★★★★	Holiday Park

Dingwall

Dingwall Camping & Caravanning Club Site	Jubilee Park Road, Dingwall, Ross-shire, IV15 9QZ	0845 1307633	★★★★	Touring Park

Dirleton

Yellowcraig Caravan Club Site	Dirleton, East Lothian, EH39 5DS	01620 850217	★★★★★	Touring Park

Dornoch

Dornoch Caravan & Camping Park	The Links, Dornoch, Sutherland, IV25 3LX	01862 810423	★★★★	Holiday Park
Dornoch Links Caravan Park	Dornoch, Sutherland, IV25 3LQ	01862 810366		Holiday Caravan
Grannies Heilan Hame Holiday Park	Embo, Dornoch, Sutherland, IV25 3QD	01862 810383	★★★★	Holiday Park
Seaview Farm Caravan Park	Seaview, Hilton, Dornoch, Sutherland, IV25 3PW	01862 810294	★★	Touring Park

Drumnadrochit

Blairbeg Caravan	Blairbeg, Drumnadrochit, Inverness-shire, IV63 6UG	01456 459350		Holiday Caravan

Drymen

Milarrochy Bay Camping & Caravanning Club Site	Balmaha, Drymen, Glasgow, G63 0AL	0845 1307633	★★★★	Touring Park
Drymen Camping	Easter Drumquhassle Farm, Gartness Road, Drymen, Stirlingshire, G63 0DN	01360 660597	★★	Camping Park

Dumfries

Barnsoul Farm	Shawhead, Irongray, Dumfries, Dumfriesshire, DG2 9SQ	01387 730249	★★★	Holiday Park
New Farm	Southwick, Dumfries, Kirkcudbrightshire, DG2 8AP	01387 780285		Holiday Caravan

Dunbar

Belhaven Bay Caravan Park	Belhaven Bay, Dunbar, East Lothian, EH42 1TU	01368 865956	★★★★	Holiday Park	♿
Dunbar Camping and Caravanning Club Site	Oxwellmains, Dunbar, East Lothian, EH42 1WG	01368 866881	Awaiting Grading		
Thurston Manor Holiday Home Park	Innerwick, Dunbar, East Lothian, EH42 1SA	01368 840643	★★★★★	Holiday Park	♿

Dunbeath

Inver Caravan Park	Houstry Road, Dunbeath, Caithness, KW6 6EH	01593 731441	★★★	Touring Park

Dundonnell

4 Camusnagaul	Dundonnell, Ross-shire, IV23 2QT	01854 633237		Holiday Caravan	
Badrallach Bothy & Camp Site	Croft No 9, Badrallach, Dundonnell, Ross-shire, IV23 2QP	01854 633281	★★★★	Camping Park	🌿

 ♿ Unassisted wheelchair access ♿ Assisted wheelchair access ♦ Access for visitors with mobility difficulties
🌿 Bronze Green Tourism Award 🌿🌿 Silver Green Tourism Award 🌿🌿🌿 Gold Green Tourism Award
For further information on our Green Tourism Business Scheme please see page 9.

Dunkeld

Erigmore House Holiday Park	Birnam, Dunkeld, Perthshire, PH8 0BJ	01350 727236	★★★★	Holiday Park
Invermill Farm Caravan Park	Inver, Dunkeld, Perthshire, PH8 0JR	01350 727477	★★★★	Touring Park

Dunnet

Dunnet Bay Caravan Club Site	Dunnet, Thurso, KW14 8XD	01847 821319	★★★★★	Touring Park

Dunoon

Hunters Quay Holiday Village	Hunters Quay, Dunoon, Argyll, PA23 8HP	01369 707772	★★★★★	Holiday Park

Dunvegan

Kinloch Campsite	Dunvegan, Isle of Skye, IV55 8WQ	01470 521210	★★★	Touring Park

East Calder

Linwater Caravan Park	West Clifton, East Calder, West Lothian, EH53 0HT	0131 333 3326	★★★★	Touring Park

Edinbane

Skye Camping & Caravanning Club Site	Borve, Mr Arnishort, Edinbane, Isle of Skye, IV51 9PS	01470 582230	Awaiting Grading	

Edinburgh

Edinburgh Caravan Club Site	Marine Drive, Edinburgh EH4 5EN	0131 312 6874	★★★★★	Touring Park	
Mortonhall Caravan Park	38 Mortonhall Gate, Frogston Road East, Edinburgh EH16 6TJ	0131 664 1533	★★★★	Holiday Park	♿

Elgin

Station Caravan Park	West Beach, Hopeman, Elgin, Morayshire, IV30 5RU	01343 830880	★★★★	Holiday Park

By Elie, East Neuk of Fife

Shell Bay Caravan	Shell Bay Caravan Park, By Elie, East Neuk of Fife, Fife, KY9 1HB	0131 605 1888	Holiday Caravan	

Eshaness

Braewick Cafe & Caravan Park	Braewick, Eshaness, Shetland, ZE2 9RS	01806 503345	★★★★	Touring Park

Ettrick

West Deloraine	Ettrick, Selkirkshire, TD7 5HR	01750 62207	Holiday Caravan	

Evanton

Black Rock Caravan Park	Balconie Street, Evanton, Ross-shire, IV16 9UN	01349 830917	★★★★★	Holiday Park

Eyemouth

Eyemouth Holiday Park	Fort Road, Eyemouth, Berwickshire, TD14 5BE	01890 751050	★★★★	Holiday Park

Fintry

Balgair Castle Park	Fintry, Stirlingshire, G63 0LP	01360 860283	★★★★	Holiday Park

♿ Unassisted wheelchair access   ♿ Assisted wheelchair access   ♿ Access for visitors with mobility difficulties
ℙ Bronze Green Tourism Award   ℙℙ Silver Green Tourism Award   ℙℙℙ Gold Green Tourism Award
For further information on our Green Tourism Business Scheme please see page 9.

372   To find out more, call 0845 22 55 121 or go to visitscotland.com.

Fishnish, Isle of Mull

Balmeanach Park	Balmeanach, Fishnish, Isle of Mull, Argyll, PA65 6BA	01680 300342	★★★★	Touring Park

Forfar

Foresterseat Caravan Park	Burnside,Arbroath Road, Forfar, Angus, DD8 2RY	01307 818880	★★★★	Touring Park
Lochlands Caravan Park	Lochlands, Dundee Road, Forfar, Angus, DD8 1XF	01307 463621	Awaiting Grading	
Lochside Caravan Park	Forfar Country Park, Craig O' Loch Road, Forfar, Angus, DD8 1BT	01307 468917	★★★★	Touring Park

By Forfar

Findhorn Bay Holiday Park	Findhorn, By Forfar, Morayshire, IV36 3TY	01309 690203	★★★	Holiday Park
Leckaway Caravan	South Leckaway Farm, By Forfar, Angus, DD8 1XF	01307 463324	Holiday Caravan	

Forres

Findhorn Sands Caravan Park	Findhorn, Forres, Morayshire, IV36 0YZ	01309 690324	★★★★★	Holiday Park

Fort Augustus

Fort Augustus Caravan and Camping Park	Market Hill, Fort Augustus, Inverness-shire, PH32 4DS	01320 366618	★★★★	Touring Park

Fort William

Glen Nevis Caravan and Camping Park	Glen Nevis, Fort William, Inverness-shire, PH33 6SX	01397 702191	★★★★★	Holiday Park
Linnhe Lochside Holidays	Corpach, Fort William, Inverness-shire, PH33 7NL	01397 772376	★★★★★	Holiday Park
Lochy Caravan Park	Camaghael, Fort William, Inverness-shire, PH33 7NF	01397 703446	★★★★	Holiday Park

Fortrose

Rosemarkie Camping & Caravanning Club Site	Ness Road East, Fortrose, Fortrose, Ross-shire, IV10 8SE	0845 1307633	★★★★	Touring Park

Fraserburgh

Esplanade Caravan Park	Harbour Road, Fraserburgh, Aberdeenshire, AB43 5EU	01346 510041	★★★	Holiday Park

Gairloch

Gairloch Caravan & Camping Park	Strath, Gairloch, Ross-shire, IV21 2BX	01445 712373	★★★★	Touring Park
Sands Caravan and Camping	Gairloch, Ross-shire, IV21 2DL	01445 712152	★★★★	Holiday Park

Gargunnock

Redhall Farm	Gargunnock, Stirlingshire, FK8 3AE	01786 860204	Holiday Caravan	

Gatehouse of Fleet

Anwoth Holiday Park	Gatehouse of Fleet, Kirkcudbrightshire, DG7 2JU	01557 814333	★★★★★	Holiday Park
Auchenlarie Holiday Park	Gatehouse of Fleet, Castle Douglas, DG7 2EX	01557 840251	★★★★★	Holiday Park
Mossyard Caravan Park	Mossyard, Gatehouse of Fleet, Kirkcudbrightshire, DG7 2ET	01557 840226	★★★★	Holiday Park

 ♿ Unassisted wheelchair access   ♿ Assisted wheelchair access   ♁ Access for visitors with mobility difficulties

🌿 Bronze Green Tourism Award 🌿🌿 Silver Green Tourism Award 🌿🌿🌿 Gold Green Tourism Award

For further information on our Green Tourism Business Scheme please see page 9.

Girvan

Bennane Shore Holiday Park	Lendalfoot, Girvan, Ayrshire, KA26 0JG	01465 891233	★★★★★	Holiday Park
Queensland Holiday Park	Barrhill, Girvan, Ayrshire, KA26 0PZ	01465 821364	★★★★	Holiday Park
Turnberry Holiday Park	Turnberry, Girvan, Ayrshire, KA26 9JW	01655 331288	★★★	Holiday Park

By Girvan

Ballantrae Holiday Park	Laggan House, Ballantrae, By Girvan, Ayrshire, KA26 0LL	01465 831229	Awaiting Grading	
Barrhill Holiday Park	Barrhill, By Girvan, Ayrshire, KA26 0PZ	01465 821355	★★★★	Holiday Park

By Glamis

Drumshademuir Caravan Park	Roundyhill, By Glamis, Angus, DD8 1QT	01575 573284	★★★★★	Holiday Park

Glasgow

Craigendmuir Park	Craigendmuir Park Business Centre, Stepps, Glasgow G33 6AF	0141 779 2973	★★★	Holiday Park

Glencoe

Invercoe Caravan & Camping Park	Invercoe, Glencoe, Argyll, PH49 4HP	01855 811210	★★★★★	Holiday Park
Red Squirrel Camp Site	Leacantuim Farm, Glencoe, Argyll, PH49 4HX	01855 811256	★★	Camping Park

Glendaruel

Glendaruel Caravan Park	Glendaruel, Argyll, PA22 3AB	01369 820267	★★★★	Holiday Park

Glenluce

Glenluce Caravan & Camping Park	Glenluce, Wigtownshire, DG8 0QR	01581 300412	★★★★	Holiday Park
Whitecairn Farm Caravan Park	Whitecairn, Glenluce, Wigtownshire, DG8 0NZ	01581 300267	★★★★	Holiday Park

Glenrothes

Balbirnie Park Caravan Club Site	Balbirnie Road, Markinch, Glenrothes, Fife, KY7 6NR	01592 759130	★★★★	Touring Park
Kingdom Caravan Park	1 Overstenton Farm, Glenrothes, Fife, KY6 2NG	01592 772226	★★★★★	Holiday Park

Grampian

Aden Caravan Park	Aden Country Park, Mintlaw, Grampian, Aberdeenshire, AB42 8FQ	01771 623460	★★★★★	Holiday Park

Grantown on Spey

Grantown on Spey Caravan Park	Seafield Avenue, Grantown on Spey, Morayshire, PH26 3JQ	01479 872474	★★★★★	Holiday Park

Gretna

Braids Caravan Park	Annan Road, Gretna, Dumfries & Galloway, DG16 5DG	01461 337409	★★★★	Touring Park

Grosebay, Isle of Harris

5 Grosebay	Grosebay, Isle of Harris HS3 3EF	01859 511246	Holiday Caravan	

♿ Unassisted wheelchair access ♿ Assisted wheelchair access 🚶 Access for visitors with mobility difficulties
Bronze Green Tourism Award Silver Green Tourism Award Gold Green Tourism Award
For further information on our Green Tourism Business Scheme please see page 9.

By Helensburgh

Rosneath Castle Caravan Park Ltd	Rosneath, By Helensburgh, Argyll & Bute, G84 0QS	01436 831208	★★★★★	Holiday Park

Huntly

Huntly Castle Caravan Park	The Meadows, Huntly, Aberdeenshire, AB54 4UJ	01466 794999	★★★★★	Holiday Park

Innerleithen

Tweedside Caravan Park	Montgomery Street, Innerleithen, Peebleshire, EH44 6JS	01896 831271	★★★	Holiday Park

Inveraray

Argyll Caravan Park	Inveraray, Argyll, PA32 8XT	01499 302285	★★★★★	Holiday Park

Inverbervie

Inverbervie Caravan Park	Kirkburn, Inverbervie, Angus, DD10 0SP	07791 678997	★★★	Holiday Park

Invergarry

Faichemard Farm Camping Site	Faichemard Farm, Invergarry, Inverness-shire, PH35 4HG	01809 501314	★★★★	Touring Park

Invermoriston

Loch Ness Caravan & Camping Park	Invermoriston, Inverness-shire, IV63 7YE	01320 351207	★★★★★	Touring Park

Inverness

Bught Caravan Park	Bught Park, Bught Lane, Inverness, Inverness-shire, IV3 5SR	01463 236920	★★★	Touring Park
The Croft	9 Leachkin, Inverness, Inverness-shire, IV3 8PN	01463 230225		Holiday Caravan

Iochdar

Anglers Retreat	1 Ardmore, Iochdar, South Uist, HS8 5QY	01870 610325		Holiday Caravan

Jedburgh

Jedburgh Camping & Caravanning Club Site	Elliot Park, Jedburgh, Roxburghshire, TD8 6EF	0845 1307633	★★★★	Touring Park
Jedwater Caravan Park	Jedburgh, Roxburghshire, TD8 6PJ	01835 869595	★★★★	Holiday Park

John O'Groats

John O'Groats Caravan Park	John O'Groats, Caithness, KW1 4YR	01955 611329	★★★	Touring Park

Johnshaven

Wairds Park Caravan Park	Beach Road, Johnshaven, Kincardineshire, DD10 0HD	01561 362395	★★★★	Holiday Park

By Kennoway

Letham Feus Caravan Park	Cupar Road, By Kennoway, Fife, KY8 4HR	01333 351900	★★★★★	Holiday Park

Kildonan

Sealshore Camp Site	Kildonan, Isle of Arran, KA27 8SL	01770 820320	★★★★	Touring Park

  ♿ Unassisted wheelchair access   ♿ Assisted wheelchair access   🏃 Access for visitors with mobility difficulties
🌿 Bronze Green Tourism Award   🌿🌿 Silver Green Tourism Award   🌿🌿🌿 Gold Green Tourism Award
For further information on our Green Tourism Business Scheme please see page 9.

Killin

Cruachan Farm Caravan & Camping Park	Cruachan, Killin, Perthshire, FK21 8TY	01567 820302	★★★	Holiday Park
Maragowan Caravan Club Site	Aberfeldy Road, Killin, Stirling, FK21 8TN	01567 820245	★★★★★	Touring Park

Kilwinning

Viewfield Manor Holiday Village	Torranard, Kilwinning, Ayrshire, KA13 7RD	01294 850286	★★★★	Holiday Park

Kinlochleven

Caolasnacon Caravan and Camping Park	Kinlochleven, Argyll, PH50 4RJ	01855 831279	★★★	Holiday Park

Kinross

Gallowhill Farm Camping and Caravan Park	Gallowhill Farm, Kinross, Kinross-shire, KY13 0RD	01577 862364	★★★	Touring Park

Kintore

Hillhead Caravan Park	Kintore, Aberdeenshire, AB51 0YX	01467 632809	★★★★	Holiday Park

Kintyre

Carradale Bay Caravan Park	Carradale, Kintyre, Argyll, PA28 6QG	01583 431665	★★★★	Holiday Park

Kippford

Kippford Holiday Park	Kippford, Kirkcudbrightshire, DG5 4LF	01556 620636	★★★★★	Holiday Park

Kirkcudbright

Brighouse Bay Holiday Park	Borgue Road, Kirkcudbright, Kirkcudbrightshire, DG6 4TS	01557 870267	★★★★★	Holiday Park	🍂🍂🍂
Seaward Caravan Park	Dhoon Bay, Kirkcudbright, Kirkcudbrighshire, DG6 4TJ	01557 331079	★★★★	Holiday Park	
Silvercraigs Caravan & Camping Site	Silvercraigs Road, Kirkcudbright, Kirkcudbrightshire, DG6 4BT	01556 503806	★★★★	Touring Park	

Kirkgunzeon

Beeswing Caravan Park	Drumjohn Moor, Kirkgunzeon, Dumfries, DG2 8JL	01387 760242	★★★★	Holiday Park

Kirkinner

Drumroamin Farm Camping & Caravan Site	1 South Balfern, Kirkinner, Newton Stewart, DG8 9DB	01988 840613	★★★★	Holiday Park

Kirkpatrick Fleming

King Robert the Bruce's Cave	Cove Estate, Kirkpatrick Fleming, Dumfriesshire, DG11 3AT	01461 800285	★★★	Holiday Park

Kirkwall

The Pickaquoy Centre Caravan Park	Pickaquoy Road, Kirkwall, Orkney, KW15 1JG	01856 879900	★★★	Touring Park

Kyle of Lochalsh

Ardelve	Dornie, Kyle of Lochalsh, Ross-shire, IV40 8DY	01599 555231		Holiday Caravan
Reraig Caravan Site	Balmacara, Kyle of Lochalsh, Ross-shire, IV40 8DH	01599 566215	★★★★	Touring Park

♿ Unassisted wheelchair access   ♿ Assisted wheelchair access   🚶 Access for visitors with mobility difficulties
🍂 Bronze Green Tourism Award   🍂🍂 Silver Green Tourism Award   🍂🍂🍂 Gold Green Tourism Award
For further information on our Green Tourism Business Scheme please see page 9.

376   To find out more, call 0845 22 55 121 or go to visitscotland.com.

Laide

The Sheiling	Achgarve, Laide, Ross-shire, IV22 2NS	01445 731487		Holiday Caravan

Lairg

Dunroamin Caravan Park	Main Street, Lairg, Sutherland, IV27 4AR	01549 402447	★★★★	Holiday Park

By Lairg

142 Oldshoremore	Rhiconich, By Lairg, Sutherland, IV27	01971 521335		Holiday Caravan

Lamlash

Dyemill House	Lamlash, Isle of Arran, KA27 8NU	01770 600419		Holiday Caravan

Langholm

Ewes Water Caravan & Camping Park	Milntown, Langholm, Dumfriesshire, DG13 0DH	013873 80386	★★★	Touring Park
Whitshiels Caravan Park	Langholm, Dumfriesshire, DG13 0HG	01387 380494	★★★★	Holiday Park

Lauder

Lauder Camping & Caravanning Club Site	Carfraemill, Oxton, Lauder, Berwickshire, TD2 6RA	0845 1307633	★★★★	Touring Park
Thirlestane Castle Caravan Park	Lauder, Berwickshire, TD2 6RU	01578 718884	★★★★	Touring Park

Laurencekirk

Dovecot Caravan Park	Northwaterbridge, Laurencekirk, Kincardineshire, AB30 1QL	01674 840630	★★★★	Holiday Park

By Laurencekirk

Brownmuir Caravan Park	Fordoun, By Laurencekirk, Aberdeenshire, AB30 1SJ	01561 320786	★★★	Holiday Park

Lerwick

Clickimin Caravan & Camping Site	Lochside, Lerwick, Shetland Isles, ZE1 0PJ	01595 741000	★★★★★	Touring Park

Liniclate, Isle of Benbecula

Shellbay Caravan & Camping Park	Liniclate, Isle of Benbecula HS7 5PJ	01870 602447	★★	Touring Park

Linlithgow

Beecraigs Caravan and Camping Site	Beecraigs Country Park, Linlithgow, West Lothian, EH49 6PL	01506 844516	★★★★	Touring Park

Loch Lomond

Ardlui Holiday Home Park	Ardlui, Loch Lomond, Argyll, G83 7EB	01301 704243	★★★★	Holiday Park
Lomond Woods Holiday Park	Balloch, Loch Lomond, Dunbartonshire, G83 8QP	01389 755000	★★★★★	Holiday Park
Luss Camping & Caravanning Club Site	Luss Camping Ground, Loch Lomond, Alexandria, G83 8NT	0845 1307633	★★★★	Touring Park

Lochboisdale, Isle of South Uist

Ocean View	410 Smerclate, Lochboisdale, Isle of South Uist HS8 5TU	01878 700383		Holiday Caravan

    ♿ Unassisted wheelchair access   ♿ Assisted wheelchair access   ✣ Access for visitors with mobility difficulties

    🄿 Bronze Green Tourism Award   🄿🄿 Silver Green Tourism Award   🄿🄿🄿 Gold Green Tourism Award

For further information on our Green Tourism Business Scheme please see page 9.

Lochearnhead

Balquhidder Braes Caravan Park	Balquhidder Station, Lochearnhead, Perthshire, FK19 8NX	01567 830293	★★★★	Holiday Park

By Lochgilphead

Stroneskar Farm	Ford, By Lochgilphead, Argyll, PA31 8RJ	01546 810286		Holiday Caravan

Lochgoilhead

Drimsynie & Kingfisher Holiday Village	Drimsynie Estate, Lochgoilhead, Argyll, PA24 8AD	01301 703312	★★★★★	Holiday Park

Lochmaben

Kirkloch Caravan & Camping Site	Kirkloch Brae, Kirkloch, Lochmaben, Dumfriesshire, DG11 1PZ	01556 503806	★★★	Touring Park

Lochwinnoch

Barnbrock Campsite	Clyde Muirshiel Regional Park, Lochwinnoch, Renfrewshire, PA10 2PZ	01505 614791	★★★	Camping Park

Lockerbie

Cressfield Caravan Park	Ecclefechan, Lockerbie, Dumfriesshire, DG11 3DR	01576 300702	★★★★	Holiday Park
Halleaths Caravan & Camping Park	Lochmaben, Lockerbie, Dumfriesshire, DG11 1NA	01387 810630	★★★★	Holiday Park
Hoddom Castle Caravan Park	Hoddom, Lockerbie, Dumfries-shire, DG11 1AS	01576 300251	★★★★★	Holiday Park

Longniddry

Seton Sands Holiday Village	Links Road, Longniddry, Longniddry, East Lothian, EH32 0QF	01875 813333	★★★★	Holiday Park
Seton Sands Holiday Village	Longniddry, East Lothian, EH32 0QF	0131 3328851		Holiday Caravan

Lower Barvas, Isle of Lewis

Lasgair	35 Lower Barvas, Lower Barvas, Isle of Lewis HS2 0QY	01851 840409		Holiday Caravan

Lundin Links

Woodland Gardens Caravan & Camping Park	Blindwell Road, Lundin Links, Fife, KY8 5QG	01333 360319	★★★★	Holiday Park

By Luss

Inverbeg Holiday Park	Inverbeg, By Luss, Dunbartonshire, G83 8PD	01436 860267	★★★★	Holiday Park

MacDuff

Myrus Holiday Park	Myrus Crossroads, MacDuff, Banffshire, AB45 3QP	01261 812845	★★★★★	Holiday Park
Wester Bonnyton Farm Caravan Site	Gamrie, MacDuff, Banffshire, AB45 3EP	01261 832470	★★★	Holiday Park

Machrihanish

Machrihanish Caravan & Camping Park	East Trodigal, Machrihanish, Campbeltown, Argyll, PA28 6PT	01586 810366	★★★★	Touring Park

Maryculter

Deeside Holiday Park	South Deeside Road, Maryculter, Aberdeenshire, AB12 5FX	01224 733860	★★★★	Holiday Park

♣ Unassisted wheelchair access ♣ Assisted wheelchair access ♟ Access for visitors with mobility difficulties
🏡 Bronze Green Tourism Award 🏡🏡 Silver Green Tourism Award 🏡🏡🏡 Gold Green Tourism Award
For further information on our Green Tourism Business Scheme please see page 9.

378   To find out more, call 0845 22 55 121 or go to visitscotland.com.

Maybole

Croyburnfoot Holiday Park	Croy Shore, Maybole, Ayrshire, KA19 8JS	01292 500239	★★★★	Holiday Park
Culzean Bay Holiday Park	Knoweside, By Croyshore, Maybole, Ayrshire, KA19 8JS	01292 500444	★★★★	Holiday Park
Culzean Castle Camping & Caravanning Club Site	Glenside, Culzean Castle, Culzean, Maybole, Ayrshire, KA19 8JX	0845 1307633	★★★★	Touring Park
Old Mill Holiday Park - Maidens	Culzean, Maybole, Ayrshire, KA19 8JZ	01581 500227		Holiday Caravan
Walled Garden Camping & Caravan Park	Kilkerran Estate, Crosshill, Maybole, Ayrshire, KA19 7SL	01655 740323	★★★★	Touring Park

By Maybole

The Ranch	Culzean Road, By Maybole, Ayrshire, KA19 8DU	01655 882446	★★★★	Holiday Park

Melrose

Gibson Park Caravan Club Site	High Street, Melrose, Roxburghshire, TD6 9RY	01896 822969	★★★★★	Touring Park

Melvich

Halladale Inn Caravan Park	Melvich, Sutherland, KW14 7YJ	01641 531282	★★★★	Touring Park

Moffat

Moffat Camping & Caravanning Club Site	Hammerland's Farm, Moffat, Dumfriesshire, DG10 9QL	0845 1307633	★★★★	Touring Park

Monifieth, By Dundee

Riverview Caravan Park	Marine Drive, Monifieth, By Dundee, Angus, DD5 4NN	01382 535471	★★★★★	Holiday Park

Montrose

South Links Caravan Park	Traill Drive, Montrose, Angus, DD10 8AJ	01674 672105	★★★★	Touring Park
St Cyrus Park	St Syrus, Montrose, Kincardineshire, DD10 0DJ	01674 850316		Awaiting Grading

By Montrose

East Bowstrips Caravan Park	St Cyrus, By Montrose, Aberdeenshire, DD10 0DE	01674 850328	★★★★★	Holiday Park

Motherwell

Strathclyde Country Park	Motherwell, North Lanarkshire, ML1 3ED	01698 402060	★★★	Touring Park

Musselburgh

Drummohr Caravan Park	Levenhall, Musselburgh, East Lothian, EH21 8JS	0131 665 6867	★★★★★	Touring Park

Nairn

Laikenbuie	Grantown Road, Nairn, Nairnshire, IV12 5QN	01667 454630		Holiday Caravan
Nairn Camping & Caravanning Club Site	Delnies Woods, Nairn, Nairnshire, IV12 5NX	0845 1307633	★★★★	Touring Park
Nairn Lochloy Holiday Park	East Beach, Nairn, Nairnshire, IV12 4PH	01667 453764	★★★★	Holiday Park

Newton Stewart

Creebridge Caravan Park	Minnigaff, Newton Stewart, Wigtownshire, DG8 6AJ	01671 402324	★★★	Holiday Park	
Creetown Caravan Park	Silver Street, Creetown, Newton Stewart, Wigtownshire, DG8 7HU	01581 500227	★★★★	Holiday Park	
East Culkae Farmhouse	Sorbie, Newton Stewart, Wigtownshire, DG8 8AS	01988 850214	Holiday Caravan		
Glentrool Holiday Park	Bargrennan, Newton Stewart, Wigtownshire, DG8 6RN	01671 840280	★★★★	Holiday Park	
Luce Bay Holiday Park & Lodges	Auchenmalg, Newton Stewart, Wigtownshire, DG8 0JT	01581 500227	★★★★	Holiday Park	
Three Lochs Holiday Park	Balminnoch, Newton Stewart, Wigtownshire, DG8 0EP	01671 830304	★★★★	Holiday Park	

By Newton Stewart

Castle Cary Holiday Park	Crewn, By Newton Stewart, Wigtownshire, DG8 7DQ	01671 820264	★★★★	Holiday Park	

Newtonmore

Invernahavon Caravan Site	Glentruim, Newtonmore, Inverness-shire, PH20 1BE	01540 673534	★★★	Touring Park	

North Berwick

Gilsland Caravan Park	Grange Road, North Berwick, East Lothian, EH39 53A	01620 892205	★★★	Holiday Park	
Tantallon Caravan Park	Dunbar Road, North Berwick, East Lothian, EH39 5NJ	01620 893348	★★★★	Holiday Park	&.

North Shawbost, Isle of Lewis

Eilean Fraoich Camp Site	North Shawbost, Isle of Lewis, Isle of Lewis, HS2 9BQ	01851 710504	★★★	Touring Park	

Oban

An Tobar	Lerags, Oban, Argyll, PA34 4SE	01631 565081	Holiday Caravan		
Oban Caravan & Camping Park	Gallanachmore Farm, Gallanach Road, Oban, Argyll, PA34 4QH	01631 562425	★★★	Touring Park	
Rose View Caravan Park	Glenshellach Road, Oban, Argyll, PA34 4QJ	01631 562755	★★★★	Touring Park	
Teanga-Bhuidhe	Glencruitten, Oban, Argyll, PA34 4QA	01631 564719	Holiday Caravan		

By Oban

North Ledaig Co Ltd	Connel, By Oban, Argyll, PA37 1RT	01631 710291	★★★★★	Touring Park	
Sunnybrae	South Cuan, Island of Luing, By Oban, Argyll, PA34 4TU	01852 314274	★★★★	Holiday Park	𝒫𝒫
Tralee Bay Purple Thistle Holidays	Benderloch, By Oban, Argyll, PA37 1QR	01631 720255	★★★★★	Holiday Park	
Bayview Caravans	13 Keil Crofts, Benderloch, By Oban, Argyll, PA37 1QS	01631 720397	Holiday Caravan		

Onich

Bunree Caravan Club Site	Onich, Inverness-shire, PH33 6SE	01855 821283	★★★★★	Touring Park	

Peebles

Crossburn Caravan Park	Edinburgh Road, Peebles, Borders, EH45 8ED	01721 720501	★★★★★	Holiday Park	

&. Unassisted wheelchair access &. Assisted wheelchair access ⃛ Access for visitors with mobility difficulties
𝒫 Bronze Green Tourism Award 𝒫𝒫 Silver Green Tourism Award 𝒫𝒫𝒫 Gold Green Tourism Award
For further information on our Green Tourism Business Scheme please see page 9.

To find out more, call 0845 22 55 121 or go to visitscotland.com.

Perth

Beech Hedge Caravan Park	Cargill, Perth, Perthshire, PH2 6DU	01250 883249	★★★	Holiday Park
Scone Camping & Caravanning Club Site	Scone Palace, Scone, Perth, Perthshire, PH2 6BB	0845 1307633	★★★★	Touring Park

Peterhead

Craighead Caravan Park	Cruden Bay, Peterhead, Aberdeenshire, AB42 0PL	01779 812251	★★★	Holiday Park
Peterhead Lido Caravan Park	The Lido, Peterhead, Grampian, AB42 2YP	01779 473358	★★★★	Holiday Park

Pitlochry

Faskally Caravan Park	Faskally, Pitlochry, Perthshire, PH16 5LA	01796 472007	★★★★	Holiday Park
Milton of Fonab Caravan Park	Bridge Road, Pitlochry, Perthshire, PH16 5NA	01796 472882	★★★★	Holiday Park
The River Tilt Park	Bridge of Tilt, Blair Atholl, Pitlochry, Perthshire, PH18 5TE	01796 481467	★★★★★	Holiday Park
Tummel Valley Holiday Park	Pitlochry, Perthshire, PH16 5SA	01882 634221	★★★★	Holiday Park

By Pitlochry

Glengoulandie Country Park	By Pitlochry, Perthshire, PH16 5NL	01887 830495	★★★	Holiday Park

Pittenweem

Grangemuir Woodland Caravan Park	Grangemuir, Pittenweem, Fife, KY10 2RB	01333 311213	★★★★	Touring Park

Poolewe

Inverewe Gardens Camping & Caravanning Club Site	Inverewe Gardens, Poolewe, Ross-shire, Highlands, IV22 2LF	0845 130 7633	★★★★	Touring Park

Port Ellen, Isle of Islay

Tigh na Suil	Lagavulin, Port Ellen, Isle of Islay PA42 7DX	01496 302483	Holiday Caravan

Portree

Torvaig Caravan & Camping Park	8 Torvaig, Portree, Isle of Skye, IV51 9HU	01478 611849	★★★	Touring Park

Portsoy

Portsoy Caravan Park	The Links, Portsoy, Grampian, AB45 2RQ	01261 842695	★★★★	Holiday Park

By Portsoy

Sandend Caravan Park	Sandend, By Portsoy, Banffshire, AB4 2UA	01261 842660	★★★★	Holiday Park

Rockcliffe

Castle Point Caravan Park	Rockcliffe, Rockcliffe, Galloway, DG5 4QL	01556 630248	★★★★	Holiday Park

Rosehearty

Rosehearty Caravan Park	The Harbour, Rosehearty, Grampian, AB43 7JQ	01346 561314	★★	Touring Park

&. Unassisted wheelchair access &. Assisted wheelchair access ⋔ Access for visitors with mobility difficulties
🄿 Bronze Green Tourism Award 🄿🄿 Silver Green Tourism Award 🄿🄿🄿 Gold Green Tourism Award
For further information on our Green Tourism Business Scheme please see page 9.

Rothesay, Isle of Bute

Roseland Caravan Park	Canada Hill, Rothesay, Isle of Bute, PA20 9EH	01700 504529	★★★★	Holiday Park

Rowardennan

Cashel Caravan & Campsite	Rowardennan, Glasgow, G63 0AW	01360 870234	★★★★	Touring Park

Roy Bridge

Bunroy Camping & Caravan Site	Bunroy Park, Roy Bridge, Inverness-shire, PH31 4AG	01397 712332	★★★★	Touring Park

Saltcoats

Sandylands Holiday Park	Auchenharvie Park, Saltcoats, Ayrshire, KA21 5JN	01294 469411	★★★	Holiday Park

Selkirk

Victoria Caravan Park	Buccleuch Road, Selkirk, Selkirkshire, TD7 5DN	01750 20897	★★★	Touring Park

Shiel Bridge

Morvich Caravan Club Site	Shiel Bridge, Ross-shire, IV40 8HQ	01599 511354	★★★★★	Touring Park

Skeld

Skeld Caravan & Camping Site	Skeld Waterfront, Skeld, Shetland, ZE2 9NL	01595 860287	Awaiting Grading	

South Uist

Crossroads	Stoneybridge, South Uist, Western Isles, HS8 5SD	01870 620321	Holiday Caravan	
Lochside Cottage	Lochboisdale, South Uist, Western Isles, HS8 5TN	01878 700472	Holiday Caravan	

Southerness

Lighthouse Leisure	Southerness, Dumfriesshire, DG2 8AZ	01387 880277	★★★★	Holiday Park	
Southerness Holiday Village	Southerness, Dumfriesshire, DG2 8AZ	01387 880256	★★★★	Holiday Park	&#x267F;

Spean Bridge

Gairlochy Holiday Park	Old Station, Gairlochy Road, Spean Bridge, Inverness-shire, PH34 4EQ	01397 712711	★★★	Holiday Park

By Spean Bridge

2 Balmaglaster	By Spean Bridge, Inverness-shire, PH34 4EB	01809 501289	Holiday Caravan	

St Andrews

Cairnsmill Caravan Park	Largo Road, St Andrews, Fife, KY16 8NN	01334 473604	★★★★	Holiday Park
Caravan C4	Kinell Braes Caravan Park, St Andrews, Fife, KY16 8PX	01698 816935	Holiday Caravan	
Clayton Caravan Park	St Andrews, Fife, KY16 9YB	01334 870242	★★★★★	Holiday Park
Craigtoun Meadows Holiday Park	Mount Melville, St Andrews, Fife, KY16 8PQ	01334 475959	★★★★★	Holiday Park
G2	Kinkell Braes Caravan Park, St Andrews, Fife, KY16 8PX	01920 461447	Holiday Caravan	

♿ Unassisted wheelchair access   Assisted wheelchair access   Access for visitors with mobility difficulties
Bronze Green Tourism Award   Silver Green Tourism Award   Gold Green Tourism Award
For further information on our Green Tourism Business Scheme please see page 9.

| Kinkell Braes Caravan Park | St Andrews, Fife, KY16 8PX | 01334 474250 | | Holiday Caravan |

Stirling

| West Drip Farm | Stirling, Stirlingshire, FK9 4UJ | 01786 472523 | | Holiday Caravan |

By Stirling

| Auchenbowie Caravan Site | Auchenbowie, By Stirling, Stirlingshire, FK7 8HE | 01324 822141 | ★★★ | Holiday Park |

Stonehaven

| Queen Elizabeth Caravan Park | Cowie, Stonehaven, Kincardineshire, AB39 2RP | 01569 764041 | ★★★ | Holiday Park |

By Stonehaven

| Cloak Caravan Park | Catterline, By Stonehaven, Kincardineshire, AB39 | 01569 750232 | | Holiday Caravan |

Stornoway

| Laxdale Holiday Park | 6 Laxdale Lane, Laxdale, Stornoway, Lewis, Western Isles, HS2 0DR | 01851 706966 | ★★★★ | Holiday Park |

Stranraer

Aird Donald Caravan Park	off London Road, Stranraer, Wigtownshire, DG9 8RN	01776 702025	★★★★	Touring Park
Clashwhannon Caravan Park	Drummore, Stranraer, Wigtownshire, DG9 9QE	01776 840632	★★	Holiday Park
Drumlochart Caravan Park	Lochnaw, Leswalt, Stranraer, Wigtownshire, DG9 0RN	01776 870232	★★★★★	Holiday Park
New England Bay Caravan Club Site	Port Logan, Stranraer, Wigtownshire, DG9 9NX	01776 860275	★★★★★	Touring Park
Sands of Luce Holiday Park	Sandhead, Stranraer, Wigtownshire, DG9 9JN	01776 830456	★★★★	Holiday Park
Wig Bay Holiday Park	Loch Ryan, Stranraer, Wigtownshire, DG9 0PS	01776 853233	★★★★	Holiday Park

By Stranraer

| Mull of Galloway Holiday Park | Drummore, By Stranraer, Wigtownshire, DG9 9RD | 01581 500227 | | Awaiting Grading |

Strathcarron

| Applecross Campsite | Applecross, Strathcarron, Ross-Shire, IV54 8ND | 01520 744268 | ★★★ | Touring Park |

Strathyre

| Immervoulin Caravan & Camping Park | Strathyre, Perthshire, FK18 8NJ | 01877 384285 | ★★★ | Touring Park |

Stromness

| Brownstown House | Stromness, Orkney, KW16 3JN | 01856 851234 | | Holiday Caravan |
| Point of Ness Caravan & Camping Site | Point of Ness, South End, Stromness, Orkney, KW16 | 01856 873535 | ★★★ | Touring Park |

Swannay

| Belmont Swanway | Swannay, Orkney, KW17 2NR | 01856 721281 | | Holiday Caravan |

  ♿ Unassisted wheelchair access   ♿ Assisted wheelchair access   🚶 Access for visitors with mobility difficulties
  🄿 Bronze Green Tourism Award   🄿🄿 Silver Green Tourism Award   🄿🄿🄿 Gold Green Tourism Award
For further information on our Green Tourism Business Scheme please see page 9.

By Tain

Dornoch Firth Caravan Park	Meikle Ferry South, By Tain, Ross-shire, IV19 1JX	01862 892292	★★★★	Holiday Park

Tarbert

Minch View Campsite	10 Drinishader, Tarbert, Isle of Harris, HS3 3DX	01859 511207	★★	Touring Park
Port Ban Holiday Park Ltd	Kilberry, Tarbert, Argyll, PA29 6YD	01880 770224	★★★	Holiday Park

By Tarbert

Point Sands	Tayinloan, By Tarbert, Argyll, PA29 6XG	01583 441263	★★★	Holiday Park

Tarbet

Loch Lomond Holiday Park	Inveruglas, Tarbet, Argyll, G83 7DW	01301 704224	★★★★★	Holiday Park

Taynuilt

Cuilreoch	Kilchrenan, Taynuilt, Argyll, PA35 1HG	01866 833236	Holiday Caravan
Curacao Holiday Caravan	Curacao, Taynuilt, Argyll, PA35 1HW	01866 822636	Holiday Caravan

Thornhill

Penpont Caravan Park	Penpont, Thornhill, Dumfries and Galloway, DG3 4BQ	01848 330470	★★★	Holiday Park

Thurso

Scrabster Caravan Park	Thurso, Caithness, KW14 8BN	01847 893524		Holiday Caravan
Thurso Caravan & Camping Park	Smith Terrace, Scrabster Road, Thurso, Caithness, KW14 7JY	01847 894631	★★	Holiday Park

Tobermory

Tobermory Campsite	Newdale, Dervaig Road, Tobermory, Isle of Mull, PA75 6QF	01688 302624	★★★	Touring Park

By Tobermory

Lochnameal	By Tobermory, Isle of Mull, PA75 6QB	01688 302364	Holiday Caravan

Turriff

Turriff Caravan Park	Station Road, Turriff, Grampian, AB53 7ER	01888 562205	★★★★	Holiday Park

Twatt

Bryameadow Farm	Twatt, Orkney, KW17 2JH	01856 841803	Holiday Caravan

Tyndrum

Strathfillan Wigwams	Auchtertyre, Tyndrum, Perthshire, FK20 8RU	01838 400251	★★★★	Camping Park

Uig

Orasay Caravan Holiday Home	14 Idrigill, Uig, Isle of Skye, IV51 9XU	01470 542316	Holiday Caravan

♿ Unassisted wheelchair access ♿ Assisted wheelchair access 🚶 Access for visitors with mobility difficulties
🅟 Bronze Green Tourism Award 🅟🅟 Silver Green Tourism Award 🅟🅟🅟 Gold Green Tourism Award
For further information on our Green Tourism Business Scheme please see page 9.

384 To find out more, call 0845 22 55 121 or go to visitscotland.com.

Uig Bay Campsite	10 Idrigill, Uig, Isle of Skye, IV51 9XU	01470 542714	★★★	Touring Park	

Upper Largo, Leven

Monturpie Caravan Park	Monturpie, Upper Largo, Leven, Fife, KY8 5QS	01333 360254	★★★	Touring Park	

Wemyss Bay

Wemyss Bay Holiday Park	Wemyss Bay, Renfrewshire, PA18 6BA	01475 520812	★★★★	Holiday Park	⌂⌂

By Wick

Wick Caravan & Camping Park	Riverside Drive, Janetstown, By Wick, Caithness, KW1 4RG	01955 605420	★★★★	Touring Park	

ᵭ Unassisted wheelchair access   Assisted wheelchair access   ⋔ Access for visitors with mobility difficulties
⌂ Bronze Green Tourism Award   ⌂⌂ Silver Green Tourism Award   ⌂⌂⌂ Gold Green Tourism Award
For further information on our Green Tourism Business Scheme please see page 9.

Thistle Award Scheme
The Thistle symbol recognises a high standard of caravan holiday home. Establishments highlighted have an advertisement in this guide.

Aberfoyle
Trossachs Holiday Park	Aberfoyle, Stirling, FK8 3SA	01877 382614	★★★★★	Holiday Park	🍃🍃🍃

Abington
Mount View Caravan Park	Station Road, Abington, South Lanarkshire, ML12 6R\	01864 502808	★★★★	Holiday Park	

By Acharacle
Resipole Farm Caravan Park	Loch Sunart, By Acharacle, Argyll, PH36 4HX	01967 431235	★★★★	Holiday Park	

Annan
Queensberry Bay Caravan Pa	Powfoot, Annan, Dumfriesshire, DG12 5PU	01461 700205	★★★★	Holiday Park	

Ayr
Craig Tara	Dunure Road, Ayr, Ayrshire, KA7 4LB	01292 265141	★★★★	Holiday Park	

By Ayr
Croft Head Caravan Park	By Ayr, Ayrshire, KA6 6EN	01292 263516	★★★★	Holiday Park	
Sundrum Castle Holiday Park	Coylton, By Ayr, Ayrshire, KA6 6HX	01292 570057(	★★★★★	Holiday Park	

Blair Atholl
Blair Castle Caravan Park	Blair Atholl, Perthshire, PH18 5SR	01796 481263	★★★★★	Holiday Park	🍃🍃

Blairgowrie
Blairgowrie Holiday Park	Rattray, Blairgowrie, Perthshire, PH10 7AL	01250 876666	★★★★★	Holiday Park	
Five Roads Caravan Park	by Alyth, Blairgowrie, Perthshire, PH11 8NB	01828 632255	★★★★	Holiday Park	

By Blairgowrie
Corriefodly Holiday Park	Bridge of Cally, By Blairgowrie, Perthshire, PH10 7JG	01250 886236	★★★★★	Holiday Park	

Boat of Garten
Boat of Garten Holiday Park	Desmar Road, Boat of Garten, Highland, PH24 3BN	01479 831652	★★★★	Holiday Park	

Cairnryan
Cairnryan Caravan Park	Cairnryan, Wigtownshire, DG9 8QX	01581 200231	★★★★	Holiday Park	

Coldingham
Scoutscroft Holiday Centre	St Abbs Road, Coldingham, Berwickshire, TD14 5NB	01890 771338	★★★★★	Holiday Park	

Crail
Sauchope Links Caravan Park	Crail, Fife, KY10 3XJ	01333 870446	★★★★★	Holiday Park	

Crianlarich
Glendochart Caravan Park	Luib, Crianlarich, Perthshire, FK20 8QT	01567 820637	★★★★	Holiday Park	

Crieff
Braidhaugh Park | South Bridgend, Crieff, Perthshire, PH7 4HP | 01764 652951 | ★★★★ | Holiday Park

Crocketford
Park of Brandedleys | Crocketford, Dumfriesshire, DG2 8RG | 01387 266700 | ★★★★ | Holiday Park

Dalbeattie
Glenearly Caravan Park | Park Farm, Dalbeattie, Kirkcudbrightshire, DG5 4NE | 01556 611393 | ★★★★ | Holiday Park

By Dalbeattie
Sandyhills Bay Leisure Park | Sandyhills, By Dalbeattie, Kirkcudbrightshire, DG5 4N | 01387 780257 | ★★★★ | Holiday Park

Dornoch
Dornoch Caravan & Camping | The Links, Dornoch, Sutherland, IV25 3LX | 01862 810423 | ★★★★ | Holiday Park

Grannies Heilan Hame Holiday | Embo, Dornoch, Sutherland, IV25 3QD | 01862 810383 | ★★★★ | Holiday Park

Dunbar
Belhaven Bay Caravan Park | Belhaven Bay, Dunbar, East Lothian, EH42 1TU | 01368 865956 | ★★★★ | Holiday Park ♿

Thurston Manor Holiday Home | Innerwick, Dunbar, East Lothian, EH42 1SA | 01368 840643 | ★★★★★ | Holiday Park ♿

Dunkeld
Erigmore House Holiday Park | Birnam, Dunkeld, Perthshire, PH8 0BJ | 01350 727236 | ★★★★ | Holiday Park

Dunoon
Hunters Quay Holiday Village | Hunters Quay, Dunoon, Argyll, PA23 8HP | 01369 707772 | ★★★★★ | Holiday Park

Edinburgh
Mortonhall Caravan Park | 38 Mortonhall Gate, Frogston Road East, Edinburgh E | 0131 664 1533 | ★★★★ | Holiday Park ♿

Evanton
Black Rock Caravan Park | Balconie Street, Evanton, Ross-shire, IV16 9UN | 01349 830917 | ★★★★★ | Holiday Park

Eyemouth
Eyemouth Holiday Park | Fort Road, Eyemouth, Berwickshire, TD14 5BE | 01890 751050 | ★★★★ | Holiday Park

Gairloch
Sands Caravan and Camping | Gairloch, Ross-shire, IV21 2DL | 01445 712152 | ★★★★ | Holiday Park

Gatehouse of Fleet
Auchenlarie Holiday Park | Gatehouse of Fleet, Castle Douglas, DG7 2EX | 01557 840251 | ★★★★★ | Holiday Park

Girvan
Bennane Shore Holiday Park | Lendalfoot, Girvan, Ayrshire, KA26 0JG | 01465 891233 | ★★★★★ | Holiday Park

♿ Unassisted wheelchair access   ♿ Assisted wheelchair access   ♿ Access for visitors with mobility difficulties
ℙ Bronze Green Tourism Award   ℙℙ Silver Green Tourism Award   ℙℙℙ Gold Green Tourism Award
For further information on our Green Tourism Business Scheme please see page 9.

Glencoe

Invercoe Caravan & Camping	Invercoe, Glencoe, Argyll, PH49 4HP	01855 811210	★★★★★	Holiday Park

Glendaruel

Glendaruel Caravan Park	Glendaruel, Argyll, PA22 3AB	01369 820267	★★★★	Holiday Park

Glenluce

Glenluce Caravan & Camping	Glenluce, Wigtownshire, DG8 0QR	01581 300412	★★★★	Holiday Park
Whitecairn Farm Caravan Park	Whitecairn, Glenluce, Wigtownshire, DG8 0NZ	01581 300267	★★★★	Holiday Park

By Helensburgh

Rosneath Castle Caravan Park	Rosneath, By Helensburgh, Argyll & Bute, G84 0QS	01436 831208	★★★★★	Holiday Park

Huntly

Huntly Castle Caravan Park	The Meadows, Huntly, Aberdeenshire, AB54 4UJ	01466 794999	★★★★★	Holiday Park

Inveraray

Argyll Caravan Park	Inveraray, Argyll, PA32 8XT	01499 302285	★★★★★	Holiday Park

Jedburgh

Jedwater Caravan Park	Jedburgh, Roxburghshire, TD8 6PJ	01835 869595	★★★★	Holiday Park

By Kennoway

Letham Feus Caravan Park	Cupar Road, By Kennoway, Fife, KY8 4HR	01333 351900	★★★★★	Holiday Park

Kintyre

Carradale Bay Caravan Park	Carradale, Kintyre, Argyll, PA28 6QG	01583 431665	★★★★	Holiday Park

Kippford

Kippford Holiday Park	Kippford, Kirkcudbrightshire, DG5 4LF	01556 620636	★★★★★	Holiday Park

Kirkcudbright

Brighouse Bay Holiday Park	Borgue Road, Kirkcudbright, Kirkcudbrightshire, DG6	01557 870267	★★★★★	Holiday Park	ᗺᗺᗺ
Seaward Caravan Park	Dhoon Bay, Kirkcudbright, Kirkcudbrighshire, DG6 4T	01557 331079	★★★★	Holiday Park	

Loch Lomond

Lomond Woods Holiday Park	Balloch, Loch Lomond, Dunbartonshire, G83 8QP	01389 755000	★★★★★	Holiday Park

Lochgoilhead

Drimsynie & Kingfisher Holiday	Drimsynie Estate, Lochgoilhead, Argyll, PA24 8AD	01301 703312	★★★★★	Holiday Park

Longniddry

Seton Sands Holiday Village	Links Road, Longniddry, Longniddry, East Lothian, EH	01875 813333	★★★★	Holiday Park

    ᗷ Unassisted wheelchair access   ᗷ Assisted wheelchair access   ♦ Access for visitors with mobility difficulties
    ᗺ Bronze Green Tourism Award   ᗺᗺ Silver Green Tourism Award   ᗺᗺᗺ Gold Green Tourism Award
    For further information on our Green Tourism Business Scheme please see page 9.

To find out more, call 0845 22 55 121 or go to visitscotland.com.

Thistle Award Scheme

The Thistle symbol recognises a high standard of caravan holiday home. Establishments highlighted have an advertisement in this guide.

By Luss

Inverbeg Holiday Park	Inverbeg, By Luss, Dunbartonshire, G83 8PD	01436 860267	★★★★	Holiday Park

Macduff

Myrus Holiday Park	Myrus Crossroads, Macduff, By Banff, AB45 3QP	01261 812845	★★★★★	Holiday Park

Maryculter

Deeside Holiday Park	South Deeside Road, Maryculter, Aberdeenshire, AB1	01224 733860	★★★★	Holiday Park

Monifieth, By Dundee

Riverview Caravan Park	Marine Drive, Monifieth, By Dundee, Angus, DD5 4NN	01382 535471	★★★★★	Holiday Park

Nairn

Nairn Lochloy Holiday Park	East Beach, Nairn, Nairnshire, IV12 4PH	01667 453764	★★★★	Holiday Park

Newton Stewart

Luce Bay Holiday Park & Lodg	Auchenmalg, Newton Stewart, Wigtownshire, DG8 0J	01581 500227	★★★★	Holiday Park
Three Lochs Holiday Park	Balminnoch, Newton Stewart, Wigtownshire, DG8 0EI	01671 830304	★★★★	Holiday Park

North Berwick

Tantallon Caravan Park	Dunbar Road, North Berwick, East Lothian, EH39 5N	01620 893348	★★★★	Holiday Park 🦽

By Oban

Tralee Bay Purple Thistle Holi	Benderloch, By Oban, Argyll, PA37 1QR	01631 720255	★★★★★	Holiday Park

Pitlochry

Milton of Fonab Caravan Park	Bridge Road, Pitlochry, Perthshire, PH16 5NA	01796 472882	★★★★	Holiday Park
The River Tilt Park	Bridge of Tilt, Blair Atholl, Pitlochry, Perthshire, PH18	01796 481467	★★★★★	Holiday Park

By Pitlochry

Tummel Valley Holiday Park	By Pitlochry, Perthshire, PH16 5SA	01882 634221	★★★★	Holiday Park

By Portsoy

Sandend Caravan Park	Sandend, By Portsoy, Banffshire, AB4 2UA	01261 842660	★★★★	Holiday Park

Southerness

Southerness Holiday Village	Southerness, Dumfriesshire, DG2 8AZ	01387 880256	★★★★	Holiday Park 🦽

St Andrews

Clayton Caravan Park	St Andrews, Fife, KY16 9YB	01334 870242	★★★★★	Holiday Park

Stornoway

Laxdale Holiday Park	6 Laxdale Lane, Laxdale, Stornoway, Lewis, Western	01851 706966	★★★★	Holiday Park

♿ Unassisted wheelchair access   🦽 Assisted wheelchair access   🚶 Access for visitors with mobility difficulties

🄿 Bronze Green Tourism Award   🄿🄿 Silver Green Tourism Award   🄿🄿🄿 Gold Green Tourism Award

For further information on our Green Tourism Business Scheme please see page 9.

Awards correct as of mid August 2008

Stranraer

Sands of Luce Holiday Park	Sandhead, Stranraer, Wigtownshire, DG9 9JN	01776 830456 ★★★★	Holiday Park

Tarbet

Loch Lomond Holiday Park	Inveruglas, Tarbet, Argyll & Bute, G83 7DW	01301 704224 ★★★★★	Holiday Park

♿ Unassisted wheelchair access   ♿ Assisted wheelchair access   ⚹ Access for visitors with mobility difficulties
Bronze Green Tourism Award   Silver Green Tourism Award   Gold Green Tourism Award
For further information on our Green Tourism Business Scheme please see page 9.

390   To find out more, call 0845 22 55 121 or go to visitscotland.com.

Aberdeen

Aberdeen Youth Hostel	8 Queens Road, Aberdeen AB10 4ZT	01224 646988	★★★★	Hostel	🌿🌿

Alexandria

Loch Lomond Youth Hostel	Arden, Alexandria, Dunbartonshire, G83 8RB	01389 850226	★★★	Hostel	🌿

Aviemore

Aviemore Bunkhouse	Dalfaber Road, Aviemore, Inverness-shire, PH22 1PU	01479 811181	★★★★	Hostel	♿	🌿
Aviemore SYHA	25 Grampian Road, Aviemore, Inverness-shire, PH22 1PR	01479 810345	★★★★	Hostel	♿	🌿🌿🌿

By Aviemore

Cairngorm Lodge (Loch Morlich)	Glenmore, By Aviemore, Inverness-shire, PH22 1QY	01479 861238	★★★★	Hostel	🚶	🌿🌿

Ballachulish

Glencoe Independent Hostel	Glencoe, Ballachulish, Argyll, PH49 4HX	01855 811906		Hostel	
Glencoe Youth Hostel	Glencoe, Ballachulish, Argyll, PA39 4HX	01855 811219	★★★	Hostel	🌿🌿

Banavie

Chase the Wild Goose Hostel	Lochiel Cresent, Banavie, Fort William, PH33 7LY	01397 772531	★★★★	Hostel	

Birsay

Birsay Outdoor Centre	(A966)Birsay, Orkney, KW17 2LY	01856 873535	★★★	Hostel	

By Blairgowrie

Blackwater Outdoor Centre	Black Lunnans, By Blairgowrie, Perthshire, PH10 7HJ	01738 477878	★★★	Group Accommodation	
Gulabin Lodge	Spittal of Glenshee, By Blairgowrie, Perthshire, PH10 7QE	01250 885255	★★★	Activity Accommodation	

Boat of Garten

Fraoch Lodge	Deshar Road, Boat of Garten, Inverness-shire, PH24 3BN	01479 831331	★★★★	Hostel	🌿🌿

Braemar

Braemar Lodge Bunkhouse	Glenshee Road, Braemar, Aberdeenshire, AB35 5YQ	013397 41627	★★★★	Hostel	
Braemar Youth Hostel	Corrie Feragie,21 Glenshee Road, Braemar, Aberdeenshire, AB35 2QL	01339 741659	★★★	Hostel	🌿🌿
Rucksacks	15 Mar Road, Braemar, Aberdeenshire, AB35 5YL	01339 74157		Hostel	

Broadford

Broadford Youth Hostel	Broadford, Isle of Skye, IV49 9AA	01471 822442	★★★	Hostel	🌿

Callander

Trossachs Backpackers	Invertrossachs Road, Callander FK17 8HW	01877 331200	★★★★	Hostel	

♿ Unassisted wheelchair access   ♿ Assisted wheelchair access   🚶 Access for visitors with mobility difficulties
🌿 Bronze Green Tourism Award   🌿🌿 Silver Green Tourism Award   🌿🌿🌿 Gold Green Tourism Award
For further information on our Green Tourism Business Scheme please see page 9.

Awards correct as of mid August 2008

By Callander

Sir Andrew Murray House	Strathayre, By Callander, Stirlingshire, FK18 8NQ	01324 562452	★★★	Group Accommodation	🚶

Cannich, Beauly

Glen Affric Youth Hostel	Allt Beithe, Glen Affric, Cannich, Beauly, Inverness-shire, IV4 7NO	01786 891400	★	Hostel	🍃🍃

Caputh

Wester Caputh Lodge	Manse Road, Caputh, Perthshire, PH1 4JH	01738 710449	★★★★	Hostel	

Carbost, Isle of Skye

But n Ben	7 Portnalong, Carbost, Isle of Skye, IV42 8SL	01478 640254	★★★★	Hostel	
Croft Bunkhouse	7 Portnalong, Carbost, Isle of Skye, IV42 8SL	01478 640254	★★★	Hostel	
Glenbrittle Youth Hostel	Glenbrittle, Carbost, Isle of Skye, IV47 8TA	01478 640278	★★★	Hostel	🍃🍃
The Waterfront Bunkhouse	The Old Inn, Carbost, Isle of Skye, IV47 8SR	01478 640205	★★★	Hostel	

Carloway, Isle of Lewis

Garenin Hostel	Garenin Village, Carloway, Isle of Lewis, Western Isles, HS2 9AL	01851 703773	★	Hostel	
No 3 Gearrannan	Gearrannan Blackhouse Village, Carloway, Isle of Lewis, Western Isles, HS2 9AL	01851 643416	★★	Group Accommodation	

Carrbridge

Slochd Mhor Lodge	Slochd, Carrbridge, Inverness-shire, PH23 3AY	01479 841666	★★★★	Hostel	♿ 🍃🍃

Castle Douglas

Galloway Activity Centre	Loch Ken, Castle Douglas DG7 ENQ	01644 420626	★★★	Activity Accommodation	

By Castle Douglas

Kendoon Youth Hostel	Dalry, By Castle Douglas DG7 3UD	01644 460680	★	Hostel	🍃

Castlebay

Dunard Hostel	Castlebay, Isle of Barra, HS9 5XA	01871 810443	★★★★	Hostel	

Cornaigmore

Millhouse Hostel	Cornaigmore, Isle of Tiree, PA77 6XA	01879 220435	★★★★	Hostel	

Crianlarich

Crianlarich Youth Hostel	Station Road, Crianlarich FK20 8QN	01838 300260	★★★	Hostel	🚶 🍃🍃

By Crieff

Comrie Croft Hostel	Braincroft, Comrie Road, By Crieff PH7 4JZ	01764 670140	★★★★	Hostel	

Cullen

Cullen Harbour Hostel	Portlong Road, Cullen, Moray, AB56 4AG	01542 841997			

  ♿ Unassisted wheelchair access ♿ Assisted wheelchair access 🚶 Access for visitors with mobility difficulties
🍃 Bronze Green Tourism Award 🍃🍃 Silver Green Tourism Award 🍃🍃🍃 Gold Green Tourism Award
For further information on our Green Tourism Business Scheme please see page 9.

Culrain

Carbisdale Castle Youth Hostel	Culrain, Sutherland, IV24 3DP	01549 921232	★★★★	Hostel	⅍	🄿

Dervaig

Dervaig Bunkrooms	Dervaig Village Hall, Dervaig, Isle of Mull, PA75 6JN	01688 400491		Hostel	

Drinishader

Drinishader Hostel	Drinishader, Isle of Harris, HS3 3DX	01859 511255	★★	Hostel	

Drumnadrochit

Loch Ness Backpackers Lodge	East Lewiston, Drumnadrochit, Inverness-shire, IV3 6UJ	01456 450807	★★★	Hostel	

By Drymen

Rowardennan Youth Hostel	Rowardennan, By Drymen G63 0AR	0870 004 1148	★★★	Hostel	⅍	🄿🄿

Dumfries

Marthrown of Mabie	Mabie Forest, Dumfries DG2 8HB	01387 247900	★★★	Hostel	

Dundee

Dundee Backpackers	71 High Street, Dundee, Angus, DD1 1SD	0131 220 2200		

Dundonnell

Badrallach Bothy	Dundonnell, Ross-shire, IV23 2QP	01854 633281		Hostel
Badrallach Bothy	Croft no 9, Badrallach, Dundonnell, Ross-Shire, IV23 2QP	01854 633281		Hostel
Sail Mhor Croft Hostel	Camusnagaul, Dundonnell, Ross-Shire, IV23 2QT	01854 633224	★★★	Hostel

By Dunoon

Bernice Farmhouse & Cottage	Bernice, By Dunoon, Argyll, PA23 8QX	01369 706337	★★ → ★★★★	Group Accommodation	⅍

Durness

Lazy Crofter	Durine, Durness, Sutherland, IV27 4PN	01971 511202	★★★	Hostel

Edinburgh

Argyle Backpackers Hotel	14 Argyle Place, Edinburgh EH9 1JL	0131 667 9991	★★★	Backpackers	
Belford Hostel	6-8 Douglas Gardens, Edinburgh EH4 3DA	0131 225 6209	★★★	Hostel	
Brodies 1	12 High Street, The Royal Mile, Edinburgh EH1 1TB	0131 556 6770	★★	Hostel	
Brodies 2	93 High Street, The Royal Mile, Edinburgh EH1 1SG	0131 5562223	★★★	Hostel	
Budget Backpackers	37-39 Cowgate, Edinburgh EH1 1JR	0131 226 6351	★★★★	Backpackers	⅍
Budget Backpackers	15 Cowgatehead, Edinburgh EH1 1JY	0131 226 6351	★★★	Backpackers	
Castle Rock Hostel	15 Johnston Terrace, Edinburgh EH1 2PW	0131 225 9666	★★	Backpackers	

     Ġ Unassisted wheelchair access   ⅍ Assisted wheelchair access   ⚦ Access for visitors with mobility difficulties
     🄿 Bronze Green Tourism Award   🄿🄿 Silver Green Tourism Award   🄿🄿🄿 Gold Green Tourism Award
     For further information on our Green Tourism Business Scheme please see page 9.

Edinburgh Backpackers	65 Cockburn Street, Edinburgh EH1 1BU	0131 220 1717	★★★	Hostel	
Edinburgh Central Youth Hostel	9 Haddington Place, Edinburgh EH7 4AL	0131 524 2090	★★★★★	Hostel	
Euro Hostels Limited	Kincaids Court, Guthrie Street, Edinburgh EH1 1JT	08454 900461	★★★	Hostel	
High Street Hostel	8 Blackfriars Street, Edinburgh EH1 1NE	0131 557 3984	★★	Backpackers	
Royal Mile Backpackers	105 High Street, Edinburgh EH1 1SG	0131 557 6120	★★	Backpackers	
Smart Apart Hostel	5 South College Street, Edinburgh EH8 9AA	0131 668 3085	★★★	Hostel	
Smart City Hostel	50 Blackfriars Street, Edinburgh EH1 1NE	0131 4669090	★★★★★	Hostel	
St Christophers Inn	9-13 Market Street, Edinburgh EH1 1DE	0131 226 1446	★★★	Backpackers	✦
The Globetrotter Inn Edinburgh Limited	Cramond Foreshore, Marine Drive, Edinburgh EH4 5EP	0131 3361030	★★★★	Hostel	
Westend Hostel	3 Clifton Terrace, Edinburgh EH12 5DR	0131 313 1031	★★★	Hostel	

Eshaness

Johnnie Notions	Hamnavoe, Eshaness, Shetland, ZE2	01595 693434		Hostel	

Fearnan

Culdees Bunkhouse	Boreland Farm, Fearnan, Perthshire, PH15 2PG	01887 830519	★★★	Hostel	

Fetlar

Aithbank Camping Bod	Fetlar, Shetland, ZE2 9DJ	01595 694688		Hostel	

Fort Augustus

Morags Lodge	Bunnoich Brae, Fort Augustus, Inverness-shire, PH32 4DG	01320 366289	★★★★	Hostel	

Fort William

Bank Street Lodge	Bank Street, Fort William, Inverness-shire, PH33 6AY	01397 700070	★★★	Hostel	
Calluna	Heathercroft, Fort William, Inverness-shire, PH33 6RE	01397 700451		Hostel	
Farr Cottage Lodge	Corpach, Fort William, Inverness-shire, PH33 7LR	01397 772315	★★★	Hostel	🅿
Fort William Backpackers	Alma Road, Fort William, Inverness-shire, PH33 6HB	01397 700711	★★	Backpackers	
Glen Nevis Youth Hostel	Glen Nevis, Fort William, Inverness-shire, PH33 6ST	01397 702336	★★★	Hostel	🅿🅿
Inchree Lodge	Onich, Fort William, Inverness-shire, PH33 6SE	01855 821287	★★★★	Hostel	
The Smiddy Bunkhouse and Blacksmiths Backpackers	Station Road, Corpach, Fort William, Inverness-shire, PH33 7JH	01397 772467		Hostel	

By Fort William

Loch Ossian Youth Hostel	Corrour, By Fort William, Inverness-shire, PH30 4AA	01397 732207	★★★	Hostel	🅿🅿🅿

Gairloch

Carn Dearg Youth Hostel	Carn Dearg, Gairloch, Rossshire, IV21 2DJ	01445 712219	★★★	Hostel	🅿🅿

♿ Unassisted wheelchair access   🦽 Assisted wheelchair access   ✦ Access for visitors with mobility difficulties
🅿 Bronze Green Tourism Award   🅿🅿 Silver Green Tourism Award   🅿🅿🅿 Gold Green Tourism Award
For further information on our Green Tourism Business Scheme please see page 9.

394   To find out more, call 0845 22 55 121 or go to visitscotland.com.

Rua Reidh Lighthouse	Melvaig, Gairloch, Ross-shire, IV21 2EA	01445 771263	★★★★	Hostel		🌿🌿🌿

Glasgow

Bunkum Backpackers	26 Hillhead Street, Glasgow G12 8PY	0141 581 4481	★★	Hostel		
Cairncross House	20 Kelvinhaugh Place, Glasgow G3 8NH	0141 330 5385	★★★	Hostel	♿	🌿
Euro Hostels	318 Clyde Street, Glasgow G1 4NR	0141 222 2828	★★★	Hostel		
Glades	142 Albert Road, Crosshill, Glasgow G42 8UF	0141 639 2601	★★★★	Hostel		
Glasgow Youth Hostel	7/8 Park Terrace, Glasgow G3 6BY	0141 332 3004	★★★★	Hostel		🌿🌿
Margaret Macdonald House	89 Buccleuch Street, Glasgow G3 6QT	0141 331 1261	★★	Hostel		🌿🌿
Murano Street Student Village	13 Caithness Street, Glasgow G20 7SB	0141 9431424	★★★	Hostel		🌿

Glen Nevis

Achintee Farm Hostel	Glen Nevis, Fort William, PH33 6TE	01397 702240	★★	Hostel	
Ben Nevis Inn	Achintee, Glen Nevis, Fort William, PH33 6TE	01397 701227		Hostel	

Glen Urquhart

The Glen Urquhart Hostel	Bearnock, Glen Urquhart, Inverness-shire, IV63 6TN	01463 230218	★★★★★	Hostel	

Glenfinnan

Glenfinnan Sleeping Car	Glenfinnan Station, Glenfinnan PH37 4LT	01397 722295		Hostel	

Glenlyon

Ben Lawers Hostel	Milton Eonan, Bridge of Balgie, Glenlyon, Perthshire, PH15 2PT	01881 866318	★★★★	Hostel	

Grantown-on-Spey

Ardenbeg Outdoor Centre	Grant Road, Grantown-on-Spey, Moray, PH26 3LD	01479 872824	★★★	Hostel	

Harris

Rhenigidale Hostel	Harris, Western Isles, HS3 3BD	01851 703773	★	Hostel	

Helmsdale

Helmsdale Hostel	Stafford Street, Helmsdale KW8 6JR	01431 821636	★★★★	Hostel	

Hoy

Hoy Centre	Moaness, Hoy, Orkney, KW15 3NJ	01856 873535	★★★★	Hostel	
Rackwick Outdoor Centre	Hoy, Orkney, KW16 3NJ	01856 873535	★★★	Hostel	

Inveraray

Inveraray Youth Hostel	Dalmally Road, Inveraray PA32 8XD	01499 302454	★★★	Hostel	🌿🌿

♿ Unassisted wheelchair access   ♿ Assisted wheelchair access   ♿ Access for visitors with mobility difficulties
🌿 Bronze Green Tourism Award   🌿🌿 Silver Green Tourism Award   🌿🌿🌿 Gold Green Tourism Award
For further information on our Green Tourism Business Scheme please see page 9.

Invergarry

Invergarry Lodge	Mandally Road, Invergarry PH35 4HP	01809 501412	★★★★	Hostel		

Invergordon

Balintraid House Backpackers & Highland	Balintraid, Invergordon, Ross-Shire, IV18 0LY	01349 854446				

Inverness

Bazpackers Hostel	4 Culduthel Road, Inverness, Inverness-shire, IV2 4AB	01463 717663	★★★	Backpackers		
Eastgate Backpackers Hostel	38 Eastgate, Inverness, Inverness-shire, IV2 3NA	01463 718756				
Inverness Millburn Youth Hostel	Victoria Drive, Inverness, Inverness-shire, IV2 3QB	01463 231771	★★★★	Hostel	♿	🍃🍃
Inverness Student Hotel	8 Culduthel Road, Inverness, Inverness-shire, IV2 4AB	01463 236556	★★	Backpackers		

By Inverness

Loch Ness Youth Hostel	Glenmoriston, By Inverness, Inverness-shire, IV63 7XD	01320 351274	★★	Hostel		🍃🍃

Isle of Colonsay

Colonsay Keepers Backpackers' Lodge	Isle of Colonsay, Argyll, PA61 7YU	01951 200312	★★	Hostel		

Isle of Eigg

Glebe Barn	Isle of Eigg PH42 4RL	01687 482417	★★★★	Hostel		🍃🍃

Isle of Harris

Lewis & Harris Youth Clubs Association	Scaladale Centre, Ardvourlie, Isle of Harris, Western Isles, HS3 3AB	01859 502502	★★★★	Activity Accommodation	🚶	
Rockview Bunkhouse	Main Street, Tarbert, Isle of Harris, Western Isles, HS3 3DJ	01859 502081	★★	Hostel		

Isle of Iona

Iona Hostel	Lagandorain, Isle of Iona, Argyll, PA76 6SW	01681 700781	★★★★	Hostel	🚶	🍃🍃🍃

Kelso

Kirk Yetholm Youth Hostel	Kirk Yetholm, Kelso, Roxburghshire, TD5 8PG	0870 155 3255	★★	Hostel		🍃🍃

Killin

Braveheart Backpackers	Lochay Lodge, Killin Hotel, Killin FK21 8TP	01567 829084		Hostel		

Kilmory

Kilmory Lodge Bunkhouse	Kilmory, Isle of Arran, KA27 8PQ	01770 870345	★★★	Group Accommodation		

Kincraig

Glen Feshie Hostel	Glen Feshie, Kincraig, Inverness-shire, PH21 1NH	01540 651323		Hostel		
Insh Hall Lodge	Loch Insh Watersports, Kincraig, Inverness-shire, PH21 1NU	01540 651272	★★★	Hostel		

♿ Unassisted wheelchair access   ♿ Assisted wheelchair access   🚶 Access for visitors with mobility difficulties
🍃 Bronze Green Tourism Award   🍃🍃 Silver Green Tourism Award   🍃🍃🍃 Gold Green Tourism Award
For further information on our Green Tourism Business Scheme please see page 9.

To find out more, call 0845 22 55 121 or go to visitscotland.com.

By Kingussie

Name	Address	Phone	Rating	Type	Access/Award
Lagganlia Outdoor Centre	Kincraig, By Kingussie, Inverness-shire, PH21 1NG	01540 651265	★★ → ★★★★	Activity Accommodation	

Kinloch Rannoch

Name	Address	Phone	Rating	Type	Access/Award
Kinloch Rannoch Centre	Kinloch Rannoch, Perthshire, PH16 5PQ	01738 477878			

Kinlochard

Name	Address	Phone	Rating	Type	Access/Award
Ledard Farm Bothies	Ledard Farm, Kinlochard FK8 3TL	01877 387219		Hostel	

Kinlochewe

Name	Address	Phone	Rating	Type	Access/Award
Kinlochewe Bunkhouse	Kinlochewe, Ross-shire, IV22 2PA	01445 760253		Hostel	

Kinlochleven

Name	Address	Phone	Rating	Type	Access/Award
Blackwater Hostel	Lab Road, Kinlochleven PH50 4SG	01855 831253	★★★★	Hostel	♿

Kirkwall

Name	Address	Phone	Rating	Type	Access/Award
Kirkwall Youth Hostel	Kirkwall, Orkney, KW15 1BB	0871 330 8533	★★	Hostel	♿ (mobility) · Bronze Green Tourism Award
Peedie Hostel	Ayre Road, Kirkwall, Orkney, KW15 1QX	01556 875477	★★★	Hostel	

Kirriemuir

Name	Address	Phone	Rating	Type	Access/Award
Glen Prosen Hostel	Glenprosen, Kirriemuir, Angus, DD8 4SA	01575 450456	★★★★	Hostel	(mobility)

By Kirriemuir

Name	Address	Phone	Rating	Type	Access/Award
The Steading Bunkhouse	Glen Clova Hotel, Glen Clova, By Kirriemuir, Angus, DD8 4QS	01575 550 350	★★★	Hostel	♿

Knoydart

Name	Address	Phone	Rating	Type	Access/Award
The Old Byre	Inverie, Knoydart, Inverness-Shire, PH41 4PL	01687 462639			

Kyle

Name	Address	Phone	Rating	Type	Access/Award
Ratagan Youth Hostel	Glenshiel, Kyle, Ross-shire, IV40 8HP	0870 0041147	★★★★	Hostel	Gold Green Tourism Award

Kyleakin

Name	Address	Phone	Rating	Type	Access/Award
Dun Caan Hostel	Pier Road, Kyleakin, Isle of Skye, IV41 8PL	01599 534087	★★★★	Hostel	
Saucy Mary's Lodge	Kyleakin, Isle of Skye, IV41 8PL	01599 534845	★★★	Hostel	
Skye Backpackers	Kyleakin, Isle of Skye, IV41 8PH	01599 534510	★★	Backpackers	

Laggan Bridge

Name	Address	Phone	Rating	Type	Access/Award
Pottery Bunkhouse	Laggan Bridge PH20 1BT	01528 544231	★★★★	Hostel	

Lairg

Name	Address	Phone	Rating	Type	Access/Award
Achmelvich Youth Hostel	Recharn, Lairg, Sutherland, IV27 4JB	01571 844480	★	Hostel	Bronze Green Tourism Award
Durness Youth Hostel	Smoo, Lairg, Sutherland, IV27 4QA	01847 891113		Hostel	Bronze Green Tourism Award

 ♿ Unassisted wheelchair access   ♿ Assisted wheelchair access   ♀ Access for visitors with mobility difficulties

Bronze Green Tourism Award   Silver Green Tourism Award   Gold Green Tourism Award

For further information on our Green Tourism Business Scheme please see page 9.

Inchnadamph Lodge Hostel	Inchnadamph, Elphin, Lairg, Sutherland, IV27 4HL	01571 822218	★★★	Hostel	

By Lairg

Tongue Youth Hostel	Tongue, By Lairg, Sutherland, IV27 4XH	1847 611789	★★★	Hostel	🍂🍂

Laxdale

Laxdale Bunkhouse	Laxdale Holiday Park, 6 Laxdale Lane, Laxdale, Isle of Lewis, HS2 0DP	01851 706966	★★★★	Hostel	🚶

Lerwick

Lerwick Youth Hostel	Islesburgh House, King Harald Street, Lerwick, Shetland, ZE1 0EQ	01595 692114	★★★★★	Hostel	

Leverburgh

Am Bothan Leverburgh Bunkhouse	Am Bothan, Leverburgh, Isle of Harris, HS5 3UA	01859 520251	★★★★★	Hostel	♿

Lochmaddy

Uist Outdoor Centre	Lochmaddy, Isle of Uist, HS6 5AE	01876 500480	★★	Hostel	

Lochranza

Lochranza Youth Hostel	Lochranza, Isle of Arran, KA27 8HL	01770 830631	★★★	Hostel	🍂🍂

Mallaig

Sheenas Backpackers Lodge	Mallaig, Inverness-shire, PH41 4PU	01687 462764	★★★	Hostel	

Melrose

Melrose Youth Hostel	Priorwood, Melrose TD6 9EF	01896 822521	★★★	Hostel	🍂

Nethy Bridge

Abernethy Bunkhouses (Nethy Station)	Station Road, Nethy Bridge PH25 3DN	01479 821370	★★	Group Accommodation	🍂
Lazy Duck Hostel	Nethy Bridge PH25 3ED	01479 821642	★★★★	Hostel	♿ 🍂🍂

New Lanark

New Lanark Youth Hostel	Wee Row, Rosedale Street, New Lanark, By Lanark, ML11 9DJ	01555 666710	★★★	Hostel	🍂🍂

Newton Stewart

Minnigaff Youth Hostel	Newton Stewart, Wigtownshire, DG8 6PL	01671 402211	★★	Hostel	🍂

Newtonmore

Craigower Lodge	Golf Course Road, Newtonmore, Inverness-shire, PH20 1AT	08450 505052	★★★	Activity Accommodation	♿
Newtonmore Hostel	Craigellachie House, Newtonmore, Inverness-shire, PH20 1DA	01540 673360	★★★	Hostel	
Strathspey Mountain Hostel	Main Street, Newtonmore, Inverness-shire, PH20 1DR	01540 673694	★★★	Hostel	♿

Oban

Corran House Hostel	1 Victoria Crescent, Oban, Argyll, PA34 5PN	01631 566040	★★★★	Hostel	

♿ Unassisted wheelchair access   ♿ Assisted wheelchair access   🚶 Access for visitors with mobility difficulties
🍂 Bronze Green Tourism Award   🍂🍂 Silver Green Tourism Award   🍂🍂🍂 Gold Green Tourism Award
For further information on our Green Tourism Business Scheme please see page 9.

     To find out more, call 0845 22 55 121 or go to visitscotland.com.

Jeremy Inglis Hostel	21 Airds Crescent, Oban, Argyll, PA34 4BA	01631 565065	★	Hostel	
Oban Backpackers	Breadalbane Street, Oban, Argyll, PA34 5NZ	01631 562107	★★	Backpackers	
Oban Youth Hostel	Esplanade, Oban, Argyll, PA34 5AF	0870 004 1144	★★★★	Hostel	𝕜 ⦿

Old Scatness
Betty Mouat's	Old Scatness, Shetland, ZE3 9JW	01595 693434		Hostel	

Onich
Corran Bunkhouse	Corran, Onich, Fort William, PH33 6SE	01855 821000	★★★★	Hostel	𝕜
Inchree Hostel	Onich, Fort William, PH33 6SE	01855 821287	★★★	Group Accommodation	

Pitlochry
Pitlochry Backpackers	134 Atholl Road, Pitlochry, Perthshire, PH16 5AB	01796 470044	★★★	Hostel	
Pitlochry Youth Hostel	Braeknowe, Knockard Road, Pitlochry, Perthshire, PH16 5HJ	01796 472308	★★★	Hostel	⦿⦿

Plockton
Plockton Station	Burnside, Plockton IV52 8TF	01599 544235		Hostel	

Portalong
Skyewalker Hostel	The Old School, Portalong, Isle of Skye, IV47 8SL	01478 640250	★★★	Hostel	

Portree
Bayfield Backpackers	Bayfield, Portree, Isle of Skye, IV51 9EW	01478 612231	★★★★	Hostel	
Dun Flodigarry Hostel	Flodigarry, Portree, Isle of Skye, IV51 9HZ	01470 552212	★★★	Hostel	
Portree Independent Hostel	Old Post Office, Portree, Isle of Skye, IV51 9BT	01478 613737	★★★	Hostel	
Uig Youth Hostel	Portree, Isle of Skye, IV51 9YD	0871 330 8556	★★★	Hostel	⦿⦿⦿

Port Charlotte
Port Charlotte Youth Hostel	Port Charlotte, Isle of Islay, PA48 7TX	01496 850385	★★★	Hostel	⦿⦿

Raasay
Raasay Youth Hostel	Creachan Cottage, Raasay, By Kyle, IV40 8NT	01478 660240	★★★	Hostel	

Rattray, Peterhead
Rattray Head Hostel	Lighthouse Cottages, Rattray, Peterhead, Aberdeenshire, AB42 3HA	01346 532236	★★	Hostel	

Rogart
Sleeperzzz.com	Rogart, Sutherland, IV28 3XA	01408 641343	★★★	Hostel	

Rousay
Rousay Hostel	Trumland Farm, Rousay, Orkney, KW17 2PU	01856 821252	★★★	Hostel	

& Unassisted wheelchair access   𝕜 Assisted wheelchair access   ⫟ Access for visitors with mobility difficulties
⦿ Bronze Green Tourism Award   ⦿⦿ Silver Green Tourism Award   ⦿⦿⦿ Gold Green Tourism Award
For further information on our Green Tourism Business Scheme please see page 9.

Awards correct as of mid August 2008

Roy Bridge

Grey Corrie Lodge	Roy Bridge, Inverness-shire, PH31 4AN	01397 712236		Hostel

Sanday

Ayres Rock Hostel	Ayre, Sanday, Orkney, KW17 2AY	01857 600410	★★★★	Hostel

Selkirk

Broadmeadows Youth Hostel	Old Broadmeadow, Yarrowford, Selkirk TD7 5LZ	0870 004 1107	★★	Hostel	🄿

Skeld

Skeld Camping Bod	Easter Skeld, Skeld, Shetland, ZE2 9NL	01595 694688		Hostel

Sligachan

Sligachan Bunkhouse	Sligachan, Isle of Skye, IV47 8SW	01478 650204	★★★	Hostel

South Galson

Galson Farm	South Galson, Isle of Lewis, HS2 0SH	01851 850492	★★★★	Hostel

Spean Bridge

Great Glen Hostel	South laggan, Spean Bridge, Inverness-shire, PH34 4EA	01809 501430	★★★	Hostel

St Margarets Hope

St Margarets Hope Backpackers	Back Road, St Margarets Hope, Orkney, KW17 2SR	01856 831225	★★★	Backpackers

Stirling

Stirling Youth Hostel	St John Street, Stirling FK8 1EA	0870 004 1149	★★★★	Hostel	🦽 🄿🄿
Willy Wallace Hostel	77 Murray Place, Stirling FK8 1AU	01786 446773	★★	Backpackers	

Stornoway

Heb Hostel	25 Kenneth Street, Stornoway, Isle of Lewis, HS1 2DR	01851 709889	★★★★	Hostel

Strathcarron

Gerry's Achnashellach Hostel	Craig, Achnashellach, Strathcarron, Wester Ross, IV54 8YU	01520 766232	★★	Hostel

Strathdon

Jenny's Bothy Crofthouse	Corgarff, Strathdon AB36 8YP	01975 651449	★★★	Hostel

Stromness

Brown's Hostel	45/47 Victoria Street, Stromness, Orkney, KW16 3BS	01856 850661	★★★	Hostel
Hamnavoe Hostel	10a North End Rd, Stromness, Orkney, KW16 3AG	01856 851202	★★★★	Hostel

Strontian

Ariundle Bunkhouse	Ariundle, Strontian PH36 4JA	01967 402279	★★★★	Hostel	♿

To find out more, call 0845 22 55 121 or go to visitscotland.com.

Thurso

Sandra's Hostel	24-26 Princes Street, Thurso, Caithness, KW14 7BQ	01847 894575	★★★★	Hostel	

Tobermory

Tobermory Youth Hostel	Main Street, Tobermory, Isle of Mull, PA75 6NU	01688 302481	★★★★	Hostel	⌒⌒⌒

Tomintoul, Ballindalloch

Tomintoul Youth Hostel	Main Street, Tomintoul, Ballindalloch, Banffshire, AB37 9EX	01479 872403	★★★★	Hostel	⌒⌒

Torridon

Torridon Youth Hostel	Torridon, Ross-shire, IV22 2EZ	01445 791284	★★★★	Hostel	⌒⌒

Twingness

The Observatory Hostel	Twingness, North Ronaldsay, KW17 2BE	01857 633200	★★★★	Hostel	

Tyndrum

By The Way Hostel	Lower Station Road, Tyndrum FK20 8RY	01838 400333	★★★★	Hostel	

Ullapool

Achininver Youth Hostel	Achiltibuie, Ullapool, Ross-shire, IV26 2YL	01854 613701	★★	Hostel	⌒⌒
Ullapool Tourist Hostel	West House, West Argyle Street, Ullapool, Ross-shire, IV26 2TY	01854 613126	★★★★	Hostel	
Ullapool Youth Hostel	Shore Street, Ullapool, Ross-shire, IV26 2UJ	01854 612254	★★★	Hostel	⌒⌒⌒

Unst

Gardiesfauld Youth Hostel	Uyeasound, Unst, Shetland, ZE2 9DW	01975 755279	★★★	Hostel	🦽
Saxa Vord Ltd	Haroldswick, Unst, Shetland Islands, ZE2 9TJ	01957 711711	★★★	Hostel	

Voe

Sail Loft	Voe, Shetland, ZE2	01595 693434		Hostel	

Waas

Voe House	Waas, Shetland, ZE2 9PB	01595 693434		Hostel	

Weisdale

Bod of Nesbister	Nesbister, Weisdale, Shetland, ZE2 9LJ	01595 694688		Hostel	

Westray

Bis Geos Hostel	Westray, Orkney, KW17 2DW	01857 677420	★★★★★	Hostel	⌒⌒⌒
The Barn	Chalmersquoy, Westray, Orkney, KW17 2BZ	01857 677214	★★★★	Hostel	

Whalsey

Grieve House	Whalsey, Shetland	01595 693434		Hostel	

& Unassisted wheelchair access &. Assisted wheelchair access ⋏ Access for visitors with mobility difficulties

⌒ Bronze Green Tourism Award ⌒⌒ Silver Green Tourism Award ⌒⌒⌒ Gold Green Tourism Award

For further information on our Green Tourism Business Scheme please see page 9.

HOSTEL ACCOMMODATION

By Wick

John O'Groats Youth Hostel	Canisbay, By Wick, Caithness, KW1 4YH	01955 611761	★★	Hostel	⭕⭕

Yell

Windhouse Lodge	Yell, Shetland	01595 693434		Hostel

♿ Unassisted wheelchair access   ♿ Assisted wheelchair access   ♁ Access for visitors with mobility difficulties
Bronze Green Tourism Award   Silver Green Tourism Award   Gold Green Tourism Award
For further information on our Green Tourism Business Scheme please see page 9.

To find out more, call 0845 22 55 121 or go to visitscotland.com.

INDEX BY LOCATION

To find out more, call 0845 22 55 121 or go to visitscotland.com.

To find out more, call 0845 22 55 121 or go to visitscotland.com.

   To find out more, call 0845 22 55 121 or go to visitscotland.com.